Lecture Notes in Computer Science 9850

Commenced Publication in 1973
Founding and Former Series Editors:
Gerhard Goos, Juris Hartmanis, and Jan van Leeuwen

Marcello La Rosa · Peter Loos
Oscar Pastor (Eds.)

Business Process Management

14th International Conference, BPM 2016
Rio de Janeiro, Brazil, September 18–22, 2016
Proceedings

 Springer

Editors
Marcello La Rosa
Queensland University of Technology
Brisbane, QLD
Australia

Peter Loos
DFKI
Universität des Saarlandes
Saarbrücken, Saarland
Germany

Oscar Pastor
Universidad Politècnica de Valencia
Valencia
Spain

ISSN 0302-9743   ISSN 1611-3349 (electronic)
Lecture Notes in Computer Science
ISBN 978-3-319-45347-7   ISBN 978-3-319-45348-4 (eBook)
DOI 10.1007/978-3-319-45348-4

Library of Congress Control Number: 2015957799

LNCS Sublibrary: SL3 – Information Systems and Applications, incl. Internet/Web, and HCI

This Springer imprint is published by Springer Nature
The registered company is Springer International Publishing AG Switzerland

Preface

The 14th International Conference on Business Process Management (BPM 2016) provided a global forum for researchers, practitioners, and developers to meet and exchange research insights and outcomes in business process management. BPM 2016 was hosted by the Federal University of the State of Rio de Janeiro, and took place during September 18–22 in Rio de Janeiro, Brazil.

We received 128 full submissions. Each paper was reviewed by at least four Program Committee (PC) members, and by one senior PC member who moderated the discussion and wrote the meta-review. Overall, the review process involved 20 senior PC members and 89 PC members. We accepted 22 papers (17.2 % acceptance rate). A subset of these papers was first conditionally accepted and underwent a thorough revision with subsequent review by a senior PC member. The rigorous review process and the high quality of the papers published in this volume attest to the leading position of the BPM Conference in this research discipline, globally.

In addition, we selected 13 papers from those that were not accepted, and invited them to the "BPM Forum." The BPM Forum is a new sub-track of the BPM Conference that aims to host innovative yet not mature research with high potential of stimulating discussions at the conference. These papers are published in a separate volume in the Springer LNBIP series.

This year we explicitly encouraged papers that report on interdisciplinary aspects of BPM and on research in emerging BPM areas, as well as papers that advance knowledge in the areas of business process analysis and improvement. Out of the submissions on these and on the traditional subject areas of BPM research, we selected a range of papers focusing on automated discovery, conformance checking, modeling foundations, understandability of process representations, runtime management, and predictive monitoring. The topics selected by the authors demonstrate the increasing interest of the research community in the area of process mining, resonated, these days, by an equally fast-growing uptake of process mining by different industry sectors.

The scientific program was complemented by three keynotes, chosen to provide a perspective from within the core BPM research community (Richard Hull, IBM T. J. Watson Research Center), from the BPM industry (Bradford Power, CXcelerator/FCB Partners), and from adjacent areas to the BPM research community (Giancarlo Guizzardi, Federal University of Espírito Santo).

We would like to thank the PC and the broader reviewer community for their dedicated commitment, and in particular the senior PC members for moderating the review process and preparing recommendations to the PC chairs. We are most grateful to all those who were involved in the realization of the conference, including the chairs of the various tracks. We would also like to congratulate the authors of all submitted and accepted papers for their high-quality work, and thank them for choosing BPM as their outlet for publication.

Finally, we would like to thank the BPM 2016 Organizing Committee and in particular the general chair, Flavia Maria Santoro, for their efforts in making this conference possible. We also thank the sponsors, Bizagi, IBM, DCR, myInvenio, UniRio, grupo A, Springer, ABPMP Brazil and SBC, for their generous support.

We hope that you will enjoy reading the papers in this volume and that you will be inspired by them to contribute to the next editions of the BPM Conference.

September 2016   Marcello La Rosa
                                                          Peter Loos
                                                          Oscar Pastor

Organization

BPM 2016 was organized by the Federal University of the State of Rio de Janeiro, and took place in Rio de Janeiro, Brazil.

Steering Committee

Wil van der Aalst (Chair)	Eindhoven University of Technology, The Netherlands
Boualem Benatallah	University of New South Wales, Australia
Jörg Desel	University of Hagen, Germany
Schahram Dustdar	Vienna University of Technology, Austria
Marlon Dumas	University of Tartu, Estonia
Manfred Reichert	University of Ulm, Germany
Stefanie Rinderle-Ma	University of Vienna, Austria
Barbara Weber	Technical University of Denmark, Denmark
Mathias Weske	HPI, University of Potsdam, Germany
Michael zur Muehlen	Stevens Institute of Technology, USA

Executive Committee

General Chair

Flavia Maria Santoro	Federal University of the State of Rio de Janeiro, Brazil

Program Chairs

Marcello La Rosa	Queensland University of Technology, Australia
Peter Loos	DFKI/Saarland University, Germany
Oscar Pastor	Universitat Politècnica de València, Spain

Industry Chairs

Claudia Cappelli	Federal University of the State of Rio de Janeiro, Brazil
Silvia Inês Dallavalle de Pádua	University of São Paulo, Brazil
André Macieira	Elo Group, Brazil
Michael Rosemann	Queensland University of Technology, Australia

Workshop Chairs

Marlon Dumas	University of Tartu, Estonia
Marcelo Fantinato	University of São Paulo, Brazil

Tutorial and Panel Chairs

Manfred Reichert	University of Ulm, Germany
Lucinéia Heloisa Thom	Federal University of Rio Grande do Sul, Brazil

Demonstration Chairs

Leonardo Azevedo   IBM Research/Federal University of Rio de Janeiro
                                                State, Brazil
Cristina Cabanillas   Vienna University of Economics and Business, Austria

Doctoral Consortium Chairs

Fernanda Baião   Federal University of the State of Rio de Janeiro, Brazil
Hajo A. Reijers   VU University Amsterdam, The Netherlands

Latin-American BPM Workshop

Juliano Lopes de Oliveira   Federal University of Goiás, Brazil
José Pino   Universidad de Chile, Chile
Pablo D. Villarreal   National Technological University, Argentina

BPM in Public Administration Panel Chair

Carina Frota Alves   Federal University of Pernambuco, Brazil

Publicity Chairs

José Ricardo Cereja   Federal University of the State of Rio de Janeiro, Brazil
Valdemar T.F. Confort   Federal University of the State of Rio de Janeiro, Brazil
Kate Revoredo   Federal University of the State of Rio de Janeiro, Brazil
Ricardo Seguel   BPM LATAM S.A., Chile

Senior Program Committee

Josep Carmona   Universitat Politècnica Catalunya, Spain
Florian Daniel   Politecnico di Milano, Italy
Jörg Desel   Fernuniversität in Hagen, Germany
Avigdor Gal   Technion, Israel
Pericles Loucopoulos   University of Manchester, UK
Heinrich C. Mayr   Alpen-Adria-Universität Klagenfurt, Austria
Massimo Mecella   SAPIENZA Università di Roma, Italy
Jan Mendling   Vienna University of Economics and Business, Austria
Andreas Oberweis   Universität Karlsruhe, Germany
Hajo A. Reijers   VU University Amsterdam, The Netherlands
Stefanie Rinderle-Ma   University of Vienna, Austria
Michael Rosemann   Queensland University of Technology, Australia
Shazia Sadiq   The University of Queensland, Australia
Pnina Soffer   University of Haifa, Israel
Jianwen Su   University of California at Santa Barbara, USA
Farouk Toumani   LIMOS/Blaise Pascal University, France
Boudewijn van Dongen   Eindhoven University of Technology, The Netherlands
Barbara Weber   Technical University of Denmark, Denmark
Matthias Weidlich   Humboldt-Universität zu Berlin, Germany
Mathias Weske   HPI, University of Potsdam, Germany

Program Committee

Mari Abe	IBM Research, Japan
Ahmed Awad	Cairo University, Egypt
Hyerim Bae	Pusan National University, Republic of Korea
Bart Baesens	KU Leuven, Belgium
Seyed-Mehdi-Reza Beheshti	University of New South Wales, Australia
Boualem Benatallah	University of New South Wales, Australia
Giorgio Bruno	Politecnico di Torino, Italy
Fabio Casati	University of Trento, Italy
Francisco Curbera	IBM Research, USA
Massimiliano de Leoni	Eindhoven University of Technology, The Netherlands
Jochen De Weerdt	KU Leuven, Belgium
Patrick Delfmann	ERCIS, Germany
Nirmit Desai	IBM T.J. Watson Research Center, USA
Remco Dijkman	Eindhoven University of Technology, The Netherlands
Marlon Dumas	University of Tartu, Estonia
Schahram Dustdar	TU Wien, Austria
Johann Eder	Alpen Adria Universität Klagenfurt, Austria
Gregor Engels	University of Paderborn, Germany
Joerg Evermann	Memorial University of Newfoundland, Canada
Dirk Fahland	Eindhoven University of Technology, The Netherlands
Marcelo Fantinato	University of São Paulo, Brazil
Peter Fettke	DFKI, Germany
Walid Gaaloul	Télécom SudParis, France
Luciano García-Bañuelos	University of Tartu, Estonia
Christian Gerth	Osnabrück University of Applied Sciences, Germany
Chiara Ghidini	FBK-irst, Italy
Guido Governatori	Data61, Australia
Sven Graupner	Hewlett-Packard Laboratories, USA
Gianluigi Greco	University of Calabria, Italy
Daniela Grigori	University of Paris-Dauphine, France
Thomas Hildebrandt	IT University of Copenhagen, Denmark
Richard Hull	IBM T.J. Watson Research Center, USA
Marta Indulska	The University of Queensland, Australia
Stefan Jablonski	University of Bayreuth, Germany
Gabriel Juhas	Slovak University of Technology, Slovakia
Leonid Kalinichenko	Russian Academy of Science, Russian Federation
Dimka Karastoyanova	University of Stuttgart, Germany
Rania Khalaf	IBM T.J. Watson Research Center, USA
Jana Koehler	Hochschule Luzern, Switzerland
Agnes Koschmider	Karlsruhe Institute of Technology, Germany
Jochen Kuester	IBM Research, Switzerland
Akhil Kumar	Penn State University, USA
Geetika Lakshmanan	Audible, USA

Moe Wynn   Queensland University of Technology, Australia
Eric Yu   University of Toronto, Canada
Liang Zhang   Fudan University, China
Michael zur Muehlen   Stevens Institute of Technology, USA

Additional Reviewers

Kevin Andrews   Annapaola Marconi
Vasilios Andrikopoulos   Alfonso Marquez-Chamorro
Abel Armas Cervantes   Alexey Mitsyuk
Nour Assy   Jorge Munoz-Gama
Vladimir Bashkin   Chun Ouyang
Dina Bayomie   Jan Recker
Khalid Belhajjame   Florian Rittmeier
Arne Bergmann   Andrey Rivkin
Mirela Madalina Botezatu   Carlos Rodriguez
Federico Chesani   Kristina Rosenthal
Jan Claes   Marco Roveri
Raffaele Conforti   Marc Schickler
Riccardo De Masellis   Alexander Schmid
Johannes De Smedt   Johannes Schobel
Adela Del Río Ortega   Stefan Schönig
Claudio Di Ciccio   Simon Schwichtenberg
Chiara Di Francescomarino   Zhe Shan
Mortada El Bana   Tijs Slaats
Jonnro Erasmus   Aleksander Slominski
Maria Fay   Sebastian Steinau
Valeria Fionda   Sergey Stupnikov
Markus Fischer   Alexander Teetz
Antonella Guzzo   Benjamin Ternes
Michael Hahn   Lucinéia Heloisa Thom
Farideh Heidari   Sanja Tumbas
Iman Helal   Han van der Aa
Vatche Ishakian   Sebastian Wagner
Anna Kalenkova   Andreas Weiß
Klaus Kammerer   Dennis Wolters
Christopher Klinkmueller   Xiwei Xu
Monika Klun   Peifeng Yin
David Knuplesch   Sira Yongchareon
Julius Köpke   Jian Yu
Sander Leemans   Nesma Zaki
Patrick Lohmann   Jelena Zdravkovic
Xixi Lu

Sponsors

Abstract of Keynotes

Don't Just Improve Work, Innovate Continuously

Bradford Power[1,2]

[1] CXcelerator, USA
[2] FCB Partners, USA
bradfordpower@gmail.com

Abstract. Process improvement (10 % incremental improvement, operational excellence, continuous improvement, the Toyota Production System, Six Sigma, Lean, kaizen, local optimization) is a strategic competency needed by every organization, but it isn't sufficient in today's competitive world. As the business world shifts from competing with physical assets and people to data and software, organizations become more and more dependent on process innovation (10X innovation, radical change, design thinking, product and service disruption, incubation, end-to-end optimization). An example to show the evolution is GE's shift from Six Sigma to Lean Six Sigma to Lean Startup to competing on software with Predix.

Historically, conventional wisdom said you could only be world class at one of three value propositions: operational excellence, customer intimacy and product leadership. Today, companies need all three to compete, particularly those that are being disrupted by software startups and big software-based companies such as Amazon, Facebook, and Google, which are in fact doing all three. How are they doing it?

This keynote will discuss the major roadblocks to transitioning legacy organizations from continuous process improvement to continuous process innovation, and shed light on how these roadblocks can be lifted.

Featured guest appearance: Gian Martinez, a startup leader using the Coca-Cola Founders Platform, will show how Coca-Cola is innovating through the example of Winnin – a social media site where young people submit recommendations that compete with each other.

Rethinking BPM in a Cognitive World: Transforming How We Learn and Perform Business Processes

Richard Hull[1] and Hamid R. Motahari Nezhad[2]

[1] IBM T.J. Watson Research Center, New York, USA
hull@us.ibm.com
[2] IBM Almaden Research Center, San Jose, USA
motahari@us.ibm.com

Abstract. If we are to believe the technology hype cycle, we are entering a new era of Cognitive Computing, enabled by advances in natural language processing, machine learning, and more broadly artificial intelligence. These advances, combined with evolutionary progress in areas such as knowledge representation, automated planning, user experience technologies, software-as-a-service and crowdsourcing, have the potential to transform many industries. In this paper, we discuss transformations of BPM that advances in the Cognitive Computing will bring. We focus on three of the most signficant aspects of this transformation, namely: (a) Cognitive Computing will enable "knowledge acquisition at scale", which will lead to a transformation in Knowledge-intensive Processes (KiP's); (b) We envision a new process meta-model will emerge that is centered around a "Plan-Act-Learn" cycle; and (c) Cognitive Computing can enable learning about processes from implicit descriptions (at both design- and run-time), opening opportunities for new levels of automation and business process support, for both traditional business processes and KiP's. We use the term *cognitive BPM* to refer to a new BPM paradigm encompassing all aspects of BPM that are impacted and enabled by Cognitive Computing. We argue that a fundamental understanding of cognitive BPM requires a new research framing of the business process ecosystem. The paper presents a conceptual framework for cognitive BPM, a brief survey of state of the art in emerging areas of Cognitive BPM, and discussion of key directions for further research.

Ontological Considerations
About the Representation of Events
and Endurants in Business Models

Giancarlo Guizzardi[1,2], Nicola Guarino[2], and João Paulo A. Almeida[1]

[1] Federal University of Espírito Santo, Vitória, Brazil
[2] ISTC-CNR Laboratory for Applied Ontology, Trento, Italy
gguizzardi@inf.ufes.br,
nicola.guarino@cnr.it, jpalmeida@ieee.org

Abstract. Different disciplines have been established to deal with the representation of entities of different ontological natures: the business process modeling discipline focuses mostly on event-like entities, and, in contrast, the (structural) conceptual modeling discipline focuses mostly on object-like entities (known as *endurants* in the ontology literature). In this paper, we discuss the impact of the event vs. endurant divide for conceptual models, showing that a rich ontological account is required to bridge this divide. Accounting for the ontological differences in events and endurants as well as their relations can lead to a more comprehensive representation of business reality.

Contents

Prediction

Keynotes

Rethinking BPM in a Cognitive World: Transforming How We Learn and Perform Business Processes

Richard Hull[1]([✉]) and Hamid R. Motahari Nezhad[2]

[1] IBM T.J. Watson Research Center, New York, USA
hull@us.ibm.com
[2] IBM Almaden Research Center, San Jose, USA
motahari@us.ibm.com

Abstract. If we are to believe the technology hype cycle, we are entering a new era of Cognitive Computing, enabled by advances in natural language processing, machine learning, and more broadly artificial intelligence. These advances, combined with evolutionary progress in areas such as knowledge representation, automated planning, user experience technologies, software-as-a-service and crowdsourcing, have the potential to transform many industries. In this paper, we discuss transformations of BPM that advances in the Cognitive Computing will bring. We focus on three of the most signficant aspects of this transformation, namely: (a) Cognitive Computing will enable "knowledge acquisition at scale", which will lead to a transformation in Knowledge-intensive Processes (KiP's); (b) We envision a new process meta-model will emerge that is centered around a "Plan-Act-Learn" cycle; and (c) Cognitive Computing can enable learning about processes from implicit descriptions (at both design- and run-time), opening opportunities for new levels of automation and business process support, for both traditional business processes and KiP's. We use the term *cognitive BPM* to refer to a new BPM paradigm encompassing all aspects of BPM that are impacted and enabled by Cognitive Computing. We argue that a fundamental understanding of cognitive BPM requires a new research framing of the business process ecosystem. The paper presents a conceptual framework for cognitive BPM, a brief survey of state of the art in emerging areas of Cognitive BPM, and discussion of key directions for further research.

1 Introduction

Business Process Management (BPM) remains a central, foundational element of running organizations today. This paper explores how BPM will be impacted by advances in *Cognitive Computing* [3,8,10,12], an emerging family of technologies that include natural language processing (NLP), machine learning, and the ability of systems to improve through experiential learning. We believe Cognitive Computing, combined with evolutionary advances in other fields including knowledge representation, automated planning, software-as-a-service, user experience technologies, and crowdsourcing, will transform the BPM ecosystem in

© Springer International Publishing Switzerland 2016
M. La Rosa et al. (Eds.): BPM 2016, LNCS 9850, pp. 3–19, 2016.
DOI: 10.1007/978-3-319-45348-4_1

fundamental ways. Cognitive Computing will enable "knowledge acquisition at scale" with the help of emerging methods for natural language understanding and machine learning at scale. It will change the nature of Knowledge-intensive Processes (KiP's) [4], including a shift in their underlying process meta-model. Advances in Cognitive Computing will enable new ways of learning and enacting processes at both design- and run-time. It will open opportunities for new levels of automation and business process support for all types of processes including KiP's.

Over the last decade BPM research has been expanded in many directions, to support more flexible business process [18], process mining [22], case management applications [13,19,23], and social BPM [1]. There has been some work around bringing AI planning into business process space [14,15] and processing textual information related to processes [21]. However, most of this research has remained close to the traditional BPM framework, with fairly clear separation between process models (or "schemas") and process instances. Less attention has been given to laying a BPM foundation for bringing the benefits of process automation over unstructured and semi-structured information, and contexts where the separation between process model and process instance is blurred or essentially non-existent. A key theme of this paper is to advance this discussion towards *Cognitive Process Enablement*, that will enable a whole new level of flexibility in business processing while nevertheless enabling traditional levels of auditing, monitoring, reporting, provenance, and also learning from experience. Important work in this direction is provided by recent exploration of KiP's [4,6]. A pioneering work is also [16], that applies cognitive techniques to learn processes as they progress, and help to guide and facilitate them along the way.

Another important, but largely unexplored, aspect of BPM is that of learning the business processes that are *implicitly described* in text or other forms rather than explicitly modeled. In [17] these have been termed "descriptive processes", as opposed to "prescriptive processes", to highlight the fact that there is no formal process model specification. Instead these processes are described by the process instances themselves, by "digital exhaust" such as communications between parties (e.g., emails, forums), and by purpose-built natural language documents (e.g., processing guidelines, best practices, regulations, and corporate policies). In the context of transaction-intensive processes that are not automated, the emerging capability for *Cognitive Process Learning* can enable a cost-effective approach for mapping the processes to formal process models and then deploying them. Furthermore, we argue that Cognitive Process Learning, together with a Plan-Act-Learn based meta-model, has the potential of enabling the formal specification and automation of many semi-structured and unstructured business processes that today are not formalized in process models. This will rely on advances in NLP and Machine Learning that hold the promise of extracting goals, best practices, actor intentions, commitments, promises, process fragments and the like from implicit descriptions, including those produced during run time.

We use the term *Cognitive BPM*[1], to refer to a new paradigm in BPM which encompass all BPM contexts and aspects of the BPM ecosystem that are impacted and enabled by the application of Cognitive Computing technologies. This paper provides a conceptual framework for Cognitive BPM in general, introduces key modeling abstractions that will be used in Cognitive BPM, discusses cognitive learning of business processes, and how Cognitive Computing will enable a new style of KiP's. We present the basis for a new process meta-model, called *Plan-Act-Learn*, which can support the full range from structured to unstructured processes in a seamless and systematic manner. The paper describes recent research advances, and identifies key research challenges going forward.

Organizationally, Sect. 2 provides the context for our discussion. Section 3 lays out a framework for Cognitive Computing and BPM, and briefly surveys how Cognitive Computing is already surfacing in the BPM marketplace. Sections 4, 5, 6 discuss, respectively, cognitive Process Model abstractions, Process Learning, and Process Enablement. Section 7 provides a summary of the discussion.

2   The Context

This section describes an overall context in which we explore the impact of Cognitive Computing on BPM. We identify three broad classes of Business Processes, and briefly discuss the emerging trends in Cognitive Computing that are relevant to BPM.

2.1   Three Classes of Business Process

Figure 1 identifies three broad types of Business Process, as follows.

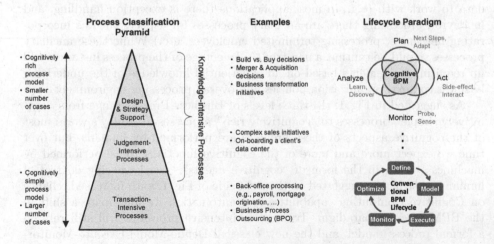

Fig. 1. Workforce pyramid and alternative BPM lifecycles

[1] The term was coined in our earlier work [17].

Transaction-intensive Processing, i.e., processes that are well-defined and are executed many times. Typical examples include week-to-week payroll processing, supply chain management, accounts receivables, etc., within the enterprise, and typical on-line purchasing and self-help in the retail and service industries.

Judgement-intensive Processes, i.e., human-driven operational work requiring many judgements involving complex information, organizations and systems. Examples include processes such as managing new sales relationships, performing project management for large scale IT or other on-boarding engagements, or investigating fraudulent activities. Adaptive Case Management has emerged to help support these kinds of operations, but in practice many of these processes are still *ad hoc,* manual procedures managed using spreadsheets.

Design and Strategy Support Processes, that involve open-ended creative collaborative work, including many decisions based on broad areas of knowledge and analysis. Examples here include the early stages of merger and acquisition explorations, of build vs. buy decisions, and also business model transformation explorations. While these processes may follow a family of best practices, they often have an unstructured and *ad hoc* nature, because of the many possible directions that may need to be explored.

Processes in the second and third categories are often referred to as "Knowledge-intensive Processes (KiP's)" [4] because of the amount and complexity of knowledge that is used, acquired, and manipulated as they progress.

Actually, most Transaction-Intensive Processes have some characteristics related to KiP's. In particular, there is a substantial amount of contextual knowledge that is relevant to the effective operation of transactional processes (e.g., the business motivations for the processes, how data flows into and out of the system, and regulations and corporate). More concretely, there are typically *ancillary processes* that are needed to ensure that the routine processes have appropriate data to work with (e.g., in most applications there is exception handling, and in Payroll processing there are ancillary processes for aspects such as incorporating new hires, processing terminated employees, etc.) While these ancillary processes should be routine, a non-trivial percentage of the process instances end up requiring judgements based on an experiential knowledge of the underlying business context, organization policies and overall processing environment.

As suggested in Fig. 1, the three levels of Business Process range from "cognitively simple" processes to "cognitively rich" processes. In today's world most of the cognitive aspects of these proceses are performed by humans, but over time we expect more and more of the cognitive functions to be performed by machines – often in the form of "cognitive agents" – with varying degrees of human oversight. As suggested on the right side of Fig. 1, with increased reliance on Cognitive Computing capabilities and automation we anticipate a shift in the BPM lifecycle paradigm. Transaction-intensive processes will still rely on a formal process model, and the now classical Define-Model-Execute-Monitor-Optimize cycle. In contrast, as suggested in the Introduction, automation of cognitively-rich KiP's will rely on a new kind of BPM lifecycle, where the separation between process model and process instance is largely blurred or nonexistant. As described in Sect. 4 below, relatively static process models will be replaced by iterative planning; monitoring will occur continuously both within individual instances and across larger families of them; and analysis will be used for learning in a range of areas, including process refinements and also about the application domain and the particular instance at hand.

2.2   Overview of Cognitive Computing

The area of Cognitive Computing is still emerging, and there is no widely accepted definition. Many companies, including IBM [10], Hewlett Packard [8], Deloitte [3], and KPMG [12], are offering visions for what Cognitive Computing is and how it will impact industry and our world. Reference [10] states that "[c]ognitive computing refers to systems that learn at scale, reason with purpose and interact with humans naturally. Rather than being explicitly programmed, they learn and reason from their interactions with us and from their experiences with their environment." This vision of Cognitive Computing is still coming into reality, but Cognitive Computing techniques are already being considered in the BPM context (see Subsect. 3.2).

For this paper, we are most interested in how key technologies considered within the Cognitive Computing umbrella will enable extending automation of traditional processes, and to support automation of less structured processes, including Judgement-Intensive and Design and Strategy Support ones, that are generally not supported by formal process models today. The technologies we focus on include: natural language understanding (both rules-based and statistical), machine learning (especially in connection with text) knowledge representation and reasoning about knowledge, planning, and experiential learning. These capabilities are becoming available both as traditional in-house functionalities and as cloud-hosted Software-as-a-Service (SaaS). We anticipate that these services will become widely available and relatively inexpensive in the coming years, enabling "always-on Cognitive Computing".

3   Towards a framework for cognitive BPM

This section provides a conceptual framework for understanding the key ways that Cognitive Computing will transform BPM in the coming years. Also included is a brief survey of emerging cognitive capabilities in the BPM industry.

3.1   Four Pillars

As shown in Fig. 2, the framework rests in part on the new kinds of information that Cognitive Computing can make sense of, including unstructured data, Internet of Things (IoT) data, new kinds of "smart" devices, and etc. Cognitive Computing will leverage and improve on human-to-human collaboration because of new capabilities to ingest and reason about natural language communication,

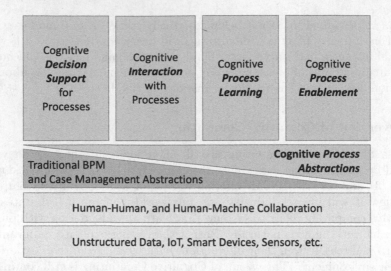

Fig. 2. A conceptual framework for cognitive BPM

and will improve on human-machine collaboration through better communication, and through machines being immensely better at understanding, reasoning about, and carrying out human goals and intentions.

The next layer of Fig. 2 highlights the fact that Cognitive Computing will be applicable in traditional BPM and Case Management contexts, and will also call for and enable new classes of Business Process not supported by process automation today. Cognitive Computing can accelerate the arrival of the next generation in BPM, by enabling the development of a fundamentally new family of process abstractions that will support much richer, more adaptive, more proactive, and more user-friendly styles of process coordination (see Sect. 4).

The four pillars across the top of Fig. 2 correspond to the primary ways that businesses and users will experience the impacts of Cognitive Computing on BPM.

Cognitive Decision Support: Many processes today, from structured to unstructured rely on human effort to make decisions based on deep experience and with reference to large volumes of unstructured data. Cognitive Computing will enable a mammoth increase in the quantity and breadth of such decisions.

Cognitive Interaction: Most human interaction with Business Process systems today is confined to screens, and often relies on constrained sequencing of steps. Advances in multi-modal human-computer interaction and in Cognitive Computing offer a rich opportunity for dramatically improving these interactions by supporting new interaction channels and devices. Importantly, these can enable new styles of collaborative work, e.g., to support collaborative goal formulation and collaborative decision making (with active participation from cognitive agents).

Cognitive Process Learning: Many processes are described only implicitly, in purpose-built documents, digital exhaust, and system logs. Across the full spectrum from structured to unstructured processes, Cognitive Computing can help to capture and codify process specifications, to enable much more automation while still retaining the requisite flexibility.

Cognitive Process Enablement: The separation of process model and process instance as found in classical BPM and Case Management is too confining for cognitively rich KiP's. The vision of Cognitive Process Enablement is to enable a vastly different style of business process support that puts the users back in charge. The underlying process model is highly event-driven, and focused on ongoing goal formation, learning of relevant knowledge including constraints, and planning and decision making.

3.2 Cognitive in Today's BPM Marketplace

KPMG's report [11] provides insights into how the industry is incorporating automation into business operations. They use the overall term *Robaotic Process Automation* to refer to three classes of automation. First is *Basic Process Automation* which focuses on the automation of manual tasks through "screen scraping" and application of rules engines on structured data. These capabilities have been available to the industry for several years. Second is *Enhanced Process Automation*, is essentially the Cognitive Decision Support pillar of Fig. 2. These applications are becoming available and are still maturing. The third stage is termed *Autonomic/Cognitive*; this is essentially the Process Learning and Process Enablement pillars of Fig. 2. The report suggests that common application of the Class 3 automation in industry is at least three to five years in the future. The report also suggests that different industries will adopt Robotic Process Automation in different time frames, with IT as the earliest adopter; Sourcing/Procurement, Finance and Accounting, Human Resources, and Supply chain/Logistics in a next wave of adoption, and Real Estate Financial Modeling and Legal after that.

There are early-stage products and offerings in Class 3, the Cognitive Process Learning and Enablement space. For example, the Amelia offering from IPsoft [9] and the Ignio product from Digitate (and offshoot of Tata Consulting) [5] apply machine learning and other Cognitive capabilities to increase automation and optimization of IT services delivery. Also, the Holmes Cognitive System from Wipro is applying cognitive computing capabilities in variety of enterprise and business process management scenarios. The Wipro Holmes web site [24] describes solutions that apply Cognitive Computing in areas such as IT Help Desk, prescription fulfillment, retail purchasing assistance, and compliance.

4   Abstractions for Cognitively-Enabled BPM

As suggested in Sect. 2, a new BPM paradigm is needed to take full advantage of Cognitive Computing. At the same time, Cognitive Computing will help to enable this new paradigm. This section identifies some of the key building blocks that are anticipated in the new paradigm. The abstractions described here are most relevant to the Judgement-Intensive and Design and Strategy Support processes discussed in Sect. 2. They may also become relevant to the more knowledge-intensive portions of Transaction-Intensive Processes.

The abstractions needed for cognitively-enabled BPM have significant overlap with those discussed in the emerging field of Knowledge-intensive Processes (KiP's). Indeed, several of the key abstractions that we highlight below are present in some form in the extensive survey of KiP requirements [4], in the KiP ontology [6], and the discussions reported in [2]. There are two points of divergence, however. The first is that Cognitive Computing brings the possibility of "knowledge at scale", because cognitive techniques can be used to automatically sift through vast amounts of unstructured data and harvest correspondingly large amounts of knowledge relevant to a process instance. The second is defining abstractions that enable systematic process support for the full spectrum from structured to unstructured processes.

4.1   Key Building Blocks

The key building blocks for cognitively-enabled business processes include the following.

Knowledge, Including Constraints: Knowledge at scale is the fundamentally new element that Cognitive Computing brings to BPM. The possibility of knowledge coming from virtually unlimited sources, and being applied to many different aspects of an on-going process instance, dramatically increases the need for highly flexible processing, that can react to unexpected new information quickly and appropriately Constraints, rules and policies on the process form an important aspect of the overall knowledge base. These may relate to costs, availability of resources, timing, allowed limits and behavior, and many other factors. The constraints may change over time, and impact decisions and planning.

Goals/Subgoals: A key concept in cognitively-enabled business processes is the notion of *goals*. Initial top-level goals may be specified in advance, and additional goals and sub-goals can be formulated dynamically, based on events in the environment, the current context, new learnings, best practices, and a myriad of other factors.

Agents (Human and Machine): Cognitively-enabled processes will be centered around both human and (automated) cognitive agents. These agents will have varying intentions, roles, and specialties. Collaboration between these agents will be rich and on-going. Communications between the agents may be captured, analyzed, and used in future aspects of a process.

Decisions: Agents will make decisions based on information and knowledge acquired through the process. These decisions may lead to new goals or the achieving of Goals, to Actions (see below), or to Plans (see below).

Actions: An action is an atomic unit of work performed by the agent. The actions in a cognitively-enabled process may side-effect the external environment and/or may lead to new learning.

Plans: A plan (or an action plan) consists of one or more related actions and is used to achieve goals, and may introduce sub-goals. The plans in cognitively-enabled processes may be revised as new information comes in and/or new decisions are made. Plans can be viewed as process model fragments, but their usage is quite different: Plans may be created frequently, modified frequently, and will generally be updated after taking action(s), within the plan, as a result of decisions made.

Events: Most cognitively-enabled processes will be highly event-driven. This is feasible in part because of the highly flexible process model (see below). It is also feasible because automated cognitive agents will be able to rapidly analyze the significance of most incoming events, thereby enabling (human or automated) decisions about whether and how to respond to them. The events may come from the external environment, from the results of information analysis or knowledge acquisition, or from decisions made by agents.

4.2 Plan-Act-Learn Cycle for Cognitively-Enabled Processes

Cognitively-enabled BPM will require a highly flexible process model, that can nevertheless support systematic monitoring and reporting, audits, provenance and explanation, and repeatability. Similar to KiP's [4], processing might range from structured to unstructured, and all points in between.

We conjecture that an appropriate process meta-model for cognitively-enabled BPM will be based on a *Plan-Act-Learn* cycle, as illustrated in Fig. 3. One part of this triad is focused on the planning and deciding portions of the process, which may be carried out by humans, by machines, or by a combination. The plans and decisions may lead to world side-effecting actions (e.g., using resources, transferring funds or goods). The plans and decisions may also lead to learning activities, e.g., the ingestion and analysis of relevant data. This will feed into an ever-expanding knowledge base. Events from the environment, and also environmental reactions to process actions, may contribute to the knowledge base. Finally, the knowledge base will lead to further decisions, goals, and plans.

In terms of more conventional BPM systems, we anticipate that the Plan-Act-Learn cycle can be supported by a kind of "universal" cognitive case management

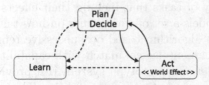

Fig. 3. The Plan-Act-Learn cycle for next-generation cognitively-enabled BPs. (Dashed lines indicate optional pathways.)

system that is integrated with a knowledge management system. In such a system, case instances might be used to manage plans and plan fragments, and also goals and sub-goals. These case instances could record progress of plans and towards goals, and also information relevant for provenance and audits. Newly arriving events could be processed by multiple of the case instances in parallel, and might also lead to the creation of new case instances. Note that a traditional BPM or Case Management process model can be supported in this framework, in essence by including the process model in the knowledge base, and having the plan-act steps repeatedly refer to that process model when deciding what to do next.

The high variability of Plan-Act-Learn-based process instances will call for a re-thinking of how to support traditional BPM capabilities such as monitoring, auditing, and improvments through analytics on history. What remains fairly constant across the highly variable ways that Plan-Act-Learn-based instances might play out? A possible answer is to shift the focus of monitoring, etc., towards the higher-level goals and also "control points", that is, business-relevant observable actions (side-effects) that need to occur in all or a substantial percentage of the process instances.

4.3   Recent Initiatives Embodying Key Abstractions

This subsection surveys three recent research systems, each of which embodies a subset of the key abstractions just described.

Citation [20] describes a system that supports the Plan-Act-Learn cycle by using a form of "universal" case management system as advocated above. The system is illustrated by using an example in city government, where advisors to a mayor collaborate to make recommendations to the mayor about various proposals. For any given proposal there may be multiple processing steps and multiple activities to gather information using a variety of (primarily manual) mechanisms. The system is implemented on top of a Guard-Stage-Milestone (GSM) business artifact system (a foundational element for modern Case Management [13]); this provides the advantage of modeling both processing steps and data as first-class citizens.

Reference [7] provides an important early step towards the rich goal-driven style of process management that will be needed for cognitively-enabled BPM. The focus of this paper is to dramatically simplify the job of business analysts when designing a business process that is intended to achieve certain goals. This research models goals as a collection of boolean conditions (in Conjuctive Normal Form), models a library of tasks that include their effects modeled as boolean conditions, and also models a set of constraints on how tasks can be sequenced. The paper describes an algorithm based on successive refinements of the goals into subgoals that yield an ontological match with capabilities of available tasks.

The SmartPM model and prototype system [14] provides on-going contextual awareness and automated planning capabilities. The system uses BPMN to provide a process model, but enables flexible adaptations to a process instance as required by incoming events or new information. The adaptation may involve the creation of a new plan, which can thereby resolve exceptions that were not designed into the original process. The family of tasks used by the system is defined at design-time, and includes pre- and post-conditions expressed in terms of data objects and attributes, also defined at design time. SmartPM provides a very important demonstration of how on-going planning can be incorporated into a buisness process system; extensions will be needed to support the incorporation of new data types and tasks during run-time, and to permit richer kinds of data and knowledge in the planning.

5   Towards Cognitive Learning of Business Process

A significant impediment to the automation of business processes today stems from the challenges of learning processes that are described only implicitly, i.e. not explicitly specified and modeled. Cognitive Computing holds the promise of automatically learning many aspects of such processes, thereby substantially reducing the cost of automation. Furthermore, as discussed in Sect. 6, in the case of Judgement-Intensive Processes and Design and Strategy Support Processes, the learning can be interleaved with process enablement to provide recommendations and guidance along the way.

Three dimensions of learning about process are considered: from structured data, from purpose-built documents, and from (unstructured) "digital exhaust". The structured and unstructured cases are considered here separately, but in practice they will be used in combination.

A variety of structured data sources may be available in connection with an implicitly described process. For the ancillary processes around Transaction-Intensive processes, system logs of the core processes can provide a wealth of information. In particular, techniques from Process Mining [22] may be applied to learn the process models that underly both the core processes, and also some of the ancillary processes. For example, the steps that were taken to insert a new hire into a payroll system might be identified by looking at log entries of tasks that involve data about the new employee at times around when that employee started work. While most process mining work is focused on process, it will be important in cognitive learning to gain a holistic understanding of the overall process, including data manipulation, and constraints on data and processing.

Similar techniques might be applied for Transaction-Intensive and Design and Strategy Support Processes, although there may be less log data available, logs may contain less- or semi-structured information and the available log data may be harder to find and extract.

We turn now to learning from unstructured data. One kind of unstructured data consists of *purpose-built documents*, that is documents that were created specifically to describe aspects of a process. These include actual natural language descriptions of (parts of) a process. These also include documents that give high-level guidelines and/or constraints about a process, including best practice descriptions, corporate policies and government regulations. The other kind of unstructured data is called here *digital exhaust*, and consists of documents and other digitally available records that are created during execution of process instances. This can include emails between process participants (and hopefully, live conversations between them), entries into process-relevant wikis or forums, the contents of trouble tickets, calendar entries, and also informally structured documents such as spreadsheets, powerpoints, etc.

Techniques are emerging for learning processes from both kinds of unstructured data. For example, [21] uses information extraction techniques to identify tasks and their sequencing from textual process descriptions, to enable comparison the text description with a formal specification (e.g., in BPMN) of the process. The text analytics is performed primarily using the Stanford Parser, which provides a rich family of rules-based capabilities for text analytics. While the approach of this paper assumes availability of a formal specification of a process, it appears that the techniques could be expanded to learn a fair amount about a process model from the text description alone.

An emerging sub-area that is gaining attention is to apply text analytics to government regulations to extract rules and constraints on processes to ensure compliance. A representative work in this area is [25]. This combines both statistical and rules-based approaches to NLP: first, statistically-based techniques are used to classify sentences that are deemed to hold regulatory information; second, these are processed using a rules-based approach, Rules relating to both industry-specific terminologies and an industry-specific ontology are also used.

Techniques are also emerging for learning process from digital exhaust, primarily email. The use of NLP techniques on email is a well-traveled field, with several tools now available that analyze email to provide personal assistance (e.g., Google Now, Microsoft Cortana, Amazon Echo). In contrast, there are only a handful of papers focused on extracting process-relevant aspects from emails, such as tasks and actions. We highlight here the eAssistant system [16], which combines both statistical and linguistic, rule-based techniques key process building blocks. The focus there is on *actionable statements*, which include both promises and requests, and *actions*, which include adding to a "to-do" list, adding to a "follow-up" list, responding to a question, scheduling a meeting, etc., and action lists (i.e., process fragments). In addition to finding these, eAssistant includes an adaptive component, that enables extensibility of feature sets being looked for, and supports online, continuous trainability. (eAssistant can also help to guide processes at runtime; see Sect. 6).

What about the accuracy of the information learned from the above techniques? The use of NLP techniques to learn BPM-relevant information is in its infancy, and so improvements will be on-going. Current techniques are essentially classification-based, and it is typical to measure accuracy in terms of precision (of the objects classifed as target what percentage are actually target objects) and recall (what percentage of target objects are classified as being target). These measures generally have an inverse relationship. Speaking broadly, automated NLP techniques typically have precision and recall in the 70 % to 95 % range. This highlights the importance of enabling humans to understand the outputs of automated learning.

6   Towards Cognitive Process Enablement

Cognitive Process Enablement refers to the ways that Cognitive Computing, taken broadly, can enhance the actual processes that carry out business operations, considered at the level of process modeling. We are focused here on how the processes themselves will be impacted by Cognitive Computing.

Cognitive Computing will impact both classical BPM (and Case Management) processes, and also processes that follow the Plan-Act-Learn meta-model. A central impact, relevant to both settings, is that Cognitive Computing will lead to processing constructs that are at a semantic level higher than those of conventional BPM – including goals, plans, policies/rules, and constraints. These constructs, called here *cognitive BPM constructs* will be both human-understandable and (directly or indirectly) machine-executable. A second key impact, relevant mainly to the Plan-Act-Learn cycle, is that the Cognitive Computing capabilities will be applied repeatedly and in near real time to provide input into the Plan/Decide step.

Although not addressed here, knowledge of implicitly described processes and the perspective provided by the cognitive BPM constructs can be used in other ways, e.g., to verify compliance of a process with regulations, or to streamline modifications of structured processes.

6.1   Classical BPM Setting

Suppose that automated learning as described in Sect. 5 is used on implicit process information in order to build a deployable process model. Because NLP techniques are generally not 100 % accurate, the learned process model will have to be vetted and revised by humans, and will also need to be tested. There is also the question of what kinds of job roles will be needed to vet, adjust, and test the learned process models (and model fragments). Effort should be made to enable Business Analysts to perform all or most of the process modeling adjustments, so that the added cost and delay of bringing in IT specialists and software engineers is minimized. It will be beneficial to present the model using both standard process constructs and cognitive BPM constructs.

These requirements help to envision an overall framework and system for cognitive enablement of the learning and deployment of classical BPM and Case Management process models. A main component is for the learning, including identification and ingestion of implicit process descriptions, logs, and etc. This component will be akin to many Data Science application frameworks, with a rich on-going combination of people and programs to learn and refine the process model, and also to help with evolution over time. Key outputs from the learning, in addition to actual process model constructs, will be *explanations* of the constructs, including, e.g., how they relate to the implicit descriptions. Another main component of the framework will be for testing and refinement. This should be aimed at Business Analysts, and should include Cognitive Computing capabilities to aid with identifying appropriate tests and process model improvements.

6.2 Plan-Act-Learn Setting

In the grand vision of Cognitive Process Enablement, a family of (automated) cognitive agents are used as smart, creative, and pro-active helpers that assist the human in the enactment of processes, and learn the human users' goals for each initiative, and learn context, preferences, and best practices over time. Cognitive agents should understand the capabilities of all resources available, including the agents (both human and automated). Agents are supported in launching new sub-activities, hypothetical explorations, trials, and conventional processes in a free form way. The cognitive agent serves as a proactive project manager, proactively suggesting ideas and approaches, providing expert advice and decision support, analyzing many what-if?scenarios, proactively performing investigations across structured and unstructured data on its own, identifying resources (including personnel), keeping track of schedules, managing and guiding collaborative activities, and recording decisions.

While this vision is some years off, there is a broad base of research to draw from, including in knowledge representation, planning, and multi-agent systems. As one illustration, the eAssistant system [16] mentioned above brings together learning about inflight processes with knowledge representation to provide run-time guidance and support for Judgement-Intensive processes. More broadly, we anticipate that cognitively-enabled processes will be founded on a Plan-Act-Learn cycle, so that they can quickly respond to new events and newly learned knowledge.

We briefly mention several of the key near- and medium-term challenges in the process management space raised by this grand vision. Advances in *goal identification* and *planning* are clearly needed. Massive amounts of application-specific knowledge acquisition creates a challenge in *knowledge representation, prioritization, and explanation*, that is, enabling agents to take advantage of knowledge that is relevant to a decision or task at hand, and ignore knowledge that is irrelevant.

Advances are needed in *process-specific knowledge acquisition*. A specific challenge relates to *event monitoring and triage*, and in particular, tools that enable appropriate response to incoming events, be they from the environment, from agents, or from newly acquired knowledge.

Cognitive Computing holds the potential of automating large swathes of the *Project Management* function, i.e., keeping track of the overall process, deadlines, shifting requirements, etc., and to alert relevant stakeholders to new events, trends, requirements, and delays.

Finally there is the challenge of *trust*. Mechanisms to encourage trust will need to be built into all levels of cognitively-enabled processes; this includes the services that can explain and support testing of essentially all of the automated decisions and plans that are made.

7 Summary and Key Steps for Cognitive BPM Research

This paper has laid out a framework for understanding how Cognitive Computing will impact the practice of BPM over the next several years, and focused primarily on emerging perspectives for cognitive process abstractions, cognitive process learning, and cognitive process enablement. Our findings are relevant to the full spectrum of business processes, from Transaction-Intensive, to Judegement-Intensive, to Design and Strategy Support.

This paper describes many of the research challenges that Cognitive Computing brings to BPM. We conclude by reiterating the most important of the research themes that are most central to the BPM community.

Automatic Learning about Business Process. This learning will be at "design time" (e.g., from purpose-built documents, historical digital exhaust, and system logs), and at "run time" (e.g., from asserted requirements and goals, fresh digital exhaust including human collaborations, and the process instance history). The learning needs to be geared towards process automation and enhancement, including semi-automated Project Management, pro-active knowledge acquisition, and guiding of human activities.

Embracing Flexibility: The Plan-Act-Learn cycle. A new kind of process meta-model is needed for KiP's in the context of "knowledge acquistion at scale". We have proposed to base this on the Plan-Act-Learn cycle. But there is a huge distance between this high-level proposal and a robust framework and technology base that can support benefits such as monitoring, provenance, auditability, and ability to refine based on previous performance.

Trust: Explanation, Testing and Manual Adjustment. Trust is essential for automation to be successful. Tools and techniques developed for cognitively-enabled BPM must include confidence-building components at many levels.

Acknowledgements. The authors wish to than several IBM colleagues for numerous inspirational discussions on the topics presented in this paper, including Currie Boyle, Robert Farrell, Janet Hunter, Matthias Kloppmann Rong Liu, Mike Marin, Manoj Mishra, Nirmal Mukhi, Jae-eun Park, Karthikeyan Ponnalagu, Michael Oland, Eniko Rozsa, Stuart Strolin, and John Vergo. The authors also thank members of the working group [2] on Knowledge-intensive Processes (KiP's) at the Dagstuhl workshop on "Fresh Approaches to Business Process Modeling" held in April, 2016, where the discussions were very stimulating and informative.

References

1. Brambilla, M., Fraternali, P., Vaca, C.: BPMN and design patterns for engineering social BPM solutions. In: Business Process Management Workshops, pp. 219–230 (2011)
2. Brucker, A., Gal, A., Herwix, A., Hull, R., Mecella, M., Nezhad, H.R.M., Santoro, F.M., Slaats, T., Wong, W.: Knowledge-intensive Processes. Unpublished manuscript created by a working group during the Dagstuhl workshop on "Fresh Approaches to Business Process Modeling", 8 May 2016

3. Deloitte. Artificial intelligence, real results. http://www2.deloitte.com/content/dam/Deloitte/global/Documents/About-Deloitte/gx-gr15-artificial-intelligence-computing-capabilities.pdf. Accessed 01 July 2016
4. Di Ciccio, C., Marrella, A., Russo, A.: Knowledge-intensive processes: characteristics, requirements and analysis of contemporary approaches. J. Data Semant. **4**(1), 29–57 (2015)
5. Ignio: Neural automation system for enterprises. https://www.digitate.com. Accessed 01 July 2016
6. dos Santos França, J.B., Netto, J.M., do E.S. Carvalho, J., Santoro, F.M., Baião, F.A., Pimentel, M.G.: KIPO: the knowledge-intensive process ontology. Softw. Syst. Model. **14**(3), 1127–1157 (2015)
7. Ghose, A.K., Narendra, N.C., Ponnalagu, K., Panda, A., Gohad, A.: Goal-driven business process derivation. In: Kappel, G., Maamar, Z., Motahari-Nezhad, H.R. (eds.) Service Oriented Computing. LNCS, vol. 7084, pp. 467–476. Springer, Heidelberg (2011)
8. Hewlett Packard. Augmented intelligence: Helping humans make smarter decisions. http://www8.hp.com/tw/zh/software-solutions/asset/software-asset-viewer.html?asset=2195447&module=1970414. Accessed 01 July 2016
9. IPSoft home page. http://www.ipsoft.com/. Accessed 01 July 2016
10. Kelley III, J.E.: Computing, cognition, and the future of knowing: how humans andmachines are forging a new age of understanding. http://www.research.ibm.com/software/IBMResearch/multimedia/Computing_Cognition_WhitePaper.pdf. Accessed 01 July 2016
11. Robotic Revolution – separating hype from reality, 5 October 2015. https://home.kpmg.com/xx/en/home/insights/2015/09/separating-hype-from-reality.html. Accessed 01 July 2016
12. KPMG. Embracing the cognitive era, February 2016. https://assets.kpmg.com/content/dam/kpmg/pdf/2016/03/embracing-the-cognitive-era.pdf. Accessed 01 July 2016
13. Marin, M., Hull, R., Vaculín, R.: Data-centric BPM the emerging Case management standard: a short survey. In: Business Process Management Workshops, pp. 24–30 (2012)
14. Marrella, A., Mecella, M., Sardiña, S.: SmartPM: an adaptive process management system through situationcalculus, indigolog, and classical planning. In: Proceedings of Conference on Principles of Knowledge Representation and Reasoning KR (2014)
15. Marrella, A., Mecella, M., Sardiña, S.: An adaptive process management system based on situation calculus, indigolog, and classical planning. In: Proceedings of International Joint Conference on Artificial Intelligence (IJCAI) (2016, to appear)
16. Nezhad, H.R.M.: Cognitive assistance at work. In: AAAI Fall Symposium Series. AAAI Publications, November 2015
17. Nezhad, H.R.M., Akkiraju, R.: Towards cognitive BPM as the next generation BPM platform for analytics-driven business processes. In: Business Process Management Workshops, pp. 158–164 (2014)
18. Reichert, M., Weber, B.: Enabling Flexibility in Process-Aware Information Systems - Challenges, Methods, Technologies. Springer, Berlin (2012)
19. Swenson, K. (ed.): Mastering the Unpredictable: How Adaptive Case Management Will Revolutionize The Way That Knowledge Workers Get Things Done. Meghan-Kiffer Press, Tampa (2010)
20. Vaculín, R., Hull, R., Vukovic, M., Heath, T., Mills, N., Sun, Y.: Supporting collaborative decision processes. In: 2013 IEEE International Conference on Services Computing, Santa Clara, CA, USA, June 28 - July 3, 2013, pp. 651–658 (2013)

21. van der Aa, H., Leopold, H., Reijers, H.A.: Detecting inconsistencies between process models and textual descriptions. In: Proceedings of International Conference on Business Process Management (BPM), pp. 90–105 (2015)
22. van der Aalst, W.M.P., et al.: Process mining manifesto. In: Business Process Management Workshops, pp. 169–194 (2011)
23. van der Aalst, W.M.P., Weske, M., Grünbauer, D.: Case handling: a new paradigm for business process support. Data Knowl. Eng. 53(2), 129–162 (2005)
24. Wipro Holmes web page. http://www.wipro.com/holmes/. Accessed 01 July 2016
25. Zhou, P., El-Gohary, N.: Ontology-based information extraction from environmental regulations for supporting environmental compliance checking. In: Computing in Civil Engineering, pp. 190–198 (2015)

Ontological Considerations About the Representation of Events and Endurants in Business Models

Giancarlo Guizzardi[1,2(✉)], Nicola Guarino[2],
and João Paulo A. Almeida[1]

[1] Federal University of Espírito Santo, Vitória, Brazil
gguizzardi@inf.ufes.br, jpalmeida@ieee.org
[2] ISTC-CNR Laboratory for Applied Ontology, Trento, Italy
nicola.guarino@cnr.it

Abstract. Different disciplines have been established to deal with the representation of entities of different ontological natures: the business process modeling discipline focuses mostly on event-like entities, and, in contrast, the (structural) conceptual modeling discipline focuses mostly on object-like entities (known as *endurants* in the ontology literature). In this paper, we discuss the impact of the event vs. endurant divide for conceptual models, showing that a rich ontological account is required to bridge this divide. Accounting for the ontological differences in events and endurants as well as their relations can lead to a more comprehensive representation of business reality.

Keywords: Events · Endurants · Reification · Conceptual modeling · Ontology

1 Introduction

"Smiles, walks, dances, weddings, explosions, hiccups, hand-waves, arrivals and departures, births and deaths, thunder and lightning: the variety of the world seems to lie not only in the assortment of its ordinary citizens—animals and physical objects, and perhaps minds, sets, abstract particulars—but also in the sort of things that happen to or are performed by them" [1]. This variety is also evident in business reality, with "processes", "activities", "tasks", "events", "occurrences", "incidents" unfolding in time, and "objects", "actors" and "resources" persisting through time. In enterprise architecture and modeling frameworks, the distinction between behavioral elements and structural elements ("how" versus "what") is often invoked to account for the different nature of these elements [2, 3]. The distinction between these categories is commonplace in philosophical literature, with the former broadly referred to as "events" and the latter broadly referred to as "objects" [1].

Different disciplines have been established to deal with the representation of these two ontological categories, each of which with a different focus: the business process modeling discipline focuses on event-like entities, and, in contrast, the (structural) conceptual modeling discipline focuses on object-like entities. In each of these

M. La Rosa et al. (Eds.): BPM 2016, LNCS 9850, pp. 20–36, 2016.
DOI: 10.1007/978-3-319-45348-4_2

disciplines, entities of one of these ontological categories are first-class citizens, while the other category plays a marginal role (if any). Some notable exceptions in the process discipline are the so-called business artifact-centric approaches [4–7], and in the structural conceptual modeling discipline, the event reification approach [8].

In this paper we investigate the ontological nature of events and object-like entities (which we will call here *endurants* in line with the philosophical literature). We discuss the impact of the event vs. endurant divide in conceptual modeling. A modeling pattern to capture events in structural conceptual models is proposed. The conceptual foundations underlying this pattern serve as the basis for establishing a suitable semantic foundation for business process models that incorporate reference to object-like entities, as well as for structural conceptual models that incorporate reference to events.

2 Ontology-Driven Modeling of Business Endurants and Events

2.1 Endurants in Structural Conceptual Models

Suppose a Person named Mr. Anderson. Mr. Anderson can genuinely change in time in a qualitative manner while still maintaining his numerical identity. For instance, suppose that Mr. Anderson weighs 70 kg at t_1 and 85 kg at t_2. This qualitative change does not alter the *identity* of Mr. Anderson. Moreover, Mr. Anderson can bear some modal properties. For instance, Mr. Anderson is *necessarily* a person but only *contingently* a computer hacker. In other words, while he instantiates the type person in all possible situations that he exists, he can cease to be a computer hacker without this change having an effect on his identity. Finally, we can perform counterfactual reasoning with Mr. Anderson. For instance, we can ponder what if Mr. Anderson had decided to study law as opposed to becoming a computer hacker? When doing this, we admit that Mr. Anderson (that in a different world is a student of law) is the *same* individual as the Mr. Anderson who in this world is a computer hacker. These are all commonly accepted characteristics of what in ontology is termed an *endurant* [9, 10].

In ontology, endurants are entities that, whenever they exist, they are wholly present, i.e., whenever they are present, they are present with all their parts. Moreover, endurants have both *essential properties* (i.e., properties they must bear in all possible situations) and *accidental properties* (properties they bear in some possible situations) [9]. In other words, endurants can qualitatively change in certain respects while maintaining their identity; they can (or could have been) different from what they actually are with respect to their accidental properties. What defines the essential and accidental properties of an individual is its kind. We mean here "kind" in a technical sense [9]: a kind is a type instantiated by an individual that provides a *principle of identity, individuation and persistence* for that individual; it defines the boundaries and parts of that individual; it supports the judgment of whether that individual is identical or not to another individual (including itself in a different situation); it provides a criteria for what qualitative changes an individual can undergo and still be the same. For instance, suppose that the kind Car provides the following criteria of identity for the legal concept of a car: *two cars are identical iff they have the same chassis number*.

So, for an individual c of kind Car, c can change all aspects (e.g., color, tires) and it will be the same car as long as it has the same chassis number.

Mr. Anderson is of the kind Person. As it is always the case for *kinds*, Mr. Anderson instantiates that kind *necessarily*, i.e., in all possible situations. This is fundamental because a principle of identity must support identity judgments in all possible situations. Thus, a principle of identity must be supplied by a type that is instantiated necessarily by its instances. However, there are types that Mr. Anderson instantiate only *contingently*. For example, he is now an Adult Man but he was once a Boy; he is an employee of company X, but he could have been a student at university Y. Types such as Adult Man, Boy, Employee or Student are contingent types, i.e., for all instances of those types, these instances instantiate them only contingently. For example, an individual x can enter or leave the extension of a type such as Boy or Student without ceasing to exist as the very same individual.

There is a difference, however, between, on the one hand Adult Man and Boy and, on the other hand, Student and Employee; namely, individuals enter or leave the extension of the former sort of types due to a change in intrinsic properties (age, in this case) while they enter or leave the extension of the latter sort of types due to a change in their relational properties (the creation or termination of enrollments and employments, respectively, in this case). Types of the former sort (i.e., contingently and relationally-independent types) are named *phases* and of the latter sorts (i.e., contingently and relationally-dependent types) are named *roles* [9].

Furthermore, we can have that both Mr. Anderson and Company X can play the roles of *renter* in a car rental. Types such as *renter* seem at first to be like a role since they are: contingently instantiated by their instances (no renter is necessarily a renter); relationally dependent (in order to be a renter someone needs to be connected to a rental). However, a role (like a phase) is what is called a *sortal*: a type whose instances are all of the same *kind*. In contrast, the type renter classifies entities that belong to multiple kinds. These are termed dispersive types or *mixins*. A mixin that is contingent and relationally dependent is termed a *role mixin* [9]. Finally, *kinds, phases, roles* and *role mixins* (among others) are sorts of types that apply to endurants, not only to objects like Mr. Anderson [11, 12]. For instance, the weight of Mr. Anderson is a *quality* (an objectified property) of Mr. Anderson that can also change while maintaining its identity. For instance, when we say: "the weight of Mr. Anderson is changing", we don't mean that 70 kg are changing! There is an entity there, localized in time and space, which can change in a qualitative way while maintaining its identity. Analogously, the employment of Mr. Anderson can change: it can go from being a non-tenured to a tenured employment (two *phases* of the employment); it can itself play the *role* of a legally recognized employment in a given jurisdiction. In summary, entities such as the weight, the hacking skills, the employment, the enrollment, the eventual marriage, the car rental are also endurants. However, different from Mr. Anderson himself, these are *existentially dependent* endurants, frequently called *qualities* [11].

In Fig. 1, we have a model partially representing a domain such as the one just described. In this domain there are only three *kinds* of objects (in dark grey), namely, *Person, Organization* and *Car*. There is one single kind of relational endurant (i.e., a *relator*), namely, *Car Rental*. These are the kinds of things that exist in this domain.

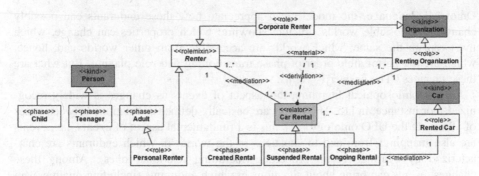

Fig. 1. Representing the possibility of change for endurants

Everything else in the model is a representation of a type that these kinds of things can instantiate contingently.

This model of Fig. 1 is represented in a conceptual modeling language termed OntoUML [9]. This language has been design to reflect the ontological distinctions and axiomatization put forth by the Unified Foundational Ontology (UFO) [9, 13]. In particular, this language has as modeling primitives those that represent ontological distinctions between all the aforementioned sorts of types (e.g., kinds, phase, roles, role mixins, relators). Figure 1 represents the possibility of change, i.e., how things could possibly be for the entities that are assumed to exist in this domain (i.e., people, organizations, cars and car rentals). In this approach, the OntoUML model of Fig. 1 can be automatically translated to knowledge representation languages such as OWL to support automated reasoning [13]. Moreover, as discussed in [13], the OntoUML approach offers a support for model validation via visual simulation. In this approach, the simulation of this model exposes its *ontological commitment* and allows us to find the possible difference between the intended state of affairs of this domain and the valid instances of this model. For instance, by simulating this model, one could find out that there is a possible instance in which an organization rents a car to itself (i.e., the roles of renter and renting organization are played by the very same entity).

One way to exclude these unintended modes is to enrich the model with formal constraints. The idea is to provide an axiomatization for the model such that set of its valid instances and the set of instances representing intended states of affairs of the domain coincide [13]. Some of these constraints are temporal constraints dealing, for example, with the life cycle of the endurants in the model. In particular, in the OntoUML approach, one can include temporal constraints (in temporal OCL) prescribing the permissible phase transitions in the model, for instance, from Child, to Teenager and (only then) to Adult, or governing the more complex transitions involved in the phases of a car rental [14].

2.2 Events in Business Process Models

As previously discussed, structural models such as in Fig. 1 represent what can possibility change and what has to remain the same in the properties of endurants, i.e., regarding matters of *necessity* and *possibility*. In the visual simulation support for the

OntoUML language, the modeler can appreciate how these endurants can possibly change in a possible worlds structure showing: which properties can change, which must remain the same; which worlds are accessible from other worlds and, hence, which are the permissible order of phase transitioning and role playing. But what are these changes? The answer is *events*.

In the philosophical literature, this aspect of events as changes is widely recognized. For instance, in [15, 16], events are basically defined as relations between states of affairs. In the UFO ontology [17], this is a fundamental aspect of events, i.e., events are also mappings from and to situations in the world, in which endurants are characterized by bearing certain properties (including relational ones). Among these changes, events can bring about situations in which endurants (including qualities) are brought into existence (i.e., are created), go out of existence (i.e., are destroyed), change their properties (via the creation and destruction of their intrinsic and relational qualities) or that they simply participate playing certain *processual roles*. For instance, in the killing of Caesar by Brutus with the dagger, we have the participation of three endurants (Caesar, Brutus, the dagger). However, their participations are of a completely different nature and it is the nature of these participations that induce their playing certain roles (victim, killer and murder instrument) in that event.

In UFO, these aspects of (i) change promoted by events and of (ii) endurant participation in events are only two among many aspects of events that receive an axiomatic treatment there. The ontology defines a fully axiomatized mereology of events (*extensional mereology*) prescribing how events relate to its parts. Moreover, it defines a theory about temporal precedence involving events, whose axiomatization incorporate the well-known *Allen Relations*. Additionally, it contemplates a *theory of causation* connecting situations brought about by events, which, in turn, trigger the occurrence of other events and so on, thus, making the world "tick". As much as for the case of endurants, events in UFO can be subject of predication. For instance, a conversation can be interesting or boring; a fight can be violent; a trip can be pleasant. Events typically also have qualities representing temporal and spatial features.

Finally, in UFO, events are manifestations of properties, in particular, of particular qualities and dispositions [17, 18]. So, for an event to unfold, the potentiality of that unfolding must exist as a concrete property of an endurant. As consequence, events are dependent on particularized properties (again, dispositions), which are in turn dependent on endurants. Ergo, events are dependent on endurants. For instance, the event of the *heart pumping* is the manifestation of the *heart's capacity to pump*; the event of the metal being attracted by the magnet is the manifestation of a number of dispositions of these entities (including the magnet's disposition to attract metallic material); Paul's Dengue Fever as a complex event is the manifestation of a number of complex dispositions that qualify that disease inhering in Paul; John & Mary's marriage as a process is the manifestation of a number of relational properties that constitute their marriage as an endurant (e.g., commitments and claims, expectations, etc.). Dispositions include propensities, capacities, capabilities, liabilities, etc. [18].

These aspects of UFO have been successfully used in the past to analyze and provide ontological foundations for Business Process Modeling languages such as ARIS [19], UML Activities Diagram [20] and BPMN [21], as well as Discrete Event Simulation approaches [22]. The results of these analyses provide for well-grounded representational mechanism that can be used to represent aspects of temporal ordering and (at least partially) aspects of object participation in events playing certain processual roles as well as aspects of event mereology. The notion of events as manifestation of dispositions inhering in certain endurants has been fundamental in our ontological analysis of the notion of *service* [23] as well as the notion of *capability* in enterprise architecture [24]. In this paper, this notion will play a key role in Sect. 3.4.

The aspect of events as changes can be represented by variations of state-machines capturing how the occurrence of events in certain conditions can promote a transition of an endurant to a different state [28]. For example, referring to model of Fig. 1, one can represent all allowed transitions between the phases of Car Rental as well as the events and conditions that promote these changes. Capturing this aspect of events is of uttermost importance and, in particular, for the case of relators. This is because the main goal of social reality (and, hence, of information systems) is to represent and control: the *life* of social relators such as enrollments, employments, contracts, rentals, allocations, presidential mandates, marriages; the social roles induced by them; and the events (including *speech acts*) that constitute their lives. We should highlight that in state-machine-like models such as in [7, 25], the events that can appear in these models are events that exist in potentially as *operations*, *functions* or *"services"* of the endurants that exist in that domain. This is conformant with a view that takes these operations, functions or "services" as dispositions (capacities, capabilities) of these endurants: they inhere in these endurants even if they are never manifested but all events that occur are manifestation of these dispositions.

In a language such as OntoUML, the possibility of change is explicitly represented in terms of contingent types such as phases and roles, and their relations. For instance, in Fig. 1, we can represent that only when an adult, a person can play the role of a Car Renter and only when a rental is ongoing we have a car associated to it. On the other hand, an OntoUML model, such as the one in this figure, explicitly identifies *phase partitions* as natural connection points for integrating behavioral models of changes (e.g., state-machines) with structural models of possibilities. In other words, OntoUML give us a clear methodological support for deciding for which types in a model of endurants we should specify a behavioral model of changes.

As discussed in this section, one of the aspects of events is that of events as changes. However, can we meaningfully talk about *changes in events*? This is a fundamental but often neglected topic in the literature of conceptual modeling. We shall address it in the next sections.

3   Events in Structural Conceptual Models

Structural conceptual models, such as the one of Fig. 1, have traditionally focused on the representation of endurants (e.g., objects, their intrinsic and relational properties, the types they instantiate, the roles they play, their parts, etc.). In fact, in classical conceptual modeling, events are rarely represented in these structural models as first-classes citizens. As a result, we can rarely represent the qualities of events as well as the underlying conceptual spaces from which these qualities can take their values. Although the representation of events as first-class citizens in structural conceptual models is openly defended in the literature [8], there is still no foundation for guiding their modeling with respect to a number of fundamental issues. Given that reference conceptual models should provide conceptual clarification and explicit characterization for notions comprising complex worldviews, and given that many of these notions refer to events, we find ourselves in a problematic situation. In this section, we address one of these fundamental issues, namely, the notion of identity, change and reference for events, exploring the consequences for the representation of events in structural conceptual models.

3.1 The Immutability of Events

Previously in this article, we talked about an endurant such as Mr. Anderson, who can: bear essential and accidental properties; qualitatively change in certain aspects while remaining the same; and, be the subject of counterfactual reasoning. Now, how shall we answer these questions regarding events? Can events genuinely change their properties while remaining the same? Can an event be the bearer of modal properties? In particular, can an event exhibit properties contingently? Can an event be different from what it is? Is there identity between events in different possible worlds?

If we look to *all classical axiomatized ontologies of events*, we would need to answer '*no*' to all these questions. According to these theories, an event is an extensional entity defined by the sum of its parts [17, 26]. It can be seen as a succession of changes in the world [15, 16], fully determined by participants, a temporal interval and the properties that are exemplified by the manifestation of the event [27, 28]. As a consequence, following these theories, an event could not been different from what it is. Had it been different, it would have different parts, it would be a different succession belonging to a different history and, hence, a different event. Furthermore, in the traditional literature, a key difference between endurants and events is that in the case of events there is nothing that endures, qualitatively changing while maintaining its identity [10]. If a discussion is peaceful at t_1 and litigious at t_2, there are different temporal parts of the discussion that bear these otherwise incompatible properties. In this view, there is nothing that is entirely present throughout the duration of the discussion. More precisely, take the branching-time possible worlds structure depicted in Fig. 2(a). Each of these branches corresponds to a *possible world as a possible history*. In these classical views, an event exists solely within one of these branches. For instance, events E_1, E_2, E_3 and E_4 are temporal parts of E'. Suppose there is another complex event E" composed by E_1, E_2, E_3 and E_5. In this case, E_1, E_2, E_3 are overlapping parts of both E' and E". However, E' and E" are distinct events.

Take, again, Mr. Anderson, our prototypical example of an endurant. While Mr. Anderson exists, there is a complex event associated with him, namely, Mr. Anderson's life (see Fig. 2(b)). Mr. Anderson's life can be seen as the successive exemplification of a number of (intrinsic and relation) properties of his. However, suppose that we are in a given point in time t_1 in which Mr. Anderson has to decide to either take the blue pill or take the red pill. If he takes the red pill, then in the moment succeeding t_1 (say, t_{1+1}) Mr. Anderson's life is a particular event E' (that includes the taking of the red pill). If instead, he takes the blue pill then, in the moment succeeding

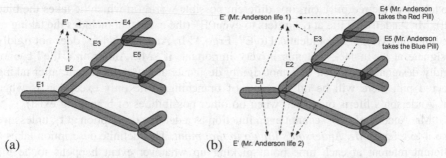

Fig. 2. (a) Events and their proper parts; (b) the life of an endurant as an event

that action, Mr. Anderson's life will be a different event E" (including the event of taking of the blue pill). Clearly, given all classical theories of events, E and E' are distinct individuals as they have different parts and incompatible properties.

3.2 The Role of Object Identifiers

In [29], Wieringa and de Jong report on a detailed study of the role of object identifiers in conceptual modeling. According to them, an object identifier should work as a *rigid designator* picking up the same individual in all possible worlds. For instance, they state that *"object identifiers (oids) are special kinds of proper names for denoting real-world objects"* and require an OID to refer in each state of the world to exactly one object. They term this requirement *singular reference* and point out that this require-ment also appears in authors such as Kent [30] (*singular* requirement for identifiers). The authors also require for an OID to remain referring to the very same object across different states of the world (in which they refer at all). They term the latter requirement *rigid reference*. As another example, in UML, the extension of a class C in a *class diagram* is a set of OIDs. These OIDs are supposed to trace the identity of the very same individual across different states.

With these requirements in mind, we should analyze Fig. 2(b). In particular, we should focus on the moment t_1 in which Mr. Anderson is pondering whether to take the red or the blue pill. As we have seen, "Mr. Anderson" should be a rigid designator, i.e., the referent of "Mr. Anderson" at a time t should be the same as the referent of "Mr. Anderson" at any time t'. Now, at time t_1, the referent of "Mr. Anderson" is the individual deliberating on what he should do regarding the pills. Whatever he does, the referent of "Mr. Anderson" at t_{1+1} is still Mr. Anderson. To see that, we can easily imagine HIM regretting his decision in t_{1+1} and thinking what HIS life (i.e., the alternative life of the SAME individual) would be like had he taken a different pill.

Now, a fundamental question is: can "Mr. Anderson's life" work as a rigid des-ignator at t_1? If the referent of "Mr. Anderson's life" is an event than the answer must be negative, since: (i) if "Mr. Anderson's life" at t_1 refers to an individual, then it must refer to the same individual in all possible worlds; (ii) in a possible world (in which he takes the red pill), Mr. Anderson's life at t_{1+1} refers to event E' (the event that includes the taking of the red pill); (iii) in a different possible world (in which he takes the blue pill), Mr. Anderson's life at t_{1+1} refers to event E'' (the event that includes the taking of the blue pill); (iv) E' is not identical to E''. Ergo, "Mr. Anderson's life" does not rigidly designate at t_1. In fact, and this is very important, if "Mr. Anderson's life" cannot rigidly designate at t_1 then it cannot rigidly designate at any point (again, after taking the red pill, there will be other points of branching). The only exception is when Mr. Anderson's life is over (i.e., when no other possibilities of branching exist).

"Mr. Anderson's life" cannot even function as a definite description at t_1, unless we take it to refer to *Mr. Anderson's life up to that point*. This definite description takes a different referent at each time point picking up whatever event happens to be the accumulation of temporal parts that is Mr. Anderson's life up to that point and in that particular world (as history). For instance, at t_{1+1} (supposing that Mr. Anderson takes the red pill), we can refer to the event of taking the red pill in a determinate way as we can refer to "Mr. Anderson's life up to t_1", which is part of "Mr. Anderson's life up to t_{1+1}". In other words, when fixing a world, "Mr. Anderson's life up to t_1" is a rigid designator picking up a determinate individual. In contrast, "Mr. Anderson's life" is not (except for when Mr. Anderson's life is over). As a consequence, while the former can serve as a candidate for an OID, the latter can't.

3.3 Ongoing Events and Object Identifiers

In the previous sections, we have established two premises, namely that: (i) events cannot change or bear modal properties; (ii) object identifiers are rigid designators. Now, if we accept premise 1 (i.e., the classical ontological theories of events in which events obey extensional mereology, cannot qualitatively change, cannot be bearer of modal properties and are locked inside a history) and premise 2 (i.e., OIDs should work as proper names obeying singular and rigid reference) then the inescapable conclusion is: we can only have OIDs referring to events after the point in which there is no possibility of branching, i.e., *we can only have OIDs referring to historical events*.

In summary, Mr. Anderson is not identical to any event that will culminate to be Mr. Anderson's life in a given world. In fact, it correlates to a set of possible lives or possible unfoldings. That is, the proper name (or OID) "Mr. Anderson" can be used to refer to the very same individual in the past and in the present and we can use it in counterfactual reasoning (e.g., what if Mr. Anderson hadn't taken that pill and continued to be a law-abiding computer programmer?; What if Mick Jagger hadn't dropped the London School of Economics and pursued a career as an economist?). In contrast, "Mr. Anderson's life at t_1" could NOT have been different from what it is. Although, the very SAME Mr. Anderson could have had a different life up to that point.

To be the best of our knowledge, this problem has not been discussed in the conceptual modeling literature up to now. When events are represented in structural conceptual models, they are always assumed to be both instantaneous and atomic [8]. Now, if events are instantaneous and atomic, they are only instantiated when they are over, i.e., all event instances are historical instances. For this reason, the aforementioned problem does not arise. However, frequently in structural conceptual models, we want to represent and refer via an OID to *ongoing events*. We want to talk about the conversation, the marriage, the employment, the presidential mandate, the football game, and the car rental as on going events that seem to somehow "change". For instance, while referring to the marriage between John and Mary, we would like to refer to it by a proper name, i.e., to use an OID that refers to something that can truly change qualitatively while remaining the same (e.g., John and Mary's marriage as a whole used to be passionate and now it is cold and distant) and to something that could have been different (e.g., John and Mary's marriage would have lasted longer hadn't they moved to Australia).

There are two possible strategies one might consider to try to escape the afore-mentioned consequences. As expected, they amount to denying at least one of the premises (1) and (2). In any case, this leads to dire consequences. If we reject premise (2), we need to replace it with a completely non-classical semantics for structural conceptual models in which OIDs do not satisfy either singular reference or rigid designation. If we reject premise (1), we need to come up with a completely non-classical ontological theory of events. One that is at odds with the commonly accepted view in linguistics [28] and in formal ontology in philosophy [26]. In par-ticular, one that is at odds with the commonly shared view of events present in the foundational ontologies that are most commonly employed in the foundations of conceptual modeling [9, 10].

In the next section, we explore a modeling alternative that accepts both premises (1) and (2), but that also allows for proper names such as "John & Mary's marriage" or "Paul's Dengue Fever" to refer to entities that can change and that can be the bearers of modal properties, namely, existentially dependent endurants.

3.4   Where Do Events Come from?

As previous discussed, we take events to be the manifestation of qualities and, in particular, of *dispositions* [11, 17, 18]. So, for an event to unfold, the potentiality of that unfolding must exist as a concrete property of an endurant. As consequence, events are dependent on particularized properties (again, qualities and dispositions), which are in turn dependent on endurants. Ergo, events are dependent on endurants. For instance, the event of the *heart pumping* is the manifestation of the *heart's capacity to pump*; the event of the metal being attracted by the magnet is the manifestation of a number of dispositions of these entities (including the magnet's disposition to attract metallic material); Paul's Dengue Fever as a process is the manifestation of a number of complex dispositions that qualify that disease inhering in Paul; John & Mary's mar-riage as a process is the manifestation of a number of relational properties that con-stitute their marriage as an endurant (e.g., commitments and claims, intentions, desires, expectations, etc.).

Since events are existentially dependent on endurants and are manifestations of particular aspects of these endurants, whenever an event unfolds, these aspects (and the endurants they inhere in) must be present. For this reason, we frequently use the same term to refer both to the event and these underlying aspects. This is a case of *systematic polysemy* [31], a phenomenon that occurs very frequently in language. Take, for instance, the sentences: (a) *this duck in the backyard is common around Europe*; (b) *this book is heavy to carry but easy to read*; (c) *we can meet in front of the bank around the corner that specializes in sub-prime loans*. In (a), we have a polysemic reference to both an individual (that duck in the backyard) and a kind (ducks in general); in (b) to a physical object (the bound volume) and an information content (the book as literary work); in (c) to a physical space (the bank's building) and to an organization. In an analogous manner, when we use the term "John & Mary's marriage" or "Paul's Dengue Fever", we sometimes refer to the endurant (a complex of particularized properties) and sometimes to the event that is the accumulated manifestation of this endurant up to a certain point, i.e., as a definite description. Given the discussion in the previous section, we claim that whenever we refer to something that is on going, that can qualitatively change and still maintain its identity, we are not referring to an event but to the endurant underlying that event. So, when we say that Paul's Dengue Fever up to now has been composed of episodes of high fever, followed by episodes of joint pain that lasted for days, we are referring to the event; when we say that Paul's Dengue Fever has changed and has become a case of Dengue Hemorrhagic Fever now, we are referring to a complex of dispositions (an endurant). Given our previous discussion, if we want to use "Paul's Dengue Fever" as an OID, it must refer to the latter endurant. That is why in Fig. 1, what is referred by the term "Car Rental" is the endurant, the relator, which can change in time, go through phases, etc. Of course, as a manifestation of the many dispositions (e.g., commitment, claims, liabilities, capacities) constituting this car rental relator, we have, in a particular unfolding of the world, a car rental complex event.

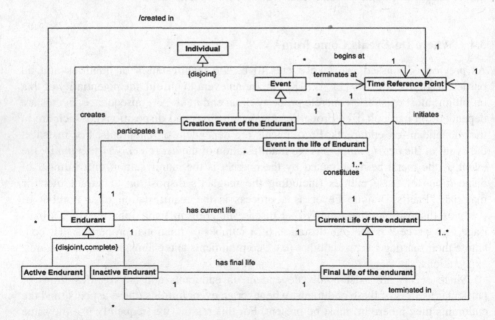

Fig. 3. A modeling pattern for representing events in structural business models

In the sequel, we propose a *modeling pattern* that captures the relation between endurants and the events whose parts accumulate as their manifestations (Fig. 3). In this pattern, endurants are *created by creation events*. As events, creation events begin and end at certain time points. The creation moment of an endurant *(created in* relation) is derived from the termination time point of its creation event. Endurants have a causally active phase (e.g., a living person, an on-going disease, an active enrollment). In this phase, the particularized properties (qualities and dispositions) of this endurant are manifested through a number of events (events in the life of endurant) that accumulate to constitute, at each point, a different process that represents the *current life of the endurant*. Endurants also have a causally inactive phase (e.g., a deceased person, a finished assignment, a legally terminated marriage). In this latter phase, the properties of that endurant can no longer be manifested and, its qualities are immutable regarding their values. Moreover, in that phase, we can refer to the *final life of the endurant* as the total accumulation of all *events in the life of the endurant*.

As an example, suppose Peter makes an appointment with Jane (his supervisor) to discuss his Ph.D. thesis in the subsequent week. After they have agreed to meet (an event), the *appointment* does not yet exist as an event, but it does exist as an aggregation of mutual commitments, individual goals, mutual expectations, etc. (again, an endurant, more precisely, a relator). So, we take the agreement event as an atomic event that creates the *appointment*. The appointment can change (they might decide to drop of the topics of the agenda), it might be postponed, its manifestation (i.e., the appointment as an event) might even not occur at all. While occurring, this appointment can be manifested through a number of events that will accumulate to be the "life of the appointment", a particular event in which Paul and Jane participate.

3.5 An Illustration

In [32], Olivé discusses the issue of relationship reification and elaborates on the connection between reified relationships and their temporal properties. He discusses the following example: suppose an employee *works in* a project. In that project, the employee has a number of worked hours per daily time interval. Moreover, for each convex time interval someone works in that project, he is connected to a single task and has a single pre-fixed deadline. Moreover, for all the non-convex time intervals that are periods in which he works in that project, the employee has the same role and the same manager. Olivé then proposes three different types of temporal relationship reifications: *(1) per instant:* a relationship r is reified into a different entity e for each time point in which r holds. In this example, for each working day in a given project, we have a different entity e which captures the worked hours in that day; *(2) per interval:* a relationship *r* is reified into a different entity *e'* for each temporal interval during which *r* holds. In this example, e' can then capture properties such as deadline and objective; *(3) per life span:* a relationship *r* (instance of *WorksIn*) is reified into a single entity *e*, which is the same during the whole life span of *r*. In this example, e'' can then capture properties such as assigned role and manager.

Given the analysis presented in this paper, the first question that comes to the mind is: what kinds of entities are being represented in these examples? If we take (1), in the solution presented by Olivé in the paper, the reified entity is termed.*Work Day* having properties such as *HoursWorked* and produced deliverable(s) (if any). Olivé highlights two meta-properties of this entity: it is instantaneous and atomic. Given the chosen name (and these meta-properties), a salient interpretation is that the reified entity represents an event, individuated by a pre-fixed time-interval. If this is the case, then an instance of this relationship corresponds to an *event*. An exemplar instance of *Work Day* is the event in which John worked 10 h and produced deliverables d_1 and d_2 in March 20th, 2013. Since events cannot change in a qualitative way, then both the attribute *HoursWorked* and the relationship with the produced deliverable(s) are immutable (and thus are marked as *readOnly* in UML).

Let us take now the case (2). In that case, Olivé's solution produces an entity termed *Assignment* connecting an Employee and a Project. An assignment, is connected to a task and a deadline and is associated to a given time convex interval. Now, in this second case, it is not obvious that Assignment is an event. Assignment can have modal properties (e.g., it can fulfilled before the deadline, it can be delayed, it can be fulfilled in time), an assignment can be manifested through a number of possible processes (for instance, being constituted by a different number of actual WorkDay instances), an assignment can change in a qualitative way (for instance, the number of current worked hours can change). Moreover, although Olivé assumes that the deadline is fixed, one can easily imagine a situation in which the deadline for an assignment can be renegotiated and, hence, possible changed. In fact, an Assignment can even fail to manifest at all (for example, if the employee fails to actually work in the project or to deliver the object of the assignment goal). However, even if this is the case, the Assignment (as a bundle of commitments and claims) holds for the entire time interval (for example, between creation and deadline, fulfillment or abandonment of the assignment) which is different from the time (sub)intervals in which the particularized properties in this assignment are actually being manifested through events. Of course, one can still assume here that what we have is a historical model that only models assignment once their manifestations are finished. Again, what we would have here would be the representation of a historical event. Once more, all properties of the relationship would be immutable (e.g., the actual number of worked hours, if the task was fulfilled or not, etc.). Finally, let us analyze case (3). In that case, Olivé's solution reifies the relationship by something (interestingly) termed Participation. Unlike in cases (1) and (2), however, a Participation is not correlated to a convex time interval. In other words, a *Participation* can be active or inactive being, hence, correlated with multiple disconnected time intervals. Once more, in case we only look at participations in hindsight, Participations can be thought as complex historical facts correlated to the mereological sum of possibly several historical events (i.e., historical participations). However, it seems that in this case the most salient interpretation is to have participation as a complex bundle of commitments (a better name could be *Project Allocation*) that can change qualitatively in many ways (e.g., the number of working hours can change, the value paid by worked hour can change), can bear modal properties (e.g., it can be active or not – I can be allocated to a project even if I am in a medical leave) and can be manifested by a number of possible processes and, hence, it can correspond to a number of possibly different participations (in the sense defended here). In these different possible manifestations of John's allocation to project P1, he can have different task assignments, which can be fulfilled or not, with different performance evaluations, in different dates with different amounts of effort, etc. In any case, in the latter (arguably more realistic) interpretation, the lifetime of the *Project Allocation* is potentially different from the sum of the time intervals in which this this relator is being manifested, i.e., different from the lifetime of the participations in the corresponding event.

Figure 4 shows a model for this scenario, revisiting Olivé's example and containing an instantiation of the pattern of Fig. 3. In this model, a *Task Assignment* is an endurant that throughout its active life is manifested through a number of *Work Day* events, which are events in the life of the *Task Assignment*. An instance of *Work Day* is also possibly a creation event for another endurant, namely, a *Deliverable*. When a *Task Assignment* is in a causally inactive phase (i.e., it has terminated), we have a complex historical process (*Task Assignment Process*), which is the final life of the *Task Assignment*, and is composed of all *Work Day* manifestations of it. As previously discussed, since events are mereological sums of their parts, all *Work Day* events

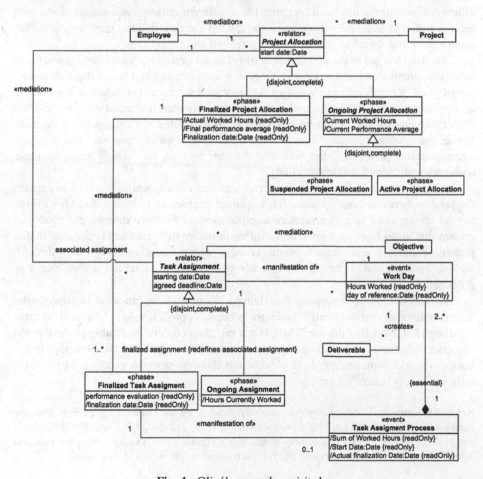

Fig. 4. Olivé's example revisited

composing a *Task Assignment Process* are essential to it. Moreover, attributes such as starting date and finalization date (for *Project Allocation* and *Task Assignment*) are specializations of the general relations of *created in* and *terminated in*, respectively (in Fig. 3). In this figure, we have the attribute day of reference in *Work Day* representing both the start and end time reference points for that event (since, by definition of work day, they are the same). The start and actual finalization dates of the *Task Assignment Process* are derived from the attributes of its constituent events, namely, the date of references of the first and last of the *Work Day* events.

4 Final Considerations

Several approaches to enterprise modeling manage the complexity of an organization by describing the organization from different perspectives. The need to relate various partial descriptions of the organization is addressed in virtually all enterprise modeling approaches and has been recognized in Zachman's early work in 1987 [2]: "each of the different descriptions has been prepared for a different reason, each stands alone, and each is different from the others, even though all the descriptions may pertain to the same object and therefore are inextricably related to one another."

This need has led to the development of *relations between architectural domains* in enterprise architecture and enterprise modeling approaches [3]. One of these domains, namely that of organizational behavior, has received significant attention in the context of business process modeling and management. Another important domain, that of object-like entities (or "structure") is strongly inter-related with the process domain. While the process domain focuses on "how" the business process activities are structured and performed, the structure domain focuses on "who" performs these activities and "what" undergoes change.

We have shown in this paper that a rich ontological account is required to explain the relation between both domains. This account enables us to understand how events can be incorporated in a structural conceptual model. We have discussed a modeling pattern that arises from dealing with the different nature of events and endurants; in this pattern, endurants and related events coexist, complementing each other through well-defined relations. The pattern extends the treatment of reified events that was proposed in [8].

We believe that the conceptual foundations discussed here can serve to improve the understanding of artifact-centric business process approaches [4–7] as well as case handling [33]. Note that the focus here is not on "data objects" but rather on real-world objects (including social objects, commitments, relationships) that are pervasive in the business world; representing these objects and their relations to events is key to capturing business reality accurately.

Acknowledgements. This research is partially funded by the Brazilian Research Funding Agencies CNPq (grants # 311313/2014-0, 485368/2013-7, 312158/2015-7 and 461777/2014-2) and FAPES (# 69382549). The authors would like to thank Roel Wieringa, Alex Borgida and John Mylopoulos for comments and fruitful discussions on the topics of this article.

References

1. Casati, R., Varzi, A.: Events. In: Zalta, E.N. (ed.) The Stanford Encyclopedia of Philosophy (2015). http://plato.stanford.edu/archives/win2015/entries/events/
2. Zachman, J.A.: A framework for information systems architecture. IBM Syst. J. **26**(3), 276–292 (1987)
3. Lankhorst, M., et al.: Enterprise Architecture at Work - Modelling, Communication, and Analysis. Springer, Heidelberg (2005)
4. Meyer, A., Weske, M.: Activity-centric and artifact-centric process model roundtrip. In: Lohmann, N., Song, M., Wohed, P. (eds.) BPM 2013. LNBIP, vol. 171, pp. 167–181. Springer, Heidelberg (2013)
5. Liu, R., Bhattacharya, K., Wu, F.Y.: Modeling business contexture and behavior using business artifacts. In: Krogstie, J., Opdahl, A.L., Sindre, G. (eds.) CAiSE 2007 and WES 2007. LNCS, vol. 4495, pp. 324–339. Springer, Heidelberg (2007)
6. Nigam, A., Caswell, N.S.: Business artifacts: an approach to operational specification. IBM Syst. J. **42**(3), 428–445 (2003)
7. Cohn, D., Hull, R.: Business artifacts: a data-centric approach to modeling business operations and processes. Bull. IEEE Comput. Soc. Tech. Committee Data Eng. **32**(3), 3–9 (2009)
8. Olivé, A., Raventós, R.: Modeling events as entities in object-oriented conceptual modeling languages. Data Knowl. Eng. **58**, 243–262 (2006)
9. Guizzardi, G.: Ontological Foundations for Structural Conceptual Models, Telematica Instituut Fundamental Research Series No. 15, The Netherlands (2005). ISBN 90-75176-81-3
10. Borgo, S., Masolo, C.: Foundational choices in DOLCE. In: Staab, S. (ed.) Handbook on Ontologies, pp. 361–381. Springer, Heidelberg (2009)
11. Guarino, N., Guizzardi, G.: Relationships and events: towards a general theory of reification and truthmaking. In: 15th International Conference of the Italian Association for Artificial Intelligence (2016, submitted)
12. Guarino, N., Guizzardi, G.: "We need to discuss the relationship": revisiting relationships as modeling constructs. In: Zdravkovic, J., Kirikova, M., Johannesson, P. (eds.) CAISE 2015. LNCS, vol. 9097, pp. 279–294. Springer, Heidelberg (2015)
13. Guizzardi, G., et al.: Towards ontological foundation for conceptual modeling: the unified foundational ontology (UFO) story. Appl. Ontol. **10**(3–4), 259–271 (2015). IOS Press
14. Guerson, J.: Representing dynamic invariants in ontologically well-founded conceptual models. Master thesis, Computer Science Department, Federal University of Espírito, Santo, Brazil (2005)
15. Lombard, L.B.: Events: A Metaphysical Study. Routledge, London (1986)
16. Bunge, M.: Treatise on Basic Philosophy the Furniture of the World Ontology I. Springer, Heidelberg (1977)
17. Guizzardi, G., Wagner, G., de Almeida Falbo, R., Guizzardi, R.S., Almeida, J.P.A.: Towards ontological foundations for the conceptual modeling of events. In: Ng, W., Storey, V.C., Trujillo, J.C. (eds.) ER 2013. LNCS, vol. 8217, pp. 327–341. Springer, Heidelberg (2013)
18. Molnar, G.: Powers: A Study in Metaphysics. Oxford University Press, Oxford (2006). Ed. by Stephen Mumford
19. Santos Jr., P.S., Almeida, J.P.A., Guizzardi, G.: An ontology-based semantic foundation for ARIS EPCs. In: 25th ACM Symposium on Applied Computing (ACM SAC 2010), Sierre, Switzerland (2010)

20. Martins, A.F., et al.: Using a Foundational Ontology to Address Ambiguity in Business Process Modeling. In: 7th Brazilian Symposium on Information Systems (SBSI 2011), Salvador, Brazil (2011). (in Portuguese)
21. Guizzardi, G., Wagner, G.: Can BPMN be used for making simulation models? In: Barjis, J., Eldabi, T., Gupta, A. (eds.) EOMAS 2011. LNBIP, vol. 88, pp. 100–115. Springer, Heidelberg (2011)
22. Guizzardi, G., Wagner, G.: Towards and ontological foundation of discrete event simulation. In: 16th International Winter Simulation Conference, Baltimore, USA (2010)
23. Nardi, J., et al.: A Commitment-Based Reference Ontology for Services Information Systems. Oxford University Press, Oxford (2015)
24. Azevedo, C., et al.: Modeling Resources and Capabilities in Enterprise Architecture: A Well-Founded Ontology-Based Proposal for ArchiMate Information Systems. Oxford University Press (OUP), Oxford (2015)
25. Estañol, M., Queralt, A., Sancho, M.R., Teniente, E.: Artifact-centric business process models in UML. In: La Rosa, M., Soffer, P. (eds.) BPM Workshops 2012. LNBIP, vol. 132, pp. 292–303. Springer, Heidelberg (2013)
26. Simons, P.M.: Parts. An Essay in Ontology. Clarendon Press, Oxford (1987)
27. Kim, J.: Events as property exemplifications. In: Action Theory, pp. 159–177. Reidel (1976)
28. Moltmann, F.: Events tropes and truthmaking. Philos. Stud. **134**, 363–403 (2007)
29. Wieringa, R., de Jonge, W.: Object identifiers, keys, and surrogates: object identifiers revisited. Theor. Pract. Object Syst. **1**(2), 101–114 (1995)
30. Kent, W.: Data and Reality. Elsevier Science Ltd, Amsterdam (1978)
31. Ravin, Y., Leacock, C.: Polysemy: Theoretical and Computational Approaches. Oxford University Press, Oxford (2002)
32. Olivé, À.: Relationship reification: a temporal view. In: Jarke, M., Oberweis, A. (eds.) CAiSE 1999. LNCS, vol. 1626, pp. 396–410. Springer, Heidelberg (1999)
33. van der Aalst, W.M.P., Weske, M.: Case handling: a new paradigm for business process support. Data Knowl. Eng. **53**(2), 129–162 (2005)

Automated Discovery

A Unified Approach for Measuring Precision and Generalization Based on Anti-alignments

B.F. van Dongen[1(✉)], J. Carmona[2], and T. Chatain[3]

[1] Eindhoven University of Technology, Eindhoven, The Netherlands
b.f.v.dongen@tue.nl
[2] Universitat Politècnica de Catalunya, Barcelona, Spain
jcarmona@cs.upc.edu
[3] LSV, ENS Cachan, CNRS, INRIA, Universit Paris-Saclay, Cachan, France
chatain@lsv.ens-cachan.fr

Abstract. The holy grail in process mining is an algorithm that, given an event log, produces fitting, precise, properly generalizing and simple process models. While there is consensus on the existence of solid metrics for fitness and simplicity, current metrics for precision and generalization have important flaws, which hamper their applicability in a general setting. In this paper, a novel approach to measure precision and generalization is presented, which relies on the notion of *anti-alignments*. An anti-alignment describes highly deviating model traces with respect to observed behavior. We propose metrics for precision and generalization that resemble the *leave-one-out cross-validation* techniques, where individual traces of the log are removed and the computed anti-alignment assess the model's capability to describe precisely or generalize the observed behavior. The metrics have been implemented in ProM and tested on several examples.

1 Introduction

The goal of *process mining* is to gain insights into the behavior of operational information systems by analyzing event logs. Often, process mining is considered synonymous to *process discovery*, which aims at describing observed behavior of a business process in the form of an (executable) process model. The behavior used as input is considered to be given in the form of an *event log* [1].

Traditionally, event logs are considered to be accurate representations of the behavior of a system in such as way that each event refers to an *activity* that was executed in the context of a *case*. By deriving a process model from such an event log, process discovery algorithms give insights into the underlying system.

There has been always a discussion on how to interpret process discovery results, i.e. how does the produced model relate to the actual, but unknown, system in four quality dimensions [2]:

Fitness quantifies how much of the observed behavior is captured by the model,
Generalization quantifies how well the model explains unobserved system behavior,

© Springer International Publishing Switzerland 2016
M. La Rosa et al. (Eds.): BPM 2016, LNCS 9850, pp. 39–56, 2016.
DOI: 10.1007/978-3-319-45348-4_3

Precision quantifies how much behavior exists in the model that was not observed, and

Simplicity quantifies the complexity of the model.

In recent years, many metrics have been developed to measure fitness, precision and generalization by comparing the event log with the generated model. For fitness, the state-of-the-art is in alignments, a technique that given a trace and a model produces the most likely explanation for that trace [3]. As the focus of this paper is not on fitness, we assume our models to be perfectly fitting. If a trace in an event log does not fit the model, we use the alignment-based explanation of that trace instead.

Measuring precision is typically done by projecting the observed traces onto the model and then count the number of ways to "escape" from the observed behavior [4]. The more "escaping edges" there are, the lower the precision. The downside of such an approach is that precision only considers the behavior of the model that is very close to the event log.

For generalization, only few metrics exist [5,6]. Some of them are again based on the projection of the log onto the model. For instance, the approach in [6] considers "frequency of use", where models are assumed to generalize if all parts of the model are used equally frequently when reproducing the event log.

In this paper, we take a fresh look at precision and generalization by using the concept of an *anti-alignment* [7]. An anti-alignment of a model with respect to a log is an execution of a model which is as different as possible from the observed log. We instruct and adapt *cross-validation*-based techniques in combination with anti-alignments to derive solid metrics that show a better estimation with respect to the state-of-the-art metrics. The following example illustrates this.

1.1   Motivating Example

Throughout the paper, we use an example of a log and several models. The example we use is taken from page 64 of [8] and consists of the simple event log shown in Table 1. The log consists of only five different traces, with various frequencies. The models in Figs. 1 through 4 are four examples of models often used to show the differences between fitness, precision and generalization. The models in

Table 1. An example event log

Trace	Frequency
$\langle A, B, D, E, I \rangle$	1207
$\langle A, C, D, G, H, F, I \rangle$	145
$\langle A, C, G, D, H, F, I \rangle$	56
$\langle A, C, H, D, F, I \rangle$	23
$\langle A, C, D, H, F, I \rangle$	28

Figs. 5, 6, 7 and 8 are models over the same set of activities with varying loop and/or parallel constructs.

The model in Fig. 1 shows the "ideal" process discovery result, i.e. the model that is fitting, fairly precise and properly generalizing. The other models are chosen such that they score poorly on at least one of the dimensions fitness, precision or generalization.

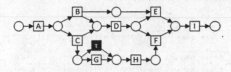

Fig. 1. The ideal model. Fitting, fairly precise and properly generalizing.

Fig. 2. Most frequent trace. Precise, but not fitting or generalizing.

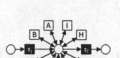

Fig. 3. The flower model. Fitting and generalizing, but very imprecise.

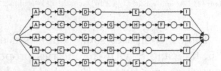

Fig. 4. All traces separate. Fitting, precise, but not generalizing.

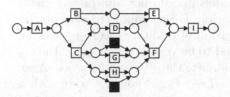

Fig. 5. A model with G and H in parallel.

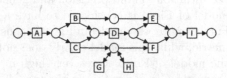

Fig. 6. A model with G and H in self-loops

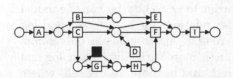

Fig. 7. A model with D in a self-loop

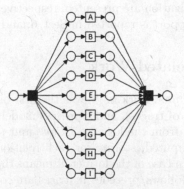

Fig. 8. A model with all transitions in parallel.

Table 2. Precision and generalization for all models

Model		P_{ET}	P_{ETC}	P_a	G_a	P_{ne}	G_{ne}	F	P_t	P_l	P	G_t	G_l	G
Figure 1	Generating model	0.992	0.994	0.982	0.585	0.995	0.594	1.000	0.886	0.857	0.871	0.270	0.143	0.206
Figure 2	Single trace	1.000	1.000	1.000	0.900	0.893	0.000	0.915	1.000	1.000	1.000	0.000	0.000	0.000
Figure 3	Flower model	0.136	0.119	0.142	0.903	0.117	1.000	1.000	0.000	0.000	0.000	1.000	1.000	1.000
Figure 4	Separate traces	1.000	0.359	1.000	0.145	0.985	0.114	1.000	1.000	1.000	1.000	0.000	0.000	0.000
Figure 5	G,H in parallel	0.894	0.936	0.947	0.511	0.950	0.615	1.000	0.800	0.800	0.800	0.268	0.183	0.225
Figure 6	G,H as self-loops	0.884	0.889	0.947	0.722	0,874	0.615	1.000	0.819	0.357	0.588	0.290	0.643	0.466
Figure 7	D as self-loop	0.763	0.760	0.797	0.728	0.720	0.619	1.000	0.688	0.357	0.523	0.485	0.643	0.564
Figure 8	All parallel	0.273	0.170	0.336	0.178	0.158	0.972	0.739	0.067	0.000	0.033	0.417	0.500	0.459
Figure 11	C,F equal loop	0.820	0.589	0.839	0.585	0.600	0.594	1.000	0.490	0.429	0.459	0.259	0.341	0.300
Figure 12	Round-robin	0.579	0.185	0.889	0.400	0.194	0.118	0.616	0.000	0.000	0.000	0.000	0.000	0.000

Table 2 compares some conformance metrics for the models in Figs. 1, 2, 3, 4, 5, 6, 7 and 8 with the metrics proposed in this paper: P (computed as the average of two metrics P_t and P_l) and G (average of G_t and G_l)[1]. The fitness value F is measured using the alignment based technique of [9] and from the same author are the values of P_a and G_a which are defined in [3]. The precision values in P_{ET} and P_{ETC} are defined in [10]. Finally, the values P_{ne} and G_{ne} denote the precision and generalization metrics from [5], respectively. Clearly, the existing metrics do not agree on all models and do not always agree with the intuition behind precision and generalization. For example, the very precise model of Fig. 4 is considered to have a precision of 0.359 by the P_{ETC} metric. Furthermore, the model in Fig. 2 is considered to be very generalizing by the G_a metric, while this model clearly does not generalize the observed behavior. Also, the model of Fig. 6 scores very high in P_{ET}-P_{ETC}-P_a, although a trace with a thousand G's is possible in the model. One can see that the metrics presented in this paper are free from the aforementioned problems.

The paper is structured as follows: in the next section a brief description of related work is provided. Preliminaries are presented in Sect. 3. The core of the paper is provided in Sects. 4 and 5, where techniques for precision and generalization are presented, respectively. Evaluation with further examples and tool support is reported in Sect. 6, and Sect. 7 concludes the paper.

2   Related Work

The seminal work in [2] was the first one in relating observed behavior (in form of a set of traces), and a process model. In order to asses how far can the model deviate from the log, the *follows* and *precedes* relations for both model and log are computed, storing for each relation whereas it *always* holds or only *sometimes*. In case of the former, it means that there is more variability. Then, log and model follows/precedes matrices are compared, and in those matrix cells where the model has a *sometimes* relation whilst the log has an *always* relation indicate

---

[1] Throughout the paper, we will use P and G letters to denote precision and generalization metrics, respectively.

that the model allows for more behavior, i.e., a lack of precision. This technique has important drawbacks: first, it is not general since in the presence of loops in the model the characterization of the relations is not accurate [2]. Second, the method requires a full state-space exploration of the model in order to compute the relations, a stringent limitation for models with large or even infinite state spaces.

In order to overcome the limitations of the aforementioned technique, a different approach was proposed in [4]. The idea is to find *escaping arcs*, denoting those situations where the model starts to deviate from the log/behavior, i.e., events allowed by the model not observed in the corresponding trace in the log. The exploration of escaping arcs is restricted by the log behavior, and hence the complexity of the method is always bounded. By counting how many escaping arcs a pair (model, log) has, one can estimate the precision of a model. Although being a practical and fast estimation for precision, it may underestimate precision when escaping arcs lead to highly deviating behavior.

In [5] the notion of *weighted artificial negative events* from a log is proposed. Given a log L, an artificial negative event is a trace $\sigma' = \sigma \cdot a$ where $\sigma \in L$, but $\sigma' \notin L$. Algorithms are proposed to weight the confidence of an artificial negative event, and they can be used to estimate the precision and generalization of a process model by computing four sets of events: i) positive events which could be replayed without error (TP), ii) negative events which could be replayed and thus erroneously permitted by the process model (FP), iii) generalized events (negative events with low confidence) which could be replayed without error and confirm model's ability to generalize (AG), and iv) generalized events which could not be replayed by the process model (DG). The formula $\frac{TP}{TP+FP}$ provides a metric for precision, whilst $\frac{AG}{AG+DG}$ provides a metric for generalization. Like in [4], by only considering one step ahead of log/model's behavior, these metrics may underestimate precision/generalization considerably. For instance, the very high generalization provided by this metric to the model of Fig. 8 (0.972, i.e., almost perfect generalization) contrast with the value provided by our metric (0.459), the latter being more in line with the real generalization of this model with respect to the log of Table 1. Furthermore, the model used to generate the log is considered more precise (0.995) than a model that only allows for a single trace (0.893), while a model with only one possible trace is as precise as it can be.

3 Preliminaries

In this paper we choose Petri nets as process modeling notation, although the theory presented is valid for any other formalism that has replay semantics.

3.1 Petri Nets and Process Mining

Definition 1 ((Labeled) Petri net). *A (labeled) Petri Net [11] is a tuple $N = \langle P, T, \mathcal{F}, m_0, m_f, \Sigma, \lambda \rangle$, where P is the set of places, T is the set of transitions (with $P \cap T = \emptyset$), $\mathcal{F} : (P \times T) \cup (T \times P) \to \{0, 1\}$ is the flow relation, m_0 is the initial marking, m_f is the final marking,*

Σ *is an alphabet of actions and* $\lambda : T \to \Sigma$ *labels every transition by an action.*

A marking is an assignment of a non-negative integer to each place. If k is assigned to place p by marking m (denoted $m(p) = k$), we say that p is marked with k tokens. Given a node $x \in P \cup T$, its pre-set and post-set are denoted by $\bullet x$ and $x \bullet$ respectively.

A transition t is *enabled* in a marking m when all places in $\bullet t$ are marked. When a transition t is enabled, it can *fire* by removing a token from each place in $\bullet t$ and putting a token to each place in $t \bullet$. A marking m' is *reachable* from m if there is a sequence of firings $t_1 t_2 \ldots t_n$ that transforms m into m', denoted by $m[t_1 t_2 \ldots t_n\rangle m'$. A sequence of actions $a_1 a_2 \ldots a_n$ is a *feasible sequence* (or *run*) if there exists a sequence of transitions $t_1 t_2 \ldots t_n$ firable from m_0 and such that for $i = 1 \ldots n$, $a_i = \lambda(t_i)$. Let $\mathcal{L}(N)$ be the set of feasible sequences of Petri net N. The set of reachable markings from m_0 is denoted by $[m_0\rangle$, and form a graph called *reachability graph*. Let $\mathcal{L}^n(N) \subseteq \mathcal{L}(N)$ be the set of complete traces of N with length n or shorter, i.e. $\mathcal{L}^n(N) = \{\sigma \in \mathcal{L}(N) \mid m_0[\sigma\rangle m_f \wedge |\sigma| \leq n\}$.

An event log is a collection of traces, where a trace may appear more than once. Formally:

Definition 2 (Event Log). *An event log* (L, ϕ) *is a set of traces* $L \subseteq \Sigma^*$ *and function denoting the occurrence frequency of each trace denoted by* $\phi : L \to \mathbb{N}$, *i.e.* $\phi(t) = 1$ *implies that trace* t *was observed once in the log. If for all* $t \in L$ *holds* $\phi(t) = 1$, *we omit* ϕ *from the notation. The number of traces in a log is denoted by* $|L|$.

Quality Dimensions. Process mining techniques aim at extracting from a log L a process model N (e.g., a Petri net) with the goal to elicit the process underlying in $\mathcal{S}$. By relating the behaviors of L, $\mathcal{L}(N)$ and $\mathcal{S}$, particular concepts can be defined [6]. A model N *fits* log L if $L \subseteq \mathcal{L}(N)$. A model is *precise* in describing a log L if $\mathcal{L}(N) \backslash L$ is small. A model N represents a *generalization* of log L with respect to system $\mathcal{S}$ if some behavior in $\mathcal{S} \backslash L$ exists in $\mathcal{L}(N)$. Finally, a model N is *simple* when it has the minimal complexity in representing $\mathcal{L}(N)$, i.e., the well-known *Occam's razor principle*.

3.2   Anti-alignments

Anti-alignments were introduced in [7]. An anti-alignment is a run of a model which differs sufficiently from all the observed traces in a log. In order to measure how much a run differs from an observed trace, one needs a notion of *distance*; actually, a mapping $d : \Sigma^* \times \Sigma^* \to [0..1]$ is sufficient to define anti-alignments: the other axioms of distance functions (symmetry, triangle inequality, . . .) are not required for the definition of anti-alignments. For a log L, we write $d(\sigma, L) = \min_{t \in L} d(\sigma, t)$. If $L = \emptyset$, then $d(\sigma, L) = 1$.

Definition 3 (Anti-alignment). *A* (n, δ)*-anti-alignment of a model* N *w.r.t. a log* L *and a distance function* d *is a run* $\sigma \in \mathcal{L}(N)$ *such that* $|\sigma| = n$ *and* $d(\sigma, L) \geq \delta$.

Choice of the Distance Function. A simple choice of a distance function, used in [7], can be constructed using the Hamming distance after truncating or padding γ to the length of σ, it simply counts the number of mismatches between the actions in the two words, i.e. the number of indices i such that $\sigma_i \neq \gamma_i$ divided by the length of σ_i. But concerning the application to process mining, Hamming distance is usually too rigid: indeed, every symbol σ_i is compared only to the exact corresponding symbol γ_i. This puts for instance the word $abababababab$ at distance 1 from $babababababa$. In process mining techniques, other distances are usually preferred (see for instance [3]), typically Levenshtein's distance (or edit distance) which counts how many replacements, deletions and insertions of symbols are needed to obtain γ projected to labeled transitions starting from σ, divided by the length of the longest trace. Unless explicitly stated otherwise, all examples in this paper use the edit distance function with equal costs for remove, replace and insert operations.

Example 1. Consider the Petri net shown in Fig. 1, and the log of Table 1. The trace $\langle A, C, G, H, D, F, I \rangle$ is a $(7, \frac{1}{7})$ anti-alignment when considering edit-distance as a distance metric: it can be obtained by inserting G in the observed trace $\langle A, C, H, D, F, I \rangle$; and the length of the longest trace is 7. Notice that for $\delta > \frac{1}{7}$ there are no anti-alignments for this example. When considering Hamming distance, the same trace is a $(7, \frac{2}{7})$ anti-alignment.

Example 2. Consider the Petri net shown in Fig. 2, and the log of Table 1. The trace $\langle A, B \rangle$ is a $(2, \frac{3}{5})$ anti-alignment for this model when considering either edit-distance or Hamming distance as a distance metric: in both case, the closest observed trace is $\langle A, B, D, E, I \rangle$.

Example 3. Consider the Petri net shown in Fig. 3, and the log of Table 1. The trace $\langle A, B, D, E, I, A, A, A, A \rangle$ is a $(9, \frac{4}{9})$ anti-alignment for either edit or Hamming distance. Given $n = 9$, the trace $\langle \tau_i, B, A, A, A, A, A, A, A, A, \tau_f \rangle$ is a $(9, 1)$ anti-alignment when considering either edit-distance or Hamming distance as a distance metric. Notice that for any $0 \leq n$ and $0 \leq \delta \leq 1$ an (n, δ) anti-alignment exists.

Example 4. Consider the Petri net shown in Fig. 4, and the log of Table 1. The trace $\langle A, C, D, G, H, F, I \rangle$ is a $(7, 0)$ anti-alignment when considering any distance metric.

In the context of process mining, discovered models typically consist of a model and an initial and final marking (where the latter is often implicit), i.e. each execution of the underlying system is assumed to be a sequence in the model from the initial to the final marking. Therefore, we define the concept of a maximal, complete anti-alignment as follows:

Definition 4 (Maximal, Complete Anti-alignments, $\Gamma_n^{d,mx}(N, L)$). *Let N be a model. We define $\Gamma_n^{d,mx}(N, L) \subseteq \mathcal{L}^n(N)$ as the set of maximal, complete anti-alignments, such that for all $\sigma \in \Gamma_n^{d,mx}(N, L)$ holds that $\nexists \sigma' \in \mathcal{L}^n(N) \setminus \Gamma_n^{d,mx}(N, L)$ with $d(\sigma', L) > d(\sigma, L)$.*

In the remainder of this paper, we write $\gamma_n^{d,mx}(N,L)$ whenever we need an arbitrary element from the set $\Gamma_n^{d,mx}(N,L)$.

Note that the set of maximal complete anti-alignments can be empty in case there is no trace in the model with length less than n. Furthermore, in this paper, we use a representative $\gamma_n^{d,mx}(N,L) \in \Gamma_n^{d,mx}(N,L)$ in case there are more maximal complete anti-alignments. One could argue that an average over the entire (by definition finite) set could be used as well. However, this is computationally expensive and for the examples covered in this paper does not add to the qualitative results.

4   Measuring Precision

As stated earlier, a model N is *precise* in describing a log L if $\mathcal{L}(N) \setminus L$ is small, i.e. if the language of the discovered model is not much larger than the observed behavior. As the behavior of model N is often infinite (when loops are present in the model) and the log L is by definition finite, directly comparing $\mathcal{L}(N)$ with L is meaningless. Therefore, classical precision metrics [4] *estimate* precision by analyzing so-called "escaping edges", i.e. the points where the model allows to deviate from observed behavior. The more deviation points there are, the lower the precision. Existing metrics however rely on an abstraction mechanism to decide how to count the deviation points and in [4] a number of abstraction mechanisms is presented, each with their own pro's and cons. Each of the abstraction mechanisms works well in one example, but not in the other and vice versa.

In this paper, we suggest a fresh view on precision, using anti-alignments. The intuition behind our metric is as follows. A very precise process model allows for exactly the observed traces to be executed and not more. Hence, if one trace is removed from the log, this trace becomes the anti-alignment for the remaining log as it is the only execution of the model that is not in the log. We use this property to estimate precision.

Definition 5 (Trace-Based Precision). *Let (L, ϕ) be an event log and N a model. We define trace-based precision as follows:*

$$P_t(N, L) = 1 - \frac{1}{|L|} \cdot \sum_{\sigma \in L} d(\sigma, \gamma_{|\sigma|}^{d,mx}(N, L \setminus \{\sigma\})).$$

We assume a perfectly fitting log, i.e. $\sigma \in \mathcal{L}^{|\sigma|}(N)$ and hence $\gamma_{|\sigma|}^{d,mx}(N, L \setminus \{\sigma\})$ exists.

For each trace σ in the log, we compute a maximal anti-alignment γ for the model N and the log without that trace $L \setminus \{\sigma\}$. This anti-alignment is guaranteed to reach the final marking m_f and hence represents an element of $\mathcal{L}(N)$. Then, we compute the distance between σ and γ which we average over the log, *not* taking into account the relative frequencies of the traces in the log. If the language of the model equals the log, then the anti-alignments γ will be equal to σ for every σ, hence the precision is 1. If for every trace σ, an anti-alignment can be produced which has maximal distance from σ, the precision is 0.

Frequencies of traces are not considered as the comparison is between the language of the model and the observed traces. Observing one trace more frequently than another should not influence the precision of the model as the amount of unobserved behavior does not change. This contrasts with current metrics for precision (e.g., [4]).

In trace-based precision, the length of the anti-alignment considered is bounded by the length of the removed trace σ. This guarantees that an anti-alignment exists in the log without trace σ, but also limits the possibility to see imprecise executions of the model that are much longer than the lengths of the observed traces. Therefore, we also define a log-based precision metric, which uses an anti-alignment of the model with respect to the entire log of a much greater length than the longest trace observed in the log.

Definition 6 (Log-Based Precision). *Let* (L, ϕ) *be an event log and* N *a model. We define Log-based precision as follows:*

$$P_l^n(N, L) = 1 - d(\gamma_n^{d,mx}(N, L), L).$$

where n *represents the maximal length of the anti-alignment, typically in the order of several times the length of the longest trace in the log.*

The log-based precision metric uses a single anti-alignment of considerable maximum length to determine the amount of behavior allowed by the model, but not observed in the event log. Our final precision metric is a weighted sum of log- and trace-based precision.

Definition 7 (Precision). *Let* (L, ϕ) *be an event log and* N *a model. We define anti-alignment based precision as follows:*

$$P(N, L) = \alpha P_t(N, L) + (1 - \alpha)P_l^n(N, L)$$

This definition is parameterized by α *and* n. *In the remainder of the paper, we choose* $\alpha = 0.5$ *and* $n = 2 \cdot \max_{\sigma \in L} |\sigma|$.

Our precision metric has two parameters, α, indicating the relative importance of the trace-based vs. the log-based part and n indicating the maximum length of the log-based anti-alignment. In this paper, we use $\alpha = 0.5$ and n equal to twice the length of the longest observed trace. Allowing for longer anti-alignments could lower the log-based precision if there are loops in the model (in the limit, log-based precision in a model with loops goes to 0). Striking the right balance between α and n in the context of real-life process discovery is beyond the scope of this paper. Instead, we focus on the qualitative aspects of our metrics more than the quantitative ones.

Example 5. Let's consider the Petri net shown in Fig. 1 again, with the log of Table 1. Earlier, we identified the trace $\langle A, C, G, H, D, F, I \rangle$ as a $(7, \frac{1}{7})$ anti-alignment. Furthermore, when leaving one trace out, we get the following anti-alignments[2]:

σ	$\gamma_{\lvert\sigma\rvert}^{d,mx}(N, L \setminus \{\sigma\})$	γ projected	$d(\gamma, \sigma)$
$\langle A, B, D, E, I \rangle$	$\langle A, B, D, E, I \rangle$	$\langle A, B, D, E, I \rangle$	0
$\langle A, C, D, G, H, F, I \rangle$	$\langle A, C, G, H, D, F, I \rangle$	$\langle A, C, G, H, D, F, I \rangle$	$\frac{2}{7}$
$\langle A, C, G, D, H, F, I \rangle$	$\langle A, C, G, H, D, F, I \rangle$	$\langle A, C, G, H, D, F, I \rangle$	$\frac{2}{7}$
$\langle A, C, H, D, F, I \rangle$	$\langle A, C, \tau, H, D, F, I \rangle$	$\langle A, C, H, D, F, I \rangle$	0
$\langle A, C, D, H, F, I \rangle$	$\langle A, C, \tau, D, H, F, I \rangle$	$\langle A, C, D, H, F, I \rangle$	0

The trace-based precision $P_t(N, L) = \dfrac{1 + \frac{5}{7} + \frac{5}{7} + 1 + 1}{5} = \frac{31}{35} = 0.886$ and the log-based precision is $P_l(N, L) = 1 - \frac{1}{7} = \frac{6}{7} = 0.857$, hence overall precision with $\alpha = 0.5$ for this model and log is $P(N, L) = 0.5 \cdot \frac{31}{35} + 0.5 \cdot \frac{6}{7} = 0.871$.

Besides precision, we can also use anti-alignments for measuring generalization.

5   Measuring Generalization

In contrast to precision, which relates the log and the model, generalization relates the system to the log and the model. Generalization aims to estimate the extent to which unobserved, but likely possible behavior, is explained by the model. In terms of process modeling, generalization is often obtained by introducing parallel structures or loops into a model when the log suggests this to be the case. Unfortunately, we do not have any knowledge of the system other than that the log forms a representation of the most common behavior in it.

In order to quantify generalizations, we consider not only the sequential behavior that is actually allowed by the model, but we also quantify how different this behavior is when considering the state space of the model. (Structured) loops and parallel structures which are most commonly used to achieve generalization when modeling a system have the tendency to allow for many different sequential traces while introducing fewer states as for structured loops, the number of states does not increase with the number of executions of the loop, while for parallel transitions, the number of states 2^n grows slower than the number of sequences $(n!)$. Therefore, in our generalization metric, we consider the notion of a recovery distance for an anti-alignment.

Definition 8 (Recovery Distance). *Let (L, ϕ) be an event log and N a model. Let $\gamma = \gamma_n^{max}(N, L)$ be an anti-alignment of length n. Let $M_\gamma = \langle m_0, \ldots, m_n \rangle$ be the sequence of states visited by γ, i.e. m_0 is the initial marking of the model, m_n is the final marking of the model and for all $0 \leq i < n$ holds $m_i[\gamma_i\rangle m_{i+1}$.*

---

[2] Note that for the edit distance between the anti-alignment and the removed trace, the trace is first projected onto labeled elements, i.e. the τ transition is removed first.

Let $S \subseteq [m_0\rangle = \{m \mid \exists\, \sigma \cdot \sigma' \in L \text{ s.t. } m_0[\sigma\rangle m\}$ be the set of states reached by L. The recovery distance is defined as:

$$d_{rec}(\gamma) = \frac{1}{|\gamma| - 1} \cdot max_{m \in M_\gamma} min_{\sigma \in \Sigma^*, m[\sigma\rangle s \in S} |\sigma|$$

i.e. the recovery distance is the maximum distance between any of the states reached in the anti-alignment and the states visited by the log.

Note that in a process mining setting, we assume that there is a single reachable final marking and that the anti-alignment guarantees to reach this final marking. Hence the length of the firing sequence to reach a previously visited marking is bounded by the length of the anti-alignment minus 1. Using the recovery distance, we define a generalization metric in a similar fashion as we did for precision, i.e. we remove one trace from the log and compute an anti-alignment for which we obtain the minimum distance to the log and the maximum recovery distance.

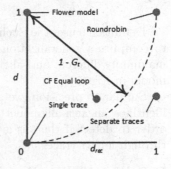

Fig. 9. Positioning of examples for trace-based generalization.

Figures 9 and 10 show the positioning of the models discussed earlier with respect to the anti-alignment distance and the recovery distance, both for the trace-based and log-based metric. Our generalization score is defined such that it favors only models that have a high anti-alignment distance and low recovery distance, i.e. models that introduce new traces without introducing new states. Recall that generalization typically occurs in structures that add fewer states than traces. If a model is properly generalizing, it is likely that the behavior observed in the log covers a significant part of the state space introduced by the generalizing structure, hence a previously unobserved trace will not introduce new states, but rather new paths between existing states, even if the introduced trace is completely different from anything observed in the log.

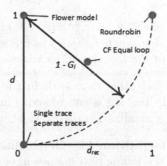

Fig. 10.   Positioning of examples for log-based generalization.

Like for precision, we first consider trace-based generalization following the same leave-one-out procedure. This way, the model is guaranteed to contain an anti-alignment of some distance (i.e. the removed trace). Not using trace-based generalization would lead us to consider all models non-generalizing if the log equals the language of the model.

Definition 9 (Trace-Based Generalization). Let (L, ϕ) be an event log and N a model. We define the trace-based generalization metric for each trace. First, for every trace $\sigma \in L$, we define:

$$G_t^\sigma(N, (L, \phi), \sigma) = 1 - ||1 - d(\gamma_\sigma, L \setminus \{\sigma\}), d_{rec}(\gamma_\sigma)||,$$

where $\gamma_\sigma = \gamma_{|\sigma|}^{d,mx}(N, L \setminus \{\sigma\})$ *and* $||a, b|| = min(1, \sqrt{a^2 + b^2})$, *i.e. the Euclidean distance from* $(0, 0)$, *bound by* 1.

Second, we define trace-based generalization as the weighted average:

$$G_t(N, (L, \phi)) = \frac{1}{\sum\limits_{\sigma \in L} \phi(\sigma)} \cdot \sum_{\sigma \in L} \phi(\sigma) \cdot G_t^\sigma(N, (L, \phi), \sigma).$$

Definition 9 uses the Euclidean distance from the perfectly generalizing model to compute a generalization score, where the perfectly generalizing model has maximally different anti-alignments without introducing new states, such as the model in Fig. 3.

Similar to precision, we also define a log-based generalization metric which identifies an anti-alignment much longer than the longest trace in the log in order to detect if there is a part of the state space which can only be reached through longer traces.

Definition 10 (Log-Based Generalization). *Let* (L, ϕ) *be an event log and* N *a model. Referring to Fig. 10, we define log-based generalization as follows:*

$$G_l^n(N, (L, \phi)) = 1 - ||1 - d(\gamma, L), d_{rec}(\gamma)||,$$

where $\gamma = \gamma_n^{d,mx}(N, L)$ *and* n *represents the maximal length of the anti-alignment, typically in the order of several times the length of the longest trace in the log. Again, we assume* $||a, b|| = min(1, \sqrt{a^2 + b^2})$

Notice that both in the two previous definitions, the frequency of traces in the log is considered. Finally, combining the trace-based and the log-based generalization metric yields our final generalization metric:

Definition 11 (Generalization). *Let* (L, ϕ) *be an event log and* N *a model. We define anti-alignment based generalization as follows:*

$$G(N, (L, \phi)) = \alpha G_t(N, (L, \phi)) + (1 - \alpha)G_l^n(N, (L, \phi)).$$

This definition is parameterized by α *and* n. *In the remainder of the paper, we choose* $\alpha = 0.5$ *and* $n = 2 \cdot \max\limits_{\sigma \in L} |\sigma|$.

Example 6. Let's once again consider the Petri net shown in Fig. 1, with the log of Table 1. Earlier, we identified the trace $\langle A, C, G, H, D, F, I \rangle$ as a $(7, \frac{1}{7})$ anti-alignment for the whole log and we measured precision to be $P(N, L) = 0.871$. The recovery distance for the trace $\langle A, C, G, H, D, F, I \rangle$ is 0 as it does not visit new states in the state space as this anti-alignment visits exactly the same set of states as the trace $\langle A, C, \tau, H, D, F, I \rangle$ which is in the log when correctly aligning the log to the model. When leaving one trace out, we got the following anti-alignments:

σ	freq.	$\gamma^{d,mx}_{|\sigma|}(N, L \setminus \{\sigma\})$	$d(\gamma, L \setminus \{\sigma\})$	$d_{rec}(\gamma)$
$\langle A,B,D,E,I \rangle$	1207	$\langle A,B,D,E,I \rangle$	$\frac{3}{6}$	$\frac{2}{4}$
$\langle A,C,D,G,H,F,I \rangle$	145	$\langle A,C,G,H,D,F,I \rangle$	$\frac{1}{7}$	0
$\langle A,C,G,D,H,F,I \rangle$	56	$\langle A,C,G,H,D,F,I \rangle$	$\frac{1}{7}$	0
$\langle A,C,H,D,F,I \rangle$	23	$\langle A,C,\tau,H,D,F,I \rangle$	$\frac{2}{6}$	$\frac{1}{6}$
$\langle A,C,D,H,F,I \rangle$	28	$\langle A,C,\tau,D,H,F,I \rangle$	$\frac{1}{6}$	0

The trace-based generalization $G_t(N, (L, \phi)) = (1207 \cdot (1 - \sqrt{\frac{9}{36} + \frac{4}{16}}) + 145 \cdot (1 - \sqrt{\frac{36}{49}}) + 56 \cdot (1 - \sqrt{\frac{36}{49}}) + 23 \cdot (1 - \sqrt{\frac{16}{36} + \frac{1}{36}}) + 28 \cdot (1 - \sqrt{\frac{25}{36}}))/1459 = 0.270$. The log-based precision is $G_l(N, (L, \phi)) = 1 - \sqrt{\frac{36}{49}} = 0.143$, hence overall generalization with $\alpha = 0.5$ for this model and log is $G(n, (L, \phi)) = 0.5 \cdot 0.270 + 0.5 \cdot 0.143 = 0.206$.

Consider again our example. The model presented in Fig. 3 (the Flower model) clearly generalizes as it allows for very different traces (high anti-alignment distance), but all within the same state space (low recovery distance).

A model like Fig. 4 (separate traces) does not generalize. If we consider the log as a whole, each anti-alignment will have distance 0 from the log and will have recovery distance 0. If we remove one trace from the log, the maximal anti-alignment found will be the removed trace, with some distance from the rest of the log, but with maximal recovery distance.

Now consider the model in Fig. 11 (CF Equal loop). This model requires transitions C and F to fire equally often in order to reach the intended final marking of one token in the sink place. This model is similar to the original, but will show a high recovery distance as the number of executions of C and F determine the part of the state space which is visited by the anti-alignment, but likely not by the rest of the log.

The models in Fig. 2 (Single trace) and Fig. 12 (Round-robin) show examples of non-fitting models which also do not generalize. After making the log fit using alignment techniques [9], Fig. 2 will have both minimal anti-alignment distance and minimal recovery distance (both 0), while the model in Fig. 12 will have maximal anti-alignment distance and maximal recovery distance. Both models however are not generalizing.

6 Evaluation and Implementation

In this section, we first consider our example log of Table 1 and the models presented in Figs. 1 through 8. Furthermore, we introduce two new models for our example log of Table 1, depicted in Figs. 11 and 12.

Table 2 shows the fitness, precision and generalization values for all models. For our precision and generalization metrics, we present both the trace-based values as well as the log-based values. The trace-based values are computed using the leave-one-out procedure presented earlier. The log-based values are computed by taking a maximal anti-alignment given the model and the entire log with maximum length equal to three times the length of the longest trace in the log.

For the models that are not fitting (Figs. 2, 8 and 12) the log is aligned to the model and then the aligned event log is used for computing precision and generalization. In case of Fig. 2 this implies that all traces in the log are equal as the model only allows for one trace and therefore, the precision is always 1 and the generalization is always 0. Figure 12 is more interesting, as this model has both poor precision and poor generalization. No matter

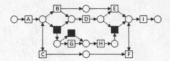

Fig. 11. A model where C and F are in a loop, but need to be executed equally often to reach the final marking.

which trace is removed from the log, there is always an anti-alignment that does not look anything like the removed trace, hence precision is 0. Furthermore, as each of the starting points of the loops generates a completely distinct subgraph in the state space, the recovery distance for an anti-alignment is always very high and hence generalization is poor, despite the fact that the model allows for many different traces.

The model of Fig. 1 has results as expected. The fitness is 1, and precision is fairly high. Furthermore, generalization is not so high as this model does not actually allow for much more behavior than observed. In fact, only the trace $\langle A, C, G, H, D, F, I \rangle$ is possible in the model, but not observed in the log. Figures 2, 3 and 4 indeed show extreme values for precision and/or generalization. As expected the self-loop model of Fig. 3 has precision 0 as it allows for many different traces, but since the recovery distance is always 0 the generalization is maximal. Figure 4 is the opposite as it does not allow for any trace not in the log, and has a maximal recovery distance.

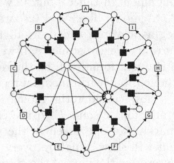

Fig. 12. Round-robin model. The outer loop can be started at any point and then exited one transition before completing the loop.

Now consider the models in Figs. 11 and 12. For Fig. 11 we consider the *relaxed-sound semantics* of this model as it was translated from a causal net as introduced in [12]. The model is constructed in such a way that transitions C and F can be executed multiple times, but equally often. This model should be considered fairly imprecise as there is a lot of behavior in the model that is not in the log. However, the automaton-based metrics for precision are unable to capture this long-term dependency and they will penalize for the fact that C *can* be executed multiple times, but not for the fact that F may *have to* be executed multiple times.

Figure 12 is a model that allows for a loop over transitions A through I to be started at any point. However, when starting the loop at a given point, the model needs to terminate after executing $8 + n \times 9$ transitions. This model again should be considered imprecise as the language of the model is very different from the language of the (aligned) log. Only the P_{ET} captures this, the others consider this model very precise.

Some differences stand out between existing metrics and our anti-alignment based metrics. Consider for example the model in Fig. 12. This model has minimal precision as it allows for much more behavior than observed in the log. However, both the P_{ET} and the P_a metric are unable to capture this since these metrics only consider behavior *directly* adjacent to the observed behavior with respect to a specific abstraction. Interestingly, the P_{ETC} metric considers the model of Fig. 4 to be imprecise, while this model allows for exactly the observed behavior and nothing more. Again, the chosen abstraction causes this effect.

Due to the nice monotonicity property of anti-alignments shown in [7], our precision metric is the only one that consistently ranks models in such a way that a model with more possible traces (of a given maximal length) is always considered less precise.

When comparing our generalization metric with the existing ones, we see a big difference in the model of Fig. 2. The behavior of this model consists of a single trace and is considered generalizing by the metric G_a since the aligned event log (the event log where non-fitting traces have been adapted to fit the model) shows great evidence of this model being the correct one for that log. In our metric however, a model that allows for only one trace will always be considered to have minimal generalization.

Interestingly, the model in Fig. 8 is considered more generalizing by our metric than by most existing ones. This is due to the fact that we consider the recovery distance as important. This model allows for more behavior than observed, but does not introduce too many new states, i.e. the recovery distance is low while the distance of the anti-alignment to the log is large. This is what we consider to be generalization. The G_{ne} metric finds this model to be almost perfectly generalizing since any label is allowed to appear at almost any position, but this metric fails to recognize that labels can only appear once in each trace.

Again, consider Figs. 11 and 12. In both cases, the various parts of the language of the models are represented by completely separated parts of the state space. In Fig. 11, the number of tokens in the place between C and F determines which part of the state space the middle part is executed, and in Fig. 12, the initial decision where to start the loop does. In both cases, once a particular part of the state space is reached which is not covered by traces observed in the log, the recovery distance is maximal, i.e. only after emptying the place between C and F in Fig. 11 or terminating the model in case of Fig. 12, a state is reached which is covered by the observed log. Therefore, these models should not be considered generalizing.

6.1 Models Found in Literature

Rather than only considering our example models, we used models found in [6] for further comparison with our approach. In [6], several process mining results are presented to illustrate the importance of fitness, precision, generalization and simplicity in process mining. The paper introduces a precision and a generalization metric which are specific for process trees, or block-structured process models. The precision metric is comparable to the P_a metric used earlier.

The generalization metric however focuses on the frequency with which each transition is executed in relation to the number of transitions in the model. Generalization is considered low if some parts of the model are infrequent in the log.

We compared our generalization and precision metrics with these models and there are some interesting observations. One of the models, depicted in Fig. 13 contains an inclusive OR block of three activities B, C and D, implying that the model allows for 15 different traces. The log used contains 10 different traces in which B, C and D are executed in parallel, but D can be

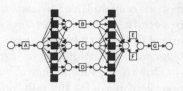

Fig. 13. Figure 9 from [6]

skipped and in [6] the model with the OR block is considered to be the fairly precise (precision 0.830). Our precision metric however identifies anti-alignments that have maximum distance of 0.5 from the removed trace or the log and therefore, our precision metric yields 0.477, which is what you would expect from a model that contains a large OR block to explain (almost) parallel behavior.

Another interesting model is model in Fig. 14 which removed the option to skip D. This model has only one trace that is not observed in the original log and this trace, when executed, does not visit any new states compared to the rest of the log. Therefore, both trace- and log-based generalization are considered low and hence our generalization metric is 0.172 while the metric used in the paper reports a generalization of 0.889. A low generalization value is in line with the intuition behind generalization, i.e. the ability of the model to predict possible but unobserved behavior. As almost all behavior of this model has been observed before, generalization should not be high.

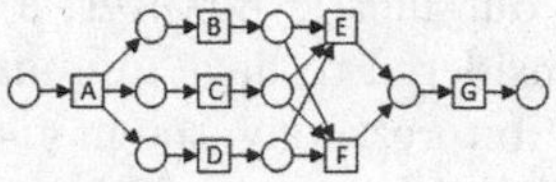

Fig. 14. Figure 5 from [6]

6.2   Implementation

The authors of [7] have shown that the problem of finding a (n, δ)-anti-alignment w.r.t. Hamming-distance is NP-complete. They have presented a way to convert this problem into a SAT problem and implemented an efficient tool in OCaml, available at http://www.lsv.ens-cachan.fr/~chatain/darksider/).

But, as discussed in Sect. 3.2, concerning the application to process mining, Hamming distance is usually too rigid. This is why, for the examples in this paper, we have chosen Levenshtein's edit distance, in spite of the higher complexity of finding anti-alignments for this distance. We have used a brute-force, depth-first search algorithm to find the anti-alignments. Since the maximum length of the anti-alignment is bounded, the size of the search space is finite which allows us to use a brute-force approach. This approach is implemented in the ProM package "anti-alignments" which can be installed through the ProM package manager available on http://www.promtools.org/. The package is included in the nightly build and in ProM 6.6.

In future work, we plan to improve the efficiency of the presented approach using heuristic implementations. Furthermore, we plan to integrate more distance metrics.

7   Conclusions

In this paper, we presented new metrics for measuring precision and generalization of a process model with respect to an event log. Both metrics rely on the concept of an anti-alignment, which is a trace of the model which is as different as possible from the event log given a certain distance function. The anti-alignments are applied using a cross-validation strategy to obtain measurements fro precision. Furthermore, we introduce the notion of recovery distance which is included in the generalization metric, basically expressing the ability of the model to recover from any deviation.

We have compared both metrics with the state-of-the-art metrics for precision and generalization on well-known examples, and the results clearly position the proposal of this paper as a significant improvement in terms of the quality of the estimations provided, albeit at the expense of a higher computational complexity.

Acknowledgments. This work has been partially supported by funds from the Spanish Ministry for Economy and Competitiveness (MINECO), the European Union (FEDER funds) under grant COMMAS (ref. TIN2013-46181-C2-1-R).

References

1. van der Aalst, W.M.P.: Process Mining - Discovery, Conformance and Enhancement of Business Processes. Springer, Berlin (2011)
2. Rozinat, A., van der Aalst, W.M.P.: Conformance checking of processes based on monitoring real behavior. Inf. Syst. **33**(1), 64–95 (2008)
3. Adriansyah, A.: Aligning observed and modeled behavior. Ph.D. thesis, Eindhoven (2014)
4. Munoz-Gama, J.: Conformance checking and diagnosis in process mining. Ph.D. thesis, Universitat Politecnica de Catalunya (2014)
5. vanden Broucke, S.K.L.M., Weerdt, J.D., Vanthienen, J., Baesens, B.: Determining process model precision and generalization with weighted artificial negative events. IEEE Trans. Knowl. Data Eng. **26**(8), 1877–1889 (2014)
6. Buijs, J., van Dongen, B.F., van der Aalst, W.M.P.: Quality dimensions in process discovery: the importance of fitness, precision, generalization and simplicity. Int. J. Cooperative Inf. Syst. **23**(1), 1440001 (2014)
7. Chatain, T., Carmona, J.: Anti-alignments in conformance checking – the dark side of process models. In: Kordon, F., Moldt, D. (eds.) PETRI NETS 2016. LNCS, vol. 9698, pp. 240–258. Springer, Heidelberg (2016). doi:10.1007/978-3-319-39086-4_15
8. Rozinat, A.: Process mining: conformance and extension. Ph.D. thesis (2010)
9. van der Aalst, W.M.P., Adriansyah, A., van Dongen, B.F.: Replaying history on process models for conformance checking and performance analysis. Wiley Interdisc. Rev.: Data Min. Knowl. Disc. **2**(2), 182–192 (2012)

10. Adriansyah, A., Munoz-Gama, J., Carmona, J., van Dongen, B.F., van der Aalst, W.M.P.: Measuring precision of modeled behavior. Inf. Syst. E-Bus. Manag. **13**(1), 37–67 (2015)
11. Murata, T.: Petri nets: Properties, analysis and applications. Proc. IEEE **77**(4), 541–574 (1989)
12. van der Aalst, W., Adriansyah, A., van Dongen, B.: Causal nets: a modeling language tailored towards process discovery. In: Katoen, J.-P., König, B. (eds.) CONCUR 2011. LNCS, vol. 6901, pp. 28–42. Springer, Heidelberg (2011)

A Stability Assessment Framework for Process Discovery Techniques

Pieter De Koninck[✉] and Jochen De Weerdt

Research Centre for Management Informatics Faculty of Economics and Business,
KU Leuven, Leuven, Belgium
{pieter.dekoninck,jochen.deweerdt}@kuleuven.be

Abstract. An extensive amount of work has addressed the evaluation of process discovery techniques and the process models they discover based on concepts like fitness, precision, generalization and simplicity. In this paper, we claim that stability could be considered as an important supplementary evaluation dimension for process discovery next to accuracy and comprehensibility, with ties to the generalization concept. As such, our core contribution is a new framework to measure stability of process discovery techniques. In this paper, the design choices of the different components of the framework are explained. Furthermore, using an experimental evaluation involving both artificial and real-life event logs, the appropriateness and relevance of the stability assessment framework is demonstrated.

Keywords: Stability · Process discovery · Conformance checking · Validity · Log perturbation

1 Introduction

In unsupervised learning, where there is no straightforward way to evaluate discovered solutions, an important question is whether or not a specific solution is valid [12]. Common domains of unsupervised learning are clustering, latent variable methods such as Gaussian Mixture Models, and certain neural network models such as Self-Organizing Maps. Applications can be found in bioinformatics, data mining and pattern recognition, among others. Process discovery, i.e. the automated construction of process models from event logs, is essentially an unsupervised learning task as well. Admittedly, discovered process models can be evaluated structurally, e.g. on soundness [21], or based on the event log through conformance checking (for an overview see [7]). Nonetheless, there is no strict variable or label to predict, hence the discovery of a process model should be considered an unsupervised learning task.

The importance of validity of unsupervised learning algorithms is addressed in [12] as follows: '*It is difficult to ascertain the validity of inferences drawn from the output of most unsupervised learning algorithms. One must resort to heuristic arguments not only for motivating the algorithms, as is often the case in*

© Springer International Publishing Switzerland 2016
M. La Rosa et al. (Eds.): BPM 2016, LNCS 9850, pp. 57–72, 2016.
DOI: 10.1007/978-3-319-45348-4_4

supervised learning as well, but also for judgements as to the quality of the results. This uncomfortable situation has led to heavy proliferation of proposed methods, since effectiveness is a matter of opinion and cannot be verified directly.'.

While validity of process discovery techniques is partially addressed by the whole plethora of conformance checking techniques, it is argued in this paper that evaluation of process discovery algorithms lacks a thorough methodology to assess the stability of these algorithms. In clustering research, a stability-based assessment of validity has received plenty of attention [12, 17]. It is argued in this paper that this stability dimension is missing to a large extent and should complement the already understood evaluation dimensions in process discovery, i.e. accuracy (recall, precision, generalization) and comprehensibility (simplicity).

Conceptually, the stability of a process discovery technique can be defined as *the consistency of process discovery solutions obtained using this technique from perturbed sets of input data or settings.* This consistency is measured as the similarity between the discovered process models for each of the perturbed data sets or deviating settings. The different constructs will be elaborated on in Sect. 2. Stability as a dimension could be further refined into different types, for instance log perturbation stability or parameter stability, depending on the method of perturbation (perturbing the event log versus perturbing the parameter settings of the discovery technique). Most likely, there is an interdependency between both: the same technique with different parameter settings could be more stable with regards to log perturbations. Parameter sensitivity of process discovery techniques has been partially addressed in [2], based on fitness and precision rather than stability.

Observe that log-perturbation stability, as it is defined and constructed here, is conceptually related to existing dimensions for the evaluation of discovered process models, specifically generalization. Generalization is defined as measuring the probability that, given an event log and a process model, a next batch of process instances not in the original event log will invalidate a process model [20]. For an overview and evaluation of existing generalization metrics, we refer to [23]. The log-perturbation could be seen as a variation on this 'next batch' of behaviour, and similarity between the discovered process model could be seen as a quantification of the validity of baseline process model.

In this paper, we propose a new framework for measuring the stability of process discovery techniques through a stability index, inspired by the approach in [15]. Although the framework could be adapted for measuring different types of stability, we focus on log perturbation stability, which is a variant with regards to repeatedly resampled or perturbed input data. The framework has been implemented as a ProM-plugin[1] and can be used by process miners to assess the stability of different process discovery techniques, given an event log of their interest.

Given this objective, the rest of this paper is structured as follows: in Sect. 2, a general approach for assessing stability is proposed. In Sect. 3, the approach

---

[1] The plugin, screenshots and additional information can be found at http://www.processmining.be/PDStability/.

is extensively evaluated considering two applications: evaluating the stability of discovered process models with regards to correctness, and evaluating the stability of process models with regards to completeness. Finally, in Sect. 4, conclusions are formulated and an outlook to future adaptations is presented.

2   A Stability Assessment Framework

The approach proposed in this paper is based on a methodology for stability-based validation of clustering solutions in [14], which was adapted for biclustering solutions in [15]. As discussed in Sect. 1, clustering is one of the most well-known unsupervised learning techniques. As such, it suffers from the same issues regarding solution validity as other unsupervised learning techniques.

In [14,15], resampling/perturbation strategies, learning algorithms, and solution similarity metrics are proposed that are specifically designed for (bi)clustering problems. In this domain, stability was shown to be an effective metric for assessing the validity of a clustering solution, e.g. with regards to cluster size or clustering technique. An advantage of the clustering domain as compared to process discovery is the existence of alternative validity indices, such as entropy or gap statistics, which can be used as a reference for comparing a stability-based approach. In process discovery, solution validity is a more complex construct, since it is already partially addressed by existing metrics. Specifically, our approach is related to the generalization sub-dimension of accuracy, as explained in the previous section. Nonetheless, we claim that a supplementary dimension to existing interpretations of process discovery validity should be considered, i.e. stability.

As such, this paper contributes by proposing a stability assessment framework for process discovery techniques. The framework is tailored to measure so-called 'log perturbation stability', however it can be reconfigured for assessing other types of stability, such as parameter stability.

In Fig. 1, our stability assessment framework is depicted. Tailoring the framework to process discovery entails the configuration of three main components, i.e. the perturbation strategy (step 1), the solution similarity computation (step 3), and a stability index calculation (step 4). In addition, a process discovery technique should be chosen (step 2).

The steps of our approach thus become:

1. **Step 1**: Given an event log L, and a log perturbation function $P()$, create n perturbed versions of the event log: $P_1(L)$ to $P_n(L)$.
2. **Step 2**: Discover a process model PM by applying a process discovery technique $PD()$ to the original event log: $PM = PD(L)$ and to the perturbed event logs: $PM_i = PD(P_i(L))$ with $i \in \{1..n\}$.
3. **Step 3**: Given a similarity index $I(PM_x, PM_y)$, quantify the similarity between the discovered process model on the original dataset and the discovered process model on the perturbed dataset as $I(PM, PM_i)$.

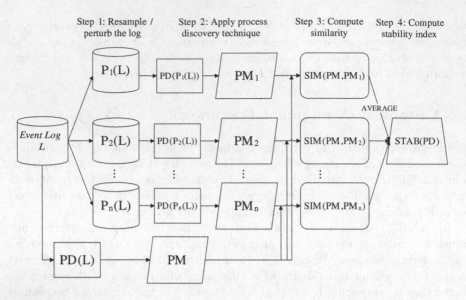

Fig. 1. A visualization of the proposed approach for calculating the stability of a discovered process model, based on a similar diagram in [15].

4. **Step 4**: Average these similarity measures to create a stability metric for event log L and discovery technique $PD()$ as

$$S^{PD} = \frac{1}{n} \sum_{i=1}^{n} I(PM, PM_i) \tag{1}$$

Observe that a higher value for S^{PD} indicates a better stability of the solution. As such, this metric can be used for evaluating a process discovery outcome. In the remainder of this section, we describe the three main components of our framework: a perturbation strategy based on resampling and noise induction (Sect. 2.1), computation of solution similarity based on process model similarity metrics (Sect. 2.2), and calculation of the stability index based on a window-based approach (Sect. 2.3).

2.1   Step 1: Log Perturbation Strategy

Perturbing event logs essentially boils down to three options: either some behaviour is removed, or some behaviour is added, or a combination of both. There are many different ways to do this. Regarding the removal of behaviour, event log perturbation can be approached through case-level resampling in a random fashion, which is closely related to classical bootstrapping [5]. Note that case-level bootstrapping an event log becomes trace-level bootstrapping. When dealing with event logs, an important consideration is whether to bootstrap process instances or distinct process instances (i.e. the effect of imbalance on the bootstrap sample). An alternative to random resampling is systematic leave-one-out cross-validation. Cross-validation has been proposed briefly in [20], in the context of generalization for process-mining techniques, where generalization is measured by leave-one-out cross-validation as follows: leave out one process instance, and count the percentage of instances that can still be replayed on the discovered process model. Observe that our approach deliberately does not incorporate any form of replay.

Secondly, regarding the addition of behaviour, small perturbations of event logs strongly relates to the idea of adding noise to the log. In [18], four types of noise were initially defined: remove head, remove tail, remove body, and swap tasks. In [6], the removal of a single task was added as a noise induction scheme, together with the combination of all previous noise types. These noise induction types were already used to evaluate robustness of process discovery techniques, for instance in [11]. However, in contrast to our paper, this work evaluated the robustness to noise of process discovery techniques directly based on traditional accuracy metrics. Here, we propose a framework for assessing the stability of process discovery techniques that is independent from the actual accuracy or comprehensibility of the outcome. As such, it is an orthogonal evaluation dimension that should be taken into account.

Taking these aspects into consideration, the log perturbation strategy underlying our stability assessment framework is as follows. First behaviour can be removed through a resampling procedure, which is essentially undersampling at the level of distinct process instances. However, to make the resampling a bit less naive, the probability that a distinct process instance is removed, is inversely proportional to the frequency with which this distinct process instance is present in the event log. Secondly, behaviour can be added through noise induction. Albeit the several noise types already available [18], we opt to include three types of noise: remove a single event, swap two events, and add a random single event (from the log activity alphabet) at a random place in the process instance. Noise addition is performed at process instance level. For both removal (undersampling at distinct process instance level) and addition (noise induction at process instance level), a percentage of affected instances should be chosen. Observe that in case both perturbation options are applied, the resampling is performed first and the noise induction is applied second.

2.2   Step 3: Solution Similarity Computation

An extensive overview of similarity metrics for the pairwise comparison of business process models is presented in [8]. Three distinct categories of similarity metrics are proposed: first, node matching similarity, where similarity is based on the labels and attributes attributed to the different elements of a process model; secondly, structural similarity, where the labels of these elements are compared as well as the topology of the process models; and thirdly, behavioural similarity, where the labels of the elements are compared as well as causal relations captured in the process model.

Given our context of process discovery from an event log, node matching similarity is irrelevant. However, both structural as well as behavioural similarity metrics can be of use within the stability assessment framework. Regarding structural similarity, a so-called graph edit distance similarity is defined in [8], based on the amount of insertions and deletions that are necessary to transform one process graph into the other. Other structural metrics such as tree edit distance are available as well [1]. Looking at behavioural similarity, a common approach relies on causal footprints [9,10], referred to as the causal footprint similarity. Other options are transition adjacency-based similarity [29], or behavioral profile-based similarity [13,24,25]. A final category of process model similarity can be described as event-log based. Such metrics are based on the principle that not all pathways in a process model are equally important, and that behaviour that is more likely given the event log should be represented as such in a similarity metrics. Examples can be found in [19].

The current stability assessment framework incorporates three similarity metrics: (1) Graph-edit Distance (GED) [8], (2) causal footprint-based similarity (CF) [9], and (3) behavioural profile-based similarity (BP) [24]. In Sect. 3, the suitability of these metrics is assessed in an experimental evaluation.

2.3   Step 4: Stability Index Computation

Finally, in step 4 of our framework, the stability index is computed as an average over a number of iterations, as detailed in Algorithm 1. Hereto, three extra input parameters are necessary: a minimal number of iterations r_{min}, a review window Δr and a maximal stability error ϵ_S. Typical values for these parameters are 20, 10, and 0.005 respectively. This iterative approach serves a double purpose: on the one hand, it ensures that the final stability is robust and sufficiently precise, by enforcing an upper bound on the stability error; on the other hand, it prevents unnecessary computation, by terminating once the stability error is sufficiently small and the minimal number of iterations have been performed.

3   Experimental Evaluation

In this section, the configurations of the proposed stability assessment framework are analyzed, together with an investigation of the effects of the level of perturbation added and the specific characteristics of an event log. The objective is to show the appropriateness of the proposed constructs for the evaluation of process discovery techniques. Therefore, this section is structured as follows: first, in Sect. 3.1, the global setup of the evaluation is discussed, with regard to the datasets, process discovery techniques, similarity metrics and perturbation strategies used. Section 3.2 discusses the effect of the level of perturbation to which the event log is exposed. Section 3.3 provides the global results, while Sect. 3.4 takes a closer look at the effects of the characteristics of the event log on the stability.

Algorithm 1. Stability evaluation

Input: L := Event log, PD := Process discovery algorithm, P:= Perturbation strategy, s := similarity metric;
Input: r_{min} := 20, Δr := 10, ϵ_S := 0.005; % Configuration
Output: S := Stability measure for the combination of event log L and discovery algorithm PD

1: **function** STABILITY(L, PD, P, s,r_{min}, Δr, ϵ_S)
2:      $r := 1$ % Iteration
3:      $PM := PD(L)$ % Baseline discovered process model
4:      $u() := \{\}$ % List of similarity results per iteration
5:      $w() := \{\}$ % List of stability results per iteration
6:      **while** $(r < r_{min}) \vee [max_{p,q}|w(p) - w(q)| > \epsilon_S; \forall p, q : r - \Delta r < p < q \leq r)]$ **do**
7:          $L_r := P_r(L)$ % Perturb the log
8:          $PM_r := PD(L_r)$ % Discovered process model from perturbed log
9:          $u(r) := s(PM, PM_r)$ % Calculate similarity with baseline model
10:         $w(r) := \frac{(r-1)*w(r-1)+u(r)}{r}$ % Calculate stability
11:         $r := r + 1$
12:     **end while**
13:     **return** $S := w(r - 1)$
14: **end function**

3.1 Setup

Five aspects of the experimental setup are of interest: the effect of characteristics of the event log on stability, the differences regarding process discovery techniques with regards to stability, the similarity metric used to compute the stability, the chosen perturbation strategy, and the level of perturbation induced by this strategy.

Firstly, the event log characteristics. We have set up experiments with 20 artificial event logs, as shown in Table 1. These datasets are taken from [3], to make our results compatible with other findings in the process mining domain. With regards to the characteristics of the event log, three measures are under scrutiny: the number of distinct process instances, the number of distinct events in the log, and the average number of events per process instance. The different activity structures on the underlying process models leveraged to create the artificial logs in [3], such as the presence loops of length 1 or 2, arbitrary or structured loops, invisible tasks are not considered here, since we are not concerned with rediscovering the artificial process model. As shown in Table 1, these characteristics vary sufficiently across the different event logs. Furthermore, we have repeated our setup on 5 real-life event logs [7], also listed in Table 1, to test whether similar results can be found using realistic event logs.

Secondly, the 8 process discovery techniques that are included in our study are the following, with default settings, and converted to Petri Nets where necessary: (1) Alpha miner [21], (2) Alpha++ miner [27], (3) Fodina [22], (4) Heuristics Miner [26], (5) ILPMiner [28], (6) Inductive Miner [16], (7) Flower miner, a technique that produces an underfitting flower model; (8) Naive [22], a discovery technique that naively models a connection between two transitions if they ever follow each other directly in the event log, unless these events overlap in time, in which case a connection is made to the closest non-overlappping transition.

Thirdly, three similarity metrics were used for comparing models discovered from perturbed event logs to the baseline discovered model, as described

Table 1. Characteristics of the artifical and real-life event logs used for the evaluation: number of process instances (#PI), distinct process instances (#DPI), number of different events (#EV) and average number of events per process instance ($\frac{\#EV}{PI}$).

Logname	#PI	#DPI	#EV	#EV/PI	Artificial	Real-life
grpd_g22pi300	300	24	26	10.32	✓	
groupedFollowsl11_500	500	29	8	11.79	✓	
grpd_g19pi300	300	32	25	13.69	✓	
grpd_g13pi300	300	35	24	16.69	✓	
grpd_g12pi300	300	38	28	16.14	✓	
grpd_g24pi300	300	46	23	13.77	✓	
grpd_g4pi300	300	48	31	19.92	✓	
grouped_g2pi300	300	65	24	15.00	✓	
grpd_g5pi300	300	66	22	20.57	✓	
driveClass_700	700	87	13	21.00	✓	
grpd_g6pi300	300	92	25	18.06	✓	
grpd_g9pi300	300	102	28	18.93	✓	
groupedFollowsparallel5_700	700	109	12	12.00	✓	
grpd_g10pi300	300	110	25	13.72	✓	
grpd_g15pi300	300	135	27	13.26	✓	
herbstFig6p37_700	700	135	20	20.00	✓	
grpd_g14pi300	300	157	26	37.80	✓	
grpd_g20pi300	300	187	23	20.64	✓	
grpd_g7pi300	300	231	31	48.17	✓	
grpd_g3pi300	300	239	31	48.66	✓	
MOA	2004	71	49	6.20		✓
KP2P	10487	76	23	9.33		✓
ICP	6407	155	18	5.99		✓
MCRM	956	212	22	11.73		✓
KIM	1541	251	18	5.62		✓

in Sect. 2.2: Graph-edit Distance [8], causal footprint based similarity [9], and behavioural profile based similarity [24]. The latter is measured as a weighted sum between exclusiveness similarity, order similarity, interleaving order similarity, extended order similarity and extended interleaving similarity, as it was implemented in *JBPT*-library.

Fourthly, three different strategies for generating perturbations are considered here. On the one hand, a resampling method, where $p\%$ distinct process instances are randomly removed from the event log. The probability of removal is the inverse of the frequency of that distinct process instance in the event log. On the other hand, a noise induction method, where $q\%$ process instances have one random event removed, added or two events swapped. One of these three perturbations is randomly chosen with equal probabilities. Finally, a third setting is included that combines both methods: first, $p\%$ distinct process instances are removed; second, $q\%$ process instances have one random event removed, added or two events swapped. Both strategies are tested with p and/or q equal to 10 %.

Finally, a small note on the specific calculations and environment of the experiments: all experiments were run on a Intel XEon E5-2699 v3 processor of a Windows Server 2012 R2. For the calculation of stability, 20 fixed iterations where taken, rather than the adaptive strategy described in Algorithm 1. The duration of 1 set of specifications (i.e. 20 iterations) was restricted to 10 min. Of the 480 configurations on artificial logs that were evaluated using three different similarity metrics, 62 did not finish the mining task within the time limit: 44 combinations with Alpha++, 16 combinations of ILP, 1 combination with Fodina and 1 combination with Inductive miner. On the real-life datasets, 120 configurations were tested of which 9 resulted in a timeout: three configurations with Alpha++ and two with Alpha, Fodina and ILP.

3.2 Effect of the Percentage of Perturbation

Figures 2 and 3 show the effects of varying percentages of noise, when using Causal Footprint similarity as an underlying metric and, respectively, Heuristics Miner and Alpha miner as process discovery algorithm. The points represent average stability over 5 of the artificial event logs. A couple of observations can be made from these figures. First, observe that, as expected, the average stability declines as it is exposed to higher percentages of noise, all other things equal. The same observation holds for resampling percentages, at least when combined with a noise percentage smaller than 40 %. Secondly, remark that the stability appears to be a lot more sensitive to the level of noise than the level of resampling. This observation should be kept in mind regarding the results in Sect. 3.3, as the same percentage of noise induction has a greater effect than the resampling. Thirdly, observe that the curve for the results using Heuristics miner (Fig. 2) declines less rapidly than the one using Alpha miner (Fig. 3). Finally, even at high levels of noise induction, the resulting stability when using Heuristics miner lies around 0.85, whereas the resulting stability using Alpha miner performs significantly worse, even at lower percentages of noise.

3.3 Results of the Experimental Evaluation

Before interpreting the results, a note should be made regarding the compatibility of the similarity metrics and some of the process discovery techniques. The technique based on behavioural profiles, for example, requires that there are no unconnected transitions. Some techniques, however, do not guarantee that no unconnected transitions will be mined. Therefore, in some combinations with BP, no result could be obtained. Specifically, for the artificial logs, this is the case in 33 configurations with Alpha miner, 12 configurations with ILP, and 2 configurations with Alpha++. For the real-life logs, this was the case in 11 combinations of Alpha with BP.

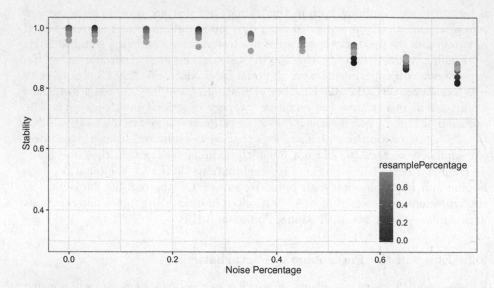

Fig. 2. Scatterplot based on noise percentage of the average stability over 5 artificial event logs using Heuristics Miner and a stability based on Causal Footprints, for resampling and noise induction percentages equal to 0 % or ranging from 5 to 75 % with 10 % intervals

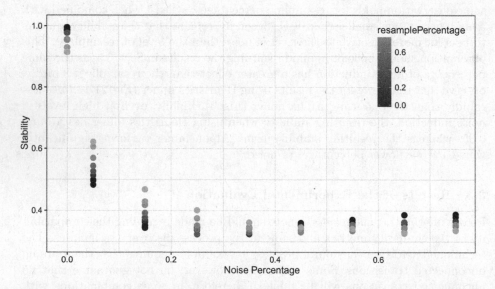

Fig. 3. Scatterplot based on noise percentage of the average stability over 5 artificial event logs using Alpha Miner and a stability based on Causal Footprints, for resampling and noise induction percentages equal to 0 % or ranging from 5 to 75 % with 10 % intervals

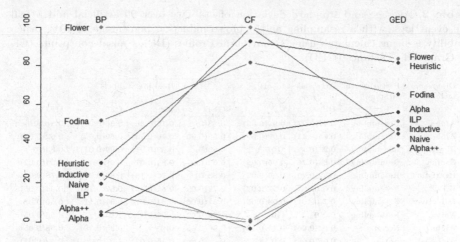

Fig. 4. Visualization of the average stability results when applying a noise induction strategy. Averages over 20 artificial event logs.

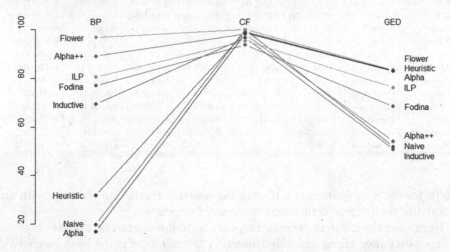

Fig. 5. Visualization of the average stability results when applying a resampling-based strategy. Averages over 20 artificial event logs.

The results can be found in Table 2. For a more intuitive representation of the results of the approaches only based on noise and only based on resampling, we refer to Figs. 4 and 5. Several observations can be made. First, it is clear that the results of the combined approach and the approach that only uses noise induction are highly similar. This was also touched upon in the previous section, and is likely due to the different impact of a 10 % noise induction compared to a 10 % resampling. Secondly, when comparing similarity metrics in Figs. 4 and 5, the ranges of the average stability appear to be similar across similarity metrics,

Table 2. Average and standard deviation of stability over 20 artificial and 5 real-life event logs, with a resampling and/or noise induction percentage of 10 %, where stability is being calculated using Behavioural Profiles (BP), Causal Footprints (CF) or Graph-edit Distance (GED).

Discovery technique	Perturbation strategy	Artificial stab(sd)			Real-life stab(sd)		
		BP	CF	GED	BP	CF	GED
Alpha	Resampling	0.17(0.27)	0.99(0.02)	0.83(0)	0.16(0.36)	0.86(0.05)	0.8(0.01)
Alpha++	Resampling	0.65(0.41)	0.99(0.02)	0.55(0.06)	0.76(0.15)	0.69(0.05)	0.62(0.09)
Flower	Resampling	0.98(0.1)	1(0)	0.83(0)	0.99(0.01)	0.99(0.01)	0.83(0)
Fodina	Resampling	0.84(0.2)	0.95(0.06)	0.69(0.05)	0.84(0.07)	0.9(0.04)	0.64(0.02)
Heuristic	Resampling	0.32(0.29)	0.99(0.02)	0.83(0)	0.72(0.16)	0.89(0.06)	0.78(0.04)
ILP	Resampling	0.5(0.49)	0.97(0.07)	0.77(0.09)	0.61(0.12)	0.62(0.18)	0.64(0.06)
Inductive	Resampling	0.7(0.15)	0.98(0.06)	0.51(0.06)	0.64(0.07)	0.91(0.1)	0.55(0.07)
Naive	Resampling	0.2(0)	1(0)	0.52(0.02)	0.21(0)	1(0)	0.53(0.05)
Alpha	Noise	0.04(0.06)	0.45(0.13)	0.56(0.05)	0(0)	0.35(0.19)	0.58(0.05)
Alpha++	Noise	0.05(0.08)	0(0.18)	0.39(0.05)	0.15(0.02)	−0.1(0.12)	0.42(0.04)
Flower	Noise	1(0)	1(0)	0.83(0)	0.83(0.05)	0.84(0.05)	0.83(0)
Fodina	Noise	0.52(0.3)	0.82(0.1)	0.65(0.06)	0.45(0.12)	0.68(0.12)	0.6(0.03)
Heuristic	Noise	0.3(0.27)	0.93(0.03)	0.81(0.01)	0.27(0.2)	0.59(0.17)	0.71(0.07)
ILP	Noise	0.14(0.23)	0.01(0.17)	0.51(0.02)	0.13(0.04)	−0.05(0.12)	0.56(0.05)
Inductive	Noise	0.24(0.08)	−0.03(0.13)	0.47(0.04)	0.35(0.1)	0(0.3)	0.51(0.02)
Naive	Noise	0.2(0.01)	1(0)	0.45(0.03)	0.2(0)	1(0)	0.51(0.04)
Alpha	Combined	0.03(0.06)	0.46(0.13)	0.56(0.05)	0(0)	0.33(0.17)	0.57(0.04)
Alpha++	Combined	0.08(0.08)	0(0.13)	0.38(0.05)	0.14(0.02)	−0.1(0.1)	0.42(0.04)
Flower	Combined	1(0)	1(0)	0.83(0)	0.82(0.04)	0.83(0.04)	0.83(0)
Fodina	Combined	0.53(0.29)	0.8(0.11)	0.64(0.06)	0.43(0.1)	0.65(0.11)	0.6(0.02)
Heuristic	Combined	0.3(0.27)	0.93(0.04)	0.81(0.01)	0.18(0.07)	0.57(0.17)	0.67(0.05)
ILP	Combined	0.13(0.19)	0.01(0.17)	0.51(0.02)	0.13(0.04)	−0.03(0.11)	0.57(0.04)
Inductive	Combined	0.24(0.07)	−0.02(0.13)	0.47(0.02)	0.34(0.11)	0.02(0.3)	0.51(0.02)
Naive	Combined	0.2(0.01)	1(0)	0.45(0.03)	0.2(0)	1(0)	0.51(0.04)

except for the combination of a resampling-based perturbation strategy with an underlying similarity metric based on causal footprints.

Regarding the different process discovery techniques, observe why we chose to incorporate flower miner and naive miner. A flower model is the least restrictive model one can imagine, where any activity can be executed in any order. It is clear that such a discovery technique should be very stable with regards to noise induction and resampling, and a very high stability is expected. Observe from Table 2 that this is indeed the case on the artificial logs. The inverse is true for the naive discovery technique, which naively incorporates any relationship between two activities seen in the log as long as they do not overlap in time. One would expect such a technique to score quite poorly on stability, which is the case when calculating its stability using behavioural profiles or Graph-edit Distance, but not using Causal Footprints. Apart from the results on the naive discovery technique, the results of the noise induction strategy are within expectations: techniques that were originally developed with robustness in mind, such as Heuristics miner and Fodina, achieve higher stability than techniques that are expected to be more sensitive to noise, such as ILP and Alpha.

Furthermore, Table 2 includes the standard deviation of the stability, which characterises the discrepancies across the 20 artificial and 5 real-life event logs, respectively. In general, the pure resampling-based perturbation strategy leads to more consistent results than the noise induction-approach. The stability based on GED appears to be the most consistent across event logs when combined with noise induction or a combined approach. When combined with resampling, the stability based on Causal Footprints and the stability based on GED perform equally consistent.

3.4   Effect of Log Characteristics

To show the effect of event log characteristics, we fit a number of regression models: a full and reduced one, for each perturbation strategy and each underlying similarity metric. All data is taken at a 10 %-level of perturbation. The full fitted models are of the form represented in Eq. 2, where x_{pd} are dummy variables indicating the process discovery technique and x_{dpi}, x_{ev}, x_{tl} are numerical variables representing the number of distinct process instances, number of distinct events and average trace length of the event log under scrutiny. In the restricted model (Eq. 3) the log characteristics are removed from the model. A lack-of-fit test is performed to show whether these log characteristics can be removed without substantial decrease in the fitness of the regression model. The results are represented in Table 3.

$$S^{pd} = \beta_0 + \sum_{pd=Alpha}^{Naive} \beta_{pd}x_{pd} + \beta_{dpi}x_{dpi} + \beta_{ev}x_{ev} + \beta_{tl}x_{tl} \qquad (2)$$

$$S^{pd} = \beta_0 + \sum_{pd=Alpha}^{Naive} \beta_{pd}x_{pd} \qquad (3)$$

Table 3. Fitness values and degrees of freedom for full and reduced linear model of stability over 20 artificial event logs, with a resampling or noise induction percentage of 10 %, with similarity being calculated using Behavioural Profiles (BP), Causal Footprints (CF) or Graph-edit Distance (GED). P values correspond to a chi-squared likelihood-ratio test on 3 degrees of freedom, and indicate whether the full model has a significantly higher goodness-of-fit than the reduced model.

Strategy	BP			CF			GED		
	R^2	LogLik	df	R^2	LogLik	df	R^2	LogLik	df
Noise: full	0.82	66	123	0.95	125.6	123	0.96	269.7	123
Noise: red	0.77	48.8	126	0.95	125	126	0.96	263.7	126
LRT: p-value		**<0.001**				0.80			**0.008**
	R^2	LogLik	df	R^2	LogLik	df	R^2	LogLik	df
Resampling: full	0.70	26	137	0.18	230	137	0.90	251	137
Resampling: red	0.65	13	140	0.15	226.8	140	0.90	248.8	140
LRT: p-value		**<0.001**				0.114			0.21

From Table 3, it is clear that excluding all log characteristics leads to a significant reduction in goodness-of-fit in the noise-induction case, except when combining this perturbation with causal footprints. This does not mean that all log characteristics are significantly related to the stability in all models: when combining noise induction with GED as similarity metric, only the average trace length is significantly related to the stability (p-value < 0.05), with a higher average trace length leading to lower stability. When combining noise induction or resampling with BP, the number of distinct activities is the only variable that is significant at a 5 %-level, with a higher number of activities leading to a lower expected stability, all other things equal.

4   Discussion and Future Work

Overview. The purpose of this paper is to propose a new dimension for the evaluation of process discovery techniques, stability, and a framework for its assessment. Specifically, a log-perturbation stability framework based on model similarity is extensively described, and its components are thoroughly evaluated using both artificial and real-life event logs. Two resampling strategies, one based on noise induction and one based on trace resampling, are proposed, and the strategy based on noise induction is shown to lead to the highest discriminating power, even at low percentages of noise induction. Three underlying similarity metrics are proposed, one based on behavioural profiles, one based on causal footprints, and one based on Graph-edit Distance.

Main Findings. Overall, there are three key takeaways from the experimental evaluation: (1) stability, as it was defined here, is a concept that can help differentiate between different process discovery techniques. (2) Different configurations of the stability framework lead to different results, however, making general conclusions about the process discovery techniques difficult. Both the type of perturbation and type of similarity metric influence these results. (3) The stability results are influenced by the specific characteristics of the event logs used, such as number of activities in this log, or the average trace length, apart from the configurations with Causal Footprints.

Limitations. Several limitations exist with regard to our framework and its evaluation, and these limitations should be addressed more thoroughly in future work. First of all, there is the question of the desirability of certain types of perturbation, especially noise induction. Although noise induction is shown to lead to interesting results, it may not be an accurate representation of reality, given that most information systems record events rather faithfully nowadays. Secondly, a limitation exists regarding the evaluation of discovery algorithms: since our approach requires a number of iterations in order to create valid results, we disregarded discovery algorithms that don't scale well (e.g. the genetic approaches of [3,6]). Moreover, it should be noted that the results presented here are valid only for the distinct configurations of the algorithms. Clearly, the results would be different for Inductive miner, for example, given that a more inclusive or exclusive configuration is be used. Therefore, 'parameter stability' and 'log perturbation stability' are interrelated concepts. Nonetheless, applying an evaluation on the default settings of an algorithm is justifiable, given that users of these implementations rarely change the default settings [4]. Thirdly, the choice of Petri nets as an underlying construct for discovered process models leads to an inherent bias, especially with regards to the conversion of techniques that produce results in an other modelling notation. Fourthly, the current implementation is limited to existing process similarity metrics. However, these metrics were not conceived with discovered process models in mind. Therefore, **future work** could look into the construction of a process similarity metric geared specifically towards stability of process discovery techniques. An alternative to this approach would be to quantify similarity in a more event-log driven way, by incorporating conformance checking metrics into the similarity. An example of this could be behavioural precision and recall as defined in [19].

Finally, two relationships should be quantified in continuing work: on the one hand, the relationship between the stability results and specific behavioural structures present in event logs, or the models used to generate these event logs, such as loops of a certain length and invisible transitions; on the other hand, the relationships between the proposed approach and related conformance checking metrics for quality metrics like cross-validation-based generalization [20].

References

1. Bae, J., Caverlee, J., Liu, L., Yan, H.: Process mining by measuring process block similarity. In: Eder, J., Dustdar, S. (eds.) BPM Workshops 2006. LNCS, vol. 4103, pp. 141–152. Springer, Heidelberg (2006)
2. Bolt, A., de Leoni, M., van der Aalst, W.M.P.: Scientific workflows for process mining: building blocks, scenarios, and implementation. Int. J. Softw. Tools Technol. Transf. 1–22 (2015). doi:10.1007/s10009-015-0399-5
3. Borja, V., Mucientes, M., Lama, M.: ProDiGen: mining complete, precise and minimal structure process models with a genetic algorithm. Inf. Sci. Innov. Appl. Artif. Neural Netw. Eng. **294**, 315–333 (2015)
4. Claes, J., Poels, G.: Process mining and the ProM framework: an exploratory survey. In: La Rosa, M., Soffer, P. (eds.) BPM Workshops 2012. LNBIP, vol. 132, pp. 187–198. Springer, Heidelberg (2013)
5. Davison, A.C., Hinkley, D.V.: Bootstrap Methods and Their Application, vol. 1. Cambridge University Press, Cambridge (1997)
6. De Medeiros, A.K.A., Weijters, A.J.M.M., Van Der Aalst, W.M.P.: Genetic process mining: an experimental evaluation. Data Min. Knowl. Discov. **14**(2), 245–304 (2007)
7. De Weerdt, J., De Backer, M., Vanthienen, J., Baesens, B.: A multi-dimensional quality assessment of state-of-the-art process discovery algorithms using real-life event logs. Inf. Syst. **37**(7), 654–676 (2012)
8. Dijkman, R., Dumas, M., Van Dongen, B., Krik, R., Mendling, J.: Similarity of business process models: metrics and evaluation. Inf. Syst. **36**(2), 498–516 (2011)
9. van Dongen, B.F., Dijkman, R.M., Mendling, J.: Measuring similarity between business process models. Adv. Inf. Syst. Eng. **5074**, 450–464 (2008)
10. van Dongen, B.F., Mendling, J., van der Aalst, W.M.P.: Structural patterns for soundness of business process models. In: 10th IEEE International Enterprise Distributed Object Computing Conference, pp. 116–128 (2006)

11. Goedertier, S., Martens, D., Vanthienen, J., Baesens, B.: Robust process discovery with artificial negative events. J. Mach. Learn. Res. **10**, 1305–1340 (2009)
12. Hastie, T., Tibshirani, R., Friedman, J.: Unsupervised learning. In: Hastie, T., Tibshirani, R., Friedman, J. (eds.) The Elements of Statistical Learning: Data Mining, Inference Prediction, 2nd edn, pp. 485–585. Springer, New York (2009)
13. Kunze, M., Weidlich, M., Weske, M.: Behavioral similarity – a proper metric. In: Rinderle-Ma, S., Toumani, F., Wolf, K. (eds.) BPM 2011. LNCS, vol. 6896, pp. 166–181. Springer, Heidelberg (2011)
14. Lange, T., Roth, V., Braun, M.L., Buhmann, J.M.: Stability-based validation of clustering solutions. Neural Comput. **16**(6), 1299–1323 (2004)
15. Lee, Y., Lee, J., Jun, C.H.: Stability-based validation of bicluster solutions. Pattern Recogn. **44**(2), 252–264 (2011)
16. Leemans, S.J.J., Fahland, D., van der Aalst, W.M.P.: Discovering block-structured process models from event logs - a constructive approach. In: Colom, J.-M., Desel, J. (eds.) PETRI NETS 2013. LNCS, vol. 7927, pp. 311–329. Springer, Heidelberg (2013)
17. Levine, E., Domany, E.: Resampling method for unsupervised estimation of cluster validity. Neural Comput. **13**(11), 2573–2593 (2001)
18. Maruster, L.: A Machine Learning Approach To Understand Business Processes. Eindhoven University of Technology, Eindhoven (2003)
19. de Medeiros, A.K.A., van der Aalst, W.M.P., Weijters, A.J.M.M.: Quantifying process equivalence based on observed behavior. Data Knowl. Eng. **64**(1), 55–74 (2008)
20. Van der Aalst, W., Adriansyah, A., Van Dongen, B.: Replaying history on process models for conformance checking and performance analysis. Wiley Interdiscip. Rev. Data Min. Knowl. Discov. **2**(2), 182–192 (2012)
21. Van Der Aalst, W., Weijters, T., Maruster, L.: Workflow mining: discovering process models from event logs. IEEE Trans. Knowl. Data Eng. **16**(9), 1128–1142 (2004)
22. Vanden Broucke, S.K.L.M.: Artificial negative events and other techniques. Ph.D. thesis, KU Leuven (2014)
23. Vanden Broucke, S.K.L.M., De Weerdt, J., Vanthienen, J., Baesens, B.: Determining process model precision and generalization with weighted artificial negative events. IEEE Trans. Knowl. Data Eng. **26**(8), 1877–1889 (2014)
24. Weidlich, M., Polyvyanyy, A., Desai, N., Mendling, J., Weske, M.: Process compliance analysis based on behavioural profiles. Inf. Syst. **36**(7), 1009–1025 (2011)
25. Weidlich, M., Polyvyanyy, A., Mendling, J., Weske, M.: Efficient computation of causal behavioural profiles using structural decomposition. In: Lilius, J., Penczek, W. (eds.) PETRI NETS 2010. LNCS, vol. 6128, pp. 63–83. Springer, Heidelberg (2010)
26. Weijters, A.J.M.M., van der Aalst, W.: Rediscovering workflow models from event-based data using little thumb. Integr. Comput. Eng. **10**, 151–162 (2003)
27. Wen, L., Van Der Aalst, W.M.P., Wang, J., Sun, J.: Mining process models with non-free-choice constructs. Data Min. Knowl. Discov. **15**(2), 145–180 (2007)
28. van der Werf, J.M.E.M., van Dongen, B.F., Hurkens, C.A.J., Serebrenik, A.: Process discovery using integer linear programming. In: van Hee, K.M., Valk, R. (eds.) PETRI NETS 2008. LNCS, vol. 5062, pp. 368–387. Springer, Heidelberg (2008)
29. Zha, H., Wang, J., Wen, L., Wang, C., Sun, J.: A workflow net similarity measure based on transition adjacency relations. Comput. Ind. **61**(5), 463–471 (2010)

Measuring the Quality of Models with Respect to the Underlying System: An Empirical Study

Gert Janssenswillen[1,2]($\boxtimes$), Toon Jouck[1], Mathijs Creemers[1],
and Benoît Depaire[1]

[1] Hasselt University, Agoralaan Bldg D, 3590 Diepenbeek, Belgium
[2] Research Foundation Flanders (FWO), Egmontstraat 5, 1060 Brussels, Belgium
{gert.janssenswillen,toon.jouck,mathijs.creemers,
benoit.depaire}@uhasselt.be

Abstract. Fitness and precision are two widely studied criteria to determine the quality of a discovered process model. These metrics measure how well a model represents the log from which it is learned. However, often the goal of discovery is not to represent the log, but the underlying system. This paper discusses the need to explicitly distinguish between a log and system perspective when interpreting the fitness and precision of a model. An empirical analysis was conducted to investigate whether the existing log-based fitness and precision measures are good estimators for system-based metrics. The analysis reveals that incompleteness and noisiness of event logs significantly impact fitness and precision measures. This makes them biased estimators of a model's ability to represent the true underlying process.

Keywords: Conformance checking · Evaluation metrics · Process model quality

1 Introduction

Due to the enormous growth of event data during the last decades, organizations are dealing with the challenge of extracting useful knowledge from it, and exploiting it to gain competitive advantages. Process mining provides ways to reach this goal, by getting a better understanding of business processes and improving them [1]. The origin of process mining dates back to the end of the previous century [5,12], and focused on discovering the process control-flow from event logs which contain recorded process behaviour. While the domain has grown much broader, control flow discovery is the most mature research track within process mining. For an overview of existing process discovery algorithms, witness [13]. In order to quantify the quality of a discovered process model, different quality dimensions have been defined [21], i.e. fitness, precision, generalization and simplicity. For each of the dimensions, several metrics have been developed and implemented, of which an overview can be found in [8].

Existing fitness and precision metrics typically measure the quality of a model with respect to the event log it was learned from. They thereby do not take into

© Springer International Publishing Switzerland 2016
M. La Rosa et al. (Eds.): BPM 2016, LNCS 9850, pp. 73–89, 2016.
DOI: 10.1007/978-3-319-45348-4_5

account that the event log is a limited sample of the real unknown process and possibly contains measurement errors. Since the underlying process is not known in real-life settings, the quality of a discovered process model as a representation of the underlying process cannot be determined directly. So far, little empirical research has been done to analyse whether the existing fitness and precision measures can be trusted as estimators of the behavioural similarity between the discovered model and the underlying system.

In this paper, the need to explicitly distinguish between a log and system perspective when interpreting the fitness and precision of a model, is highlighted. Experiments are conducted to examine whether the quality of a model with respect to the event log can be used as an unbiased estimator for the quality of the model with respect to the underlying process. Both the metrics their ability to estimated the quality of models unbiasedly, as their ability to unbiasedly rank a given collection of models from worst to best will be investigated.

The next section introduces the evaluation framework. Section 3 describes the experimental set-up. The results of this experiment are discussed in Sect. 4. Section 5 discusses the role of generalization and its link with the proposed framework. Finally, Sect. 6 provides an overview or related work and Sect. 7 concludes the paper.

2 Different Perspectives in Measuring Model Quality

The four classical quality dimensions are fitness, precision, generalization and simplicity [1]. Fitness, precision and generalization can be visualized using a Venn diagram [9], as is shown in Fig. 1.[1] In this figure, M, L and S refer to the *process behaviour* which belongs to the model, event log and system, respectively. It therefore abstracts from the representational language of the model. According to the author [9], the system S refers to the context of the process, e.g., the organization, rules, economy, etc.

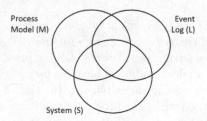

Fig. 1. Venn diagram representing the behaviour in the process model (M), event log (L) and system (S) [9].

In this paper, a slightly more tangible definition of *system* will be used. It will refer to the behaviour which is *real*, i.e. the underlying process. This process,

---

[1] In this paper, the simplicity dimension will not be taken into account, as it is not directly related to the behaviour of the discovered model.

generally unknown, defines the actual way in which work can be done. Note that the system is broader than only a prescriptive model used for the configuration of an information system, but can also include certain unwritten rules or customs. Everything which appears in the event log but is not part of the system is regarded as noise. Examples are measurement errors resulting from system outages. On the other hand, real though infrequent behaviour will not be perceived as noise in this paper.

Figure 1 points out that a discrepancy exists between the system and the event log. Process discovery tasks can thus be conducted using different objectives. Firstly, business users might be interested in the relation between the discovered model and the event log. In such a case, the objective will be to find a model which perfectly mimics the behaviour in the event log. Secondly, one might be interested in the relationship between the discovered model and the true underlying system. To understand the way work is actually be done, the objective will be to learn a model that exactly represents the system behaviour.

Following the well-known definitions of fitness and precision [10], it is evident that both dimensions try to tell something about the relationship between event log and model. Generalization, being defined in [9] as *the likelihood of previously unseen but allowed behaviour being supported by the process model*, appears to aim at assessing the relationship between the model and the system. However, the effectiveness of existing measures in achieving these goals remains unexplored.

In the remainder of this section, we articulate four alternative quality dimensions based on Fig. 1 and the work in [9]. Two of these dimensions measure the *distance* between a model and an event log, and correspond to the classical dimensions of fitness and precision. The other two quantify the distance between a model and a system. The four dimensions will be defined conceptually in terms of L, M and S, after some preliminary notations have been introduced.

2.1 Preliminaries

Definition 1 (Activity Sequences). *We define $\mathcal{A}$ as the activity alphabet. $\mathcal{A}^*$ is the set of all finite sequences over $\mathcal{A}$, representing the universe of traces. A trace $\sigma_j \in \mathcal{A}^*$ is a finite sequence of activities.*

Definition 2 (Event Log, Model, System). *An event log L is a multiset of traces, i.e. $L \in \mathbb{B}(\mathcal{A}^*)$, where $\mathbb{B}(\mathcal{A}^*)$ is the set of all mutlisets of $\mathcal{A}$.*

Definition 3 (Model, System). *A model M and a system S are subsets of the universe of traces, i.e. $M \in \mathbb{P}(\mathcal{A}^*)$ and $S \in \mathbb{P}(\mathcal{A}^*)$, where $\mathbb{P}(\mathcal{A}^*)$ is the power set of $\mathcal{A}^*$. $\mathbf{M}$ and $\mathbf{S}$ represent the domain of all possible models and systems, respectively, whereby $\mathbf{M} = \mathbf{S} = \mathbb{P}(\mathcal{A}^*)$. $\mathbf{L}$ represents the domain of all possible logs, whereby $\mathbf{L} = \mathbb{B}(\mathcal{A}^*)$.*

2.2 Model-Log Distance

The fit between an event log and a process model is monitored by two ratios [9], corresponding to the known concepts of fitness and precision. Given event log L, the log-fitness and log-precision of a model M can be defined as follows.

Definition 4 (Log-Fitness). *Log-fitness is a function* $F : \mathbf{M} \times \mathbf{L} \to [0, 1]$, *which quantifies how much of the behaviour in the event log is captured by the model. This can be defined as [9]:*

$$F(M, L) = \frac{|L \cap M|}{|L|} \qquad (1)$$

Definition 5 (Log-Precision). *Log-precision is a function* $P : \mathbf{M} \times \mathbf{L} \to [0, 1]$, *which quantifies how much of the behaviour in the model was observed in the event log. This can be defined as [9]:*

$$P(M, L) = \frac{|L \cap M|}{|M|} \qquad (2)$$

Only when both log-fitness and log-precision are equal to 1, then $L = M$, i.e. the event log and the model represent exactly the same behaviour. These metrics are orthogonal to each other, making it possible to construct models which score poorly on one criterion and excellent on the other. Acting as complementary forces, maximizing log-fitness and log-precision simultaneously maximizes the *fit* between the model and the event log.

2.3 Model-System Distance

By drawing the analogy, it is evident that two similar dimensions are needed to quantify the match between the model and the system. Firstly, there is a need for a metric that ensures the selection of models that contain all possible real behaviour. Secondly, a metric that favors the selection of models that only contain real behaviour is needed. Therefore, given the system S, the system-fitness and system-precision of a model M can be defined as:

Definition 6 (System-Fitness). *System-fitness is a function* $F : \mathbf{M} \times \mathbf{S} \to [0, 1]$, *which quantifies how much of the behaviour in the system is captured by the model. This can be defined as [9]:*

$$F(M, S) = \frac{|S \cap M|}{|S|} \qquad (3)$$

Definition 7 (System-Precision). *System-precision is a function* $P : \mathbf{M} \times \mathbf{S} \to [0, 1]$, *which quantifies how much of the behaviour in the model is part of the system. This can be defined as [9]:*

$$P(M, S) = \frac{|S \cap M|}{|M|} \qquad (4)$$

When event logs are incomplete and contain noise, log-based and system-based metrics will diverge. Depending on the goal, business users should then direct their attention to one pair of metrics. Note that the above formulas are rather coarse-grained. While in reality more fine-grained measures are preferred, these formulas suffice to distinguish the different concepts.

3   Experimental Analysis

3.1   Goal of the Experiments

The goal of the experiments conducted in this paper is twofold. Firstly, the goal is to analyse whether existing metrics are unbiased estimators of the true system fitness and precision. Secondly, the goal is to analyse whether the ranking of a set of models, based on existing metrics, also represents the true ranking in representing the underlying system.

Note that both abilities - estimation and ranking - have different impacts: when the quality of models with respect to the system is consistently overestimated, the ranking of the models will remain valid. However, when the biases are highly variable among models, also the ranking of models will be perturbed.

Unbiased Estimation. For the first goal of the experiment the quality of a set of models was measured both with respect to the event log it was learned from and the underlying system that generated the event log. The fitness value obtained from replaying event log L onto model M is represented as $F(M, L)$ for any fitness-measure. Conversely the fitness value obtained when comparing the system S with model M is represented as $F(M, S)$. Equivalently, we can compute $P(M, L)$ and $P(M, S)$ for any precision metric. Note that $F(M, L)$ and $P(M, L)$ represent log-fitness and log-precision, as defined in Eqs. 1 and 2, respectively, while $F(M, S)$ and $P(M, S)$ represent system-fitness and system-precision as expressed in Eqs. 3 and 4, respectively.

To investigate whether $F(M, L)$ and $P(M, L)$ are unbaised estimates of $F(M, S)$ and $P(M, S)$, respectively, we define the difference between these values for both fitness and precision as follows.

$$\Delta F(M, L, S) = F(M, L) - F(M, S) \tag{5}$$

$$\Delta P(M, L, S) = P(M, L) - P(M, S) \tag{6}$$

For example, $F^{ab}(M, L)$, the log-fitness as measured by the Alignment Based Fitness metric will be an unbiased estimator of $F^{ab}(M, S)$, if $E[\Delta F^{ab}] = 0$. When this value is positive, $F^{ab}(M, L)$ is said to overestimate $F^{ab}(M, S)$. Both ΔF and ΔP will be analysed for logs with and without noise, and with varying levels of completeness.

Unbiased Ranking. In order to examine whether the ranking which log-based metrics define on a set of models represent the true ranking of these models with respect to the underlying system, a second analysis will be done. Even when existing metrics are biased estimators, if they still rank different models accurately, they can still be used to compare the quality of models. In order to investigate this, a limited set of discovered models will be compared with a collection of event logs generated by the same system. These event logs will have different levels of completeness and noise. The actual set up of the experiments will be discussed in the following paragraph.

3.2   Set up

The set up of the experiments was based on the framework for comparing process mining algorithms in [22]. The design is explained in more detail below. Table 1 shows an overview of the key-characteristics of the experiment, including the overall scale of the experiment.

1. Generate 10 systems, which will act as ground truth process models.
2. Estimate the number of different traces which can be generated by the systems, in order to target the completeness of the logs to be simulated.
3. Simulate the enactment of each system to produce artificial event logs with different levels of noise and completeness. Furthermore, simulate a ground truth event log for each system.
4. For each log, mine a set of process models using discovery algorithms.
5. Compute the quality of the models using the selected metrics
   a. For each model, compute process quality metrics both in relation to the log it was discovered from, and in relation to the ground truth event log.
   b. For a set of randomly selected models for each system, compute the quality metrics in relation to all the event logs generated by that system.

Table 1. Experimental set up.

Characteristic	Value
Number of systems	10
Completeness levels	100 %, 75 %, 50 %, 25 %
Noise levels	0 %, 5 %, 10 %, 15 %
Number of event logs for each combination	5
Discovery algorithms	Heuristics [24]
	Inductive [18]
	ILP [10]
Fitness metrics	Alignment based fitness [3] (*ab*)
	Negative event recall [7] (*ne*)
	Token-based fitness [20] (*tb*)
Precision metrics	Alignment based precision [3] (*ab*)
	Best align etc precision [4] (*ba*)
	Negative event precision [7] (*ne*)
	One align etc precision [4] (*oa*)
Generalization metrics	Alignment based generalization [3] (*ab*)
	Negative event generalization [7] (*ne*)
Total number of event logs	800 logs
Total number of models	2400 models

Generation of Systems. In total 10 random models were artificially generated, in order to be used as systems, using the methodology in [17]. The generated systems were process trees. Each system has been generated according to its own characteristics, i.e. the expected number of activities, the different types of process operators (sequence, choice, parallel, etc.), the occurrence of silent activities and the occurrence of duplicate tasks.

Determine Number of Paths. In order to target the completeness of event logs during log simulation, the number of unique activity sequences in each model was computed using the algorithm in [16]. In order to cope with loops, a maximum number of iterations was taken into account for this calculation. This can be justified by adapting a so-called *fairness assumption*, which states that a task of a process cannot be postponed indefinitely. The assumption therefore rules out infinite behaviours that are considered unrealistic [6].

Simulation of Event Logs. Each of the artificial systems was used to simulate event logs with different levels of completeness and noise. Both the completeness and noise level of the logs were controlled explicitly during the simulation. The amount of noise as well as the amount of completeness has been defined at the level of activity sequences. Four different levels were defined for each characteristic, resulting in 16 different types of logs. For each type, 5 different logs were simulated, amounting to a total of 80 logs per system. Next to these, a ground truth event log, with perfect completeness and without noise is created for each system.

The levels of completeness are 100 %, 75 %, 50 % and 25 %. A log of 100 % completeness is obtained by simulating the system until the simulated event log contains the same number of unique paths as calculated in the previous step, say n. A log of 75 % is obtained by simulating the system until $0.75n$ different paths have been seen, etc.

The levels of noise have been defined at 0 %, 5 %, 10 % and 15 %. A log with 5 % noise is created by taking $0.05/0.95 = 5.26$ % of the traces of a noise-free log. To this subset of traces, different types of noise are added: missing head, missing body, missing tail or missing activity [19]. These noisy traces are then added to the original event log. The resulting event log consequently has $n(1 + 0.0526)$ traces, of which $0.0526n$ are noisy. The noise level will thus be 5 %.

Model Discovery. For each log, several process models are discovered using process discovery algorithms. ProM 6.5 was used for the discovery of the process models. Default values were used for all parameters.

Conformance Checking. Regarding the first goal of the experiment, the quality of each of the discovered models was examined both with respect to the event log from which the model was discovered, and with respect to the ground truth event log. Furthermore, concerning the second goal, for a randomly selected

set of 10 discovered models for each system, the quality with respect to all event
logs generated by that system was measured. Table 1 shows the measures that
were used in the analysis. Each measure was given a short label for simplicity.
All calculations were performed using the benchmarking framework CoBeFra [8].

4   Results

4.1   Estimation Biases

In order to visually analyse estimation biases of fitness metrics, Fig. 2 show the
distribution of ΔF as boxplots for the different fitness measures, conditioned on
the completeness and noisiness of the event logs. Note that, next to the ideal
levels of noise and completeness, only the 15 % noise level and 50 % completeness
level are depicted due to space limitations. Nevertheless, these levels of noise and
completeness seem to be representative for real-life event logs [19, 25]. Note that
the asterisks represent the mean difference, while the middle horizontal lines of
the boxplots represent the median values.

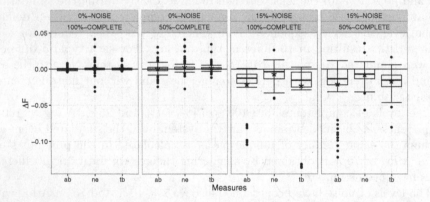

Fig. 2. Distribution of ΔF for fitness measures

It can be observed that noise causes the average difference between log and
system-based measurement of fitness metrics to be negative, which means that
the fitness-measures generally underestimate the real system-fitness. In these
cases, models are presumably being punished because they cannot replay behaviour that is not even real. On the other hand, the incompleteness of event logs
does not seem to bias the fitness measures significantly, although for some measures it clearly decreases its precision as an estimator. Note that variability in the
case when completeness is 100 % and noise is 0 % is the mere result of sampling
variability in the composition of the event logs.

Figure 3 shows the same graph for precision metrics. In contrast to system-
fitness, system-precision appears to be slightly underestimated by most precision

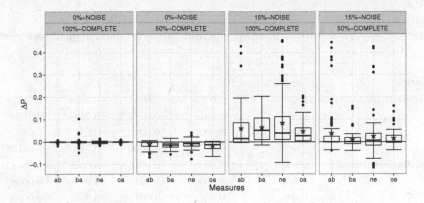

Fig. 3. Distribution of ΔP^z for precision measures

metrics when the event log is incomplete. Indeed, when event logs contain less behaviour, each model's log-precision will decrease, while the system-precision is independent of log completeness. Furthermore, the presence of noise seems to have an adverse effect.

In addition to the visual analysis, a Kruskal-Wallis test was done for each fitness and precision metric, to see whether there are statistically significant differences between ΔF or ΔP for different levels of noise and completeness. It can be observed in Table 2 that for all the metrics, the hypothesis that there are no significant differences among the groups, is rejected.

Table 2. Results of Kruskal-Wallis rank sum test by completeness and noise

Fitness metrics	Kruskal-Wallis χ^2	Precision metrics	Kruskal-Wallis χ^2
Alignment based fitness	120.7946***	Alignment based precision	1114.2523***
Negative event recall	352.5966***	Negative event precision	1006.2333***
Token-based fitness	320.5694***	Best align precision	587.7634***
		One align precision	1276.3387***

Note: *p < 0.1; **p < 0.05; ***p < 0.01

In order to further understand these differences, Tables 3 and 4 show the average difference between log and system measures, for fitness and precision metrics, respectively. The levels of statistical significance indicated in these table reflect whether this mean is different from zero. Since the data suffers from non-normality, the non-parametric Wilcoxon signed rank test was used.

Note that for each metric, 16 different tests were done. In order to limit the family-wise error to 5 %,, the Bonferonni correction was applied. Therefore, aach

Table 3. Mean ΔF for fitness metrics under differing noise and completeness levels.

Metric	Completeness	Noise			
		0 %	5 %	10 %	15 %
Alignment based fitness	100 %	-0.0003^{**}	-0.0061^{+}	-0.0124^{+}	-0.0179^{+}
	75 %	-0.0017^{***}	-0.0072^{+}	-0.0134^{+}	-0.0185^{+}
	50 %	-0.0007	-0.0062^{+}	-0.012^{+}	-0.018^{+}
	25 %	0.0000	-0.0059^{+}	-0.013^{+}	-0.0179^{+}
Negative event recall	100 %	0.0005	-0.0016^{+}	-0.0039^{+}	-0.0058^{+}
	75 %	0.0000	-0.0018^{+}	-0.0039^{+}	-0.0058^{+}
	50 %	0.0011^{**}	-0.0017^{+}	-0.0035^{+}	-0.0059^{+}
	25 %	0.0017^{**}	-0.0001^{**}	-0.0043^{+}	-0.0048^{+}
Token-based fitness	100 %	0.0004	-0.0048^{+}	-0.0109^{+}	-0.0161^{+}
	75 %	0.0007^{*}	-0.0035^{+}	-0.0078^{+}	-0.0135^{+}
	50 %	0.0009^{**}	-0.0028^{+}	-0.0079^{+}	-0.0115^{+}
	25 %	0.0016	-0.0012^{+}	-0.0044^{+}	-0.0056^{+}

Note: $^{*}p < 0.1$; $^{**}p < 0.05$; $^{***}p < 0.01$; $^{+}p < 0.0032$
Based on Wilcoxon signed rank test with continuity correction

Table 4. Mean ΔP for precision metrics under differing noise and completeness levels.

Metric	Completeness	Noise			
		0 %	5 %	10 %	15 %
Alignment based precision	100 %	-0.0004	0.0726^{+}	0.093^{+}	0.0989^{+}
	75 %	-0.0025^{+}	0.0539^{+}	0.0729^{+}	0.0895^{+}
	50 %	-0.008^{+}	0.0343^{+}	0.0617^{+}	0.0653^{+}
	25 %	-0.0195^{+}	0.0069	0.0162^{+}	0.0239^{+}
Best align precision	100 %	0.0004	0.064^{+}	0.0827^{+}	0.1008^{+}
	75 %	-0.004^{+}	0.0401^{+}	0.0508^{+}	0.0609^{+}
	50 %	-0.0098^{+}	0.0233^{+}	0.04^{+}	0.0446^{+}
	25 %	-0.0261^{+}	-0.0042	0.0137	0.01
Negative event precision	100 %	-0.0009^{+}	0.0786^{+}	0.0887^{+}	0.1076^{+}
	75 %	-0.0056^{+}	0.0398^{+}	0.0637^{+}	0.0803^{+}
	50 %	-0.0102^{+}	0.0228^{+}	0.0392^{+}	0.0518^{+}
	25 %	-0.0255^{+}	-0.0062^{+}	-0.0074^{**}	0.0082
One align precision	100 %	-0.0002^{**}	0.0637^{+}	0.0873^{+}	0.0872^{+}
	75 %	-0.0036^{+}	0.0456^{+}	0.0615^{+}	0.0752^{+}
	50 %	-0.0111^{+}	0.0224^{+}	0.0485^{+}	0.0506^{+}
	25 %	-0.0286^{+}	-0.0014	0.0079^{*}	0.0174^{+}

Note: $^{*}p < 0.1$; $^{**}p < 0.05$; $^{***}p < 0.01$; $^{+}p < 0.0032$
Based on Wilcoxon signed rank test with continuity correction

individual test has to be at a signficance level of $1 - 0.95^{(1/16)} = 0.0032$, annotated with the $^{+}$ symbol in Tables 3 and 4. It can be seen that for fitness metrics, there is indeed a bias for noisy logs. The bias for noise-free but incomplete logs is less prevalent and not significant at a 0.32% significance level. However, it must be observed that this corrected significance level is very restrictive, as the Kruskall-Wallis test already pointed out that biases do exist. Notwithstanding the statistical significance, the real impact of the bias is limited.

For precision metrics, it is clear that both noisiness and incompleteness of event log creates significant biases for the quality metrics. It is remarkable that ΔP was found to be significantly different from zero for the Negative Event Precision and One-Align Precision metrics under the condition of noise-free and complete logs. Further experiments have to be conducted to see whether this result is reproducible.

It is clear that precision measures, and to a lesser extent fitness measures, are not always unbiased nor reliable estimators of the system-alignment, as they fail to adequately estimate a model's system-fitness and system-precision. However, if these estimation errors are consistent among all models, the correct ranking of models will be preserved. It is therefore essential to investigate how the effects of noise and completeness differ among models.

4.2   Ranking Biases

In order to investigate ranking biases, 10 of the discovered models for each system were randomly chosen. Subsequently, the quality of these models with respect to all event logs generated from this system was measured. The relationship between the value of these metrics and the level of noise and completeness were subsequently analyzed. Figure 4 shows the relationship between the level of completeness and the fitness and precision values. Note that only noise-free logs were considered in this graph, in order to isolate the effect of (in)completeness.

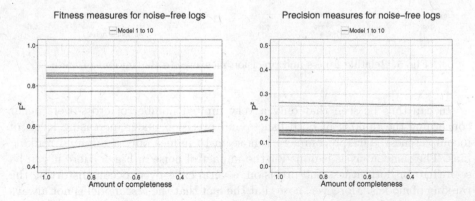

Fig. 4. Relating fitness and precision measures to the completeness of logs

Each line in this Figure represents one of the 10 models, and its height represents the average fitness (precision) value at a given level of completeness. These values were averaged over all logs at the given completeness level and over all fitness (precision) metrics. Since fitness (precision) metrics were largely correlated, they are not longer individually distinguished from each other. Moreover, the graphs for individual metrics were found to be similar. Note that the mapping between each of the lines and the models is irrelevant for our purpose. Also observe that this figure only shows the results for one of the systems, though the results for other systems were found to be similar.

When one would draw a vertical line at a certain level of completeness, the intersections with the lines of the graph define a ranking on the models. The intersection with the highest line refers to the model which is perceived the best, while the lowest intersection will point out which model is the worst. Consequently, when the lines of two different models cross one another, the ranking between these two models will change. The intersections with the y-axis reflect to correct ranking of the models with respect to the underlying system, as logs are complete and noise-free at this point. Under such circumstances, metrics are unbiased estimators of system-quality, as was demonstrated in Sect. 4.1. The more cross-overs that take place between lines when moving rightwards, the more the true ranking is distorted.

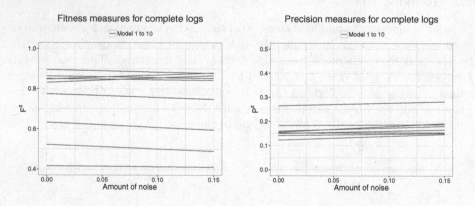

Fig. 5. Relating fitness and precision measures to the amount of noise

In can thus be seen that only a very limited number of cross-overs occur concerning the ranking of both fitness and precision under increasing levels of incompleteness. Thus, incomplete logs seem to induce only a minimal ranking bias. The same analysis is done for the impact of noise in Fig. 5. Here it can be seen that for both fitness and precision, several cross-overs occur, distorting the ranking of models. Moreover, note that the fact that the *best* model is not always impacted by the perturbations in the ranking, does not solve the problem. After all, there is no guarantee that this *best* model will always be found.

It can be concluded that the existence of noise impacts the measurement of fitness and precision. Not only do they fail at estimating the quality of models correctly under these circumstances, the impact varies greatly among different models, which in turn significantly confuses their ranking. On the other hand, incompleteness of event logs only slightly biases the existing fitness and precision metrics when assessing a models quality with respect to the underlying system.

5   The Role of Generalization

It can be argued that the generalization quality dimension somewhat matches the system-based perspective, in particular system-fitness. In order to conduct a thorough analysis, we therefore also investigate the distance between the generalization measures ab and ne on the one hand, and both system-fitness and system-precision on the other hand.

This distance, for each log and model is defined as $\Delta G_F(M, L, S) = G(M, L) - F^{ab}(M, S)$ for system-fitness, and $\Delta G_P(M, L, S) = G(M, L) - P^{ab}(M, S)$ for system-precision. For the sake of clarity, generalization measures were only compared with one system-fitness and one system-precision measure, i.e. F^{ab} and P^{ab}. These measures where chosen because of their relatively intuitive interpretations. The distribution of ΔG_F and ΔG_P can then be analyzed as before, for both the *alignment based* and *negative event* generalization metrics. This was done in Fig. 6.

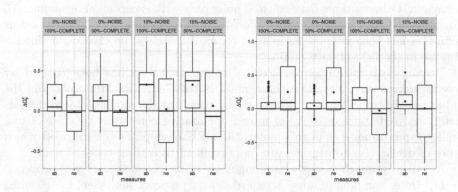

Fig. 6. Distribution of ΔG_F^z and ΔG_P^z

It can be observed that G^{ne} is a relatively good estimator of system-fitness, although it is biased when logs are both noisy and incomplete. On the other hand, there does not seem to be any relationship with system-precision, as one would expect based on the definition of generalization. However, G^{ab} is not a good predictor of system-fitness, nor system-precision. Moreover, it should be noted that the generalization measures were hardly correlated (0.176), which confirms the fact that generalization remains a vague and ambiguous concept, both regarding its definition and its implementations.

6   Related Work

Over time, many challenges within the field of process discovery, such as dealing with duplicate tasks and non-free choice constructs have been tackled [13]. Consequently, new process discovery algorithms increasingly focus on outperforming existing algorithms rather than tackling new challenges. This shift in research requires an agreed-upon and scientifically sound evaluation framework to compare different process mining algorithms. Recently, first attempts towards the development of an evaluation framework have been made [8, 10, 21]. The set of evaluation measures is the area which has received most attention so far.

In [2], the author states that "process discovery and conformance checking aim to tell something about the unknown real process rather than the example traces in the event log". The author therefore claims that, the one and only goal of process discovery would be to represent the true underlying process. However, existing quality metrics are mostly focussed on the relationship between the model and the event log. Furthermore, little empirical evidence exists so far.

The problem of log incompleteness is well acknowledged in literature. In [25], the authors defined different estimators of log completeness. The application of these on several real-life data sets showed that the estimated coverage of event logs is only about 50 %, bearing in mind that the estimators were even found to be over-estimating the coverage when tested on artificial event logs.

Noise has been defined less unambiguously. According to [15], noise covers the occurrence of errors, the incompleteness of the event log, as well as exceptional behaviour. Other authors have equated noise only with exceptional behaviour [1]. Finally, some authors have defined noise as measurement errors [23]. The latter definition has been adopted in this paper, as it matches the classical definition of noise in the field of data mining.

Dealing with incomplete as well as noisy event logs has been tackled by several process discovery algorithms, notably the Heuristics Miner [24] and the Inductive Miner [18]. In the field of declarative process models, [14] systematically analysed the sensitivity of mined declarative constrains to noise. Using similar types of noise as in this paper, the authors empirically confirmed which types of declarative constraints are (not) resilient to certain types of noise.

Another approach towards handling noise in process discovery was proposed in [11]. Here, handling of noise is regarded as a preprocessing step, i.e. *cleaning* the log, before discovery algorithms are applied. While this view on managing noise in event logs definitely has its merits, more research is needed on how to distinguish noise in an event log, and how to do this in an automatic way.

Despite the efforts towards handling noise in process discovery, the concepts of noise and log-incompleteness are not incorporated in most process quality measures. As a result, one must be cautious to use the same quality measures when the goal is rather to describe the underlying process. A notable exception has been the work on artificial negative events [7]. The induction of negative events explicitly supports the fact that event logs are not complete. The negative events aim at delineating the system by defining its complement S^c. The related quality metrics are thus expected to be more suitable for measuring a process model's alignment with the system rather than the event log, although this is not exactly clear from the analyses.

7 Conclusions and Future Work

This papers suggest that there are different objectives within process discovery. To gain information on how work is done in a business process, the objective of process discovery is to learn a model which provides a good representation of the underlying process, i.e. the system. However, when process discovery is used for auditing purposes, the mere objective might be to discover a model which is limited to the behaviour described in the event log.

Although discovery algorithms have been able to tackle noisiness and incompleteness of event logs, existing quality measures are predominantly focused on the event log as the unmistaken truth. In order to examine whether these measures still perform well in case of noisy and incomplete event logs, their sensitivity to these issues was investigate. The results show that both fitness and precision measures are very sensitive to noise, which makes them biased estimators of system-precision. Moreover, when event logs are incomplete, the variability of the measurements increase. Under these circumstances, there is no guarantee that the metrics will be able to correctly assess a models quality with respect to the underlying system, and rank different models accordingly. Furthermore, it is unclear what existing generalization measures quantify. Moreover, the two generalization measures under consideration were found to be hardly correlated.

Ranking biases clearly need to be further investigated from a more statistical point of view. Further research concerning the existing generalization measures is also needed to uncover their added value. Moreover, it should be investigated how existing measures can be corrected in order to remove their bias as estimator for system-fitness and system-precision in the presence of noise and incomplete event logs, which is especially needed for precision measures. Also, the need for confidence intervals for quality metrics should be further investigated, in order to assess the reliability of their results.

Acknowledgments. The computational resources and services used in this work for both process discovery and process conformance tasks were provided by the VSC (Flemish Supercomputer Center), funded by the Research Foundation - Flanders (FWO) and the Flemish Government.

References

1. van der Aalst, W.M.P.: Process mining: discovery, conformance and enhancement of business processes. Springer, Heidelberg (2011)
2. van der Aalst, W.M.P.: Mediating between modeled and observed behavior: the quest for the Right process. In: IEEE Computing Society, pp. 31–43 (2013)
3. van der Aalst, W.M.P., Adriansyah, A., van Dongen, B.: Replaying history on process models for conformance checking and performance analysis. Wiley Interdisc. Rev.: Data Min. Knowl. Discov. **2**(2), 182–192 (2012)

4. Adriansyah, A., Munoz-Gama, J., Carmona, J., van Dongen, B.F., van der Aalst, W.M.P.: Alignment based precision checking. In: La Rosa, M., Soffer, P. (eds.) BPM Workshops 2012. LNBIP, vol. 132, pp. 137–149. Springer, Heidelberg (2013)
5. Agrawal, R., Gunopulos, D., Leymann, F.: Mining process models from workflow logs. In: Schek, H.-J., Saltor, F., Ramos, I., Alonso, G. (eds.) EDBT 1998. LNCS, vol. 1377, pp. 467–483. Springer, Heidelberg (1998)
6. Baier, C., Katoen, J.P., et al.: Principles of Model Checking, vol. 26202649. MIT Press, Cambridge (2008)
7. vanden Broucke, S.K.L.M., De Weerdt, J., Vanthienen, J.B., Baesens, B.: Determining process model precision and generalization with weighted artificial negative events. IEEE Trans. Knowl. Data Eng. 26(8), 1877–1889 (2014)
8. vanden Broucke, S.K.L.M., De Weerdt, J., Vanthienen, J., Baesens, B.: A Comprehensive Benchmarking Framework (CoBeFra) for conformance analysis between procedural process models and event logs in ProM. In: 2013 IEEE Symposium on Computational Intelligence and Data Mining (CIDM), pp. 254–261. IEEE (2013)
9. Buijs, J.: Flexible evolutionary algorithms for mining structured process models. Ph.D. thesis, Technische Universiteit Eindhoven, Eindhoven (2014)
10. Buijs, J.C.A.M., van Dongen, B.F., van der Aalst, W.M.P.: On the role of fitness, precision, generalization and simplicity in process discovery. In: Meersman, R. (ed.) OTM 2012, Part I. LNCS, vol. 7565, pp. 305–322. Springer, Heidelberg (2012)
11. Cheng, H.J., Kumar, A.: Process mining on noisy logs can log sanitization help to improve performance? Decis. Support Syst. 79, 138–149 (2015)
12. Cook, J.E., Wolf, A.L.: Software process validation: quantitatively measuring the correspondence of a process to a model. ACM Trans. Softw. Eng. Methodol. (TOSEM) 8(2), 147–176 (1999)
13. De Weerdt, J., De Backer, M., Vanthienen, J., Baesens, B.: A multi-dimensional quality assessment of state-of-the-art process discovery algorithms using real-life event logs. Inf. Syst. 37(7), 654–676 (2012)
14. Di Ciccio, C., Mecella, M., Mendling, J.: The effect of noise on mined declarative constraints. In: Ceravolo, P., Accorsi, R., Cudre-Mauroux, P. (eds.) SIMPDA 2013. LNBIP, vol. 203, pp. 1–24. Springer, Heidelberg (2015)
15. Folino, F., Greco, G., Guzzo, A., Pontieri, L.: Discovering expressive process models from noised log data. In: Proceedings of the 2009 International Database Engineering and Applications Symposium, pp. 162–172. ACM (2009)
16. Janssenswillen, G., Depaire, B., Jouck, T.: Calculating the number of unique paths in a block-structured process model. In: Algorithms and Theories for the Analysis of Event Data (2016)
17. Jouck, T., Depaire, B.: Generating artificial data for empirical analysis of process discovery algorithms: a process tree and log generator. Technical report, Universiteit Hasselt, Universiteit Hasselt, March 2016
18. Leemans, S.J.J., Fahland, D., van der Aalst, W.M.P.: Discovering block-structured process models from event logs containing infrequent behaviour. In: Lohmann, N., Song, M., Wohed, P. (eds.) BPM 2013 Workshops. LNBIP, vol. 171, pp. 66–78. Springer, Heidelberg (2014)
19. de Medeiros, A.K.A.: Genetic process mining. Ph.D. thesis, Technische Universiteit Eindhoven, Eindhoven (2006)
20. Rozinat, A., van der Aalst, W.M.P.: Conformance checking of processes based on monitoring real behavior. Inf. Syst. 33(1), 64–95 (2008)
21. Rozinat, A., De Medeiros, A.K.A., Günther, C.W., Weijters, A.J.M.M., van der Aalst, W.M.P.: Towards an evaluation framework for process mining algorithms. In: Beta, Research School for Operations Management and Logistics (2007)

22. Weber, P., Bordbar, B., Tiňo, P., Majeed, B.: A framework for comparing process mining algorithms. In: GCC Conference and Exhibition (GCC), 2011 IEEE, pp. 625–628. IEEE (2011)
23. Weijters, A., van der Aalst, W.M.P.: Rediscovering workflow models from event-based data. In: Proceedings of the 11th Dutch-Belgian Conference on Machine Learning (Benelearn 2001), pp. 93–100. Citeseer (2001)
24. Weijters, A., van der Aalst, W.M.P., De Medeiros, A.K.A.: Process mining with the heuristics miner-algorithm. Technische Universiteit Eindhoven, Technical report WP 166, pp. 1–34 (2006)
25. Yang, H., van Dongen, B., ter Hofstede, A., Wynn, M., Wang, J.: Estimating completeness of event logs. BPM Center Report, 12 April 2012

Handling Duplicated Tasks in Process Discovery by Refining Event Labels

Xixi Lu[1](✉), Dirk Fahland[1], Frank J.H.M. van den Biggelaar[2],
and Wil M.P. van der Aalst[1]

[1] Eindhoven University of Technology, Eindhoven, The Netherlands
{x.lu,d.fahland,w.m.p.v.d.aalst}@tue.nl
[2] Maastricht University Medical Center, Maastricht, The Netherlands
f.vanden.biggelaar@mumc.nl

Abstract. Processes may require to execute the same *activity* in different stages of the process. A human modeler can express this by creating two different *task* nodes labeled with the same activity name (thus *duplicating* the task). However, as events in an event log often are labeled with the activity name, discovery algorithms that derive tasks based on labels only cannot discover models with duplicate labels rendering the results imprecise. For example, for a log where "payment" events occur at the beginning and the end of a process, a modeler would create two different "payment" tasks, whereas a discovery algorithm introduces a loop around a single "payment" task. In this paper, we present a general approach for refining labels of events based on their context in the event log as a preprocessing step. The refined log can be input for any discovery algorithm. The approach is implemented in ProM and was evaluated in a controlled setting. We were able to improve the quality of up to 42 % of the models compared to using a log with imprecise labeling using default parameters and up to 87 % using adaptive parameters. Moreover, using our refinement approach significantly increased the similarity of the discovered model to the original process with duplicate labels allowing for better rediscoverability. We also report on a case study conducted for a Dutch hospital.

1 Introduction

Real-life processes may require that the same *activity* occurs at different stages or branches of the process [1–4]. A human modeler would use different *nodes* in a model (e.g., different transitions in a Petri net) labeled with the same activity to express different occurrences of an activity in the process. We call each node labeled with an activity a *task*. Thus, there could be many tasks referring to the same activity, which are known as *duplicated tasks*. In a log, events are usually labeled with activity names instead of tasks. As a result, two different events with the same activity label may originate from the same task or from different tasks, i.e., the labeling in the event log is *imprecise*.

Process discovery aims at creating an accurate representation of the real process from an event log helping users to understand the executed process [3,5].

© Springer International Publishing Switzerland 2016
M. La Rosa et al. (Eds.): BPM 2016, LNCS 9850, pp. 90–107, 2016.
DOI: 10.1007/978-3-319-45348-4_6

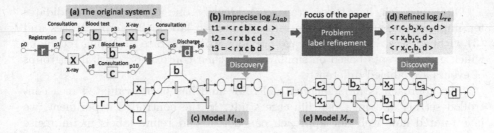

Fig. 1. The imprecise label problem settings and the running example.

However, most existing discovery algorithms assume the labels of events to be precise and consider for each label as one task represented by a single task node in the model. In case of event logs with imprecise labels, these discovery algorithms tend to return over-generalized models that allow much more behavior than in the event log [2,3]. Such models may be misleading or even incorrect, obstructing users to use the models for understanding the real processes or performing accurate process analysis. A better solution would be to discover models where two tasks carry the same label, i.e., *duplicate* tasks [1,2].

We exemplify the problem using an example shown in Fig. 1. The original system (a) has five activities "r", "d", "c", "b" and "x" and ten tasks; activities "c", "b" and "x" occur at multiple different tasks, which result in an imprecise log (b), in which the events only refer to activities "c", "b" and "x" rather than the different tasks in the system. Using a standard discovery algorithm, we discover for the imprecise log (b) an imprecise model (c) that states "b" could be skipped and has a loop that allows "c" and "x" to be executed an arbitrary number of times, even though every trace in the log has an event labeled "b" and only one event labeled "x". Overall, model (c) is imprecise as it contains many behaviors neither seen in the log (b), nor in the original system (a). Refining the labels of events could yield the refined log (d), from which a refined model (e) can be discovered that corresponds to the original model (a) while using the same discovery algorithm. However, the trivial refinement where each event gets its own unique label is not desired as it would lead to models that overfit the event log. Thus, our goal is to refine an imprecise log in such a way that a discovery algorithm finds a better model which is more precise and closer to the original model.

In this paper, we investigate the problem of imprecise labels of events for process discovery and propose an approach to resolve the problem through log preprocessing. In particular, we introduce an approach for refining labels and relabeling events in the log such that any existing or future process discovery algorithm can infer duplicated tasks from the refined labels. As the optimal refined log or model may be unknown, our approach aims at adding more alternative representations of a process into the solution space of process discovery algorithms to help users find better models systematically.

Our approach has three steps: (1) identify one or multiple candidates for imprecise event labels; then refine imprecise labels (2) across traces and (3) within traces. Here, we leverage previous work on trace matching technique which groups events based on similarities in their context [6]; dissimilar groups of events are labeled differently.

The approach is implemented in ProM[1] and has been evaluated in a controlled setting and in a real life case study. In the controlled experiment, we investigated how well our approach can detect and refine labels in imprecise event logs generated from a large set of synthetic process models with duplicated tasks. We analyzed model quality with respect to the event log and the similarity to the original model. For 87% of the processes having duplicated tasks outside of loops, our approach automatically refined imprecise logs so that a discovery algorithm returned a more precise model. For processes having duplicated tasks in a loop, label refinement improved precision for 61% of the imprecise logs.

In the remainder, we first discuss related work in Sect. 2. In Sect. 3, we recall the concepts used for defining the problem, the measures used in the evaluation, and the methods used in the approach. In Sect. 4, we formalize problems and aims. Section 5 explains the proposed approach. The evaluation results are presented in Sect. 6, and Sect. 7 concludes the paper.

2   Related Work

Process Model Elements Labeling or Relabeling. Many studies have investigated the problem of labeling or relabeling process elements (e.g., activities, flow relations) in process models [7,8]. These works assume that a collection of structurally correct process models is available and use additional domain knowledge or other semantically correct labels to then suggest or revise the incorrect labels of elements in these models. Here, we assume no models to be available and operate solely on event logs, in order to discover structurally correct models. One then may apply [7,8] on the discovered models to revise and improve their labels.

Process Discovery and Duplicated Tasks. Process discovery algorithms aim at discovering "good" models from an event log to help users to understand real-life processes. Most existing discovery algorithms map each unique event label to one task, making it impossible to discover processes with two tasks with the same label. Some discovery algorithms can refine labels during model construction to some extent [1,2,4,5,9]. However, these internal mechanism to handle duplicated tasks can not be used in other discovery algorithms. Moreover, these algorithms have other limitations such as they do not guarantee sound models or fitting models. To be able to benefit from current and future progress in process discovery techniques [10,11], we propose to refine labels in the event log itself, which then can be used by any process discovery algorithm.

Trace Clustering and Clone Detection. As duplicated tasks may also manifest themselves as multiple variants of executing a set of activities within the same process, trace clustering was proposed as a way to distinguish these variants [12,13]. However, clustering techniques always consider entire traces and thus also unnecessary duplicate tasks which are the same in all variants. In [14], the authors proposed a top-down approach that clusters the traces, discovers models for each cluster separately and uses clone detection to find tasks that are the same in all variants, preventing unnecessary duplicating tasks [15]. However, trace clustering techniques are unable to distinguish two events having the same label within a trace or a variant [12]. In this paper, we aim at tackling both problems.

Data Quality and Noise/Deviation Filtering. Imprecise labels could also be seen as data quality problem, i.e., events having incorrect labels. To the best of our knowledge, no existing work investigated this problem from this point of view. Other existing work on log preprocessing such as noise/deviation filtering would change input logs, both structurally and behaviorally, e.g., by removing events [6]. Such changes would also affect fitness of the discovered model with respect to the original log as a process discovery algorithm can only guarantee fitness for the filtered log. In this paper, we propose to not change the event log but only the labeling of events, which help us to preserve fitness if the discovery algorithm has such a guarantee.

Model Quality of Discovered Models. Dozens criteria and measures have been proposed for assessing the quality of discovered models, which may be discussed in three categories. Measures that evaluate the quality of the model using the input log often consider fitness, precision, and generalization [3,5]; we use the fitness defined in [16] and precision in [17]. In the context of controlled experiments, the quality of a discovered model can be evaluated against the original system in terms of how much of the behavior of the system can be reproduced by the discovered model and how precise the model describes the system [18]. When evaluating the quality of model irrespective of the log, then soundness and simplicity are often considered [5,19]. In the next section, we further discuss the measures used in this paper.

3   Preliminaries

In this section, we present (1) the input for our approach, (2) the quality measures used, and (3) the key concepts of a technique for finding events with a similar context.

Event, Label, and Event Log. Let $\mathcal{E}$ be the universe of unique events, i.e., the set of all possible event identifiers. A trace $\sigma \in \mathcal{E}^*$ is a finite sequence of events. An event log $C = \{\sigma_1, \sigma_2, \cdots, \sigma_n\} \subseteq \mathcal{E}^*$ is a set of traces. Here we assume no event appears twice in the same trace nor in different traces. We use E_C for the set of events in log C. Let A be a set of activities and C a log. A *labeling* function

$l : E_C \rightarrow A$ is surjective and assigns to each event $e \in E_C$ a label $l(e) = a \in A$. We call $L = (C, l)$ a *labeled event log* over activities A.

Process Discovery and Model Quality. Let $L = (C, l)$ be a labeled log over A. A discovery algorithm D returns a model M (i.e. $D(L) = M$) such that the activities $\mathcal{A}(M)$ occurring in model M are A, i.e., $\mathcal{A}(M) = A$. The quality of the discovered model $D(L) = M$ may be evaluated in two ways. First, with respect to the input log L, the $log\_fitness(L, M)$ and $log\_precision(L, M)$ of the model can be computed, for which we use the measures defined in [16,17], respectively. Both return a value between 0 and 1: if $log\_fitness(L, M) = 1$, every trace in the log can be replayed by the model perfectly. When $log\_precision(L, M)$ is close to 1, most (alternative) behavior allowed by the model is also observed in the log.

In addition, we compare the discovered $M = D(L)$ to the original system in terms of *system recall* and *system precision* to evaluate the generalization and discoverability of our approach. Let S be the system that generated L. The system recall $sys\_recall(S, M, L)$ and system precision $sys\_precision(S, M, L)$ of the discovered model are computed according to [18]. For example, in Fig. 1(b), after executing events "r" and "x" in trace t_2, tasks "b" and "c" are enabled in the original system; in model (c), "b" and "c" but also "x" are enabled, which has 100 % recalled all enabled activities in the system but is less precise (an additional "x" not enabled in the system); a trace model would only allow "b" (the next event in the trace), which is precise but has bad recall. Note that the recall with respect to system thus also captures the aforementioned generalization quality [5]. Furthermore, note that the system precision is different from the log precision, as the system could be imprecise with respect to the log (when the log is incomplete), but system is always precise with respect to to itself.

Similar Events, Mapping, and Cost Function. We build on existing concepts [6] to identify events that carry the same label but occur in different contexts. Let σ, σ' be two traces. A *mapping* $\lambda_{(\sigma,\sigma')} \subseteq E_\sigma \times E_{\sigma'}$ between σ and σ' is a binary, injective relation; $(e, e') \in \lambda_{(\sigma,\sigma')}$ is a *matched pair*. We write $\overline{\lambda}_{(\sigma,\sigma')}$ for the set of events having not match in $\lambda_{(\sigma,\sigma')}$, i.e. $\overline{\lambda}_{(\sigma,\sigma')} = \{e \in E \mid \neg\exists e' \in E' : (e, e') \in \lambda_{(\sigma,\sigma')}\} \cup \{e' \in E' \mid \neg\exists e \in E : (e, e') \in \lambda_{(\sigma,\sigma')}\}$. In this paper, we assume for all $(e, e') \in \lambda_{(\sigma,\sigma')}$, $l(e) = l(e')$.

Given any two traces σ and σ', there are many possible mappings between them. An optimal mapping that maximizes the pairs of mapped events with large similarity in their context can be selected using a cost function with three weighted components: (1) the differences in the (direct or indirect) neighbors of the matched pairs (using $cost_{Matched}$), (2) the differences in the distances between a matched pair (e, e') and other matched pairs (using $cost_{Struc}$), and (3) the non-matched events $e \in \overline{\lambda}$ (using $cost_{NoMatch}$). Formally, $cost(\sigma, \sigma', \lambda) = w_M * \sum_{(e,e')\in\lambda} cost_{Matched}(e, e', \lambda) + w_S * \sum_{(e,e')\in\lambda} cost_{Struc}(e, e', \lambda) + w_N *$

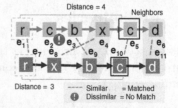

Fig. 2. An example of a mapping between two traces.

$\sum_{e\in\overline{\lambda}} cost_{NoMatch}(e)$, in which w_M, w_S, w_N are the weights for the components. Figure 2 shows an example of a mapping between traces t_1 and t_2 of log L_{lab} of Fig. 1 (see [6] for a detailed explanation). As the traces σ and σ' are finite, one may simply enumerate all possible mappings between two traces, compute the cost of each mapping, and select the optimal ones. In [6], a greedy algorithm is proposed to find a locally optimal mapping in polynomial time. The results of this paper have been obtained with the greedy variant.

4   Problem Definition and Analysis

In this section, we first formally define our research problem and then discuss the related complications and our design decisions. In essence, given an imprecisely labeled log $L = (C, l_A)$ over the set of activities A, we would like to return a more *refined labeling function* l_B for the events E_C in order to help a discovery algorithm find better models.

Definition 1 (Refined Labeling Function). *For a labeled log L_A over the set of labels A, the log L_B over an arbitrary set of labels B is a* refined log *iff (1) they have the same traces, i.e., $L_A = (C, l_A), L_B = (C, l_B)$, and (2) for each two events $e, e' \in E_c$, e and e' can only have the same label according to l_B, if they also have the same label by l_A, i.e., $(l_B(e) = l_B(e')) \Rightarrow (l_A(e) = l_A(e'))$. We call l_B a* refined labeling function *for L_A.*

Note that the model M_B discovered from L_B has a different set of activity labels (i.e., $\mathcal{A}(M_B) = B$) than the model M_A discovered from L_A (i.e., $\mathcal{A}(M_A) = A$). However, for comparing M_A and M_B w.r.t. various measures, both models should have the same set of activities. To allow for this comparison, we introduce some notions that allow replacing the refined labels B of M_B with the original labels in A. Each refined log $L_B = (C, l_B)$ of $L_A = (C, l_A)$ induces the *label abstraction* function $\beta : B \rightarrow A$ with $\beta = \bigcup_{e\in E}\{l_B(e) \mapsto l_A(e)\}$. The inverse $\beta^{-1}(a) = \{b \in B | \beta(b) = a\}$ gives the set of refined labels for original label $a \in A$. Note that $\beta(l_B(e)) = l_A(e)$ for all events $e \in E$. For example, in Fig. 1, the refined log L_{re} of L_{lab} induces the abstraction $\beta = \{r \rightarrow r, c_1 \rightarrow c, c_2 \rightarrow c, c_3 \rightarrow c, b_1 \rightarrow b, b_2 \rightarrow b, x_1 \rightarrow x, x_2 \rightarrow x, d \rightarrow d\}$, label c is refined into the set $\beta^{-1}(c) = \{c_1, c_2, c_3\}$.

Using β, we can abstract model M_B by replacing each label b in M_B with $\beta(b)$. Let $\beta(M_B)$ denote the resulting model. Lemma 1 then follows immediately from the definitions.

Lemma 1 (M_B and $\beta(M_B)$ have the Same Behaviors). *Let L_A be an event log and L_B be a refined log of L_A. Let M_B be a model discovered from L_B such that each trace of L_B is a trace of M_B. Let β be the label abstraction induced by L_B. Then each trace of L_A is a trace of $\beta(M_B)$.*

Through β we can now compare models M_A and $\beta(M_B)$ respectively discovered from both original log L_A and refined log L_B and formally define our problem.

Problem Definition. Let $L_{lab} = (C, l)$ be an (imprecisely) labeled event log over the set of activities A. Let S denote the system model that generated L_{lab} with $\mathcal{A}(S) = A$. Given discovery algorithm D, let $M_{lab} = D(L_{lab})$ be the model discovered on the labeled log. We would like to find a *refined labeling function l'* of l that with induced label abstraction β such that for the refined log $L_{re} = (C, l')$ and the discovered, abstracted model $M_{re} = \beta(D(L_{re}))$ over A, the following properties hold:

(1) Fitness and precision of M_{re} improves over M_{lab} w.r.t. the given labeled log:
   - $log\_precision(M_{re}, L_{lab}) \geq log\_precision(M_{lab}, L_{lab})$ and
   - $log\_fitness(M_{re}, L_{lab}) \geq log\_fitness(M_{lab}, L_{lab})$
(2) Recall and precision of behavior of M_{re} should be higher than M_{lab} w.r.t. S, i.e.,
   - $sys\_precision(S, M_{re}, L_{lab}) \geq sys\_precision(S, M_{lab}, L_{lab})$ and
   - $sys\_recall(S, M_{re}, L_{lab}) \geq sys\_recall(S, M_{lab}, L_{lab})$

When the system S is unknown, we consider our third aim as providing different refined labeling functions that satisfy the first requirement which allows users to explore different representations of the input log.

Related Issues and Design Decisions. We discuss three complications related to the research problem to motivate our design decisions and assumption. First, there is a large combinatorial number of possible solutions, since in principle any label can be refined into an arbitrary number of refined labels. In addition, we have no criteria nor metrics that define when a refinement is optimal for the algorithm D. This depends on the discovery algorithm used. Furthermore, when the system is unknown, the same process may have different equally good representations depending on the stakeholder, the context, and decisions made in the formalization of the model. Since one can not deduce the optimal log nor the optimal model, we have to base the decisions for refining event labels on the behavioral structure of the event log and some basic principles and heuristics we discuss later.

The second complication is posed by the discovery algorithms and measures used for evaluation. Ideally, a more precise log would result in a more precise model, independent of the discovery algorithm and the measures we applied. However, this is not the case. A discovery algorithm may return a less precise model while the log is more refined (for example to avoid overfitting). Therefore, we decided to propose a backup plan. If $log\_precision(M_{re}, L_{lab}) < log\_precision(M_{lab}, L_{lab})$, we simply return the log with its imprecise labeling. This guarantees that at least using the refined log would not lead to discovering a model worse than using the imprecise log.

Finally, in this paper, we assume the discovered model is sound and fitting for the following reasons. Most state-of-art measures assume a fitting log when evaluating the quality of a model. We observed in our own experiments that the measures become rather unreliable and difficult to compare or to understand the improvements when the models are not sound and fitting. Moreover, as fitness is defined in terms of the number of events that can be replayed by a model and we are not adding or removing any events (which would have direct influence on the fitness), changes in fitness are merely a quality of the discovery algorithms used. For example, if the algorithm guarantees to return a fitting model, relabeling events would not change this property.

5 Approach

We decompose the label refinement problem into three subproblems. First, we identify one or multiple labels as candidates for imprecise labels. Then, we consider a group of traces that have *similar behavior* to be a *variant* of the process and refine the imprecise label candidates (horizontally) into different variants and (vertically) within a variant. Figure 3 shows an overview of the three subproblems using an example.

5.1 Detecting Imprecise Labels

The first step is to identify one or multiple candidates for imprecise labels. This step helps to limit the search scope to those events that have an imprecise label and to avoid splitting non-duplicated tasks. Furthermore, it helps to consolidate the context information of events with imprecise labels. One may also consider all labels, however, this may unnecessarily complicate the label refinement process.

Formally, we define the problem as follows. Let $L = (C, l_A)$ be a labeled event log and A the set of labels used. We would like to identify a subset of labels $A' \subseteq A$ and consider them as candidates for imprecise labels. In other words, the labels in $A \setminus A'$ are precise labels, and there is no need to refine them, i.e., for $e \in E_C$ and $l_A(e) = a \in A \setminus A'$, any refined labeling function l_B of l_A with its β implies $l_B(e) = a$, and $\beta^{-1}(a) = \{a\}$.

There are many different ways to detect imprecise labels. We discuss two methods (used in the evaluation) and consider other possibilities as future work. The optimal case is to have an oracle that returns the truly imprecise labels as candidates. For example, domain experts indicate a particular label to be imprecise. In the remainder, we refer to this as Oracle Detection (OD).

Besides having an oracle, we propose an automated method that uses properties of Inductive Miner (IM) [11]. IM systematically parses an event log and

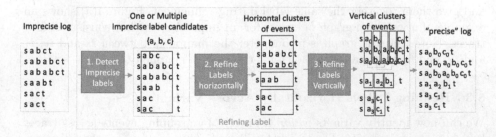

Fig. 3. The proposed approach for refining imprecise label as log preprocessing.

finds a locally optimal "subprocess" recursively. If IM fails to find an accurate subprocess, it returns a generic subprocess that can replay any trace over the events in the corresponding sublog (i.e., a local "flower loop"). In this paper, we consider this type of subprocess to be imprecise. We choose to select the smallest imprecise subprocess (i.e., local "flower loop") and return the activity labels in the subprocess as imprecise label candidates. For instance, applying IM on the running example, IM returns a process model of Fig. 1(c) containing a flower loop with activity labels c, b and x, and this set $\{c, b, x\}$ is returned as candidates for imprecise labels. We use the IM Detection (IMD) to refer to this method. In principle, any subprocess or multiple subprocesses can be selected.

5.2   Intermediate Step - Matching Events

After finding imprecise label candidates, we propose an intermediate step before refining these labels. The objective of this intermediate step is to identify similarities between events across traces. Similar events should carry the same refined label whereas dissimilar events should carry a different label.

In essence, the procedure for computing the similarity of events of different traces uses the existing trace matching technique of Sect. 3 and goes as follows. Given a labeled log $L = (C, l)$, for each two traces $\sigma, \sigma' \in C$, we find an optimal mapping $\lambda_{\sigma,\sigma'} \in E_\sigma \times E_{\sigma'}$ between their events for a given cost function. This way we get the distance between any two traces σ and σ' as $cost(\sigma, \sigma', \lambda_{\sigma,\sigma'})$. This distance can be normalized w.r.t. the highest cost $maxCost = \max_{\sigma,\sigma' \in C} cost(\sigma, \sigma', \lambda_{\sigma,\sigma'})$.

To obtain the distance between any two events, we project the normalized distance between traces onto the individual pairs of events. Formally, we construct an undirected weighted graph $G = (E_C, R, l, w)$ where nodes E_C are the events of $L = (C, l)$ with labeling l. For each pair (σ, σ') of traces in L and a best matching $\lambda_{\sigma,\sigma'}$ and for each pair $(e, e') \in \lambda_{\sigma,\sigma'}$ of events, we add the edge (e, e') to R with weight $w(e, e') = cost(\sigma, \sigma', \lambda_{\sigma,\sigma'})/maxCost$. Note that in G a single event may have many weighted edges describing how close it is to the most similar event in other traces. When mapping the costs from pairs of traces to pairs of events in G, any edge between events with a precise label a (i.e., $a \notin A'$) gets cost 0. This way, we will enforce that these labels are not refined. The higher the cost between two events, the more likely that they receive different labels. Searching for a mapping with least cost ensures we group the most similar events and give them together the same label during refinement. Figure 4(a) shows an example of a weighted graph of events for an imprecise log that consists of four traces. Note that the graph is incomplete; the mappings between t_0 and t_2, t_1 and t_3, and t_0 and t_3 are not shown for the sake of simplicity.

5.3   Refining Labels Horizontally Across Variants

We can now identify variants *within* a process by grouping events across traces based on their similarity. The reason for distinguishing variants is the following. If two very different variants of a part of the process are considered together, a

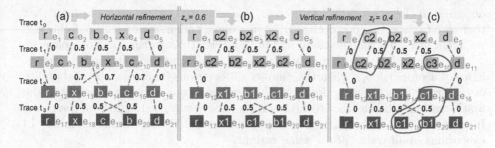

Fig. 4. A graph of labeled events with weighted edges denoting the dissimilarity (a), for which the labels are refined horizontally (b) and then vertically (c).

discovery algorithm may return a more general structure than exists in reality. Consider for example the two traces $\sigma = \langle ..., c, b, x, ... \rangle$ and $\sigma' = \langle ..., x, b, c, ... \rangle$. One may consider them a single variant and return for example a model with activities b, c and x in parallel (i.e. can be executed in any order). However, an alternative would be having a precise model that only allows these two variants. The "optimal" model depends on the particular case. When the original model for the system is unknown, we cannot claim one of them is better, therefore we simply want to add the alternative with both variants to the solution space of existing discovery algorithms allowing user to explore both representations. Label refinement allows us to achieve this systematically.

The similarity measure enables us to be flexible when considering which variants to split by introducing a variant threshold z_v. We say, two traces σ and σ' are *in the same variant*, written $\sigma \sim \sigma'$ iff their normalized $cost(\sigma, \sigma', \lambda_{\sigma, \sigma'})/maxCost \leq z_v$ or there exists σ'' with $\sigma \sim \sigma'' \sim \sigma'$. Note that $\sim$ is an equivalence relation where two very dissimilar traces may become equivalent if there is a "chain" of similar traces between them. Thus, two events $e \in \sigma, e' \in \sigma'$ that have imprecise labels (i.e., $l(e), l(e') \in A'$) *are in the same variant* iff $\sigma \sim \sigma'$. In our graph G, we materialize (dis-)similarity by removing any edge (e, e') with weight $w(e, e') > z_v$. As all mappings between events of the same two traces σ and σ' carry the same weight, all events of a trace are kept in the same variant. Note that edges between the events that carry precise labels have weight 0 and are not split into multiple variants.

For example, setting the variant threshold for the event distance graph G of Fig. 4(a) to 0.6 yields the graph G' of Fig. 4(b) showing two variants in the part of the process involving labels c, b, x. Labels r and d are not refined into multiple variants.

5.4 Refining Labels Vertically Within Variant

After refining labels horizontally to distinguish different variants, there can still be multiple events carrying the same label within a single variant indicating either a loop or different tasks. Assuming in 50 % of cases activity c is executed once and in the other 50 % of the cases, c is executed twice, we could infer that there are two c tasks (one optional), or just one c task in a loop. In the following, we again use label refinement to add both alternatives to the solution space.

For refining labels within a single variant, we assume the following character-istics of a proper loop: when the number of iterations increases, the probability of executing this iteration decreases. For example, one may always execute the first iteration, whereas the second iteration is only executed in 20 % of the cases. In contrast, a duplicated task in a sequence would show similar numbers of executions in all traces of the same variant.

Based on this assumption, we introduce an *unfolding threshold* parameter z_f. For each imprecise label candidate $a \in A'$, let $G_a^1, ..., G_a^m$ be the connected components of G in which all events have label a. G_a^i and G_a^j are in the same variant iff for any two events $e^i \in G_a^i$ and $e^j \in G_a^j$, e^i and e^j *are in the same variant* (see Sect. 5.3). For example, Fig. 4(c) highlights for imprecise label c the three connected components $G_c^1 = \{e_2, e_7\}$, $G_c^2 = \{e_{10}\}$, $G_c^3 = \{e_{15}, e_{19}\}$, in which G_c^1 and G_c^2 in the same variant. Next, let $\#G_a^i$ denote the average position of the events of $\#G_a^i$ in their respective traces. Let $G_a^1 ... G_a^k$ be in the same variant ordered by $\#G_a^i$. Let $maxSize = max_{1 \leq i \leq k} |G_a^i|$ be the size of largest component (w.r.t. its events). For $1 \leq i \leq k$, if $i = 1$ or $|G_a^i| \geq v_f * maxSize$, then all events in G_a^i get a new label, otherwise G_a^i get the label of the events of G_a^{i-1}. For example, for imprecise label c, for the two connected components $G_c^1 = \{e_2, e_7\}$ and $G_c^2 = \{e_{10}\}$ that are in the same variant, $\#G_c^1 = 2$, $\#G_c^2 = 5$, and $maxSize = 2$. Therefore, if the *unfolding threshold* v_f is 0.6, then the events in G_c^2 get the same label as the events in G_c^1. If v_f is 0.4, then both G_c^1 and G_c^2 each get a new label.

6   Experimental Evaluation and Case Study

We implemented the techniques of Sect. 5 in the process mining toolkit ProM and conducted controlled experiments and a real-life case study to evaluate our approach. Plugins and experiments are available in the *TraceMatching* package of ProM. We first explain the experimental setup and then discuss the result.

Experimental Setup. The experimental setup is shown in Fig. 5. We randomly generated block structured models as systems with n number of visible tasks. Each system has k tasks that have the same activity label (here we consider just one duplicated label). For each system, we generate one imprecisely labeled log $L_{lab} = (C, l_{lab})$ of a 1000 cases each. From the imprecise log L_{lab}, we discover $M_{lab} = D(L_{lab})$. For the same log, we also apply our approach of Sect. 5 to obtain a refined log $L_{re} = (C, l_{re})$ (note that $\beta(L_{re}) = L_{lab}$), for which we dis-cover model M_{re}. Two algorithms are used: IM [11], i.e., $M_{re,IM} = \beta(D_{IM}(L_{re}))$, and ILP [10], i.e., $M_{re,ILP} = \beta(D_{ILP}(L_{re}))$. The quality of each of the models is compared with the corresponding model M_{lab} for evaluating to what extent our aims has been achieved. In all experiments, the same cost configuration is used for matching events. To speed up the experiments, the events that have precise

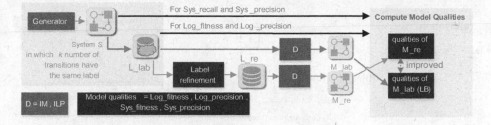

Fig. 5. An overview of the experimental design.

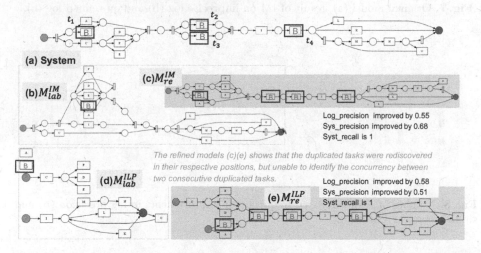

Fig. 6. Original model with duplicate tasks (a), results of IM on imprecise log (b) and on refined log (c), same for ILP (d) and (e).

labels, i.e. $l(e) = l(e') \notin A'$, are matched naively based on their labels and ordering in their respective traces. All models, logs and results can be downloaded[2].

(Exp. 1) When Imprecise Labels are not in a Loop, What are the Improvements? In this experiment, we used the default parameters: the variant threshold z_v is 0.05 and the unfolding threshold z_f is 0.60 for all models. We generated for size $n = [10, 15, 20]$ 200 models (600 models in total). For each model, there are $k = 4$ transitions having the same label and that are not in a loop.

We show two examples of the refined models compared to their imprecise models in Figs. 6 and 7 to illustrate our results: Fig. 6 shows an improvement in *log_precision* of more than 0.50 and Fig. 7 an improvement of 0.10. In Fig. 6, the original model (a) has four duplicated tasks labeled "*B*"; applying IM and ILP on the imprecise log respectively results in discovering an imprecise model (b), which has a flower subprocess consisting of 5 activities, or an imprecise

2 doi:10.4121/uuid:ea90c4be-64b6-4f4b-b27c-10ede28da6b6
  or https://svn.win.tue.nl/repos/prom/Documentation/TraceMatching/BPM2016.zip.

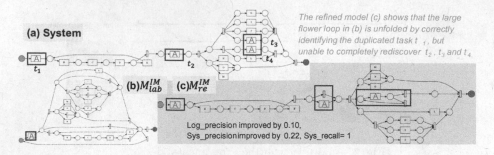

Fig. 7. Original model (a), result of IM on imprecise log (b) and on refined log (c).

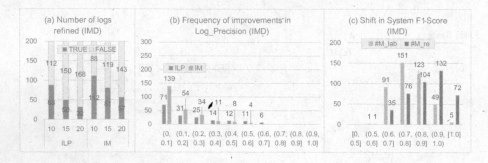

Fig. 8. Number of refined log (a), frequency of improvements in log precision (b) and shifts in system scores (c).

model (d), which has two unconnected activities; on the refined log, for both ILP and IM, the refined models (c) and (e) shows that the four duplicated tasks were correctly discovered in their respective positions in the process, however, our approach is unable to identify the concurrency between two consecutive duplicated tasks t_2 and and t_3 in (a).

Overall, Fig. 8(a) shows the number of systems for which our approach was able to find a refinement for its log that leads to discovering a better model with a higher log precision, while using automated detection of imprecise labels (IMD). In general, in 35 % (420 of 1200) of the logs, we were able to find a refinement with default parameters using IMD; using domain knowledge (OD) increased this number by 3 %. For 42 % of the refined logs, IM discovered an improved model, which is 14 % more than for ILP.

Figure 8(b) shows the histogram of frequencies of actual *log_precision* improvements using IMD. As can be seen, for both ILP and IM, our approach is able to help discover models with significant improvements. For ILP, the approach was able to find for 99 out of 600 models an improvement between 0.1 and 0.7 (using OD, this number increased by 9 %); similar for IM, 111 out of 600 refined models had such an improvement (using OD, this number is increased by 20 %). The average log precision is increased by 0.15.

Figure 8(c) shows the absolute $F1$-score (which is the harmony average of *sys_precision* and *sys_recall*) for M_{lab} (discovered on imprecise logs) versus M_{re} (discovered on the successfully refined logs using IM and ILP); our refinement clearly shifts the F1-score towards 1. When using automated detection (IMD), 16 % (67 out of 420) of the improved logs were refined in such way that $F1$-score becomes 1, which indicates that the resulting model have exactly the same alternative behavior as the original system enabled by the log (using OD we obtain 77 out of 516). Performance-wise, the average running time for computing one refined log varies between 8 and 14 s. depending on the model size.

(Exp. 2) Influence of Our Parameters. Next, we investigated whether adjusting parameters improves the quality of label refinement and whether such parameters can be found automatically for each model. For this, we repeated the above experiment for IM and OD and changed variant threshold (from 0.08 to 0.00 in steps of 0.01) and unfolding threshold (from 0.00 to 0.60 in steps of 0.10). We stopped when getting a log where M_{re} had higher log precision than M_{lab}. The average running time for computing one such refined log has increased to between 53 and 111 sec. depending on the model size.

Figure 9(a) shows the number of imprecise logs improved, (b) shows the actual improvements in *log_precision*, and (c) shows the F1-scores of *sys_recall* and *sys_precision*. It is worthwhile to note that, using the adaptive parameters, for 87 % of the imprecise logs, we were able to refine the log helping IM discover a better model. The average log precision is increased by 0.12. Compared to the

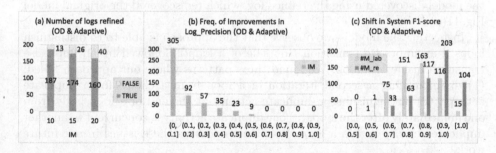

Fig. 9. The same types of result as Fig. 8 when using adaptive parameters.

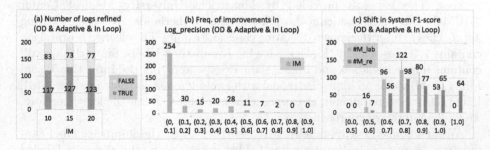

Fig. 10. The same types of result as Fig. 8, if a duplicated task is found in a loop.

46 % (when using default parameters and OD), the number is increased by more than 89 %. Another notable result is that the number of M_{re} that has an increase in *log_precision* between 0.2 and 0.7 is also increased by 72.2 % compared to the default parameter. This states for over one out of five logs, the adaptive approach is able to find a rather significant improvement, if the imprecise labels are not in a loop.

We manually inspected the models that could not be improved by using adjusted parameters. We found that this mostly concerned models that either have a large loop or have duplicated tasks concurrent to many other tasks. The difference in the corresponding components (i.e. such loops increase the cost of structure and such concurrency increases the cost of neighbors) becomes dominant in the cost returned by trace matching, resulting in splitting the imprecise labels wrongly even though the matching may be correct.

(Exp. 3) What if Imprecise Labels Appear in a Loop? We again generated 600 models, 200 for each $n = 10, 15, 20$. We used OD and set $k = 2$ transitions that have imprecise label: one inside and one outside of a loop. We used adaptive parameter selection and IM as discovery algorithm. Figure 10 shows the results. In 60.5 % of the models, the approach could find an improvement (32 % less compared to the results when no duplicated task is in a loop), which indicates that the approach has more difficulties to distinguish imprecise labels in loops. Another interesting result is that although the approach could improve fewer logs, the improvements achieved were considerable in some cases; 20 models have increased log precision by more than 0.5. Figure 11 shows an example of the model discovered using the refined log, which rediscovered the original model Fig. 11(a).

Inspecting the models, we observe that the approach is able to to distinguish loops if an imprecise transition t outside of a loop is followed by an imprecise transition inside of a loop. We found three patterns where our approach failed: (1) distinguishing a second iteration of a loop from a choice for a duplicate activity, (2) distinguishing a duplicate activity at the end of a loop body from one immediately after the loop, (3) one duplicate activity is concurrent to another duplicate activity within a loop. We plan to address these issues in our future work.

Real-Life Case Study. We conducted a case study involving a healthcare process. The log was provided by Maastricht University Medical Center (MUMC+), a large academic hospital in the Netherlands. We used existing approaches to filter the known deviating cases and events. The cleaned hospital log contains 1039 cases and 6213 events having five distinct labels. Since the log still contains imprecise labels and misses some events, applying the Inductive Visual Miner (IvM) yields an imprecise model with two self loops, as shown in Fig. 12(a). Using the default parameter, the approach was unable to refine the log. Therefore, we took an iterative approach.

We first refined events labeled with "surgery", i.e., the imprecise label candidate is "surgery". In the second and third iteration we refined events labeled with "consultation". The resulting model shows the sequential behavior expected

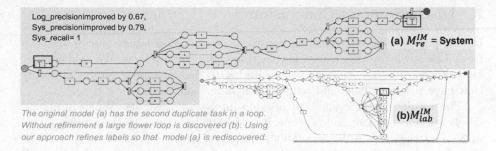

Fig. 11. Original model with duplicate tasks and rediscovered by IM on refined log (a), result of IM on imprecise log (b).

by domain experts. An interesting result is that after refining the labels, the discovered model is now suitable for computing performance. For example, a domain expert stated that within 2 months after the measurements, the first surgery should be executed, and the model shows on avg. 59 days. After the first surgery, a post-surgery consultation should take place within a week, and the model shows on avg. 8 days. If a second surgery should take place, then it should be performed after two weeks, and the model shows on avg. 14 days. Note that such performance diagnostics are difficult to obtain using the model discovered from the imprecise log Fig. 12(a).

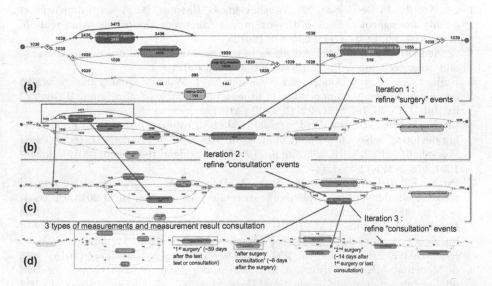

Fig. 12. Real-life log obtained from a Dutch hospital that was refined our approach; the resulting model better reflects reality and can be used to diagnose performance.

7   Discussion and Conclusion

In this paper, we investigated the problem of imprecise labels and proposed a fresh look at the problem from a log preprocessing point of view. We used context and structural information of events in a log to find dissimilar groups of events that have the same label and refined their labels accordingly.

The results of our evaluation provide interesting insights. When imprecise labels are not in a loop, our approach is able to improve logs by refining labels in 35 % of the cases using a default parameter, which increased to 87 % if the parameter is automatically adapted to the log and the discovery algorithm. If one imprecise label is in a loop, we could still improve 61 % of the logs. The case study demonstrated that the approach can be used iteratively (i.e., refining labels in multiple steps) in practice to obtain more accurate and precise models. Interestingly, such a model can be used to derive reliable performance diagnostic. Future research aims at investigating and tackling the limitations of the approach found during the experiments.

References

1. Herbst, J.: A machine learning approach to workflow management. In: Proceedings 11th European Conference on Machine Learning, pp. 183–194 (2000)
2. van der Aalst, W.M.P., Rubin, V., Verbeek, H.M.W., van Dongen, B.F., Kindler, E., Günther, C.W.: Process mining: a two-step approach to balance between under-fitting and overfitting. Soft. Syst. Model. **9**(1), 87–111 (2010)
3. De Weerdt, J., De Backer, M., Vanthienen, J., Baesens, B.: A multi-dimensional quality assessment of state-of-the-art process discovery algorithms using real-life event logs. Inf. Syst. **37**(7), 654–676 (2012)
4. vanden Broucke, S.K.L.M.: Advances in process mining: artificial negative events and other techniques. Ph.D. thesis, KU Leuven (2014)
5. Buijs, J.C.A.M., van Dongen, B.F., van der Aalst, W.M.P.: Quality dimensions in process discovery: the importance of fitness, precision, generalization and simplicity. Int. J. Coop. Inf. Syst. **23**(1), 1–39 (2014)
6. Lu, X., Fahland, D., van den Biggelaar, F.J.H.M., van der Aalst, W.M.P.: Detecting deviating behaviors without models. In: Reichert, M., Reijers, H. (eds.) BPM Workshops 2015. LNBIP, vol. 256, pp. 126–139. Springer, Heidelberg (2016). doi:10.1007/978-3-319-42887-1_11
7. Pittke, F., Richetti, P.H.P., Mendling, J., Baião, F.A.: Context-sensitive textual recommendations for incomplete process model elements. In: BPM 2015, Proceedings, pp. 189–197 (2015)
8. Koschmider, A., Ullrich, M., Heine, A., Oberweis, A.: Revising the vocabulary of business process element labels. In: Zdravkovic, J., Kirikova, M., Johannesson, P. (eds.) CAiSE 2015. LNCS, vol. 9097, pp. 69–83. Springer, Heidelberg (2015)
9. de Medeiros, A.K.A., Weijters, A.J.M.M., van der Aalst, W.M.P.: Genetic process mining: an experimental evaluation. Data Min. Knowl. Discov. **14**(2), 245–304 (2007)
10. van Zelst, S.J., van Dongen, B.F., van der Aalst, W.M.P.: ILP-based process discovery using hybrid regions. In: Proceedings of the International Workshop on Algorithms and Theories for the Analysis of Event Data, ATAED 2015, pp. 47–61 (2015)

11. Leemans, S.J.J., Fahland, D., van der Aalst, W.M.P.: Discovering block-structured process models from event logs - a constructive approach. In: Colom, J.-M., Desel, J. (eds.) PETRI NETS 2013. LNCS, vol. 7927, pp. 311–329. Springer, Heidelberg (2013)

12. Greco, G., Guzzo, A., Pontieri, L., Saccà, D.: Discovering expressive process models by clustering log traces. IEEE Trans. Knowl. Data Eng. 18(8), 1010–1027 (2006)

13. De Weerdt, J., vanden Broucke, S.K.L.M., Vanthienen, J., Baesens, B.: Active trace clustering for improved process discovery. IEEE Trans. Knowl. Data Eng. 25(12), 2708–2720 (2013)

14. García-Bañuelos, L., Dumas, M., La Rosa, M., De Weerdt, J., Ekanayake, C.C.: Controlled automated discovery of collections of business process models. Inf. Syst. 46, 85–101 (2014)

15. La Rosa, M., Dumas, M., Ekanayake, C.C., García-Bañuelos, L., Recker, J., ter Hofstede, A.H.M.: Detecting approximate clones in business process model repositories. Inf. Syst. 49, 102–125 (2015)

16. van der Aalst, W.M.P., Adriansyah, A., van Dongen, B.F.: Replaying history on process models for conformance checking and performance analysis. Wiley Interdisc. Rev.: Data Min. Knowl. Discov. 2(2), 182–192 (2012)

17. Munoz-Gama, J.: Conformance checking and diagnosis in process mining. Ph.D. thesis, Universitat Politècnica de Catalunya (2014)

18. van der Aalst, W.M.P., de Medeiros, A.K.A., Weijters, A.J.M.M.T.: Process equivalence: comparing two process models based on observed behavior. In: Dustdar, S., Fiadeiro, J.L., Sheth, A.P. (eds.) BPM 2006. LNCS, vol. 4102, pp. 129–144. Springer, Heidelberg (2006)

19. van der Aalst, W.M.P., van Hee, K.M., ter Hofstede, A.H.M., Sidorova, N., Verbeek, H.M.W., Voorhoeve, M., Wynn, M.T.: Soundness of workflow nets: classification, decidability, and analysis. Formal Aspects Comput. 23(3), 333–363 (2011)

Discovering Duplicate Tasks in Transition Systems for the Simplification of Process Models

Javier de San Pedro[(⊠)] and Jordi Cortadella

Department of Computer Science, Universitat Politècnica de Catalunya,
Barcelona, Spain
jspedro@cs.upc.edu

Abstract. This work presents a set of methods to improve the under-standability of process models. Traditionally, simplification methods trade off quality metrics, such as fitness or precision. Conversely, the methods proposed in this paper produce simplified models while preserving or even increasing fidelity metrics. The first problem addressed in the paper is the discovery of duplicate tasks. A new method is proposed that avoids overfitting by working on the transition system generated by the log. The method is able to discover duplicate tasks even in the presence of concurrency and choice. The second problem is the structural simpli-fication of the model by identifying optional and repetitive tasks. The tasks are substituted by annotated events that allow the removal of silent tasks and reduce the complexity of the model. An important feature of the methods proposed in this paper is that they are independent from the actual miner used for process discovery.

1 Introduction

Many factors can reduce the usefulness of a process model. Good quality models need to find a balance between all the common metrics by which a model can be evaluated against a log: *fitness, precision, simplicity* and *generalization* [1]. For example, an open problem in process mining is finding a middle point between *overfitting* and *underfitting* models [2]. Overfitting models only allow the behav-ior that has been observed, and thus may trade off simplicity and generaliza-tion, while underfitting models allow for more behavior, sacrificing precision. An unnecessarily overfit model may prevent the user from distilling more insight about the behavior of the process.

This paper presents a set of techniques to explore the trade off between *simplicity* and *precision*. More specifically, by introducing a small number of new elements, the proposed techniques result in tangible improvements in precision. They can work in combination with any existing discovery (mining) algorithm. While some of the techniques can be applied to different formal models, this work will focus on Petri nets.

The first technique enables the discovery of duplicate tasks in process models. Duplicate tasks allow several nodes to refer to the same activity in the event log. While this is not a new concept in Process Mining [3–6], our proposal is novel in

© Springer International Publishing Switzerland 2016
M. La Rosa et al. (Eds.): BPM 2016, LNCS 9850, pp. 108–124, 2016.
DOI: 10.1007/978-3-319-45348-4_7

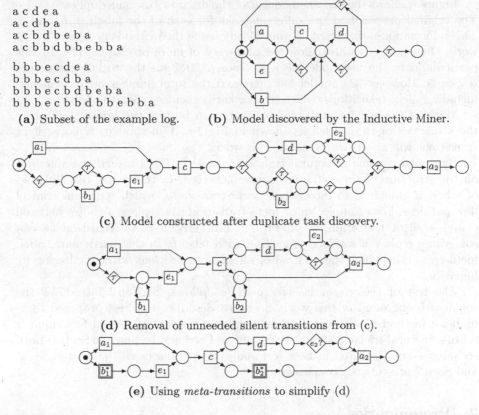

```
acdea
acdba
acbdbeba
acbbdbbebba

bbbecdea
bbbecdba
bbbecbdbeba
bbbecbbdbbebba
```

(a) Subset of the example log.   (b) Model discovered by the Inductive Miner.

(c) Model constructed after duplicate task discovery.

(d) Removal of unneeded silent transitions from (c).

(e) Using *meta-transitions* to simplify (d)

Fig. 1. Applying the method presented in this paper to a sample model discovered by the Inductive Miner.

that the splitting criteria is based on properties of Labeled Transition Systems, thus allowing more precision than other existing techniques.

The second technique performs structural simplifications that do not modify the semantics of the model, thus preserving the quality metrics. We introduce extensions to the formalism that allow single nodes to represent more complex control-flow structures, such as loops or optional tasks.

1.1 Motivating Example

Figure 1 will be used to illustrate the main contributions of this paper. We start from a simple log, a subset of which is shown in Fig. 1a. Figure 1b shows the model discovered by the Inductive Miner [7]. This model is highly imprecise (50 %): while it is not a pure flower model, almost all the words are recognized.

The reason many discovery algorithms generate such a low-precision model is the presence of *duplicate tasks* in the original process. These may be introduced if, for example, different tasks have been improperly tagged with the same label.

Figure 1c shows the process model after the discovery of some duplicate tasks. The original process had two different tasks for each of the labels a, b, and e. This information is discovered automatically using the methods proposed in this work. Duplicate tasks also allow the discovery of more precise models. In this particular case, the new model has a precision of 90 % and the workflow structure is clearer. However, the model has increased the total number of components, including silent transitions, which unnecessarily increase cognitive load.

Many of the silent transitions in Fig. 1c can be removed without affecting the semantics of the model, as shown in Fig. 1d. A method to remove silent transitions will also be presented in this work.

By applying some structural transformations to Fig. 1d, further reductions on the structure of the Petri net can be achieved. In this work, the alphabet of labels is enhanced to incorporate *meta-transitions*, which represent control flow patterns. For example, an e? meta-transition can replace a choice between e and a silent transition, as in Fig. 1d. Similarly, a meta-transition $b*$ can sometimes replace a self-loop transition with label b. In this particular model, meta-transitions allow the removal of all silent transitions without altering its behavior.

The rest of this paper is structured as follows. Section 2 introduces the required background of this work. Section 3 describes the first proposed technique: a method to discover discover duplicate tasks. The second technique, a set of structural transformations to simplify a Petri net, is shown in Sect. 4. Both techniques are evaluated in Sect. 5. Finally, Sect. 6 discusses the related work, and Sect. 7 presents the conclusions.

2 Preliminaries

2.1 Process Mining

Let Σ be an alphabet of *events*. A *trace* is a word $\sigma \in \Sigma^*$ that represents a finite sequence of events. An *event log* $L \in \mathcal{B}(\Sigma^*)$ is a multiset of traces[1]. Event logs are the starting point to apply process mining techniques, guided towards the discovery, analysis or extension of process models. *Process discovery* is an important discipline in process mining, concerned with learning a process model (e.g., a Petri net) from a log. Several discovery techniques are summarized in [1].

Process models are usually evaluated in four quality dimensions: *replay fitness*, *simplicity*, *precision*, and *generalization* [1]. A model with perfect replay fitness can replay all the traces in the log. On the other hand, a precise model does not replay any trace other than those contained in the log.

Among the different formalisms for process models, Petri nets are perhaps the most popular, due to its well-defined semantics. This paper focuses on Petri nets, although the work may be adapted to other formalisms.

---

[1] $\mathcal{B}(A)$ denotes the set of all multisets over A.

2.2   Petri Nets

A labeled Petri Net [8] is a tuple $N = \langle P, \Sigma, T, \mathcal{L}, \mathcal{F}, m_0 \rangle$, where P is the set of places, Σ is the alphabet of labels (corresponding to events), T is the set of transitions, $\mathcal{L} : T \rightarrow \Sigma \cup \{\tau\}$ assigns a label (or the empty label τ) to every transition, $\mathcal{F} : (P \times T) \cup (T \times P) \rightarrow \{0, 1\}$ is the flow relation, and m_0 is the initial marking. A marking $m : P \mapsto \mathbb{N}$ is an assignment of a non-negative integer to each place. If $m(p) = k$, we say that p is marked with k tokens. Given a node $x \in P \cup T$, its pre-set and post-set are denoted by ${}^{\bullet}x$ and $x^{\bullet}$ respectively.

A transition t is *enabled* in a marking m when all places in ${}^{\bullet}t$ are marked. When t is enabled, it can *fire* by removing a token from each place in ${}^{\bullet}t$ and putting a token to each place in $t^{\bullet}$. A marking m' is *reachable* from m if there is a sequence of firings $t_1 t_2 \ldots t_n$ that transforms m into m', denoted by $m[t_1 t_2 \ldots t_n \rangle m'$. A sequence $t_1 t_2 \ldots t_n$ is *feasible* if it is firable from m_0. A trace σ *fits* N if there exists a feasible sequence in N with the same labels.

A transition labeled with the empty label τ is called a *silent* transition. A *duplicate* task is a transition with the same label as some other transitions in N.

2.3   Transition Systems

A finite labeled transition system is a tuple $A = (S, \Sigma, T, s_0)$ where S is a finite set of states, Σ is the alphabet of labels, $T \in S \times \Sigma \times S$ are the transition relations between states, labeled with Σ, and s_0 is the initial state.

We use $s \xrightarrow{e} s'$ as a shorthand for the arc $(s, e, s') \in T$. A trace $\sigma = e_1 e_2 \ldots e_n$ *fits* A if there exists $s_1, s_2, \ldots, s_n \in S$ with $s_0 \xrightarrow{e_1} s_1 \xrightarrow{\ldots} s_{n-1} \xrightarrow{e_n} s_n$. An event $e \in \Sigma$ is enabled in a state $s_1 \in S$ if there exists $s_2 \in S$ with $s_1 \xrightarrow{e} s_2$.

Given two states s_1 and s_2 with $s_1 \xrightarrow{e} s_2 \in T$, we say e *triggers* another event f iff f is enabled in s_2, but not in s_1. In a sense, e triggering f implies a causality relation between the two events.

Excitation Sets. For a given LTS $A = (S, \Sigma, T, s_0)$ and event $e \in \Sigma$, we define the *Excitation Set* of e as the set of states in which e is enabled, i.e., $ES(e) = \{s \in S \mid \exists s' \in S : s \xrightarrow{e} s'\}$.

Figure 2b shows an LTS constructed from the process in Fig. 2a. Notice how $ES(a)$ contains the states in which the three duplicate tasks of a are enabled. The concept of *local excitation set* distinguishes each such instance of a:

Definition 1 (Local Excitation Set). Given LTS $A = (S, \Sigma, T, s_0)$ and event $e \in \Sigma$, the *local excitation sets* of e, $LES(e)_1, \ldots, LES(e)_k$ are the maximally connected subsets of $ES(e)$ such that, $\forall s_1 \xrightarrow{e} s_2 \in A$, if $s_1 \in LES(e)_i$ and $s_2 \in LES(e)_j$, then $i \neq j$.

Notice that the definition does not allow both the source and target states of a transition with label e to be in the same $LES(e)_i$. The set of LES of an event can be efficiently computed with a simple algorithm, illustrated in Fig. 2c for event a. The algorithm has the following steps: (1) calculate $ES(a)$, (2) remove the transitions with label a from the LTS, (3) identify all $LES(a)$ as the maximally connected subsets of $ES(a)$ after the removal of the a-transitions.

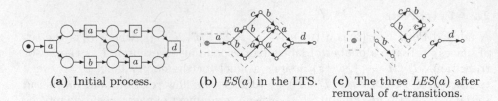

(a) Initial process.   **(b)** $ES(a)$ in the LTS.   **(c)** The three $LES(a)$ after removal of a-transitions.

Fig. 2. Calculation of local excitation sets.

3   Discovering Duplicate Tasks

This section introduces a method that automatically discovers which events from an event log correspond most likely to duplicate tasks, i.e. should be represented by more than one task in order to enhance the quality of the model. The technique works with the LTS constructed from a log and can be combined with any discovery algorithm. By adding new tasks, the method slightly increases the element count of the model but results in tangible improvements in precision.

Given a log L, the goal of this procedure is to generate, for every activity $a \in L$, a *partition* of all the events in L referring to a. When mining a process model, every different partition will be represented by a different task. We will generally refer to each task by $a_1, a_2, \ldots, a_n$. A partition that, for every activity a, maps all events into a single task a_1 results in a model with no duplicate tasks. Figure 3b shows an example partition for the log in Fig. 1a.

An overview of the proposed method is shown in Fig. 3a. At the core of the proposal lies a clustering process that generates a small set of candidate partitions. An existing mining algorithm is used to generate a process model for each of these partitions, and the best model is selected out of these discovered models. This way, the method adapts to the subtleties of the different mining

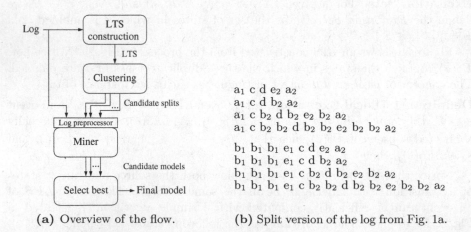

(a) Overview of the flow.   **(b)** Split version of the log from Fig. 1a.

Fig. 3. Summary of the duplicate task discovery process.

algorithms. Even for miners that automatically discover duplicate tasks, the proposed method may help improving the results.

The clustering method uses a bottom-up (*agglomerative*) approach: starting from the trivial partition which maps every event to a different task, the procedure iteratively selects pairs of *similar* events, grouping them into the same task. To find similar events, the algorithm uses causality relationships between events as discovered in a LTS, instead of using log information directly (e.g. direct predecessors or successors of an event). An LTS can be built from the log with a variety of methods [2]. Section 3.1 describes how the procedure finds similar events in the LTS, while Sect. 3.2 details the actual clustering algorithm.

3.1   Partitioning Based on Excitation Sets

A significant difference between this proposal and previous approaches to duplicate tasks is that the proposed method works at the Transition System level. The log is firstly converted into an LTS, and the clustering procedure generates a partition *based on causality relationships between excitation sets in this LTS*, rather than directly using the preceding and successor events in the log. Because of this, the approach is resilient to processes where duplicate tasks are combined with concurrency and choice. The use of clustering-based methods [9] and similarity metrics rather than looking for exact matches also allow the proposed flow to gracefully handle noise and incompleteness in the log.

Let us use an example to show the benefits of using ESs. Figure 4a shows the LTS constructed from the log in Fig. 1a, with no duplicate task detection

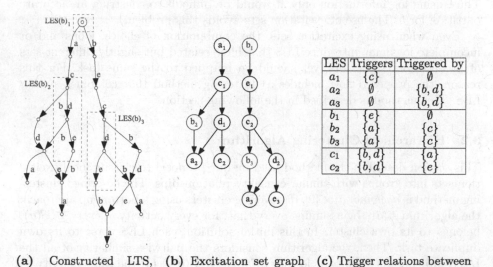

(a)   Constructed LTS, highlighting all *LES*(*b*). (b) Excitation set graph of the LTS in (a). (c) Trigger relations between LES.

Fig. 4. Example excitation set graph of a subset of Fig. 1a (loops removed).

performed. For simplicity, loops have been removed (allowing one iteration only). As per the definition of LES, there are 3 LESs for activity b, shown in Fig. 4a.

Notice how the LESs of b provide an intuitive view of the correct partition for activity b (as shown in Fig. 3b): $LES(b)_1$ corresponds to the events of task b_1, while $LES(b)_2 \cup LES(b)_3$ would correspond to b_2. Our proposal classifies these LES by their relationships with other LES. The *excitation set graph* represents all the LES of a TS as well as the causality relationships between those:

Definition 2 (Excitation Set Graph). Given a Labeled Transition System $A = (S, \Sigma, T, s_0)$, the excitation set graph of A is a graph $ESG(A)$ where:

- The set of vertices $V(ESG(A))$ corresponds to the set of LES of A.
- For every pair $(LES(a)_i, LES(b)_j)$ of A, with $a, b \in \Sigma$, there is an edge $(LES(a)_i, LES(b)_j) \in E(ESG(A))$ iff for any $s_1 \in LES(a)_i$ and $s_2 \in LES(b)_j$, $s_1 \xrightarrow{a} s_2$ triggers b.

Figure 4b shows the corresponding excitation set graph of the example LTS, while Fig. 4c summarizes the immediate trigger relations. Notice how this information allows us to trivially distinguish between $LES(b)_1$ and $\{LES(b)_2, LES(b)_3\}$, since $LES(b)_1$ triggers a different set of events.

Compare this to using predecessor and successor information from the log directly, without constructing an LTS first. It is difficult to distinguish events of b by looking at the immediately following event. For example, an event b followed by e may indicate an instance of task b_1 as discovered in the previous section, but it may also be caused by an instance of b_2, since it is concurrent with e. Thus, using log information only, it would be difficult to construct an accurate partition for b. The use of excitation sets avoids this problem.

Even when using excitation sets, the combination of choice, loops and/or incomplete logs may introduce LES that have related but slightly different sets of predecessors/successors, yet should be mapped to the same task. For this reason, the proposed flow includes a clustering method that combines *similar* LES. This method is described in the following section.

3.2   Hierarchical Clustering Algorithm

This section describes the method used by our proposal to classify local excitation sets into groups with similar causality relationships. The described clustering method is *agglomerative* [9], discovering clusters using a bottom up approach: the algorithm starts by assuming every that, for every activity a, every $LES(a)_i$ belongs to its own cluster. In this initial solution, each LES maps to its own duplicate task. Then, the algorithm considers the pairwise similarity of all the LES, and combines the two closest $(LES(a)_i, LES(a)_j)$ (of the same activity a) into the same task a_i. The entire process iterates until no further clustering can be performed. On every iteration, the algorithm explores a solution with exactly one duplicate task less than the previous solution.

Algorithm 1. Discovery flow with duplicate tasks

1: **function** DUPLICATETASKDISCOVERY(L, M)
   ▷ L is the input log, M is a miner algorithm.
2:    $A \leftarrow$ CONSTRUCTLTS(L)
3:    $G \leftarrow$ ESG(A)
4:    $R \leftarrow M(L_i)$ ▷ Stores the best result (process model) discovered so far
5:    **while** $|V(G)| > |Activities(A)|$ **do**   ▷ While there is some duplicate task
6:       $v_i, v_j \leftarrow$ FINDMOSTSIMILARNODES(G)
7:       merge v_i, v_j into single node in G
8:       $L_i \leftarrow$ TAGLOG(L, G) ▷ Tag events in the log according to current partition
9:       $N_i \leftarrow M(L_i)$ ▷ Discover a temporary model for evaluation
10:      **if** N_i is better than R **then**
11:         $R \leftarrow N_i$
12:    **return** R

The full discovery algorithm can be seen in Algorithm 1. The input is a log L. A is an LTS constructed from L (for example using the methods described in [2]), while G is the initial ESG, constructed using the rules seen in Definition 2. The output R is a process model with duplicate tasks.

In every iteration, procedure FINDMOSTSIMILARNODES selects two vertices of G with the most similar *context vectors*, a numeric way to represent their causality relations which will be explained in the following section. The selected vertices are then merged into a single new vertex, representing the new cluster, which inherits the causality relationships of the merged vertices. Note that only vertices with the same activity label will be selected. The loop ends when there is only vertex in G for every activity, i.e. there are no duplicate tasks.

To select which partition of tasks will be returned by our procedure, we construct a temporary process model N_i at every iteration. The provided miner is called using a log where events have been tagged according to the currently evaluated partition. The details of how models are compared will be described in a later section. Note that the total maximum number of models to evaluate (i.e. the number of iterations in the procedure) is limited by the number of excitation sets in the LTS. However, most processes contain only a few duplicate tasks. Limiting to 4 or 5 tasks per activity reduces the number of models that need to be evaluated to a few, depending on the number of different activities.

Figure 5 visualizes the clustering procedure. The initial solution, where every LES is partitioned into its own duplicate task, is shown at the bottom row. The following row represents one iteration of the clustering process, in which a_2, a_3 were the most similar LES and were merged. Thus, the number of duplicate tasks, in the first column, is reduced by 1. The top row shows the result after all nodes have been merged and thus there are no duplicate tasks left. Columns 2 and 3 show sample metrics of the evaluation model for each row: Petri net size and precision. The selected model has the best precision and smallest size.

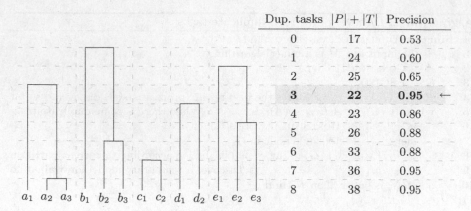

Dup. tasks	$|P| + |T|$	Precision
0	17	0.53
1	24	0.60
2	25	0.65
3	**22**	**0.95** ←
4	23	0.86
5	26	0.88
6	33	0.88
7	36	0.95
8	38	0.95

Fig. 5. Dendogram showing clustering of LTS in Fig. 4a.

Representing Excitation Set Relations in Vector Space. In order to find the closest two groups of LES, a distance metric capable of evaluating the similarity of the relationships of two LES is required. For this, we will first provide a way to represent, as a numeric vector, the causality relationships of a given vertex (representing a LES or cluster of LES) in a ESG.

This representation needs to satisfy several requirements: (a) it needs to be normalized, allowing meaningful comparisons between different vertices, (b) it needs to distinguish vertices by their immediate predecessors/successors, but also more distant neighbors. Otherwise, duplicate tasks sharing the same set of immediate predecessors or successors would not be distinguishable. However, similarity of closer neighbors should have more weight than distant neighbors.

Definition 3 (Context Vector). Given LTS A, $ESG(A)$, and a vertex $v \in ESG(A)$, the *forward context vector* of v, $\overrightarrow{C_v}$, is a function $E \mapsto \mathbb{R}$ that maps an activity $e \in \Sigma$ to

$$\overrightarrow{C_v}(e) = \frac{|\operatorname{Succ}(v,e)|}{2|\operatorname{Succ}(v)|} + \frac{\sum_{v' \in \operatorname{Succ}(v)} \overrightarrow{C_{v'}}(e)}{4|\operatorname{Succ}(v)|}$$

where $\operatorname{Succ}(v)$ is the set of immediate successors of v and $\operatorname{Succ}(v,e)$ is the set of immediate successors of v of activities with label e. Similarly, we can define the *backwards context vector*, $\overleftarrow{C_v}$, using predecessors instead of successors.

For a given vertex v and event e, the value of $\overrightarrow{C_v}(e)$ depends on the number of e-successors of v relative to the total number of successors of v. Notice the function gives decreasing weight to more distant successors using the pattern $\frac{1}{2} + \frac{1}{4} + \frac{1}{8} + \ldots$. Thus, the function is normalized between $[0 \ldots 1)$, allowing for numeric comparisons between different vectors.

Imposing a limit k to the recursion depth, context vectors are easy to compute with a single pass over the graph. As the weight of successors decreases with

Table 1. Context vectors for the ESG in Fig. 4b.

LES	Forward					Backward				
	a	b	c	d	e	a	b	c	d	e
a_1	0	$1/8$	$1/2$	$1/8$	0	0	0	0	0	0
a_2	0	0	0	0	0	0	$1/4$	0	$1/8 + 1/8$	$1/4$
a_3	0	0	0	0	0	0	$1/4$	0	$1/8 + 1/8$	$1/4$
b_1	0	0	$1/4$	0	$1/2$	0	0	0	0	0
b_2	$1/2$	0	0	0	0	$1/4$	0	$1/2$	0	0
b_3	$1/2$	0	0	0	0	0	0	$1/2$	0	$1/4$
c_1	$1/16 + 2/16$	$1/4$	0	$1/4$	$1/16$	$1/2$	0	0	0	0
c_2	$1/16 + 2/16$	$1/4$	0	$1/4$	$1/16$	0	$1/4$	0	0	$1/2$

distance, this limit does not impact the quality of the metric. An example list of context vectors for the graph in Fig. 4b is shown in Table 1, assuming $k = 2$.

Distance Function. To measure the similarity (distance) between two vertices $v_1, v_2 \in ESG(A)$, the following formula is used, where d is the Euclidean distance:

$$\text{dist}(v_1, v_2) = \min(\text{d}(\overrightarrow{C_{v_1}}, \overrightarrow{C_{v_2}}), \text{d}(\overleftarrow{C_{v_1}}, \overleftarrow{C_{v_2}}))$$

Using the minimal distance between the forward and backward vectors allows proper detection of duplicate tasks in the first and last iterations of loops. For tasks in a loop, several LESs may exist in the LTS for different iterations of the same task. The causality relations of the LESs corresponding to the first and last iterations will be different of those from inner iterations. For example, only the LES corresponding to the last iteration will not trigger other LESs of the same task. By centering on either the backward or forward context vector, depending on which pair is the closest, these LESs will still be clustered into a single task.

Comparing Candidate Models. Traditional hierarchical clustering algorithms use various criteria to determine which clustering solution is more suited to the data, such as for example the *elbow* criteria [10]. However, the flow proposed in this work produces more than one candidate model, allowing the exploration of the trade-off between precision and simplicity. By limiting the maximum number of allowed duplicate tasks, the set of candidate models can be kept under manageable sizes. Therefore, conventional conformance checking strategies may be used to accurately compare the candidate models, e.g. measuring fitness, precision, generalization or simplicity. Generally, a combination of these parameters will be used, depending on user preference. For example, maximizing precision while constraining the simplicity to a minimum threshold value.

Figure 5 shows that the precision increases with every duplicate task until 95 % with 3 duplicate tasks, and then decreases, revealing that more duplicate tasks introduce unnecessary choices and are not necessary for this process. The result, with 3 duplicate tasks, exactly matches the model shown in Fig. 1c.

4   Structural Simplification

This section introduces the structural simplifications proposed in this work:substituting common control flow patterns with special *meta-tasks* that represent optional or iterative behavior.

The simplifications are especially suitable for Petri nets. They reduce the complexity of the net while still allowing the expressiveness of Petri nets. In addition, the proposed simplifications exactly preserve the semantics of the models, and thus, conformance metrics such as fitness and precision.

The simplifications center on two aspects. First, the removal of unnecessary silent transitions. While silent transitions are a useful construct, many mining algorithms or conversions from other modeling languages often generate silent transitions that may be unnecessary [11]. Second, we introduce a series of *meta-transitions* which extend the language of Petri nets and represent simple flow control operations such as optional or iterative behavior.

Removal of Silent Transitions. Our proposal removes unnecessary silent transitions by following the transformations shown in Fig. 6. The objective of these transformations is to eliminate as many silent transitions as possible without impacting the semantics of the Petri net, so that the set of traces fitting the original net is identical to the traces fitting the transformed Petri net. The transformations proposed are similar to the liveness and safeness-preserving transformations proposed in [8], that have been already used in previous work [11,12]

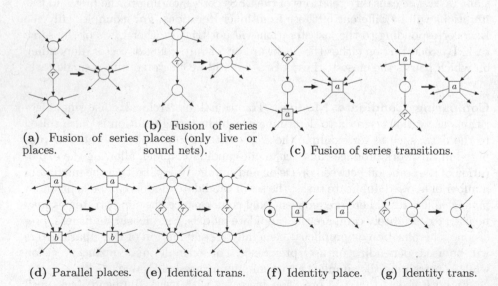

(a) Fusion of series places.

(b) Fusion of series places (only live or sound nets).

(c) Fusion of series transitions.

(d) Parallel places.   (e) Identical trans.   (f) Identity place.   (g) Identity trans.

Fig. 6. Reduction rules for behavior-preserving removal of silent transitions.

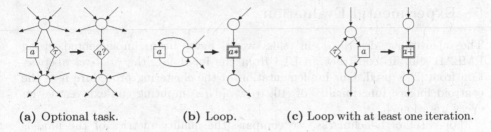

(a) Optional task.   (b) Loop.   (c) Loop with at least one iteration.

Fig. 7. Rules for transformation using *meta-transitions*.

also with the goal of removing silent transitions. However, the existing set of transformations is not exhaustive. For example, it is not possible to remove all the silent transitions from the model in Fig. 1c using only the rules defined in [8].

By centering on a commonly used structural type of Petri nets, sound workflow nets [13], we are able to introduce additional transformations covering the removal of more silent transitions. For example, Fig. 6b proposes that fusion of serial places can be performed even if the first place has other outgoing arcs. However, this transformation does not fully preserve the behavior of general Petri nets, as it may remove deadlocks present in the original Petri net. Full preservation of behavior, including liveness, is only guaranteed in the case of live Petri nets or nets with deadlocks only on specific states, such as sound workflow nets. For the former subtype of Petri nets, deadlocks only appear in states where the output sink place is marked [13], and the output place will never be modified by the transformation rule.

Meta-Transitions. A *meta-transition* replaces common a Petri net substructure (e.g., a self-loop) with a single transition that is defined to have identical behavior. By transforming a Petri net, replacing instances of these structures by meta-transitions, the element count of a Petri net can be reduced while completely preserving its behavior. The transformed net will fit exactly the same traces as the original net. In addition, the transformation may open the door to further simplifications such as removal of additional silent transitions.

In Fig. 7 we show the proposed new meta-transitions, as well as the behavior represented by each meta-transition. These specific patterns have been selected because of their high frequency in real-life processes. In addition, the well-known regular expression-like syntax used in the meta-transitions makes their meaning familiar.

The first meta-transition, $a?$, models an *optional* event: it is equivalent to a choice between the empty label τ and trace a. The other two meta-transitions represent iterative behavior. $a*$ is equivalent to a self-loop. Thus, it fits the empty trace, but also $\{a, aa, aaa, \dots\}$. Meta-transition $a+$ similarly represents a loop of a, but requires at least one iteration.

5   Experimental Evaluation

The algorithms described in this work have been implemented using PMLAB [14]. To construct an LTS from the input log, the *multiset* abstraction from [2] is used. Our implementation of the clustering procedure uses the centroid linkage functionality of [10] to avoid recomputing context vectors on every iteration.

For a set of benchmarks, we compare the quality metrics of the models obtained with and without the proposed duplicate task discovery algorithm, as well as the reduction in complexity after the structural simplifications and use of meta-transitions. All benchmarks are available at http://www.cs.upc.edu/~jspedro/pnsimpl/. In order to demonstrate the ability of the proposal to work with multiple miners, two different miners will be used: Inductive Miner [7] (IM) and Petrify [15]. While the current version of the Inductive Miner does not support duplicate tasks, Petrify contains some support for automatic discovery of duplicate tasks [4]. Thus, models discovered by Petrify may already contain duplicate task before the clustering method proposed in this article takes place.

Precision and generalization are measured using the available ProM plugins [16,17]. To measure complexity, we will show the size of the Petri nets. For non-workflow Petri nets, such as those generated by Petrify, we will also use a complexity metric closely related to the concept of planarity: the minimal number of *crossings* required to embed the graph on a plane. This number is estimated using GraphViz [18].

The method used to select a model from the list of candidates produced by the duplicate task discovery method depends on the miner used. When using the IM, the smallest model (in terms of places and transitions) out of all models with highest precision will be selected. When using Petrify, the model with lowest number of crossings, out of those with highest precision, is used instead.

Artificial Benchmarks. To evaluate our duplicate task discovery workflow and compare to the results presented by previous work, we reuse an existing dataset comprising a combination of logs [5,6,19] whose source processes are well-known and reproduce behavior commonly found in real-life. Because these benchmarks have no noise, the miners were configured to generate perfectly fitting models.

Table 2 summarizes the results. For every benchmark, there are three different runs: in the first one, the log is mined with the default miner configuration. In the second run, the flow with duplicate task discovery as presented in this work is used. In the third result, we apply structural simplifications (silent transition elimination and meta-transitions) on top of the model discovered on the second run. For each run, we evaluate the size of the model (number of places, transitions and silent (τ) transitions) as well as its precision and generalization.

The proposed method significantly increases the precision on all the benchmarks. In some examples, generalization is reduced, yet still shows that the method results in models that are not overfitting. In tests with the Inductive Miner, using duplicate tasks allows removing most of the silent transitions, and

Table 2. Comparison using artificial benchmarks.

	Inductive Miner					With duplicate tasks					After simpl.		
	|P|	|T|	|τ|	Prec.	Gen.	|P|	|T|	|τ|	Prec.	Gen.		|P|	|T|	|τ|
alpha	11	17	6	68%	100%	11	16	4	70%	100%	†	9	13	1
betaSimpl	14	21	8	62%	86%	14	16	1	94%	73%		14	15	0
Fig5p19	9	14	6	67%	89%	12	14	5	85%	76%		12	12	3
Fig5p1AND	9	8	3	83%	28%	10	8	2	100%	0%		9	7	1
Fig5p1OR	5	6	1	70%	33%	6	6	0	100%	0%		6	6	0
Fig6p10	15	24	13	63%	100%	19	25	10	77%	100%		18	19	4
Fig6p25	22	35	14	76%	100%	24	35	12	84%	100%		23	27	4
Fig6p31	6	10	1	63%	72%	9	11	0	100%	42%		9	11	0
Fig6p33	7	11	1	67%	70%	10	12	0	100%	38%		10	12	0
Fig6p34	17	24	12	58%	100%	19	20	4	93%	100%		17	18	2
Fig6p38	13	11	4	62%	84%	12	14	6	66%	87%		11	11	3
Fig6p39	12	12	5	90%	94%	12	12	5	90%	94%	†	10	9	2
Fig6p42	7	18	4	23%	100%	26	32	12	75%	96%	†	24	29	9
Fig6p9	10	15	8	67%	82%	9	12	3	83%	72%		9	9	0
flightCar	10	14	4	67%	64%	10	14	4	67%	64%	†	11	9	1
RelProc	21	28	12	71%	100%	21	28	11	74%	100%	†	19	21	4

	Petrify					With duplicate tasks					After simpl.		
	|P|	|T|	Cros.	Prec.	Gen.	|P|	|T|	Cros.	Prec.	Gen.		|P|	|T|	Cros.
alpha	13	11	11	92%	100%	12	12	1	92%	100%	†	12	12	1
betaSimpl	11	13	1	80%	77%	14	15	0	97%	39%		15	15	0
Fig5p19	8	8	2	100%	74%	9	9	1	100%	58%		9	9	1
Fig5p1AND	8	5	0	100%	0%	7	6	0	100%	0%		7	6	0
Fig5p1OR	5	5	3	100%	0%	5	6	0	100%	0%		5	6	0
Fig6p10	7	11	1	39%	100%	13	15	1	91%	100%		13	15	1
Fig6p25	14	21	6	80%	100%	14	23	0	80%	100%		18	23	0
Fig6p31	7	9	12	100%	42%	8	11	0	100%	42%		8	11	0
Fig6p33	8	10	7	100%	38%	9	12	0	100%	38%		9	12	0
Fig6p34	9	12	4	39%	100%	14	16	0	89%	100%		14	16	0
Fig6p38	8	7	0	71%	85%	10	8	0	100%	64%		10	8	0
Fig6p39	6	7	0	72%	98%	7	8	1	86%	86%	†	8	8	0
Fig6p42	11	14	20	37%	98%	21	23	3	96%	94%	†	21	23	3
Fig6p9	9	7	9	100%	54%	8	9	0	100%	54%		8	9	0
flightCar	6	8	0	58%	72%	6	8	0	58%	72%	†	7	8	0
RelProc	16	16	11	87%	100%	15	17	2	87%	100%	†	15	17	2

thus the overall complexity of the model decreases. Using meta-transitions, additional silent tasks can be removed. On the other hand, when combining our discovery flow with Petrify, the discovery of duplicate tasks allows for models with fewer crossings. However, results after simplification are not as remarkable as with the IM, since Petrify does not discover silent transitions.

For the majority of benchmarks, the partition of tasks discovered by the proposed flow exactly matched the duplicate tasks in the original process. The exceptions are marked with †. These cases are usually situations where, e.g., duplicate tasks are concurrent with themselves. Despite the fact that the partition is not exactly correct, the increase in quality metrics is still significant.

Logs with Noise. An additional experiment shows the resilience of the proposed method to noise. We used Process Log Generator (PLG) [20] to generate a set of 3 random processes using a process depth of 3 and uniform probabilities for all control flow operators. Then, for each of these processes, we generated 10 logs containing 1000 traces each. In each log a different amount of random control-flow noise was injected using PLG, ranging from 0 % to 10 %.

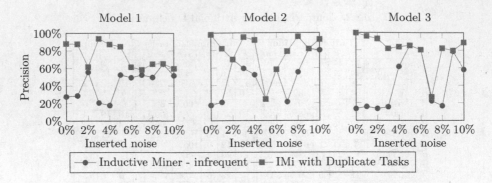

Fig. 8. Resilience of duplicate task discovery to different artificial noise levels.

Figure 8 compares the precision of the models obtained using the Inductive Miner – infrequent [7] (IMi) miner, configured with a 20 % threshold, with the models obtained by the combination of our duplicate task discovery flow and the IMi. For the 3 evaluated processes, our flow can discover duplicate tasks and thus increase the precision even when confronted with noise. The differences in fitness were always smaller than 5 % between both versions.

On a Intel Core i5-2520m, our implementation of the clustering procedure is able to provide a set of candidate partitions in less than 4 seconds, even for the largest of these logs. The runtime of the miner, required to evaluate each candidate, is usually much larger than the clustering process. However, the number of candidates to be evaluated can be limited by setting an upper bound to the number of allowed duplicate tasks per label.

6   Related Work

Several methods already exist for duplicate task detection. In [6], a set of heuristics creates a candidate set of duplicate tasks, which is then explored by a local search procedure working in tandem with an arbitrary mining algorithm. The method produces high-quality results in combination with advanced miners. However, since the miner influences the direction of the search, it is difficult to predict the runtime of the discovery process. In this work, the miner algorithm is only used to evaluate the set of candidate results. The number of results is exactly bounded by the maximum number of allowed duplicate tasks per event. The work in [5] proposes a clustering approach based on the context of events similar to the one described in this work. Analogously, finding repeating patterns in the log [21] may be used to discover potential duplicate tasks. However, our work uses excitation sets to identify the context of events, which allows for more accurate detection that using the log directly.

A different family of methods to perform duplicate task detection are tied to specific mining technologies. For example, Fodina [22], Genetic Miner [3], AGNEs [23], InWoLvE [19], region theory [4], α^*-algorithm [24]. The proposal in this work works with any mining algorithm, and does not require e.g. workflow nets or other specific process models.

For the second proposal in this work, structural simplifications, a potential comparable work is the use of other process modeling notations, such as BPMN [1]. The formalisms presented in this paper still allow the expressiveness of Petri nets, yet hide the complexity of common flow control operators. Other methods to simplify Petri nets do so at the cost of accuracy [25,26].

7 Conclusions

This work has presented methods for simplification of process models that improve the quality of discovered models, in both simplicity and precision, while using different mining algorithms.

As future work, we envision methods that work even in the presence of concurrent duplicate tasks, which are currently handled with unsatisfactory results. In addition, the language of structural tasks can be extended, for example, to allow simple regular expressions in nodes, e.g., $(a|bc)*$.

Acknowledgments. This work has been partially supported by funds from the Spanish Ministry for Economy and Competitiveness and the European Union (FEDER funds) under grant TIN2013-46181-C2-1-R, and the Generalitat de Catalunya (2014 SGR 1034 and FI-DGR 2015).

References

1. van der Aalst, W.M.P.: Process Mining - Discovery: Conformance and Enhancement of Business Processes. Springer, Heidelberg (2011)
2. van der Aalst, W., Rubin, V., Verbeek, H., van Dongen, B., Kindler, E., Gnther, C.: Process mining: a two-step approach to balance between underfitting and overfitting. Softw. & Syst. Model. **9**(1), 87–111 (2010)
3. de Medeiros, A.K.A.: Genetic process mining. Ph.D. thesis, Technische Universiteit Eindhoven, Eindhoven, The Netherlands (2006)
4. Carmona, J.: The label splitting problem. In: Jensen, K., van der Aalst, W.M., Ajmone Marsan, M., Franceschinis, G., Kleijn, J., Kristensen, L.M. (eds.) Transactions on Petri Nets and Other Models of Concurrency VI. LNCS, vol. 7400, pp. 1–23. Springer, Heidelberg (2012)
5. Song, J.L., Luo, T.J., Chen, S., Liu, W.: A clustering based method to solve duplicate tasks problem. J. Univ. Chin. Acad. Sci. **26**(1), 107 (2009)
6. Vázquez-Barreiros, B., Mucientes, M., Lama, M.: Mining duplicate tasks from discovered processes. In: Proceedings of Algorithms and Theories for the Analysis of Event Data, vol. 1371, Brussels, Belgium, CEUR, pp. 78–82 June 2015
7. Leemans, S.J.J., Fahland, D., van der Aalst, W.M.P.: Discovering block-structured process models from incomplete event logs. In: Ciardo, G., Kindler, E. (eds.) PETRI NETS 2014. LNCS, vol. 8489, pp. 91–110. Springer, Heidelberg (2014)
8. Murata, T.: Petri nets: properties, analysis and applications. Proc. IEEE **77**(4), 541–574 (1989)

9. Johnson, S.C.: Hierarchical clustering schemes. Psychometrika **32**(3), 241–254 (1967)
10. Jones, E., Oliphant, T., Peterson, P., et al.: SciPy: open source scientific tools for Python (2001) . Accessed 18 Mar 2016
11. van der Aalst, W.M.P., Dumas, M., Ouyang, C., Rozinat, A., Verbeek, E.: Conformance checking of service behavior. ACM Trans. Internet Technol. **8**(3), 1–13 (2008)
12. van Dongen, B.F., de Medeiros, A.K.A., Verbeek, H.M.W.E., Weijters, A.J.M.M.T., van der Aalst, W.M.P.: The ProM framework: a new era in process mining tool support. In: Ciardo, G., Darondeau, P. (eds.) ICATPN 2005. LNCS, vol. 3536, pp. 444–454. Springer, Heidelberg (2005)
13. van der Aalst, W.M.P., van Hee, K.M., ter Hofstede, A.H.M., Sidorova, N., Verbeek, H.M.W., Voorhoeve, M., Wynn, M.T.: Soundness of workflow nets: classification, decidability, and analysis. Formal Aspects Comput. **23**(3), 333–363 (2011)
14. Carmona, J., Sol, M.: PMLAB: an scripting environment for process mining. In: Proceedings of the BPM Demo Sessions 2014, pp. 16–21 (2014)
15. Carmona, J.A., Cortadella, J., Kishinevsky, M.: A region-based algorithm for discovering petri nets from event logs. In: Dumas, M., Reichert, M., Shan, M.-C. (eds.) BPM 2008. LNCS, vol. 5240, pp. 358–373. Springer, Heidelberg (2008)
16. Adriansyah, A., Munoz-Gama, J., Carmona, J., van Dongen, B., van der Aalst, W.: Measuring precision of modeled behavior. Inf. Syst. e-Bus. Manag. **13**(1), 37–67 (2015)
17. Buijs, J.C.A.M., van Dongen, B.F., van der Aalst, W.M.P.: On the role of fitness, precision, generalization and simplicity in process discovery. In: Meersman, R., Panetto, H., Dillon, T., Rinderle-Ma, S., Dadam, P., Zhou, X., Pearson, S., Ferscha, A., Bergamaschi, S., Cruz, I.F. (eds.) OTM 2012, Part I. LNCS, vol. 7565, pp. 305–322. Springer, Heidelberg (2012)
18. Gansner, E.R., Koutsofios, E., North, S.C., Vo, K.: A technique for drawing directed graphs. IEEE Trans. Softw. Eng. **19**(3), 214–230 (1993)
19. Herbst, J., Karagiannis, D.: Workflow mining with InWoLvE. Comput. Ind. **53**(3), 245–264 (2004). Process / Workflow Mining
20. Burattin, A., Sperduti, A.: PLG: a framework for the generation of business process models and their execution logs. In: Muehlen, M., Su, J. (eds.) BPM 2010 Workshops. LNBIP, vol. 66, pp. 214–219. Springer, Heidelberg (2011)
21. Bose, R.: Process mining in the large: preprocessing, discovery, and diagnostics. Ph.D. thesis, Technische Universiteit Eindhoven (2012)
22. van den Broucke, S.K.L.M.: Advances in Process Mining. Ph.D., Katholieke Universiteit Leuven (2014)
23. Goedertier, S., Martens, D., Vanthienen, J., Baesens, B.: Robust process discovery with artificial negative events. J. Mach. Learn. Res. **10**, 1305–1340 (2009)
24. Li, J., Liu, D., Yang, B.: Process mining: extending α-algorithm to mine duplicate tasks in process logs. In: Chang, K.C.-C., Wang, W., Chen, L., Ellis, C.A., Hsu, C.-H., Tsoi, A.C., Wang, H. (eds.) APWeb/WAIM 2007. LNCS, vol. 4537, pp. 396–407. Springer, Heidelberg (2007)
25. De San Pedro, J., Carmona, J., Cortadella, J.: Log-based simplification of process models. In: Motahari-Nezhad, H.R., Recker, J., Weidlich, M. (eds.) BPM 2015. LNCS, vol. 9253, pp. 457–474. Springer International Publishing, Heidelberg (2015)
26. Fahland, D., van der Aalst, W.M.P.: Simplifying discovered process models in a controlled manner. Inf. Syst. **38**(4), 585–605 (2013)

From Low-Level Events to Activities - A Pattern-Based Approach

Felix Mannhardt[1]([⊠]), Massimiliano de Leoni[1], Hajo A. Reijers[1,2],
Wil M.P. van der Aalst[1], and Pieter J. Toussaint[3]

[1] Eindhoven University of Technology, Eindhoven, The Netherlands
{f.mannhardt,m.d.leoni,h.a.reijers,w.m.p.v.d.aalst}@tue.nl
[2] Vrije Universiteit Amsterdam, Amsterdam, The Netherlands
[3] Norwegian University of Science and Technology, Trondheim, Norway
pieter@idi.ntnu.no

Abstract. Process mining techniques analyze processes based on event data. A crucial assumption for process analysis is that events correspond to occurrences of meaningful activities. Often, low-level events recorded by information systems do not directly correspond to these. Abstraction methods, which provide a mapping from the recorded events to activities recognizable by process workers, are needed. Existing supervised abstraction methods require a full model of the entire process as input and cannot handle noise. This paper proposes a supervised abstraction method based on behavioral activity patterns that capture domain knowledge on the relation between activities and events. Through an alignment between the activity patterns and the low-level event logs an abstracted event log is obtained. Events in the abstracted event log correspond to instantiations of recognizable activities. The method is evaluated with domain experts of a Norwegian hospital using an event log from their digital whiteboard system. The evaluation shows that state-of-the art process mining methods provide valuable insights on the usage of the system when using the abstracted event log, but fail when using the original lower level event log.

Keywords: Process mining · Supervised abstraction · Event log · Alignment

1 Introduction

Organizations use information systems to support their work. Often, information about the usage of those systems by workers is recorded in event logs [1]. Process mining techniques use such event data to analyze processes of organizations. It is assumed that recorded events correspond to meaningful activities in instances of a process (i.e., cases). This information about recorded executions of activities can then be used, e.g., to *discover* models describing the observed behavior or to check *conformance* with existing process documentation. The ability to identify executions of activities based on events is crucial for any process mining technique. Events that do not directly correspond to activities recognizable for process workers are unsuitable for process analytics since their semantics are not clear to domain experts. However, events recorded

© Springer International Publishing Switzerland 2016
M. La Rosa et al. (Eds.): BPM 2016, LNCS 9850, pp. 125–141, 2016.
DOI: 10.1007/978-3-319-45348-4_8

by information systems often do not directly correspond to recognizable executions of activities [2]. Generally, there can be an n:m-relation between recorded events and activities [2,3], i.e., one higher level activity may create multiple low level events and one such event possibly relates to multiple activities. There are proposals for unsupervised abstraction methods that try to determine this relation based on identifying subsequences and machine learning methods [2,4–7], as well as proposals for supervised methods based on existing process documentation and constraint satisfaction [3,8–11]. Unsupervised abstraction methods, clearly, do not take existing knowledge into account and may fail to provide meaningful labels for discovered event clusters. Existing supervised abstraction methods [3,8–11] assume knowledge about a single model for the overall process. They resolve to clustering methods and heuristics when challenged with event logs from processes that feature *n:m event-activity relations*, *concurrent* activities, and *noise* (i.e., erroneous or missing events).

This paper proposes a supervised event abstraction method. We use behavioral *activity patterns* to capture domain knowledge about the conjectured relation between high-level activities and recorded low-level events. We *align* the behavior defined by these activity patterns with the observed behavior in the event log. Our technique uses alignment techniques, and, hence, is able to find an optimal mapping between low-level events and activity patterns even for event logs that contain noise. In this way, we obtain a reliable *abstraction mapping* from low-level events to activity patterns. This mapping is used to create an abstracted event log. This log contains only high-level events at the desired level of abstraction, which relate directly to executions of high-level activities. We applied the proposed method together with domain experts from a Norwegian hospital to an event log retrieved from a digital whiteboard system at the observation ward of the hospital. Through observation and interviews with people working at the hospital we were able to identify activity patterns for 18 recognizable activities, which, together, explained 91 % of the recorded behavior. Using the abstracted event log, we were able to analyze how nurses use the digital whiteboard system in their daily work. We obtained process models that relate to their actual work in a meaningful way.

The remainder of this paper is structured as follows. First, we describe the event abstraction problem in more detail (Sect. 2). Then, we present the five main steps of our abstraction method (Sect. 3). We evaluate the proposed method using the results obtained for the digital whiteboard event log (Sect. 4), and conclude with a summary and a sketch of future work (Sect. 5).

2   Problem Description

We start with a definition of event logs. An event log stores information about activities that were recorded by one or more information systems while supporting the execution of a process. Each execution of a *process instance* results in a sequence of events.

Definition 1 (Event Log). *Given universes of attributes A and values U, we define an event log as* $(E, \Sigma, \#, \mathscr{E})$ *with:*

- *E is a set of unique event identifiers;*
- $\Sigma \subseteq U$ *is a set of activities;*

Table 1. Excerpt of a trace $\sigma_L \in \mathscr{E}_L$ from a low-level event log with identifiers **Id** and attributes **Activity**, **Time**, **Instance**, and **Nurse**. Symbol $\perp$ denotes that the attribute was not recorded. The last columns show those high-level activities, which caused the event.

Id	Activity	Time	Instance	Nurse	High-level activity	High-level instance
e_{12}	NurseChanged	122	12	NurseA	Shift	1
e_{13}	CallSignal1	122	13	$\perp$	Shift	1
e_{14}	CallSignal0	124	14	$\perp$	Shift	1
...	...	...	...	...	...	...
e_{20}	CallSignal4	185	20	$\perp$	Alarm	2
e_{21}	CallSignal1	197	21	$\perp$	Alarm	2
...	...	...	...	...	...	...
e_{29}	NurseChanged	250	29	NurseB	Handover	3
e_{30}	CallSignal4	310	30	$\perp$	Alarm	4
e_{31}	CallSignal1	311	31	$\perp$	Alarm	4
e_{32}	NurseChanged	312	32	NurseC	Handover	5
e_{33}	CallSignal0	315	33	$\perp$	Alarm	4

- $\#: E \to (A \nrightarrow U)$ *is a function that obtains attribute values recorded for an event;*
- $\mathscr{E} \subseteq E^*$ *is the set of traces over E. A trace $\sigma \in \mathscr{E}$ records the sequence of events for one process instance. Each event identifier occurs only in a single trace.*

Given an event $e \in E$ in the event log $\mathscr{E}$, we write $\#_a(e) \in A \nrightarrow U$ to obtain the value $u \in U$ recorded for attribute $a \in A$. Three mandatory attributes are recorded by each event: $\#_{act}(e) \in \Sigma$, the **name of the activity** that caused the event; $\#_{time}(e) \in U$, the **time** when the event occurred; $\#_{ai}(e) \in U$, the **activity instance**, i.e., an identifier linking multiple events, which are related to the same execution of a single activity.

Example 1. Table 1 shows an excerpt of a trace $\sigma_L \in \mathscr{E}_L$ obtained from a low-level event log $(E_L, \Sigma_L, \#^L, \mathscr{E}_L)$ that is recorded by a digital whiteboard, which supports the work of nurses in a hospital. Each row represents an unique event $e \in E_L$ together with the produced data (i.e., attributes) created by a change in the system. For confidentiality reasons, we show only some events of an artificial trace that resembles the real data. The initial events are omitted. After 122 min low-level activity NurseChanged (*NC*) occurs resulting in event e_{12}. Attribute Nurse is recorded as $\#^L_{\text{Nurse}}(e_{12}) = NurseA$. Next, two low-level activities CallSignal1 (*CS1*) and CallSignal0 (*CS0*) are registered as events e_{13} and e_{14} by a call signal system, which is integrated with the whiteboard. An hour later the call signal system records the activity CallSignal4 (*CS4*) as event e_{20} and, again, activity *CS1* as event e_{21}. Some further low-level events follow.

Often, not all events $e \in E_L$ represent work at the same level of abstraction [1,4]. The execution of some high-level activities might result in multiple low-level events being recorded during their execution. Those events only store the names of low-level activities Σ_L, i.e., $\#^L_{act}(e) \in \Sigma_L$ instead of names of recognizable high-level activities. *Event abstraction* can be seen as the problem of transforming such an event

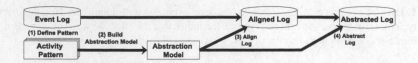

Fig. 1. Overview of the proposed event abstraction method

log $(E_L, \Sigma_L, \#^L, \mathscr{E}_L)$ at a lower or mixed level of abstraction, into a new event log $(E_H, \Sigma_H, \#^H, \mathscr{E}_H)$ with events E_H that record executions of activities Σ_H at the desired, higher level of abstraction. We need to determine how low-level events E_L are related to **high-level events** E_H, i.e., we need to find an **abstraction mapping** $\pi \subseteq E_L \times E_H$.

Please note that determining a good abstraction mapping π (i.e., one that reflects what really happened) is difficult for several reasons. Low-level events mapped to more than one high-level activity, i.e., *shared functionality* [3] need to be disambiguated. It is difficult to differentiate between *reoccurring* and *concurrent* activities [3]. Also, the low-level event log might contain *noise*: Erroneous events that should not have been recorded or missing events that should have been recorded.

Example 2. Event log $\mathscr{E}_L$ shown in Table 1 contains low-level events. The various `CallSignal` events do not directly correspond to high-level activities. Moreover, depending on the context, those events correspond to different high-level activities. The last two columns in Table 1 list the corresponding names of high-level activities that caused the low-level events as well as an identifier uniquely identifying the execution of the activity, i.e., the activity instance. For example, we know that in the context of a shift change events *CS1* and *CS0* are recorded when the patient is visited in the normal routine, i.e., events e_{12}, e_{13}, e_{14} correspond to one execution (i.e., instance 1) of the high-level activity `Shift`. This mapping between low-level events and high-level activity instances cannot be solely done on the activity names. For example, when *CS1* and *CS0* are preceded by event *CS4* they correspond to an alarm triggered by the patient, i.e., events e_{30}, e_{31}, e_{33} were caused by instance 4 of high-level activity `Alarm`.

3 Pattern-Based Abstraction of Event Logs

We present a method that takes an event log $(E_L, \Sigma_L, \#^L, \mathscr{E}_L)$ at a lower level of abstraction and transforms it to an event log $(E_H, \Sigma_H, \#^H, \mathscr{E}_H)$ at the desired level of abstraction. We establish an abstraction mapping π from events E_L to the events E_H. Our method can deal with noise, reoccurring and concurrent behavior, and shared functionality. The proposed method consists of four steps (Fig. 1):

1. We encode the low-level behavior of activities in *activity patterns* (Sect. 3.1).
2. We compose activity patterns in an *abstraction model* (Sect. 3.2).
3. We align the behavior of the *abstraction model* and the low-level event log (Sect. 3.3).
4. We create an *abstracted* event log using the alignment information (Sect. 3.4).

We describe these steps in the following sections. Note that activity patterns represent domain knowledge on the behavior of high level activities in terms of low-level events.

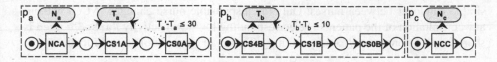

Fig. 2. Three activity patterns $p_a, p_b, p_c \in P$ for the example in DPN notation

3.1 Define Activity Patterns

In the reminder of this paper, we use process models to capture behavior. Generally, our abstraction method is independent of the particular formalism (e.g., Petri nets, UML, Declare, BPMN) used to model processes. We represent knowledge about the relation between low-level events and given high-level activities Σ_H in *activity patterns*. Each activity pattern is a process model describing those events that are expected to be seen in the event log for one instance of the corresponding high-level activity.

Definition 2 (Activity Pattern). *Given a set of low-level activity names Σ_L, process moves Σ_M, process attributes A and values U. Let $S = (\Sigma_M \times (A \nrightarrow U))$ be the set of all possible process steps. Let $\#_{name} : \Sigma_M \rightarrow \Sigma_L$ be a labeling function that returns the low-level activity name of a process move. An activity pattern $p \subseteq S^*$ captures sequences corresponding to an execution of one instance of a high-level activity. Steps $s \in \sigma$ in process traces $\sigma \in p$ correspond to low-level activities executed as part of the high-level activity. We denote with $P = \{p \subseteq S^*\}$ the set of all activity patterns.*

In the remainder, we require that process moves are not shared between activity patterns, i.e., given two different patterns $p_1, p_2 \in P$ and sequences $\sigma_1 \in p_1, \sigma_2 \in p_2$ we require for any steps $(m_1, w_1) \in \sigma_1, (m_2, w_2) \in \sigma_2$ that $m_1 \neq m_2$. Given a step, we can uniquely identify to which pattern it belongs. However, process moves from different patterns may be associated with the same activity name, i.e., $\#_{name}(m_1) = \#_{name}(m_2)$.

Example 3. Fig. 2 shows three activity patterns p_a, p_b and p_c defined for the event log in Table 1, implemented as Data Petri Nets (DPNs) [12]. We implement activity patterns by using DPN as notation with well-defined semantics, which can express the control-flow as well as the data-, resource- and time-perspective of a pattern. We refer to [12] for an introduction to DPNs. We use transitions of the DPN to model process moves. We name transitions uniquely by using the abbreviated low-level activity name concatenated with the pattern name, e.g., transition *CS1A* models activity CallSignal1 in pattern p_a. Therefore, we can easily obtain the activity name (i.e., $\#_{name}(x)$) for each transition x. The *first pattern* p_a describes a shift change. First, the nurse responsible for the patient changes (*NCA*) and the name of the nurse is recorded (N_a). Within 30 min ($T_a' - T_a \leq 30$), the responsible nurse visits the patient and the call signal system records a button press (*CS1A*). Finally, the nurse leaves the room and another button press is registered (*CS0A*) resetting the status. The *second pattern* p_b describes a similar sequence (i.e., transitions *CS1B* and *CS0B*), but represents a different high-level activity: The patient is attended outside of the normal routine. Transition *CS4B* has to be executed at most 10 min beforehand (i.e., $T_b' - T_b \leq 10$). The low-level activity corresponding to *CS4B* is an *alarm* triggered by the patient. The *third pattern* describes a simple handover between nurses: Only the responsible nurse changes (*NCC*) without any consultation of the patient. The corresponding low-level activity NurseChanged is shared with a transition *NCA* of pattern p_a. This is an example of shared functionality.

Using domain knowledge about the high-level activities of the process at hand we define such an *activity pattern* for every activity of interest. *Activity patterns* represent the knowledge about how high-level activities are reflected by low-level events in the event log. Please note that we do not expect an *activity pattern* to be an exact representations of every possible way a high-level activity manifests itself in the event log. Later, in Sect. 3.3 we show that our method is able to deal with approximate matches.

3.2 Build an Composed Abstraction Model

With a set of activity patterns for the process under analysis at hand, we can compose their behavior into an integrated *abstraction model*.

Definition 3 (Composition Function). *A composition function* $f : 2^P \rightarrow P$ *combines the behavior activity patterns* $p_1, \ldots, p_n$ *into an (composite) activity pattern* $cp \in P$, *i.e.,* $f(p_1, \ldots, p_n) = cp$. *We denote with* $F \subseteq 2^P \rightarrow P$ *the set of all composition functions.*

We provide the semantics for five basic composition functions: *sequence, choice, parallel, interleaving* and *cardinality*. Our abstraction method is not restricted to these functions. Further composition functions can be added. We introduce some necessary notations for sequences. Given a sequence $\sigma \in S^*$ and a subset $X \subseteq S$, $\sigma|_X$ is the *projection* of σ on X. For example, $\langle w, o, r, d \rangle|_{\{o,r\}} = \langle o, r \rangle$. $\sigma_1 \cdot \sigma_2 \in S^*$ *concatenates* two sequences, e.g., $\langle w, o \rangle \cdot \langle r, d \rangle = \langle w, o, r, d \rangle$. Given activity patterns $p_i \in P$ with $p_i \subseteq S_i^*$ and $i \in \mathbb{N}$, we define the following functions:

– **Sequence** composition $\odot \in F$:

$$p_1 \odot p_2 = \{\sigma \in S^* \mid \sigma_1 \in p_1 \wedge \sigma_2 \in p_2 \wedge \sigma = \sigma_1 \cdot \sigma_2\}.$$

Binary operation $\odot$ is associative. We write $\odot_{1 \leq i \leq n} p_i = p_1 \odot p_2 \odot \ldots \odot p_n$ to compose ordered collections of patterns in sequence. We define $\odot_{1 \leq i \leq 0} p_i = \{\langle \rangle\}$.

– **Choice** composition $\otimes \in F$:

$$p_1 \otimes p_2 = p_1 \cup p_2.$$

Binary operation $\otimes$ is commutative and associative. We write $\otimes_{1 \leq i \leq n} p_i = p_1 \otimes p_2 \otimes \ldots \otimes p_n$ to compose sets of patterns in choice.

– **Parallel** composition $\diamond \in F$:

$$p_1 \diamond p_2 = \{\sigma \in (S_1 \cup S_2)^* : \sigma|_{S_1} \in p_1 \wedge \sigma|_{S_2} \in p_2\}.$$

Binary operation $\diamond$ is commutative and associative. We write $\diamond_{1 \leq i \leq n} p_i = p_1 \diamond p_2 \diamond \ldots \diamond p_n$ to compose sets of patterns in parallel.

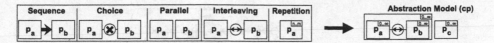

Fig. 3. Overview of the graphical notation of the supported composition functions and an example of their usage in an composed pattern. Patterns are depicted as plain boxes for better legibility.

- **Interleaving** composition $\leftrightarrow \in F$ with $p(n)$ denoting the set of all permutations of numbers $\{1, \ldots, n\}$:

$$\leftrightarrow (p_1, \ldots, p_n) = \bigotimes_{(i_1, \ldots, i_n) \in p(n)} \bigodot_{1 \leq k \leq n} p_{i_k}.$$

- **Repetition** composition $[n, m] \in F$ with $n \in \mathbb{N}_0, m \in \mathbb{N} \cup \{\infty\}$, and $n \leq m$:

$$p_1^{[n,m]} = \bigotimes_{n \leq i \leq m} \bigodot_{1 \leq k \leq i} p_1.$$

We build an overall abstraction model with a formula that contains all patterns of interest. The resulting composed pattern $cp \in S^*$ should include the overall behavior that we expect to observe for the execution of *all* high-level activities.

Example 4. Given the activity patterns p_a, p_b and p_c shown in Fig. 2, we can compose their behavior to $cp = (\leftrightarrow (p_a^{[0,\infty]}, p_b^{[0,\infty]}))^{[0,\infty]} \diamond p_c^{[0,\infty]}$. We allow indefinite repetition of all activity patterns using the repetition composition. We allow the absence of patterns using the repetition composition as the corresponding high-level activities might not have been executed in every process instance. We restrict cp to only contain the interleaving of patterns p_a and p_b as there is only one responsible nurse per patient. Therefore, the activities expressed by p_a and p_b can occur in any order but should not happen in parallel. We add p_c using the parallel composition as handovers can take place in parallel to p_a and p_b. In the remainder of this example, we omit the attribute assignments w from steps $(t, w) \in S$ for improved legibility. The result of this composition is the abstraction model cp. Model cp corresponds to all behavior that could be observed for executions of the three high-level activities. For example, $\langle NCA, CS1A, NCC, CS0A \rangle \in cp$ is expected, whereas $\langle NCA, CS1A, CS4B, CS0A \rangle \notin cp$ is not expected.

We designed a graphical representation for each composition function, which can be used to design abstraction models in the implementation of our approach. Figure 3 shows the graphical notation for each of the composition functions. Moreover, the graphical representation of the composition of activity patterns p_a, p_b, p_c as defined in Example 4 is shown. Because the repetition composition is unary, we attach its graphical representation directly to patterns. Parallel composition is the least restrictive composition. Unless otherwise specified, we assume that patterns are composed in parallel. We draw a box around composed patterns if necessary to clarify the precedence of operations. For example, patterns p_a and p_b are first interleaved and then composed in parallel with p_c. We implemented the composition of activity patterns using

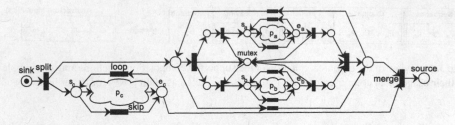

Fig. 4. DPN created by our implementation for the abstraction model cp. Activity patterns p_a, p_b, p_c are depicted as clouds with source places s_a, s_b, s_c and sink places e_a, e_b, e_c. Black transitions are invisible routing transitions, which are not recorded in any event log.

Table 2. The top three rows show an alignment of the running example log trace and abstraction model. Low-level events (L. Event) e are aligned to process moves (P. Move) m that relate to the same low-level activity (L. Activity). Write operations are omitted for better legibility. One process move could not be aligned to an event, symbol $\gg$ is used in this case. The bottom five rows show the high-level event returned by the abstraction method described in this paper.

L. Event (e)	e_{12}	e_{13}	e_{14}	...	e_{20}	e_{21}	$\gg$	...	e_{29}	e_{30}	e_{31}	e_{32}	e_{33}
L. Activity	NC	CS1	CS0	...	CS4	CS1		...	NC	CS4	CS1	NC	CS0
P. Move (m)	NCA	CS1A	CS0A	...	CS4B	CS1B	CS0B	...	NCC	CS4B	CS1B	NCC	CS0B
H. Activity	Shift		Shift	...	Alarm		Alarm	...	Handover	Alarm		Handover	Alarm
Life-cycle	Start		Complete	...	Start		Complete	...	Complete	Start		Complete	Complete
Instance	3		3	...	6		6	...	10	11		12	11
Time	122		124	...	185		197	...	250	310		312	315
H. Event	$\hat{e}_5$		$\hat{e}_6$	...	$\hat{e}_{11}$		$\hat{e}_{12}$	...	$\hat{e}_{20}$	$\hat{e}_{21}$		$\hat{e}_{22}$	$\hat{e}_{23}$

the DPN notation. To simplify the composition, we assume that the DPNs of activity patterns have a single source place and a single sink place. Figure 3 shows the DPN encoding of $cp = (\leftrightarrow (p_a^{[0,\infty]}, p_b^{[0,\infty]}))^{[0,\infty]} \diamond p_c^{[0,\infty]}$. The implementation of all compositions using DPN is available in a technical report [13].

Example 5. Figure 4 depicts the DPN implementation of abstraction model cp. The abstraction model starts with a single sink place $\texttt{sink}$ and ends with a single source place $\texttt{source}$. We model the parallel composition of $p_c^{[0,\infty]}$ with $\leftrightarrow (p_a^{[0,\infty]}, p_b^{[0,\infty]})^{[0,\infty]}$ by adding invisible transitions $\texttt{split}$ and $\texttt{merge}$, which realize a parallel split and join. Invisible transitions cannot be observed; they are only added for routing purposes. We use place $\texttt{mutex}$ to model the mutual exclusion constraint of the interleaving composition of patterns $p_a^{[0,\infty]}$ and $p_b^{[0,\infty]}$. Place $\texttt{mutex}$ guarantees that only either p_a or p_b can be executed at the same time, yielding the interleaving of p_a and p_b. Each repetition composition is implemented by adding two invisible transitions $\texttt{loop}$ and $\texttt{skip}$, which allow to repeat the pattern indefinitely or to skip its execution, respectively.

3.3   Alignment of Patterns Behavior and the Event Log

With an abstraction model at hand, we need to relate the behavior in the low-level event log to process traces defined by the abstraction model. More specifically, we need to determine the mapping between low-level events in the event log and process steps of the abstraction model. We use existing **alignment** techniques [12] that establish a mapping between log traces and process traces. The top three rows of Table 2 show such an alignment between the example log trace (Table 1) and a process trace of the example abstraction model cp (Fig. 3). The alignment in Table 2 consists of *moves* $(e,s) \in (E_L \cup \{\gg\}) \times (S \cup \{\gg\})$ that relate low-level events e to process steps s in the abstraction model. Events e can only be mapped to process steps $s = (m,w)$ that refer to the same low-level activity, i.e., $\#_{act}(e) = \#_{name}(m)$. It may not be possible to align all events and process steps. These deviating events and process steps are mapped to $\gg$ (e.g., $(\gg,(CS0B,w))$ in Table 2). Alignments find an optimal mapping, which minimizes the number of such deviations. They return the most likely mapping between events and process steps. Moreover, an alignment guarantees that its sequence of model steps without $\gg$-steps is a process trace defined by the model. For example, the third row in Table 2 is a process trace of abstraction model cp. Pattern p_a is executed once, i.e., $\langle NCA, CS1A, CS0A \rangle$ is a sub-sequence. Patterns p_b and p_c are both repeated twice, i.e., there are two sub-sequences $\langle CS4B, CS1B, CS0B \rangle$ and two sub-sequences $\langle NCC \rangle$. We can uniquely identify sub-sequences of initial activity pattern since we required that process moves are unique among activity patterns.

3.4   Build the Abstracted Event Log Using the Alignment

We describe how to build the high-level event log $(E_H, \Sigma_H, \#^H, \mathscr{E}_H)$ and the abstraction mapping π using an alignment of the low-level event log with the abstraction model.

The bottom four rows of Table 2 show how we obtain the high-level event log from the information provided by the alignment. We align each trace of the low-level event log with the abstraction model. Doing so, we obtain an alignment as shown in the first three rows for each trace in the low-level log. Given the alignment, we use two mappings to build the high-level log:

- $\mu : \Sigma_M \to \Sigma_H$, a mapping between process moves and high-level activities.
- $\lambda : \Sigma_M \nrightarrow L$, a mapping between process moves and life-cycle transitions.

Mapping function μ can be obtained from the initially defined activity patterns. Each activity patterns models exactly one high-level activity and each process move belongs to exactly one activity patterns, thus, the corresponding high-level activity can be uniquely determined for each process move. For example, we use $\mu(NCA) = Shift$ and $\mu(NCC) = Handover$. Mapping function λ defines which process moves correspond to transitions in the life-cycle of activities. Mapping λ is motivated by the observation that activities rarely happen instantaneously. Activities have *life-cycles* [1]. The set of life-cycle transitions L and mapping function λ is specified by the user. In the case-study we use $L = \{start, complete\}$ and define λ such that the first process move of an activity pattern is mapped to the *start* transition and the last process move is mapped to the *complete* transition. The other process moves are not mapped, i.e., they are not in the domain of λ. For example, we use $\lambda(NCA) = start$ and $\lambda(CS0A) = complete$.

We add new high-level events e_H to E_H (i.e., $E_H = E_H \cup \{e_H\}$) for those alignment moves (e,s) for which process steps $s = (m,w)$ are not mapped to $\gg$ (i.e., $s \neq \gg$) and process move m is mapped to a life-cycle transition $\lambda(m)$ (i.e., $m \in dom(\lambda))$[1]. In this manner, we create a high-level trace in $\mathscr{E}_H$ for each low-level trace in $\mathscr{E}_L$. We obtain the high-level log $(E_H, \Sigma_H, \#^H, \mathscr{E}_H)$ and a mapping between low-level events e and the new high-level events e_H. We include (e, e_H) in the abstraction mapping π when event e is not mapped to $\gg$ (i.e., $e \neq \gg$). For example, events $\hat{e}_5$ and $\hat{e}_6$ in Table 2 are created based on the alignment of low-level events e_{12} and e_{14} to process moves NCA and $CSOA$, i.e., $(e_{12}, \hat{e}_5) \in \pi$ and $(e_{14}, \hat{e}_6) \in \pi$. We assign event $\hat{e}_5$ the activity name $Shift$ (i.e., $\#^H_{act}(\hat{e}_5) = Shift$) and the life-cycle transition $start$ (i.e., $\#^H_{cycle}(\hat{e}_5) = start$). Event $\hat{e}_6$ is assigned the same activity name $Shift$, but a different life-cycle transition: $complete$.

Then, the high-level events E_H are enriched with additional information: *activity instance* and *timestamp*. A unique instance identifier is added for each execution of an activity pattern. For example, event $\hat{e}_{21}$ and event $\hat{e}_{23}$ are both assigned instance identifier 11 (i.e., $\#^H_{ai}(\hat{e}_{21}) = \#^H_{ai}(\hat{e}_{23}) = 11$). Both are aligned to process steps in the same execution of activity pattern p_b (*Alarm*). Instance 11 of the activity *Alarm* was started by event $\hat{e}_{21}$ and completed by event $\hat{e}_{23}$. Regarding the timestamp, there are two cases depending on the alignment move (e, s): (1) The process step was aligned to a low-level event e and (2) the process step was mapped to $e = \gg$. In the first case, we use the timestamp of the aligned low-level event (e.g., $\#^H_{time}(\hat{e}_{11}) = \#^H_{time}(e_{20}) = 185$). In the second case, we cannot directly obtain a timestamp. For example, event $\hat{e}_{12}$ in Table 2 is missing a low-level event: $e = \gg$. There are multiple methods to determine the most likely timestamp for $\hat{e}_{12}$. For the case study (Sect. 4), we use timestamps of neighboring low-level events that are mapped to the same activity instance, e.g., we use the timestamp from event e_{21} for the high-level event $\hat{e}_{12}$ (i.e., $\#^H_{time}(e_{21}) = 197$).

In general, there might be scenarios where one event could be mapped to several activity instances. We simplified the discussion by assuming that events are only mapped to single activity instances. This is not a limitation, as described by Baier et al. [3]: Those events can be duplicated in a pre-processing step beforehand.

Finally, we define two quality measures for the abstraction mapping. First, we use **fitness** as a measure for how well the entire event log matches the behavior imposed by the abstraction model. In this context, a fitness measure such the one defined in [12] for alignments of DPNs can be seen as measure for the quality of the used abstraction model. A low fitness indicates that there are many events that cannot be correctly matched, thus, the abstraction model does not capture the whole process correctly. Second, we define a **matching error** $\varepsilon : \Sigma_H \to [0, 1]$ on the level of each recognized high-level activity. Some process steps in the alignment are not matched to an event in the log, i.e., the event is missing. For example, in Table 2 one execution of process activity $CSOB$ is mapped to $\gg$. Given a high-level activity $h \in \Sigma_H$ (e.g., *Alarm*) and the subset of process activities $M \subset \Sigma_M$ that are mapped to the activity pattern defined for the high-level activity (e.g., $CS4B$, $CS1B$ and $CSOB$). We determine the number of those alignment moves $(e, (m, w))$ with process activities $m \in M$, for which the event is missing, i.e., $e = \gg$. The matching error $\varepsilon(h)$ is the fraction of such erroneous alignment moves over the total number of alignment moves with process move m. For example, $\varepsilon(Alarm) = \frac{5}{6}$ for the alignment in Table 2. The matching error can be used to exclude unreliable matches, which exceed a certain ε-threshold.

---

[1] $dom(f)$ denotes the domain of a function f.

4   Evaluation

We evaluate the proposed abstraction method by conducting a case study using event data that was obtained from a digital whiteboard system[2]. The whiteboard supports the daily work of nurses in the observation unit of a Norwegian hospital. Our method is implemented as plug-in of the open-source process mining framework ProM[3].

4.1   Case and Dataset

Digital whiteboard systems are used to improve health care processes by raising situation awareness among nurses and to support coordination of care [14]. In our case, the whiteboard is used to manage information about admitted patients. The information is displayed in a tabular manner, where each row shows information about a single patient. The cells are used for various purposes, such as displaying logistical and medical information about the patient. A call signal system, which allows patients to trigger an alarm, is integrated with the whiteboard. Alarms are shown on the whiteboard. Generally, there are few constraints on how the whiteboard is actually used.

We obtained an event log with *8,487 cases* and *286,000 events* recorded by the whiteboard of the observation unit between 04/2014 and 12/2015. Each case records events for the visit of a single patient. On average, traces contain 34 events. Events are recorded for changes of single cells of the whiteboard. This very fine grained logging leads to a low-level event log. Events in the log do not directly represent recognizable activities. In total, there are 42 distinct low-level activity names in the log. Moreover, varying work practices among nurses lead to different events being recorded for the same high-level activity. The event log is unsuitable for any kind of process analytics as the semantics of results are not clear to process workers.

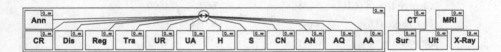

Fig. 5. Abstraction model used in the case study. Most activities can only interleave as there is only one nurse assigned to a patient.

We created an abstraction model with 18 activity patterns as shown in Fig. 5. The activity patterns are based on information on the whiteboard system and interviews with a domain expert from the hospital, who observed the actual work of nurses. In this case study, we do not use all composition functions that our framework provides, as some do not apply to the whiteboard system. However, we believe that the unused functions are useful in many different settings. All 18 activity patterns are listed in Table 3 together with the number of process activities and the name of the modeled high-level activity. The examples introduced in Fig. 2 correspond to the activities *Shift* (p_a), *Alarm Normal* (p_b) and *Handover* (p_c) in the case study.

---

[2] The used whiteboard system is *Imatis Visi*: http://www.imatis.com.

[3] Plug-in *Log Abstraction* of the ProM package *LogEnhancement*: http://promtools.org.

4.2   Results and Discussion

We applied the proposed abstraction method to the event log and successfully obtained a smaller abstracted event log with 206,054 high-level events for 103,027 activity instances (i.e., each instance has a *start* and a *complete* event). The computation of the abstracted event log took one hour and used 6 GB of memory. We decomposed the DPN of the abstraction model into two smaller DPNs that did not share labels. The overall fitness with regard to the log was 0.91, which indicates that most of the observations could be explained. Even though 9 % of the events did not match, this is a good result for further analysis as we can expect the event log to contain noise, i.e., events unrelated to any modeled high-level activity. The abstracted event log contains 25 high-level activities: 18 activities were obtained through abstraction and 7 further activities were already at the appropriate level of abstraction. Table 3 shows the resulting number of activity instances that were matched, as well as the corresponding matching error. It should be noted that the relatively high error for the activity *Surgery* stems from the fact that this activity is sometimes recorded in a different manner, i.e., one event is missing. Regarding the error for activity *Alarm Assist* we found that the *assist* button can be pressed without a prior alarm by the patient, which is different from our initial assumption.

Table 3. Activity patterns used in the digital whiteboard case study. For each pattern we list the number of process activities, the number of low-level activity names shared with other patterns, and the results of our method: the number of recognized activity instances and the matching error.

Activity name	Transitions (shared)	Matches	Matching error (ε)
Announcement (Ann)	8 (6)	29	0.02
Change Room (CR)	5 (4)	662	0.09
Discharge (Dis)	7 (4)	8,054	0.0
Registration (Reg)	6 (6)	9,855	0.01
Transfer (Tra)	6 (6)	575	0.09
Update Report (UR)	4 (0)	6,912	0.0
Update Arrival (UA)	5 (1)	4,626	0.0
Handover (H)	1 (1)	24,228	0.0
Shift (S)	3 (3)	405	0.04
Call Nurse (CN)	2 (2)	12,416	0.08
Alarm Normal (AN)	3 (3)	8,842	0.02
Alarm Quick (AQ)	2 (2)	12,730	0.0
Alarm assist (AA)	5 (3)	32	0.17
CT	4 (2)	1,443	0.0
MRI	4 (2)	124	0.0
Surgery (Sur)	3 (3)	297	0.17
Ultrasound (Ult)	5 (3)	1,164	0.0
X-Ray	4 (2)	1,117	0.0

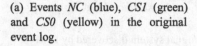

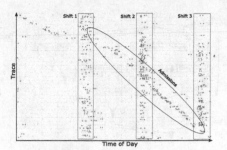

(a) Events *NC* (blue), *CS1* (green) and *CS0* (yellow) in the original event log.

(b) Abstracted event log only showing the high-level *Shift* events captured by pattern p_a.

Fig. 6. Dotted charts of events related to the activity *Shift*. Traces are shown on the y-axis and sorted by the time of day of the first event in a trace. (Color figure online)

The activities under consideration can be grouped into three categories: (1) actions related to patient logistics, (2) actions related to the call signal system and handover between the nurses, and (3) actions related to ordered examinations and surgeries. Given the absence of a perfectly abstracted event log as ground truth, we evaluate our method by comparing the results obtained using three process analytics techniques *with* and *without* the abstraction. Using the abstracted event log, we obtained several insights into work practices of nurses in clinical processes. A domain expert from the hospital stated that the analysis: *"[... gives insight beyond the usual reports and analysis that we have access to. It gives a fresh and "new" perspective on how we understand the processes involved in running a ward or department."* By contrast, we show that using the low-level event log directly does not lead to any insights for stakeholders, because the semantics of low-level events are unclear. We used the ProM plug-ins *Log Projection* (LP), *Inductive Visual Miner* (IVM), and *Multi-perspective Explorer* (MPE).

Log Projection (LP). Fig. 6 shows two dotted charts created with LP. Figure 6(a) is created using the original event log. It shows the distribution of events *NC*, *CS1* and *CS0* over the course of a day. As expected, the *NC* event (i.e., the responsible nurse changed) mostly occurs when a patient is admitted (i.e., on the blue diagonal) and during one of the three shift changes (i.e., the three blue vertical lines). Still, the responsible nurse also changes between those well-defined times. Yet, from Fig. 6(a) it is not evident whether nurses use the call signal system when visiting a patient after their shift started. Looking at Fig. 6(b), which shows only the event *Shift* (p_a) from the abstracted event log, it is clearly visible that our assumption was correct. Activity pattern p_a captured a meaningful high-level activity. Figure 6(b) shows that nurses do use the call signal system to indicate their presence in the room of the patient after taking responsibility for a patient. In contrast to the dotted chart in Fig. 6(a), event *Shift* only occurs after admissions (dots on the main diagonal) and after shift changes (three vertical lines). Still, by comparing the number of activity instances in Table 3 it is clear that activity

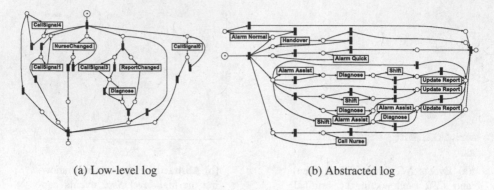

(a) Low-level log   (b) Abstracted log

Fig. 7. Petri nets of the nurse handover and call signal system discovered by IVM

Shift (405 times) happens rarely in comparison to activity *Handover* (24,228 times). Two likely reasons for this are that nurses do either not attend the patient after a shift change, or that they do not use the system to indicate their presence. This is a valuable insight on how the whiteboard system is used in practice. Notably, this could not be concluded without the use of our abstraction method.

Inductive Visual Miner (IVM). We analyzed two parts of the whiteboard system by discovering process models with IVM [15]. We used only those events from the original event log that are used in the respective activity patterns. This indicates what results could be obtained by only filtering the original log based on some knowledge about the low-level events. Figure 7 shows Petri nets discovered using IVM for events related to *nurse handovers and the call signal system based* on the original event log (Fig. 7(a)), and the abstracted event log (Fig. 7(b)). The model in Fig. 7(a) gives little insights into the usage of the call signal system. Most events can be repeated in any order, expect for *CallSignal3*, *Diagnose*, and *ReportChanged* which may only occur once. The model in Fig. 7(b), instead, contains recognizable activities that can be used to investigate the usage of the call signal system further. The model indicates that activities *Shift* and *Alarm Assist* occur together, recording a *diagnose* and updating the report cell (*Update Report*) that is used to store medical information about patients. This finding deserves further investigation. Regarding the other variants of using the call signal system (*Alarm Quick*, *Alarm Normal*, and *Call Nurse*), no specific ordering among the high-level activities is discovered. This could be expected given the flexible nature of the whiteboard system. Moreover, we compared models discovered for low-level and high-level events related to *examinations and patient logistics* (Fig. 8). Again, the model that is discovered from the low-level event log, shown in Fig. 8(a), does not offer insights into the work at the observation unit. The only visible structure is that event *TreatmentChanged*, which is related to some examination, is executed in parallel with the event *Abdom. Pain*. Figure 8(b) shows the process model discovered by IVM *with* the abstracted event log. The control-flow structure of this model is more specific than the model shown in Fig. 8(a). It shows several interesting structures that could be used to investigate further with people working in the hospital. For example, for multiple patients the planning and

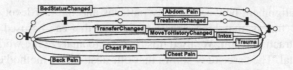

(a) Low-level log

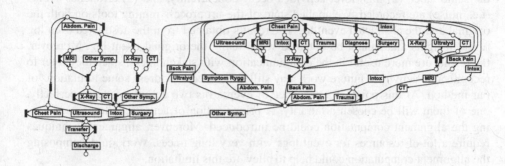

(b) Abstracted log

Fig. 8. Petri nets of the examinations and patient logistics discovered by IVM

execution of *surgeries* and updating the *diagnose* occur together in parallel. One path reveals that 300 patients with chest pain receive an *X-Ray*. Another path shows that for 1,300 patients with abdominal pain no examinations are ordered. By using activities on the same abstraction level, the process model in Fig. 8(b) offers a better insight into the process. Moreover, it allows to discuss the observations with process workers. Please note that the high-level model in Fig. 8(b) contains more activities since the same event is shared among multiple, high-level activities.

Multi-Perspective Explorer (MPE). Finally, we used the MPE to analyze differences between the different ways nurses respond to patient-initiated call signals. It was found that the assumed activities *Alarm Normal* (AN) and *Alarm Quick* (AQ), indeed, correspond to different work practices by nurses. For activity AN the nurse first indicates her presence in the room by using a button on the call signal system, after which she attends the patient. However, within activity AQ nurses do not use this functionality. The average service time for activity AN (7.3 min) is longer than for activity AQ (1.5 min). A hypothesis is that nurses do not use the full functionality of the call signal system for minor tasks, which may be important for the hospital to investigate further.

5   Conclusion

We presented a new method for supervised *event abstraction* using behavioral activity patterns. Activity patterns encode assumptions on how high-level activities manifest themselves in terms of recorded low-level events. We obtain an abstracted event log based on an alignment between activity patterns and the low-level event log. Two quality measures (fitness, matching error) are defined that can be used to evaluate the quality of the abstraction result. We used this method to analyze the work of nurses in a Norwegian hospital. The case study shows that our abstraction method can be successfully applied in complex real-life environments. We obtained an abstracted event log from a system, in which (1) multiple high-level activities share low-level events with the same label, (2) high-level activities occur concurrently, and (3) erroneous events (i.e., noise) are recorded. We applied state-of-the-art process mining tools on both the original and the abstracted event log The results obtained from the abstracted even log reveal insights that cannot be obtained when using the original event log. Moreover, the results are more useful in the communication with stakeholders, since they refer to recognizable activities. Future work may still be needed to address some limitations of our method. At this point, if a sequence of events fits two activity patterns perfectly, one of them will be chosen arbitrarily. A prioritization of activity patterns used during the alignment computation could be introduced. Moreover, alignment techniques require a lot of resources for event logs with very long traces. Work on decomposing the alignment computation could help to alleviate this limitation.

Acknowledgments. We would like to thank Ivar Myrstad for his valuable insights on the digital whiteboard and his help with the case study.

References

1. van der Aalst, W.M.P.: Process Mining - Discovery, Conformance and Enhancement of Business Processes. Springer, Berlin (2011)
2. Günther, C.W., Rozinat, A., van der Aalst, W.M.P.: Activity mining by global trace segmentation. In: Rinderle-Ma, S., Sadiq, S., Leymann, F. (eds.) BPM 2009. LNBIP, vol. 43, pp. 128–139. Springer, Heidelberg (2010)
3. Baier, T., Mendling, J., Weske, M.: Bridging abstraction layers in process mining. Inf. Syst. **46**, 123–139 (2014)
4. Jagadeesh Chandra Bose, R.P., van der Aalst, W.M.P.: Abstractions in process mining: a taxonomy of patterns. In: Dayal, U., Eder, J., Koehler, J., Reijers, H.A. (eds.) BPM 2009. LNCS, vol. 5701, pp. 159–175. Springer, Heidelberg (2009)
5. Cook, D.J., Krishnan, N.C., Rashidi, P.: Activity discovery and activity recognition: a new partnership. IEEE Trans. Cybern. **43**(3), 820–828 (2013)
6. Ferreira, D.R., Szimanski, F., Ralha, C.G.: Improving process models by mining mappings of low-level events to high-level activities. J. Intell. Inf. Syst. **43**(2), 379–407 (2014)
7. Folino, F., Guarascio, M., Pontieri, L.: Mining multi-variant process models from low-level logs. In: Abramowicz, W. (ed.) BIS 2015. LNBIP, vol. 208, pp. 165–177. Springer, Heidelberg (2015)
8. Baier, T., Rogge-Solti, A., Mendling, J., Weske, M.: Matching of events and activities: an approach based on behavioral constraint satisfaction. In: SAC, pp. 1225–1230. ACM (2015)
9. Ferreira, D.R., Szimanski, F., Ralha, C.G.: Mining the low-level behaviour of agents in high-level business processes. IJBPIM **6**(2), 146–166 (2013)
10. Fazzinga, B., Flesca, S., Furfaro, F., Masciari, E., Pontieri, L.: A probabilistic unified framework for event abstraction and process detection from log data. In: Debruyne, C., Panetto, H., Meersman, R., Dillon, T., Weichhart, G., An, Y., Ardagna, C.A. (eds.) OTM 2015 Conferences. LNCS, vol. 9415, pp. 320–328. Springer, Heidelberg (2015)

11. Baier, T.: Matching events and activities. Ph.D. thesis, Universität Potsdam (2015)
12. Mannhardt, F., de Leoni, M., Reijers, H.A., van der Aalst, W.M.P.: Balanced multi-perspective checking of process conformance. Computing **98**(4), 407–437 (2016)
13. Mannhardt, F., de Leoni, M., Reijers, H.A., van der Aalst, W.M.P., Toussaint, P.J.: From low-level events to activities - a pattern-based approach. Technical report, BPMcenter.org, BPM Center Report BPM-02-06 (2016)
14. Wong, H.J., Caesar, M., Bandali, S., Agnew, J., Abrams, H.: Electronic inpatient whiteboards: improving multidisciplinary communication and coordination of care. Int. J. Med. Inform. **78**(4), 239–247 (2009)
15. Leemans, S.J.J., Fahland, D., van der Aalst, W.M.P.: Using life cycle information in process discovery. In: Reichert, M., Reijers, H. (eds.) BPM Workshops 2015. LNBIP, vol. 256, pp. 204–217. Springer, Heidelberg (2016)

Discovering and Exploring State-Based Models for Multi-perspective Processes

Maikel L. van Eck[✉], Natalia Sidorova, and Wil M.P. van der Aalst

Eindhoven University of Technology, Eindhoven, The Netherlands
{m.l.v.eck,n.sidorova,w.m.p.v.d.aalst}@tue.nl

Abstract. Process mining provides fact-based insights into process behaviour captured in event data. In this work we aim to discover models for processes where different facets, or perspectives, of the process can be identified. Instead of focussing on the events or activities that are executed in the context of a particular process, we concentrate on the states of the different perspectives and discover how they are related. We present a formalisation of these relations and an approach to discover state-based models highlighting them. The approach has been implemented using the process mining framework ProM and provides a highly interactive visualisation of the multi-perspective state-based models. This tool has been evaluated on the BPI Challenge 2012 data of a loan application process and on product user behaviour data gathered by Philips during the development of a smart baby bottle equipped with various sensors.

1 Introduction

The aim of process mining is to provide fact-based insights into the execution of processes [1,11,13]. An important aspect of this is the discovery of process models based on behaviour captured in event data. These models generally show the activities that can be executed during the process and how they are ordered [15].

One of the most important aspects of process discovery is to deduce the states of the operational process in the log [1]. Many mining algorithms only have an implicit notion of state, i.e. the focus is on learning the ordering of activities [11,16]. However, process state information may actually be present explicitly in information systems. Examples of such explicit state information are the diagnosis of a patient in a healthcare process or the status of an order in a purchasing process. In this paper we focus on analysing such state information instead of merely focussing on the activities that are executed during a process.

A single process can have different facets, or *perspectives*, each with their own state space. For example, consider the homeostatic process in a person, parts of which regulate sleep and nutrition. From the perspective of sleep the state of a

---

M.L. van Eck—This research was performed in the context of the IMPULS collaboration project of Eindhoven University of Technology and Philips: "Mine your own body".

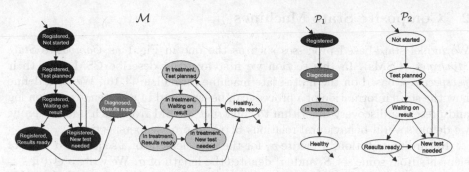

Fig. 1. A model of a simple healthcare process $\mathcal{M}$ and its two perspectives $\mathcal{P}_1$ and $\mathcal{P}_2$. Each state in the process is a combination of a state from each perspective.

person can be e.g. awake or asleep, while the state of the nutrition perspective can be e.g. eating or sated. These perspectives have individual process cycles, but there are interdependencies between states from different perspectives, e.g. people are awake while eating. The state of a person is the composition of the state of both perspectives, and we aim to study such multi-perspective processes.

In Fig. 1 we present a simple healthcare process, which we use as a running example. This composite process $\mathcal{M}$ has two distinct perspectives: $\mathcal{P}_1$, related to the status of the patient being treated, and $\mathcal{P}_2$, related to the status of lab tests of the patient. The initial states are marked with an incoming arrow and the final states are marked with an outgoing arrow.

The healthcare process starts when the patient is registered, after which a lab test is planned to diagnose the patient. If the patient misses their appointment or if the results are inconclusive then a new test is planned, but if the test results are ready then the treatment can proceed. During the treatment additional tests may be required, until the patient is healthy again and the process ends. Note that the composite process is smaller than the Cartesian product of the perspectives ($4 \times 5 = 20$ states) because not all state combinations can be observed due to interdependencies. For example, once the patient is healthy no extra lab tests are needed. Such dependencies between perspectives can be interesting to analyse.

In this paper we present an approach to provide insights into processes that can be considered from multiple state-based perspectives, like the ones described above. The models of these processes quickly become complex as the number of perspectives or the number of states per perspective increases, and it is difficult to interpret the relations between states from different perspectives. Therefore, our approach focusses on visualising and quantifying these relations and empowering the user through interactive exploration of the discovered process models.

The structure of the paper is as follows. In Sect. 2 we formally define state-based models for multi-perspective processes. In Sect. 3 we discuss operations that simplify these models. In Sect. 4 we introduce metrics to quantify the relations between perspectives and we show how they can be visualised. In Sect. 5 we discuss an evaluation of the approach on two real-life data sets. Finally, we present the related work in Sect. 6, and conclusions and future work in Sect. 7.

2   Composite State Machines

We model state-based processes such as the one in Fig. 1 as *Composite State Machines* (CSMs). In this section we first formally describe CSMs and their *perspectives*, based on the finite-state machine formalism [4,10]. We then define how the state information of a process can be captured in a system execution log and present a discovery algorithm to construct a CSM from such a log. Finally, we define several behavioural relations between process perspectives.

Regarding notation, we write σ_i for the i-th element of a sequence $\sigma \in S^*$ of elements from some set S, and $|\sigma|$ denotes the length of σ. We write $s \in \sigma$ if $s = \sigma_i$ for some i. Additionally, for an element s of a cartesian product $S_1 \times \ldots \times S_n$ we write $s(i)$ for the value of the i-th component of s ($i \in \{1, \ldots, n\}$).

2.1   State Machines and Perspectives

We define *State Machines* (SMs) as follows:

Definition 1. *A State Machine $\mathcal{M}$ is a tuple (S, T, S_0, S_F) where S is the set of states, $T \subseteq S \times S$ is the set of transitions, $S_0 \subseteq S$ is the set of initial states, and $S_F \subseteq S$ is the set of final states. $(s, s') \in T$ is also denoted as $(s \rightarrow s')$.*

An *execution sequence* of a state machine is a sequence of states starting from an initial state and ending in a final state such that every state change is allowed by the transitions of the SM. The set of all valid execution sequences of an SM represents the possible behaviour of the process modelled by that SM.

Definition 2. *An execution sequence $\sigma \in S^*$ of an SM $\mathcal{M} = (S, T, S_0, S_F)$ is a sequence of states such that $\sigma_1 \in S_0$, $\sigma_{|\sigma|} \in S_F$, and $(\sigma_i, \sigma_{i+1}) \in T$ for $i \in \{1, \ldots, |\sigma| - 1\}$. The set $\Sigma_{\mathcal{M}}$ is the set of all the execution sequences of $\mathcal{M}$.*

A CSM describes a process with a number of *perspectives*. A state of a CSM is defined as the composition of the states of its perspectives, i.e. it is a vector of states. The set S of all possible states of a CSM is a subset of the cartesian product $S_1 \times \ldots \times S_n$ of the sets of states of its perspectives, as not all combinations of perspective states are necessarily present. Each transition in a CSM represents a change in the state of at least one perspective; therefore we do not consider self loops. Formally:

Definition 3. *A Composite State Machine $\mathcal{M} = (S, T, S_0, S_F)$ is a state machine where $S \subseteq (S_1 \times \ldots \times S_n)$, with $S_1, \ldots, S_n$ being sets of perspective states, and for all $(s, s') \in T$ it holds that $s \neq s'$.*

Perspectives of CSMs can be interpreted as projections of a CSM, as seen in Fig. 1. Two states s_i, s'_i of a perspective P_i are connected by a transition iff there is a transition from some state s to a state s' in the CSM that changes the value of the i-th state component from s_i to s'_i. Again, self loops are not considered because transitions represent state changes. Formally:

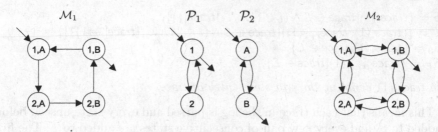

Fig. 2. Two CSMs $\mathcal{M}_1$ and $\mathcal{M}_2$ with $S = \{1,2\} \times \{A,B\}$, $S_0 = \{(1,A)\}$, $S_F = \{(1,B)\}$. Both have the same two perspectives $\mathcal{P}_1$ and $\mathcal{P}_2$.

Definition 4. *Perspective* $\mathcal{P}_i$ ($i \in \{1,\ldots,n\}$) *of a CSM* $\mathcal{M} = (S,T,S_0,S_F)$ *with* $S \subseteq (S_1 \times \ldots \times S_n)$ *is a state machine* $\mathcal{P}_i = (S_i, T_i, S_{i0}, S_{iF})$ *with* $S_{i0} = \{s(i)|s \in S_0\}$, $S_{iF} = \{s(i)|s \in S_F\}$, *and* $T_i \subseteq S_i \times S_i$ *such that:* $(s_i, s_i') \in T_i$ *iff* $s_i \neq s_i' \wedge \exists (s,s') \in T : s(i) = s_i \wedge s'(i) = s_i'$.

Figure 2 shows two different CSMs, $\mathcal{M}_1$ and $\mathcal{M}_2$, both having identical perspectives. However, the possibility of changes of the states w.r.t. one perspective of $\mathcal{M}_1$ depends on the state of the other perspective, while in $\mathcal{M}_2$ these changes only depend on the state of a single perspective. E.g. the transition from state 1 to state 2 in perspective $\mathcal{P}_1$ is only possible when $\mathcal{M}_1$ is in state A in perspective $\mathcal{P}_2$, while this transition is independent of perspective $\mathcal{P}_2$ in $\mathcal{M}_2$. This type of dependency shows a relation between the states of different perspectives.

2.2   State Logs and CSM Discovery

The executions of the behaviour of a process can be recorded in a log [1,3–5]. A *state log* describes a collection of sequences with each sequence consisting of the points in time where a process entered a new state. Hence, a *state entry* in the log indicates that the given process has a specific state from the corresponding point in time onwards, until the next *different* state is entered.

Definition 5. *A* trace $\in (S \times \mathbb{T})^*$ *over the state set* S *is a timed sequence of state entries with time domain* $\mathbb{T}$ *such that subsequent state entries differ in their states. A state log* $\mathcal{L} \in \mathbb{N}^{(S \times \mathbb{T})^*}$ *is a multiset of traces over* S.

Given a state log of a process, with every state entry being the product of the states of all perspectives, i.e. entries $(s_1 \times \ldots \times s_n \times t)$, we can discover a CSM describing the process behaviour. We interpret the sequence of state entries in each trace in the log as an execution sequence of the SM being discovered. Time is not used in the discovery of the model, only in the calculation of statistics for the visualisation later. The discovery algorithm is defined as follows:

Definition 6. *Discovery algorithm* $\mathcal{D}(\mathcal{L})$ *takes a state log* $\mathcal{L} \in \mathbb{N}^{(S \times \mathbb{T})^*}$ *over the set of states* $S = S_1 \times \ldots \times S_n$ *and produces a CSM* $\mathcal{M} = (\widehat{S}, T, S_0, S_F)$ *such that:*

- $\widehat{S} - \{trace_i(1)| trace \in \mathcal{L} \wedge (i \in \{1, \ldots, |trace|\})\}$,
- $T = \{(trace_i(1), trace_{i+1}(1))| trace \in \mathcal{L} \wedge (i \in \{1, \ldots, |trace| - 1\})\}$,
- $S_0 = \{trace_1(1)| trace \in \mathcal{L}\}$,
- $S_F = \{trace_{|trace|}(1)| trace \in \mathcal{L}\}$,

with $trace_i(1)$ denoting the i-th state entry of trace.

This means that each trace in the log is parsed and every state unseen before is added to $\widehat{S}$, and every new pair of consecutive states are added to T. The first state entry in every trace is added to S_0 and the last state entry is added to S_F. The perspectives of the CSM discovered in this way are obtained by projecting the sets of states and transitions, as defined above.

This discovery algorithm corresponds to the first step of the approach presented in [1]. The algorithm in [1] takes an *event* log as input and constructs a transition system. Several different possible abstractions are described that can be used to infer *implicit* states from the events recorded in the log. However, we defined our state log to contain the *explicit* state information of our process, so we do not need to use these abstractions. In fact, mining the log with a horizon limited to single transitions produces a CSM like the algorithm above.

2.3   Behavioural Relations Between Perspectives

Once we have obtained a CSM, we can consider several types of behavioural relations to analyse. Traditional process discovery primarily aims to discover causal relations, i.e. which activity (eventually) follows another [11,16]. In that context it is more difficult to analyse relations like the expected waiting time between two activity occurrences because of the implicit state notion. However, with an explicit state notion the calculation of time statistics is much easier, while the causal relations are still expressed as transitions between states.

In addition, there are also specific insights that can be of interest related to the interdependencies between perspectives in a multi-perspective process. E.g. for the healthcare process in Fig. 1 one can compare the time required to obtain a result when the patient is not yet diagnosed versus the time required for that when the patient is already in treatment. To enable this, it is necessary to know which states and transitions from different perspectives can be observed to *co-occur*, for which additional statistics can then be calculated.

For a given state of a perspective we consider three relations defining with which states and transitions of another perspective it can co-occur:

Definition 7. Let $\mathcal{M} = (S, T, S_0, S_F)$ be a CSM with $S \subseteq S_1 \times \ldots \times S_n$ and $\mathcal{P}_1, \ldots, \mathcal{P}_n$ its perspectives. For a state $s_i \in S_i$ of perspective $\mathcal{P}_i$ ($i \in \{1, \ldots, n\}$),

- the co-occurring CSM states are $CMS_i(s_i) = \{s \in S|s(i) = s_i\}$
- the co-occurring states of perspective $\mathcal{P}_j$, $j \neq i$ are $CPS_{ij}(s_i) = \{s_j \in S_j|\exists s \in S : s(i) = s_i \wedge s(j) = s_j\}$
- and the state's co-occurring transitions of perspective $\mathcal{P}_j$, $j \neq i$ are $SCPT_{ij}(s_i) = \{(s_j, s'_j) \in T_j|\exists(s, s') \in T : s(i) = s_i \wedge s'(i) = s_i \wedge s(j) = s_j \wedge s'(j) = s'_j\}$.

The CMS and CPS relations show which combinations of states from different perspectives can be observed in a CSM. For the CSM $\mathcal{M}$ in Fig. 1, e.g. $\mathrm{CMS}_1(Diagnosed) = \{(Diagnosed,\ Results\ ready)\}$, while the other $\mathcal{P}_2$ states do not occur together with the $Diagnosed$ state. The SCPT relation similarly shows which transitions in a specific perspective can be observed when in a given state of another perspective. E.g. $\mathrm{SCPT}_{21}(Results\ ready) = \{(Registered{\rightarrow}Diagnosed),\ (Diagnosed{\rightarrow}In\ treatment),\ (In\ treat\text{-}ment{\rightarrow}Healthy)\}$, so all transitions of perspective $\mathcal{P}_1$ are possible when perspective $\mathcal{P}_2$ is in the $Results\ ready$ state.

For a given transition of a perspective we consider three relations linking the transitions of a perspective to the transitions of the CSM and to the states and transitions of other perspectives:

Definition 8. *Let $\mathcal{M} = (S, T, S_0, S_F)$ be a CSM with $S \subseteq S_1 \times \ldots \times S_n$ and $\mathcal{P}_1, \ldots, \mathcal{P}_n$ its perspectives. For a transition $(s_i, s_i') \in T_i$ of perspective $\mathcal{P}_i$ $(i \in \{1, \ldots, n\})$,*

- *the co-occurring CSM transitions are $CMT_i(s_i, s_i') = \{(s, s') \in T | s(i) = s_i \wedge s'(i) = s_i'\}$,*
- *the co-occurring transitions of perspective $\mathcal{P}_j$, $j \neq i$ are $CPT_{ij}(s_i, s_i') = \{(s_j, s_j') \in T_j | \exists (s, s') \in T : s(i) = s_i \wedge s'(i) = s_i' \wedge s(j) = s_j \wedge s'(j) = s_j'\}$*
- *and the transition's co-occurring states of perspective $\mathcal{P}_j$, $j \neq i$ are $TCPS_{ij}(s_i, s_i') = \{s_j \in S_j | \exists (s, s') \in T : s(i) = s_i \wedge s'(i) = s_i' \wedge s(j) = s_j \wedge s'(j) = s_j\}$.*

The CMT relation gives the set of transitions that contain a specific state change in a given perspective. E.g. in Fig. 1, $\mathrm{CMT}_2((Test\ planned{\rightarrow}New\ test\ needed)) = \{((Registered,\ Test\ planned){\rightarrow}(Registered,\ New\ test\ needed)),\ ((In\ treatment,\ Test\ planned){\rightarrow}(In\ treatment,\ New\ test\ needed))\}$, so the transition from $Test\ planned$ to $New\ test\ needed$ is possible at two points in $\mathcal{M}$. The CPT relation gives the transitions that can be observed simultaneously. So, $\mathrm{CPT}_{12}((In\ treatment{\rightarrow}Healthy)) = \{(Waiting\ on\ result{\rightarrow}Results\ ready)\}$. Finally, the TCPS relation shows all the states in a perspective where it is possible to observe a specific transition in another perspective. For example, $\mathrm{TCPS}_{21}((Test\ planned{\rightarrow}New\ test\ needed)) = \{Registered,\ In\ treatment\}$.

3 Creating Simplified Views for CSMs

The CSMs that are discovered on real life process can be quite complex. Thus it can be desirable to simplify the model in order to focus the analysis on the parts of interest. Therefore, we consider three different operations that create a simplified view on a state machine, i.e. the CSM as a whole or one of the perspectives. These operations take an SM and create a new SM, so multiple operations can be applied in sequence to create a final view.

The first operation removes a given transition from a state machine. This simplifies the model in the sense that the number of arcs is decreased.

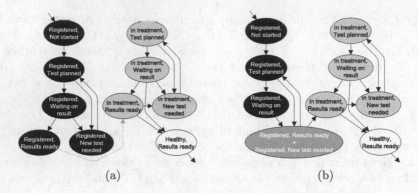

(a)   (b)

Fig. 3. Two views of $\mathcal{M}$ from Fig. 1. In view (a) the (*Diagnosed, Results ready*) state is abstracted from and in view (b) (*Registered, Results ready*) and (*Registered, New test needed*) are aggregated in addition.

When creating a view for a perspective of a CSM it is assumed that a similar view is also created for the CSM as a whole. So, if a transition (s_i, s_i') is removed from perspective $\mathcal{P}_i$ then all transitions from $\mathrm{CMT}_i(s_i, s_i')$ are also removed.

Removing transitions from an SM affects its behaviour, i.e. the set of allowed execution sequences is reduced. For example, removing the transition (*Waiting on result→New test needed*) from perspective $\mathcal{P}_2$ in Fig. 1 implies that the result of the test is never inconclusive. Note that the transitions ((*Registered, Waiting on result*)→(*Registered, New test needed*)) and ((*In treatment, Waiting on result*)→(*In treatment, New test needed*)) should also be removed from $\mathcal{M}$ in Fig. 1 to keep $\mathcal{P}_2$ consistent with $\mathcal{M}$.

The second operation abstracts from a given state in a state machine, simplifying the model by decreasing the number of states. This means that the state is removed, but other states that were connected by transitions through this state should remain connected. In addition, if the abstracted state was an initial or final state then the states that could directly follow or precede this state respectively become initial or final states as well. As an example, Fig. 3a shows the abstraction of the (*Diagnosed, Results ready*) state from $\mathcal{M}$ in Fig. 1. In this view there is now a new transition from (*Registered, Results ready*) to (*In treatment, Results ready*).

Abstracting from states is not guaranteed to simplify the model. If a state is highly connected with many incoming and outgoing transitions then abstracting from this state can result in the addition of many new transitions that make the model more complex.

The third operation aggregates two given states into a single new state, simplifying the model by decreasing both the number of states and transitions. The two old states are removed from the model and a new state is added representing the combination of the two, so all the transitions to and from the old states are also added to the new state (omitting self-loops). If either of the old states was an initial or final state, then the new state is also an initial or final state,

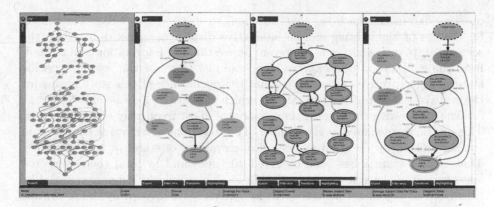

Fig. 4. The interactive visualisation of a discovered CSM. The selected state is denoted with a red box and its co-occurring states and transitions are highlighted in the other perspectives and the overall view based on their *confidence*. Additional statistics are displayed for the highlighted states and transitions.

respectively. In Fig. 3b the aggregation of the states (*Registered, Results ready*) and (*Registered, New test needed*) from the CSM of Fig. 3a is shown.

Although no behaviour is removed during aggregation due to the preservation of transitions, new behaviour may be added. For example, in the CSM in Fig. 3b it is now possible to go from the state *Registered* to the state *In treatment* without going through the state (*Registered, Waiting on result*), while this was not possible before.

4   Exploring Composite State Machines

In this section we introduce the metrics of *support, confidence* and *lift* to quantify the behavioural relations between perspectives. These metrics come from the field of association rule learning [9] and they enable us to highlight relations of potential interest. We also discuss the metric visualisation in the implementation of our approach as a plug-in[1] in the process mining framework ProM.

The visualisation of the discovered CSMs is shown in Fig. 4. The CSM is shown on the left and its perspectives are displayed next to it. Initial states are marked with a dashed border and final states with a double border. Statistics such as the number of observations, are displayed at the bottom for the selected state or transition. The operations from Sect. 3 can be applied to simplify the discovered models. For example, the user can filter arcs based on the amount of observations and iteratively select the states to abstract from or to aggregate.

The behavioural relations introduced in Sect. 2.3 are highlighted and quantified for the selected state or transition. These statistics are calculated from the

---

[1] Contained in the *CSMMiner* package of the ProM 6 nightly build and the ProM 6.6 release, available at http://www.promtools.org/.

observations in the state log that was used to discover the CSM. The reason for the use of highlighting and an interactive display of statistics based on the selected state or transition is to prevent an overload of information and to facilitate the exploration of scenario's. For example, the user can select a specific state in a perspective and evaluate what the occurrence of this state means for the state of the rest of the process and which transitions may be enabled.

The states with the highest *support* are the most frequently observed states. This metric is calculated as the number of observations of a state or transition in the log divided by the total number of observations of states or transitions [9]. That is, if a state s has been observed 40 times and in total there were 100 state entries in the state log then $Supp(s) = \frac{40}{100}$. Similarly, support can also be calculated as the time that was spent in a given state divided by the total time covered by the log. For transitions the support is only defined over the number of observations, as a transition is assumed to happen instantaneously.

The *confidence* metric is defined over pairs of state or transitions, expressing the estimated conditional probability of the occurrence of one, given the occurrence of the other [9]. E.g. if a state s_i from perspective $\mathcal{P}_i$ co-occurs with two states $CPS_{ij}(s_i) = \{s_j, s'_j\}$ from perspective $\mathcal{P}_j$, and if the co-occurrence of s_i with s_j is observed 30 times and the co-occurrence of s_i with s'_j is observed 10 times, then $Conf(s_i, s_j) = \frac{30}{40}$ and $Conf(s_i, s'_j) = \frac{10}{40}$. Confidence for co-occurring states can also be calculated based on the amount of time that was spent in the related states. For pairs of transitions the computation is comparable.

We define the confidence metric slightly differently for the co-occurrence of a state with a transition. For a given state's co-occurring transitions the confidence expresses the expected conditional probability of observing the transition, given that the CSM is in this specific state *and* a transition occurs. For example, a state s_i from perspective $\mathcal{P}_i$ co-occurs with two transitions $SCPT_{ij}(s_i) = \{(s_j, s'_j), (s_j, s''_j)\}$ from perspective $\mathcal{P}_j$. Then the confidence $Conf(s_i, (s_j, s'_j))$ is the estimated conditional probability of observing transition (s_j, s'_j), given that the CSM is in s_i and s_j and a transition occurs. That is, if (s_j, s'_j) has been observed 8 times while in state s_i and (s_j, s''_j) has been observed 2 times while in state s_i then $Conf(s_i, (s_j, s'_j)) = \frac{8}{10}$ and $Conf(s_i, (s_j, s''_j)) = \frac{2}{10}$. The confidence of observing a transition's co-occurring state is the expected conditional probability of being in that specific state, given that the transition is observed.

The *lift* metric is also defined over pairs of states or transitions and it expresses how much the confidence differs from the expected confidence [9]. For the co-occurrence of two states s_i and s_j, given that the CSM is in state s_i in perspective $\mathcal{P}_i$, the lift is computed as the ratio of the confidence $Conf(s_i, s_j)$ over the unconditional probability of being in s_j in perspective $\mathcal{P}_j$. E.g. if $Conf(s_i, s_j) = \frac{30}{40} = 0.75$ and the probability of being in s_j in perspective $\mathcal{P}_j$ (i.e. its support) is $\frac{40}{100} = 0.4$, then $Lift(s_i, s_j) = \frac{0.75}{0.4} = 1.875$. This indicates that the probability of being in state s_j in perspective $\mathcal{P}_j$ is 1.875 times higher than expected when in s_i in perspective $\mathcal{P}_i$. In other words, the lift quantifies whether being in s_i provides information on the likelihood of being in s_j and expresses whether the relation is unexpected and hence potentially interesting.

5   Evaluation

The tool introduced in Sect. 4 has been used to analyse two data sets recorded for two real-life processes. One is the BPI Challange 2012 data of a loan application process [6] and the other is product user behaviour data for a smart baby bottle equipped with various sensors that was developed by Philips.

5.1   BPI Challenge 2012

The BPI Challenge 2012 data set (BPI 2012) is a real-life event log that was obtained from a Dutch financial institute [6]. The log contains 262.200 events distributed over 13.087 process instances. The process described in this log concerns applications for a personal loan or overdraft at the financial institute. The events recorded in this log are related to three interrelated sub-processes, which we take as our perspectives. Artificial initial and final states were added to each process instance in the log[2] to ensure correct calculations of state sojourn times for all three perspectives.

The first perspective concerns the state of the application (A-events), the second relates to the work-items performed by the bank's employees (W-events), and the third concerns the state of the institute's offers to the applicant (O-events). Although the BPI 2012 log is presented as an event log, the A and O-events actually specify changes in the state of the application or an offer. This means that they can be interpreted as state entries in a state log as defined in Sect. 2.2. On the other hand, the W-events are clearly identifiable as activities. These activities are enabled at some point in the process, indicated with a single *schedule* event, after which the *start* and *completion* of each instance of this activity is recorded whenever it is performed. At most one activity is performed per application at a time, so we study the process from the viewpoint that the states of the work-item perspective indicate either the type of activity currently being executed (i.e. indicated by a start event) or the type of activity that was most recently completed (i.e. indicated by a complete event).

The interrelation of these three perspectives introduces complex behaviour that makes it difficult for traditional process discovery algorithms to discover informative models. Figure 5 shows a process model discovered by the Inductive visual Miner (IvM) [11]. This flower model provides very little insights into the application process and no relations between the three perspectives. On the other hand, models such as the one shown in Fig. 6, discovered with the Flexible Heuristics Miner (FHM) [16], do show these relations, but they provide little structure and they are difficult to interpret.

Applying the CSM Miner on the BPI 2012 results in the models shown in Fig. 4. The discovered CSM is shown as the leftmost model and, like the result from the FHM, it is very difficult to interpret. However, the three models for the individual perspectives are well structured and easy to comprehend. Mining such structured models is also possible with traditional process discovery algorithms if

---

[2] Available at http://svn.win.tue.nl/repos/prom/Packages/CSMMiner/Logs/.

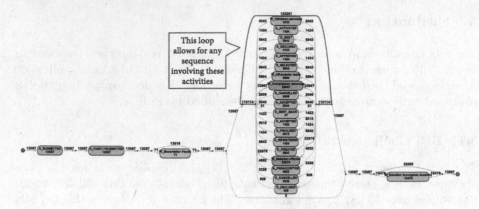

Fig. 5. The result of applying the IvM [11] on the BPI 2012 data. The relations between the events from different perspectives are not visible in this model.

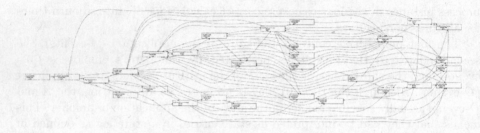

Fig. 6. The result of applying the FHM [16] on the BPI 2012 data. The general flow of the process cannot easily be inferred from this model.

the log is filtered for a specific perspective. *However, the resulting models would not show any of the interrelations between the perspectives.* The CSM Miner does show these relations when the user explores the models interactively.

Another reason why the CSM Miner results are easier to interpret is that they can be simplified using the transformation operations from Sect. 3. E.g. the BPI 2012 process starts with the submission of the application, shown in Fig. 7a. This is always immediately followed by a state indicating that the application is not completed yet, i.e. partly submitted. Based on the fact that the time spent in the first state is negligible, this state can be abstracted from.

Figure 7b also shows a transformation simplifying the application perspective. It contains the end of the application process for successfully accepted applications, which are approved, registered and the loan is activated. The model structure and state statistics indicate that these states occur in arbitrary order and that the process immediately ends afterwards (i.e. the state sojourn time is 0). Hence, these states can be merged into a single one representing a successful application.

Exploring the discovered CSM provides several interesting insights. For example, when inspecting the declined applications that co-occur with automatic processing (Fig. 8a) and comparing them to the declined applications that

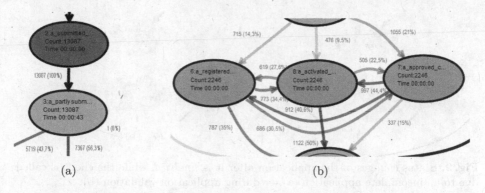

Fig. 7. Part of the *application* perspective with *a_submitted* marked for abstraction, and *a_registered*, *a_activated* and *a_approved* marked for aggregation.

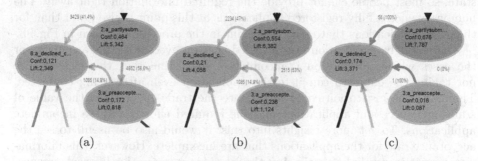

Fig. 8. The decline of applications by the institution, highlighted to show statistics for the co-occurrence with automatic application submission (a), manual handling of leads (b), and fraud detection (c).

co-occur with manual handling of the leads (Fig. 8b). These statistics show that the rate of declined applications is very similar for both type of applications. So, this suggests that perhaps the guidelines for declining applications are uniform, but some applications may come in through a channel where it is not possible to automatically evaluate them on the application.

Exploration of the CSM also shows that some applications are declined while the institution is investigating potential fraud, shown in Fig. 8c. In the 75 cases where fraud is investigated for applications that have not been validated, 57 were declined (76 %). However, after application validation there were also 33 cases where potential fraud was investigated, but none of these were declined. Therefore, the validation appears to be successful at filtering out fraud and it suggests that they only investigate applications that have not been validated for which they already have a suspicion of possible fraud.

Finally, it is also possible that an application is declined after it has been validated and the offer sent to the applicant. This appears to be related to unresponsive applicants or incomplete applications. In Fig. 9a the co-occurrence statistics are shown for the state where the client is called because of an incomplete application. While on the phone, only $\frac{86+193+127}{1647} = 25\%$ cases changed

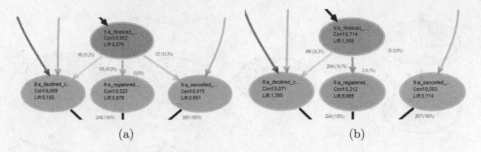

Fig. 9. Status changes of the application after it is *finalized*, while the client is called due to an incomplete application (a), or during application validation (b).

state, so most people cannot provide the required information right away. The number of successfully registered applications at this point is also lower than for the other applications that reach this point in the process, as shown in Fig. 9b.

Interestingly, exploration also revealed that on average 7 calls are made for the cases where information is incomplete, suggesting that these clients are not taking the effort to complete the application even after being contacted. Therefore, the institution could investigate the trade-off between the value of additional successful applications and the required effort for these incomplete applications. To get more insights into this, it would also be useful to see the acceptance rate for the applications that are incomplete. However, this information cannot currently be obtained as the relations between the different perspectives are limited to co-occurrence and do not show (long term) dependencies.

5.2   Smart Product User Behaviour

This data set was obtained from Philips during a study where Philips worked on the design of a smart baby bottle equipped with various sensors. The goal of the study was to investigate the characteristics of the data obtained during the use of the bottle, and to explore potential product improvements or ideas for related services based on analysis of this data.

The data set used during this evaluation concerns 358 instances of baby feedings that resulted in 8369 state entries in a state log. There are two perspectives used in the analysis: a temperature sensor and an accelerometer measuring bottle movement. The states in this log correspond to the state of the sensor signals of these two sensors and their product-specific interpretation. They were obtained by clustering the sensor measurement values and labelling the cluster centroids. The resulting CSM is shown in Fig. 10 The main challenge of analysing this sensor data is the recognition of user behaviour and its effects on the measurements.

One of the basic assumptions on user behaviour for this smart bottle is that a feeding is started soon after the bottle has been heated. Figure 11a shows the bottle movement states, highlighted to indicate their co-occurrence with the state of the bottle having just been heated. The high lift of the state

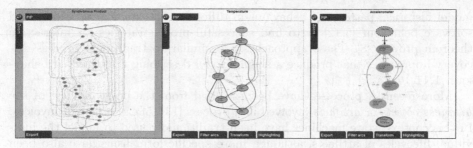

Fig. 10. The result of applying the CSM Miner on the Philips data set.

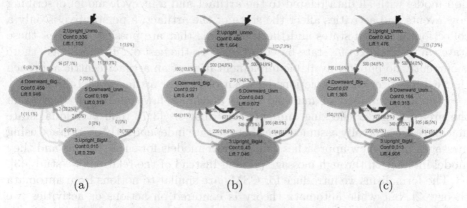

Fig. 11. States in the *accelerometer* perspective, highlighted for the co-occurrence with the bottle heating (a), cooling (b), and small temperature increases (c).

Downward_BigMove shows that the feedings are indeed generally started soon after heating, as this state is an important indicator for the start of a feeding.

Similarly, Fig. 11b shows the co-occurrence of bottle movement states with the transition from a warm bottle to a cold bottle through a big decrease in temperature. Here the lift of the state *Upright_BigMove* is high, indicating a relation with this indicator of the feeding having ended. This shows that the bottle is usually cleaned soon after a feeding has ended.

Interestingly, there is also a strong relation between a small temperature increase and the *Upright_BigMove* state, as shown in Fig. 11c. This occurs because during the feeding the warm food was further away from the sensor than when the bottle was in a stationary position, resulting in fluctuating temperatures. The product designers inferred from this that the temperature sensor was not in the correct position to measure the temperature accurately during the feeding.

6   Related Work

The discovery of state-based models from logs of behavioural data is not a recent idea [4,5]. Finite state machines have been found to be convenient to model historical patterns of behaviour in different contexts, e.g. to understand software behaviour [5,12] or to find successful proof strategies for interactive theorem provers [8]. These approaches are similar to traditional process discovery approaches that produce a single model describing the observed behaviour [1,11,16].

More recently, processes have been studied from the point of view of the *business objects* or *artifacts* involved in a process [13–15],e.g. orders or invoices. In this context, state machines have been traditionally used to model the individual lifecycles of artifacts, although more specific formalisms have also been developed [14]. While artifacts are generally defined to include both an information model with all data related to the artifact and a lifecycle model describing how events and activities affect the state of the artifact, a perspective is only a collection of related states and the transitions that are possible between these states in the context of a state-based process. To the best of our knowledge, there is currently no publicly available implementation of an artifact-centric approach that can discover the interactions between objects or artifacts [13,14].

Systems composed of multiple state machines have also been studied in the areas of model checking and software analysis [3,7]. The individual state machines are generally assumed to either operate independently or interact using messages [2,10]. Few approaches can discover models for such systems and they model interaction through message passing instead of the relations we study [3].

The formalisms we introduce for CSMs are similar to notions from automata theory [2], but while automata theory is centered on actions or activities, we deviate from the dominating activity view in process mining and utilize available state information explicitly. In automata theory notions of e.g. product automata can be used to build up a system of multiple automata based on synchronised transitions [2], which can be reduced to create a minimal automata, i.e. bottom-up construction. However, a CSM cannot be built up from its perspectives as there is no information in the data of individual perspectives to synchronise on. This information is only available in the log of the entire process, which is mined to directly create a composite model that is minimal by definition.

7   Conclusion

This paper presented an approach to discover state-based process models that can be interactively explored. We first formally defined the notion of a Composite State Machine as a way to model multi-perspective processes that can be learned from event logs. As the resulting models can be quite complex, we provided three different operations that can be used to create simplified views on state machines.

To explore the discovered models we have developed an interactive visualisation tool that is available as a plug-in for ProM. The tool highlights interesting relations between states and transitions graphically and quantifies them in terms of *support, confidence* and *lift*. This tool has been evaluated on two real-life data sets, demonstrating that valuable and novel insights can be obtained.

Future work we plan to do in this area aims at improving practical usability. For example, the view creation operations could be automatically evaluated to provide the user with feedback on the changes in process model quality when creating a new view. Based on the existing metrics or on concurrency detection there could also be automatic suggestions for candidate transitions and states for removal or aggregation. Finally, the approach should be extended to support more types of behavioural relations between the perspectives. In addition to co-occurrence, it is also interesting to look at the dependencies between perspectives that occur before or after reaching a given state.

References

1. van der Aalst, W.M.P., Rubin, V., Verbeek, H.M.W., van Dongen, B.F., Kindler, E., Günther, C.W.: Process mining: a two-step approach to balance between under-fitting and overfitting. Softw. Syst. Model. **9**(1), 87–111 (2010)
2. Baier, C., Katoen, J.: Principles of Model Checking. MIT Press, Cambridge (2008)
3. Beschastnikh, I., Brun, Y., Ernst, M.D., Krishnamurthy, A.: Inferring models of concurrent systems from logs of their behavior with CSight. In: 36th International Conference on Software Engineering, ICSE 2014, pp. 468–479 (2014)
4. Biermann, A.W., Feldman, J.A.: On the synthesis of finite-state machines from samples of their behavior. IEEE Trans. Comput. **21**(6), 592–597 (1972)
5. Cook, J.E., Wolf, A.L.: Discovering models of software processes from event-based data. ACM Trans. Softw. Eng. Methodol. **7**(3), 215–249 (1998)
6. van Dongen, B.F.: BPI Challenge 2012 (2012). http://dx.doi.org/10.4121/uuid:3926db30-f712-4394-aebc-75976070e91f
7. Fisler, K., Krishnamurthi, S.: Modular verification of collaboration-based software designs. In: Proceedings of 8th European Software Engineering Conference 2001, pp. 152–163 (2001)
8. Gransden, T., Walkinshaw, N., Raman, R.: Mining state-based models from proof corpora. In: Watt, S.M., Davenport, J.H., Sexton, A.P., Sojka, P., Urban, J. (eds.) CICM 2014. LNCS, vol. 8543, pp. 282–297. Springer, Heidelberg (2014)
9. Hastie, T., Tibshirani, R., Friedman, J.: The Elements of Statistical Learning: Data Mining, Inference and Prediction. Springer, New York (2001)
10. Kam, T., Villa, T., Brayton, R.K., Sangiovanni-Vincentelli, A.: Synthesis of Finite State Machines: Functional Optimization. Springer Science and Business Media, New York (2013)
11. Leemans, S.J.J., Fahland, D., van der Aalst, W.M.P.: Exploring processes and deviations. In: Fournier, F., Mendling, J. (eds.) BPM 2014 Workshops. LNBIP, vol. 202, pp. 304–316. Springer, Heidelberg (2015)
12. Lorenzoli, D., Mariani, L., Pezzè, M.: Automatic generation of software behavioral models. In: 30th International Conference on Software Engineering (ICSE 2008), pp. 501–510 (2008)
13. Lu, X., Nagelkerke, M., van de Wiel, D., Fahland, D.: Discovering interacting artifacts from ERP systems. IEEE Trans. Serv. Comput. **8**(6), 861–873 (2015)
14. Popova, V., Fahland, D., Dumas, M.: Artifact lifecycle discovery. Int. J. Coop. Inf. Syst. **24**(1), 144 (2015)
15. Ryndina, K., Küster, J.M., Gall, H.C.: Consistency of business process models and object life cycles. In: Kühne, T. (ed.) MoDELS 2006. LNCS, vol. 4364, pp. 80–90. Springer, Heidelberg (2007)
16. Weijters, A.J.M.M., Ribeiro, J.T.S.: Flexible heuristics miner (FHM). In: Proceedings of IEEE Symposium on Computational Intelligence and Data Mining, CIDM 2011, pp. 310–317 (2011)

Semantical Vacuity Detection in Declarative Process Mining

Fabrizio Maria Maggi[1], Marco Montali[2], Claudio Di Ciccio[3]($\boxtimes$), and Jan Mendling[3]

[1] University of Tartu, Tartu, Estonia
f.m.maggi@ut.ee
[2] Free University of Bozen-Bolzano, Bolzano, Italy
montali@inf.unibz.it
[3] Vienna University of Economics and Business, Vienna, Austria
{claudio.di.ciccio,jan.mendling}@wu.ac.at

Abstract. A large share of the literature on process mining based on declarative process modeling languages, like DECLARE, relies on the notion of *constraint activation* to distinguish between the case in which a process execution recorded in event data "vacuously" satisfies a constraint, or satisfies the constraint in an "interesting way". This fine-grained indicator is then used to decide whether a candidate constraint supported by the analyzed event log is indeed relevant or not. Unfortunately, this notion of relevance has never been formally defined, and all the proposals existing in the literature use ad-hoc definitions that are only applicable to a pre-defined set of constraint patterns. This makes existing declarative process mining technique inapplicable when the target constraint language is extensible and may contain formulae that go beyond pre-defined patterns. In this paper, we tackle this hot, open challenge and show how the notion of constraint activation and vacuous satisfaction can be captured semantically, in the case of constraints expressed in arbitrary temporal logics over finite traces. We then extend the standard automata-based approach so as to incorporate relevance-related information. We finally report on an implementation and experimentation of the approach that confirms the advantages and feasibility of our solution.

Keywords: Vacuity detection · Declarative process mining · Constraint activation

1 Introduction

The increasing availability of event data recorded by information systems, electronic devices, web services, and sensor networks provides detailed information about the actual processes in systems and organizations. Process mining techniques can use such event data to discover process models and check the conformance of process executions. When a process works in a flexible and knowledge-intensive setting, it is desirable to describe it in terms of a constraint-based

© Springer International Publishing Switzerland 2016
M. La Rosa et al. (Eds.): BPM 2016, LNCS 9850, pp. 158–175, 2016.
DOI: 10.1007/978-3-319-45348-4_10

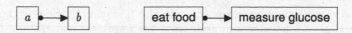

Fig. 1. Response template and a possible instantiation

declarative process model rather than of a detailed procedural model. Consider, for instance, a physician in a hospital confronted with a variety of patients that need to be handled in a flexible manner but, at the same time, following some general regulations and guidelines. In such cases, declarative process models are more effective than procedural models [1, 27, 28]. Instead of explicitly specifying all possible sequences of tasks in a process, declarative models implicitly specify the allowed behavior of the process with *constraints*, i.e., rules that must be followed during the process executions.

In [1, 26], the authors introduce a declarative process modeling language called DECLARE. DECLARE is characterized by a user-friendly graphical representation with formal semantics grounded in LTL over finite traces (LTL$_f$ [8,9]). For example, the response constraint in Fig. 1 means that every action eat food must eventually be followed by action measure glucose, and this can be formalized with the LTL$_f$ formula $\Box$(eat food $\rightarrow$ $\Diamond$measure glucose). DECLARE has been fruitfully applied in the context of process discovery [5, 13, 14, 18, 20, 22] and compliance/conformance checking [2, 4, 6, 16, 19, 23, 25]. In both tasks, when execution traces are analyzed so as to check whether they satisfy a given DECLARE constraint, it is not sufficient to obtain a yes/no answer, but it becomes crucial to understand whether the trace is *relevant*, in the sense that it *actively interacts* with the constraint.

For this reason, most of the existing process mining techniques based on DECLARE rely on the notion of *constraint activation*. This notion is, in general, useful to assess the "degree of adherence" of a process execution with respect to a constraint. In particular, in process discovery, it becomes crucial to define interestingness metrics (like support and confidence [13,20]) to select the most relevant constraints to be discovered among a set of candidates that can be, in some cases, extremely large. In the context of conformance checking, constraint activations are useful to define a set of "health indicators" to measure the *healthiness* of a process execution by evaluating the proportion of constraint activations that lead to a violation and the proportion of constraint activations that lead to a fulfillment [4,19,21,25]. This quantitative analysis would not be possible without the notion of constraint activation.

In spite of the huge interest in this problem, the notion of constraint activation has never been formally defined, and all the papers so far have worked with ad-hoc definitions, explicitly spelled out for each of the DECLARE constraints. This poses a twofold issue. On the one hand, the lack of a general, formal approach to this problem makes it extremely difficult to understand whether ad-hoc approaches are indeed correct, when the constraints under study go beyond simple patterns like the aforementioned *response*. On the other hand, ad-hoc and pattern-based definitions of relevance make existing declarative process mining technique inapplicable when the target constraint language is extensible and may contain formulae that go beyond pre-defined patterns. The goal of this paper is to overcome these issues, by proposing for the first time a general, systematic characterization of relevance and activation for temporal constraints. Our approach is formally-grounded, and at the same time it is by and large compatible with the human intuition exploited in the previous literature.

The notion of constraint activation is related to the notion of *vacuity detection* in model checking. In the *response* example of Fig. 1, if eat food never occurs in a trace, then the constraint is "vacuously" satisfied, that is, satisfied without showing any form of interaction with the trace. However, existing techniques for vacuity detection (i.e., for determining whether a given trace is a relevant, *interesting witness* for the formula of interest) [3,17] present two key limitations in our context. First, they focus on temporal formulae over infinite traces (standard LTL in particular), whereas we are interested in finite traces only (as customary in BPM). Second, they suffer from *syntax sensitivity*. This implies that expressing a constraint through two semantically equivalent but syntactically different formulae could lead to a different judgement for the same trace.

By leveraging a finite-trace semantics for constraints, we move from a syntax-dependent to a fully semantical characterization of constraint activation and, in turn, vacuity detection. Our approach is grounded on the RV-LTL 4-valued semantics [2], which is adapted to the finite-trace setting in accordance with existing literature [7,21]. RV-LTL is exploited to provide a fine-grained characterization of the "constraint activation state" in a given execution context. The relationship between activation states is then explored to identify when the execution of a given task results in a "relevant" transition. We abstractly formulate this theory of relevance at the logical level, but then we concretize it by leveraging the automata-theoretic approach for temporal logics over finite-traces. In particular, we show how the finite-state automaton characterizing the constraint of interest can be enriched with activation-related information without affecting the complexity of its construction. We finally report on implementation and experimentation of our solution, confirming its advantages and feasibility.

The paper is structured as follows. In Sect. 2, we introduce some preliminary notions. In Sect. 3, we describe the motivation behind our contribution. In Sect. 4, we give the definition of constraint activation. Section 5 shows how to check constraint activations using automata. In Sect. 7, we evaluate our approach on two real-life logs. Section 7 concludes the paper and spells out directions for future work.

2 Preliminaries

We start by introducing the necessary preliminary notions used in the rest of the paper. We fix a finite set Σ of tasks, i.e., atomic units of work in the process. This set provides the alphabet on top of which process execution traces are defined.

Definition 1 (Execution trace). *An* (execution) *trace over Σ is a possibly empty, finite sequence of tasks $\langle t_1, \ldots, t_n \rangle$ belonging to the set Σ^* of finite sequences over Σ. We use ε to denote the empty trace.*

We use the standard *concatenation* operator over traces: given two traces $\tau_1 = \langle t_1^1, \ldots, t_m^1 \rangle$ and $\tau_2 = \langle t_1^2, \ldots, t_n^2 \rangle$, we have that a trace τ_3 is the *concatenation* of τ_1 and τ_2, written $\tau_1 \cdot \tau_2$, if $\tau_3 = \langle t_1^1, \ldots, t_m^1, t_1^2, \ldots, t_n^2 \rangle$. We also use notation $\tau \cdot t$ as a shortcut for $\tau \cdot \langle t \rangle$.

Intuitively, constraints are used to declaratively describe which traces are considered *compliant*, and which instead are forbidden. Typically, this intuitive notion of conformance is formally expressed using the notion of logical consequence over temporal logics, whose models are indeed traces [24]. The most widely used logic for declarative process modeling is LTL over finite traces (LTL$_f$). This logic is at the basis of concrete constraint modeling languages such as DECLARE. As pointed out in [7], the most widely adopted approach to reason about and execute declarative process models is to leverage the automata-theoretic approach for temporal logics, exploiting the well-known result that every LTL$_f$ formula can be captured by a corresponding (deterministic) finite-state automaton (FSA). However, FSAs are actually richer than LTL$_f$, and in fact capture sophisticated constraints expressed in monadic second-order logic over finite traces (MSO$_f$), a logic that is expressively equivalent to regular expressions, and also to linear-dynamic logic over finite traces (LDL$_f$). Interestingly, LDL$_f$ has been recently applied to monitor business constraints going beyond the typical DECLARE patterns [7]. To abstract away from the specific logic of interest, in this paper we employ the generic term *(business) constraint* as a way to refer to a (closed) formula in any of the logics mentioned above. We use LTL$_f$ in our examples just for presentation purposes. As pointed out above, all such logics can be characterized using DFAs. We call *constraint automaton* the DFA corresponding to a constraint of interest.

Definition 2 (Constraint Automaton). *Let φ be a constraint over Σ. The constraint automaton $\mathcal{A}_\varphi$ of φ is a DFA $\langle \Sigma, S, s_0, \delta, F \rangle$, where: (i) Σ is the input alphabet (which corresponds to the set of tasks); (ii) S is a finite set of states; (iii) $s_0 \in S$ is the initial state; (iv) $\delta : S \times \Sigma \to S$ is the (task-labeled) state-transition function; (v) $F \subseteq S$ is the set of accepting states. $\mathcal{A}_\varphi$ has the property of precisely accepting those traces $\sigma \in \Sigma^*$ that satisfy φ. Without loss of generality we assume that $\mathcal{A}_\varphi$ is not trimmed, i.e., for every state $s \in S$ and every task $t \in \Sigma$, $\delta(s, t)$ is defined.*

Examples of algorithms that produce the constraint automaton given a constraint expressed in LDL$_f$ or LTL$_f$ can be found in [7,9,15].

Given a constraint automaton $\mathcal{A} = \langle \Sigma, S, s_0, \delta, F \rangle$ and two states $s_1, s_2 \in S$, we say that s_2 *is reachable from* s_1 *in* $\mathcal{A}$, written $\delta^*(s_1, s_2)$, if $s_1 = s_2$ or there exists a trace that leads from s_1 to s_2 according to δ. We say that $\mathcal{A}$ *accepts a trace* τ, or equivalently that τ *complies with* $\mathcal{A}$, if there exists a path that reaches an accepting state starting from the initial state, such that for $i \in \{0, \ldots, |\tau|\}$, the i-th transition in the path matches with the i-th task in τ.

Figure 2 shows the constraint automata representing the following LTL$_f$ DECLARE templates, grounded on two tasks a and b:

- *Precedence* ($\varphi_p = \neg b\,\mathcal{U}a$) - each b must be preceded by a;
- *Response*($\varphi_r = \square(a \rightarrow \Diamond b)$) - each a must be eventually followed by b;
- *Succession* ($\varphi_p \wedge \varphi_r$) - combination of precedence and response.

For compactness, in the figure, we graphically employ sophisticated labels as a shortcut for multiple transitions connecting two states with different task-labels. For example, a transition labeled with !a is a shortcut for a set of transitions between the same two states, each one labeled with a task taken from $\Sigma \setminus$ a. A transition labeled with "−" is a shortcut for a set of transitions between the same two states, one per task in Σ. Notably, this compact notation allows us to use the same automaton regardless of Σ (assuming just that Σ contains the tasks mentioned by the constraint, plus at least one additional, "other" task). Following Definition 2, in Fig. 2, we do not *trim* the automata, i.e., we explicitly maintain all states, even the trap states that cannot reach any accepting state (like state 2 in Fig. 2(a) and 2(c)). Our approach seamlessly works for trimmed automata as well.

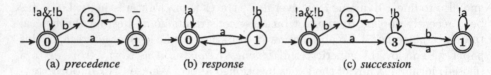

(a) *precedence*   (b) *response*   (c) *succession*

Fig. 2. Automata for the *precedence*, *response* and *succession* DECLARE constraints

3   Background and Motivation

When checking whether a process execution complies with a constraint, one among two outcomes arises: the execution may *violate* the constraint, or it may *satisfy* it. In the latter case, however, the reason for satisfaction may be twofold. On the one hand, it could be the case that the trace interacts with the constraint, ensuring that the constraint is satisfied at the time the trace is completed. On the other hand, it could be the case that the constraint is trivially satisfied because there is no interaction with the trace. Consider again the *response* constraint in Fig. 1. This constraint is satisfied when food is eaten and then the glucose is eventually measured; this is in fact an interesting situation. However, this constraint is also satisfied by those traces where no food is ever eaten. In this latter case, we say that the constraint is *vacuously satisfied*. Traces where a constraint is *non*-vacuously satisfied are called *interesting witnesses* for that constraint. As pointed out in the introduction, discriminating between these two situations is crucial in a variety of (declarative) process mining tasks, such as conformance checking and declarative process discovery. In this section, we deepen the discussion provided in the introduction, by considering the two main limitations of existing approaches when it comes to interesting witnesses: syntax-dependence and ad-hoc definitions.

3.1 Syntax-Dependent Vacuity Detection

In [17], the authors introduce an approach for vacuity detection in temporal model checking for LTL (over infinite traces), so as to determine whether a given trace is an interesting witness for an LTL formula; they provide a method for extending an LTL formula φ to a new formula $witness(\varphi)$ that, when satisfied, ensures that the original formula φ is non-vacuously satisfied. In particular, $witness(\varphi)$ is generated by considering that a path π satisfies φ non-vacuously (and then is an interesting witness for φ), if π satisfies φ and π satisfies a set of additional conditions that guarantee that every subformula of φ does really affect the truth value of φ in π. We call these conditions *vacuity detection conditions* of φ. They correspond to the formulae $\neg\varphi[\psi \leftarrow \bot]$ where, for all the subformulae ψ of φ, $\varphi[\psi \leftarrow \bot]$ is obtained from φ by replacing ψ by false or true, depending on whether ψ is in the scope of an even or an odd number of negations. Then, $witness(\varphi)$ is the conjunction of φ and all the formulae $\neg\varphi[\psi \leftarrow \bot]$ with ψ subformula of φ:

$$witness(\varphi) = \varphi \wedge \bigwedge \neg\varphi[\psi \leftarrow \bot]. \tag{1}$$

Consider, e.g., the response constraint $\Box(\text{eat food} \to \Diamond\text{measure glucose})$. The vacuity detection condition is $\Diamond\text{eat food}$, so that the interesting witnesses for this constraint are all traces where $\Box(\text{eat food} \to \Diamond\text{measure glucose}) \wedge \Diamond\text{eat food}$ is satisfied.

This approach was applied to DECLARE in [22] for vacuity detection in the context of process discovery. However, the algorithm introduced in [17] can generate different results for equivalent LTL_f formulae. Consider, for instance, the following equivalent formulae (expressing a DECLARE *alternate response* constraint):

$$\varphi = \Box(a \to \Diamond b) \wedge \Box(a \to \bigcirc((\neg a\,\mathcal{U}\,b) \vee \Box(\neg b)))$$
$$\varphi' = \Box(a \to \bigcirc(\neg a\,\mathcal{U}\,b))$$

When we apply (1) to φ and φ', we obtain that $witness(\varphi) \neq witness(\varphi')$.

We focus on φ. Since $\varphi = \Box(\neg a \vee \Diamond b) \wedge \Box(\neg a \vee \bigcirc((\neg a\,\mathcal{U}\,b) \vee \Box(\neg b)))$, one of the subformulae of φ is $\psi = \Box(\neg b)$. Since ψ is in the scope of an even number of negations, the corresponding vacuity detection condition is

$$\neg(\Box(\neg a \vee \Diamond b) \wedge \Box(\neg a \vee \bigcirc((\neg a\,\mathcal{U}\,b) \vee \mathit{false}))) \equiv \neg(\Box(\neg a \vee \Diamond b) \vee \Diamond(a \wedge \neg\bigcirc(\neg a\,\mathcal{U}\,b))$$

Considering that $\neg(\Box(\neg a \vee \Diamond b)$ and $\Diamond(a \wedge \neg\bigcirc(\neg a\,\mathcal{U}\,b))$ are always false in conjunction with φ, this vacuity detection condition is always false in conjunction with φ. This is sufficient to conclude that $witness(\varphi) = \mathit{false}$.

We now focus on φ'. Since $\varphi' = \Box(\neg a \vee \bigcirc(\neg a\,\mathcal{U}\,b))$, its subformulae are

$$\psi'_1 = \varphi' \qquad \psi'_2 = \neg a \vee \bigcirc(\neg a\,\mathcal{U}\,b) \qquad \psi'_3 = a(1)$$
$$\psi'_4 = \bigcirc(\neg a\,\mathcal{U}\,b) \qquad \psi'_5 = \neg a\,\mathcal{U}\,b \qquad \psi'_6 = a(2) \qquad \psi'_7 = b.$$

The corresponding vacuity detection conditions are: *(i)* true for ψ'_1 and ψ'_2; *(ii)* $\neg(\Box(\bigcirc(\neg a\,\mathcal{U}\,b))) \equiv \Diamond(\neg\bigcirc(\neg a\,\mathcal{U}\,b))$ for ψ'_3; *(iii)* $\neg(\Box(\neg a \vee \mathit{false})) \equiv \Diamond a$ for ψ'_4 and ψ'_5; *(iv)* $\neg(\Box(\neg a \vee \bigcirc(\mathit{false}\,\mathcal{U}\,b))) \equiv \Diamond(a \wedge \neg\bigcirc(b))$ for ψ'_6.

Constraint-based declarative languages like DECLARE are used to describe requirements to the process behavior. In this case, each LTL$_f$ rule describes a specific constraint with clear semantics. Therefore, we need a *univocal*, syntax-independent and intuitive way to diagnose vacuously compliant behavior in constraint-based processes.

3.2 Ad-Hoc Approaches

An alternative approach to the syntax-dependent vacuity detection recalled in Sect. 3.1 is to restrict the constraint language, considering a pre-defined family of constraint patterns rather than a full-fledged temporal logic. This is the case, e.g., of DECLARE. [11,20] take advantage from this feature of DECLARE, and provide an ad-hoc definition of constraint activation and vacuity, explicitly handling each templates. However, this approach fails when DECLARE is extended with new templates, a feature that has been deemed essential since the very first seminal papers on this approach [26]. The following example introduces a quite interesting template that cannot be expressed by using the core templates of DECLARE.

Example 1. We call *progression* of a tuple of tasks $\langle t_1, \ldots, t_n \rangle$ a trace that contains $t_1, \ldots, t_n$ in the proper order (possibly with other tasks in between), and ends with t_n. We use this notion to introduce a *progression response* constraint that extends the DECLARE *response* as follows: given two tuples $U = \langle u_1, \ldots, u_k \rangle$ and $V = \langle v_1, \ldots, v_m \rangle$ of source and target task tuples, the progression response constraint states that, whenever a progression of the source U is observed, then a progression of the target V must be observed in the future; if this happens, the constraint goes back checking whether a new progression of the source is observed. This constraint can be used, e.g., to specify that whenever an order is finalized *and then* paid, the future course of execution must contain an order delivery *followed by* the emission of a receipt. The LTL$_f$ formalization of this constraint is overly complex. Given a tuple $T = \langle t_1, \ldots, t_n \rangle$, we call *progression formula* the LTL$_f$ formula $\Phi_{prog}^T = \Diamond(t_1 \land \Diamond(t_2 \land (\cdots \land \Diamond t_n)))$. With this notion at hand, in the general case, the *progression response from U to V* can be formally captured in LTL$_f$ as $\Box\left(\neg\Phi_{prog}^U \lor \Phi_{prog}^{\langle U,V \rangle}\right)$, where $\langle U, V \rangle$ is the tuple of tasks that appends V after U. For example, by using tasks fin, pay, del, rec to respectively denote the order finalization, its payment, its delivery, and the emission of a receipt, the aforementioned progression response is formalized in LTL$_f$ as:

$$\Box\left(\neg\Diamond(\mathsf{fin} \land \Diamond\mathsf{pay}) \lor \Diamond(\mathsf{fin} \land \Diamond(\mathsf{pay} \land \Diamond(\mathsf{del} \land \Diamond\mathsf{rec})))\right) \qquad \blacksquare$$

The definition of vacuous satisfaction for such a constraint, and the corresponding notion of constraint activation, cannot be easily hijacked from that of DECLARE patterns, nor it is easy to extract using human ingenuity. In contrast, our goal is to provide a semantical, general treatment of vacuity and activation, making it possible to seamlessly apply declarative process mining techniques also on new constraint patterns such as the progression response of Example 1, without requiring human intervention.

4   Activation of Constraints

This section discusses the core contribution of this paper, i.e., how to determine whether an execution trace *activates* a constraint or not. Our approach has three distinctive features. (1) It is *fully semantical*, in the sense that it detects when a trace is an interesting witness for a constraint, in a way that is completely independent from the specific syntactic form of the constraint. (2) It is *general*, in the sense that it does not focus on specific constraint languages such as DECLARE, but seamlessly work for all the temporal logics mentioned in Sect. 2, including MSO_f, LDL_f, regular expressions, and LTL_f. (3) It *seamlessly applies at run-time or a posteriori*, i.e., it can also be used to assess relevance of running, evolving traces.

Our approach consists of three steps. In the first step, we gain more details about the different states in which a constraint can be, going beyond the coarse-grained characterization of satisfied vs violated. In the second step, we leverage these additional details to semantically characterize the notion of "interesting witness", which in turn constitutes the basis for understanding whether a constraint is activated by a trace or not. In the last step, we mirror this approach into the automata-based characterization of the aforementioned logics, consequently obtaining a concrete technique to check whether a trace activates a constraint or not (this is subject of Sect. 5).

4.1   Activation States and Relevant Task Executions

To understand in details how a trace relates to a constraint, we leverage on the four truth values provided by RV-LTL [2], which considers LTL in the light of runtime verification. This approach has been already extensively adopted in the recent past for conformance checking and monitoring of LTL_f and LDL_f constraints [7,21,23]. RV-LTL brings two main advantages in the context of this paper. On the one hand, it makes our approach working also in a monitoring setting. On the other hand, it provides the basis to check whether an execution trace actively interacts with the constraint or not.

Definition 3 (RV-LTL truth values). *Given a constraint φ over Σ, and an execution trace τ over Σ^*, we say that:*

- *τ permanently satisfies φ, written $[\tau \models \varphi]_{RV} = ps$, if φ the constraint is satisfied by the current trace (i.e., $\tau \models \varphi$ in the standard logical sense), and will remain satisfied for every possible continuation of the trace: for every τ' over Σ^*, we have $\tau \cdot \tau' \models \varphi$;*
- *τ permanently violates φ, written $[\tau \models \varphi]_{RV} = pv$, if φ is violated by the current trace (i.e., $\tau \not\models \varphi$ in the standard logical sense), and will remain violated for every possible continuation of the trace: for every τ' over Σ^*, we have $\tau \cdot \tau' \not\models \varphi$;*

- τ temporarily satisfies φ, written $[\tau \models \varphi]_{RV} = \mathtt{ts}$, if φ is satisfied by the current trace (i.e., $\tau \models \varphi$), but there exists at least one continuation of the trace leading to violation: there exists τ' over Σ^* such that $\tau \cdot \tau' \not\models \varphi$;
- τ temporarily violates φ, written $[\tau \models \varphi]_{RV} = \mathtt{tv}$, if φ is violated by the current trace (i.e., $\tau \not\models \varphi$), but there exists at least one continuation of the trace leading to satisfaction: there exists τ' over Σ^* such that $\tau \cdot \tau' \models \varphi$.

We also say that τ complies with φ if $[\tau \models \varphi]_{RV} = \mathtt{ps}$ or $[\tau \models \varphi]_{RV} = \mathtt{ts}$.

Why do we care about such RV-LTL *truth values?* The intuition is that once a constraint becomes permanently satisfied ($\mathtt{ps}$) or permanently violated ($\mathtt{pv}$), then what happens next in the trace is irrelevant for the constraint, since such truth values are indeed unmodifiable. Temporary states instead are those for which interesting task executions may still happen.

The RV-LTL truth values can be used to identify, given an execution trace, which tasks are permitted (or forbidden) next.

Definition 4 (Forbidden/permitted task). *Let φ be a constraint over Σ, and τ an execution trace over Σ^*. We say that task $\mathtt{t}$ is* forbidden *by φ after τ, if executing $\mathtt{t}$ next leads to a permanent violation state: $[\tau \cdot \mathtt{t} \models \varphi]_{RV} = \mathtt{pv}$. If this is not the case, then $\mathtt{t}$ is said to be* permitted *by φ after τ.*

Notice that, by definition, if a constraint is permanently satisfied (respectively, violated) by a trace, then every task is permitted (respectively, forbidden). *Why do we care about permitted tasks?* Intuitively, considering the set of permitted tasks and how it evolves over time helps when the RV-LTL characterization alone is not informative. Specifically, whenever a task execution does not trigger any change in the RV-LTL truth value of a constraint, we can assess relevance by checking whether it causes at least a relevant change in the set of permitted tasks.

We now combine the notions of RV-LTL truth value and of permitted task so as to identify when a task execution is relevant for a constraint. This combination gives rise to the notion of activation state.

Definition 5 (Activation state). *An* activation state over Σ is a pair $\langle V, \Lambda \rangle$, *where V is one of the four truth values in RV-LTL, i.e., $V \in \{\mathtt{ps}, \mathtt{pv}, \mathtt{ts}, \mathtt{tv}\}$, and $\Lambda \subseteq \Sigma$ is a set of* permitted *tasks.*

Due to Definitions 3 and 4, not all activation states are meaningful. For example, we know that if the current RV-LTL value is $\mathtt{pv}$, then no task is permitted. We systematize this notion by identifying those activation states that are "legal".

Definition 6 (Legal activation state). *An activation state over Σ is* legal *if it is of one of the following forms:*

- $\langle \mathtt{ps}, \Sigma \rangle$ *(every task is permitted if the constraint is permanently satisfied);*
- $\langle \mathtt{pv}, \emptyset \rangle$ *(if the constraint is permanently violated, nothing is permitted);*
- $\langle \mathtt{ts}, \Lambda \rangle$*, with $\emptyset \subset \Lambda \subseteq \Sigma$ (if the constraint is temporarily satisfied, there must be at least one permitted task that triggers a change towards violation);*

– $\langle \mathtt{tv}, \Lambda \rangle$, with $\emptyset \subset \Lambda \subseteq \Sigma$ (if the constraint is temporarily violated, there must be at least one permitted task that triggers a change towards satisfaction).

We denote by $\mathbb{S}_\Sigma$ the set of possible legal activation states over Σ.

Definition 7 (Trace activation state). Let φ be a constraint over Σ, and τ an execution trace over Σ^*. The trace activation state of φ in τ, written $actState_\varphi(\tau)$, is the activation state $\langle V, \Lambda \rangle$, where: (1) $V = v$ iff $[\tau \models \varphi]_{RV} = v$ (cf. Definition 3); (2) for every $\mathtt{t} \in \Sigma$, we have $\mathtt{t} \in \Lambda$ iff $\mathtt{t}$ is permitted by φ after τ (cf. Definition 4). The initial activation state is the activation state computed for $\tau = \varepsilon$.

Trace activation states enjoy the following property.

Lemma 1. For every constraint φ over Σ and every trace τ over Σ^*, the trace activation state of φ in τ is legal, i.e., $actState_\varphi(\tau) \in \mathbb{S}_\Sigma$.

Proof. Immediate from the definitions of trace and legal activation states.   □

Example 2. Consider the DECLARE *response* constraint $\varphi_r = \Box(\mathtt{a} \to \Diamond \mathtt{b})$ over Σ. The initial activation state of φ_r is $\langle \mathtt{ts}, \Sigma \rangle$: all tasks are permitted, and φ_r is temporarily satisfied, since there are traces culminating in the violation of the constraint. Consider now the trace $\langle \mathtt{a} \rangle$: we get $actState_{\varphi_r}(\mathtt{a}) = \langle \mathtt{tv}, \Sigma \rangle$. In fact, all tasks are still permitted, but the constraint is temporarily violated because it requires the future presence of $\mathtt{b}$.   ■

The execution of a task induces a transition in the trace activation state. By considering the combination of the current and next trace activation states, we can understand whether the induced transition is relevant for the constraint or not. This is done by formalizing the intuitions discussed in Sect. 4.1.

Definition 8 (Relevant task execution). Let φ be a constraint over Σ, $\mathtt{t} \in \Sigma$ be a task, and τ an execution trace over Σ^*. Let $\langle V, \Lambda \rangle = actState_\varphi(\tau)$ and $\langle V', \Lambda' \rangle = actState_\varphi(\tau \cdot \mathtt{t})$ respectively be the trace activation states of φ in τ and the one obtained as the result of executing $\mathtt{t}$ after τ. We say that $\mathtt{t}$ is a relevant execution for φ after τ (or equivalently that $\mathtt{t}$ is a relevant execution for φ in $actState_\varphi(\tau)$) if $V \neq V'$ or $\Lambda \neq \Lambda'$.

4.2   Interesting Witnesses, Activation and Vacuity

Definition 8 provides the basis to assess whether a task execution is relevant to a constraint in a given execution context (characterized by the current activation state). We now lift this notion to a trace as a whole.

Definition 9 (Activation/Interesting witness). A constraint φ over Σ is activated by a trace τ over Σ^* if there exists $\mathtt{t} \in \Sigma$ s.t.: (1) $\tau = \tau_{pre}\, \mathtt{t}\, \tau_{suf}$; (2) $\mathtt{t}$ is a relevant execution for φ after τ_{pre} (cf. Definition 8). If so, we also say that τ is an interesting witness for φ.

Example 3. Consider the *response* constraint of Example 2, and the execution trace $\tau = \langle c, b, a, b, b, a, a, b \rangle$. By making trace activation states along τ explicit, we get:

$$\langle ts, \Sigma \rangle \; c \; \langle ts, \Sigma \rangle \; b \; \langle ts, \Sigma \rangle \; a \; \langle tv, \Sigma \rangle \; b \; \langle ts, \Sigma \rangle \; b \; \langle ts, \Sigma \rangle \; a \; \langle tv, \Sigma \rangle \; a \; \langle tv, \Sigma \rangle \; b \; \langle ts, \Sigma \rangle$$
$$\qquad \qquad \uparrow \qquad \qquad \uparrow \qquad \qquad \qquad \qquad \uparrow \qquad \qquad \qquad \qquad \uparrow$$

Arrows indicate the relevant task executions. In fact, the first relevant task execution is a, because it is the one that leads to switch the RV-LTL truth value of the constraint from temporarily satisfied to temporarily violated. The following task b is also relevant, because it triggers the opposite change. The second following b, instead, is irrelevant, because it keeps the activation state unchanged. A similar pattern can be recognized for the following two as: the first one is relevant, the second one is not. Notice that τ complies with φ_r. Now, consider the *not coexistence* constraint $\varphi_{nc} = \neg(\Diamond a \wedge \Diamond b)$, and the same execution trace τ as before. We obtain:

$$\langle ts, \Sigma \rangle \; c \; \langle ts, \Sigma \rangle \; b \langle ts, \Sigma \setminus \{a\} \rangle \; a \; \langle pv, \emptyset \rangle \; b \; \langle pv, \emptyset \rangle \; b \; \langle pv, \emptyset \rangle \; \dots \; \langle pv, \emptyset \rangle$$
$$\qquad \qquad \uparrow \qquad \qquad \qquad \qquad \uparrow$$

The constraint is in fact initially temporarily satisfied, and remains so until one between a or b is executed. This happens in the second position of τ, where the relevant execution of b introduces a restrictive change that does not affect the truth value of the constraint, but reduces the set of permitted tasks. The consequent execution of a is also relevant, because it causes a permanent violation of the constraint. A permanent violation corresponds to an irreversible activation state, and therefore independently on how the trace continues, all consequent task executions are irrelevant.   ∎

In Example 3, the same trace is an interesting witness for two constraints, but for a very different reason. In one case, the trace contains relevant task executions and satisfies the constraint, whereas in the second case the trace violates the constraint. For "reasonable" constraints, i.e., constraints that admit at least one satisfying trace, every trace that violates the constraint is an interesting witness, since it necessarily contains one execution causing the trace activation state to become $\langle pv, \emptyset \rangle$. In the case of satisfaction, two cases may arise: either the trace satisfies the constraint and is relevant, or the trace satisfies the constraint without ever activating it. We systematize this intuition, obtaining a *fully semantical characterization of vacuity* for temporal formulae over finite traces.

Definition 10 (Interesting/vacuous satisfaction). *Let φ be a constraint over Σ, and τ a trace over Σ^* that complies with φ (cf. Definition 3). If τ is an interesting witness for φ (cf. Definition 9), then τ interestingly satisfies φ, otherwise τ vacuously satisfies φ.*

Example 4. In Example 3, trace τ activates both the *response* (φ_r) and *not coexistence* (φ_{nc}) constraints. Now consider the execution trace $\tau_2 = \langle c, c, b, c, b \rangle$. Since τ_2 contains b, it is an interesting witness for φ_{nc}: when the first occurrence of b happens, the set of permitted tasks moves from the whole Σ to $\Sigma \setminus a$. Furthermore, τ_2 does not contain both a and b, and hence it complies with φ_{nc}. Consequently, we have that τ_2 interestingly satisfies φ_{nc}. As for the *response* constraint, since τ_2 does not contain occurrences of a, it does not activate the constraint. More specifically, τ_2 never changes the initial activation state of φ_r, which corresponds to $\langle \mathtt{ts}, \Sigma \rangle$. This also shows that τ_2 complies with φ_r and, in turn, that τ_2 vacuously satisfies φ_r. ∎

5 Checking Constraint Activation Using Automata

We now make the notion of activation operational, leveraging the automata-theoretic approach for constraints expressed in MSO_f or LDL_f (which, recall, are expressively equivalent and strictly subsume LTL_f). We consider in particular LDL_f, for which automata-based techniques have been extensively studied [7,9]. Towards our goal, we exploit a combination of the automata construction technique in [7] with the notion of *colored automata* [21]. Colored automata augment FSAs with state-labels that reflect the RV-LTL truth value of the corresponding formulae. We further extend such automata in two directions. On the one hand, each automaton state is also labeled with the set of permitted tasks, thus obtaining full information about the corresponding activation states; on the other hand, relevant executions are marked in the automaton by "coloring" their corresponding transitions. We consequently obtain the following type of automaton.

Definition 11 (Activation-Aware Automaton). *The* activation-aware *automaton $\mathcal{A}_\varphi^{act}$ of an LDL_f formula φ over Σ is a tuple $\langle \Sigma, S, s_0, \delta, F, \alpha, \rho \rangle$, where:*

- *$\langle \Sigma, S, s_0, \delta, F \rangle$ is the constraint automaton for φ (cf. Definition 2 and [7]);*
- *$\alpha : S \longrightarrow \mathbb{S}_\Sigma$ is the function that maps each state $s \in S$ to the corresponding activation state $\alpha(s) = \langle V, \Lambda \rangle$, where:*
  - *$V = \mathtt{ts}$ iff $s \in F$ and there exists state $s \in S$ s.t. $\delta^*(s, s')$ and $s' \notin F$;*
  - *$V = \mathtt{ps}$ iff $s \in F$ and for every state $s' \in S$ s.t. $\delta^*(s, s')$, we have $s' \in F$;*
  - *$V = \mathtt{tv}$ iff $s \notin F$ and there exists state $s' \in S$ s.t. $\delta^*(s, s')$ and $s' \in F$;*
  - *$V = \mathtt{pv}$ iff $s \notin F$ and for every state $s' \in S$ s.t. $\delta^*(s, s')$, we have $s' \notin F$;*
  - *Λ contains task $\mathtt{t} \in \Sigma$ iff there exists $s' \in S$ s.t. $s' = \delta(s, \mathtt{t})$ and $\alpha(s')$ has an RV-LTL truth value different from $\mathtt{pv}$.*
- *$\rho \subseteq Domain(\delta)$ is the set of transitions in δ that are relevant for φ, i.e.:*
  $\rho = \{\langle s, \mathtt{t} \rangle \mid \langle s, \mathtt{t} \rangle \in Domain(\delta) \text{ and } \mathtt{t} \text{ is a relevant execution for } \varphi \text{ in } \alpha(s)\}$

Notably, such an activation-aware automaton correctly reconstructs the notions of activation and relevance as defined in Sect. 4.2.

Theorem 1. *Let φ be an LDL_f formula over Σ, and $\mathcal{A}_\varphi^{act} = \langle \Sigma, S, s_0, \delta, F, \alpha, \rho \rangle$ the activation-aware automaton for φ. Let $\tau = \langle \mathtt{t}_1 \cdots \mathtt{t}_n \rangle$ be a non-empty, finite trace over Σ, and $s_0 \cdots s_n$ the sequence of states such that $\delta(s_{i-1}, \mathtt{t}_i) = s_i$ for $i \in \{1, \ldots, n\}$.[1] Then, the following holds: (1) $\mathrm{atr}_\varphi(\tau) = \alpha(s_0) \cdots \alpha(s_n)$; (2) for every $i \in \{1, \ldots, n\}$, $\langle s_{i-1}, \mathtt{t}_i \rangle \in \rho$ if and only if $\mathtt{t}_i$ is a relevant task execution for φ after $\langle \mathtt{t}_1, \ldots, \mathtt{t}_{i-1} \rangle$.*

---

[1] Recall that, since $\mathcal{A}_\varphi^{act}$ is not trimmed, then it can replay any trace from Σ^*.

Table 1. Extended constraint automata for some DECLARE patterns

Proof. From the correctness of the constraint automaton construction (cf. Definition 2 and [7]), we know that τ satisfies φ iff it is accepted by $\mathcal{A}_\varphi^{act}$ (i.e., iff $s_n \in F$). This corresponds to the notion of conformance in Definition 3. The proof of the first claim is then obtained by observing that all tests in Definition 11, which characterize the RV-LTL values and permitted tasks of the automaton states, perfectly mirror Definitions 3 and 4. In particular, notice that the labeling of states with RV-LTL values agrees with the construction of "local colored automata" in [21], proven to be correct in [7]. The second claim immediately follows from the first one, by observing that Definition 11 define ρ by directly employing the notion of relevance in a given activation state as defined in Definition 8.   □

We close this section by observing that Definition 11 can be directly implemented to build the activation-aware automaton of an LDL$_f$ formula φ. Notably, such extended information does not impact on the computational complexity of the automaton construction. This is done in three steps. (1) The constraint automaton $\mathcal{A}_\varphi$ for φ is built by applying the LDL$_f$2NFA procedure of [7], and then the standard determinization procedure for the obtained automaton (thus getting a DFA). (2) Function α is constructed in two iterations. In the first iteration, the RV-LTL truth value of each state in $\mathcal{A}_\varphi$ is computed, by iterating once through each state of the automaton, and checking whether it may reach a final state or not. This can be done in PTIME in the size of the automaton. The second iteration goes over each state of $\mathcal{A}_\varphi$, and calculates the permitted tasks by considering the RV-LTL value of the neighbor states. This can be done, again, in PTIME. (3) Function ρ is built in PTIME by considering all pairs of states in $\mathcal{A}_\varphi$, and by applying the explicit definition of relevant execution. Table 1 and Fig. 3 respectively list the activation-aware automata for some standard DECLARE

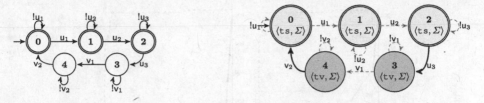

Fig. 3. Constraint automaton and activation-aware automaton for the *progression response* constraint (with three sources and two targets)

patterns, and the activation-aware automaton for a progression response. State colors reflect the RV-LTL truth value they are associated to. Dashed, gray transitions are irrelevant, whereas the black, solid ones are relevant in the sense of Definition 8. Interestingly, relevant transitions for the progression response are those that "close" a proper progression of the source or target tasks. This reflect human intuition, but is obtained automatically from our semantical approach.

6   Evaluation

In order to validate our approach, we have embedded it into a prototype software codified in Java for the discovery of constraints from an event log (based on the algorithm presented in [22]).[2] The approach has been run on two real-life event logs taken from the collection of the IEEE Task Force on Process Mining, i.e., the log used for the BPI challenge 2013[3] and a log pertaining to a road traffic fines management process[4]. The tests have been conducted on a machine equipped with an Intel Core processor i5-3320M, CPU at 2.60 GHz, quad-core, Ubuntu Linux 12.04 operating system. In our experiments, for the discovery task, we have considered four templates belonging to the repertoire of standard DECLARE, i.e., *existence, alt. precedence, co-existence,* and *neg. chain succession,* and three variants of the *progression response* with numbers of sources and targets respectively equal to 2 and 1, 2 and 2, and 3 and 2. In the remainder, we call these templates *prog. resp2:1, prog. resp2:2,* and *prog. resp3:2,* respectively.

Figure 4 shows the trends of the number of progression response constraints discovered from the BPI challenge 2013 log with respect to the number of traces (vacuously and interestingly) satisfying them. Figs. 4(a)–4(c) relate to progression response templates with an increasing number of parameters. On the abscissae of each plot lies the number of traces where the constraints are satisfied. The number of discovered constraints lies on the ordinates. The analysis of the results shows how crucial the strive for vacuity detection is, in order to avoid the business analyst to be overwhelmed by a huge number of uninteresting constraints. The discovery algorithm detected indeed that 66 *prog. resp2:1,* 139 *prog. resp2:2,* and

---

[2] The tool is available at https://github.com/cdc08x/MINERful/blob/master/ run-MINERful-vacuityCheck.sh.

[3] DOI: 10.4121/c2c3b154-ab26-4b31-a0e8-8f2350ddac11.

[4] DOI: 10.4121/uuid:270fd440-1057-4fb9-89a9-b699b47990f5.

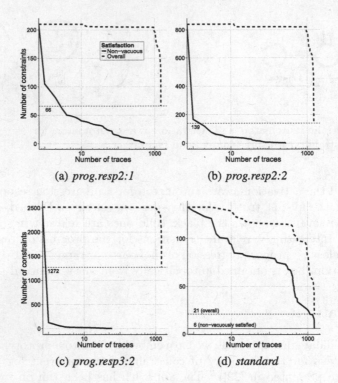

(a) *prog.resp2:1*   (b) *prog.resp2:2*

(c) *prog.resp3:2*   (d) *standard*

Fig. 4. Trends of the number of the discovered constraints with respect to the number of traces satisfying them

1,272 *prog.resp3:2* were vacuously satisfied in the entire log. The reason why the number of irrelevant returned constraints is higher for *prog.resp3:2* than for *prog.resp2:1* and *prog.resp2:2* is twofold. On the one hand, this is because the first one can only be activated when three different tasks occur sequentially, whereas the second and the third one only require two tasks to occur one after another to be activated. Another reason is that the implemented algorithm checks the validity in the event log of a set of candidate constraints obtained by instantiating each template with all the possible combinations of the tasks available in the log. Therefore, the higher number of parameters of *prog.resp3:2* leads to a higher number of candidate constraints. Figure 4(d) shows the same trend when using the standard DECLARE templates mentioned above for the discovery. Overall, the computation took 9.442 s, out of which 426 ms were spent to build the automata, and the remaining 9,016 ms to check the log.

We show that our technique is sound, by comparing the results obtained from the road traffic fines management log using our implemented prototype with the constraints discovered by the MINERful declarative miner [14] and the DECLARE Miner [22]. The comparison has been conducted using a minimum threshold of 100 % of interesting witnesses in the log. The discovered constraints are:

- Existence(Create Fine)
- Alt. precedence(Create Fine, Add penalty)
- Neg. chain succession(Create Fine, Add penalty)
- Alt. precedence(Create Fine, Appeal to Judge)
- Alt. precedence(Create Fine, Insert Date Appeal to Prefecture)
- Alt. precedence(Create Fine, Insert Fine Notification)
- Neg. chain succession(Create Fine, Insert Fine Notification)
- Alt. precedence(Create Fine, Notify Result Appeal to Offender)
- Neg. chain succession(Create Fine, Notify Result Appeal to Offender)
- Alt. precedence(Create Fine, Receive Result Appeal from Prefecture)
- Neg. chain succession(Create Fine, Receive Result Appeal from Prefecture)
- Alt. precedence(Create Fine, Send Appeal to Prefecture)
- Neg. chain succession(Create Fine, Send Appeal to Prefecture)
- Alt. precedence(Create Fine, Send Fine)
- Alt. precedence(Create Fine, Send for Credit Collection)
- Neg. chain succession(Create Fine, Send for Credit Collection)

Such constraints are a subset of the ones returned by MINERful using the same templates, since MINERful has no vacuity detection mechanism, and coincide with the ones returned by the DECLARE Miner. The derived constraints suggest that "Create fine" occurs in every trace and precedes many other activities. In addition, some activities cannot directly follow "Create fine". Also, we discovered that the following progression response constraints are interestingly satisfied by around 53 % of traces:

- Prog.resp2:1((Create Fine, Insert Fine Notification), Add penalty)
- Prog.resp2:1((Send Fine, Insert Fine Notification), Add penalty)
- Prog.resp2:1((Create Fine, Send Fine), Add penalty)
- Prog.resp2:1((Create Fine, Send Fine), Insert Fine Notification)
- Prog.resp2:2((Create Fine, Send Fine, Insert Fine Notification), Add penalty)

Although not always activated, the first two in the list are never violated. The last three are instead violated by approximately 26 % of the traces. Similar results cannot be obtained neither with MINERful that is not designed to discover non-standard DECLARE constraints nor with the DECLARE Miner that offers such facility, but only provides an ad-hoc mechanism for vacuity detection.

7   Conclusion

To the best of our knowledge, this paper presents the first semantical characterization of activation and relevance for declarative business constraints expressed with temporal logics over finite traces. As a side result, we also obtain a semantical notion of vacuous satisfaction for such logics. Our characterization comes with a concrete approach to monitor and check activation and relevance on running or complete traces, achieved by suitably extending the standard automata-theoretic approach for (finite trace) temporal logics. The carried experimental evaluation confirms the benefits of our approach, and paves the way towards a more extensive study on mining declarative constraints going (far) beyond the DECLARE patterns.

The presented solution generalizes the ad-hoc approaches previously proposed in the literature to tackle conformance checking and discovery of DECLARE constraints [14,20,22]. However, it is also compatible with human intuition, in the sense that it by and large agrees with such ad-hoc approaches when applied to the DECLARE patterns.

An interesting line of research is to extend our approach towards the possibility of "counting" activations. This becomes crucial when declarative process discovery is tuned so as to extract constraints that do not have full support in the log. In this case, "relevance heuristics" must be devised so as to rank candidate constraints, and these are typically based on various notions of activation counting [12]. However, providing a systematic theory of counting is far from trivial. Our intuition is that this theory can be developed only by making constraints data-aware, which in turn requires to adopt first-order variants of temporal logics for their formalization [10]. In fact, data-aware constraints can express *task correlation* [10,25], an essential feature towards counting.

References

1. van der Aalst, W., Pesic, M., Schonenberg, H.: Declarative workflows: balancing between flexibility and support. Comput. Sci. - R&D **23**, 99–113 (2009)
2. Bauer, A., Leucker, M., Schallhart, C.: Runtime verification for LTL and TLTL. ACM Trans. Softw. Eng. Methodol. **20**(4), 14 (2011)
3. Beer, I., Eisner, C.: Efficient detection of vacuity in temporal model checking. Formal Meth. Syst. Des. **18**(2), 141–163 (2001)
4. Burattin, A., Maggi, F.M., van der Aalst, W.M.P., Sperduti, A.: Techniques for a posteriori analysis of declarative processes. In: Proceedings of EDOC. IEEE (2012)
5. Chesani, F., Lamma, E., Mello, P., Montali, M., Riguzzi, F., Storari, S.: Exploiting inductive logic programming techniques for declarative process mining. In: Jensen, K., van der Alast, W.M.P. (eds.) Transactions on Petri Nets and Other Models of Concurrency II. LNCS, vol. 5460, pp. 278–295. Springer, Heidelberg (2009)
6. Damaggio, E., Deutsch, A., Hull, R., Vianu, V.: Automatic verification of data-centric business processes. In: Rinderle-Ma, S., Toumani, F., Wolf, K. (eds.) BPM 2011. LNCS, vol. 6896, pp. 3–16. Springer, Heidelberg (2011)
7. De Giacomo, G., De Masellis, R., Grasso, M., Maggi, F.M., Montali, M.: Monitoring business metaconstraints based on LTL and LDL for finite traces. In: Sadiq, S., Soffer, P., Völzer, H. (eds.) BPM 2014. LNCS, vol. 8659, pp. 1–17. Springer, Heidelberg (2014)
8. De Giacomo, G., De Masellis, R., Montali, M.: Reasoning on LTL on finite traces: insensitivity to infiniteness. In: Proceedings of AAAI (2014)
9. De Giacomo, G., Vardi, M.Y.: Linear temporal logic and linear dynamic logic on finite traces. In: Proceedings of IJCAI. AAAI (2013)
10. De Masellis, R., Maggi, F.M., Montali, M.: Monitoring data-aware business constraints with finite state automata. In: Proceedings of ICSSP. ACM (2014)
11. Di Ciccio, C., Maggi, F.M., Mendling, J.: Efficient discovery of target-branched declare constraints. Inf. Syst. **56**, 258–283 (2016)
12. Di Ciccio, C., Maggi, F.M., Montali, M., Mendling, J.: Ensuring model consistency in declarative process discovery. In: Motahari-Nezhad, H.R., Recker, J., Weidlich, M. (eds.) BPM 2015. LNCS, vol. 9253, pp. 144–159. Springer, Heidelberg (2015)
13. Di Ciccio, C., Mecella, M.: A two-step fast algorithm for the automated discovery of declarative workflows. In: Proceedings of CIDM. IEEE (2013)
14. Di Ciccio, C., Mecella, M.: On the discovery of declarative control flows for artful processes. ACM Trans. Manag. Inf. Syst. **5**(4), 24 (2015)
15. Giannakopoulou, D., Havelund, K.: Automata-based verification of temporal properties on running programs. In: Proceedings of ASE. IEEE (2001)

16. Knuplesch, D., Ly, L.T., Rinderle-Ma, S., Pfeifer, H., Dadam, P.: On enabling data-aware compliance checking of business process models. In: Parsons, J., Saeki, M., Shoval, P., Woo, C., Wand, Y. (eds.) ER 2010. LNCS, vol. 6412, pp. 332–346. Springer, Heidelberg (2010)

17. Kupferman, O., Vardi, M.Y.: Vacuity detection in temporal model checking. Int. J. Softw. Tools Technol. Transf. **4**, 224–233 (2003)

18. Lamma, E., Mello, P., Montali, M., Riguzzi, F., Storari, S.: Inducing declarative logic-based models from labeled traces. In: Alonso, G., Dadam, P., Rosemann, M. (eds.) BPM 2007. LNCS, vol. 4714, pp. 344–359. Springer, Heidelberg (2007)

19. de Leoni, M., Maggi, F.M., van der Aalst, W.M.P.: An alignment-based framework to check the conformance of declarative process models and to preprocess event-log data. Inf. Syst. **47**, 258–277 (2015)

20. Maggi, F.M., Bose, R.P.J.C., van der Aalst, W.M.P.: Efficient discovery of understandable declarative process models from event logs. In: Ralyté, J., Franch, X., Brinkkemper, S., Wrycza, S. (eds.) CAiSE 2012. LNCS, vol. 7328, pp. 270–285. Springer, Heidelberg (2012)

21. Maggi, F.M., Montali, M., Westergaard, M., van der Aalst, W.M.P.: Monitoring business constraints with linear temporal logic: an approach based on colored automata. In: Rinderle-Ma, S., Toumani, F., Wolf, K. (eds.) BPM 2011. LNCS, vol. 6896, pp. 132–147. Springer, Heidelberg (2011)

22. Maggi, F.M., Mooij, A.J., van der Aalst, W.M.P.: User-guided discovery of declarative process models. In: Proceedings of CIDM (2011)

23. Maggi, F.M., Westergaard, M., Montali, M., van der Aalst, W.M.P.: Runtime verification of LTL-based declarative process models. In: Khurshid, S., Sen, K. (eds.) RV 2011. LNCS, vol. 7186, pp. 131–146. Springer, Heidelberg (2012)

24. Montali, M.: Declarative open interaction models. In: Montali, M. (ed.) Specification and Verification of Declarative Open Interaction Models. LNBIP, vol. 56, pp. 11–45. Springer, Heidelberg (2010)

25. Montali, M., Maggi, F.M., Chesani, F., Mello, P., van der Aalst, W.M.P.: Monitoring business constraints with the event calculus. ACM Trans. Intell. Syst. Technol. **5**(1), 17 (2013)

26. Pesic, M., Schonenberg, H., van der Aalst, W.: DECLARE: full support for loosely-structured processes. In: Proceedings of EDOC. IEEE (2007)

27. Pichler, P., Weber, B., Zugal, S., Pinggera, J., Mendling, J., Reijers, H.A.: Imperative versus declarative process modeling languages: an empirical investigation. In: Daniel, F., Barkaoui, K., Dustdar, S. (eds.) BPM Workshops 2011, Part I. LNBIP, vol. 99, pp. 383–394. Springer, Heidelberg (2012)

28. Zugal, S., Pinggera, J., Weber, B.: The impact of testcases on the maintainability of declarative process models. In: Halpin, T., Nurcan, S., Krogstie, J., Soffer, P., Proper, E., Schmidt, R., Bider, I. (eds.) BPMDS 2011 and EMMSAD 2011. LNBIP, vol. 81, pp. 163–177. Springer, Heidelberg (2011)

Conformance Checking

In Log and Model We Trust?
A Generalized Conformance Checking Framework

Andreas Rogge-Solti[1]([✉]), Arik Senderovich[2], Matthias Weidlich[3],
Jan Mendling[1], and Avigdor Gal[2]

[1] Vienna University of Economics and Business, Vienna, Austria
{andreas.rogge-solti,jan.mendling}@wu.ac.at
[2] Technion–Israel Institute of Technology, Haifa, Israel
sariks@tx.technion.ac.il, avigal@ie.technion.ac.il
[3] Humboldt University zu Berlin, Berlin, Germany
matthias.weidlich@hu-berlin.de

Abstract. While models and event logs are readily available in modern organizations, their quality can seldom be trusted. Raw event recordings are often noisy, incomplete, and contain erroneous recordings. The quality of process models, both conceptual and data-driven, heavily depends on the inputs and parameters that shape these models, such as domain expertise of the modelers and the quality of execution data. The mentioned quality issues are specifically a challenge for conformance checking. Conformance checking is the process mining task that aims at coping with low model or log quality by comparing the model against the corresponding log, or vice versa. The prevalent assumption in the literature is that at least one of the two can be fully trusted. In this work, we propose a *generalized conformance checking* framework that caters for the common case, when one does neither fully trust the log nor the model. In our experiments we show that our proposed framework balances the trust in model and log as a generalization of state-of-the-art conformance checking techniques.

Keywords: Process mining · Conformance checking · Model repair · Log repair

1 Introduction

Business process management plays an important role in modern organizations that aim at improving the effectiveness and efficiency of their processes. To assist in reaching this goal, the research area of process mining offers multitude of techniques to analyze event logs that carry data from business processes. Such techniques can be classified into *process discovery* that sheds light into the behavior captured in event logs by searching for a model that best reflects the encountered behavior [3], *conformance checking* that highlights differences between a given

© Springer International Publishing Switzerland 2016
M. La Rosa et al. (Eds.): BPM 2016, LNCS 9850, pp. 179–196, 2016.
DOI: 10.1007/978-3-319-45348-4_11

process model and an event log [2,19], *model repair* that attempts to update a process model by adding behavior that is between model and log [6,9], and *anomaly detection* that identifies anomalies in event logs with respect to expected behavior to locate sources of errors in business processes [17].

Process mining investigates the interplay among reality (*system*), its reported observations (*event log*), and a corresponding *process model* [5]. While reality is typically unknown, we are left with the need to reconcile the event log and the process model, where evidence of a certain behavior may only be present in one but not in the other.

Current conformance checking techniques are not capable of defining levels of trust for model and log to cater for uncertainty. Therefore, in this paper we consider the problem of optimally reconciling an event log with a process model, given an input event log and a model (if such exist) and our degree of trust in each. We outline that various process mining tasks can actually be regarded as special cases of this generic problem formulation. Specifically, we define the problem of *generalized conformance checking* (GenCon). It goes beyond locating misalignments between a process model and an event log by providing explanations of misalignments and categorizing them as one of (a) anomalies in an event log, (b) modeling errors, and (c) unresolvable inconsistencies. This generalized conformance checking problem can be seen as the unification of conformance checking, model repair, and anomaly detection.

The contribution of this paper is threefold. First, we introduce a formalization of generalized conformance checking, i.e., the GenCon problem. It is cast as an optimization problem that incorporates distance measures for logs, for models, and for pairs of a log and a model. Second, to demonstrate our approach, we consider a specific instantiation of this problem, using process trees as a formalism to capture models along with distance measures based on (log or tree) edit operations and alignments between a log and a model. For this problem instance, we propose a divide-and-conquer approach that exploits heuristic search in the model space to transform a given model-log pair into their improved counterparts. Third, we provide a thorough evaluation of the approach based on three real-world datasets. Our experiments show that the GenCon problem setting has an empirical grounding, and outline its potential to complement existing process mining techniques.

The remainder of this paper is structured as follows. Section 2 motivates and describes the general problem setting, formalizes the GenCon problem, and relates it to common process mining tasks. In Sect. 3, we introduce the required notation for a particular instantiation of this problem, i.e., event logs, process trees, and related distance measures. Section 4 then presents a divide-and-conquer approach to address this particular problem instance. Section 5 empirically evaluates our approach in comparison with alternative techniques. Section 6 concludes the paper.

2   The Setting of Generalized Conformance Checking

Buijs et. al [5] define the truly executed business process as the *system* and analyze logs and models with respect to it. An event log may be noisy, with events that occurred in the system yet not recorded (missing events), and also events that did not occur in real-life (log errors) [18]. Discovering models from noisy event logs may result in under-fitting models with respect to the system, or alternatively models that allow impossible behavior. In symmetry, an external process model may allow excess behavior that cannot happen in the system, or it can under-represent behavior that actually occur [5].

Such quality issues gave rise to two process mining tasks, namely *model repair* and *log repair*. Model repair techniques consider the event log as the best evidence a system may produce, and adjust the model accordingly [9]. In contrast, log repair methods trust a given model from which the log deviates and repair the log [18]. Orthogonal to tasks that aim at changing either the log or the model, conformance checking compares models and logs to detect deviations between the two [1]. For example, the alignment technique proposed in [2] receives an event log and a process model, as well as costs of deviations in log and in model. Based on the costs, the alignment finds an optimal mapping between traces and possible paths through the model that minimizes the total deviation costs. An alignment shows where the model and the log perform unsynchronized moves. For each such move either the model or the log could be blamed and considered for repair.

Generalized conformance checking unites the three tasks of model repair, log repair, and conformance checking under a common roof. Specifically, it aims at altering both model and log such that control-flow discrepancies, which are measured via standard conformance checking, are reduced. The underlying assumption is that the log and the model are not 'wrong' for the same fragments of the system, and their joint repair is beneficial. Under this assumption, generalized conformance checking results in a pair of event log and model that are both better representatives of the originating system, and are tightly aligned together. The assumption on how beneficial it is to correct the model based on the log, or vice versa, stems from trust levels, which are associated with the initial model and log.

2.1   Formalization of the GenCon Problem

We now define generalized conformance checking by formalizing its primitives, and formulating an optimization problem that result in a joint of model and log. Let $\mathcal{L}$ be the universe of event logs, and let $\mathcal{M}$ be the universe of process models. We are given an event log $L \in \mathcal{L}$ and a process model $M \in \mathcal{M}$, as well as their corresponding trust levels $\tau_L, \tau_M \in [0, 1]$ (with 0 corresponding to zero trust, and 1 being full trust). A trust level is predefined for both model and log. Model trust can be related to the experience of the modeler, or the validity of a discovery algorithm that was used to extract the model. Log trust corresponds to the veracity of the data. For example, the data that we use for our experiments in Sect. 5 comes from real-time locating system (RTLS) sensors. These sensors typically come with a known error range, and measurement quality issues. The latter can be used to construct a prior of trust.

We distinguish the following distance functions:

○ the function $\delta_{\mathcal{L}^2} : \mathcal{L} \times \mathcal{L} \to [0, 1]$ measures the distance between two event logs.
○ the function $\delta_{\mathcal{M}^2} : \mathcal{M} \times \mathcal{M} \to [0, 1]$ measures the distance between two models.
○ the function $\delta_{\mathcal{LM}} : \mathcal{L} \times \mathcal{M} \to [0, 1]$ measures the distance (alignment) between an event log and a process model;

We are now ready to formulate the GenCon optimization problem.

Problem 1 (Generalized Conformance Checking (GenCon) Problem).
Given the input tuple $\langle L, M, \delta_{\mathcal{L}^2}, \delta_{\mathcal{M}^2}, \delta_{\mathcal{LM}}, \tau_L, \tau_M \rangle$ of initial log, initial model, the distance functions and the two trust levels, find a pair $(L^*, M^*) \in \mathcal{L} \times \mathcal{M}$ such that

$$(L^*, M^*) = \underset{(L', M') \in \mathcal{L} \times \mathcal{M}}{\arg\min} \ \langle \delta_{\mathcal{L}^2}(L, L'), \delta_{\mathcal{M}^2}(M, M'), \delta_{\mathcal{LM}}(L', M') \rangle.$$

$$\text{(subject to} : \delta_{\mathcal{L}^2}(L, L') \leq 1 - \tau_L, \text{ and } \delta_{\mathcal{M}^2}(M, M') \leq 1 - \tau_M)$$

(1)

We aim at a pair (L^*, M^*) that is in a trust-based proximity to the original pair of log and model, as well as aligned with each other. Note that the abstract framing of the problem, rather than binding the concepts to specific distance notions and specific process models, creates a framework that is general enough to cover several process mining problems. To operationalize generalized conformance checking, we require the definition of the functions $\delta_{\mathcal{L}^2}$, $\delta_{\mathcal{M}^2}$, and $\delta_{\mathcal{LM}}$, based on suitable data structures. We later provide one such example, introducing distance measures over logs and models.

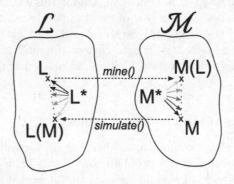

Fig. 1. Conceptual sketch of the problem setting.

Figure 1 illustrates the setting of generalized conformance checking. On the left, the universe of logs $\mathcal{L}$; on the right, the universe of models $\mathcal{M}$ is scetched. Given are the input log L and input model M. We can mine a model from L, to obtain a fitting $M(L)$; and simulate M to get a fitting log $L(M)$. Conceptually, the optimal log L^* can move closer to the image of the model, and also the optimal model M^* can be closer to the mined model. This depends on the respective trust levels, indicated by the grayscale of the arrows (darker for more trust, lighter for less). It is worth to highlight that the arrows labeled *mine()* and *simulate()* do not specify functions, as there can be countable infinite sets of simulated logs or mined models.

2.2 Related Work

Table 1 maps process mining tasks and respective techniques to the GenCon problem. In a nutshell, previous work on process discovery and conformance checking can be viewed as special cases of our approach. Regarding conformance checking, setting $\tau_L = 1$, and $0 < \tau_M < 1$, the GenCon problem corresponds to *model repair*. For $0 < \tau_L < 1$, and $\tau_M = 1$, we are facing *log repair*. When both trust levels are 1, GenCon corresponds to standard *conformance checking* (e.g., model-log alignment). Hence, GenCon extends existing approaches for process

Table 1. Some process mining tasks cast as problem instances.

Process mining task	Log trust	Model trust
Classical Process Discovery finds a model that best fits to the entire event log, e.g., the alpha algorithm [3]	$\pi_L = 1$	$\pi_M = 0$
Heuristic Process Discovery algorithms apply preprocessing to the event log by discarding infrequent patterns [10,23]	$0 < \pi_L < 1$	$\pi_M = 0$
Model Repair fixes deficient models due to e.g., a change in the system that is reflected in the log. For example [9]	$\pi_L = 1$	$0 < \pi_M < 1$
Conformance Checking. This task tries to find misalignments between event log and model. Example works include [2,19,20]	$\pi_L = 1$	$\pi_M = 1$
Log Repair. Given a trusted model and a noisy log, we modify the log until it conforms to the model [17,18,21]	$0 < \pi_L < 1$	$\pi_M = 1$
"Happy Path" Simulation is complementary to heuristic process discovery. It is a theoretical use case where we do not trust infrequent parts of the model [15].	$\pi_L = 0$	$0 < \pi_M < 1$
Process Simulation is complementary to process discovery, where we are given an untrustworthy empty log and a fully trustworthy model	$\pi_L = 0$	$\pi_M = 1$
Garbage In, Garbage Out. When both the model and the log are untrustworthy, the best log and model tuple that fits them is any pair of model and log that fits each other, including an empty log and an empty model	$\pi_L = 0$	$\pi_M = 0$
Generalized Conformance Checking is the focus of this paper. Instead of only detecting the misalignments, as in conformance checking, we also provide, where the model would best be adopted, and where the log would best be adopted for a better overall fit	$0 < \pi_L$	$0 < \pi_M$

discovery and conformance checking in that it not only finds the deviations between a log and a model, but it also identifies if deviations between the two stem from the log, or from the model.

Process discovery is yet another special case of our approach, where the model trust is set to be zero. Recently proposed process discovery algorithms optimally balance model quality measures such as fitness, precision, and generalization [1, 5]. Specifically, in [4] minimal values of those quality measures are used as inputs for the evolutionary tree miner (ETM), which finds a model that balances all quality measures. Similarly to our approach, a normative model can be assumed as an input to the ETM, and the resulting model is guaranteed to be in proximity to the normative model. However, since the ETM is an evolutionary approach, it has no termination guarantees [24], and real-life log discovery takes a long time to terminate, if at all [13]. Other discovery algorithms are based on log filtering to balance the quality measures. These algorithms neither return an aligned log, nor do they provide guarantees on the quality of the resulting model [10,13]. Therefore, generalized conformance checking extends process mining in that it does not impose $\tau_M = 0$, and returns both a process model and a repaired log.

3 Model

To give the necessary background for a specific instantiation of the GenCon problem, this section recalls notions of event logs, process trees, and related distance measures.

Event Logs. We adopt a common model of event logs that is grounded in sequences of activity labels that denote the activity executions as part of a single process instance (aka case). Let $\mathcal{A}$ be a universe of *activity labels* (*activities* for short). A *trace* $\sigma = \langle a_1, \ldots, a_n \rangle \in \mathcal{A}^*$ is a finite sequence of activities with a cardinality $|\sigma| = n$. The universe of traces is denoted by $\mathcal{T}$. An *event log* $L : \mathcal{T} \to \mathbb{N}$ is a multi-set of traces. A flattened representation $\bar{L}$ of a log L associates each trace with an identity such that $\bar{L} \in \mathcal{T}^*$ is a sequence of traces, and each trace $\sigma \in L$ is contained $L(\sigma)$ times in $\bar{L}$. The order of traces in $\bar{L}$ is arbitrary and $|\bar{L}|$ represents $\bar{L}$'s cardinality.

For example, an event log $L = \{\langle a, b, c \rangle^3, \langle b, c \rangle^1\}$ of three traces $\langle a, b, c \rangle$ and one trace $\langle b, c \rangle$ is flattened to $\bar{L} = \langle \langle a, b, c \rangle, \langle a, b, c \rangle, \langle a, b, c \rangle, \langle b, c \rangle \rangle$ with four distinct traces.

Process Trees. To represent process models, we adopt the notion of a process tree [12]. A process tree is a rooted tree, in which the leaf nodes are activities and all non-leaf nodes are control-flow operators. Common control-flow operators include sequences of activities ($\to$), exclusives choice ($\times$), concurrent execution ($\wedge$), and structured loops ($\circlearrowright$). Process trees are defined recursively, as follows. Let $\Psi = \{\to, \times, \wedge, \circlearrowright\}$ be a set of *operators* and $\tau \notin \mathcal{A}$ be the *silent activity*. Then, $a \in \mathcal{A} \cup \{\tau\}$ is a *process tree*; and $\psi(T_1, \ldots, T_n)$, $n > 0$, with $T_1, \ldots, T_n$ being process trees and $\psi \in \Psi$ being an operator is a *process tree* ($n > 1$ if $\psi = \circlearrowright$). The universe of process trees is denoted by $\mathcal{M}_T$.

The semantics of a process tree T is defined by a set of traces, which is also constructed recursively: A function $\iota : \mathcal{M}_T \rightarrow \wp(T)$ assigns a set of traces to a process tree. Trivially, $\iota(a) = \{\langle a \rangle\}$ for $a \in \mathcal{A}$ and $\iota(\tau) = \{\langle\rangle\}$. The interpretation of an operator $\psi \in \Psi$ is grounded in a specific language join function $\psi_l : \wp(T) \times \ldots \times \wp(T) \rightarrow \wp(T)$. Then, the semantics of a process tree $\psi(T_1, \ldots, T_n)$ is defined as $\iota(\psi(T_1, \ldots, T_n)) = \psi_l(\iota(T_1), \ldots, \iota(T_n))$. For instance, the trace set of the exclusive choice operator $\times_l(L_1, \ldots, L_n)$ is given by the union of the trace sets of its children $\bigcup_{1 \leq i \leq n} L_i$. See [12] for the formal execution semantics of all operators in Ψ.

A fitting tree model to the example log L above would be T:

Process tree T describes a sequence of a choice between a and a *silent activity* τ, followed by activity b, and then c.

Distance of Logs. We quantify the distance of event logs based on the weighted, normalized string edit distance of their traces. For two traces $\sigma, \sigma' \in \mathcal{A}^*$, we first define their normalized distance as $\delta_t(\sigma, \sigma') = \frac{d(\sigma, \sigma')}{\max(|\sigma|, |\sigma'|)}$ with $d(\sigma, \sigma')$ as the string edit distance, i.e., the minimal number of atomic activity operations (insert, delete, update) needed to transform one trace into another. Given two event logs in their flattened representation $\bar{L}, \bar{L}'$, let $\bar{L}^\epsilon = \bar{L} \cup \{\epsilon\}$ and $\bar{L}'^\epsilon = \bar{L}' \cup \{\epsilon\}$ with ϵ being the empty trace. Then, we define a mapping $\mu \subseteq \bar{L}^\epsilon \times \bar{L}'^\epsilon$, requiring that it is left-total, right-total, injective, and surjective when ignoring empty traces, i.e., for all $x \in \bar{L}$ there exists $y \in \bar{L}'^\epsilon$ such that $(x, y) \in \mu$; for all $y \in \bar{L}'$ there exists $x \in \bar{L}^\epsilon$ such that $(x, y) \in \mu$; for all $(x, x'), (y, y') \in (\mu \cap (\bar{L} \times \bar{L}))$ it holds that $x = y \Leftrightarrow x' = y'$.

The cost of such a mapping is defined as $\delta_m(\mu) = \sum_{(\sigma, \sigma') \in \mu} \delta_t(\sigma, \sigma')$. Then, the distance between two event logs L, L is defined based on the optimal mapping between their flattened representations $\bar{L}, \bar{L}'$ as follows:

$$\delta_{\mathcal{L}^2}(L, L') = \min_{\mu \subseteq \bar{L}^\epsilon \times \bar{L}'^\epsilon} \delta_m(\mu).$$

Distance of Models. To quantify the distance of process models, we exploit the fact that models are given as process trees and employ the tree edit distance [16]. Latter is, given two process trees T, T', the minimum cost sequence of node edit operations that transforms T into T'. Node edit operations are node deletion (connecting its children to its a parent maintaining the order); node insertion (between an existing node and a consecutive subsequence of its children); and node relabeling. Each of these node edit operations is assigned a cost.

When applying node edit operations to process trees, insertion and relabeling needs to respect the syntax of the model: inserted/relabeled nodes need to be activities if the node is a leaf; and control-flow operators otherwise. Further, we observe that the impact of node relabeling on the semantics of a process tree depends on the position of the relabeled node in the tree—intuitively, the higher the node is in the tree, the larger the effect on the language of the process tree would be. We define a relabeling cost for a node of a process tree as the number of leaf nodes of the subtree that is rooted in this node. Therefore, for a trivial process tree a with $a \in \mathcal{A} \cup \{\tau\}$, the node edit cost is $c(a) = 1$; for a process tree $\psi(T_1, \ldots, T_n)$, $n > 0$, the cost is $c(\psi(T_1, \ldots, T_n)) = \sum_{1 \leq i \leq n} c(T_i)$. For node insertion and deletion, we employ unit costs.

Using this cost model, we define a normalized distance for process trees. As a normalization factor, we take the sum of the tree sizes: the size $|a|$ of a trivial process tree is defined as $|a| = 1$; for a process tree $\psi(T_1, \ldots, T_n)$, the size is defined as $|\psi(T_1, \ldots, T_n)| = 1 + \sum_{1 \leq i \leq n} |T_i|$. Given two process trees T, T', we define the normalized distance as:

$$\delta_{\mathcal{M}^2}(T, T') = \frac{\delta_d(T, T')}{|T| + |T'|}, \text{ where } \delta_d(T, T') \text{ is the tree edit distance of } T \text{ and } T'.$$

Distance of Log and Model. As a distance measure between a log and a process model we consider different dimensions of the relation of logs and process models [5]: fitness (can a model show the behavior of a log?), precision (does a model allow for precisely the behavior of a log?), and generalization (does a model generalise over the behavior of a log?). We employ measures that are grounded in the notion of an *alignment* [2]. It is defined based on steps $(x, y) \in \mathcal{A}^\perp \times \mathcal{A}^\perp$, where $\mathcal{A}^\perp = \mathcal{A} \cup \{\perp\}$ is constructed from the universe of activities and a symbol $\perp \notin \mathcal{A}$. A step (x, y) is legal if $x \in \mathcal{A}$ or $y \in \mathcal{A}$ and is interpreted such that an alignment is said to 'move in both' traces $((x, y) \in \mathcal{A} \times \mathcal{A})$, 'move in first' $(y = \perp)$, or 'move in second' $(x = \perp)$. Given two traces σ, σ', an alignment is a sequence of legal steps, such that the projection on the first step component (modulo $\perp$) yields σ and the projection on the second step component (modulo $\perp$) yields σ'.

Each step is assigned a cost and a common cost model assigns unit cost if either $x = \perp$ or $y = \perp$; zero cost if $x = y$; and infinite cost if $x \neq y$. An alignment is a sequence of steps and the alignment cost is the sum of the costs of its steps. An alignment between two traces σ, σ' is optimal if it has the smallest possible cost.

Fitness is quantified by finding for each log trace $\sigma \in \text{dom}(L)$, a trace $\sigma' \in \iota(T)$ of model T for which the optimal alignment has minimal cost regarding all traces in $\iota(T)$. We denote this alignment cost as $\delta_a(\sigma, T)$. Costs per log trace are then aggregated, weighted by the trace frequency in the log, and normalized by the maximal possible cost:

$$\delta_{fit}(L, T) = \sum_{\sigma \in \text{dom}(L)} L(\sigma) \frac{\delta_a(\sigma, T)}{|\sigma| + \min_{\sigma' \in \iota(T)} |\sigma'|}.$$

To quantify precision, we apply the measure proposed by Buijs et. al [5]. It is grounded in the transition system underlying the model T. Given an alignment of a log L and model T, let $state(L, T)$ be all states of this transition system that are visited when replaying all alignment steps of all traces $\sigma \in dom(L)$ (ignoring steps with $\perp$ for the component of the model trace). Further, let $out(s)$ be the number of outgoing transitions of state $s \in state(L, T)$ and $taken(s, L)$ the number of these transitions that are taken during the replay of the log traces. Then, precision quantifies the additional allowed behavior of model T as

$$\delta_{pre}(L, T) = \frac{\displaystyle\sum_{s \in state(L,T)} (out(s) - taken(s, L))}{\displaystyle\sum_{s \in state(L,T)} out(s)}.$$

The replay of steps of an alignment is also used to quantify generalisation, directly on the model structure. Such a measure can be based on how often a node of a process tree is visited during replay [5]. Let $N(T)$ be the set of all nodes of a process tree T. Then, given L, let $visit(n, L)$ be the number of visits of node $n \in N(T)$ during replay of all alignment steps of all traces $\sigma \in dom(L)$. Generalisation is defined as:

$$\delta_{gen}(L, T) = \frac{1}{|T|} \sum_{n \in N(T)} \left(\sqrt{visit(n, L)} \right)^{-1}.$$

Taking into account the above dimensions, we define the distance between a log L and a model T as follows:

$$\delta_{\mathcal{LM}}(L, T) = \frac{1}{3} \left(\delta_{fit}(L, T) + \delta_{pre}(L, T) + \delta_{gen}(L, T) \right).$$

4 A Divide-and-Conquer Approach for the GenCon Problem

In this section, we propose a two-step divide-and-conquer approach for addressing Problem 1, when the problem is instantiated for the model introduced in the previous section. The main idea of this approach is to avoid the inherent complexity of the problem induced by the freedom to change the model or the log by sequentialization: first identifying changes in the model, before turning to changes applied to the log.

Our solution is outlined in Fig. 2. The first step consists of two parts, denoted by 1a) and 1b). In 1a), we lift the problem into the model space (i.e., process trees) by representing event logs as their discovered counterparts. Then, in 1b), we approximate T^* by applying a greedy heuristic search. In the second step, we use the approximation for T^* to transform L into the approximated L^* via an alignment-based technique. Specifically, we align the input log with the originating model, and make moves in L until an approximation of L^* is reached.

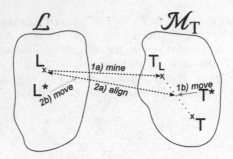

Fig. 2. Conceptual sketch of the heuristic proposed to solve the problem.

4.1   A Quest for T^*

Log Lifting. The formulation of Problem 1 involves a search for (L^*, T^*) in two spaces: space of logs and space of models. To ease the search for (L^*, T^*) we lift the log L to its model representation by applying process discovery. This enables us to search for T^* in the model space without considering the log space. This step is agnostic to the specific discovery technique used for obtaining T_L. Aiming at efficient discovery of fitting process trees, in this work, we rely on the Inductive Miner [12].

Further, we denote the resulting process tree as T_L, and approximate T^* by an interpolation between T and T_L (step 1b) in Fig. 2). To this end, we apply a greedy heuristic that is based on the behavioral similarity of intermediate models, T', and T'_L.

Heuristic Search. We quantify the tree-edit distance between T and T_L, which results in a cost-minimal set of tree-edit operations $\mathcal{E}$ with a a corresponding total tree-edit cost $C_{\mathcal{E}}$. Operating all edit operations in $\mathcal{E}$ to T transforms it into T_L. However, we do not always reach T_L, since we have a (possibly) non-zero trust in the originating model, and a (possibly) non-zero mistrust in the input log, L. Thus, the number of allowed edit operations depends on τ_L and τ_M.

We define the proportion of the total mistrust in both M and L, as

$$\gamma_{mistrust} = \min(1, 1 - \tau_M + 1 - \tau_L) = \min(1, 2 - \tau_M - \tau_L).$$

Consequently, we allow the algorithm to repair a total cost proportion of the model or the log that is at most $\gamma_{mistrust}$ of the entire cost $C_{\mathcal{E}}$.

However, since in this step, we only move from T towards T_L, we quantify the number of allowed repair operations on T. Denote the proportion of model repair operations out of the allowed $\gamma_{mistrust}$ by γ_{model}. The latter is defined as:

$$\gamma_{model} = \frac{1 - \tau_M}{2 - \tau_M - \tau_L} \gamma_{mistrust}.$$

Hence, the quest for T^* problem boils down to finding a set of edit operations $E \in 2^{\mathcal{E}}$ such that the total tree-edit cost of E is at most $\gamma_{model} C_{\mathcal{E}}$.

Our heuristic search contains the following steps. Initially, we consider $E = \emptyset$. We search for a tree-edit operation on T, $e \in \mathcal{E} \setminus E$ that maximizes the behavioral similarity of the resulting model T_E and T_L. The set must not violate the cost bound of $\gamma_{model} C_{\mathcal{E}}$. In practice, we consider several behavioral similarity functions, including behavioural profile-based similarity [11], and behavioural footprints [3].

If such e exists, we update E to be $E \cup \{e\}$ and consider further edit operations out of the remaining set, namely $\mathcal{E} \setminus E$. Selection of edit operations stops if there are no further candidates to enter E. In other words, one of the following condition holds: (1) the algorithm reached the mined model T_L, or (2) applying any repair operation in the set $\mathcal{E} \setminus E$ is beyond the allowed repair bound γ_{model}. Operating all tree-edit operations in E transforms T into a process tree T_E, which is our approximation of T^*.

4.2   Approximating L^*

Once an approximation for T^* is obtained, we turn to search for L^*. In this step, we assume that T^* is correct, and adjust the log to better fit T^*. Here, we rely on the alignment between log and model [2] that yields the minimal edit operations per trace. Specifically, the edit operations can be: (1) move in model (i.e., an activity in the model is missing an event counterpart in the trace), (2) move in log (i.e., the event has no corresponding part in the model), and (3) synchronous move (i.e., the event has a matching representation in the current state of the model).

Based on the assumption that model T^* is optimal, we assume that all remaining misalignments stem from the event log L. Analogously to the greedy heuristic for finding T^*, we greedily repair L towards a log that perfectly fits T^*. As before, we do not allow repairing the log beyond the trust level τ_L. To this end, we sort the misaligned candidates according to their frequency in the alignment result, and apply repair operations sequentially, until the distance of the current log L' to L is smaller than $(1-\tau_L)$. The result of this step is L^*. Finally, we return the approximated optimal pair (L^*, T^*).

The run-time complexity of the entire method is dominated by optimal alignments, which are in worst-case exponential in the length of the alignment [14]. The inductive miner that is used for discovery is polynomial in the number of activities [13], and tree-edit distance using a greedy heuristic has worst-case complexity of $O(|T|^2)$ with $|T|$ being the size of the larger tree [16]. Last, the heuristic search for T^* is also quadratic in the size of the tree, because the behavioral footprint needs to be read from each candidate tree (linear) when applying one operation, and there are maximum $|T|$ operations. The heuristic search for L^* is dominated by the alignment, as the remaining steps are sorting ($O(n \log n)$ where n is the number of activities in the model) and greedily picking the misalignment with the highest occurrence count (linear in the number of misalignments).[1]

---

[1] The approach has been implemented in the `GeneralizedConformance` plugin in ProM. A screencast demonstrating the usage of the plugin is provided here: http://andreas.solti.de/generalized-conformance-checking/.

Note that the problem is symmetric by nature, and we could also approach it the other way around. In that case, we would first align the input log L to the input model T, and move the log toward a better fit with respect to τ_L. This results in L^* first. Based on this, we would mine a representation of L^* in the model space, i.e., discover T_{L^*}. And last, we would move the input model toward the discovered model with respect to trust level τ_M, to derive T^*.

5   Evaluation

We evaluated the benefits of generalized conformance checking in general, and the proposed approach to address a specific instantiation of the GenCon problem, by answering the following questions:

Effect of Trust (EoT): How do the trust levels τ_L and τ_M affect the quality of the resulting log and model pair? We use this step to explore the range of possible solutions.

Model Repair Quality (MRQ): Can the proposed solution compete with state-of-the-art (specialized) model repair algorithms?

Log Repair Quality (LRQ): How does our technique affect the quality of models when we repair the log?

Below, we first outline our experimental setup and present the event logs and models used as inputs to the experiments. Then, we provide an overview of the main results.

5.1   Experiment Setup

To evaluate our approach we consider event logs and process trees as detailed in Sect. 3. For process tree discovery, we use the Inductive Miner [12]. For model search (see Sect. 4.1), we consider the following greedy heuristics:

○ Simple heuristic – prioritizes delete operations, then applies add operations, and lastly renames nodes.
○ Random heuristic – applies edit operations in random order.
○ Footprints heuristic – uses a similarity measure based on behavioral footprints (as in [3]) to select the next edit operation.
○ Behavioral profiles heuristic – uses a similarity measure based on behavioral profiles (as in [11]) to select the next edit operation.

Due to space limitation, we present the results for the heuristic that yielded the best results, namely the footprints heuristic. In the remainder of the experimental setup, we specify the controlled variables and the responses that we measure to answer the three aforementioned questions.

Controlled Variables. The experiments vary on the trust levels (τ_L, τ_M). First, for assessing the effect of trust (EoT) we vary for each event log and a corresponding model, both trust levels. For the model repair quality (MRQ) experiment, we fix the input trust in the log to $\tau_L = 1$, and vary the trust in the model τ_M between 0 and 1. Similarly, to evaluate the log repair quality (LRQ) we fix $\tau_M = 1$ and vary the trust in the log.

Response Variables. As our response in the EoT experiments we consider the three-way similarity (TWS) as follows. For each of the experiments we calculated the inverts of the three quality measures that we consider in Problem 1, namely $1 - \delta_{\mathcal{L}^2}(L^*, L)$, $1 - \delta_{\mathcal{LM}}(L^*, T^*)$ and $1 - \delta_{\mathcal{M}^2}(T, T^*)$, turning distances into similarities. The TWS response is the average of these similarity measures. For the MRQ and LRQ experiments we measured replay fitness, precision, and generalization as presented in Sect. 3.

5.2   Input Logs and Models

Event Logs. We use the following sample of event logs to evaluate the approach:

(a) Real-World Data of DayHospital. DayHospital is an outpatient clinic located in the United States. Approximately 250 patients arrive daily to receive treatment from 300 healthcare providers. Patients stay in the hospital for an average time of 4.4 h and typically go through vital signs collection performed by a Clinical Assistant (CA) and an Infusion performed by an infusion nurse (InfRN). The log contains 4, 281 traces with a total of 26, 286 events and 17 event classes (single month of data). Traces are sequences of roles that correspond to the aforementioned activity. The most frequent trace $\langle Arrival, CA, InfRN, End \rangle$ appears 943 times and represents 22 % of the event log.

(b) Student data from an e-Learning platform. The second data set corresponds to an event log from a university. The university records whenever students take course exams. Specifically, students need to select two specializations (SBWLs). Each of the SBWLs consists of five courses. Exams for these courses can be taken individually (Courses I to V) or for multiple of the five at once (Examination) [22]. This event log contains 2, 777 traces with a total of 10, 590 events, and 6 event types (one for each type of the courses). The most frequent trace is Course I, Course V, Examination with 499 occurrences that amount to almost 18 % of the traces.

(c) The Loan Application Process BPIC 2012. This log is taken from the BPI challenge of 2012 [8]. The log stems from a financial company handling a loan application process. We only consider the top level process, i.e., we apply a log filter to retain only the events whose labels start with "A-". This results in 13, 087 traces with a total of 60, 849 events, 10 distinct event types, and 15 trace variants. Further, most cases (43.7 %) are declined and emit the trace $\langle A{-}SUBMITTED, A{-}PARTLYSUBMITTED, A{-}DECLINED \rangle$.

Corresponding Models. In all our experiments, the input models, T, are constructed as follows. In order to avoid a fully aligned pair of model and log, we set the input model to be the "happy path" model, that is, the process tree capturing the sequence ($\rightarrow$) of the events in the log that corresponds to the

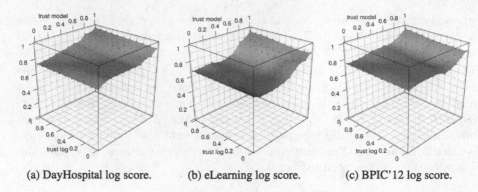

(a) DayHospital log score.   (b) eLearning log score.   (c) BPIC'12 log score.

Fig. 3. Depending on the different trust levels the weighted average score of log similarity, model similarity and log-model alignment is shown on the vertical axis. The controlled trust levels are presenting on the remaining two axes.

most frequent trace $\sigma^* = \arg\max_{\sigma \in L} L(\sigma)$. Note that these models correspond to business process models as captured by process analysts in their first modeling attempt.

5.3   Results

On the Effect of Trusts (EoT). Fig. 3 shows the three surfaces (one for each log) that represent the TWS as function of the two trust levels. Each point on the surface corresponds to two trust levels, and the resulting similarity average. We observe that the best scores are achieved by assigning full trust levels $\tau_L = \tau_M = 1$. Here, we start with small "happy path" models that represent the most frequent behavior in the log. With full trusts in model and log, we return the input log-model pair and therefore, $\delta_{\mathcal{L}^2}$ and $\delta_{\mathcal{M}^2}$ are zero. The distance between a "happy path" model and the event log is also not high (although fitness is not optimal, precision and generalization are high). Therefore, the result is a high TWS score. Note that there is a general deterioration as the trust in the log and the model decreases. This yields a new pair of model-log that may have any similarity between 0 and 1, especially because any change to a small model is a relatively costly.

An interesting result is depicted in Fig. 3b. One may expect a monotonic decline of the TWS when going from full trust levels and no-trust levels. However, in Fig. 3b we observe that when lowering trust levels in the model, we pass a valley in quality to later reach again better results. Therefore, one may have to move away from a current local optimal solution, through a set of sub-optimal solutions to reach an optimum. This provides evidence in favor of the trust-based setting that we propose in the GenCon problem, using trust levels to parameterize our search for optimal log/model matching.

On Model Repair Quality (MRQ). Fig. 4 presents the model repair quality evaluation with respect to replay fitness, precision, generalization and their

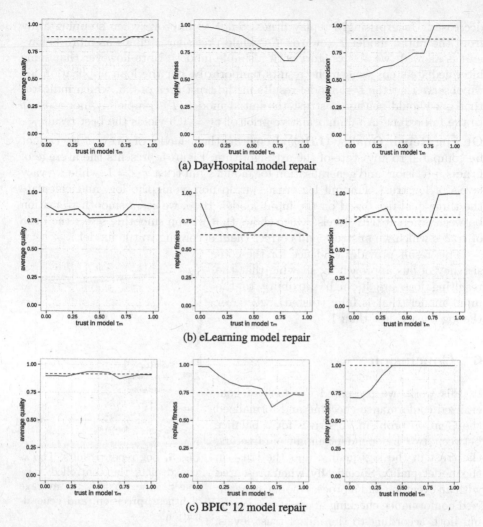

Fig. 4. Model repair with different trust levels. The graphs show the resulting averages for (left to right): (1) average of fitness, precision, generalization, (2) replay fitness, and (3) precision. Dashed lines show competing results based on applying [9].

average. Specifically, it shows the results for setting trust in the log $\tau_L = 1$ and controlling only trust in the model τ_M between 1 to 0. We compare the quality of our approach to a state-of-the-art model repair technique with default settings as presented in [9]. The average quality (leftmost chart for all logs) is the average of the three measures, namely fitness, precision, and generalization. We also present fitness (middle) and precision (right). The generalization remained steady at 1.0 for all models.

We see that the average quality is comparable to the model repair technique from [9], with a slight deterioration for the hospital log as the trust in model decreases. Unsurprisingly, replay fitness tends to improve when stepping away from the initial model T towards T_L, while precision declines as more behaviour is allowed (we always start with a simple model). Note however that some intermediate steps worsen the results temporarily. For the loan application log we observe that the best model results in the trust area of 0.5, which indicates that one should neither mistrust the initial model (T) completely, nor trust it to the full extent. An uninformative prior of $\tau_M = 0.5$ yields the best result.

On Log Repair Quality (LRQ). Repairing the behavior of an event log cannot be compared to any state-of-the-art algorithm. Figure 5 presents the average of fitness, precision, and generalisation for model's full trust $\tau_M = 1$, while we vary levels of log trust. For full log trust, we do not repair the log, and calculate the three qualities based on the input model. Here, we see a smooth transition between different trust levels, which shows that we can smoothly select the ratio of traces which we mistrust and correct them according to the model.

This result provides evidence for the consistency of our approach by showing that the resulting logs are in high proximity to the input model (that is fully trusted), whenever the log trust is less than 1.

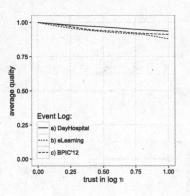

6   Conclusion

In this work, we presented the task of generalized conformance checking and formalized the GenCon problem. It strives for a balance between two independent input parameters: the trust in the log quality, and the trust in the model quality. Specifically, when presented with an event log and a process model, generalized conformance checking attempts at repairing both according to the initial trust levels, and returns an improved log-model pair.

Fig. 5. Log repair results. The x-axis depicts the controlled variable τ_L; the y-axis is the average of fitness, precision, and generalization.

We instantiated the GenCon problem with process trees, and with distance measures based on (log or tree) edit operations and alignments between a log and a process tree. Further, we proposed a technique to obtain the improved log-model pair by first lifting the log into the model space, and applying a greedy heuristic to search for the best model in the model space. The improved event log is obtained by aligning it to the resulting best model. An evaluation with real-world datasets demonstrates evidence in favor of the proposed trust-based approach. Further, generalized conformance checking is comparable to state-of-the-art model repair techniques in model quality measures.

One limitation of our approach is that we use a sub-optimal search for the best model. Although state-of-the-art techniques for optimal search are notorious for their steep run-time costs, recent ideas in the direction of automated planning demonstrate positive empirical results with respect to time complexity [7]. In future work, we aim at applying these techniques to the model search problem. Further, a key insight from our experiments is that process trees are overly conservative in their allowed behavior. A more flexible model representation might allow finer grained model repairs, even for high levels of model trust. Therefore, we aim at addressing the GenCon problem for other model spaces, e.g. workflow nets. Last, we plan to lift generalized conformance checking to operational process models, such as Generalized Stochastic Petri Nets.

Acknowledgments. This work was partially supported by the European Union's Seventh Framework Programme (FP7/2007-2013) grant 612052 (SERAMIS) and the German Research Foundation (DFG), grant WE 4891/1-1.

References

1. van der Aalst, W.M.P.: Process Mining: Discovery, Conformance Checking and Enhancement of Business Processes. Springer Science & Business Media, Berlin (2011)
2. van der Aalst, W.M.P., Adriansyah, A., van Dongen, B.F.: Replaying history on process models for conformance checking and performance analysis. WIREs. Data Min. Knowl. Discov. **2**, 182–192 (2012)
3. van der Aalst, W.M.P., Weijters, T., Maruster, L.: Workflow mining: discovering process models from event logs. IEEE Trans. Knowl. Data Eng. **16**(9), 1128–1142 (2004)
4. Buijs, J.C.A.M., van Dongen, B.F., van der Aalst, W.M.P.: A genetic algorithm for discovering process trees. In: Evolutionary Computation (CEC 2012), pp. 1–8. IEEE (2012)
5. Buijs, J.C.A.M., van Dongen, B.F., van der Aalst, W.M.P.: Quality dimensions in process discovery: the importance of fitness, precision, generalization and simplicity. Int. J. Coop. Inf. Syst. **23**(01), 1440001 (2014)
6. Buijs, J.C.A.M., La Rosa, M., Reijers, H.A., van Dongen, B.F., van der Aalst, W.M.P.: Improving business process models using observed behavior. In: Cudre-Mauroux, P., Ceravolo, P., Gašević, D. (eds.) SIMPDA 2012. LNBIP, vol. 162, pp. 44–59. Springer, Heidelberg (2013)
7. Domshlak, C., Mirkis, V.: Deterministic oversubscription planning as heuristic search: abstractions and reformulations. J. Artif. Intell. Res. (JAIR) **52**, 97–169 (2015)
8. van Dongen, B.: BPI Challenge 2012 (2012). http://dx.doi.org/10.4121/uuid: 3926db30-f712-4394-aebc-75976070e91f
9. Fahland, D., van der Aalst, W.M.P.: Model repair — aligning process models to reality. Inf. Syst. **47**, 220–243 (2015)
10. Günther, C.W., van der Aalst, W.M.P.: Fuzzy mining – adaptive process simplification based on multi-perspective metrics. In: Alonso, G., Dadam, P., Rosemann, M. (eds.) BPM 2007. LNCS, vol. 4714, pp. 328–343. Springer, Heidelberg (2007)
11. Kunze, M., Weidlich, M., Weske, M.: Behavioral similarity – a proper metric. In: Rinderle-Ma, S., Toumani, F., Wolf, K. (eds.) BPM 2011. LNCS, vol. 6896, pp. 166–181. Springer, Heidelberg (2011)
12. Leemans, S.J.J., Fahland, D., van der Aalst, W.M.P.: Discovering block-structured process models from event logs - a constructive approach. In: Colom, J.-M., Desel, J. (eds.) PETRI NETS 2013. LNCS, vol. 7927, pp. 311–329. Springer, Heidelberg (2013)

13. Leemans, S.J.J., Fahland, D., van der Aalst, W.M.P.: Discovering block-structured process models from event logs containing infrequent behaviour. In: Lohmann, N., Song, M., Wohed, P. (eds.) BPM 2013. LNBIP, vol. 171, pp. 66–78. Springer, Heidelberg (2013)
14. Mannhardt, F., de Leoni, M., Reijers, H.A., van der Aalst, W.M.P.: Balanced multi-perspective checking of process conformance. Computing **98**(4), 407–437 (2016)
15. Marquard, M., Shahzad, M., Slaats, T.: Web-based modelling and collaborative simulation of declarative processes. In: Motahari-Nezhad, H.R., Recker, J., Weidlich, M. (eds.) BPM 2015. LNCS, vol. 9253, pp. 209–225. Springer, Heidelberg (2015)
16. Pawlik, M., Augsten, N.: Tree edit distance: robust and memory-efficient. Inf. Syst. **56**, 157–173 (2016)
17. Rogge-Solti, A., Kasneci, G.: Temporal anomaly detection in business processes. In: Sadiq, S., Soffer, P., Völzer, H. (eds.) BPM 2014. LNCS, vol. 8659, pp. 234–249. Springer, Heidelberg (2014)
18. Rogge-Solti, A., Mans, R.S., van der Aalst, W.M.P., Weske, M.: Improving documentation by repairing event logs. In: Grabis, J., Kirikova, M., Zdravkovic, J., Stirna, J. (eds.) PoEM 2013. LNBIP, vol. 165, pp. 129–144. Springer, Heidelberg (2013)
19. Rozinat, A., van der Aalst, W.M.P.: Conformance checking of processes based on monitoring real behavior. Inf. Syst. **33**(1), 64–95 (2008)
20. Senderovich, A., Weidlich, M., Yedidsion, L., Gal, A., Mandelbaum, A., Kadish, S., Bunnell, C.A.: Conformance checking and performance improvement in scheduled processes: a queueing-network perspective. Inf. Syst. (2016, forthcoming)
21. Wang, J., Song, S., Lin, X., Zhu, X., Pei, J.: Cleaning structured event logs: a graph repair approach. In: Data Engineering (ICDE 2015), pp. 30–41. IEEE (2015)
22. Weber, I., Farshchi, M., Mendling, J., Schneider, J.: Mining processes with multi-instantiation. In: 30th Annual ACM Symposium on Applied Computing, pp. 1231–1237 (2015)
23. Weijters, A., van der Aalst, W.M.P., De Medeiros, A.K.A.: Process mining with the heuristics miner-algorithm. Technical report, 166. Technische Universiteit Eindhoven (2006)
24. Whitley, D.: An overview of evolutionary algorithms: practical issues and common pitfalls. Inf. Softw. Technol. **43**(14), 817–831 (2001)

A Recursive Paradigm for Aligning Observed Behavior of Large Structured Process Models

Farbod Taymouri[✉] and Josep Carmona

Universitat Politècnica de Catalunya, Barcelona, Spain
{taymouri,jcarmona}@cs.upc.edu

Abstract. The alignment of observed and modeled behavior is a crucial problem in process mining, since it opens the door for conformance checking and enhancement of process models. The state of the art techniques for the computation of alignments rely on a full exploration of the combination of the model state space and the observed behavior (an event log), which hampers their applicability for large instances. This paper presents a fresh view to the alignment problem: the computation of alignments is casted as the resolution of Integer Linear Programming models, where the user can decide the granularity of the alignment steps. Moreover, a novel recursive strategy is used to split the problem into small pieces, exponentially reducing the complexity of the ILP models to be solved. The contributions of this paper represent a promising alternative to fight the inherent complexity of computing alignments for large instances.

1 Introduction

As business processes become more complex and change frequently, companies and organizations use information systems to handle the processing and execution of their business transactions. These systems generate *event logs* which are the footprints left by process executions. *Process mining* is an emerging field that focuses on analyzing these event logs with the purpose of extracting, analyzing and enhancing evidence-based process models [13].

One of the current challenges for process mining techniques is the computation of an *alignment* of a process model with respect to observed behavior [1]. Intuitively, given a trace representing a real process execution, an optimal alignment provides the best trace the process model can provide to mimic the observed behavior. Then observed and model traces are rendered in a two-row matrix denoting the synchronous/asynchronous moves between individual activities of model and log, respectively. Alignments are extremely important in the context of process mining, since they open the door to evaluate the metrics that asses the quality of a process model to represent observed behavior: *fitness* and *generalization* [1] and precision [2]. Additionally, alignments are a necessary step to enhance the information provided in a process model [13].

Unfortunately, the current algorithmic support to compute alignments is defined as search for a minimal path on the product of the state space of the

© Springer International Publishing Switzerland 2016
M. La Rosa et al. (Eds.): BPM 2016, LNCS 9850, pp. 197–214, 2016.
DOI: 10.1007/978-3-319-45348-4_12

process model and the observed behavior, an object that is worst-case exponential with respect to the size of the model. This hampers the application of these techniques for medium/large instances. Hence, in the process mining field we are facing an interesting paradox: while the current research for process discovery is capable to be applied to large inputs (e.g., [7]), the obtained models often cannot be optimally aligned due to their size. Addressing this paradox is the main motivation of the work presented in this paper.

This paper presents a technique to compute a particular type of alignments, called *approximate alignments*. In an approximate alignment, the granularity of the moves is user-defined (from singletons like in the original definition of alignments, to non-unitary sets of activities), thus allowing for an abstract view, in terms of *step-sequences*, of the model capability of reproducing observed behavior. The implications of generalizing the concept of alignment to non-singleton steps are manifold: conformance checking techniques can be discretized to a desired (time) granularity, e.g., when the ordering of activities in a period is not important for the diagnosis. Also, other techniques like *model repair* [6] may be guided to only repair coarse-grain deviating model parts. Finally, in domains where a fine-grained ordering of activities is not needed approximate alignments can play an important role (e.g., health care [9]).

We assume the input models to be specified as Petri nets. This is without loss of generality, since there exist transformations from other notations to Petri nets. Given a Petri net and a trace representing the observed behavior, we use the *structural theory* of Petri nets [12] to find an approximate alignment. This means that at the end we solve *Integer Linear Programming* (ILP) models whose resolution provide a model firing sequence that mimics the observed behavior. Importantly, these ILP models are extended with a cost function that guarantees (under certain structural conditions on the process model) a global optimality criteria: the obtained firing sequence is mostly similar to the observed trace in terms of the number of firings of each transition. This optimality capability represents one clear difference with respect to current distributed approaches for conformance checking which focus on the decisional problem of checking fitness, but not to compute optimal alignments [10, 14].

Since ILP is NP-hard, casting the problem of computing approximate alignments as the resolution of ILP models is not sufficient for alleviating the complexity of the problem. As the complexity of ILP is dominated by the number of variables and constraints, we present a recursive framework to compute approximate alignments that transforms the initial ILP encoding into several smaller and bounded ILP encodings. This approach reduces drastically both the memory and the CPU time required for computing approximate alignments. Remarkably, it can be applied not only with the ILP encoding used in this paper, but also in combination with current techniques for computing alignments.

The organization of this paper is as follow, related work is presented in Sect. 2. Preliminaries will be presented in Sect. 3. The formalization of approximate alignments is described in Sect. 4. Section 5 describes the ILP encoding for computing approximate alignments, while Sect. 6 presents the recursive framework. Experiments, conclusions and future work are presented in Sects. 7 and 8 respectively.

2   Related Work

The seminal work in [1] proposed the notion of alignment, and developed a technique to compute optimal alignments for a particular class of process models. For each trace σ in the log, the approach consists on exploring the synchronous product of model's state space and σ. In the exploration, the shortest path is computed using the A^* algorithm, once costs for model and log moves are defined. The approach is implemented in ProM, and can be considered as the state-of-the-art technique for computing alignments. Several optimizations have been proposed to the basic approach: for instance, the use of ILP techniques on each visited state to prune the search space [1]. In contrast to the technique of this paper, these ILP techniques only alleviate the search space while in our case they form the basis to compute an alignment. Alignment techniques from [1] have been extended recently in [3] for the case of *process trees*, presenting techniques for the state space reduction with *stubborn sets*[1]. Also, high-level deviations are proposed in [1] in form of *deviation patterns* that, as the work in this paper, aim at providing less detailed diagnostics.

Decompositional techniques have been presented [10, 14] that instead of computing optimal alignments, they focus on the *decisional problem* of whereas a given trace fits or not a process model. The underlying idea is to split the model into a particular set of transition-bordered fragments which satisfy certain conditions, and local alignments can be computed for each one of the fragments, thus providing a upper bound on the cost of an alignment. In contrast, the technique presented in this paper does not split the model, hence enabling the computation of alignments at a global (model) level.

Finally, the work in [8, 9] focuses on dealing with partially ordered information, a common situation in contexts like health care. The notion of *partially ordered alignment* is introduced, and a variation of the techniques presented in [1] described.

3   Preliminaries

3.1   Petri Nets, Process Mining and Step Sequences

A Petri Net [11] is a 3-tuple $N = \langle P, T, \mathcal{F} \rangle$, where P is the set of places, T is the set of transitions, $P \cap T = \emptyset$, $\mathcal{F} : (P \times T) \cup (T \times P) \rightarrow \{0, 1\}$ is the flow relation. A marking is an assignment of non-negative integers to places. If k is assigned to place p by marking m (denoted $m(p) = k$), we say that p is marked with k tokens. Given a node $x \in P \cup T$, its pre-set and post-set (in graph adjacency terms) are denoted by $^\bullet x$ and $x^\bullet$ respectively. A transition t is *enabled* in a marking m when all places in $^\bullet t$ are marked. When a transition t is enabled, it can *fire* by removing a token from each place in $^\bullet t$ and putting a token to each place in $t^\bullet$. A marking m' is *reachable* from m if there is a sequence

---

[1] There is no fundamental difference between aligning Petri nets or process trees: only the latter allows for a slightly better memory representation.

of firings $t_1 t_2 \ldots t_n$ that transforms m into m', denoted by $m[t_1 t_2 \ldots t_n\rangle m'$. A sequence of transitions $t_1 t_2 \ldots t_n$ is a *feasible sequence* if it is firable from the initial marking m_0.

Definition 1 (Trace, Event Log, Parikh vector). *Given an alphabet of events* $T = \{t_1, \ldots, t_n\}$, *a trace is a word* $\sigma \in T^*$ *that represents a finite sequence of events. An* event log $L \in \mathcal{B}(T^*)$ *is a multiset of traces[2].* $|\sigma|_a$ *represents the number of occurrences of a in* σ. *The Parikh vector of a sequence of events* σ *is a function* $\widehat{\ } : T^* \to \mathbb{N}^n$ *defined as* $\widehat{\sigma} = (|\sigma|_{t_1}, \ldots, |\sigma|_{t_n})$. *For simplicity, we will also represent* $|\sigma|_{t_i}$ *as* $\widehat{\sigma}(t_i)$. *The support of a Parikh vector* $\widehat{\sigma}$, *denoted by* $supp(\widehat{\sigma})$ *is the set* $\{t_i | \widehat{\sigma}(t_i) > 0\}$. *Finally, given a multiset m,* $tr(m)$ *provides a trace* σ *such that* $supp(\widehat{\sigma}) = \{x | m(x) > 0\}$.

Workflow processes can be represented in a simple way by using Workflow Nets (WF-nets). A WF-net is a Petri net where there is a place *start* (denoting the initial state of the system) with no incoming arcs and a place *end* (denoting the final state of the system) with no outgoing arcs, and every other node is within a path between *start* and *end*. The transitions in a WF-net represent tasks. For the sake of simplicity, the techniques of this paper assume models are specified with WF-nets[3].

In this paper we are interested not only in sequential observations of a model, but also in *steps*. A step is a sequence of multisets of activities. The following definitions relate the classical semantics of models and its correspondence to step semantics. Likewise, we lift the traditional notion of *fitness* to this context.

Definition 2 (System Net, Full Firing Sequences). *A system net is a tuple* $SN = (N, m_{start}, m_{end})$, *where* N *is a WF-net and the two last elements define the initial and final marking of the net, respectively. The set* $\{\sigma \mid (N, m_{start})[\sigma\rangle(N, m_{end})\}$ *denotes all the full firing sequences of SN.*

Definition 3 (Full Model Step-Sequence). *A step-sequence* $\bar{\sigma}$ *is a sequence of multisets of transitions. Formally, given an alphabet* T: $\bar{\sigma} = V_1 V_2 \ldots V_n$, *with* $V_i \in \mathcal{B}(T)$. *Given a system net* $N = (\langle P, T, \mathcal{F} \rangle, m_{start}, m_{end})$, *a full step-sequence in* N *is a step-sequence* $V_1 V_2 \ldots V_n$ *such that there exists a full firing sequence* $\sigma_1 \sigma_2 \ldots \sigma_n$ *in* N *such that* $\widehat{\sigma}_i = V_i$ *for* $1 \le i \le n$.

The main metric in this paper to asses the adequacy of a model in describing a log is *fitness* [13], which is based on the reproducibility of a trace in a model:

Definition 4 (Fitting Trace). *A trace* $\sigma \in T^*$ *fits* $SN = (N, m_{start}, m_{end})$ *if* σ *coincides with a full firing sequence of SN, i.e.,*$(N, m_{start})[\sigma\rangle(N, m_{end})$.

Definition 5 (Step-Fitting Trace). *A trace* $\sigma_1 \sigma_2 \ldots \sigma_n \in T^*$ *step-fits* SN *if there exists full model step-sequence* $V_1 V_2 \ldots V_n$ *of SN such that* $V_i = \widehat{\sigma}_i$ *for* $1 \le i \le n$.

---

[2] $\mathcal{B}(A)$ denotes the set of all multisets of the set A.

[3] The theory of this paper can deal with models having *silent* transitions $\widehat{\ }$. For the sake of simplicity, we do not consider them in the formalization.

3.2 Petri Nets and Linear Algebra

Let $N = \langle P, T, \mathcal{F} \rangle$ be a Petri net with initial marking m_0. Given a feasible sequence $m_0 \xrightarrow{\sigma} m$, the number of tokens for a place p in m is equal to the tokens of p in m_0 plus the tokens added by the input transitions of p in σ minus the tokens removed by the output transitions of p in σ:

$$m(p) = m_0(p) + \sum_{t \in {}^\bullet p} |\sigma|_t \, \mathcal{F}(t, p) - \sum_{t \in p^\bullet} |\sigma|_t \, \mathcal{F}(p, t)$$

The marking equations for all the places in the net can be written in the following matrix form (see Fig. 1(c)): $m = m_0 + \mathbf{N} \cdot \widehat{\sigma}$, where $\mathbf{N} \in \mathbb{Z}^{P \times T}$ is the *incidence matrix* of the net: $\mathbf{N}(p, t) = \mathcal{F}(t, p) - \mathcal{F}(p, t)$. If a marking m is reachable from m_0, then there exists a sequence σ such that $m_0 \xrightarrow{\sigma} m$, and the following system of equations has at least the solution $X = \widehat{\sigma}$

$$m = m_0 + \mathbf{N} \cdot X \tag{1}$$

If (1) is infeasible, then m is not reachable from m_0. The inverse does not hold in general: there are markings satisfying (1) which are not reachable. Those markings (and the corresponding Parikh vectors) are said to be *spurious* [12]. Figure 1(a)-(c) presents an example of a net with spurious markings: the Parikh vector $\widehat{\sigma} = (2, 1, 0, 0, 1, 0)$ and the marking $m = (0, 0, 1, 1, 0)$ are a solution to the marking equation, as is shown in Fig. 1(c). However, m is not reachable by any feasible sequence. Figure 1(b) depicts the graph containing the reachable markings and the spurious markings (shadowed). The numbers inside the states

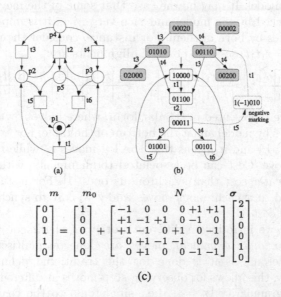

(c)

Fig. 1. (a) Petri net, (b) Potential reachability graph, (c) Marking equation.

represent the tokens at each place $(p_1, \ldots, p_5)$. This graph is called the *potential reachability graph*. The initial marking is represented by the state $(1, 0, 0, 0, 0)$. The marking $(0, 0, 1, 1, 0)$ is only reachable from the initial state by visiting a negative marking through the sequence $t_1 t_2 t_5 t_1$, as shown in Fig. 1(b). Therefore, equation (1) provides only a sufficient condition for reachability of a marking and replayability for a solution of (1).

For well-structured Petri nets classes equation (1) characterizes reachability. The largest class is *free-choice* [11], *live*, bounded and *reversible* nets. For this class, equation (1) together with a collection of sets of places (called *traps*) of the system completely characterizes reachability [4]. For the rest of cases, the problem of the spurious solutions can be palliated by the use of traps [5], or by the addition of some special places named *cutting implicit places* [12] to the original Petri net that remove spurious solutions from the original marking equation.

4   Approximate Alignment of Observed Behavior

As outlined above, the fitness dimension requires an *alignment* of trace and model, i.e., transitions or events of the trace need to be related to elements of the model and vice versa. Such an alignment reveals how the given trace can be replayed on the process model. The classical notation of

Fig. 2. Process model

aligning event log and process model was introduced by [1]. To achieve an alignment between process model and event log we need to relate *moves* in the trace to *moves* in the model. It may be the case that some of the moves in the trace can not be mimicked by the model and vice versa, i.e., it is impossible to have synchronous moves by both of them. For instance, consider the model in Fig. 2 and the trace $\sigma = t_1 t_1 t_4 t_2$; some possible alignments are:

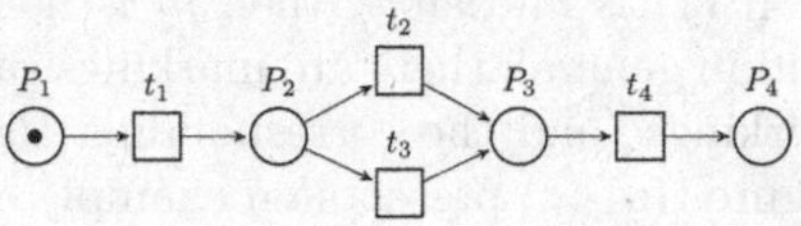

$$\gamma_1 = \frac{\begin{array}{|c|c|c|c|c|} t_1 & t_1 & \bot & t_4 & t_2 \\ \hline t_1 & \bot & t_2 & t_4 & \bot \end{array}}{} \quad \gamma_2 = \frac{\begin{array}{|c|c|c|c|c|} t_1 & t_1 & \bot & t_4 & t_2 \\ \hline \bot & t_1 & t_2 & t_4 & \bot \end{array}}{} \quad \gamma_3 = \frac{\begin{array}{|c|c|c|c|c|} t_1 & t_1 & t_4 & t_2 & \bot \\ \hline t_1 & \bot & \bot & t_2 & t_4 \end{array}}{} \quad \gamma_4 = \frac{\begin{array}{|c|c|c|c|c|} t_1 & t_1 & t_4 & t_2 & \bot \\ \hline \bot & t_1 & \bot & t_2 & t_4 \end{array}}{}$$

The moves are represented in tabular form, where moves by trace log are at the top and moves by model are at the bottom of the table. For example the first move in γ_2 is $(t_1, \bot)$ and it means that the log moves t_1 while the model does not make any move. Cost can be associated to alignments, with asynchronous moves having greater cost than synchronous ones [1]. For instance, if unitary costs are assigned to asynchronous moves and zero cost to synchronous moves, alignment γ_2 has cost 3.

In this paper we introduce a different notion of alignment. In our notion, denoted as *approximate alignment*, moves are done on multisets of activities (instead of singletons, as it is done for the traditional definition of alignment). Intuitively, this allows for observing step-moves at different granularities, from the finest granularity ($\eta = 1$, i.e., singletons) to the coarse granularity, ($\eta = |\sigma|$, i.e., the Parikh vector of the model's trace). To illustrate the notion of approximate alignment, consider again the process model in Fig. 2 and trace $\sigma = t_1 t_1 t_4 t_2$. Some possible approximate alignments with different level of granularities are:

$$\alpha_1 = \left|\frac{\{t_1,t_1,t_4,t_2\}}{\{t_2,t_1,t_4\}}\right| \quad \alpha_2 = \left|\frac{t_1}{t_1}\right|\frac{t_1}{\bot}\left|\frac{\{t_4,t_2\}}{\{t_4,t_2\}}\right| \quad \alpha_3 = \left|\frac{t_1}{\bot}\right|\frac{t_1}{t_1}\left|\frac{t_4}{\bot}\right|\frac{t_2}{t_2}\left|\frac{\bot}{t_4}\right|$$

For instance, approximate alignment α_2 computes a step-sequence $t_1\{t_4,t_2\}$, meaning that to reproduce σ, the model first fires t_1 and then the step $\{t_4, t_2\}$ is computed, i.e., the order of the firings of the transitions of this step is not specified.

Definition 6 (Approximate Alignment). *Let A_M and A_L be the set of transitions in the model and the log, respectively, and $\bot$ denote the empty multiset.*

- *(X, Y) is a synchronous move if $X \in \mathcal{B}(A_L)$, $Y \in \mathcal{B}(A_M)$ and $Y = X$*
- *(X, Y) is a move in log if $X \in \mathcal{B}(A_L)$ and $Y = \bot$.*
- *(X, Y) is a move in model if $X = \bot$ and $Y \in \mathcal{B}(A_M)$.*
- *(X, Y) is a approximate move if $X \in \mathcal{B}(A_L)$, $Y \in \mathcal{B}(A_M)$, $X \neq \bot$, $Y \neq \bot$, $X \neq Y$, and $X \cap Y \neq \bot$*
- *(X, Y) is an illegal move, otherwise.*

The set of all legal moves is denoted as A_{LM}. Given a trace σ, an approximate alignment is a sequence $\alpha \in A_{LM}^*$. The projection of the first element (ignoring $\bot$ and reordering the transitions in each move as the ordering in σ) results in the observed trace σ, and projecting the second element (ignoring $\bot$) results in a step-sequence.

Similar to the classical alignment, for a given trace different alignments can be defined with respect to the level of agreement with the trace. Hence, a distance function $\Psi : \mathcal{B}(A_L) \times \mathcal{B}(A_M) \to N$ must be defined for this goal. We propose the following implementation of the function: $\Psi(X, Y) = |X \Delta Y|$, although other possibilities could be considered[4]. For example $\Psi(\alpha_2) = \Psi(\{t_1\}, \{t_1\}) + \Psi(\{t_1\}, \bot) + \Psi(\{t_2, t_4\}, \{t_2, t_4\}) = 0 + 1 + 0 = 1$. For the other approximate alignments $\Psi(\alpha_1) = 0$ and $\Psi(\alpha_2) = 3$. Notice that the optimality (according to the distance function) of an approximate alignment depends on the granularity allowed.

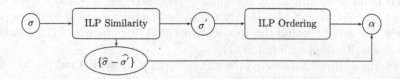

Fig. 3. Schematic of ILP approach for computing approximate alignments.

---

[4] $X \Delta Y = (X \setminus Y) \cup (Y \setminus X)$.

5   Structural Computation of Approximate Alignments

Given an observed trace σ, in this paper we will compute approximate alignments using the structural theory introduced in Sect. 3.2. The technique will perform the computation of approximate alignments in two pipelined phases, each phase considering the resolution of an Integer Linear Programming (ILP) model containing the marking equation of the net corresponding to the model. The overall approach is described in Fig. 3. In the first ILP model (ILP Similarity) a solution (the Parikh vector of a full firing sequence of the model) is computed that maximizes the similarity to $\widehat{\sigma}$. Elements in σ that cannot be replayed by the model in the Parikh vector found are removed for the next ILP, resulting in the projected sequence σ'. These elements are identified as *moves on log* cf. Definition 6, and will be inserted in the approximate alignment computed α. In the second ILP model (ILP Ordering), it is guaranteed that a feasible solution containing at least the elements in σ' exists. The goal of this second ILP model is to compute the approximate alignment given a user-defined granularity: it can be computed from the finest level ($\eta = 1$) to the most coarse level ($\eta = |\sigma|$).

5.1   ILP for Similarity: Seeking for an Optimal Parikh Vector

This stage will be centered on the marking equation of the input Petri net. Let $J = T \cap \mathrm{supp}(\widehat{\sigma})$, the following ILP model computes a solution that is as similar as possible with respect to the firing of the activities appearing in the observed trace:

$$\text{Minimize} \sum_{t \in J} X^s[t] - \sum_{t \in J} X[t], \text{ Subject to:}$$

$$m_{end} = m_{start} + \mathbf{N}.X \tag{2}$$

$$\forall t \in J: \quad \widehat{\sigma}[t] = X[t] + X^s[t]$$

$$X, X^s \geq \mathbf{0}$$

Hence, the model searches for a vector X that both is a solution to the marking equation and maximizes the similarity with respect to $\widehat{\sigma}$. Notice that the ILP problem has an additional set of variables $X^s \in \mathbb{N}^{|J|}$, and represents the slack variables needed when a solution for a given activity cannot equal the observed number of firings. By minimizing the variables X^s, and the variables X^s (negated), solutions to (2) clearly try to both assign zeros as much as possible to the X^s variables, and the opposite for the X variables in J (i.e., variables denoting activities appearing in σ).

Given an optimal solution X to (2), activities a_i such that $X[i] < \widehat{\sigma}(a_i)$ are removed from σ; in the simplest case, when $X[i] = 0$ and $\widehat{\sigma}(a_i) > 0$, every occurrence of a_i in σ will not appear in σ'. However, if $X[i] > 0$ and $X[i] < \widehat{\sigma}(a_i)$, all possibilities of removal should be checked when computing σ'^5.

---

[5] In our experiments, only the simplest cases were encountered.

5.2   ILP for Ordering: Computing an Aligned Step-Sequence

The schematic view of the ILP model for the ordering step is shown in Fig. 4. Given a granularity η, $\lambda = \lceil \frac{|\sigma'|}{\eta} \rceil$ steps are required for a step-sequence in the model that is aligned with σ'. Accordingly, the ILP model has variables $X_1 \ldots X_\lambda$ with $X_i \in \mathbb{N}^{|T|}$ to encode the λ steps of the marking equation, and variables $X_1^s \ldots X_\lambda^s$, with $X_i^s \in \mathbb{N}^{|J|}$ and $J = T \cap \operatorname{supp}(\sigma')$, to encode situations where the model cannot reproduce observed behavior in some of these steps. We now describe the ILP model in detail.

Objective Function. The goal is to compute a step-sequence which resembles as much as possible to σ'. Therefore transitions in $\operatorname{supp}(\sigma')$ have cost 0 in each step X_i whilst the rest have cost 1. Also, the slack variables X_i^s have cost 1.

Marking Equation Constraints. The computation of a model's step-sequence $m_0 \xrightarrow{X_1} m_1 \xrightarrow{X_2} m_2 \ldots m_{\lambda-1} \xrightarrow{X_\lambda} m_{end}$ is enforced by using a chain of λ connected marking equations.

Parikh Equality Constraints. To enforce the similarity of the Parikh vectors $X_1 \ldots X_\lambda$ with respect to $\widehat{\sigma'}$, this constraints require the sum of the assignments to variables X_i and X_i^s for every variable $t \in J$ should be greater or equal to $\widehat{\sigma'}(t)$. Given the cost function, solutions that minimize the assignment for the X_i^s variables are preferred.

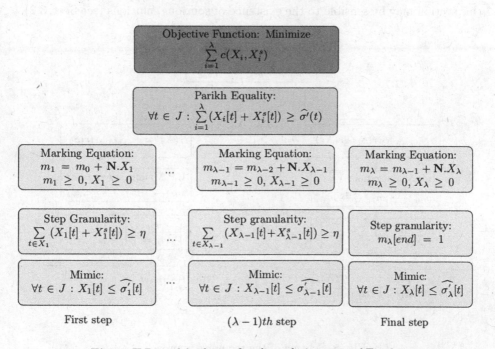

Fig. 4. ILP model schema for the ordering step of Fig. 3.

Step Granularity Constraints. Require that the sum of model's steps X_i and the slack variables X_i^s is lower bounded by the given granularity η. Since the cost of variables X_i is lesser than the cost of X_i^s variables, the solutions will tend to assign as much as possible to X_i. Last step X_λ is not constrained in order to ensure the feasibility of reaching the final marking m_{end}.

Mimic Constraints. The input sequence σ' is split into λ consecutive chunks, i.e., $\sigma' = \sigma'_1\sigma'_2\ldots\sigma'_\lambda$, with $|\sigma'_i| = \eta$, for $1 \leq i < \lambda$. This set of constraints require at each step that the multiset of observed transitions (X_i) must only happen if it has happened in the corresponding chunk σ'_i. It is worth to note that events with multiple occurrences are distinguished based on their positions.

Once the two steps of Fig. 3 are performed, the gathered information is sufficient to obtain an approximate alignment: on the one hand, the removed activities from the ILP model (2) are inserted as "moves in the log". On the other hand, the solution obtained from the ILP model of Fig. 4 provide the steps that can be appended to construct the final approximate alignment.

A Note on Completeness and Optimality. The global optimality guarantee provided in the approach of this paper is with respect to the similarity between the Parikh vectors of the computed and the observed trace. Informally, the technique searches for traces as similar as possible (c.f., ILP models (2)) and then computes the ordering (with respect to a given granularity). However, as the reader may have realized, by relying on the marking equation the approach presented in this section may be sensible to the existence of spurious solutions (see Sect. 3.2).

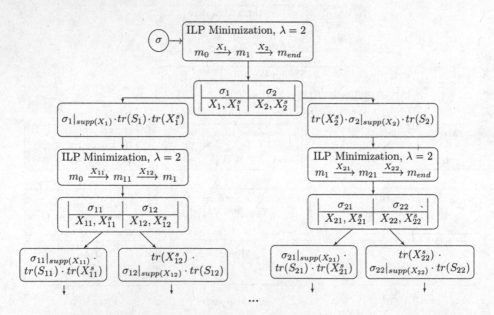

Fig. 5. Schema of the recursive approach.

This may have negative consequences since the marking computed may not be possible in the model, and/or the Parikh vectors may not correspond to a real model trace. For the former problem (marking reachability), in case of free-choice, live, bounded and reversible nets, this problem does not exists since the structural theory completely characterizes reachability [12]. For non-structured process models (e.g., spaghetti-like) or when the Parikh vector is spurious, the technique of this paper may still be applied, if the results obtained are verified a-posteriori by replaying the step-sequence computed. In Sect. 7 an evaluation over both well-structured and unstructured process models is reported, showing the potentials of the technique in practice for both situations.

6   The Recursive Algorithm

Section 5 shows how to compute approximate alignments using the structural theory of Petri nets through the marking equation. The complexity of the approach, which is NP-hard, can be measured by the size of the ILP formulation in the minimization step, in terms of number of variables: given a trace σ and a model with $|T|$ transitions and $|P|$ places, $(|T| + |J| + |P|) \cdot (|\sigma|/\eta)$ variables are needed, where η is the desired granularity and $J = T \cap \mathrm{supp}(\widehat{\sigma})$. This poses a problem for handling medium/large process models.

In this section we will present a way to fight the aforementioned complexity, by using a recursive strategy that will alleviate significantly the approach presented in the previous section. The first step will be done as before, so we will focus on the second step (Ordering), and will assume that σ is the input sequence for this step. The overall idea is, instead of solving a large ILP instance, solve several small ILP instances that combined represent a feasible solution of the initial problem. Figure 5 illustrates the recursive approach: given a trace σ, on the top level of the recursion a couple of Parikh vectors X_1, X_2 are computed such that $m_0 \xrightarrow{X_1} m_1 \xrightarrow{X_2} m_{end}$, by using the Ordering ILP strategy of the previous section with granularity $|\sigma|/2$, with $\sigma = \sigma_1\sigma_2$. Some crucial observations can now be made:

1. X_1 and X_2 represent the optimal Parikh vectors for the model to mimic the observed behavior *in two steps*.
2. Elements from X_1 precede elements from X_2, but no knowledge on the orderings within X_1 or within X_2 is known yet.
3. Marking m_1 is the intermediate marking, being the final marking of X_1, and the initial marking of X_2.
4. Elements in $\mathrm{supp}(X_1) \cap \mathrm{supp}(\widehat{\sigma_1})$ denote those elements in σ_1 that can be reproduced by the model if one step of size $|\sigma|/2$ was considered.
5. Elements in $S_1 = X_1 \setminus \mathrm{supp}(\sigma_1|_{\mathrm{supp}(X_1)})$, denote the additional transitions in the net that are inserted to compute the final ordering. They will denote skipped "model moves" in the final alignment.
6. Elements in $\mathrm{supp}(X_1^s)$ denote those elements in σ_2 that the model needs to fire in the first part (but they were observed in the second part). They will denote asynchronous "model moves" in the final alignment.
7. 4, 5, and 6 hold symmetrically for X_2, X_2^s and σ_2.

The combination of these observations implies the independence between the computation of an approximate alignment for $\sigma_1|_{\text{supp}(X_1)} \cdot \text{tr}(S_1) \cdot \text{tr}(X_1^s)$ and $\text{tr}(X_2^s) \cdot \sigma_2|_{\text{supp}(X_2)} \cdot \text{tr}(S_2)$, if the intermediate marking m_1 is used as connecting marking between these two independent problems[6]. This gives rise to the recursion step: each one of these two problems can be recursively divided into two intermediate sequences, e.g., $m_0 \overset{X_{11}}{\to} m_{11} \overset{X_{12}}{\to} m_1$, and $m_1 \overset{X_{21}}{\to} m_{21} \overset{X_{22}}{\to} m_{end}$, with $X_1 = X_{11} \cup X_{12}$ and $X_2 = X_{21} \cup X_{22}$. By consecutive recursive calls, more precedence relations are computed, thus progressing towards finding the full step sequence of the model.

Now the complexity analysis of the recursive approach can be measured: at the top level of the recursion one ILP problem consisting of $(|T| + |J_1|) \cdot 2 + |P|$ variables is solved, with $J_1 = T \cap \text{supp}(\widehat{\sigma})$. In the second level, two ILP problems consisting of at most $(|T| + |J_2|) \cdot 2 + |P|$ variables, with $J_2 = \max(T \cap (\text{supp}(\widehat{\sigma_1}) \cup X_1 \cup X_1^s), T \cap (\text{supp}(\widehat{\sigma_2})) \cup X_2 \cup X_2^s)$. Hence as long as the recursion goes deeper, the ILP models have less variables. The depth of the recursion is bounded by $\log(|\sigma|)$, but in practice we limit the depth in order to solve instances that are small enough.

Let us show how the method works step by step for an example. Consider the model in Fig. 6 and a given non-fitting trace like $\sigma = t_5 t_1 t_3 t_4 t_4 t_3 t_4 t_3$. On this trace ILP model (2) will not remove any activity from σ. We then concentrate on the recursive ordering

Fig. 6. Example with loop

step. First at the top level of Fig. 5 the solutions X_1, X_1^s, X_2 and X_2^s will be computed, with $\lambda = 2$.

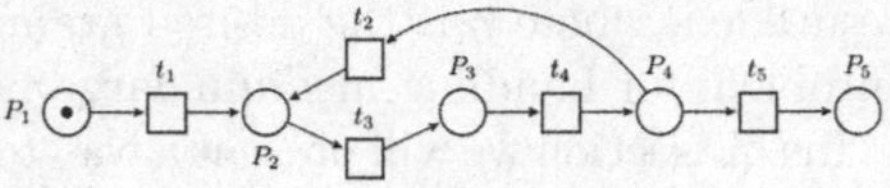

$$\alpha_0 = \begin{array}{c|c|c} & \sigma_1 = t_5 t_1 t_3 t_4 & \sigma_2 = t_4 t_3 t_4 t_3 \\ \hline X_1 \cup X_1^s = \{t_1, t_3, t_4, t_2\} & X_2 \cup X_2^s = \{t_3, t_3, t_4, t_5^s, t_2, t_4\} \end{array}$$

Notice that when seeking for an optimal ordering, t_5 does not appears in X_1 since then its firing will empty the net, and hence it appears in X_2^s (to guarantee reaching the final marking). The intermediate marking computed is $m_1 = \{P_2\}$. Accordingly, $\sigma_1|_{\text{supp}(X_1)} \cdot \text{tr}(S_1) \cdot \text{tr}(X_1^s) = t_1 t_3 t_4 \cdot t_2 \cdot \emptyset$, and $\sigma_2|_{\text{supp}(X_2)} \cdot \text{tr}(X_2^s) = t_5 \cdot t_4 t_3 t_4 t_3 \cdot t_2$. Let us assume the recursion stops with subtraces of length less than 5, and then the ILP approach (with granularity 1 in this example) is applied. The left part will then stop the recursion, providing the optimal approximate alignment:

$$\begin{array}{|c|c|c|c|c|} \hline t_5 & t_1 & t_3 & t_4 & \bot \\ \hline \bot & t_1 & t_3 & t_4 & t_2 \\ \hline \end{array}$$

---

[6] Note the different way the traces are obtained, e.g., in the right part $\text{tr}(X_2^s)$ is the leftmost part since it denotes log moves that the model can produce on the left step.

For the subtrace on the right part, i.e., $t_5t_4t_3t_4t_3t_2$ the recursion continues. Applying again the ILP with two steps, with $m_1 = \{P_2\}$ as initial marking, results in the following optimal approximate alignment:

$$\alpha_1 = \begin{array}{|c|c|} \sigma_{21} = t_5t_4t_3 & \sigma_{22} = t_4t_3t_2 \\ \hline X_{21} \cup X_{21}^s = \{t_3, t_4, t_2\} & X_{22} \cup X_{22}^s = \{t_4, t_3, t_5^s\} \end{array}$$

With $m_1 = \{P_2\}$ as intermediate marking. Whenever the recursion goes deeper, transitions are re-arranged accordingly in the solutions computed (e.g., t_2 moves to the left part of α_1, whilst t_5 moves to the right part). The new two subtraces induced from α_1 are $t_4t_3t_2$ and $t_5t_4t_3$. Since the length of both is less than 5, the recursion stops and the ILP model with granularity 1 is applied for each one, resulting in the solutions:

$$\alpha_{31} = \begin{array}{|c|c|c|} t_4 & t_3 & \bot \\ \hline \bot & \{t_3, t_4\} & t_2 \end{array} \quad \alpha_{32} = \begin{array}{|c|c|c|} t_4 & t_3 & \bot \\ \hline \bot & \{t_3, t_4\} & t_5 \end{array}$$

So the final optimal approximate alignment can be computed by concatenating the individual alignments found in preorder traversal:

$$\alpha = \begin{array}{|c|c|c|c|c|c|c|c|c|c|} t_5 & t_1 & t_3 & t_4 & \bot & t_4 & t_3 & \bot & t_4 & t_3 & \bot \\ \hline \bot & t_1 & t_3 & t_4 & t_2 & \bot & \{t_3, t_4\} & t_2 & \bot & \{t_3, t_4\} & t_5 \end{array}$$

which represents the step-sequence $\bar{\sigma} = t_1t_3t_4t_2\{t_3, t_4\}t_2\{t_3, t_4\}t_5$ from the model of Fig. 6. Informally, the final approximate alignment reports that two activities t_2 were skipped in the trace, the ordering of two consecutive pair of events (t_4t_3) was wrong, and transition t_5 was observed in the wrong order. Also, as mentioned in previous sections, the result of proposed method is an approximation to the corresponding optimal alignment, since some moves have non-singleton multisets (e.g., $\{t_3, t_4\}$). For these moves, the exact ordering is not computed although the relative position is known.

7   Experiments

The techniques of this paper have been implemented in Python as prototype tool that uses Gurobi for ILP resolution[7]. The tool has been evaluated over two different families of examples: on the one hand, large and well-structured synthetic benchmarks used in [10] for the distributed evaluation of fitness (see Table 1). On the other hand, a collection of large realistic examples from the literature has been also considered, some of them very unstructured (see Table 2). We compare our technique over $\eta = 1$ with the reference three approaches for computing

---

[7] The experiments have been done on a desktop computer with Intel Core i7-2.20 GHz, and 5 GB of RAM. Source code and benchmarks can be provided by contacting the first author.

Table 1. BPM2013 artificial benchmark datasets

Model	$|P|$	$|T|$	$|Arc|$	Cases	Fitting	$|\sigma|_{avg}$
prAm6	363	347	846	1200	No	31
prBm6	317	317	752	1200	Yes	43
prCm6	317	317	752	500	No	43
prDm6	529	429	1140	1200	No	248
prEm6	277	275	652	1200	No	98
prFm6	362	299	772	1200	No	240
prGm6	357	335	826	1200	No	143

Table 2. Real benchmark datasets

Model	$|P|$	$|T|$	$|Arc|$	Cases	Fitting	$|\sigma|_{avg}$
Banktransfer	121	114	276	2000	No	58
Documentflow	334	447	2059	12391	No	5
Documentflow2	337	456	2025	12391	No	5
BPIC15_ 2	78	420	848	832	No	53
BPIC15_ 4	178	464	954	1053	No	44
BPIC15_ 5	45	277	558	1156	No	51

optimal alignments from [1][8]: With or without ILP state space pruning, and the swap+replacement aware[9].

Comparison for Well-Structured and Synthetic Models. Figure 7 provides the comparison in CPU time for the two families of approaches. One can see that for event logs with many short traces the approach from [1] takes advantage of the optimizations done in the implementation, e.g., caching and similar. Notice that those optimizations can also be implemented in our setting. But clearly, in large models and event logs with many long traces (*prDm6*, *prFm6* and *prGm6*) the three approaches from [1] either provide a solution in more than 12 hours or crash due to memory problems (N/A in the figure), while the recursive technique of this paper is able to find approximate alignments in a reasonable time. We have monitored the memory usage: our techniques use an order of magnitude less

---

[8] In spite of using $\eta = 1$, still the objects computed by our technique and the technique from [1] are different, and hence this comparison is only meant to provide an estimation on the speedup/memory/quality one can obtain by opting for approximate alignments.

[9] The plugin "Replay a log on Petri net for conformance analysis" from ProM with parameters "A^* cost-based fitness express with/without ILP and being/not being swap+replacement aware". We instructed the techniques from [1] to compute *one-optimal* alignment.

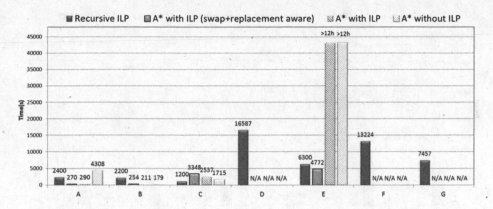

Fig. 7. Comparison of computation time for well-structured synthetic benchmarks.

memory than the techniques from [1]. Finally, for these well-structured benchmarks, the approach presented in this technique never found spurious solutions.

Comparison for Realistic Benchmarks. Figure 8 provides the comparison for the realistic examples from Table 2. The figure is split into structured and unstructured models[10]. Benchmark Banktransfer is taken from [15] and Documentflow benchmarks are taken from [16]. Some event logs from the last edition of the *BPI Challenge* were used, for which the models BPIC15_ 2, BPIC15_ 4, BPIC15_ 2 were generated using Inductive Miner plugin of ProM with noise threshold 0.99, 0.5 and 0.2, respectively. For the structural realistic models, the tendency of the previous structured benchmarks is preserved. For the two unstructured benchmarks, the technique of this paper is able to produce approximate alignments in considerably less time than the family of A^*-based techniques. Moreover, for the benchmarks from the BPI challenge, the A^*-based techniques crashes due to memory problems, whilst our technique again can handle these instances. The memory usage of our technique is again one order of magnitude less than the compared A^*-based techniques, but for the unstructured models spurious solutions were found.

Quality of Approximate Alignments.
Table 3 reports the evaluation of the quality of the results obtained by the two approaches for the cases where [1] provides a solution. We considered two different comparisons: (i) fine-grained comparison between the sequences computed by [1] and the step-sequences of our approach, and (ii) coarse-grained comparison

Table 3. Quality comparison.

Model/ Case	ED	Jaccard	MSE
prAm6	0.25	0	0.0002
prBm6	0	0	0
prCm6	2.99	0.01	0.0093
prEm6	0	0	0
Banktransfer	4.30	0.04	0.0400
Documentflow	3.16	0.27	0.0310
Documentflow2	3.17	0.29	0.0330

---

[10] Most of the realistic benchmarks in Table 2 have silent transitions.

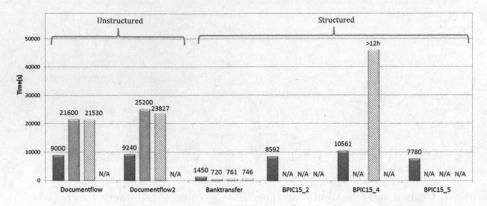

Fig. 8. Comparison of computation time for realistic benchmarks.

between the fitness value of the two approaches. For (i), we considered two possibilities: using the *Edit* or *Jaccard* distances. For the first, given a trace σ and a step-sequence $\bar{\gamma}$, we simply take the minimal edit distance between σ and any of the linearizations of $\bar{\gamma}$. For the Jaccard distance, which measures similarities between sets, we considered both objects as sets and used this metric to measure their similarity. In the table, we provide the average of these two metrics per trace, e.g. for prAm6 the two approaches are less than 1 edit operation (0.25) different on average. For measuring ii), the *Mean Square Root* (MSE) over the fitness values provided by both metrics is reported. Overall, one can see that both in fine-grained and coarse-grained comparisons, the approach of this paper is very close to the optimal solutions computed by [1], specially for well-structured models.

8   Conclusions and Future Work

Approximate alignments generalize the notion of alignment by allowing moves to be non-unitary, thus providing a user-defined mechanism to decide the granularity for observing deviations of a model with respect to observed behavior. A novel technique for the computation of approximate alignments has been presented in this paper, based on a divide-and-conquer strategy that uses ILP models both as splitting criteria and for obtaining partial alignments. The technique has been implemented as a prototype tool and the evaluation shows promising capabilities to handle large instances.

As future work, we see many possibilities. On the one hand, a thorough evaluation of the quality of the obtained results over a large set of benchmarks will be carried out. Second, extending the current theory to deal with models having duplicate transitions will be considered. Also, the incorporation of natural optimizations like parallelization and caching would have an strong impact.

Finally, as the recursive method presented in this paper can be used as a high-level strategy for partitioning the alignment computations, we plan to combine it with the A^* approach from [1] for computing partial alignments on the leafs of the recursion.

Acknowledgments. This work was supported by the Spanish Ministry for Economy and Competitiveness (MINECO) and the European Union (FEDER funds) under grant COMMAS (ref. TIN2013-46181-C2-1-R).

References

1. Adriansyah, A.: Aligning observed and modeled behavior. Ph.D. thesis, Technische Universiteit Eindhoven (2014)
2. Adriansyah, A., Munoz-Gama, J., Carmona, J., van Dongen, B.F., van der Aalst, W.M.P.: Measuring precision of modeled behavior. Inf. Syst. E-Bus. Manag. **13**(1), 37–67 (2015)
3. Buijs, J.C.A.M.: Flexible evolutionary algorithms for mining structured process models. Ph.D. thesis, Technische Universiteit Eindhoven (2014)
4. Desel, J., Esparza, J.: Reachability in cyclic extended free-choice systems. TCS **114**, 93–118 (1993). Elsevier Science Publishers B.V
5. Esparza, J., Melzer, S.: Verification of safety properties using integer programming: beyond the state equation. Formal Methods Syst. Des. **16**, 159–189 (2000)
6. Fahland, D., van der Aalst, W.M.P.: Model repair - aligning process models to reality. Inf. Syst. **47**, 220–243 (2015)
7. Leemans, S.J.J., Fahland, D., van der Aalst, W.M.P.: Scalable process discovery with guarantees. In: Gaaloul, K., Schmidt, R., Nurcan, S., Guerreiro, S., Ma, Q. (eds.) BPMDS 2015 and EMMSAD 2015. LNBIP, vol. 214, pp. 85–101. Springer, Heidelberg (2015)
8. Xixi, L., Fahland, D., van der Aalst, W.M.P.: Conformance checking based on partially ordered event data. In: Business Process Management Workshops - BPM 2014 International Workshops, Eindhoven, The Netherlands, 7–8 September 2014, Revised Papers, pp. 75–88 (2014)
9. Xixi, L., Mans, R., Fahland, D., van der Aalst, W.M.P.: Conformance checking in healthcare based on partially ordered event data. In: Proceedings of the 2014 IEEE Emerging Technology and Factory Automation, ETFA 2014, Barcelona, Spain, 16–19 September 2014, pp. 1–8 (2014)
10. Munoz-Gama, J., Carmona, J., van der Aalst, W.M.P.: Single-entry single-exit decomposed conformance checking. Inf. Syst. **46**, 102–122 (2014)
11. Murata, T.: Petri nets: Properties, analysis and applications. Proc. IEEE **77**(4), 541–574 (1989)
12. Silva, M., Teruel, E., Colom, J.M.: Linear algebraic and linear programming techniques for the analysis of place/transition net systems. In: Reisig, W., Rozenberg, G. (eds.) APN 1998. LNCS, vol. 1491. Springer, Heidelberg (1998)
13. van der Aalst, W.M.P.: Process Mining - Discovery: Conformance and Enhancement of Business Processes. Springer, Heidelberg (2011)
14. van der Aalst, W.M.P.: Decomposing petri nets for process mining: a generic approach. Distrib. Parallel Databases **31**(4), 471–507 (2013)

15. vanden Broucke, S.K.L.M., Munoz-Gama, J., Carmona, J., Baesens, B., Vanthienen, J.: Event-based real-time decomposed conformance analysis. In: Meersman, R., Panetto, H., Dillon, T., Missikoff, M., Liu, L., Pastor, O., Cuzzocrea, A., Sellis, T. (eds.) OTM 2014. LNCS, vol. 8841, pp. 345–363. Springer, Heidelberg (2014)

16. De Weerdt, J., vanden Broucke, K.L.M., Vanthienen, J., Baesens, B.: Active trace clustering for improved process discovery. IEEE Trans. Knowl. Data Eng. **25**(12), 2708–2720 (2013)

Modeling Foundations

Semantics and Analysis of DMN Decision Tables

Diego Calvanese[1], Marlon Dumas[2], Ülari Laurson[2], Fabrizio M. Maggi[2(✉)],
Marco Montali[1], and Irene Teinemaa[2]

[1] Free University of Bozen-Bolzano, Bolzano, Italy
[2] University of Tartu, Tartu, Estonia
f.m.maggi@ut.ee

Abstract. The Decision Model and Notation (DMN) is a standard notation to capture decision logic in business applications in general and
business processes in particular. A central construct in DMN is that of
a decision table. The increasing use of DMN decision tables to capture
critical business knowledge raises the need to support analysis tasks on
these tables such as correctness and completeness checking. This paper
provides a formal semantics for DMN tables, a formal definition of key
analysis tasks and scalable algorithms to tackle two such tasks, i.e., detection of overlapping rules and of missing rules. The algorithms are based
on a geometric interpretation of decision tables that can be used to support other analysis tasks by tapping into geometric algorithms. The algorithms have been implemented in an open-source DMN editor and tested
on large decision tables derived from a credit lending dataset.

Keywords: Decision model and notation · Decision table · Sweep
algorithm

1 Introduction

Business process models often incorporate decision logic of varying complexity,
typically via conditional expressions attached either to outgoing flows of decision gateways or to conditional events. The need to separate this decision logic
from the control-flow logic [2] and to capture it at a higher level of abstraction
has motivated the emergence of the Decision Model and Notation (DMN) [8].
A central construct of DMN is that of a decision table, which stems from the
notion of decision table proposed in the context of program decision logic specification in the 1960s [10]. A DMN decision table consists of columns representing
the inputs and outputs of a decision, and rows denoting rules. Each rule is a
conjunction of basic expressions captured in an expression language known as
S-FEEL (Simplified Friendly Enough Expression Language).

The use of DMN decision tables as a specification vehicle for critical business
decisions raises the question of ensuring the correctness of these tables, in particular the detection of inconsistent or incomplete DMN decision tables. Indeed,
detecting errors in DMN tables at specification time may prevent costly defects
down the road during business process implementation and execution.

© Springer International Publishing Switzerland 2016
M. La Rosa et al. (Eds.): BPM 2016, LNCS 9850, pp. 217–233, 2016.
DOI: 10.1007/978-3-319-45348-4_13

This paper provides a foundation for analyzing the correctness of DMN tables. The contributions of the paper are: (i) a formal semantics of DMN tables; (ii) a formalization of correctness criteria for DMN tables; and (iii) scalable algorithms for two basic correctness checking tasks over DMN tables, i.e., detection of overlapping rules and detection of missing rules (i.e., incompleteness). The latter algorithms are based on a novel geometric interpretation of DMN tables, wherein each rule in a table is mapped to an iso-oriented hyper-rectangle in an N-dimensional space (where N is the number of columns). Accordingly, the problem of detecting overlapping rules is mapped to that of detecting overlapping hyper-rectangles. Meanwhile, the problem of detecting missing rules is mapped to that of computing the difference between the N-dimensional universe defined by the domains of the N columns of a DMN table, and the set of hyper-rectangles induced by its rules. Based on this geometric interpretation and inspired by sweep-based spatial join algorithms [1], the paper presents scalable algorithms for these two analysis tasks. The algorithms have been implemented atop the dmn-js editor and evaluated over decision tables of varying sizes derived from a credit lending dataset.

The rest of the paper is structured as follows. Section 2 introduces DMN and discusses related work. Section 3 presents the formalization of DMN tables and their associated correctness criteria. Section 4 presents the algorithms for correctness analysis while Sect. 5 discusses their empirical evaluation. Finally, Sect. 6 summarizes the contributions and outlines future work directions.

2   Background and Related Work

2.1   Overview of DMN Decision Tables

A DMN table consists of columns corresponding to input or output attributes, and rows corresponding to rules. Each column has a type (e.g., a string, a number, or a date), and optionally to a more specific domain of possible values, which we hereby call a *facet*. Each row has an identifier, one expression for each input column (a.k.a. the *input entries*), and one specific value for each output column

Table 1. Sample decision table with its constitutive elements

(the *output entries*). For example, Table 1 shows a DMN table with two input columns, one output column and four rules.

Given an input configuration consisting of a vector of values (one entry per column), if every input entry of a row holds true for this input vector, then the vector *matches* the row and the output entries of the row are evaluated. For example, vector $\langle 500, 4230 \rangle$ matches rule B in Table 1, thus yielding G in the output configuration. To specify how output configurations are computed from input ones, a DMN table has a *hit indicator* and a *completeness indicator*. The hit indicator specifies whether only one or multiple rows of the table may match a given input, and if multiple rules match an input, how should the output be computed. The completeness indicator specifies whether every input must match at least one rule or potentially none. If an input configuration matches multiple rules, this may contradict the hit policy. Similarly, if no rule matches an input configuration, this may contradict the completeness indicator. The former contradiction is called *overlapping rules* while the latter is called *missing rule*.

2.2 Analysis of DMN Decision Tables

The need to analyze decision tables from the perspective of completeness (i.e., detecting missing rules) as well as consistency and non-redundancy (i.e., detecting overlapping rules) is widely recognized [3]. These two analysis tasks have been tackled using rough sets [9]. However, this approach requires that the domains of the input attributes are boolean or categorical. Numerical attributes need to be previously discretized into intervals and in such a way that no two intervals over any column overlap. For example, approaches based on rough sets cannot handle situations where multiple overlapping intervals appear along the same attribute (e.g., [151..300] and [200..250]). Instead, the table needs to be expanded so that these intervals do not overlap (e.g., intervals [151..300] and [200..250] need to be broken down into [151..200], [201..250] and [251..300]) and this expansion can in the worst case increase the size of the table exponentially.

Prologa [11,12] is a tool for modeling and executing classical decision tables. It supports the construction of decision tables in a way that prevents overlapping or missing rules. It also supports the simplification of decision tables via rule merging: two rules are merged when all but one of their input entries are identical, and their output entries are also identical. However, Prologa has the same intrinsic limitation as the rough set approach: it requires columns to have categorical domains. Numerical domains need to be broken down into elementary non-overlapping intervals as explained above. The same limitations hold in other techniques for detecting overlapping and missing rules [7,13] and algorithms for simplifying decision tables [6]. In other words, while the verification and simplification of decision tables with discrete or discretized domains has received much attention, the case where the columns have both discrete domains and numeric domains with arbitrary interval expressions has not been considered in the literature.

Signavio's DMN editor[1] detects overlapping and missing rules without imposing discretization of numeric domains. However, the employed techniques are
undisclosed and no empirical evaluation thereof has been reported. Also, the
diagnosis of overlapping and missing rules produced by Signavio is unnecessarily
large: it often reports the same rule overlap multiple times. This behavior will
be further explained in Sect. 5.

OpenRules[2] uses constraint satisfaction techniques to analyze business rules,
in particular rules encoded in decision tables. While using a general solver to
analyze decision tables is an option (e.g., an SMT solver such as Z3 [4]), this
approach leads to a boolean output (is the set of rules satisfiable?), and cannot
natively highlight specific sets of rules that need to be added to a table (missing
rules), nor specific overlaps between pairs of rules that need to be resolved.

3   Formalization

In this section, we provide a formalization of DMN decision tables, unambiguously defining their input/output semantics, and at the same time introducing
several analysis tasks focused on correctness checking. As a concrete specification language for input entries, we consider the S-FEEL language introduced in
the DMN standard itself.

Our formalization is based on classical predicate logic extended with data
types, which are needed to capture conditions that employ domain-specific predicates such as comparisons interpreted over the total order of natural numbers.
Such formalization is important per sè, as it defines a clear, unambiguous semantics of decision tables, and also as an interlingua supporting the comparison of
different analysis techniques.

3.1   Data Types and S-FEEL Conditions

We first introduce the building blocks of decision tables, i.e., the types of the
modeled attributes, and conditions over such types expressed using the S-FEEL
language. A data type T is a tuple $\langle \Delta_T, \Sigma_T \rangle$, where Δ_T is an *object domain*,
and $\Sigma_T = \Sigma_T^P \uplus \Sigma_T^F$ is a *signature*, constituted by a set Σ_T^P of *predicate symbols*,
and a set Σ_T^F of *function symbols* (disjoint from Σ_T^P). Each predicate symbol
$R \in \Sigma_T^P$ comes with its own arity n, and with an n-ary predicate $R^T \subseteq \Delta_T^n$ that
rigidly defines its semantics. Each function symbol $f \in \Sigma_T^F$ comes with its own
arity m, and with a function $\Delta_T^m \to \Delta_T$ that defines its semantics. To make the
arity explicit in predicate and function symbols, we use the standard notation
R/n and f/m. As usual, we assume that every data type is equipped *equality*
as a predefined, binary predicate interpreted as the identity on the underlying
domain. Hence, we will not explicitly mention equality in the signatures of data
types. In the following, we show some of the S-FEEL data types[3]:

---

[1] http://www.signavio.com.

[2] http://openrules.com/.

[3] Date/time data types are also supported but can be considered as simple numeric
  attributes.

- $\mathcal{T}_{\mathbb{S}} = \langle \mathbb{S}, \emptyset, \emptyset \rangle$ – strings.
- $\mathcal{T}_{\mathbb{B}} = \langle \{\text{true}, \text{false}\}, \emptyset, \emptyset \rangle$ – boolean attributes.
- $\mathcal{T}_{\mathbb{Z}} = \langle \mathbb{Z}, \{\mathbf{0}/0, \mathbf{1}/0, </2, >/2\}, \{+/2, -/2, \cdot/2, \div/2\} \rangle$ – integer numbers equipped with the usual comparison predicates and binary operations;
- $\mathcal{T}_{\mathbb{R}}$ (defined as $\mathcal{T}_{\mathbb{Z}}$ by replacing the domain $\mathbb{Z}$ with $\mathbb{R}$, and by reinterpreting all predicates and functions accordingly) – real numbers equipped with the usual comparison predicates and binary operations.

The set of all such types is denoted by $\mathfrak{T}$. Since decision tables do not support conditions that combine multiple data types, we can assume that the *object domains of all types in $\mathfrak{T}$ are pairwise disjoint.*

S-FEEL allows one to formulate conditions over types. These conditions constitute the basic building blocks for facets and rules, which in turn are the core of decision tables. The syntax of an *(S-FEEL) condition $\mathcal{Q}$* over type is:

$$\mathcal{Q} ::= \text{``$-$''} \mid Term \mid \text{``not(''} Term \text{``)''} \mid Comparison \mid Interval \mid \mathcal{Q}_1, \mathcal{Q}_2$$
$$Comparison ::= COp\ Term$$
$$COp ::= \text{``$=$''} \mid \text{``$<$''} \mid \text{``$>$''} \mid \text{``$\leq$''} \mid \text{``$\geq$''}$$
$$Interval ::= (\text{``(''} \mid \text{``[''})\ Term_1 \text{``..''}\ Term_2\ (\text{``)''} \mid \text{``]''})$$
$$Term ::= v \mid f(Term_1, \dots, Term_m)$$

where v is an object and f is an m-ary function.

S-FEEL supports the following conditions on a given data type $\mathcal{T} = \langle \Delta_{\mathcal{T}}, \Sigma_{\mathcal{T}} \rangle$: *(i)* "$-$" indicates *any value*, i.e., it holds for every object in $\Delta_{\mathcal{T}}$. *(ii)* "$= Term$" indicates a *matching expression*, which holds for the object in $\Delta_{\mathcal{T}}$ that corresponds to the result denoted by term *Term*. A term, in turn, corresponds either to a specific object in $\Delta_{\mathcal{T}}$, or to the recursive application of an m-ary function in $\Sigma_{\mathcal{T}}$ to m terms. It is worth noting that, in the actual S-FEEL standard, the symbol " $=$ " is usually omitted, that is, when resolving the scope symbol $\mathcal{Q}$, *Term* is interpreted as a shortcut notation for "$= Term$". *(iii) Comparison* is only applicable when $\mathcal{T}$ is a numeric data type, and indicates a *comparison condition*, which holds for all objects that are related via the employed comparison predicate to the object resulting from expression *Term*. *(iv) Interval* is only applicable when $\mathcal{T}$ is numeric, and allows the modeler to capture membership conditions that tests whether an input object belongs to the modeled interval. *(v)* "$\mathcal{Q}_1, \mathcal{Q}_2$" indicates an *alternative condition*, which holds whenever one of the two conditions $\mathcal{Q}_1$ and $\mathcal{Q}_2$ holds.

Example 1. The fact that a risk category is either high, medium or low can be expressed by the following condition over $\mathcal{T}_{\mathbb{S}}$: "$\text{high}, \text{medium}, \text{low}$". By using $\mathcal{T}_{\mathbb{Z}}$ to denote the age of persons (in years), the group of people that are underage or old (i.e., having at least 70 years) is captured by condition "$[0..18], \geq 70$". ∎

3.2 Decision Tables

We are now in the position of defining DMN decision tables. See Table 1 for a reference example. A *decision table* $\mathcal{D}$ is a tuple $\langle T, I, O, \text{Type}, \text{Facet}, R, \text{Priority}, C, H \rangle$, where:

- T is the *table name*.
- I and O are disjoint, finite sets of *input* and *output attributes* (represented as strings).[4]
- Type : $I \uplus O \to \mathfrak{T}$ is a *typing function* that associates each input/output attribute to its corresponding data type.
- Facet is a *facet function* that associates each input/output attribute $\mathbf{a} \in I \uplus O$ to a condition over Type($\mathbf{a}$), defining the *acceptable objects* for that attribute. Facet functions are depicted as "optional lists of values" in Table 1.
- R is a finite set of *rules* $\{r_1, \ldots, r_p\}$. Each rule r_k is a pair $\langle \mathsf{If}_k, \mathsf{Then}_k \rangle$, where If_k is an *input entry function* that associates each input attribute $\mathbf{a}^{\mathbf{in}} \in I$ to a condition over Type($\mathbf{a}^{\mathbf{in}}$), and Then_k is an *output entry function* that associates each output attribute $\mathbf{a}^{\mathbf{out}} \in O$ an object in Type($\mathbf{a}^{\mathbf{out}}$).
- Priority : $R \to \{1, \ldots, |R|\}$ is a *priority function* injectively mapping rules in R to a corresponding rule number defining its priority. If no priority is explicitly given, in accordance with the standard we assume that the priority is implicitly defined by the graphical ordering in which rule entries appear inside the decision table.
- $C \in \{\mathsf{c}, \mathsf{i}\}$ is the *completeness indicator*, where c is the default value and stands for *complete* table, while i stands for *incomplete* table.
- $H \in \{\mathsf{u}, \mathsf{a}, \mathsf{p}, \mathsf{f}\}$ is the *(single) hit indicator* defining the policy for the rule application, where: *(i)* u is the default value and stands for *unique hit policy*, *(ii)* $H = \mathsf{a}$ stands for *any hit policy*, *(iii)* $H = \mathsf{p}$ stands for *priority hit policy*, and *(iv)* $H = \mathsf{f}$ stands for *first hit policy*.

We now informally review the intuitive semantics of rules and of completeness/hit indicators in DMN, moving to the formalization in Sect. 3.3.

Rule Semantics. Intuitively, rules follow the standard "if-then" interpretation. Rules are matched against *input configurations*, which map the input attributes to objects in such a way that each object *(i)* belongs to the type of the corresponding input attribute, and *(ii)* satisfies the corresponding facet. If, for every input attribute, the assigned object satisfies the condition imposed by the rule on that type, then the rule *triggers*, and bounds the output attributes to the actual objects mentioned by the rule.

Example 2. Consider the decision table in Table 1. The input configuration where **Income** is 500 and **Loan** is 4230, triggers rule B. ∎

Completeness Indicator. When the table is declared to be complete, the intention is that every possible input configuration must trigger at least one rule. Incomplete tables, instead, have input configurations with no matching rule.

---

[4] These are called "expressions" in the DMN standard, but we prefer the term "attribute" as it is less ambiguous.

Hit Policies. Hit policies specify how to handle the case where multiple rules are triggered by an input configuration. In particular:

- "Unique hit" indicates that at most one rule can be triggered by a given input configuration, thus avoiding the need of handling how to compute the output objects in the case of multiple triggered rules.
- "Any hit" indicates that when multiple rules are triggered, they must agree on the output objects, thus guaranteeing that the output is unambiguous.
- "Priority hit" indicates that whenever multiple rules trigger, then the output is unambiguously computed by only considering the contribution of the triggered rule that has highest priority.
- "First hit" can be understood as a variant of the priority hit, in which priority is implicitly obtained from the ordering in which rules appear in the decision table. Hence, this case is subsumed by that of priority hit.
- "Collect" implies that multiple rules can match an input configuration and when this is the case, all matching rules are fired the resulting output configurations are aggregated. Aggregation is orthogonal to correctness checking, and thus we leave the "Collect" policy outside the scope of the formalization below.

3.3 Formalization of Rule Semantics and of Analysis Tasks

We first define how conditions map to corresponding formulae. Since each condition is applied to a single input attribute, the corresponding formula has a single free variable corresponding to that attribute. Given a condition Q over type $\mathcal{T} = \langle \Delta_\mathcal{T}, \Sigma_\mathcal{T} \rangle$, the *condition formula for* Q, written Φ_Q, is a formula using predicates/functions in $\Sigma_\mathcal{T}$ and objects from $\Delta_\mathcal{T}$, and possibly mentioning a single free variable, constructed as follows:

$$
\Phi_Q \triangleq
\begin{cases}
true & \text{if } Q = \text{``}-\text{''} \\
\neg \Phi_{Term} & \text{if } Q = \text{``}\texttt{not}(\,Term)\text{''} \\
x = Term & \text{if } Q = Term \\
x \; COp \; Term & \text{if } Q = \text{``}COp \; Term\text{''} \text{ and } COp \in \{<, >, \le, \ge\} \\
x > \Phi_{Term_1} \wedge x < \Phi_{Term_2} & \text{if } Q = \text{``}(Term_1..Term_2)\text{''} \\
x > \Phi_{Term_1} \wedge x \le \Phi_{Term_2} & \text{if } Q = \text{``}(Term_1..Term_2]\text{''} \\
x \ge \Phi_{Term_1} \wedge x < \Phi_{Term_2} & \text{if } Q = \text{``}[Term_1..Term_2)\text{''} \\
x \ge \Phi_{Term_1} \wedge x \le \Phi_{Term_2} & \text{if } Q = \text{``}[Term_1..Term_2]\text{''} \\
\Phi_{Q_1} x \vee \Phi_{Q_2} x & \text{if } Q = \text{``}Q_1, Q_2\text{''}
\end{cases}
$$

As usual, we also use notation $\Phi_Q(x)$ to explicitly mention the free variable of the condition formula.

Example 3. Consider the S-FEEL conditions in Example 1. The condition over the risk category is $Risk = \texttt{high} \vee Risk = \texttt{medium} \vee Risk = \texttt{low}$. The condition formula person ages is instead: $(Age \ge 0 \wedge Age \le 18) \vee Age \ge 70$. ∎

With this notion at hand, we now formalize the notions of correctness of rule specifications, semantics of rules, and semantics of completeness and hit indicators. These notions are building blocks for an overall notion of *table correctness*.

Let $\mathcal{D} = \langle T, I, O, \mathsf{Type}, \mathsf{Facet}, R, \mathsf{Priority}, C, H \rangle$ be a decision table with m input attributes $I = \{\mathbf{a_1}, \ldots, \mathbf{a_m}\}$, n output attributes $O = \{\mathbf{b_1}, \ldots, \mathbf{b_n}\}$, and p rules $R = \{r_1, \ldots, r_p\}$. We use variables $x_1, \ldots, x_m$ for objects matching the input attributes, and variables $y_1, \ldots, y_n$ for those matching the output attributes.

Facet Correctness. We first consider the *Facet correctness* of $\mathcal{D}$, which intuitively amounts to check whether all the mentioned input conditions and output objects are compatible with their corresponding attribute facets. Given an attribute $\mathbf{a} \in I \cup O$ and a corresponding input variable x, we can identify whether *a condition Q over $\mathbf{a}$ is compatible with $\mathbf{a}$*, i.e., whether the condition is specified in such a way that can potentially trigger, or is instead contradictory with the facet attached to $\mathbf{a}$:

$$Compatible_{\mathbf{a}}^{Q} \triangleq \exists x. \Phi_{\mathsf{Facet}(\mathbf{a})}(x) \wedge \Phi_{Q}(x)$$

Rule Semantics. A rule $r = \langle \mathsf{If}, \mathsf{Then} \rangle \in R$ is *triggered by* a configuration $x_1, \ldots, x_m$ of input objects whenever each such object matches with the corresponding input condition:

$$TriggeredBy_r(x_1, \ldots, x_m) \triangleq \bigwedge_{i \in \{1, \ldots, m\}} Matches_{\mathbf{a_i}}^{\mathsf{If}(\mathbf{a_i})}(x_i)$$

Two configurations $\vec{x}$ and $y_1, \ldots, y_n$ of input and output objects are *input-output related* by a rule $r = \langle \mathsf{If}, \mathsf{Then} \rangle \in R$ if the rule is triggered by the input configuration, and binds the output as specified by the output configuration:

$$IORel_r(\vec{x}, y_1, \ldots, y_n) \triangleq TriggeredBy_r(\vec{x}) \wedge \bigwedge_{j \in \{1, \ldots, n\}} Matches_{\mathbf{b_j}}^{\mathsf{Then}(\mathbf{b_j})}(y_j)$$

Completeness. When declaring that a table is (in)complete, there is no guarantee that the specified rules guarantee this property. To check whether this is indeed the case, we introduce a formula that holds whenever each possible input configuration triggers at least one rule:

$$Complete_{\mathcal{D}} \triangleq \forall x_1, \ldots, x_m. \bigvee_{k \in \{1, \ldots, p\}} TriggeredBy_{r_k}(x_1, \ldots, x_m)$$

Hit Policies. We start with the unique hit policy, which requires that each input configuration triggers at most one rule. This can be formalized as follows:

$$Unique_{\mathcal{D}} \triangleq \forall \vec{x}. \bigwedge_{i \in \{1, \ldots, p\}} \left(TriggeredBy_{r_i}(\vec{x}) \rightarrow \bigwedge_{j \in \{1, \ldots, p\} \setminus \{i\}} \neg TriggeredBy_{r_j}(\vec{x}) \right)$$

We then continue with the any hit policy. Here multiple rules may be triggered by the same input configuration, but if so, then they must agree on the output. This can be formalized as follows:

$$AgreesOnOutput_{\mathcal{D}} \triangleq \bigwedge_{i,j \in \{1,...,p\}, i \neq j} (\forall \vec{x} \forall \vec{y}.\ TriggeredBy_{r_i}(\vec{x})$$
$$\wedge\ TriggeredBy_{r_j}(\vec{x}) \rightarrow IORel_{r_i}(\vec{x}, \vec{y})$$
$$\wedge\ IORel_{r_j}(\vec{x}, \vec{y}))$$

We now consider the case of priority hit policy. This requires to reformulate the rule semantics, so as to consider the whole decision table and the priority of the rules. In particular, with this hit policy a rule $r \in R$ is *triggered with priority* by an input configuration $\vec{x}$ if it is triggered by $\vec{x}$ in the sense specified above, and no rule of higher priority is triggered by the same input $\vec{x}$:

$$TriggeredWithPriorityBy_r(\vec{x}) \triangleq TriggeredBy_r(\vec{x}) \wedge \bigwedge_{r_h \in \{r' | r' \in R \text{ and } Priority(r') > Priority(r)\}} \neg TriggeredBy_{r'}(\vec{x})$$

Finally, we observe that the priority hit policy may create a situation in which some rules are never triggered. This happens when other rules of higher priority have more general input conditions. We formalize this notion by introducing a formula dedicated to check when a rule $r_1 \in R$ *is masked* by another rule $r_2 \in R$:

$$MaskedBy_{r_1}^{r_2} \triangleq \mathsf{Priority}(r_2) > \mathsf{Priority}(r_1) \wedge \forall \vec{x}.\ TriggeredBy_{r_1}(\vec{x}) \rightarrow TriggeredBy_{r_2}(\vec{x})$$

Correctness Formula. We now combine the previously defined formulae into a single formula that captures the overall correctness of a decision table.

We say that $\mathcal{D}$ is *correct* if the following conditions hold:

1. Every table cell, i.e., every input condition or output object, is legal for the corresponding attribute (considering the attribute type and facet).
2. The completeness indicator corresponds to c iff the table is indeed complete.
3. The rules are compatible with the hit policy indicator:
   (a) if the hit policy is u, each input configuration triggers at most one rule;
   (b) if the hit policy is a, all overlapping rules (i.e., rules that could simultaneously trigger) have the same output;
   (c) if the hit policy is p, all rules are "useful", i.e., no rule is masked by a rule with higher priority.

Based on the previously introduced formulae, we formalize correctness as:

$$Correct_{\mathcal{D}} \triangleq \bigwedge_{\langle \mathsf{If, Then} \rangle \in R} \left(\bigwedge_{a \in I} Compatible_a^{\mathsf{If}(a)} \wedge \bigwedge_{b \in O} Compatible_b^{\mathsf{Then}(b)} \right)$$
$$\wedge \left((C = \mathsf{c}) \leftrightarrow Complete_{\mathcal{D}} \right)$$
$$\wedge \left((H = \mathsf{u}) \rightarrow Unique_{\mathcal{D}} \right)$$
$$\wedge \left((H = \mathsf{a}) \rightarrow AgreesOnOutput_{\mathcal{D}} \right)$$
$$\wedge \left((H = \mathsf{p}) \rightarrow \bigwedge_{r_1, r_2 \in R} \neg MaskedBy_{r_1}^{r_2} \right)$$

Global Input-Output Formula. We combine the previously defined formulae into a single formula that captures the overall input-output relation induced by $\mathcal{D}$. This is done by exploiting the notion of input-output related configurations by a rule, so as to cover the entire table. Specifically we say that an input configuration $\vec{x}$ and an output configuration $\vec{y}$ are *input-output related* by $\mathcal{D}$ if:

1. The hit policy is either u or a, and there exists a rule that relates $\vec{x}$ to $\vec{y}$ (in the case of any hit policy, there could be many, but they establish the same input-output relation, so it is sufficient to pick one of them);
2. The hit policy is p, and there exists a rule relating $\vec{x}$ to $\vec{y}$ without any other rule of higher priority that is triggered by $\vec{x}$ (if such a rule exists, then it is such rule that has to be selected to relate input-output).

This is formalized as follows:

$$IORel_{\mathcal{D}}(\vec{x}, \vec{y}) \triangleq \left((H = \text{u} \vee H = \text{a}) \to \bigvee_{r \in R} IORel_r(\vec{x}, \vec{y}) \right)$$

$$\wedge \left((H = \text{p}) \to \bigvee_{r = \langle \text{If,Then} \rangle \in R} \begin{array}{l} TriggeredWithPriorityBy_r(\vec{x}) \\ \wedge \bigwedge_{j \in \{1,\ldots,n\}} Matches_{\text{b}_\text{j}}^{\text{Then}(\text{b}_\text{j})}(y_j) \end{array} \right)$$

4   Algorithms

We now introduce algorithms to handle the two main analysis tasks introduced in the previous section: detecting overlapping rules and (in)completeness. The proposed algorithms rely on a geometric interpretation of a DMN table. Every rule in a table is seen as an iso-oriented hyper-rectangle in an N-dimensional space (where N is a number of columns). Indeed, an input entry in a rule can be seen a constraint over one of the columns (i.e., dimensions). In the case of a numerical column, an input entry is an interval (potentially with an infinite upper or lower bound) and thus it defines a segment or line over the dimension corresponding to that column. In the case of a categorical column, we can map each value of the column's domain to a disjoint interval – e.g., "Refinancing" to $[0..1)$, "Card payoff" to $[1..2)$, "Car leasing" to $[2..3)$, etc. – and we can see an input entry under this column as defining a segment (or set of segments) over the dimension corresponding to the column in question. The conjunction of the entries of a row hence defines a hyper-rectangle, or potentially multiple hyper-rectangles in the case of a multi-valued categorical input entry (e.g., {"Refinancing", "Car leasing"}). The hyper-rectangles are iso-oriented because only constraints of the form "attribute operator literal" are allowed in S-FEEL and such constraints define iso-oriented lines or segments.

For example, the geometric interpretation of Table 1 is shown in Fig. 1.[5] The two dimensions, x and y, represent the two input columns (*Annual income* and

---

[5] For simplicity, the figure is purely schematic and does not preserve the scale along the axes.

Loan size) respectively. The table contains 4 rules: A, B, C, and D. Some of them are overlapping. For example, rule A overlaps with rule C. Their intersection is the rectangle $[500, 1000] \times [500, 1000]$. The table also contains missing values. For example, vector $\langle 200, 2000 \rangle$ does not match any rule in Table 1.

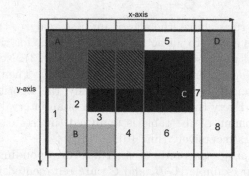

Fig. 1. Geometric representation of the DMN table shown in Table 1

The algorithms are presented for numeric columns. Minor adaptations (not discussed here) allow these algorithms to handle categorical columns as well.

4.1 Finding Overlapping Rules

Algorithm 1 finds overlapping rules in a DMN table. This algorithm is an extension of line-sweep algorithm for two-dimensional spatial joins proposed in [1]. The idea of this latter algorithm is to pick one dimension (e.g., x-axis), project all hyper-rectangles into this dimension, and then sweep an imaginary line orthogonal to this axis (i.e., parallel to the y-axis). The line stops at every point in the x-axis where either an hyper-rectangle starts or ends. When the line makes a "stop", we gather all hyper-rectangles that intersect the line (the *active list*). These hyper-rectangles overlap along their x-axis projection. In [1], it is then checked if the hyper-rectangles also overlap in the y-axis, and if so they are added to the result set (i.e., the hyper-rectangles overlap). Algorithm 1 extends this idea to N dimensions. The algorithm takes as input:

1. ruleList, containing all rules of the input DMN table;
2. i, containing the index of the column under scrutiny;
3. N, representing the total number of columns;
4. OverlappingRuleList, storing the rules that overlap.

The algorithm starts analyzing the first column of the table (axis x). All rules are projected over this column. Note that the projection of a rule on a column is an interval. We indicate the projection of rule K over axes x and y with I_K^x and I_K^y respectively. All the intervals are represented in terms of upper and lower bounds. The bounds are sorted in ascending order (line 7). The algorithm iterates over the list of sorted bounds (line 8). In the case of Fig. 1, the rules projected over the x axis correspond are:

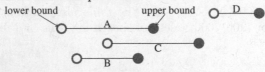

Considering the rules above, the algorithm first analyzes the lower bound of I_A^x. Therefore, I_A^x is added to an active list of intervals for the first column x, $\mathcal{L}_x$, since the bound processed is a lower bound (line 13). Next, the algorithm processes the lower bound of I_B^x and I_B^x is added to $\mathcal{L}_x$. Then, the lower bound of I_C^x is processed and I_C^x is added to $\mathcal{L}_x$. Finally, the algorithm processes the upper bound of I_B^x. Every time an upper bound of an interval is processed (line 9), the following column of the table is analyzed (in this case y) by invoking *findOverlappingRules* recursively (line 10).

All the interval projections on y of the rules corresponding to intervals contained in $\mathcal{L}_x$ (in our example A, B, and C) are represented in terms of upper bounds and lower bounds as depicted below:

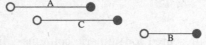

The bounds are sorted in ascending order. The algorithm iterates over the list of sorted bounds. Considering the intervals above, the algorithm first encounters the lower bound of I_A^y. Therefore, I_A^y is added to the active list of intervals for the second column y, $\mathcal{L}_y$. Next, the algorithm processes the lower bound of I_C^y and adds I_C^y to $\mathcal{L}_y$. Then, the upper bound of I_C^y is processed. Since there is no other column in the table, this means that all the rules corresponding to the intervals in $\mathcal{L}_y$ overlap. At the end of each recursion, the interval corresponding to the current bound is removed from the current active list (line 11). In addition, when the last column of the table is processed (line 1), the algorithm checks whether the identified set of overlapping rules is contained in one of the other sets produced in a previous recursion (lines 3). If this is not the case, the new set of overlapping rules is added to the output list overlappingRuleList (line 4). In this way, the procedure outputs maximal sets of overlapping rules having a non-empty intersection stored in overlappingRuleList (line 14).

4.2 Finding Missing Rules

Algorithm 2 describes the procedure for finding missing rules, which is also based on the line-sweep principle. The algorithm takes as inputs 5 parameters:

1. ruleList, containing all rules of the input DMN table;
2. missingIntervals, storing the current missing intervals;
3. i, containing the index of the column under scrutiny;
4. N, representing the total number of columns;
5. MissingRuleList, storing the missing rules.

Algorithm 1. Procedure findOverlappingRules.

Input: *ruleList*; *i*; *N*; *overlappingRuleList*.

```
1  if i == N then
2      define current overlap currentOverlapRules; /* it contains the list of rules that overlap
        up to the current point */ ;
3      if !overlappingRuleList.includes(currentOverlapRules) then
4          overlappingRuleList.put(currentOverlapRules);
5  else
6      define the current list of bounds L_{x_i};
7      sortedListAllBounds = ruleList.sort(i);
8      foreach currentBound ∈ sortedListAllBoundaries do
9          if !currentBound.isLower() then
10             findOverlappingRules(L_{x_i}, i +1, N, overlappingRuleList); /* recursive call */
11             L_{x_i}.delete(currentBound);
12         else
13             L_{x_i}.put(currentBound);

14  return overlappingRuleList;
```

The algorithm starts analyzing the first column of the table (axis x). Consider again the projection of the table in Fig. 1 on x:

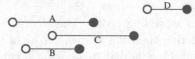

Upper and lower bounds of each interval are sorted in ascending order (line 3). The algorithm iterates over the list of sorted bounds (line 5).

Considering the rules above, the algorithm first analyzes the lower bound of I_A^x. Therefore, I_A^x is added to an active list of intervals for the first column x, $\mathcal{L}_x$. An interval is added to the active list only if its lower bound is processed (line 16). If the upper bound of an interval is processed, the interval is removed from the list (line 18). Next, the algorithm processes the lower bound of I_B^x. Since $\mathcal{L}_x$ is not empty, I_B^x is not added to $\mathcal{L}_x$ yet (line 12). Starting from the interval $\mathcal{I}_{A,B}$ (line 13) having the lower bound of I_A^x as lower bound and the lower bound of I_B^x as upper bound, the following column of the table is analyzed (in this case y) by invoking *findMissingRules* recursively (line 14). All the interval projections on y of the rules corresponding to intervals contained in $\mathcal{L}_x$ (in our example only A) are represented in terms of upper and lower bounds, obtaining in this case the following simple situation:

The bounds are sorted in ascending order. The algorithm iterates over the list of sorted bounds. The first bound taken into consideration is the lower bound of I_A^y so that I_A^y is added to $\mathcal{L}_y$ (since $\mathcal{L}_y$ is empty). Since this bound corresponds to the minimum possible value for y, there are no missing values between the minimum possible value for y and the lower bound of I_A^y (line 6). Next, the algorithm processes the second bound in $\mathcal{L}_y$ that is the upper bound of I_A^y. Considering that the upper bound of I_A^y is the last one in $\mathcal{L}_y$, the algorithm checks if this value corresponds to the maximum possible value for y (line 6). Since this is not the case, this means that there are missing values in the area between the upper bound of I_A^y and the next bound over the same column (in this case area 1). The algorithm checks if the identified area is contiguous to an area of missing values previously found (line 8). If this is the case the two areas are merged (line 9). If this is not the case, the area is added to a list of missing value areas (line 11). In our case, area 1 is added to a list of missing value areas. Note that the algorithm merges two areas of missing values only when the intervals corresponding to one column are contiguous and the ones corresponding to all the other columns are exactly the same. In the example in Fig. 1, areas 4 and 6 are merged.

At this point, the recursion ends and the algorithm proceeds analyzing the intervals in the projection along the x axis. The last bound processed was the lower bound of I_B^x, so that I_B^x is added to $\mathcal{L}_x$. Next, the algorithm processes the lower bound of I_C^x (since $\mathcal{L}_x$ is not empty, I_C^x is not added to $\mathcal{L}_x$ yet). Starting from the interval $\mathcal{I}_{B,C}$ having the lower bound of I_B^x as lower bound and the lower bound of I_C^x as upper bound, the following column of the table is analyzed (in this case y) again through recursion.

All intervals projections on y of the rules corresponding to intervals contained in $\mathcal{L}_x$ (in this case A and B) are represented in terms of upper and lower bounds:

The bounds are sorted in ascending order. The algorithm iterates over the list of sorted bounds. Considering the rules above, the algorithm first processes the lower bound of I_A^y so that I_A^y is added to $\mathcal{L}_y$ ($\mathcal{L}_y$ is empty). Then, the upper bound of I_A^y is processed. When the algorithm reaches the upper bound of an interval in a certain column the interval is removed from the corresponding active list. Therefore, I_A^y is removed from $\mathcal{L}_y$. Next, the lower bound of I_B^y is processed. Since $\mathcal{L}_y$ is empty, the algorithm checks if the previous processed bound is contiguous with the current one (line 6). Since this is not the case, this means that there are missing values in the area between the upper bound of I_A^y and the next bound over the same column (in this case area 2). The algorithm checks if the identified area is contiguous to an area of missing values previously found. If this is the case, the two areas are merged. If this is not the case, the area is added to a list of missing value areas (in our case area 2 is added to a list of missing value areas). The list of missing areas stored in missingRuleList is returned by the algorithm (line 20).

5   Evaluation

We implemented the algorithms on top of dmn-js: an open-source rendering and editing toolkit for DMN tables.[6] In it current version, dmn-js does not support correctness verification. Our dmn-js extension with verification features can be found at https://github.com/ulaurson/dmn-js and a deployed version is available for testing at http://dmn.cs.ut.ee.

---

[6] https://github.com/bpmn-io/dmn-js.

Algorithm 2. Procedure findMissingRules.

Input: *ruleList*; *missingIntervals*; *i*; *N*; *missingRuleList*.

```
 1  if i > N then
 2  |   define the current list of boundaries 𝓛ₓᵢ;
 3  |   sortedListAllBoundaries = ruleList.sort(i);
 4  |   lastBound = 0;
 5  |   foreach currentBound ∈ sortedListAllBoundaries do
 6  |   |   if !areContiguous(lastBound, currentBound) then
 7  |   |   |   missingIntervals[i] = constructInterval(lastBound, currentBound);
 8  |   |   |   if missingRuleList.canBeMerged(missingIntervals); then
 9  |   |   |   |   missingRuleList.merge(missingIntervals);
10  |   |   |   else
11  |   |   |   |_  missingRuleList.add(missingIntervals);
        |
12  |   |   if !𝓛ₓᵢ.isEmpty() ) then
13  |   |   |   missingIntervals [i] = constructInterval(lastBound, currentBound);
14  |   |   |   findMissingRules(𝓛ₓᵢ,missingIntervals,i +1, N, missingRuleList); /*
        |   |   |_  recursive invocation */
        |
15  |   |   if currentBound.isLower() then
16  |   |   |   𝓛ₓᵢ.put(currentBound);
17  |   |   else
18  |   |   |_  𝓛ₓᵢ.delete(currentBound);
        |
19  |   |_  lastBound = currentBound;

20  return missingRuleList;
```

For the evaluation, we created decision tables from a loan dataset of Lend-ingClub – a peer-to-peer lending marketplace.[7] The employed dataset contains data about all loans issued in 2013–2014 (23 5629 loans). For each loan, there are attributes of the loan itself (e.g., amount, purpose), of the lender (e.g., income, family status, property ownership), and a credit grade (A, B, C, D, E, F, G).

Using Weka [5], we trained decision trees to classify the grade of each loan from a subset of the loan attributes. We then translated each trained decision tree into a DMN table by mapping each path from the root to a leaf of the tree into a rule. Using different attributes and pruning parameters in the decision tree discovery, we generated DMN tables containing approx. 500, 1000 and 1500 rules and 3, 5 and 7 columns (nine tables in total). The 3-dimensional (i.e., 3-column) tables have one categorical and two numerical input columns; the 5-dimensional tables have two categorical and three numerical input columns, and the 7-dimensional tables has two categorical and five numerical input columns.

By construction, the generated tables do not contain overlapping or missing rules. To introduce missing rules in a table, we selected 10 % of the rules. For each of them, we then randomly selected one column, and we injected noise into the input entry in the cell in the selected column by decreasing its lower bound and increasing its upper bound in the case of a numerical domain (e.g., interval [3..6] becomes [2..7]) and by adding one value in the case of a categorical domain (e.g., { Refinancing, CreditCardPayoff } becomes { Refinancing, CreditCard-Payoff, Leasing }). These modifications make it that the rule will overlap others. Conversely, to introduce missing rule errors, we selected 10 % of the rules, picked a random column for each row and "shrank" the corresponding input entry.

---

[7] https://www.lendingclub.com/info/download-data.action.

We checked each generated table both for missing and incomplete rules and measured execution times averaged over 5 runs on a single core of a 64-bit 2.2 GHz Intel Core i5-5200U processor with 16 GB of RAM. The results are shown in Table 2. Execution times for missing rules detection are under 2 s, except for the 7-columns tables with 1000–1500 rules. The detection of overlapping rules leads to higher execution times, due to the need to detect sets of overlapping rules and ensure maximality. The execution times for overlapping rules detection on the 3-columns tables is higher than on the 5-columns tables because the 5-columns tables have less rule overlaps, which in turn is due to the fact that the 5-columns tables have proportionally less categorical columns than the 3-columns ones.

In addition to implementing our algorithms, we implemented algorithms designed to produce the same output as Signavio. In Signavio, if multiple rules have a joint intersection (e.g., rules {r1, r2, r3}) the output contains an overlap entry for the triplet {r1, r2, r3} but also for the pairs {r1, r2}, {r2, r3} and {r1, r3} (i.e., subsets of the overlapping set). Furthermore, the overlap of pair {r1, r2} may be reported multiple times if r3 breaks $r1 \cap r2$ into multiple hyper-rectangles (and same for {r2, r3} and {r1, r3}). Meanwhile, our approach produces only maximal sets of overlapping rules with a non-empty intersection.

Table 3 shows the number of sets of overlapping rules and the number of missing rules identified by our approach vs. Signavio's one. In all runs, both the number of overlapping and missing rules is drastically lower in our approach.

Table 2. Execution times (in milliseconds)

	3 COLUMNS			5 COLUMNS			7 COLUMNS		
#rules	499	998	1 492	505	1 000	1 506	502	1 019	1 496
Overlapping time	297 ms	6 475 ms	24 530 ms	200 ms	1 621 ms	5 374 ms	5 715 ms	6 793 ms	30 736 ms
Missing time	160 ms	611 ms	1 672 ms	163 ms	820 ms	1 942 ms	2 173 ms	7 029 ms	18 263 ms

Table 3. Number of reported errors of type "overlapping rules" and "missing rule"

		3 COLUMNS			5 COLUMNS			7 COLUMNS		
#rules		499	998	1 492	505	1 000	1 506	502	1 019	1 496
#overlapping rule sets	Our approach	131	447	812	110	225	378	139	227	371
	Signavio	1 226	10 920	23 115	679	3 692	8 921	23 175	22 002	62 217
#missing rules	Our approach	117	330	726	136	254	462	134	322	518
	Signavio	668	2 655	5 386	563	2 022	4 832	5 201	18 076	43 552

6   Conclusion and Future Work

This paper presented a formal semantics of DMN decision tables, a notion of DMN table correctness, and algorithms that operationalize two core elements of this correctness notion: the detection of overlapping rules and of missing rules. The algorithms have been implemented atop the DMN toolkit dmn-js. An empirical evaluation on large decision tables has shown the potential for scalability of the proposed algorithms and their ability to generate non-redundant feedback that is more concise than the one generated by the Signavio DMN editor.

The proposed algorithms rely on a geometric interpretation of rules in decision tables, which we foresee could be used to tackle other analysis problems. In particular, we foresee that the problem of simplification of decision tables (rule merging) could be approached from a geometric standpoint. Indeed, if we see the rules as hyperrectangles, the problem of table simplification can be mapped to one of finding an optimal way of merging hyperrectangles with respect to some optimality notion. Another direction for future work is to extend the proposed formal semantics to encompass other aspects of the DMN standard, such as the concept of Decision Requirements Graphs (DRGs), which allow multiple decision tables to be linked in various ways.

Acknowledgement. This research was partly funded by an Institutional Grant of the Estonian Research Council.

References

1. Arge, L., Procopiuc, O., Ramaswamy, S., Suel, T., Vitter, J.S.: Scalable sweeping-based spatial join. In: VLDB (1998)
2. Batoulis, K., Meyer, A., Bazhenova, E., Decker, G., Weske, M.: Extracting decision logic from process models. In: Zdravkovic, J., Kirikova, M., Johannesson, P. (eds.) CAiSE 2015. LNCS, vol. 9097, pp. 349–366. Springer, Heidelberg (2015)
3. CODASYL Decision Table Task Group: A modern appraisal of decision tables: a CODASYL report. ACM (1982)
4. de Moura, L., Bjørner, N.S.: Z3: an efficient SMT solver. In: Ramakrishnan, C.R., Rehof, J. (eds.) TACAS 2008. LNCS, vol. 4963, pp. 337–340. Springer, Heidelberg (2008)
5. Hall, M.A., Frank, E., Holmes, G., Pfahringer, B., Reutemann, P., Witten, I.H.: The WEKA data mining software: an update. SIGKDD Explor. **11**(1), 10–18 (2009)
6. Hewett, R., Leuchner, J.: Restructuring decision tables for elucidation of knowledge. Data Knowl. Eng. **46**(3), 271–290 (2003)
7. Hoover, D.N., Chen, Z.: Tablewise, a decision table tool. In: Proceedings of COMPASS, pp. 97–108 (1995)
8. Object Management Group: Decision Model and Notation (DMN) 1.0 (2015)
9. Pawlak, Z.: Decision tables - a rough set approach. Bull. EATCS **33**, 85–95 (1987)
10. Pooch, U.W.: Translation of decision tables. Compt. Surv. **6**(2), 125–151 (1974)
11. Vanthienen, J., Dries, E.: Illustration of a decision table tool for specifying and implementing knowledge based systems. Int. J. Artif. Intell. Tools **3**(2), 267–288 (1994)
12. Vanthienen, J., Mues, C., Aerts, A.: An illustration of verification and validation in the modelling phase of KBS development. Data Knowl. Eng. **27**(3), 337–352 (1998)
13. Zaidi, A.K., Levis, A.H.: Validation and verification of decision making rules. Automatica **33**(2), 155–169 (1997)

Dynamic Skipping and Blocking and Dead Path Elimination for Cyclic Workflows

Dirk Fahland[1]([⊠]) and Hagen Völzer[2]

[1] Eindhoven University of Technology, Eindhoven, The Netherlands
d.fahland@tue.nl
[2] IBM Research - Zurich, Zurich, Switzerland
hvo@ibm.zurich.com

Abstract. We propose and study dynamic versions of the classical flexibility constructs skip and block and motivate and define a formal semantics for them. We show that our semantics for dynamic blocking is a generalization of classical dead-path-elimination and solves the long-standing open problem to define dead-path elimination for cyclic workflows. This gives rise to a simple and fully local semantics for inclusive gateways.

1 Introduction

One of the challenges in process management is striking a balance between the clarity of a process model on one hand and its ability to support a large variety of process flows on the other hand (also called process flexibility). A model can express flexibility in different ways: by design, by deviation, by underspecification, and by change [13, 14]. Flexibility *by design* faces the above challenge directly: including many different possible paths in a model tends to increase its complexity.

A public service process from a Dutch municipality [3] illustrates the problem; the process model (Fig. 1) has 80 process steps (white) and 20 routing constructs (grey). As 65 % of the process steps are optional under some condition, the model also contains 52 explicit paths for skipping 38 single process steps (black) or 13 segments of multiple process steps (red). Paths for skipping are not mutually exclusive but overlap as indicated by the highlighted segment in the middle of Fig. 1. The complex routing logic is relevant: in 481 cases over a period of over 1 year, each case required steps to be skipped, amounting to 3087 skipped steps for 11846 executed steps (26 %). Other municipalities running the same process face similar dynamics [3], their share of optional process steps ranges between 50 % and 63 % to allow for 516/5363 to 1574/7684 skips in 1 year. Creating, understanding, and

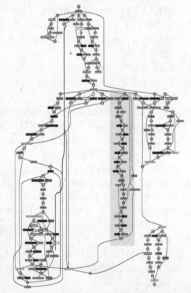

Fig. 1. Model of a flexible process (Color figure online)

© Springer International Publishing Switzerland 2016
M. La Rosa et al. (Eds.): BPM 2016, LNCS 9850, pp. 234–251, 2016.
DOI: 10.1007/978-3-319-45348-4_14

maintaining models for such flexible processes with explicit design constructs is tedious.

The classical concepts to *skip* tasks and to *block* a path can be used to express flexibility by design. They have been used predominantly for *static* flexibility, i.e., to remove tasks or paths from the model *before* deployment through process model configuration [7]. However, in many processes, skipping and blocking dynamically depend on user input or dynamically computed data, e.g., Fig. 1 [3]. Such *dynamic* skipping and blocking can be expressed to some extent in WS-BPEL by setting the status of a *link* through a combination of transition conditions, join conditions, suppressing join failure, and dead path elimination - however, mapping classical skip and block to their implementation in BPEL is not straight-forward. Furthermore, the link status can carry only the values 'true' or 'false', but this binary value can have many different causes, which merges the concepts of flexibility through data conditions, flexibility through alternate joining of paths, join failure, elimination of paths that were deliberately not taken in the process logic, and elimination of paths that are blocked through activity failure. This prevents the free combination of these concepts and can create unintended side effects [15,18]. Moreover, BPEL restricts these constructs to acyclic control-flow graphs.

In this paper, we study dynamic skipping and blocking in the context of BPMN with the following contributions:

1. We define dynamic skipping and blocking for BPMN-like languages, each with a dedicated local semantics, such that they can be used independently from each other or freely combined. We define the semantics for general control-flow graphs, including cyclic graphs.
2. We show that the proposed dynamic blocking generalizes the Dead-Path-Elimination (DPE) concept [18], which so far was limited to acyclic control flow.
3. We show that dynamic blocking is equivalent to having no control-flow on the edge. This allows a modeler to comprehend the semantics of 'block' flows as their intended concept: absence of flow. Therefore, dynamic blocking is closely related with the semantics of inclusive gateways (aka synchronizing merge pattern, OR-join semantics). Our generalization of DPE to cyclic flow graphs gives rise to a purely local semantics for inclusive joins. As a result, our semantics does not entail semantic anomalies such as 'vicious cycles' (see, e.g. [9]). In comparison with existing semantics, it can be enacted faster, i.e., in constant time, it is compositional for more models and therefore easier to understand and use, and it permits more refactoring operations for process models.

We start by discussing concepts for dynamic skipping and blocking based on literature for static skipping and blocking in Sect. 2. In Sect. 3, we generalize dead path elimination to all sound workflow graphs. The resulting local semantics for inclusive gateways is discussed in Sect. 4 in the context of the larger body of literature on inclusive join semantics. We conclude in Sect. 5 where we also compare conceptual and subtle differences of our approach to the literature.

2   Dynamic Skipping and Blocking

In this section, we present dynamic versions of task skipping and path blocking together with modeling examples. These constructs are inspired by their well-known static counterparts. For example, the approach by Gottschalk et al. [7] allows to make a model configurable by adding visual annotations for 'execute', 'hide', and 'block' to tasks and to inputs and outputs of control-flow nodes. 'Execute' leaves the task as is, 'hide' removes the task, whereas 'block' removes the task and the entire flow after it until the next flow merge.

Our exposition is partially based on the view that a process is a synchronization of state machines. We start by explaining that view.

2.1   Workflow Graphs as Synchronized State Machines

We work with *workflow graphs* [5] as the model of the core constructs of business process models. Other modeling elements, e.g., BPMN events, can be added orthogonally and are out of scope of this paper. We use the following definitions.

A *two-terminal graph* is a directed graph (multiple edges between a pair of nodes are allowed) such that (i) there is a unique source and a unique sink and (ii) every node is on a path from the source to the sink. A *workflow graph* is a two-terminal graph with four types of nodes: *task*, *exclusive gateway*, *parallel gateway*, and *dummy* such that (i) the source and the sink are exactly the dummy nodes such that the source has a unique outgoing edge, called the *source edge* and the sink has a unique incoming edge, called the *sink edge* and (ii) each task has at most one input and at most one output edge. Further, each outgoing edge e of an exclusive gateway has a guarding expression $\gamma(e)$. We use the BPMN [11] semantics and visualization for workflow graphs. We will restrict to *sound* workflow graphs, which are defined in Sect. 3.3.

A natural way to understand a workflow graph is to view it as a synchronization of *state machines*, or *threads*, also called *S-components* or *P-components* in Petri net theory. An S-components represents purely sequential behavior, e.g., the lifecycle of a business object such as a purchase order or a payment document. Multiple objects may be completely synchronized, i.e., have exactly the same life cycle represented by the same S-component. Otherwise, different S-components are synchronized through parallel gateways. For example, Fig. 2 shows a decomposition of a simple workflow graph into two S-components A and B, which are synchronized in the black part. A more complex example is shown in Fig. 8.

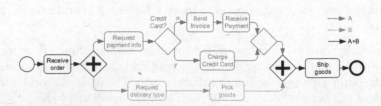

Fig. 2. A workflow graph with two S-components A (red and black) and B (blue and black) (Color figure online)

More formally, a subgraph G' of a workflow graph G is said to be *sequential* if for every parallel gateway, at most one incoming and at most one outgoing edge belongs to G'. G' is an *S-component* of G if (i) G' contains the source and the sink of G and in G', every node is on a path from the source to the sink, and (ii) every exclusive gateway has all its incoming and all its outgoing edges in G'. A set of S-components of G is called a *state machine decomposition* of G if the union of all S-components yields G. Note that every sound workflow graph has a state machine decomposition, which can be computed in cubic time [8]. An important property of S-components is that each S-component is always marked with exactly one token.

2.2 Dynamic Skip

Both constructs that we define, i.e., the *dynamic skip* and the *dynamic block*, allow the control flow of a process to skip one or more activities on its path depending on the evaluation of a dynamic data condition. More precisely, a *data expression* is a Boolean-valued expression that may contain variables that represent data objects of the business process, e.g., $amount > 1000$, *isGoldCustomer(client)*. A *guard* is a data expression associated with a point of the control flow of the workflow graph, which we model as a separate node with a single incoming and a single outgoing edge, depicted as a mini-diamond, cf. the grey mini-diamonds in Fig. 3. This is similar to the data conditions (white mini-diamonds) in BPMN [11].

A token flowing through a guard triggers the evaluation of the guard. Only if the guard evaluates to true, then the subsequent activities in the *scope* of the guard will be executed. Hence the guard can be considered as a precondition for the activities in scope. Informally, the scope of a *skip guard g* is from g until the next guard (of any type) in the S-component.

A simple application of a skip guard (grey mini-diamond) is shown in Fig. 3(a), where two activities are skipped when the data condition $amount > 1000$ evaluates to false. This is of course equivalent to the graph fragment shown in Fig. 3(b), however Fig. 3(a) represents the same behavior more compactly while still indicating the two cases of the flow graphically. This allows a modeler to represent more complex behavior more succinctly. The first guard can 'switch off' the corresponding S-component, the second guard switches it back on in order to make sure that the third activity 'Inform customer' is executed in any case.

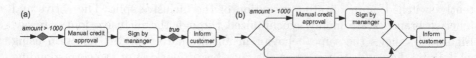

Fig. 3. (a) A simple example for skip guards. (b) Its corresponding explicit representation.

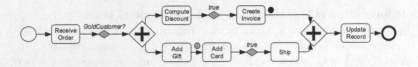

Fig. 4. A workflow graph with three skip guards, a grey and a black token.

A more complex example for skip guards is shown in Fig. 4, which models a part of an order fulfillment process. There are two S-components which split up in the center – the upper is concerned with the invoice whereas the lower is concerned with the physical items to be shipped. Both of these two components behave differently in case the item is shipped to a gold customer. Hence the guard is placed already before the parallel split. If the customer is not a gold customer, then the activities 'Compute discount', 'Add gift' and 'Add card' are skipped.

We formalize the effect of guards using token colors. The normal token color is *black*. The workflow starts with a single black token on the source. A black token flowing through a skip guard remains black if the guard evaluates to true and turns into a *grey* token otherwise. Similarly, a grey token flowing through a skip guard turns black if the guard evaluates to true and remains grey otherwise. A black token flowing through an activity executes the activity, a grey token skips the activity. An activity does not change the color of a token flowing through it. Likewise, the token color does not change through split gateways and exclusive joins. A parallel join emits a black token iff at least one of its inputs is black, otherwise it emits a grey token. Hence, a skip guard evaluating to false switches off the S-component until it is switched on again by another skip guard or by synchronizing with another S-component that is switched on. Figure 4 shows a reachable marking of the corresponding graph with one black and one grey token.

2.3   Dynamic Block

A skip guard can switch on or off an S-component repeatedly. In contrast, a *block guard* blocks an S-component persistently, i.e., after a blocking, the S-component cannot be switched on again by another guard. Thus any activity on the S-component is skipped until the S-component synchronizes with another S-component that is still active. This behavior is known from the synchronizing split/merge control-flow pattern, which is also known as the inclusive split and join, cf. Fig. 5(a). Each of the branches, i.e., S-components is either persistently switched on or off after execution of the inclusive split. The active and inactive branches are finally synchronized through the inclusive join gateway. Figure 5(b) shows the same behavior in an alternative BPMN notation using white mini-diamonds to represent the data-based blocking of the corresponding branch. Hence we use the BPMN white mini-diamond to represent a block guard as shown in Fig. 5(c).

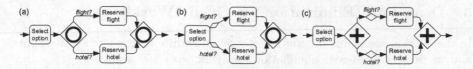

Fig. 5. (a) Inclusive split and -join, (b) Inclusive split with BPMN mini-diamond, (c) Proposed notation with block guards

Figure 6 shows a more elaborate example for the use of block guards. Similarly to Fig. 5, a subset of the branches can be activated. However, the upper branch is always taken, which does not need any guard. The lower branch is also always taken, and hence the activity 'Add standard travel insurance' is always executed - however this branch, i.e., S-component, is switched off subsequently by the block guard whenever an optional emergency insurance is not selected, which means that all remaining activities before the parallel join will be skipped. Since all those activities are skipped whenever a preceding block guard evaluates to false, the guard can again be viewed as a precondition to those activities.

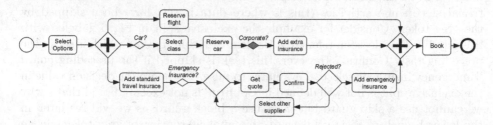

Fig. 6. A more complex example for a block guard

To formalize block guards, we introduce *white* tokens. A black or grey token entering a block guard g turns white when g evaluates to false, otherwise it retains its color. A white token flowing through a block guard, skip guard, or an exclusive gateway always retains its color, hence the guard does not need to be evaluated in that case. If a white token flows through an activity, the activity is not executed and the color of the token does not change. Likewise, a white token entering a parallel split produces only white tokens on the outgoing edges of the parallel split. A parallel split emits a black token iff at least one of its inputs is black, it emits a grey token iff none of its inputs is black but at least one is grey, and it emits a white token iff all its inputs are white.

Note that, so far, the difference between a skip and a block guard is merely that blocking is more permanent than skipping, i.e., a grey token can easily be turned into a black one whereas a white token cannot. However, we will introduce another crucial difference in Sect. 3.2.

3   Dead Path Elimination for Cyclic Workflows

In this section, we define the routing of grey and white tokens in exclusive splits, and we present dead-path elimination for cyclic workflow graphs.

3.1   Grey Tokens in Exclusive Splits

How should we route a grey or white token in an exclusive split? Both token colors represent inactive S-components – recall that all incoming and outgoing edges of an exclusive gateway belong to the same S-components. However, while a white token cannot execute any activity on any of the outgoing branches of the exclusive split since it cannot become black, a grey token can become black, and it will in general execute different activities on different outgoing branches just as a black token can. Therefore, it matters how we route a grey token and we route it as a black token, i.e., according to the evaluation of the data expression in the exclusive split – firmly controlled by the modeler.

This requires care since the data variables that the exclusive split refers to must be in an expected state, in particular must be defined at all. This is not trivial since some activities (this is where data is set) have been skipped by the grey token. Consider for example the exclusive split in Fig. 6, labeled with 'Rejected?'. This decision refers to a Boolean variable *rejected* which is set in the preceding task 'Confirm'. However, this task is skipped if the preceding guard 'Emergency insurance selected' evaluates to false. Therefore the decision value in the exclusive split is not well defined if 'Confirm' is not executed (and that's why we cannot use a skip guard but must use a block guard–as we will see later–in the lower branch of Fig. 6). Likewise, this explicit routing of grey tokens in an exclusive split must be carefully designed by the modeler if the split represents the exit condition of a loop to make sure that the process eventually exits the loop to be able to terminate.

This extra care will not be necessary when using white tokens as we show below. On the other hand, grey tokens, i.e., skip guards, provide greater flexibility than block guards. In particular, the explicit control of routing grey tokens in exclusive splits can be leveraged to model different skipping behavior in different branches of the S-component. For example, Fig. 7 models that all *GoldCustomers* receive an immediate prioritization of picking their goods; the upper alternative branch is taken for members living in an area where delivery via drone is offered, but only *GoldCustomers* get their picked goods scheduled for delivery via drone (for non-*GoldCustomers* this activity is still skipped); for any customer (Gold or regular) living in a different area the lower branch is taken and a flyer about alternative rapid delivery options is added to their shipment.

3.2   White Tokens in Exclusive Splits and Dead Path Elimination

In contrast to the explicit routing of grey tokens, we can route a white token implicitly at an exclusive split. Intuitively, the routing of a white token does not

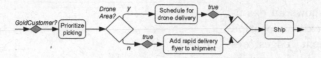

Fig. 7. Flexible skipping in different branches of an S-component

matter, because the S-component is dead anyway – neither of the branches can be executed because a white token remains white, hence all activities on each of the branches are skipped. In particular, we do not need to evaluate the data condition at an exclusive split if a white token arrives at it, which is important, because it may not be well defined – as we have seen in Fig. 6.

Still we have to make sure that a white token arrives at the next synchronization point, i.e., 'eliminates the dead path', even or in particular in the presence of cycles as in Fig. 6, where we have to make sure that the white token is not following a cycle infinitely often and prevents termination of the process. We can do that by implicitly 'flushing out' the white tokens, i.e., route them automatically towards the sink, thereby providing a form of dead path elimination for cyclic workflow graphs. We operationalize such a behavior by help of an *exit allocation*.

Definition 1. *Call any outgoing edge of an exclusive split a* choice edge *of the workflow graph. An* exit allocation *is a mapping ϕ that assigns to each exclusive split v one of its choice edges $\phi(v)$, called the* exit edge, *such that, for each edge e of the workflow graph there exists a path from e to the sink such that each choice edge on the path is an exit edge.*

The intuition behind Definition 1 is that white tokens will get flushed out of the graph by routing them via exit edges. The exit edges are statically fixed and can be considered as 'providing a compass' to the sink. To justify this definition, we first observe:

Theorem 1. *An exit allocation exists for each workflow graph and it can be computed in time $O(|E| + |V| \cdot \log |V|)$.*

Proof. Note that a workflow graph is equivalent to a corresponding isomorphic free-choice Petri net [5]. Therefore, we can directly apply the theory of free-choice Petri nets to workflow graphs. An exit allocation is an *allocation pointing to* the sink in the sense of [1, Definition 6.4]. Existence follows from [1, Lemma 6.5 (1)]. We can use Dijkstras algorithm to compute, for each node the shortest path to the sink. We allocate a choice edge of an exclusive split v as exit edge if it starts the shortest path from v to the sink. It follows that, for each edge e, every choice edge on the shortest path from e to the sink is an exit edge.

Figure 8 shows an example of an exit allocation where the exit edges are shown in bold. A white token produced by the block guard g_1 will be routed at the exclusive splits d_1 and d_2 towards the parallel join j_2, where it is joined with either a black token or a white token produced by block guard g_2. A white token arriving at d_3 is routed

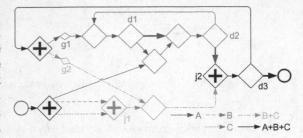

Fig. 8. A workflow graph decomposed into three S-components A (red and black), B (orange, green, and black) and C (blue, green, and black). An exit allocation is shown in bold. (Color figure online)

directly to the sink. Note that an exit allocation for the graph in Fig. 8 is not unique. We could have chosen also the other choice edge of d_1 (but not for d_2 or d_3).

An exit allocation defines the routing of white and only white tokens at an exclusive split and it does not need to be defined by the modeler – it is implicitly there, i.e., the compiler or execution engine provides the dead path elimination automatically. However, since an exit allocation is not unique and the modeler does not choose it, how does the modeler understand and control the behavior of the workflow graph? To this end, we prove that the particular choice of the exit allocation does not matter, i.e., all exit allocations and even more general, all *fair* routings of white tokens produce essentially the same behavior. Therefore any exit allocation operationalizes the same abstract behavior of dead path elimination.

Before we formally prove this, we have to formalize our extended model of workflow graphs and their semantics.

3.3   Multipolar Workflow Graphs

In this section, we present the formal concepts for our model, which we named *multipolar workflow graph* based on the bipolar synchronization schemes of [6] which introduced true/false tokens for graphs without choices; see [4, Appendix A] for a rigorous formalization of our model.

A *multipolar workflow graph* G consists of a workflow graph with two additional nodes types *skip guard* (small grey diamond) and *block guard* (small white diamond); $°v$ and $v°$ denote the input and output edges of node v, respectively. Each guard v has one incoming and one outgoing edge and is annotated with an expression $\gamma(v)$ over some data variables, where the data is accessed during process and updated during task execution. A *marking m* assigns to each edge a nonnegative number of *tokens*, where each token has a *color* $c \in C = \{black, grey, white\}$. We write $m[e, c]$ for the number of tokens of color $c \in C$ on e and $m[e] = \sum_{c \in C} m[e, c]$ for the number of all tokens of any color in m on e; m is *safe* iff $m[e] \leq 1$ for each edge e. The marking with exactly one black token on the source edge and no token elsewhere is called the *initial*

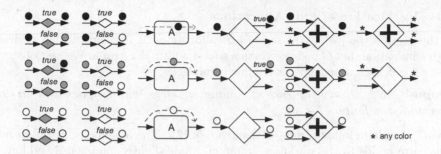

Fig. 9. Possible transitions of nodes in a multipolar workflow graph.

marking of G. A marking that has a single token of any color on the sink edge and no token elsewhere is called a *final marking* of G.

Nodes are *enabled* as in classical workflow graphs: a task, exclusive gateway, or guard v needs a token (of any color) on some edge $e^- \in {}^\circ v$; a parallel gateway v needs a token on each edge $e^- \in {}^\circ v$. Each node v defines several *transitions* t that distinguish the possible colors of input tokens consumed and output tokens produced in a step $m \xrightarrow{t} m'$ as illustrated in Fig. 9; see [4, Appendix A] for the formalization.

A step $m \xrightarrow{t} m'$ of G is called an *elimination* step, denoted $m \dashrightarrow^{t} m'$ if all tokens consumed (and produced) by t are white, otherwise it is a *normal* step. If m' can be reached from m through zero or more elimination steps, we write $m \dashrightarrow^{*} m'$. We write $m \xrightarrow{\text{max}}^{*} m^*$ if $m \dashrightarrow^{*} m^*$ and m^* does not enable any further elimination step. Given an exit allocation ϕ for G, we say that an elimination step $m \dashrightarrow^{t} m'$ *complies with* ϕ if the white token is produced on $e^+ = \phi(v)$ whenever t is a step of an exclusive split v.

A *trace* of G is a sequence $\sigma = m_0, t_1, m_1, \ldots$ of markings and transitions s.t. m_0 is the initial marking of G and $m_i \xrightarrow{t_{i+1}} m_{i+1}$ for each $i \geq 0$; σ is *maximal* if it is either infinite or ends in a marking m_n such that no transition is enabled in m_n. A trace σ is *fair* with respect to a choice edge e of an exclusive split v of G if the following holds: If v is executed infinitely often in σ, then e is marked infinitely often in σ.

A node v (edge e) is *dead* in m if no marking reachable from m enables v (marks e). A node or edge x is *live* in m if x is not dead in each marking reachable from m. A *local deadlock* is a marking in which a node v other than the sink is dead and an edge $e \in {}^\circ v$ is marked. G is *live* if no marking reachable from the initial marking m_0 is a local deadlock. G is *safe* if each marking reachable from m_0 is safe. G is *sound* if G is safe and live. Equivalently, G is sound iff G is safe, the sink edge is live in m_0 and only a final marking is a reachable marking that marks the sink edge. Soundness guarantees that each maximal and fair trace of G terminates in a final marking of G.

3.4 Justification of Exit Allocations

In this section, we justify the use of exit allocations as implementation of dead path elimination. Let G be henceforth a sound multipolar graph. We first observe that an exit allocation implements fair behavior:

Proposition 1. *Every sequence of elimination steps that complies with an exit allocation ϕ is finite.*

Proof. The claim follows from [1, Lemma 6.5, (2)]: The free-choice workflow net that corresponds to the workflow graph, cf. [5], is slightly modified by adding a transition, called the *return transition*, that consumes a token from the sink and produces a token on the source. This version is called the *connected version*. It is strongly connected and the exit allocation points to the return transition in the sense of [1]. Furthermore, each reachable marking of a sound workflow graph is bounded. [1, Lemma 6.5, (2)] now implies that an infinite elimination sequence implies infinitely many firings of the return transition, which implies the claim.

In the following, we will prove that all exit allocations generate essentially the same behavior. We prove first that two maximal elimination sequences that comply with the same exit allocation end in the same marking:

Lemma 1. *Let m_0 be a reachable marking, ϕ be an exit allocation and $m_0 \overset{max}{\dashrightarrow} m_1$ and $m_0 \overset{max}{\dashrightarrow} m_2$ be two maximal elimination sequences that comply with ϕ. Then we have $m_1 = m_2$.*

Proof. Every elimination step that is enabled in m_0 will be executed in a maximal elimination sequence because it cannot be disabled by another elimination step. Therefore, it can be shown by induction that each maximal elimination sequence contains the same steps, i.e., one maximal sequence is a permutation of the other. The marking equation for Petri nets (cf. [1]) implies that both sequences end in the same marking.

As a result, we can consider two elimination sequences both starting in m_0 and ending in $m_1 = m_2$ to be equivalent, as neither executes any activities. An even stronger result holds: any two fair, maximal elimination sequences starting in m_0 necessarily reach the same marking even if they do not comply with a particular exit allocation.

Lemma 2. *Let m_0 be a reachable marking, $m_0 \overset{max}{\dashrightarrow} m_1$ and $m_0 \overset{max}{\dashrightarrow} m_2$ be two fair maximal elimination sequences. Then we have $m_1 = m_2$.*

Proof (Sketch). In the state-machine decomposition of the sound WFG, any S-component contains exactly one token. During elimination steps, the single white token only travels edges of 'its' S-component until reaching a parallel join. Two different sequences reaching two different markings $m_1 \neq m_2$ would reach different parallel joins. But then one would cause either a local deadlock or an *improper termination*, i.e., a reachable marking that has a token on the sink edge and another token elsewhere. Both cases contradict soundness of the WFG. The detailed proof is given in [4, Appendix B]

We can now prove that the behavior of the WFG does not depend on the choice of a particular exit allocation, and hence *the behavior of the WFG does not depend on the routing of white tokens.* In other words, routing white tokens in exclusive splits in a fair but otherwise nondeterministic way suffices to reach a unique marking after finite elimination steps. We do not prove the result in full generality, i.e., for the most general behavioral equivalence possible, as the necessary technical overhead would not justify the additional insight within the scope of this paper. In a technically simplified form, we assume that the WFG is executed with *eager* elimination, i.e., after each normal step, we execute a sequence of maximal elimination steps before we execute the next normal step.

Theorem 2. *Let σ and σ' be two eager traces of a sound multipolar WFG, i.e., they are of the form $m_0 \xrightarrow{t_1} m_1 \xdashrightarrow{max} m_2 \xrightarrow{t_2} \dots$ where m_0 is the initial marking of the WFG, and*

1. *$t_i, i > 0$ are normal steps such that for any two markings m_i, m_j of σ and σ', we have $m_i = m_j$ implies $t_{i+1} = t_{j+1}$, i.e. the program behaves deterministically from a given marking, and*
2. *$m_i \xdashrightarrow{max} m_{i+1}$ are fair and maximal elimination sequences.*

Then, σ and σ' have the same sequence of normal steps and in particular the same sequence of executed activities.

Proof. The theorem follows directly from Lemma 2.

Note that the proof of Theorem 2 rests on the essential property of white tokes, i.e., that a white token always remains white. This property allows us to route them automatically.

We have shown that a modeler can abstract from the behavior of white tokens and consider block guards as a means to disable control-flow along the subsequent path as if no token is present. As any fair routing of white tokens is permissible, the compiler or execution engine can choose an exit allocation that optimizes some cost measure, e.g., the average number of elimination steps, to implement the fair routing. Control-flow will consistently and predictably re-emerge at parallel joins with black tokens. Next, we show that this property allows us to give inclusive gateways a simple and fully local semantics.

4   Dynamic Blocking as Inclusive Gateway Semantics

We have argued already in Sect. 2.3 that parallel gateways in combination with block guards with their semantics of white tokens and dead path elimination provide a generalization of inclusive gateways. This allows us to propose to use the semantics proposed above as an inclusive join semantics. Since we only use the existing constructs of parallel gateways and white mini-diamonds, the new semantics would allow us to use inclusive gateways merely as syntactic sugar for parallel gateways with block guards or to abolish the inclusive gateways altogether. Next, we discuss such a proposal in more detail.

Many papers on the inclusive join semantics (aka Or-join semantics) problem have been published, for a survey see [17]. In this section, we compare our proposal with existing semantics from the literature with respect to various properties.

Enactment. Existing semantics that do not restrict to a subset of workflow graphs are *non-local*, i.e., the enablement of an inclusive join there depends not only on the tokens of the incoming edges of the join but also on the presence of tokens on other edges of the graph. Two kinds of non-local semantics have been proposed: In the first, the enablement can depend on the entire state space of the workflow graph, e.g., [9]. Therefore, enactment takes exponential time. In the second kind of non-local semantics, which includes the current BPMN semantics [11], the enablement depends on the existence of paths from other tokens in the graph to the inclusive join [2, 17]. It can be determined in linear [17] or quadratic time [2] respectively whether a particular inclusive join is enabled. The run time can be reduced in both cases by trading time for space, i.e., by creating data structures of quadratic size.

The local semantics presented in this paper has a small constant overhead for storing the additional token colors. It can be determined in constant time whether a particular inclusive join is enabled under the assumption that the in-degree of nodes is bounded by a constant.

Compositionality. A process model can be better understood if it is composed out of simpler patterns or modules. However this is only the case when the simple module can be understood in isolation, i.e., independent from the context it will be embedded in. Note that many textbooks explain the semantics of BPMN gateways, in particular the inclusive gateway by help of simple patterns.

One of the simplest and most popular notions of module is a single-entry-single-exit fragment, cf. e.g. [16]. Figure 10 shows such a fragment (shaded) nested in another fragment. Considered in isolation, each fragment has the expected intuitive and sound behavior in the BPMN semantics, cf. [11, 17]. However, if we compose them in the way shown, the composed workflow graph has a deadlock (the marking shown in Fig. 10) in the BPMN semantics. This is due to the non-local semantics of the inclusive join in BPMN where the synchronization behavior can depend on tokens outside the containing fragment.

In our local semantics, the behavior of any subgraph G depends only on the tokens it exchanges at its border, i.e., the behavior of a composed graph is

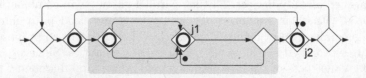

Fig. 10. The current BPMN semantics for inclusive joins is not fully compositional w.r.t. single-entry-single-exit fragments.

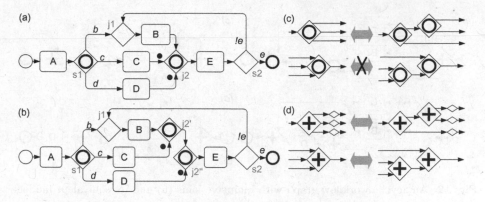

Fig. 11. The BPMN inclusive join semantics is not robust under node splitting (a) and (b). The corresponding refactoring rule (c) is valid in our semantics (d).

the composition of the behaviors of its constituent graphs. Even the non-local property of soundness is compositional for single-entry-single-exit-fragments in the local semantics, i.e., a composition is sound if and only if all its constituent fragments are sound [16]. The example in Fig. 10 shows that the non-local BPMN semantics [11,17] is not compositional in general in this sense.

Refactoring. Compositionality supports refactoring, i.e., maintenance of a process model. A fragment can be extracted from a process model, outsourced into a separate process and then called from different places without changing the behavior. There are other well-known refactoring operations that preserve the local semantics, viz. various structural transformation rules originally stated for Petri nets [10], but which apply to workflow graphs as well. For example, the two patterns shown in Fig. 11(d) are equivalent in any context in our local semantics as this is a well-known rule for parallel gateways. Note that the combination of colors in a parallel join can be seen as a form of disjunction or maximum operation. In particular, it is commutative and associative. However, the corresponding rule for the non-local semantics for inclusive gateways in BPMN is not valid (Fig. 11(c)). As a counterexample, we consider the model Fig. 11(b) that is obtained by applying the rule for inclusive joins from Fig. 11(c) on join j_2 of the model of Fig. 11(a). The workflow graph in Fig. 11(b) is not sound – the marking shown is a deadlock in the non-local semantics of BPMN, whereas the workflow graph of Fig. 11(a) is sound. Therefore, for that semantics, the rule in Fig. 11(c) is not a valid refactoring rule. Whether a deadlock occurs or not depends in our local semantics only on whether all incoming edges are live (a black, grey, or white token will eventually arrive) or whether one edge is dead (there may no token arrive). Transformation rules such as the one of Fig. 11(d) preserve whether an edge is live or dead, and hence can be applied in any situation. How to express the model of Fig. 11(a) in our semantics is discussed next; Fig. 13 shows the result.

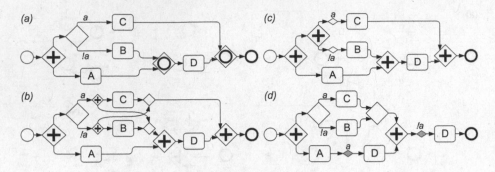

Fig. 12. An acyclic workflow graph with inclusive joins (a) and its equivalent models (b–d)

Expressiveness. A semantics is preferable to another if it can model more (realistic) process behaviors than the other in a concise way. The best documented modeling use case for inclusive gateways is the structured synchronizing merge pattern, cf. Fig. 5(a). Figure 5(c) already showed that this case can be modeled isomorphically with parallel gateways and block guards.

Another well-understood context for the use of inclusive joins are acyclic workflow graphs. There is little debate what semantics inclusive joins should have in acyclic graphs, only how to express that semantics such that it generalizes to a semantics for general workflow graphs. Figure 12(a) shows a paradigmatic example, where a task D is executed after concurrent tasks A and B, but B is executed only when the condition a is false. Often, but not always, all inclusive joins can be replaced by parallel joins [5], at the price of introducing additional auxiliary paths called *bridges*, cf. Fig. 12(b). However, each acyclic graph in BPMN semantics is equivalent when each inclusive and exclusive split is replaced with a parallel split with block guards and each exclusive and inclusive join is replaced with a parallel join, which follows from [17, Theorem 2]. The resulting workflow graph is a BPEL flow with DPE semantics. For the graph in Fig. 12(a), the resulting graph is shown Fig. 12(c). Note that we can also re-model the graph in Fig. 12(a) into a well-structured graph, i.e., a graph where the gateways are matching pairs of split and join, cf. Fig. 12(d). We do this by using skip guards at the expense of duplicating the conditions a and $!a$ and the task D.

Acyclic workflow graphs can be composed by single-entry-single-exit nesting with arbitrary sequential workflow graphs. For the resulting workflow graphs, the BPMN semantics and our local semantics here agree, which follows from the theorems in [17]. Only for workflow graphs that cannot be obtained in this way, the two semantics disagree. A few such graphs with sound behavior have been documented for technical discussion [2,17]; the model of Fig. 11(a) is an example. We have verified that these workflow graphs documented there can be easily equivalently modeled with our local semantics, again by adding bridges. Figure 13 shows the model of Fig. 11(a) in our semantics. The bridges producing white

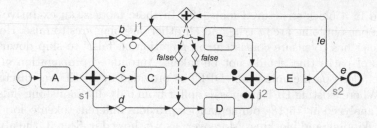

Fig. 13. Representation of the unstructured loop with inclusive gateways of Fig. 11(a) in our semantics.

tokens (by the 'false' block guards) can be merged anywhere along the c and d branches. In summary, the rare modeling cases where concurrency and loops cannot be separated by single-entry-single-exit decomposition can still easily be supported by the local semantics at the expense of extra bridges. The extra bridges for rare models are a small price to pay for faster execution across all models and the other advantages of the local semantics discussed above.

Note that the default outgoing edge of inclusive splits as defined in BPMN [11] to ensure a token in the sink upon termination is not necessary in the local semantics, because the white tokens that are sent take care of these issues.

5   Conclusion

We have defined dynamic versions of task skipping and path blocking together with a local semantics which supports efficient execution. Dynamic path blocking comes with dead path elimination, which we have generalized to work for all sound workflow graphs. We argued that when inclusive gateways in BPMN are semantically replaced with parallel gateways with block guards, the advantages outweigh the disadvantages. Note also that workflow graphs with a fully local semantics can be easier and more naturally mapped to Petri nets where a wealth of tools and algorithms is available for their analysis. In particular, verifying soundness can be done in polynomial time for the local semantics, whereas no polynomial-time algorithm is known to verify soundness under the non-local BPMN semantics for inclusive joins.

Further related work. We already discussed in Sect. 2 how our semantics for dynamic skipping and blocking originates from ideas of configurable process models, e.g. [7]. In Sect. 4 we extensively discussed our semantics wrt. works on the inclusive join semantics. Another way to support dynamic skipping and blocking is to give each task an explicit *activation condition* (over process data and control-flow) that, when evaluated to false, leads to *skipping* of the activity [20]; the modeler can choose to further propagate 'true' or 'false' control-flow values by a corresponding start condition [19, p. 55]. This model was restricted to acylic processes, but can be generalized to models where 'false' flows are contained in a block-structured loop [12]. In these models, an exclusive choice evaluates one outgoing arc to true and all other outgoing arcs to false. However, the modeler has to ensure consistent propagation of 'false' to skip downstream activities of paths that should not be taken. Automated propagation of 'false' edges, i.e., dead path elimination (DPE) as provided by BPEL was discussed in Sect. 1. Where existing DPE proposals suffer from only distinguishing 'false' and 'true' as analyzed in [15,18], our semantics provides different token colors to distinguish skipping and blocking. Moreover, as we showed in Sect. 3, the ability to also route skipping and blocking flow across exclusive choices (rather than propagating 'false'), makes our approach applicable to any model, including cyclic ones.

Additional remarks. We have assumed a unique sink only for simplicity of the presentation. Multiple sinks can be easily admitted as they are equivalent to an implicit inclusive join that merges all sinks into one. The use of blocking for paths that lead to a sink is compatible with that view and our definition of blocking.

References

1. Desel, J., Esparza, J.: Free Choice Petri Nets. Cambridge University Press, New York (1995)
2. Dumas, M., Grosskopf, A., Hettel, T., Wynn, M.T.: Semantics of standard process models with OR-joins. In: Meersman, R., Tari, Z. (eds.) OTM 2007, Part I. LNCS, vol. 4803, pp. 41–58. Springer, Heidelberg (2007)
3. Fahland, D., van der Aalst, W.M.P.: Model repair - aligning process models to reality. Inf. Syst. **47**, 220–243 (2015)
4. Fahland, D., Völzer, H.: Dynamic Skipping and Blocking and Dead Path Elimination for Cyclic Workflows (Ext. Version). BPM Center Report BPM-16-05 (2016). http://bpmcenter.org
5. Favre, C., Fahland, D., Völzer, H.: The relationship between workflow graphs and free-choice workflow nets. Inf. Syst. **47**, 197–219 (2015)
6. Genrich, H.J., Thiagarajan, P.S.: A theory of bipolar synchronization schemes. Theor. Comput. Sci. **30**, 241–318 (1984)
7. Gottschalk, F., van der Aalst, W.M.P., Jansen-Vullers, M.H., La Rosa, M.: Configurable workflow models. Int. J. Coop. Inf. Syst. **17**(2), 177–221 (2008)
8. Kemper, P., Bause, F.: An efficient polynomial-time algorithm to decide liveness and boundedness of free-choice nets. In: Jensen, K. (ed.) ICATPN 1992. LNCS, vol. 616, pp. 263–278. Springer, Heidelberg (1992)
9. Kindler, E.: On the semantics of EPCs: resolving the vicious circle. Data Knowl. Eng. **56**(1), 23–40 (2006)
10. Murata, T.: Petri nets: properties, analysis and applications. Proc. IEEE **77**(4), 541–580 (1989)
11. OMG: Business process model and notation (BPMN) version 2.0, OMG document number dtc/2010-05-03. Technical report (2010)
12. Reichert, M., Dadam, P.: ADEPT$_{flex}$-supporting dynamic changes of workflows without losing control. J. Intell. Inf. Syst. **10**(2), 93–129 (1998)

13. Reichert, M., Weber, B.: Enabling Flexibility in Process-Aware Information Systems - Challenges, Methods, Technologies. Springer, Heidelberg (2012)
14. La Rosa, M., van der Aalst, W.M.P., Dumas, M., Milani, F.P.: Business process variability modeling: a survey. QUT e-Print 61842, QUT, Australia (2013)
15. van Breugel, F., Koshkina, M.: Dead-path-elimination in BPEL4WS. In: Fifth International Conference on Application of Concurrency to System Design (ACSD 2005), 6–9 June 2005, St. Malo, France, pp. 192–201. IEEE Computer Society (2005)
16. Vanhatalo, J., Völzer, H., Leymann, F.: Faster and more focused control-flow analysis for business process models through SESE decomposition. In: Krämer, B.J., Lin, K.-J., Narasimhan, P. (eds.) ICSOC 2007. LNCS, vol. 4749, pp. 43–55. Springer, Heidelberg (2007)
17. Völzer, H.: A new semantics for the inclusive converging gateway in safe processes. In: Hull, R., Mendling, J., Tai, S. (eds.) BPM 2010. LNCS, vol. 6336, pp. 294–309. Springer, Heidelberg (2010)
18. Weidlich, M., Großkopf, A., Barros, A.P.: Realising dead path elimination in BPMN. In: 2009 IEEE Conference on Commerce and Enterprise Computing, CEC 2009, Vienna, Austria, 20–23 July 2009, pp. 345–352. IEEE Computer Society (2009)
19. Weske, M.: Workflow management systems: formal foundation, conceptual design, implementation aspects. Habilitationsschrift Fachbereich Mathematik und Informatik, Universität Münster (2000)
20. Weske, M.: Formal foundation and conceptual design of dynamic adaptations in a workflow management system. In: 34th Annual Hawaii International Conference on System Sciences (HICSS-34), 3–6 January 2001, Maui, Hawaii, USA. IEEE Computer Society (2001)

The Complexity of Deadline Analysis
for Workflow Graphs with Multiple Resources

Mirela Botezatu[1,2]([⊠]), Hagen Völzer[1], and Lothar Thiele[2]

[1] IBM Research, Zürich, Switzerland
mirela.botezatu@gmail.com
[2] ETH, Zürich, Switzerland

Abstract. We study whether the executions of a time-annotated sound workflow graph (WFG) meet a given deadline when an unbounded number of resources (i.e., executing agents) is available. We present polynomial-time algorithms and NP-hardness results for different cases. In particular, we show that it can be decided in polynomial time whether some executions of a sound workflow graph meet the deadline. For acyclic sound workflow graphs, it can be decided in linear time whether some or all executions meet the deadline. Furthermore, we show that it is NP-hard to compute the expected duration of a sound workflow graph for unbounded resources, which is contrasting the earlier result that the expected duration of a workflow graph executed by a single resource can be computed in cubic time. We also propose an algorithm for computing the maximum concurrency of the workflow graph, which helps to determine the optimal number of resources needed to execute the workflow graph.

1 Introduction

A workflow graph can capture the main control flow of processes modeled in languages such as BPMN, UML-Activity Diagrams, and Event Process Chains, cf. [11]. That is, the core routing constructs of these languages can be mapped to the routing constructs of workflow graphs, which are alternative choice and merge, and concurrent fork and join. Figure 1 shows an example of a workflow graph modeling a ticket resolution workflow. After a task to categorize the ticket ("Label ticket"), there is a choice $s1$ whether the ticket documents a database issue (DB) or a disk issue (HDD). Following the case of HDD, there is a preliminary step to fetch the disk logs followed by a fork $f2$ that spawns two concurrent threads. One thread follows "Consistency check", the other thread follows "Analyze HDD logs". Then each thread is merged with the corresponding thread of the case DB through the merge gateways $m1$ and $m2$. After merging, there are some additional tasks "Identify error" and "Report usage pattern", before the threads are synchronized at the join $j1$. Finally there are some wrap-up tasks, common to both cases.

A workflow graph is equivalent to a two-terminal free-choice Petri net i.e., a connected net with a unique source and sink, which is also called a *free-choice workflow net* [6]. A workflow graph can be seen as a compact representation of

© Springer International Publishing Switzerland 2016
M. La Rosa et al. (Eds.): BPM 2016, LNCS 9850, pp. 252–268, 2016.
DOI: 10.1007/978-3-319-45348-4_15

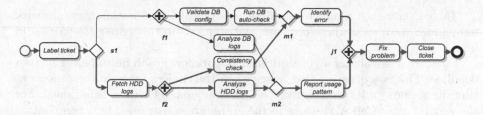

Fig. 1. An example of a workflow graph and one of its executions (red) (Color figure online)

the corresponding free-choice net. Therefore, the theory of free-choice Petri nets directly applies to workflow graphs.

A workflow graph may contain a local deadlock or exhibit *lack of synchronization*. The latter corresponds to unsafeness in Petri nets. The absence of local deadlock and lack of synchronization has been termed *soundness*, which can be decided in cubic time by help of the rank theorem for free-choice Petri nets [5], also cf. [1].

In this paper, we analyze whether the executions of a sound workflow graph meet a given deadline, where tasks, or, equivalently, edges are annotated with execution times. We are not aware of any similar work for the model class we investigate. In our previous work [3], we considered the case where the workflow graph is executed by a single resource (i.e., executing agent). In this work, we provide results for the case where the workflow graph is executed by an unbounded number of resources. We also discuss the case of a fixed number $n > 1$ of resources in Sect. 6.

General workflow graphs can of course be analyzed for timing behavior in terms of their reachability graph, and there are various techniques and tools that support this [9,10,18]. This holds also for non-Petri-net like models, e.g., timed automata where the minimum cost reachability problem is addressed through exponential branch-and-bound based algorithms [13]. Since the construction of the reachability graph incurs an exponential blowup, these techniques do not run in polynomial time in the size of the workflow graph. In this paper, we show that some deadline analysis problems for workflow graphs can nevertheless be solved in polynomial time.

Table 1. Overview of results; new contributions in bold

	1. All executions	2. Some execution	3. Probability of transgression	4. Expected duration	5. Min. nr. resources
A. Sound WFG	NP-hard	$O(|V||E|)$	NP-hard	**NP-hard**	**Open**[a]
B. Acyclic sound WFG	$O(|V| + |E|)$	$O(|V| + |E|)$	NP-hard	**NP-hard**	**Open**[a]
C. Regular WFG	$O(|V| + |E|)$	$O(|V| + |E|)$	NP-hard	**NP-hard**	$O(|V| + |E|)$

[a] We give a heuristic for this in Sect. 5

Table 1 shows the results for deadline analysis of sound workflow graphs with unbounded resources, where our new contributions in this paper are written in bold.

First, we ask whether all executions of a workflow graph finish before a given deadline. This is a question that arises when the choices made in the process at runtime are not under our control. This corresponds to Column 1 in Table 1. For the general case (Cell A.1), loops in the graph are constrained by a termination order. The complexity result for this case follows directly from Theorem 2 in our previous paper [3]. For acyclic workflow graphs, this question can be answered in linear time (Cell B.1) and we provide an algorithm for this in Sect. 3. For *regular graphs*, which are workflow graphs that can be generated by a regular expression, i.e., every split corresponds to a join of the same logic (see Fig. 3 for an example), the solutions consist of simple recursive algorithms that run in linear time (Cell C.1).

Next, we assume we have control over the choices made in the process at runtime. Therefore, we ask the question whether there exists an instantiation of the process – an execution – that meets a given deadline. This corresponds to Column 2 in Table 1. In particular, as one of our main contributions, we show that for general sound workflow graphs, finding the minimum duration over all executions can be solved in polynomial time (Cell A.2). When restricting to acyclic workflow graphs (Cell B.2, similarly as for Cell B.1), the problem can be solved in linear time. As above, for regular graphs, the minimum duration of an execution can be computed recursively in linear time.

Suppose not all executions meet a given deadline but only some. We can then ask whether the probability of a deadline transgression exceeds a given threshold - Column 3 in Table 1. Results carry over from our previous work [3] where we have proven that computing whether the probability of an execution with a single resource terminating before the deadline exceeds a given threshold is NP-hard (Cells A.3, B.3 and C.3).

Also in the probabilistic framework, another valuable information is the expected duration of an execution of a given workflow graph. The results related to this question map to Column 4 in Table 1. We show that computing the expected duration is NP-hard even for regular graphs. This is in contrast to the execution with a single resource where, the expected duration can be computed in cubic time for general sound workflow graphs [3].

Finally, we ask what is the optimal number of resources for the workflow graph where optimal means the minimum number k of resources such that each execution achieves its minimal execution time under k resources (Column 5 in Table 1). We propose an algorithm for computing the maximum concurrency of a workflow graph in Sect. 5, which is an upper bound for the optimal number of resources.

2   Preliminaries

In this section, we define the necessary fundamental notions, which include workflow graphs and their semantics.

A *weighted, directed multi-graph* $G = (V, E, c, w)$ consists of a set of nodes V, a set of edges E, a mapping $c : E \to V \times V$ that maps each edge to an ordered pair of nodes and a mapping $w : E \to \mathbb{N}$ that maps each edge to a nonnegative integer, called its *weight* or *duration*. For each edge e with $c(e) = (v, z)$, we assume $v \neq z$ for simplicity throughout the paper.

A *workflow graph* $\Gamma = (V, E, c, l, w)$, is a weighted multi-graph $G = (V, E, c, w)$ with distinct and unique source and sink nodes, denoted v_{source} and v_{sink}, respectively, equipped with an additional mapping $l : V \setminus \{v_{source}, v_{sink}\} \to \{\text{XOR}, \text{AND}\}$ that associates a *branching logic* with every node, except for the source and the sink. Furthermore, we assume that every node is on a path from the source to the sink, that the source has a unique outgoing edge, called the *source edge* (e_{source}), and that the sink has a unique incoming edge, called the *sink edge* (e_{sink}). For each node v, we define the *pre-set* of v, $\bullet v = \{e \in E \mid \exists z \in V : c(e) = (z, v)\}$ and the post-set of v, $v^\bullet = \{e \in E \mid \exists z \in V : c(e) = (v, z)\}$. A node with a single incoming edge and multiple outgoing edges is called a *split*. A node with multiple incoming edges and a single outgoing edge is called a *join*. We don't allow nodes that have multiple incoming edges as well as multiple outgoing edges. Note that this is not restrictive as such a node can be converted into a join followed by a split without changing the semantics.

Figure 1 shows a workflow graph in BPMN notation: An XOR gateway is depicted as a diamond, an AND gateway as a diamond decorated with a plus sign. Source and sink are depicted as circles. A node that is neither a join, split, nor source or sink is usually called a *task*. A task is shown as a rounded rectangle in Fig. 1. It is natural to assign durations to tasks. Tasks are executed by *resources*: non-preemptive, identical agents, and we assume an unbounded number of these. We will henceforth omit tasks for simplicity and annotate each edge with a duration $w(e)$ as formalized above.

Let A be a set. A *multi-set* over A is a mapping $m : A \to \mathbb{N}$. For two multi-sets m_1, m_2, and each $x \in A$, we have: $(m_1 + m_2)(x) = m_1(x) + m_2(x)$ and $(m_1 - m_2)(x) = m_1(x) - m_2(x)$.

A *marking* $m : E \to \mathbb{N}$ of a workflow graph is a multi-set over E. If $m(e) = i$, we say that there are i *tokens* on edge e. The marking with exactly one token on the source edge and no token elsewhere is called the *initial marking*, denoted by m_s. The marking with exactly one token on the sink edge and no token elsewhere is called the *final marking* of the workflow graph, denoted by m_f.

The *semantics* of workflow graphs is defined as a token game as it is in Petri nets. A comprehensive analysis of the relationship between workflow graphs and free-choice workflow nets (a subclass of Petri nets) can be found in [6]. The execution of a node with an AND-logic removes one token from each of its incoming edges and adds one token to each of the outgoing edges. The execution of a node with a XOR-logic removes non-deterministically a token from one of its incoming edges that has a token, then non-deterministically adds one token to one of the outgoing edges. Although we omit tasks, we allow nodes with just one incoming and one outgoing edge for technical reasons. For such nodes, XOR- and AND-logic behave the same.

A triple $T = (E_1, v, E_2)$ is called a *transition* of Γ if $v \in V$, $E_1 \subseteq {}^\bullet v$, and $E_2 \subseteq v^\bullet$. A transition (E_1, v, E_2) is *enabled* in a marking m if for each edge $e \in E_1$ we have $m(e) > 0$ and any of the following propositions:

- $l(v) = \text{AND}$, $E_1 = {}^\bullet v$, and $E_2 = v^\bullet$, or
- $l(v) = \text{XOR}$, there exists an edge e such that $E_1 = \{e\}$, and there exists an edge e' such that $E_2 = \{e'\}$.

We will use ${}^\bullet T$ to denote E_1 and $T^\bullet$ to denote E_2.

A transition T can be executed in a marking m if T is enabled in m. When T is executed in m, a marking m' results such that $m' = m - E_1 + E_2$. We write $m \to m'$ if there exists a transition T, enabled in a marking m and its execution results in a marking m'. We write $m \xrightarrow{T} m'$ when the transition T is enabled in a marking m and its execution results in the marking m'. We use $\xrightarrow{*}$ to denote the transitive and reflexive closure of $\to$. We say m' is *reachable from a marking* m if $m \xrightarrow{*} m'$. We say m' is a *reachable marking* of Γ if $m_s \xrightarrow{*} m'$.

An *execution* of Γ is an alternate sequence $\sigma = \langle m_s, T_0, m_1, T_1, \cdots \rangle$ of markings m_i of Γ and transitions T_i such that $m_i \xrightarrow{T_i} m_{i+1}$, for each $i \geq 0$. We will be using also the shorter notation $\sigma = \langle m_s, m_1, \cdots \rangle$ to denote an execution.

An execution σ is *maximal* if either σ is of infinite length or σ ends in a marking from which no other marking can be reached.

We say an edge e is *taken* at i if $\exists\, T_i$ such that $e \in T_i^\bullet$.

A maximal execution is *fair* if for each XOR-split v, that is executed infinitely often in σ, each edge $e \in v^\bullet$ is taken infinitely often in σ.

If $\sigma = \langle m_0, T_0, m_1, T_1, \cdots, T_n, m_{n+1} \rangle$ is an execution, then $\tau_\sigma = \langle T_0, T_1, \cdots, T_n \rangle$ is a *transition sequence* leading from m_0 to m_{n+1} and we write $m_0 \xrightarrow{\tau_\sigma} m_{n+1}$.

A reachable marking m is a *local deadlock* if m has a token on an incoming edge e of an AND-join such that each marking reachable from m also contains a token on e. A reachable marking m is *unsafe* or exhibits *lack of synchronization* if one edge has more than one token in m. A workflow graph is said to be *sound* if it has no *local deadlock* and no unsafe reachable marking. Soundness guarantees that every fair execution terminates in the final marking of Γ. Soundness has various equivalent characterizations and can be decided in polynomial time [1,5].

We now equip each token with an integer-valued clock initialized to zero. Then the *state* of the workflow graph is given by the tuple (m, c) where m is the marking and $c : m \to \mathbb{N}$ (note that for safe workflow graphs, $m : E \to \{0, 1\}$, hence m is a subset of E). We carry over the token-game semantics for clocks and we set $(m, c) \xrightarrow{T} (m', c')$, when $m \xrightarrow{T} m'$ and $c'(e) = c(e)$ for $e \in m' \setminus T^\bullet$ and $c'(e) = w(e) + \max\{\, c(e') \mid e' \in {}^\bullet T \}$ for $e \in T^\bullet$.

In the initial marking, the state of the workflow graph is given by (m_s, c_s), where $c_s(e_{source}) = w(e_{source})$. Similarly, in the final marking, the state of the workflow graph is given by (m_f, c_f). We then define the *duration of an execution* σ as $c_f(e_{sink})$, where σ ends in the final marking m_f.

Let Γ be a WFG; Γ is *sequential* if it contains no AND-split and no -join. It is *acyclic* if the underlying graph has no cycles. A *regular* workflow graph is a

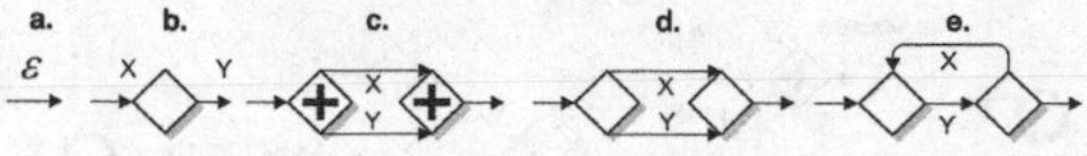

Fig. 2. Regular patterns 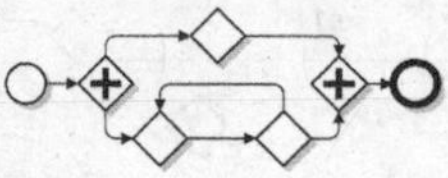   **Fig. 3.** Regular graph

workflow graph that can be generated from a regular expression as follows. Let ϵ be a constant symbolizing an edge and X, Y variables for workflow graphs. Then a regular workflow graph expression is the smallest set such that ϵ is a regular workflow graph, and if X and Y are regular workflow graphs, then X ; Y, X AND Y, X XOR Y, and X LOOP Y are also regular workflow graphs. From each regular workflow graph expression, we can generate a workflow graph, where each expression type corresponds to one of the graph fragment patterns shown in Fig. 2 and composition is done by replacing an edge labeled with a variable by another pattern. For example, the expression $((\epsilon;\epsilon)$ AND $(\epsilon$ $LOOP$ $\epsilon))$ generates the graph shown in Fig. 3. Note that the loop construct has two loop bodies. It can be viewed as a combination of a while and a repeat loop, one loop body before the loop condition one after it. It can be decided in linear time whether a workflow graph is a regular workflow graph using graph parsing techniques [14].

3 Workflow Graphs with Nondeterministic Choice

In this section, we present our first main contribution, a polynomial time algorithm that computes the minimum execution time of a workflow graph, which can be used to determine whether some fair execution of a time annotated workflow graph with an unbounded number of resources meets the deadline.

3.1 The Minimum Duration of a Workflow Graph

We start by presenting several preliminary notions that are necessary for the algorithm. We introduce the *accumulated cost associated with an edge* in a fair execution. Based on our definition of the accumulated cost associated with an edge, the cost accumulated on the *source* edge represents the cost of a fair execution. Next, we present an algorithm to compute the *minimum* cost accumulated on the *source* edge, this equals the *minimum* cost of a fair execution of a given workflow graph and prove its correctness.

In the following, let Γ be a sound workflow graph.

To facilitate the computation of the cost accumulated on an edge in a fair execution σ, we express the execution as the sequence of edges that get marked in σ. To introduce an unambiguous representation, we use $\tau_\sigma = \langle T_0, T_1, \cdots, T_n \rangle$, the transition sequence that corresponds to σ. The sequence of edges that get marked in σ is given by $\langle e_{source}, T_0^\bullet, T_1^\bullet, \cdots, T_n^\bullet \rangle$, where each set $T_k^\bullet$ such that

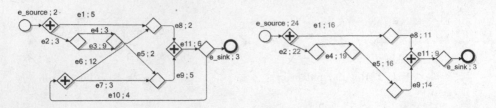

Fig. 4. Workflow graph with edge weights

Fig. 5. Minimum duration execution and the accumulated costs

$|T_k^\bullet| > 1$ is ordered in a fixed predefined order (e.g., alphabetic). We use the notation $\sigma = \langle e_{source}, \cdots, e_i, \cdots, e_{sink} \rangle$. Since we are interested in fair executions (and we assume soundness), the sequence of edges is finite and ends with e_{sink}.

Having the sequence of edges that are marked in σ, we traverse the sequence backwards, from the last to the first edge in the sequence and *update* the cost of an edge $e \in {}^\bullet v$ at position i in the sequence based on the cost already computed for the edges in the sequence that belong to $v^\bullet$.

As an example, consider the workflow graph in Fig. 4. In Fig. 4, edges are labeled (e.g. $e8$; 2) with an edge name ($e8$) and a duration (2). Figure 5 represents the workflow graph restricted to the elements that are contained in the fair execution with minimum duration, i.e., it is a representation of the minimum duration execution. Each edge in Fig. 5 is labeled with the accumulated cost for reaching the sink in that execution.

For e_{11}, the accumulated cost to reach the sink is: $w(e_{11})$ to which we add the cost of e_{sink} therefore, $6 + 3 = 9$. Based on our update rule for AND-join nodes, the cost associated to e_9 becomes $w(e_9)$ plus the cost of e_{11} and we obtain 14 and the cost associated to e_8 becomes $w(e_8)$ plus the cost of e_{11}, and we get $2 + 9 = 11$. For edges e_5 and e_1, we update the cost by adding the edge weight to the accumulated cost on the outgoing edge of the XOR-split, and we obtain costs 16 ($11 + 5$) for $e1$ and 16 ($14 + 2$) for e_5. We apply the same rule for e_4 and we obtain an accumulated cost of 19 ($16+3$) and subsequently also for e_2 and we obtain 22 ($19 + 3$). Now we can compute the cost of the execution. Note that the AND-join we are about to process spawns two threads. The cost of the execution is decided by the longest thread (in terms of duration). Therefore, we update the cost accumulated on e_{source} to be equal to $w(e_{source}) + max(16, 22)$ which equals 24 and this equals the cost of the execution.

Now we present formally how to compute the accumulated cost associated with an edge for a given execution. Let e^i be the edge at position i in the sequence of edges that get marked in the execution.

Since we update based on the edges in $v^\bullet$, for the XOR nodes, we define a function $next_\sigma(e^i)$ such that for the edge at position i, $e^i \in {}^\bullet v$, it returns the edge in $v^\bullet$ that get marked next after e^i gets marked.

For each position i in the sequence of edges that get marked in the execution, starting from the last index, we update the cost of the edge e^i, which we denote by $d_\sigma(e^i)$:

$$d_\sigma(e^i) = \begin{cases} w(e^i) & \text{if } e^i = e_{sink} \\ w(e^i) + d_\sigma(next_\sigma(e^i)) & \text{if } l(v) = \text{XOR} \\ w(e^i) + \max\{d_\sigma(e') \mid e' \in v^\bullet\} & \text{if } l(v) = \text{AND and } |v^\bullet| > 1 \\ w(e^i) + d_\sigma(e') & \text{if } l(v) = \text{AND and } \{e'\} = v^\bullet \end{cases}$$

Note that this procedure may update the cost of an edge e multiple times in case the execution is cyclic, i.e. executes an edge multiple times. As the final accumulated cost associated with the edge e in σ, we take the value of $d_\sigma(e)$ after the last update.

Since e_{source} is always the first edge in the sequence of edges that get marked in a fair execution, it follows that $e^0 = e_{source}$ and $d_\sigma(e^0) = d_\sigma(e_{source})$. Since the computation of $d_\sigma(e)$ follows the semantics of workflow graphs, it is easy to see that $d_\sigma(e_{source}) = c(\sigma)$, the duration of the execution σ.

The algorithm for computing the minimum duration of a fair execution of a workflow graph with an unbounded number of resources, Algorithm 1, is given below. It works on a weighted workflow graph, and for each node v, and each edge $e \in {}^\bullet v$, it updates a value $\delta(e)$ that represents the currently known *minimum cost* to reach the sink from e based on relaxation rules specific to each node type (see Algorithm 3). All edge costs are updated at most $|V|$ times for a cyclic workflow graph (see Algorithm 1) and only once for an acyclic workflow graph (see Algorithm 2). Upon termination of our algorithm, the value associated to e_{source}, $\delta(e_{source})$, represents the duration of the minimum duration execution.

The outer loop of the algorithm is similar to the Bellman-Ford algorithm [2] for sequential graphs, but the parallel constructs entail a different relaxation procedure to reflect the semantics of sound workflow graphs. In addition, the correctness proofs are more complex due to the characteristics of workflow graphs.

Next, we will show the correctness of the algorithm. For this we introduce the definition of the *minimum cost* that can be accumulated on an edge. This is necessary for the proofs, as we will demonstrate that the algorithm computes the minimum cost accumulated on the source edge.

Let e be an edge of Γ and v a node of Γ such that $e \in {}^\bullet v$. We define the *edge enabling marking* m_e, as the reachable marking for which $m_e(e) = 1$, v is enabled in m_e and no other node is enabled in m_e. It has been shown [8] that for a sound workflow graph, the edge enabling marking is unique.

We define $d^*(e)$, *the minimum cost downstream from* e, as follows:

$$d^*(e) = \min\{d_\sigma(e) \mid \sigma \text{ is a fair execution that starts in } m_e\}. \tag{1}$$

Because Γ is sound, note that since m_e is a reachable marking, it holds that $m_e \xrightarrow{*} m_f$.

Since $d_\sigma(e_{source})$ represents the cost of a fair execution σ, $d^*(e_{source})$ represents the duration of the minimum duration execution.

Algorithm 1. Minimum duration

```
1: function WFGMIN( V, E)
2:     for e ∈ E \ {e_sink} do
3:         δ(e) ← ∞
4:     end for
5:     δ(e_sink) ← w(e_sink)
6:     for i = 1 : |V| do
7:         for all e ∈ E do
8:             u, v ← nodes s.t. e = c(u, v)
9:             RELAX(e,v)
10:        end for
11:    end for
12: end function
```

Algorithm 2. Min duration, acyclic

```
1: function ACYCLICWFGMIN(V, E)
2:     for e ∈ E \ {e_sink} do
3:         δ(e) ← ∞
4:     end for
5:     δ(e_sink) ← w(e_sink)
6:     TOPOLOGICALSORT(Γ)
7:     while V ≠ ∅ do
8:         Select v ∈ V s.t. v is maximal
    with respect to the topological sort
9:         V ← {V \ v}
10:        for all e ∈ •v do
11:            RELAX(e,v)
12:        end for
13:    end while
14: end function
```

Algorithm 3. Relaxation of an edge $e \in \,^{\bullet}v$

```
1: function RELAX(e,v)
2:     if l(v) = XOR and {e'} = v• then
3:         if δ(e) > w(e) + δ(e') then
4:             δ(e) ← w(e) + δ(e')
5:         end if
6:     end if
7:     if l(v) = XOR and |v•| > 1 then
8:         if δ(e) > w(e) + min_{e'∈v•}(δ(e'))
    then
9:             δ(e) ← w(e) + min_{e'∈v•}(δ(e'))
10:        end if
11:    end if
12:    if l(v) = AND and {e'} = v• then
13:        if δ(e) > w(e) + δ(e') then
14:            δ(e) ← w(e) + δ(e')
15:        end if
16:    end if
17:    if l(v)= AND and |v•| > 1 then
18:        if δ(e) > w(e) + max{δ(e') | e' ∈
    v•} then
19:            δ(e) ← w(e) + max{δ(e') | e' ∈
    v•}
20:        end if
21:    end if
22: end function
```

Lemma 1. *Let e be an edge and v a node such that $e \in \,^{\bullet}v$. We always have $\delta(e) \geq d^*(e)$.*

The proof of Lemma 1 is presented in [4].

Lemma 2. *Let e be an edge. Let σ be a fair execution such that $d_\sigma(e) = d^*(e)$. Let $S = \langle e_{i-1}, \cdots, e_{sink} \rangle$ be the sequence edges that get marked after e gets marked for the last time in σ. Each sequence of calls of $Relax(e, v)$ that has the property that edges $e_{sink}, \cdots, e_{i-1}, e$ have been relaxed in this order, after the sequence of calls to $Relax(e, v)$ we have $\delta(e) = d^*(e)$.*

The proof of Lemma 2 is presented in [4].

Definition 1. *A fair execution σ of Γ, is a loop-free execution if no node is executed more than once in σ, and therefore no edge is marked more than once in σ.*

Lemma 3. *Some fair execution of Γ with minimum duration is loop-free.*

The proof of Lemma 3 is presented in [4].

For a workflow graph Γ and a fair, loop-free execution σ of Γ, we define Γ_σ as the workflow graph Γ restricted to σ such that it contains only the nodes of Γ that are executed in σ and the edges of Γ such that $\sigma(e) = 1$. For a fair, loop-free execution σ of Γ, it follows that Γ_σ is an acyclic workflow graph.

The elements of an acyclic workflow graph are in a partial order defined by the flow of the graph: Let $G = (V, E, c)$ be an acyclic multi-graph. If x_1, x_2 are two elements in $V \cup E$ such that there is a path from x_1 to x_2, then we say that x_1 precedes x_2, denoted $x_1 \preceq x_2$, and x_2 follows x_1.

Lemma 4. *For a sound workflow graph, after running the Algorithm 1, it holds that $\delta(e_{source}) = d^*(e_{source})$.*

Proof: Lemma 3 states that some fair execution of Γ, with minimum duration, is loop-free (i). Recall that for a given fair execution σ, $d_\sigma(e_{source})$ represents the duration of execution of σ (ii). From (i) and (ii) it follows that some execution that minimizes $d_\sigma(e_{source})$ is loop-free (iii).

Note that m_s is the edge enabling marking for e_{source}.

Using (iii) and the definition for $d^*(e)$ instantiated to e_{source}, we obtain: $d^*(e_{source}) = \min\{d_\sigma(e_{source}) \mid \sigma$ is a fair execution that starts in m_s $\}$. It follows that some σ^* for which $d_{\sigma^*}(e_{source}) = d^*(e_{source})$, is a fair, loop-free execution.

Since σ^* is loop-free, it means that at most $|V|$ nodes are executed in σ^*. In each complete relaxation step (one iteration of the loop in line 6 in Algorithm 1), we relax all the edges. Therefore, at the $|V|$-th iteration we have relaxed all the edges, in decreasing order with respect to the partial order on the edges of Γ_{σ^*}. It means that at the $|V|$-th iteration, we will have relaxed all the edges that get marked after e gets marked in σ^*. Therefore, from Lemma 2, $\delta(e) = d^*(e)$.

Therefore, we computed the duration of the minimum duration execution of the workflow graph, which is $d^*(e_{source})$.

For Algorithm 1, the initialization of the edge costs takes $O(|V|)$ time and each of the $|V|$ iterations over the edges of the workflow graph is performed in $O(|E|)$ time. The cost update is performed in constant time. Hence, we have proven the following:

Theorem 1. *The minimum duration execution of a sound workflow graph with unbounded number of resources can be computed in time $O(|V||E|)$.*

3.2 Regular and Acyclic Workflow Graphs

In the following, we briefly present the ideas for computing the maximum duration of execution for regular and acyclic workflow graphs.

As presented in [3], for a regular workflow graph with a structured cycle, i.e., a while or repeat loop, or more general, of the form X LOOP Y, the computation of the maximum duration requires the specification of the maximal number of iterations for each loop. If we assume that the backedge of each loop (i.e., edge "x" in Fig. 2) of the regular graph is annotated with a positive integer k that represents the maximum number of times the backedge can be traversed, then the maximum duration of X LOOP Y is $(k+1) \cdot d_X + k \cdot d_Y$ where d_X denotes the maximum duration of the loop body X, and d_Y represents the maximal duration associated to reentering the loop. For computing the minimum duration we take $k = 0$ and the minimum duration of the loop body. We still obtain the minimum/maximum duration of such an annotated regular workflow graph in linear time (Cell C.1, C.2 of Table 1).

For acyclic workflow graphs, we can use the algorithm for the cyclic case but without the need to perform $|V|$ iterations. Instead we exploit the fact that the elements of an acyclic workflow graph are in a partial order defined by the flow of the graph. Therefore, in order to make sure that the edges are relaxed respecting the partial order, first, the graph is sorted topologically - $O(|V|+|E|)$. Secondly, the edges are relaxed in descending order with respect to the topological sorting in $O(|E|)$ time. The algorithm that formalizes this idea is Algorithm 2.

Theorem 2. *The minimum duration execution of a sound acyclic workflow graph with unbounded number of resources can be computed in time $O(|V|+|E|)$.*

Note that, in the acyclic case, for computing the maximum duration execution, one only needs to select the maximum instead of the minimum in the $Relax(e, v)$ procedure when $l(v) = $ XOR and $|v^\bullet| > 1$.

4 Workflow Graphs with Probabilistic Choice

If not all fair executions of a workflow graph meet the deadline, we could ask whether at least a large portion of the fair executions does. We approach this question by assuming that decisions are resolved through a coin flip, i.e., each XOR-node v is assigned a distribution $\mu : v^\bullet \to [0, 1]$ such that $\mu(e) > 0$ for each $e \in v^\bullet$ and $\sum_{e \in v^\bullet} = 1$. Although some fair executions may not terminate, their probability[1] is zero. We can then take the duration of an execution as a random variable and ask whether the probability of an execution terminating before the deadline exceeds a given threshold.

4.1 Expected Duration

In the following, we will present our result for the complexity of computing the expected duration of a workflow graph.

---

[1] We do not explicitly construct the probability space here on which the development of this chapter is formally based on. As workflow graphs contain concurrency, we need to consider maximal partial-order executions to obtain a single probability space and to avoid the notion of an adversary as in Markov decision processes. Note that a probabilistic workflow graph does not contain real non-determinism, just concurrency. The construction of such a probability space is provided elsewhere [16, 17], e.g. for Petri nets and in fact rests on the assumption that the Petri net is free-choice. In this paper, we are only concerned with the duration of an execution, which is independent of the interleaving, i.e., the ordering of concurrent events.

Theorem 3. *Given a regular, acyclic probabilistic workflow graph Γ, computing the expected duration of Γ executed by an unbounded set of resources is NP-hard.*

The proof consists of a reduction from the *subset sum problem* which is the problem: given a set $D = \{d_1, \cdots, d_n\}$ of integers and an integer S, to determine whether any non-empty subset $D' \subseteq D$ sums up to exactly S. This problem is known to be NP-hard. This is equivalent to solving a problem where all the values $d_1, \cdots, d_n, S$ are multiples of 4 (this statement will be used in the proof later on). For the proof, we use the class of (regular, acyclic) probabilistic workflow graphs $\Gamma_{\epsilon,n}$ in Fig. 6, where each decision outcome has probability 0.5.

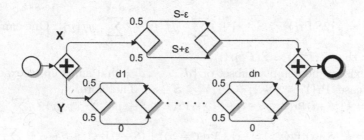

Fig. 6. A probabilistic workflow graph

Proof. Let X, Y be random variables that denote the duration of each of the two parallel flows of $\Gamma_{\epsilon,n}$. The expected duration of the workflow graph $\Gamma_{\epsilon,n}$ is:

$$\mathbb{E}(\Gamma_{\epsilon,n}) = \mathbb{E}(max(X,Y))$$
$$\mathbb{E}(\Gamma_{\epsilon,n}) = \tfrac{1}{2}\mathbb{E}(max(S - \epsilon, Y)) + \tfrac{1}{2}\mathbb{E}(max(S + \epsilon, Y))$$

Let f be the probability distribution of Y. We rewrite the terms of $\mathbb{E}(\Gamma_{\epsilon,n})$ as follows:

$$\mathbb{E}(max(Y, S - \epsilon)) = (S - \epsilon)\Pr(Y \le S - \epsilon) + \sum_{y > S - \epsilon} yf(y) \qquad (2)$$

$$\mathbb{E}(max(Y, S + \epsilon)) = (S + \epsilon)\Pr(Y \le S + \epsilon) + \sum_{y > S + \epsilon} yf(y) \qquad (3)$$

By using Eqs. (2), (3) we obtain the following expression for $\mathbb{E}(\Gamma_{\epsilon,n})$:

$$\mathbb{E}(\Gamma_{\epsilon,n}) = \frac{1}{2}\Big[(S+\epsilon)\Pr(Y \le S+\epsilon) + \sum_{y > S+\epsilon} yf(y) + (S-\epsilon)\Pr(Y \le S-\epsilon) + \sum_{y > S-\epsilon} yf(y)\Big].$$

Let us choose $\epsilon > 0$ such that no subset of $\{d_1, \cdots, d_n\}$ has sum in $[S - \epsilon, S)$ nor in $(S, S + \epsilon]$. Note that the sum, can still potentially equal exactly S. Such ϵ is easy to find. It is enough to choose $\epsilon = 2$ as all the numbers $d1, \cdots, d_n, S$ are multiples of 4.

We will show that $\mathbb{E}(\Gamma_{\epsilon,n}) = \mathbb{E}(\Gamma_{\frac{\epsilon}{2}})$ if there is no non-empty subset of $\{d_1, \cdots, d_n\}$ that sums up to exactly S (i), and $\mathbb{E}(\Gamma_{\epsilon,n}) \neq \mathbb{E}(\Gamma_{\frac{\epsilon}{2}})$ otherwise (ii). If we can compute the expected duration of a workflow graph with unbounded resources in polynomial time we can solve the subset sum problem in polynomial time. Note that both ϵ and $\epsilon/2$ are integers, so we are always considering workflow graphs with integer weights.

(i) There is no non-empty subset of $\{d_1, \cdots, d_n\}$ that sums up to exactly S. In this case, it holds that $\Pr(Y \leq S - \epsilon) = \Pr(Y \leq S + \epsilon)$. Therefore we update the equation for $\mathbb{E}(\Gamma_{\epsilon,n})$):

$$\mathbb{E}(\Gamma_{\epsilon,n}) = \tfrac{1}{2}\Big[\Pr(Y \leq S + \epsilon)(S + \epsilon + S - \epsilon) + \sum_{y > S - \epsilon} yf(y) + \sum_{y > S + \epsilon} yf(y)\Big].$$

$$\mathbb{E}(\Gamma_{\epsilon,n}) = \tfrac{1}{2}\Big[2S\Pr(Y \leq S + \epsilon) + \sum_{y > S - \epsilon} yf(y) + \sum_{y > S + \epsilon} yf(y)\Big]. \text{ One can easily}$$

observe that $\mathbb{E}(\Gamma_{\epsilon,n}) = \mathbb{E}(\Gamma_{\frac{\epsilon}{2}})$.

(ii) There exists a non-empty subset of $\{d_1, \cdots, d_n\}$ that sums up to exactly S. In this case, $\Pr(Y \leq S - \epsilon) \neq \Pr(Y \leq S + \epsilon)$. Therefore,

$$\mathbb{E}(\Gamma_{\epsilon,n}) = \tfrac{1}{2}\Big[(S + \epsilon)\Pr(Y \leq S + \epsilon) + (S - \epsilon)\Pr(Y \leq S - \epsilon) + \sum_{y > S - \epsilon} yf(y) + \sum_{y > S + \epsilon} yf(y)\Big].$$

$$\mathbb{E}(\Gamma_{\epsilon,n}) = \tfrac{1}{2}\Big[(S + \epsilon)(\Pr(Y \leq S - \epsilon) + \Pr(Y = S)) + (S - \epsilon)\Pr(Y \leq S - \epsilon) + \sum_{y > S - \epsilon} yf(y)$$
$$+ \sum_{y > S + \epsilon} yf(y)\Big].$$

$$\mathbb{E}(\Gamma_{\epsilon,n}) = \tfrac{1}{2}\Big[\underbrace{2S\Pr(Y \leq S - \epsilon)}_{T_1} + \underbrace{(S + \epsilon)\Pr(Y = S)}_{T_2} + \underbrace{\sum_{y > S - \epsilon} yf(y) + \sum_{y > S + \epsilon} yf(y)}_{T_3}\Big].$$

Please note that term T_2 has different value for $\mathbb{E}(\Gamma_{\epsilon,n})$ and $\mathbb{E}(\Gamma_{\frac{\epsilon}{2}})$, while T_1 and T_3 have the same value for $\mathbb{E}(\Gamma_{\epsilon,n})$ and $\mathbb{E}(\Gamma_{\frac{\epsilon}{2}})$. Therefore, $\mathbb{E}(\Gamma_{\epsilon,n}) \neq \mathbb{E}(\Gamma_{\frac{\epsilon}{2}})$.

5   Minimum Number of Resources

In this section, we compute the maximum *degree of concurrency* of Γ, i.e., the maximum number of tokens that can exist in the graph in a reachable marking. This can help in answering a natural question that arises in the quantitative timing analysis of a business process. What is the minimum number k^* of resources one needs, such that each execution achieves its minimal execution time? This means there does not exist any execution for which the duration could be decreased by having more than k^* resources. The maximum number of tokens that can exist in the graph is an upper bound for k^*. There are cases where tighter bounds can be given, as illustrated in Fig. 7 where the maximum number of tokens is 3, obtained in the marking that marks edges e_2, e_3 and e_4 but 2 resources would suffice for reaching the minimum duration, i.e., 15.

Before presenting the algorithm we need to introduce one more subclass of workflow graphs.

A workflow graph Γ is a *marked graph* if any node $v \in \Gamma \setminus \{v_{source}, v_{sink}\}$ is either an AND-node or an XOR-node with a single incoming and a single outgoing edge.

There is an EXPTIME algorithm for computing the maximum degree of concurrency for general worklfow graphs. It is based on computing the reachability graph of Γ, which is the transition relation $\rightarrow$ restricted to its reachable markings. Note that for sound workflow graphs the reachability graph is finite, but exponential in the size of Γ. Each reachable marking is visited to compute the maximum concurrency degree.

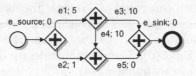

Fig. 7. Tighter bound example

However, efficient algorithms are known for subclasses such as marked graphs, regular or sequential worklfow graphs. Therefore, we propose to leverage this fact and tackle the problem through a *divide and conquer* strategy. This approach has the potential of speeding up the computation of the maximum degree of concurrency of a work in practice.

In order to divide the problem into smaller parts, we compute the Refined Process Structure Tree (RPST) [14] of the workflow graph. The RPST represents a decomposition of a workflow graph into a hierarchy of sub-workflows that are subgraphs with a single entry and a single exit of control called *fragments* (see e.g., Fig. 8(a)). The decomposition results in a parse tree which reflects the containment relationship of the fragments.

The algorithm for computing the maximum degree of concurrency works as follows: (1) divide the problem of computing the maximum degree of concurrency to subproblems by decomposing the workflow graph into its fragments. These fragments are labeled with their corresponding subclass (e.g., marked graph). (2) conquer the problem by computing the maximum degree of concurrency of the workflow graph based on the maximum degree of concurrency computed for its fragments. Note that we omit here trivial fragments consisting of a single edge.

The complexity of the algorithm depends on the subclass of the fragment f, as follows. It runs in linear time for sequential workflow graphs, where the returned value is the maximum weight of an edge of this fragment. Similarly it runs in linear time for regular fragments. For regular fragments modeling concurrency (cf. Fig. 2c) the maximum degree of concurrency is the *sum* of the weights of the edges. For regular fragments modeling choice (cf. Fig. 2b, d, e) the maximum degree of concurrency is the *maximum* of the weights of the edges. The computation of the concurrency degree runs in polynomial time for marked graphs and in exponential time for the *complex fragments* – the fragments which are not regular nor marked-graphs nor state-machines.

An example for how our algorithm works is provided in Fig. 8. In Fig. 8, edge weights represent the concurrency degree. The root fragment is *Sequence Fragment 2* and the tree has one leaf – the *Marked Graph Fragment*, Fig. 8(a). After computing the concurrency degree of the marked graph (value 3) the work is updated as shown in Fig. 8(b). In the next iteration, the wor is reduced to the e

wo composed of a regular fragment contained in a sequence fragment, as shown
in Fig. 8(c). The concurrency degree of the regular fragment is computed (we
obtain $3 + 1 = 4$), we update the he w and we are left with a sequence fragment
Fig. 8(d). The maximum degree of concurrency of the is the concurrency degree
of this fragment (4).

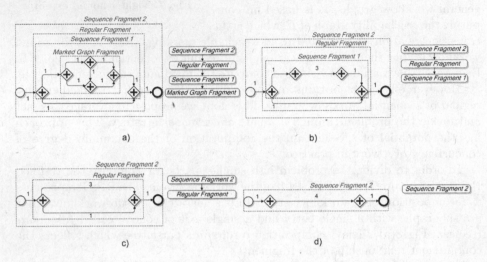

Fig. 8. An example of a work decomposition into its fragments and its corresponding
RPST (a), the wor and RPST after computing the concurrency degree for the *Marked
Graph Fragment* (b) the e wo and RPST after computing the concurrency degree for
Sequence Fragment 1 (c) the he w and RPST before the algorithm ends (d)

In the following, we present the approaches for computing the maximum
degree of concurrency for marked graphs and for complex fragments.

Let w denote a $|E| \times 1$ column vector representing the degree of concurrency
associated with each edge of Γ. Finding the maximum degree of concurrency of
a marked graph Γ, $deg(\Gamma)$, can be formulated as:

$$deg(\Gamma) = max\{m \cdot w \mid m \text{ is a marking reachable from } m_0\} \qquad (4)$$

The solution we propose for computing $\deg(\Gamma)$ in a marked graph is identical
to the computation of the maximum weighted sum of tokens in [12]. In [12]
the author formulates this problem as an integer programming (IP) problem
with integer data and totally unimodular constraint matrix. Note that any IP
problem with integer data and totally unimodular constraint matrix is solvable
in polynomial time.

The complexity of the algorithm is therefore dominated by complex fragments, for which we resort to the EXPTIME algorithm. Since complex fragments
are rare in practice, this approach can be efficient in computing the maximum
degree of concurrency. In a previous study documented in [15] on 645 industrial

business process which were translated to workflow graphs, only about 4 % of the total of their corresponding fragments were complex with an average number of edges between 21 and 32.

6   Conclusion

We presented new results on the deadline analysis of workflow graphs with an unbounded number of resources.

The same questions can be asked in settings with a fixed number $n > 1$ of resources. This constraint leads to problems that can not be solved in polynomial time. The probability of deadline transgression and the expected duration remain NP-hard which is easy to see from our justifications in the current work. For the maximum duration – the worst case execution time is attained when we require all the

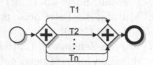

Fig. 9. Regular WFG with n parallel threads

tasks to be executed by a single resource, which we have studied in [3]. What is different, is the fact that computing the minimum duration of execution becomes NP-hard for a fixed number $n > 1$ of resources. For example, for a simple workflow graph as the one in Fig. 9, let's assume we need to complete n tasks $T_1, \cdots, T_n$ and we have k identical agents to solve them. Finding an assignment of the tasks to the agents such that the duration of execution (*makespan*) is minimized is NP-hard as one can reduce 2-PARTITION to finding the minimum duration when there are exactly two resources available [7].

In future work, we would like to investigate further whether computing the maximum degree of concurrency of a WFG is NP-hard or a polynomial time algorithm exists.

References

1. van der Aalst, W.M.P., Hirnschall, A., Verbeek, H.M.W.E.: An alternative way to analyze workflow graphs. In: Pidduck, A.B., Mylopoulos, J., Woo, C.C., Ozsu, M.T. (eds.) CAiSE 2002. LNCS, vol. 2348, pp. 535–552. Springer, Heidelberg (2002)
2. Bellman, R.: On a routing problem. Q. Appl. Math. **16**, 87–90 (1958)
3. Botezatu, M., Völzer, H., Thiele, L.: The complexity of deadline analysis for workflow graphs with a single resource. In: Proceedings of the 20th IEEE ICECCS Conference, December 2015
4. Botezatu, M., Völzer, H., Thiele, L.: The complexity of deadline analysis for workflow graphs with multiple resources. Technical report RZ3896, IBM (2016)
5. Desel, J., Esparza, J.: Free Choice Petri Nets. Cambridge University Press, New York (1995)
6. Favre, C., Fahland, D., Völzer, H.: The relationship between workflow graphs and free-choice workflow nets. Inf. Syst. **47**, 197–219 (2015)
7. Garey, M.R., Johnson, D.S.: Computers and Intractability: A Guide to the Theory of NP-Completeness. W. H. Freeman & Co., New York (1979)

268 M. Botezatu et al.

8. Gaujal, B., Haar, S., Mairesse, J.: Blocking a transition in a free choice net and what it tells about its throughput. J. Comput. Syst. Sci. **66**(3), 515–548 (2003)
9. Hansson, H., Jonsson, B.: A framework for reasoning about time and reliability. In: Proceedings of the Real Time Systems Symposium, 1989, pp. 102–111, December 1989
10. Kwiatkowska, M., Norman, G., Parker, D.: PRISM 4.0: verification of probabilistic real-time systems. In: Gopalakrishnan, G., Qadeer, S. (eds.) CAV 2011. LNCS, vol. 6806, pp. 585–591. Springer, Heidelberg (2011)
11. Mili, H., Tremblay, G., Jaoude, G., Lefebvre, É., Elabed, L., El Boussaidi, G.: Business process modeling languages: sorting through the alphabet soup. ACM Comput. Surv. **43**(1), 4:1–4:56 (2010)
12. Murata, T.: Petri nets: properties, analysis and applications. Proc. IEEE **77**(4), 541–580 (1989)
13. Popova-Zeugmann, L., Heiner, M.: Worst-case analysis of concurrent systems with duration interval petri nets. In: BTU COTTBUS, pp. 162–179 (1996)
14. Vanhatalo, J., Völzer, H., Koehler, J.: The refined process structure tree. Data Knowl. Eng. **68**(9), 793–818 (2009)
15. Vanhatalo, J., Völzer, H., Leymann, F.: Faster and more focused control-flow analysis for business process models through SESE decomposition. In: Krämer, B.J., Lin, K.-J., Narasimhan, P. (eds.) ICSOC 2007. LNCS, vol. 4749, pp. 43–55. Springer, Heidelberg (2007)
16. Varacca, D., Völzer, H., Winskel, G.: Probabilistic event structures and domains. Theor. Comput. Sci. **358**(2–3), 173–199 (2006)
17. Völzer, H.: Randomized non-sequential processes. In: Larsen, K.G., Nielsen, M. (eds.) CONCUR 2001. LNCS, vol. 2154, pp. 184–201. Springer, Heidelberg (2001)
18. Wan, M., Ciardo, G.: Symbolic reachability analysis of integer timed Petri nets. In: Nielsen, M., Kučera, A., Miltersen, P.B., Palamidessi, C., Tůma, P., Valencia, F. (eds.) SOFSEM 2009. LNCS, vol. 5404, pp. 595–608. Springer, Heidelberg (2009)

Understandability of Process Representations

Dealing with Behavioral Ambiguity in Textual Process Descriptions

Han van der Aa[1](✉), Henrik Leopold[1], and Hajo A. Reijers[1,2]

[1] Department of Computer Sciences, VU University Amsterdam,
Amsterdam, The Netherlands
{j.h.vander.aa,h.leopold}@vu.nl
[2] Department of Mathematics and Computer Science,
Eindhoven University of Technology, Eindhoven, The Netherlands
h.a.reijers@vu.nl

Abstract. Textual process descriptions are widely used in organizations since they can be created and understood by virtually everyone. The inherent ambiguity of natural language, however, impedes the automated analysis of textual process descriptions. While human readers can use their context knowledge to correctly understand statements with multiple possible interpretations, automated analysis techniques currently have to make assumptions about the correct meaning. As a result, automated analysis techniques are prone to draw incorrect conclusions about the correct execution of a process. To overcome this issue, we introduce the concept of a *behavioral space* as a means to deal with behavioral ambiguity in textual process descriptions. A behavioral space captures all possible interpretations of a textual process description in a systematic manner. Thus, it avoids the problem of focusing on a single interpretation. We use a compliance checking scenario and a quantitative evaluation with a set of 47 textual process descriptions to demonstrate the usefulness of a behavioral space for reasoning about a process described by a text. Our evaluation demonstrates that a behavioral space strikes a balance between ignoring ambiguous statements and imposing fixed interpretations on them.

1 Introduction

Automated techniques for the analysis of business processes provide a wide range of valuable opportunities for organizations. Among others, they allow to check for business process compliance [12], to identify redundant activities within an organization [11], and to identify operational overlap between two business processes [5]. What all these techniques have in common is that they rely on *process models* as input. That is, they build on the formally specified relationships between the activities of process models to perform their analyses. Thus, these techniques cannot be applied to less structured forms of process documentation such as textual process descriptions.

The relevance and widespread use of textual process descriptions as source for process analysis has been emphasized in various contexts [1,6,10,18]. However, the inherent ambiguity of textual process descriptions is a challenge to

M. La Rosa et al. (Eds.): BPM 2016, LNCS 9850, pp. 271–288, 2016.
DOI: 10.1007/978-3-319-45348-4_16

their utilization for analysis purposes. A simple natural language statement such as *"in parallel to the latter steps"* leaves considerable room for interpretation. Whether the word *"latter"* refers to the preceding two, three, or even more activities mentioned in the textual description is, in many cases, impossible to infer with certainty. While human readers can use their context knowledge to make sense of such statements, it is hardly possible for automated analysis approaches to resolve such cases. In prior work, techniques for automatically extracting process models from textual process descriptions circumvented this problem by introducing interpretation heuristics [6, 8, 19]. In this way, they obtained a single process-oriented interpretation of the text. This interpretation, however, contains assumptions on the correct interpretation of undecidable ambiguity issues. So, there is always the risk that the derived interpretation conflicts with the proper way to execute the process. As a result, the focus on a single interpretation can lead to incorrect outcomes when reasoning about a business process, e.g. incorrect assessments on its compliance to regulations or expectations.

To provide a rigorous solution for these reasoning problems, we introduce a novel concept we refer to as *behavioral space*. A behavioral space formally captures all possible behavioral interpretations of a textual process description. The behavioral space clearly defines which behavior is within and which behavior is outside the reasonable bounds of interpretation. Therefore, it allows us to reason about, for example, compliance without the need to impose assumptions on the correct interpretation of a text.

The remainder of the paper is structured as follows. Section 2 motivates the problem of reasoning under behavioral ambiguity in textual process descriptions. Section 3 introduces the notion of a behavioral space to capture behavioral ambiguity and Sect. 4 describes how these can be obtained from a text. Section 5 illustrates the usage of behavioral spaces for compliance checking. In Sect. 6 we demonstrate the importance of behavioral spaces through a quantitative evaluation. Section 7 discusses streams of related work. Finally, we conclude the paper and discuss directions for future research in Sect. 8.

2   Behavioral Ambiguity in Textual Process Descriptions

In this section, we illustrate the problem of reasoning about business processes based on textual process descriptions. The key challenge in this context is the ambiguity of textual process descriptions, in particular with respect to how the text describes the ordering relations between activities. In the remainder, we refer to such ambiguity as *behavioral ambiguity*. Figure 1 illustrates the problem of behavioral ambiguity by showing a simplified description of a claims handling process. The description uses typical patterns to describe ordering relations, as observed in process descriptions obtained from practice and research [6].

At first glance, the description from Fig. 1 appears to be clear. However, on closer inspection, it turn outs that the description does not provide conclusive answers to several questions regarding the proper execution of the described process. For instance:

After a claim is received, a claim officer reviews the request and records the claim information. The claim officer then validates the claim documents before writing a settlement recommendation. A senior officer then checks this recommendation. The senior officer can request further information from the claimant, or reject or accept the claim. In the former case, the previous steps must be repeated once the requested information arrives. If a claim is rejected, the claim is archived and the process finishes. If a claim is accepted, the claim officer calculates the payable amount. Afterwards, the claims officer records the settlement information and archives the claim. In the meantime, the financial department takes care of the payment.

Fig. 1. Exemplary description of a claims handling process.

Q1. Is it allowed that the claims officer records the claim information before reviewing the request?

Q2. Which steps must be repeated upon receipt of additional information from the claimant?

Q3. When can the financial department start taking care of the payment?

Based on the information provided in the textual description, these questions are not clearly decidable. This lack of decidability results from two forms of behavioral ambiguity: type ambiguity and scope ambiguity. *Type ambiguity* occurs when a textual description does not clearly specify the type of order relationship between two activities. For instance, the relation between the "*review request*" and "*record claim information*" activities in the first sentence is unclear. The term "*and*" simply does not allow us to determine whether these activities must be executed sequentially or can be executed in an arbitrary order. *Scope ambiguity* occurs when statements in a textual description underspecify to which activity or activities they precisely refer. This type of ambiguity particularly relates to repetitions and parallelism. For instance, the statement that "*the previous steps must be repeated*" does not clearly specify which activities must be performed again. Similarly, the expression "*in the meantime*" does not define when the financial department can start performing its activities.

As a result of such ambiguities, there are different views on how to properly carry out the described process. When deriving a single structured interpretation from a textual process description, as is done by process model generation techniques (cf. [6,8,19]), there is thus always the risk that a derived interpretation conflicts with the proper way to execute the process. The focus on a single interpretation can, therefore, lead to wrong conclusions when reasoning about a business process. This can, for instance, result in a loss of efficiency by not allowing for parallel execution where possible (Q3). Furthermore, it can even result in noncompliance to regulations, for example, by failing to impose necessary ordering restrictions (Q1) or by not repeating the required steps when dealing with the receipt of new claim information (Q2).

To avoid the problems associated with fixed interpretations, automated reasoning techniques should take into account all reasonable interpretations of a textual process description. For this reason, we use this paper to introduce the concept of a *behavioral space*. A behavioral space allows us to capture the full range of semantics possibly implied by textual descriptions in a structured manner. As such, it provides the basis to safely reason about described processes.

3   Capturing Behavioral Ambiguity Using Behavioral Spaces

In this section, we introduce and define the concept of a *behavioral space*. The notion of a behavioral space provides the foundation to reason about properties such as conformance and similarity for behaviorally ambiguous process descriptions. The general idea of the notion is to represent the causes and effects of behavioral ambiguity in a structured manner. Behavioral ambiguity leads to different views on how to properly execute a business process. To capture these views, we first conceptualize a single view or *interpretation* of the process behavior described in a text. For the purposes of this paper, we express this behavior using the *behavioral profile* relations from [22].

Behavioral profile relations capture the ordering restrictions that are in effect between activities. Three different behavioral profile relations can exist for an activity pair (a_i, a_j). The *strict order* relation $a_i \leadsto a_j$ is used to express that activity a_i cannot be executed after the execution of activity a_j. The *exclusiveness* relation $a_i + a_j$ denotes that either activity a_i or activity a_j can be executed in a single process instance. Finally, the *interleaving order* relation $a_i \parallel a_j$ states that a_i and a_j can be executed in an arbitrary order. Based on these behavioral profile relations, we define a *behavioral interpretation* of a textual process description as follows:

Definition 1 (Behavioral Interpretation). *Given a textual process description T and the set of behavioral profile relations $\mathcal{R} = \{\leadsto, +, \parallel\}$, we define a behavioral interpretation as a tuple $BI = (A_T, BP)$, with:*

- *A_T: the set of activities described in the textual process description T;*
- *$BP : A_T \times A_T \nrightarrow \mathcal{R}$: a partial function that assigns a behavioral profile relation from $\mathcal{R}$ to a pair of activities from A_T, if any.*

Multiple behavioral interpretations for the same textual process description occur when the text contains statements about behavioral relations that can be interpreted in different ways. We refer to such statements as *behavioral statements*. Each behavioral statement consists of a single or several words and describes pair-wise relations between one or more activity pairs. An ambiguous relational statement can result in multiple, conflicting sets of pair-wise relations. For instance, the statement *"a claim officer reviews the request and records the claim information"*, results in two different interpretations because it is unclear whether this statement implies a strict order or an interleaving order between the two described activities. Using the activity identifiers specified in Table 1, this results in two sets of behavioral relations, namely $\{a_2 \leadsto a_3\}$ and $\{a_2 \parallel a_3\}$. Given the set S_T of the behavioral statements in a text T, the set of possible

Table 1. Activities in the running example

ID	Activity	ID	Activity
a_1	Receive claim	a_8	Reject claim
a_2	Review request	a_9	Accept claim
a_3	Record claim information	a_{10}	Receive requested information
a_4	Validate documents	a_{11}	Calculate payable amount
a_5	Write settlement recommendation	a_{12}	Record settlement information
a_6	Check recommendation	a_{13}	Archive claim
a_7	Request further information	a_{14}	Arrange payment

behavioral interpretations $\mathcal{BI}_T$, follows naturally as the set of possible combinations of interpretations of statements in S_T. This results in a three-dimensional view on the behavioral relations that exist between activities, as visualized in Fig. 2.

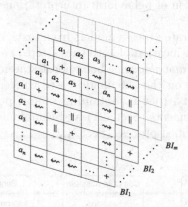

Fig. 2. A behavioral space as a collection of m behavioral interpretations

The behavioral space captures this spectrum of possible behavioral interpretations for a textual process description, as given by Definition 2.

Definition 2 (Behavioral Space). *Given a textual process description T and the behavioral profile relations $\mathcal{R} = \{\rightsquigarrow, +, ||\}$, we define a behavioral space as a tuple $\mathcal{S}_T = (A_T, S_T, \mathcal{BI}, \delta)$, with:*

- *A_T: the set of activities described in the textual process description T;*
- *S_T: the set of behavioral statements contained in the textual process description T;*
- *$\mathcal{BI}$: the set of behavioral interpretations of a textual process description T;*
- *$\delta : A_T \times A_T \rightarrow \mathcal{P}(S_T \times \mathcal{R})$, as a function that links the behavioral profile relations that can exist between activity pairs to sets of behavioral statements.*

In Definition 2, the function δ provides traceability between behavioral statements and the behavioral profile relations included in the behavioral interpretations for activities. This traceability can be used to provide diagnostic information when reasoning about compliance. We furthermore use $R(a_i, a_j) \subseteq \mathcal{R}$ as a short-hand to refer to the set of behavioral profile relations that can exist between activities a_i and a_j, e.g. $R(a_2, a_3) = \{\rightsquigarrow, \|\}$.

4 Obtaining Behavioral Spaces

The procedure to obtain a behavioral space from a textual process description consists of three main steps, as visualized in Fig. 3. First, we identify the process activities described in the text T. This results in an activity set A_T, as shown in Table 1 for the claims handling example. Second, we identify the behavioral relations that exist among these activities. This step involves both the extraction of behavioral relations for unambiguous behavioral statements, as well as the extraction of sets of possible behavioral relations for ambiguous behavioral statements. Third, we combine the different interpretations of individual ambiguous statements into a collection of behavioral interpretations $\mathcal{BI}$ in order to obtain a behavioral space.

Approaches that generate process models from texts, cf. [6], address the challenges related to the identification of activities (step 1) and to the extraction of behavioral relations for *unambiguous* behavioral statements (part of step 2). Therefore, we focus here on the yet unaddressed challenges related to dealing with behavioral ambiguity, that is, obtaining sets of possible behavioral relations for *ambiguous* statements (Sect. 4.1) and combining these into behavioral interpretations of a described process (Sect. 4.2).

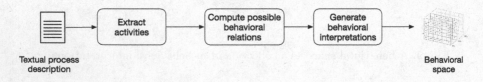

Fig. 3. Steps involved to obtain a behavioral space from a textual description

4.1 Computing Possible Behavioral Relations

Approaches that generate process models from textual descriptions use heuristics-based techniques to identify and analyze behavioral statements in a text. These techniques mainly build on predefined sets of indicators that pinpoint the different types of relations, e.g. "*then*" as well as "*afterwards*" for strict order relations and "*while*" as well as "*meanwhile*" for parallel or interleaving order relations. To identify ambiguous behavioral statements, we isolated a subset of these indicators that result or can result in behaviorally ambiguous statements. For example, the usage of *"meanwhile"* or *"in the meantime"* to indicate interleaving order relations results in statements with scope ambiguity. By contrast, this is not the case for *"while"* because this indicator is naturally accompanied by a scope specifier, e.g. *"while the claim is being archived"*. Once a statement with behavioral ambiguity has been identified, we generate possible interpretations for these statements. Here, we treat statements with type and with scope ambiguity differently, since they result in different sets of behavioral relations.

Statements with Type Ambiguity. A behavioral statement with type ambiguity describes that there exists a relation among a specific set of activities, but does not clearly state the type of relationship. For example, the first sentence of the running example does not clearly specify whether the order is important when executing the activities a_2 and a_3. To capture these different possibilities in the behavioral space, we generate an interpretation of this statement for each of the possible relation types, i.e. strict order and interleaving order. This results in two sets of relations that are linked to the ambiguous behavioral statement s_1: $\{a_2 \rightsquigarrow a_3\}$ and $\{a_2 \parallel a_3\}$.

Statements with Scope Ambiguity. Dealing with behavioral statements with scope ambiguity is more complex. These statements describe the existence of a relation, but do not specify between which activities this relationship holds. For example, the statement *"the previous steps must be repeated, once the requested information arrives"*, which we shall refer to as s_2, does not state which activities should be repeated. Though such statements are highly problematic, we do not have to be completely unaware about their meaning, i.e. about the possible sets of activities that the statements can refer to. In particular, we can utilize the notion that statements such as *"the previous steps"* and *"in the meantime"* relate to distinct parts of a process. This means that the set of activities to which these statements refer *cannot* be any arbitrary combination of activities. The activities in the set must rather have something in common, such as activities that are all executed by the same person.

For this reason, we generate interpretations for statements with scope ambiguity based on sets of activities that have a certain commonality. In particular, given a textual process description, we can identify sets of subsequently described activities that are (i) performed by the same resource, (ii) performed on or with the same (business) object, or (iii) are part of the same discourse statement (i.e. a choice in the process). Based on this, we can recognize that *"the previous steps"* in s_2, can refer to either:

1. The activities performed by the *senior claims officer*, i.e. $\{a_6, a_7, a_8, a_9\}$;
2. The activities related to the *settlement recommendation*, i.e. $\{a_5, a_6\}$;
3. All previous activities of the process, i.e. $\{a_1, a_2, a_3, a_4, a_5, a_6, a_7, a_8, a_9\}$.

These three possibilities result in three sets of relations that can follow from the same behavioral statement. In the same way, we can obtain different interpretations for the statement s_3: "*In the meantime, the financial department takes care of the payment*". This statement can refer to the following sets of activities:

1. The activities performed by the *claims officer*, after a senior claims officer has accepted the claim, i.e. $\{a_{11}, a_{12}, a_{13}\}$;
2. The activities related to the *claim* object, i.e. $\{a_{13}\}$;
3. The last mentioned activity before the statement, i.e. $\{a_{13}\}$.

The last interpretation here differs from the third interpretation of statement s_2 because, unlike for s_2, statement s_3 can also refer to a single activity. In that case, "*in the meantime*" is interpreted to simply refer to the preceding activity. Recognizing that the two latter interpretations of statement s_3 encompass the same set of activities, this results in two instead of three possible interpretations of s_3.

4.2   Generating Behavioral Interpretations

Based on the relations extracted from unambiguous behavioral statements and the sets of possible relations for ambiguous behavioral statements, we can generate a set of behavioral interpretations $\mathcal{BI}$ for the entire textual description. As considered in the previous section, the claims handling process contains three ambiguous statements with, respectively, two, three, and two possible interpretations. We obtain behavioral interpretations by combining the interpretations of individual statements in all possible manners. For the claims handling process, this results in a behavioral space with 12 ($2 \times 3 \times 2$) possible interpretations in $\mathcal{BI}$. To complete the full behavioral profile relations for a behavioral interpretation, we make use of the transitivity of the strict order and interleaving order relations [20]. In this way, we can obtain relations beyond those pair-wise relations that we extracted from a textual description. For example, if a text specifies that activity a_i is followed by a_j and a_j is followed by a_k, i.e. $a_i \rightsquigarrow a_j$ and $a_j \rightsquigarrow a_k$, then a_i is also followed by a_k, i.e. $a_i \rightsquigarrow a_k$.

Once the behavioral interpretations have been constructed, the behavioral space is complete. Table 2 visualizes the possible behavioral relations for a

Table 2. Possible behavioral relations for activities of the claims handling process.

	a_9	a_{10}	a_{11}	a_{12}	a_{13}	a_{14}
a_9	$+$	$\rightsquigarrow$	$\rightsquigarrow$	$\rightsquigarrow$	$\rightsquigarrow$	$\rightsquigarrow$
a_{10}		$\|\|$	$\rightsquigarrow$	$\rightsquigarrow$	$\rightsquigarrow$	$\rightsquigarrow$
a_{11}			$+$	$\rightsquigarrow$	$\rightsquigarrow$	$\|\|/\rightsquigarrow$
a_{12}				$+$	$\rightsquigarrow$	$\|\|/\rightsquigarrow$
a_{13}					$+$	$\|\|$
a_{14}						$+$

fraction of the activities in the running example. The table illustrates that many of the relations are known with certainty. Still, due to the ambiguous behavioral statement s_3, the relations between, on the one hand, activities a_{11} and a_{12}, and, on the other, activity a_{14} can be both strict orders or interleaving orders. Finally, it is interesting to note that although the relation between a_{13} and a_{14} is affected by the ambiguous statement s_3, its relation type is known with certainty. This is because all possible interpretations of s_3 include the relation $a_{13} \parallel a_{14}$.

5   Reasoning Using Behavioral Spaces

By capturing behavioral ambiguity in a structured manner, behavioral spaces allow us to reason about behavioral properties without the need to arbitrarily settle ambiguity. Similar to behavioral profiles and process models, suitable reasoning tasks include similarity analysis, matching, and compliance checking. In this section, we show the usefulness of behavioral spaces for such reasoning tasks. To achieve this, we describe the specific use case of checking the compliance between a behavioral space and an execution trace.

The goal of compliance checking is to determine whether the behavior captured in an execution trace is allowed by the behavioral specification of a business process. The key difference between traditional compliance checking and compliance checking using behavioral spaces lies in the potential outcomes of a check. In traditional compliance checking, a trace is either *compliant* or it is *non-compliant* with a business process. By contrast, due to the behavioral ambiguity captured in behavioral spaces, a trace can be either compliant, non-compliant, but also *potentially compliant* with a behavioral space. The latter outcome occurs for traces that comply with one or more behavioral interpretations in a behavioral space, but not to all of them.

5.1   Behavioral Interpretation Compliance

Compliance checking of a trace t against a behavioral space $\mathcal{S}$ builds on the compliance checking of t against individual behavioral interpretations in $\mathcal{BI}_\mathcal{S}$. This is equal to the compliance check of a trace and a behavioral profile, as obtained from a process model (see [23]). This check builds on a comparison of the behavioral profile of a trace BP_t to the behavioral profile relations of behavioral interpretation BI. The behavioral profile BP_t captures the strict order and interleaving order relations for the set of activities A_t in a trace t. Given an activity pair $(a_i, a_j) \in (A_t \times A_t)$, BP_t contains the strict order relation $a_i \rightsquigarrow_t a_j$ iff at least one occurrence of activity a_i precedes an occurrence of activity a_j in t, and no occurrence of a_j precedes an occurrence of a_i in t. BP_t contains the interleaving order relation $a_i \parallel a_j$ iff at least one occurrence of a_i precedes an occurrence of a_j in t, and at least one occurrence of a_j precedes an occurrence of a_i in t.

Given a behavioral profile of a trace BP_t and a behavioral interpretation BI, we can determine if t is compliant to BI by checking if the relations in

BP_t do not violate the behavioral relations in BI. Specifically, t is compliant
to BI if all relations in BP_t are *subsumed* by the relations in BI. A relation
type $R \in \mathcal{R}$ is subsumed by relation type $R' \in \mathcal{R}$ if the relation types are equal,
i.e. $R = R'$, or if R' is less restrictive than R. The latter captures the notion that
when an activity pair (a_i, a_j) is in a strict order or reverse strict order relation
in $\mathcal{B}_t$, this does not violate an interleaving order relation in $\mathcal{B}_I$. In other words,
$a_i \rightsquigarrow a_j \in BP_t$ is subsumed by the relation $a_i \parallel a_j \in BI$.

Based on the notion of subsumption, we define compliance between a trace
and a behavioral interpretation in Definition 3. Here, for brevity we say that an
activity pair (a_i, a_j) is in *reverse strict order*, denoted by $a_i \rightsquigarrow_t^{-1} a_j$, if and only
if $a_j \rightsquigarrow_t a_i$.

Definition 3 (Trace to Behavioral Interpretation Compliance). *Let*
$t = e_1, \ldots, e_m$ *be a trace with an activity set A_t and $BI \in \mathcal{BI}_\mathcal{S}$ a behavioral*
interpretation in the behavioral space $\mathcal{S}$, with $A_t \subseteq A_\mathcal{S}$.

- *For an activity pair $(x, y) \in (A_t \times A_t)$, the relation $xRy \in \mathcal{B}_t \cup \{\rightsquigarrow_t^{-1}\}$ is*
  subsumed by relation $xR'y \in \mathcal{B}_I \cup \{\rightsquigarrow_I^{-1}\}$, i.e. the subsumption predicate
  $sub(R, R')$ is satisfied, iff $R = R'$ or $R' = \parallel$.
- *Trace t complies to behavioral interpretation BI if for each activity pair $(x, y) \in$*
  $(A_t \times A_t)$ the relation in t is subsumed by the relation in BI, i.e. the compliance
  predicate $compl(t, BI)$ is satisfied, iff $\forall R \in \mathcal{B}_t \cup \{\rightsquigarrow_t^{-1}\}, \mathcal{B}_I \cup \{\rightsquigarrow_I^{-1}\}$, it holds
  $(xRy \land xR'y) \implies sub(R, R')$.

5.2   Behavioral Space Compliance

Based on the compliance check between a trace and individual behavioral interpretations, we can determine the compliance of a trace to the full behavioral
space. In particular, we can quantify the *support* of the behavioral space for a
trace and extract the conditions under which this trace complies to the textual
process description. We define the support of a behavioral space $\mathcal{S}$ for a trace t
as the ratio between the number of interpretations to which t is compliant and
the total number of interpretations in $\mathcal{BI}_\mathcal{S}$:

$$\text{supp}(t, \mathcal{S}) = \frac{|\{BI \in \mathcal{BI}_\mathcal{S} \mid compl(t, BI)\}|}{|\mathcal{BI}_\mathcal{S}|} \tag{1}$$

The support metric quantifies the fraction of interpretations that allow for
a trace to occur. A support value of 1.0 indicates that a trace is without any
doubt compliant to the behavioral space, i.e. independent of the chosen interpretation. A support of 0.0 shows that there is no interpretation under which a
trace complies to the behavioral space. Therefore, it can be said with certainty
that the trace is non-compliant to $\mathcal{S}$. Finally, any trace t with a support value
$0.0 < \text{supp}(t, \mathcal{S}) < 1.0$ is potentially compliant to $\mathcal{S}$. This implies that there are
certain interpretations of the textual description to which the trace complies.
To illustrate the usefulness of the support metric and the additional compliance
information that behavioral spaces can provide, consider the following three partial execution traces of the running example:

- Trace $t_1 = < a_1, a_2, a_3, a_4, a_5 >$;
- Trace $t_2 = < a_1, a_3, a_2, a_4, a_5 >$;
- Trace $t_3 = < a_{11}, a_{14}, a_{12}, a_{13} >$.

The traces t_1 and t_2 both describe an execution sequence for the first part of the claim handling process. The difference between the two is that in t_1 activity a_2 occurs before a_3, whereas these are executed in reverse order in t_2, i.e. $a_2 \leadsto a_3 \in BP_{t_1}$ and $a_2 \leadsto^{-1} a_3 \in BP_{t_2}$. Furthermore, recall that the behavioral relation between these two activities is given by the ambiguous behavioral statement s_2. Depending on the interpretation of s_2, there either exists a strict order or an interleaving order relation between a_2 and a_3, i.e. $R(a_2, a_3) = \{\leadsto, ||\}$. The relation $a_2 \leadsto_{t_1} a_3$ from t_1 is subsumed by both possible interpretations included in the behavioral space, since $\mathrm{sub}(\leadsto, \leadsto)$ and $\mathrm{sub}(\leadsto, ||)$ are both satisfied. Therefore, t_1 is compliant to all interpretations in $\mathcal{BI}$ and, thus, has a support value of 1.0. By contrast, while $a_2 \leadsto_{t_2}^{-1} a_3$ in trace t_2 is subsumed by relation $a_2 || a_3$, this relation is not subsumed by $a_2 \leadsto a_3$. Therefore, t_2 does not comply to half of the behavioral interpretations in $\mathcal{BI}$. This results in $\mathrm{supp}(t_2, \mathcal{S}) = 0.5$.

Aside from providing information on the (fraction of) behavioral interpretations to which a trace is compliant, behavioral spaces allow us to obtain further diagnostic information from this compliance check. In particular, we can utilize the function δ, which relates behavioral statements to relations, to gain insights into the conditions under which a trace is compliant to a process description. For example, we can learn under which interpretations of the statement s_3, "*In the meantime, the financial department takes care of the payment*", trace t_3 is compliant. In t_3, the financial department pays the settlement amount (a_{14}) before the claims officer records the settlement information (a_{12}). This complies with one of two interpretations of statement s_3 and, therefore, results in a support value of 0.5. Furthermore, we know that this trace is compliant, if and only if "*in the meantime*" means "*while the claims officer is performing its tasks*" and not "*while the claims officer is archiving the claim*". Such diagnostic information can be useful when interpreting the support values for a trace or when aiming to resolve the ambiguity contained in a textual description.

6   Evaluation

To demonstrate the importance of behavioral spaces for automated reasoning about textual process descriptions, we conduct a quantitative evaluation that assesses the impact of behavioral ambiguity on compliance checking. The goal of this evaluation is to learn how well behavioral spaces provide a balance between loose and restricted ways of dealing with behavioral ambiguity. In Sect. 6.1, we introduce the test collection used for the evaluation. Section 6.2 describes the details of the evaluation setup. Finally, we present and discuss the evaluation results in Sect. 6.3.

6.1 Test Collection

To perform the evaluation, we use the collection of textual process descriptions from the evaluation of the text to process model generation approach by Friedrich et al [6]. The collection contains 47 process descriptions obtained from various industrial and scholarly sources. The included texts differ greatly in size, ranging from 3 to 40 sentences. Furthermore, they differ in the average length of sentences and in terms of how explicitly and unambiguously they describe process behavior. Among others, this results from the variety of authors that created the textual descriptions. Hence, we believe that the collection is well-suited for achieving a high external validity of the results.

6.2 Setup

To conduct the evaluation, we implemented a prototype to generate behavioral spaces from textual process descriptions. To achieve this, we build on the state-of-the-art text to process model generation approach by Friedrich et al. [6]. In particular, the Java prototype builds on a library that is part of the RefMod-Miner[1], which implements a process model generation approach in a stand-alone tool. We use the library to automatically identify activities and extract behavioral profile relations that exist between the activities. Subsequently, we identify and remove those behavioral relations that result from ambiguous behavioral statements. Instead, we replace these relations by generating a behavioral space with the different possible interpretations, following the approach described in Sect. 4.

To demonstrate the importance of behavioral spaces, we compare the behavior they capture to two alternative ways of dealing with behavioral ambiguity. On the one end of the spectrum, instead of capturing behavioral ambiguity, a possibility is to focus only on the behavioral relations that can be extracted with certainty. For unclear behavioral relations, we take the least restrictive relation, i.e. the interleaving order. We shall refer to the behavioral profile that implements this way of dealing with behavioral ambiguity as a *minimally restricted* behavioral model. On the opposite end, it is possible to impose assumptions on ambiguous statements, resulting in a single interpretation of the described behavior. This is the approach that text-to-process-model generation techniques use to deal with behavioral ambiguity. We refer to this as a *fully interpreted* behavioral model. Together with a behavioral space, we therefore generate three behavioral models for each of 47 textual process descriptions:

1. **Minimally restricted behavioral profile:** This behavioral profile only captures the behavioral relations that can be extracted with certainty from the textual process description, i.e. we removed all behavioral relations obtained by the process model generation algorithm from [6] that result from ambiguous behavioral statements. We refer to the minimally restricted behavioral profile of a text T as BP_T^{min}.

---

[1] http://refmod-miner.dfki.de.

2. **Fully interpreted behavioral profile:** The behavioral profile that is extracted from the process model generated by the process model generation approach from [6]. We refer to the fully interpreted behavioral profile of a text T with BP_T^{full}.
3. **Behavioral space:** The behavioral space generated for the textual description in accordance with the interpretation generation method described in Sect. 4. We refer to the behavioral space of a text T as $\mathcal{S}_T$.

The goal of the evaluation is to show that a behavioral space provides a balance between the minimally restricted model BP_T^{min}, which takes an agnostic view on ambiguous statements, and a fully restricted behavioral profile BP_T^{full}, obtained by imposing assumptions to arbitrarily settle behavioral ambiguity. We illustrate this by comparing the size of the sets of traces that are (potentially) compliant with the three behavioral models, in accordance to the definitions provided in Sect. 5.[2] Using $\mathcal{C}(BM)$ to refer to the collection of traces that are compliant or potentially compliant to a behavioral model BM, we quantify the differences using for a textual description T using the following two metrics:

$$R_1(T) = \frac{\mid \mathcal{C}(\mathcal{S}_T) \mid}{\mid \mathcal{C}(BP_T^{full}) \mid} \tag{2}$$

$$R_2(T) = \frac{\mid \mathcal{C}(BP_T^{min}) \mid}{\mid \mathcal{C}(\mathcal{S}_T) \mid} \tag{3}$$

R_1 quantifies the ratio between the number of traces allowed by a behavioral space and a minimally restricted behavioral profile. Its purpose is to illustrate how much behavior that certainly does not conform to the business process description, is allowed by a model that ignores statements with behavioral ambiguity. R_2 quantifies the ratio between the number of traces allowed by a behavioral space and those allowed by a fully interpreted behavioral profile. Its purpose is to illustrate how much behavior that is not unequivocally non-compliant to a process specification, is removed from consideration when imposing assumptions on the interpretation of a textual process description.

6.3 Results

Table 3 summarizes the evaluation results for the textual process descriptions with behavioral ambiguity. The first interesting thing to note is how common textual process descriptions with behavioral ambiguity are. In total, 32 of the 47 textual process descriptions (70 %) contained one or more ambiguous phrases. The majority, 28 cases, included just phrases with type ambiguity. Four cases contain statements with scope ambiguity, 3 of which also contain behavioral statements with type ambiguity.

For processes with just type ambiguity in their descriptions, there is a clear difference between the behavior allowed by fully interpreted behavioral profiles

---

[2] For processes that contain loops, we only include traces with at most one repetition.

Table 3. Evaluation results

Collection	P	S_{type}	S_{scope}	A	$|\mathcal{BI}|$	R_1	R_2
Only type ambiguity	28	64	0	19.6	11.0	100.0 %	37.8 %
With scope ambiguity	4	13	4	24.0	76.5	16.4 %	0.5 %
Total	32	77	4	20.2	19.1	89.5 %	33.7 %

Legend: P = number of processes, S_{type} = statements with type ambiguity, S_{scope} = statements with scope ambiguity, A = extracted activities per process (avg.), $|\mathcal{BI}|$ = interpretations per behavioral space.

$\mathcal{C}(BP^{full})$ and the behavior allowed by behavioral spaces $\mathcal{C}(\mathcal{S})$. As indicated by metric R_2, the fully interpreted behavioral profiles allow for only 37.8 % of the behavior allowed by the behavioral space. The remaining 62.2 % represent traces for which it *cannot* be said with certainty that these do not comply to the process described in the text. This difference results from ordering restrictions that the text-to-model generation algorithm imposes on activities, even when these ordering restrictions may not exist. Behavioral spaces do not impose such restrictions and, thus, mark traces that exhibit such execution flexibility as potentially compliant. Though these cases already illustrate the impact of imposing assumptions on the interpretation of textual process descriptions, this impact is much more severe for cases that also contain statements with scope ambiguity.

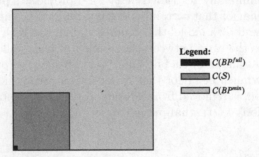

Fig. 4. Visualization of three sets of compliant traces for cases with scope ambiguity.

The behavioral models for the 4 cases with scope ambiguity show considerable differences among the behavior they allow. We visualize the relative sizes of the three sets of compliant traces in Fig. 4. There, the light-gray area denotes the set of traces compliant with BP^{min}, i.e. the set of traces that remain when treating ambiguous statements as undecidable. The behavior allowed by the behavioral space, represented by the dark-gray area, is considerably smaller, as also indicated by the R_1 score of 16.4 %. This number reveals that 83.6% of the traces in $\mathcal{C}(BP^{min})$ represent traces that are not compliant with any reasonable interpretation of the statements with scope ambiguity. For instance, for the running example, this set would include traces where the financial department pays a settlement for an insurance claim, *before* the claim has been accepted. Figure 4 also shows the considerable impact that the usage of single interpretations has on the number of compliant traces. The tiny black area in the figure and the R_2 score of 0.5 % indicate that, for the cases with scope ambiguity, the fully interpreted behavior profiles allow for only a very small fraction of the behavior that is (potentially) compliant to a behavioral space. Again, the remaining 99.5 % represent traces that do not with certainty conflict with behavior specified in a textual process description.

The evaluation results show the impact both of ignoring ambiguous statements and of imposing single interpretations on them. As visualized by Fig. 4, behavioral spaces provide a balance between these loosely restricted and too restricted behavioral models. In summary, behavioral spaces exclude a large number of nonsensical traces that can be excluded by generating proper interpretations for ambiguous statements. Still, they allow for much more traces than the restricted models obtained by imposing assumptions on the ambiguous statements in textual descriptions.

A point to consider for these evaluations results is that some of the statements with type ambiguity are ambiguous to automated approaches, but not for human interpreters. For instance, the meaning of the phrase *"sign and send contract"* can be inferred by human readers, because of the implicit order that exists between *signing* and *sending* of a document. Nevertheless, the decision to treat such statements as ambiguous for automated approaches is justified, because state-of-the-art automated approaches do not succeed in making such inferences.

7   Related Work

The work presented in this paper primarily relates to two major research streams: the analysis of textual process descriptions and the representation of data uncertainty.

The majority of works that consider the analysis of textual process models and other texts related to business processes, focus on the automated derivation of process models from natural language texts. Such techniques have been designed for textual process descriptions [6,7], group stories [8], use case descriptions [19] and textual methodologies [21]. Out of these, the text-to-process-model generation techniques by Friedrich et al. [6], on which we build our prototype and use as benchmark in our evaluation, is recognized as the state-of-the-art [16]. Although these works do not mention the problem of behavioral ambiguity explicitly, all of the presented techniques impose assumptions on the interpretation of ambiguous behavioral statements. This results in a single interpretation, i.e. a process model, for a text. However, as shown in the evaluation, this comes at the great disadvantage that the behavior allowed by this representation is much more strict than the behavior specified in the textual description. Our earlier work on the comparison of textual process descriptions to process models [2], faces similar issues when reasoning about the consistency of the two artifacts.

Similar to behavioral ambiguity inherent to natural language descriptions, uncertain data is also inherent to other application contexts. In the cases, uncertainty can be caused by, among others, data randomness, incompleteness, and limitations of measuring equipment [13]. This has created a need for algorithms and applications for uncertain data managements [4]. As a result, the modeling of uncertain data has been studied extensively, cf. [3,9,14,17]. Our notion of a behavioral space builds on concepts related to those used in uncertain data models. For instance, similar to the behavioral interpretations captured in a behavioral space, the model presented by Das Sarma et al. [17] uses a set of *possible instances* to represent the spectrum of possible interpretations for an uncertain relation. Furthermore, the model described in [3] uses conditions to capture dependencies between uncertain values. This notion has the same result as the sets of behavioral relations we derive from uncertain behavioral statements and convert into different behavioral interpretations. Still, the technical aspects and application contexts of these uncertain data models, mostly querying and data integration [4], differ considerably from the process-oriented view of behavioral spaces.

8   Conclusions

In this paper, we introduced the concept of a behavioral space to deal with the ambiguity in textual process descriptions. A behavioral space captures all possible interpretations of a textual process description and thus avoids the issue of focusing on a single process-oriented interpretation of a text. We demonstrated that a behavioral space is a useful concept for reasoning about a process described by a text. In particular, we used a quantitative evaluation with a set of 47 textual process descriptions and a compliance checking setting to illustrate that a behavioral space strikes a reasonable balance between ignoring ambiguous statements and imposing fixed interpretations on them.

While we defined the behavioral space concept based on textual process descriptions, we would like to point out that its use is not limited to texts. A behavioral space can help to capture the full behavior of different types of process descriptions that contain (ambiguous) natural language text. Consider, for instance, process models containing activities that describe several streams of actions by using ambiguous behavioral statements such as "*and*". It has been found that such *non-atomic* activities can result in different interpretations of how to properly execute the process [15]. A behavioral space is also useful for application scenarios beyond compliance checking. Among others, it can serve as a basis for computing process similarity and conducting process matching.

In future work, we set out to explore these usage scenarios of behavioral spaces in more detail. What is more, we plan to investigate how we can prune a behavioral space in a systematic fashion.

References

1. Van der Aa, H., Leopold, H., Mannhardt, F., Reijers, H.A.: On the fragmentation of process information: challenges, solutions, and outlook. In: Gaaloul, K., Schmidt, R., Nurcan, S., Guerreiro, S., Ma, Q. (eds.) BPMDS 2015 and EMMSAD 2015. LNBIP, vol. 214, pp. 3–18. Springer, Heidelberg (2015)
2. Van der Aa, H., Leopold, H., Reijers, H.A.: Detecting inconsistencies between process models and textual descriptions. In: Motahari-Nezhad, H.R., Recker, J., Weidlich, M. (eds.) BPM 2015. LNCS, vol. 9253, pp. 90–105. Springer, Heidelberg (2015)
3. Abiteboul, S., Kanellakis, P., Grahne, G.: On the representation and querying of sets of possible worlds, vol. 16. ACM (1987)
4. Aggarwal, C.C., Yu, P.S.: A survey of uncertain data algorithms and applications. IEEE Trans. Knowl. Data Eng. **21**(5), 609–623 (2009)
5. Dijkman, R., Dumas, M., García-Bañuelos, L.: Graph matching algorithms for business process model similarity search. In: Dayal, U., Eder, J., Koehler, J., Reijers, H.A. (eds.) BPM 2009. LNCS, vol. 5701, pp. 48–63. Springer, Heidelberg (2009)
6. Friedrich, F., Mendling, J., Puhlmann, F.: Process model generation from natural language text. In: Mouratidis, H., Rolland, C. (eds.) CAiSE 2011. LNCS, vol. 6741, pp. 482–496. Springer, Heidelberg (2011)
7. Ghose, A., Koliadis, G., Chueng, A.: Process discovery from model and text artefacts. In: 2007 IEEE Congress on Services, pp. 167–174. IEEE (2007)
8. de AR Gonçalves, J.C., Santoro, F.M., Baiao, F.A.: Business process mining from group stories. In: 13th International Conference on Computer Supported Cooperative Work in Design, CSCWD 2009, pp. 161–166. IEEE (2009)
9. Imieliński, T., Lipski Jr., W.: Incomplete information in relational databases. J. ACM (JACM) **31**(4), 761–791 (1984)
10. Leopold, H., Mendling, J., Polyvyanyy, A.: Supporting process model validation through natural language generation. IEEE Trans. Software Eng. **40**(8), 818–840 (2014)
11. Leopold, H., Pittke, F., Mendling, J.: Automatic service derivation from business process model repositories via semantic technology. J. Syst. Softw. **108**, 134–147 (2015)
12. Liu, Y., Muller, S., Xu, K.: A static compliance-checking framework for business process models. IBM Syst. J. **46**(2), 335–361 (2007)
13. Pei, J., Jiang, B., Lin, X., Yuan, Y.: Probabilistic skylines on uncertain data. In: Proceedings of the 33rd International Conference on Very Large Data Bases, pp. 15–26 (2007)
14. Peng, L., Diao, Y.: Supporting data uncertainty in array databases. In: ACM SIGMOD International Conference on Management of Data, pp. 545–560. ACM (2015)
15. Pittke, F., Leopold, H., Mendling, J.: When language meets language: anti patterns resulting from mixing natural and modeling language. In: Fournier, F., Mendling, J. (eds.) BPM 2014 Workshops. LNBIP, vol. 202, pp. 118–129. Springer, Heidelberg (2015)
16. Riefer, M., Ternis, S.F., Thaler, T.: Mining process models from natural language text: a state-of-the-art analysis. In: Multikonferenz Wirtschaftsinformatik (MKWI-16), March 9–11, Illmenau, Germany. Universität Illmenau (2016)
17. Sarma, A.D., Benjelloun, O., Halevy, A., Widom, J.: Working models for uncertain data. In: 22nd International Conference on Data Engineering, p. 7. IEEE (2006)

18. Selway, M., Grossmann, G., Mayer, W., Stumptner, M.: Formalising natural language specifications using a cognitive linguistic/configuration based approach. Inf. Syst. **54**, 191–208 (2015)
19. Sinha, A., Paradkar, A.: Use cases to process specifications in Business Process Modeling Notation. In: IEEE International Conference on Web Services, pp. 473–480 (2010)
20. Smirnov, S., Weidlich, M., Mendling, J.: Business process model abstraction based on behavioral profiles. In: Weske, M., Yang, J., Fantinato, M., Maglio, P.P. (eds.) ICSOC 2010. LNCS, vol. 6470, pp. 1–16. Springer, Heidelberg (2010)
21. Viorica Epure, E., Martin-Rodilla, P., Hug, C., Deneckere, R., Salinesi, C.: Automatic process model discovery from textual methodologies. In: 2015 IEEE 9th International Conference on Research Challenges in Information Science (RCIS), pp. 19–30. IEEE (2015)
22. Weidlich, M., Mendling, J., Weske, M.: Efficient consistency measurement based on behavioral profiles of process models. IEEE Trans. Software Eng. **37**(3), 410–429 (2011)
23. Weidlich, M., Polyvyanyy, A., Desai, N., Mendling, J., Weske, M.: Process compliance analysis based on behavioural profiles. Inf. Syst. **36**(7), 1009–1025 (2011)

The Effect of Modularity Representation and Presentation Medium on the Understandability of Business Process Models in BPMN

Oktay Turetken[1(✉)], Tessa Rompen[2], Irene Vanderfeesten[1],
Ahmet Dikici[3], and Jan van Moll[2]

[1] Eindhoven University of Technology,
Eindhoven, The Netherlands
{o.turetken,i.t.p.vanderfeesten}@tue.nl
[2] Philips Health Tech, Best, The Netherlands
{tessa.rompen,jan.van.moll}@philips.com
[3] TÜBİTAK BİLGEM Software Technologies Research Institute,
Ankara, Turkey
ahmet.dikici@tubitak.gov.tr

Abstract. Many factors influence the creation of understandable business process models for an appropriate audience. Understandability of process models becomes critical particularly when a process is complex and its model is large in structure. Using modularization to represent such models hierarchically (e.g. using sub-processes) is considered to contribute to the understandability of these models. To investigate this assumption, we conducted an experiment that involved 2 large-scale real-life business process models that were modeled using BPMN v2.0 (Business Process Model and Notation). Each process was modeled in 3 modularity forms: fully-flattened, flattened where activities are clustered using BPMN groups, and modularized using separately viewed BPMN sub-processes. The objective is to investigate if and how different forms of modularity representation in BPMN collaboration diagrams influence the understandability of process models. In addition to the forms of modularity representation, we also looked into the presentation medium (paper vs. computer) as a factor that potentially influences model comprehension. Sixty business practitioners from a large organization participated in the experiment. The results of our experiment indicate that for business practitioners, to optimally understand a BPMN model in the form of a collaboration diagram, it is best to present the model in a 'fully-flattened' fashion (without using collapsed sub-processes in BPMN) in the 'paper' format.

Keywords: Business process model · Understandability · Comprehension · Modularity · BPMN · Sub-process · Group

© Springer International Publishing Switzerland 2016
M. La Rosa et al. (Eds.): BPM 2016, LNCS 9850, pp. 289–307, 2016.
DOI: 10.1007/978-3-319-45348-4_17

1 Introduction

Business process modeling is an essential component of successful business process management (BPM). It is a fundamental activity to understand and communicate process information, and often a prerequisite for conducting process analysis, redesign and automation [1]. However, in order for process models to successfully serve for their potential uses, they should be perceived as understandable by their audience.

Process model understandability (or comprehension) can be defined as the degree to which information contained in a process model can be easily understood by a reader of that model [2]. It is typically associated with the ease of use and the effort required for reading and correctly interpreting a process model [3].

The increasing complexity of real-life processes leads to an increase also in size and complexity of the models that represent them. These two factors are known to impair understandability [4, 5]. Hierarchy through the use of sub-processes has widely been considered as a practical means to deal with the size and complexity of models [6, 7]. Many modeling languages allow for the design of hierarchical structures (e.g. sub-processes in BPMN and EPCs). Hiding less relevant information in sub-models is expected to decrease the mental effort (cognitive load) needed to understand the model [8], whereas fragmentation due to modularization increases the mental effort by forcing the reader to switch attention between different fragments (so called the split attention effect [6]). In consequence, the discussions about the proper way of using modularity and its implications on the understandability of models are not conclusive [6, 9, 10]. This also leads to a lack of theoretically grounded guidelines for modularizing process models into sub-processes. In particular, the influence of using different forms of modularization in BPMN v2.0 (e.g. sub-processes, groups) on the understandability of process models has not been investigated.

Another factor that has not been addressed in the literature is the medium used to present the models to their audience. Although the paper is usually the preferred means for interacting with model readers in practice [7], the models are typically designed using software applications (particularly when the objective is process automation), and communicated through an online environment (e.g. web portal, company intranet) across the organization and beyond. Therefore, it is important to explore if using paper or a computer environment has any effect on model understandability.

Accordingly, the objective of this study is *to investigate the influence of using different forms of modularity and presentation medium on the understandability of processes modeled in BPMN*. To this end, we conducted an experiment with the participation of 60 practitioners working in a large organization. For the experiment, we used models of two business processes of the organization, which are of similar size and structure, and can be considered large in scale.

The remainder of the paper is structured as follows. Section 2 discusses briefly the related work on the effect of modularity on process model understandability. Section 3 presents the research design including the research model that we tested, and the setup of the experiment. In Sect. 4, we report and discuss the results of our analyses. Finally, Sect. 5 presents our conclusions and future research directions.

2 Related Work

Although modularity in business process models is considered to have benefits in various dimensions, such as increased reuse, maintainability and scalability [11, 12], its influence on the understandability is not well understood [9, 13, 14]. The findings of empirical studies that investigate the effect of modularization (decomposition, or structuring in a hierarchy) on the understandability hardly converge into a validated set of practical guidelines for applying modularization in process modeling.

The works by Reijers et al. [7, 9] test the influence of using sub-processes on the understandability of two real-life processes that are modeled using Workflow Nets in two forms: modular and flattened. The participants (28 consultants) were asked to answer a set of (control-flow related) understandability questions regarding these models (to measure effectiveness). For the first process model, the experiment did not result in a significant difference between the modular and flattened versions, but a positive influence of modularity on understandability was found for the second model. The authors attribute this to the difference in the degree of modularization applied in these models. As the second model had more sub-processes, they sparingly conclude that 'modularity appears to have a positive connection with process understanding'.

Zugal et al. [6] tests the effect of modularization on the understandability of *declarative* process models. Four processes were modeled in two forms (modular and flattened) using a declarative language ConDec. The understandability is measured using the number of correct answers given for the questions (all related to process activities and their ordering/control flow), and the (perceived) mental effort. The results suggest that modularization decreases perceived mental effort but has no influence with respect to the number of correct answers. The limited number of participants (9 respondents) is reported as a threat to the validity of the findings.

The technique used for modularizing process models also plays a role in the effect of modularity on understandability [9]. Applying different modularization methods could yield different structures, in turn different levels of influence on comprehension. The study by Johannsen et al. [15] uses eEPC process models and tests the use of Wand and Weber's five decomposition conditions [16], which are considered to yield well-decomposed models. The models are modularized in three forms with respect to their level of adherence to these conditions. The results indicate that models that are structured in full adherence to these conditions are more understandable than those that violate them. However, the study does not compare the performance of modularized models against their flattened counterparts.

The study by Figl et al. [10] uses expert evaluation approach (with 15 process modeling experts) to determine whether some visualization strategies provide a better fit for representing process model hierarchies than others. Accordingly, the experts prefer to navigate in the hierarchy with the help of an *overview + detail* strategy (where sub-processes are shown as separate models detached from the context of the higher level model) instead of a *focus + context* strategy (where sub-processes are expanded in the higher-level model directly within their context). The 'overview + detail' view was considered to simplify the design and provide undistorted views on focus and context.

In a closely relevant domain of software modeling, Cruz-Lemus et al. [17] presents a family of experiments investigating the effect of hierarchy on the understandability of UML statechart diagrams (which are used not only to model software but also business processes). The results indicate insignificant or varied effects of hierarchy on understandability. Moreover, the understandability worsens with the increase of the nesting level (depth of hierarchy).

This diversity in the results can be attributed to the outcome of two opposing effects of modularization: *abstraction* (information hiding) and *split-attention effect* (browsing costs) [9, 18]. Using sub-processes might increase reader's understanding of a complex model by abstracting away less relevant information (and thereby reducing complexity). However, additional cost (increased cognitive load) incurred in browsing through and integrating fragmented pieces of models can counter-balance this gain [10].

The existing research as discussed above calls for further empirical studies to contribute to a better understanding of the impact of modularization. In particular, there is a lack of studies on the effect of modularity that involve BPMN - de-facto process modeling notation in practice [19]. BPMN v2.0 has specific elements and techniques for representing modularity (e.g. collapsed/expanded sub-processes, groups) which have not been addressed in the research concerning process model understandability. In addition, to the best of our knowledge, no empirical work has studied the effect of the presentation medium on the understandability of process models.

3   Research Design

We used a *between-groups* design for our experiment where separate groups of participants for each of the different conditions in the experiment were tested once only [20]. Aligned with our research question, there are two main *independent* variables: *modularity representation* (in 3 forms) and *presentation medium* (paper vs. computer). We describe these variables in detail later in this section. In addition, we asked participants about their experience in process modeling (following [21]), knowledge on process modeling and BPMN, and familiarity with the domain to investigate the potential effects of these *personal factors*.

We used *two process models* as the objects of our experiment. These processes are taking place in a large corporation headquartered in The Netherlands (which employs more than 115,000 employees and operates in over 100 countries worldwide). The experiment took place in a division in the headquarters in June 2015.

Figure 1 presents the research model that we tested in our experiment. The model proposes that the understandability of process models (in terms of understandability task effectiveness and efficiency, and perceived usefulness and ease of understanding) is influenced by the modularity technique applied in modeling the process and the medium used for its presentation. Accordingly, we can draw two groups of hypotheses:

- *H1.* The form of modularity representation has a significant influence on the understandability factors, i.e.: *(a)* understandability task effectiveness, *(b)* understandability task efficiency, *(c)* perceived usefulness for understandability, and *(d)* perceived ease of understanding.

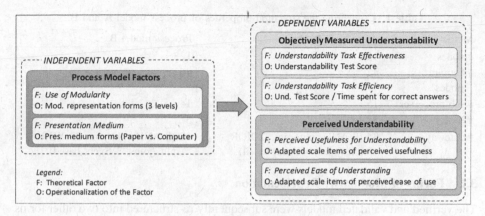

Fig. 1. Research model.

- *H2.* The medium used for presenting process models has a significant influence on the understandability factors (as listed above).

In the sections that follow, we explain the details regarding the process models and forms of modularity representations used, dependent and independent variables as well as their operationalization, and the design of the experiment.

3.1 Process Models Used for the Experiment

Among several processes in the quality management system of the company, two processes of similar size and nature were selected by the company representatives taking into account their criticality in the business domain in which the company operates. The processes can be considered as large and rich in terms of the interaction taking place between different departments and divisions of the company. The selected processes were initially modelled in BPMN v2.0 using sub-processes where applicable (based on existing process documentation, and interviews with process owners and participants). The resulting models were BPMN collaboration diagrams, where the interaction between process participants was explicitly modeled using message flows. (Signavio.com was used for modeling processes, however only static images of models were used for the experiment, as explained in Sect. 3.3.)

The models were subsequently reviewed by process modeling experts for syntactical correctness, and validated for their correctness (including the choice of modularization) by the domain experts in the company, who were also knowledgeable about process modeling. The basic metrics used to measure the structural properties of process models show that these models are comparable in terms of size and complexity (see Table 1).

Table 1. Comparing the structural properties of process model A and B.

Metric	Process model A	Process model B
#Nodes	133	122
#Activity nodes	47	46
#Sub-processes	15	14
#Pools	5	5
#Gateways	34 (8 AND split/join; 22 XOR splits/joins; 4 Event-based)	38 (8 AND split/join; 27 XOR splits/joins; 3 Event-based)

3.2   Forms of Modularity Representation

The verified and validated models were subsequently re-structured into two other forms using different modularity representations in BPMN v2.0, leading to three forms of representation to be tested. Figure 2 illustrates these forms. The first form (Repr1) is the *fully-flattened* representation of the process models. This type acts as the reference model which offers the possibility to draw conclusions about whether the use of any modularity technique has an influence on the understandability. (Note that, re-structuring models does not affect the business logic in a semantic sense, but may influence the extent of information provided in the models. For instance, the sub-process information disappears in the fully-flattened models.)

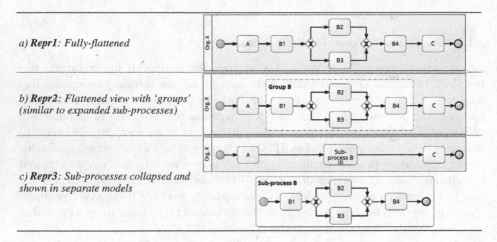

a) **Repr1**: Fully-flattened

b) **Repr2**: Flattened view with 'groups' (similar to expanded sub-processes)

c) **Repr3**: Sub-processes collapsed and shown in separate models

Fig. 2. Three modularity representations: *(a)* Fully-flattened [Repr1], *(b)* Flattened view with groups [Repr2], and *(c)* Sub-processes collapsed and shown in separate models [Repr3].

The second form of representation (Repr2) combines the fully-flattened form with *groups* that informally cluster a logically related set of activities. We used groups in a way similar to the use of 'expanded sub-processes' in BPMN (but without the use of additional start/end events for each sub-process). This form shows some characteristics of a 'focus + context' view (as in Figl et al. [10]), which is considered to require less cognitive load of the user, who usually has to integrate model parts again when sub-processes are extracted from the main model as separate models (i.e. in 'overview + detail' view). However, in this form, the complexity of the full-flattened model is inherited and amplified by the additional information on process groupings.

The third form (Repr3) is the initial representation, which addresses the size and complexity with the use of collapsed sub-processes in BPMN. The sub-processes are hidden in the higher level (main) process model, but can be accessed as a separate model whenever the user is interested in the information it contains.

Figure 3 shows example models of the processes A and B in two representation forms (Repr2 and Repr3), respectively. (Note that the figure is provided to give an

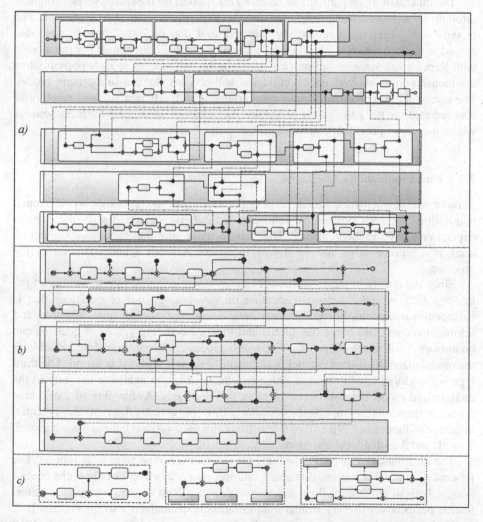

Fig. 3. The process models in two forms of modularity representation: *(a) Process A in Repr2* (flattened with groups of activities), *(b) Process B in Repr3* (with collapsed sub-processes), (c) Few of the *sub-process models* of Process B in *Repr3*. *(The process models and the questionnaire used for the experiment are available online at:* https://goo.gl/0mUOFc.

indication of the size and structure of the models, and labels of all process elements that existed in the experiment are removed here.)

3.3 Presentation Medium for the Process Models

We experimented with two alternative presentation mediums: paper and computer. Half of the participants were provided with the models on A3 size papers, which allowed for adequate readability. The sub-processes in Repr3 were also printed on separate A3 size papers with 6 sub-processes on each.

The other half of the participants received the models on the computer environment through an online website developed for the experiment (see also Sect. 3.7). The models with Repr1 and Repr2 (fully-flattened, and flattened with groups) were displayed as images, which can be zoomed and navigated in all directions. For the models with Repr3 (with separate sub-process models), the sub-process models pop-up when the mouse pointer hoovers on the collapsed sub-process element in the main model. The potential effect of using computer environment with different size and resolutions was reduced, as the participants performed the experiment in their business settings where they were provided with standard computer facilities.

3.4 Understandability Questions

In order to evaluate participants' level of understanding of the processes, we developed 9 questions for each process by following an iterative approach with the domain experts employed in the company. This was to make sure that each question can be used as a representative and valid way to assess someone's understanding of the processes.

Since the quality of these questions has significant influence on the validity of the findings [22], we paid particular attention on developing a set of questions that is balanced in relation to different *process perspectives* (i.e. control flow, resource, and information/data), and *scope* (i.e. global and local). Accordingly, a *local* question can be answered within the scope of a single sub-process, while information available in the modularized (high-level) model is sufficient to answer a *global* question. The third type is the *global-local* questions which require information available not only in the modularized model but also in one or more sub-processes. Availability of these three types of questions is important particularly for the investigation of the potential influence of modularity [9]. Out of 9 questions (for each process), there were 3 global, 3 local, and 3 global-local questions.

The distribution of questions with regard to process perspectives is as follows: For Process A, out of 9 questions, 3 relates to all process perspectives, 2 only to the control flow, 1 both to the control flow and resource, and 3 both to the resource and information perspectives. A very similar configuration is maintained also for Process B.

Each question has a multiple-choice design, where respondents are provided with 5 choices – the last one always being 'I don't know' (i.e. unable to tell). An example question for Process A is given below. For instance, this question is a *local* question that relates to all three perspectives: control-flow (cnt), resource (res), information (inf).

> *Q: Who will know that the AB Request is accepted after a positive opinion of the*
> *Review Board?*
> *a) Only AB Manager   b) Only AB Owner   c) Only Requester*
> *d) Both AB Manager and Requester   e) I don't know* (unable to tell)

3.5   Dependent Variables

As illustrated in our research model (in Fig. 1), we identified four dependent variables concerning process model understandability. The first two relate to the (objectively measurable) level of understanding that the participants can demonstrate with respect to each model [14, 9]. These are as follows:

- *Understandability Task Effectiveness* is operationalized by the understandability test *score*, i.e. the number of correctly answered understandability questions.
- *Understandability Task Efficiency* indicates the degree of cognitive resources spent by the reader in understanding the model [21]. It is operationalized by dividing the test score to the total time spent by a participant for the questions that he/she correctly answered.

The remaining two variables are based on the two constructs of the Technology Acceptance Model (TAM) [23] (i.e. perceived usefulness and perceived ease of use) and concern users' perception of the models in terms of their usefulness for understandability and ease of understanding:

- *Perceived Usefulness for Understandability (PUU)* indicates users' perception on the utility of a process model structured in a particular form in providing gains to the user in terms of understandability.
- *Perceived Ease of Understanding (PEU)* indicates the degree to which a person believes that understanding a model is free from mental effort (as also in [14]).

TAM and its derivatives (e.g. [24]) are the commonly referred theories that predict and explain the acceptance and use of design artefacts, such as IS methods and models [25, 26]. In TAM, the two constructs (perceived usefulness and ease of use) are believed to be strong determinants of users' intentions to use a design artefact. For the experiment, the variables that are adopted are operationalized using multiple indicators (scale items), which have been evaluated for reliability and validity in previous research [23, 25]. Following [24], we used 4 items for each construct, where the wording of the items was modified to accommodate this research. Below are two example items:

- *PUU-1: Using this type of process models would make it more easy to communicate business processes to end-users.*
- *PUE-1: I found the way the process is represented as clear and easy to understand.*

The participants expressed their level of agreement with each statement on a 7-point Likert scale, ranging from 1 (strongly disagree) to 7 (strongly agree).

3.6   Experiment Blocks

The experiment was designed to have six blocks (as shown in Table 2). Each participant went through a single block, where he/she was given two process models (A and B) in sequence. In each block, the models were shown using different forms of modularity representation but either on paper or in a computer environment.

Table 2. Experimental block-design

Exp.	Representation		Presentation
Block	Process A	Process B	Medium
1	Repr1	Repr2	Paper
2	Repr1	Repr3	Computer
3	Repr2	Repr1	Computer
4	Repr2	Repr3	Paper
5	Repr3	Repr1	Paper
6	Repr3	Repr2	Computer

3.7   Questionnaire

The questionnaire for the experiment was provided through an online web environment, which was developed using a software application available for creating online surveys (Sawtooth Software SSI WEB 8.4.6). The questionnaire consisted of 5 parts. The *first* part involved questions related to the personal factors, where participants were asked to give their opinion about their experience and knowledge on process modeling and BPMN, and familiarity with the process and its domain. In the *second* part, the participants were given Process A in a particular form and on a medium depending on the experiment block that they were assigned to. They were expected to answer 9 understandability questions (each placed on a separate online webpage in sequence). In the blocks where computers were used, the process models were embedded in the questionnaire environment in such a way that the question and model were presented on the same page. The *third* part gathers users' perceptions on the particular representation form and medium used to represent the model for Process A. The *fourth* and the *fifth* parts of the questionnaire had the same structure as the second and third parts, but this time for Process B.

All participants (whether they received the models on paper or on computer) received the questions through the *online* environment. This was particularly necessary for accurately tracking the time it took for participants to answer each understandability question, and for computing metrics regarding the *understandability task efficiency*. The participants were informed upfront that they were time-tracked.

Before the actual experiment took place, the questionnaire was pre-tested as a final step by 6 people (4 graduate students, and 2 PhD students). This also gave an indication about the required time-frame for the experiment. As a result of the pre-test, several ambiguities and minor mistakes were corrected in the final version.

3.8 Participants

The company representatives initially selected 74 employees working in 13 departments of the division (where the experiment took place), who had already taken or might potentially take part in the execution of one of these processes. Ultimately, 60 employees participated in the experiment, leading to a response rate of around 81 %. All participants have at least a university degree - majority with an engineering background. Out of 60, 26 employees had previously taken part in the execution of one of these processes or were moderately familiar with their execution.

The participants were randomly assigned to each experiment block with the exception of the 26 employees that had certain degree of familiarity with the domain and process models. These were evenly assigned to the blocks (4 or 5 participants per experiment block). Each participant was sent an invitation with practical guidelines on accessing the online experiment site, including a username which also determined the experimental block that the participant was assigned to.

4   Results and Discussions

Figure 4 presents the distribution of participants based on their opinion about how frequently they encounter process models in practice, and what their level of knowledge on process modeling and BPMN is. Accordingly, around half of the participants encountered process models less than once a month, while the majority of the rest (33 % in total) encountered process models more than once a month. About 72 % of the participants stated that they are knowledgeable or somewhat knowledgeable about process modeling. However, they had no or limited knowledge about BPMN. In the overall, we can consider majority of the participants to be fairly novice in terms of general BPM skills and capabilities.

As each participant tested two process models in different forms, the experiment led to 120 observations distributed largely in a uniform way over different modularity

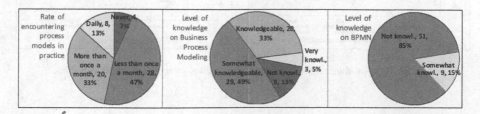

Fig. 4. Participants' background information about process modeling.

Table 3. Descriptive statistics.

Independent variable/levels	N	Unders. task effectiveness (Scale: 0–9)[a]		Unders. task efficiency (in Score/Hour)		Perceived usefulness (Scale: 4–28)[b]		Perceived ease of und.ing (Scale: 4–28)[b]	
		Mean	S.Dev.	Mean	S.Dev.	Mean	S.Dev.	Mean	S.Dev.
Repr1 (fully-flattened)	39	6.2	1.5	33.2	21.0	20.7	5.6	23.2	5.1
Repr2 (flat with groups)	41	5.9	1.5	33.1	12.9	18.3	6.0	20.1	5.6
Repr3 (with sub-processes)	40	5.3	1.6	40.5	24.9	15.8	6.2	18.6	6.3
Paper	62	6.0	1.5	38.4	24.2	20.0	5.4	21.6	5.8
Computer	58	5.6	1.6	32.6	14.9	16.3	6.5	19.6	5.9

[a]Each correctly answered question counts for 1 point for the Score, totaling to 9 points max for 9 questions.
[b]Four items to be answered in a 7-point Likert scale, totaling to a min value of 4, max value of 28 (4 × 7).

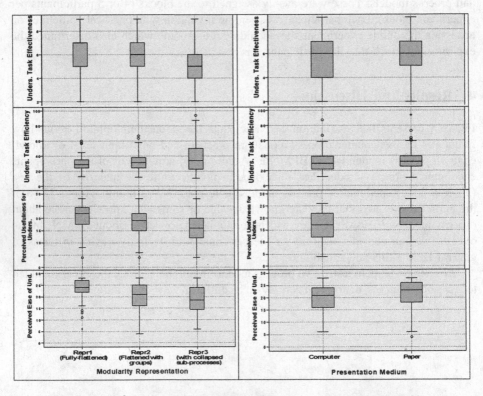

Fig. 5. Boxplot diagrams for dependent variables over independent variables.

representations and presentation mediums. Table 3 presents the descriptive statistics for the variables tested in the experiment. The boxplot diagrams for the dependent variables over the modularity representation and presentation medium are shown in Fig. 5.

To test our hypotheses, we first analyzed the data for conformance with the assumptions of the statistical tests that can be used. The results of our initial analysis showed that there are clear deviations from *normality* for the measures of all dependent variables over independent variables (Kolmogorov–Smirnov test of normality, all with $p < 0.02$). Therefore, we forewent the predictive power of parametric tests and applied their non-parametric counterparts, in particular the Kruskal-Wallis test (with stepwise step-down multiple comparison) [27] to evaluate our hypotheses (using SPSS v.23).

4.1 Testing the Hypotheses on the Forms of Modularity Representation

We argued in our first group of hypotheses that different forms of modularity representation in BPMN significantly influences process understandability. Table 4 shows the results of our tests regarding this set of hypotheses. Accordingly, modularity representation has significant impact on three of the four understandability factors.

Table 4. Results of the Kruskal-Wallis statistical tests.

Independent variables	Unders. task effectiveness		Unders. task efficiency		Perceived usefulness		Perceived ease of und. ing	
	H	p	H	p	H	p	H	p
Modularity representation	8.49	*0.014**	9.67	0.208	13.12	*0.001**	13.59	*0.001**
Presentation medium	1.89	0.169	2.24	0.134	9.54	*0.002**	4.32	*0.038**

Understandability Task Effectiveness. The results of the Kruskal-Wallis tests indicate that the understandability task effectiveness measured by the *score* achieved from the understandability questions, is influenced by the modularity form [H(2): 8.49, $p = 0.014$]. According to stepwise multiple comparison, the scores attained with fully-flattened models (Repr1) and with models where BPMN groups are used (Repr2) are *significantly higher* than the score with models where sub-processes (Repr3) are used. The scores with Repr1 and Repr2 do not differ significantly. Hence, the flattened models (with or without the use of groups) lead to a higher effectiveness than the models where sub-processes are used.

We performed further tests to investigate if the scores obtained from questions regarding different *process perspectives* (cnt/res/inf) and *scope* (global/local) show any major difference. The results indicate that, the scores concerning different *process perspectives* do not differ significantly. However, in line with the results obtained with the overall score values, the scores from *local* questions (which involve information only about sub-processes) are significantly higher in Repr1 and Repr2 than in Repr3 [H(2): 10.32, $p = 0.006$]. For the *global* questions (where answering requires information only about the main/modularized model) and *global-local* questions (where answering requires information about both modularized model and one or more sub-processes), the differences in the scores for each form of modularity representation are not significant (p = 0.757 and p = 0.459, respectively).

Based on these results, we can infer that for *local* questions, modularization degrades effectiveness when *overview + detail* strategy is used (as in Repr3, where sub-processes are shown separately, detached from their context). This is likely due to the increased browsing costs (split-attention effect) in Repr3 and *insignificant* cost of complexity in flattened models (Repr1) even with the group information (Repr2). This may further indicate that the context -where a sub-process takes place, plays an important role in understanding (sub-)process information. On the other hand, the use of modularization in which the sub-processes are displayed directly within the context of the higher level model (as in Repr2) doesn't offer any advantage for effectiveness.

For *global* and *global-local* questions, the modularization does not have significant effect on effectiveness. This implies that the understandability gain acquired in abstracting away less relevant information through modularization is insignificant in these types of process models.

Understandability Task Efficiency. Although the average understandability task efficiency (i.e. the number of correctly answered questions divided by the time spent for answering them) is higher for Repr3, our statistical analysis does not indicate a *significant* difference for the three forms of modularity representations [H(2): 9.67, p = 0.208]. A relatively high dispersion of the efficiency values for Repr3 is also worth mentioning. The results are in line also with respect to the efficiency obtained for questions concerning different process perspectives and scope (i.e. there is no significant difference with respect to the forms of modularity representation).

Perceived Usefulness for Understandability. Participant's view on the usefulness of three modularity representation forms differs significantly [H(2): 13.12, p = 0.001]. Although the stepwise multiple comparisons indicate no statistically significant difference between Repr1 and Repr2, and Rep2 and Repr3, the difference between Repr1 and Repr3 is significant. Accordingly, participants found Repr1 significantly more useful in fostering understandability than Repr3. Hence, fully flattened models in BPMN (collaboration) diagrams are considered more useful in providing gains to the user in terms of understandability in comparison with the models with sub-processes.

Perceived Ease of Understanding. Similar to usefulness, the attitude on the ease of understanding also differs significantly with respect to the forms of modularity representation [H(2): 13.59, p = 0.001]. However, in this case, Repr1 is considered easier to understand than *both* modular forms, i.e. Repr2 and Repr3. This indicates that, fully flattened models are regarded as easier to understand than any of their modularized form. Given that the only difference between Repr1 and Repr2 is the grouping information, we can deduce that any additional information on the process model can be perceived to increase the difficulty of understanding.

4.2 Testing the Hypotheses on the Presentation Medium

The second group of hypotheses argued for the influence of the medium used to present process models on the understandability. The results of the tests regarding this set of hypotheses are shown in Table 4 (second row). The results indicate that the presentation medium does not have significant influence on the understandability task effectiveness or efficiency, but is regarded as critical from users' point of view.

Understandability Task Effectiveness and Efficiency. The statistical tests indicate that the use of paper or computer for presenting process models does not lead to a significant difference on the understandability task effectiveness or efficiency [H(1): 1.89, p = 0.169] and [H(1): 2.24, p = 0.134], respectively. Similarly, the results of the analyses on the scores gained from questions concerning different process perspectives and scope (local/global) do not show any significant difference.

Perceived Usefulness for Understandability and Ease of Understanding. The participants consider models presented on paper easier to understand and more useful (from understandability's point of view) than the ones presented on the computer [H(1): 4.32, p = 0.038] and [H(1): 9.54, p = 0.002], respectively.

The analysis on the effect of presentation medium indicates that using paper or computer influences only the perceived understandability when it comes to the models of this type, structure and complexity. We observed that the participants that received models on paper studied them using their fingers, which can be more difficult on the screen. However, very few of the participants took notes directly on the printed models.

4.3 Testing the Influence of Personal Factors and Using Different Process Models

As mentioned, we gathered information about participants' experience and level of knowledge in process modeling and BPMN, as well as their familiarity with the processes. We used this information to test the direct or moderating effects of these factors on the understandability. Our statistical analyses did not yield any significant effect of these factors. Additional research is required to better operationalize these factors and investigate their influence.

As we used *different* sets of understandability questions for the two process models we used in our experiment, it would not be plausible to compare the average score and efficiency values regarding these models. However, we checked the perceived understandability variables (PUU, PEU) and were not able to find a significant difference between the results obtained for these two models. Separate results for these two models are in line with the general findings discussed above.

5 Conclusions

Business process models are important elements at various phases of the BPM lifecycle. As such, their understandability for their intended audience is crucial. In this paper, we have described the design and conduct of an experimental study to

Table 5. Summary of hypotheses tests.

Hypothesis	Result	Description
H1- Forms of modularity representation has a significant influence on:		
(a) Understandability task effectiveness	*Supported*	Effectiveness is higher with *flattened* BPMN models (with or without groups) than with modularized models with sub-processes
(b) Understandability task efficiency	*Not supported*	Efficiency is not different with models in any form (flattened or modularized using groups/sub-processes)
(c) Perceived usefulness for understandability	*Supported*	Fully-flattened models are considered more useful (in terms of facilitating understanding) than models with sub-processes
(d) Perceived ease of understanding	*Supported*	Fully-flattened models are perceived easier to understand than models that are modularized (using groups or sub-processes)
H2- Presentation medium has a significant influence on:		
(a) Understandability task effectiveness	*Not supported*	Presenting models on paper or on computer does not influence effectiveness
(b) Understandability task efficiency	*Not supported*	Medium (paper, computer) does not influence efficiency significantly
(c) Perceived usefulness for understandability	*Supported*	Paper is considered more useful (in terms of facilitating understanding) as a presentation medium
(d) Perceived ease of understanding	*Supported*	The models on paper are considered easier to understand than models on computer

investigate two factors that potentially influence process model understandability. We have examined if and how different forms of modularity representation and the medium used for the presentation influence the understandability of process models that are in the form of BPMN collaboration diagrams. To contribute to the generalizability of our findings, we used two real-life processes as the objects of our experiment and 60 practitioners as our participants. The participants were employees of a large organization and potential audience of the models tested. The majority had some degree of BPM knowledge but relatively limited familiarity with the BPMN.

Table 5 summarizes our hypotheses and findings. Overall, we found that using sub-processes in BPMN (where sub-processes are shown as separate models) negatively influences understandability effectiveness without any contribution to efficiency (when compared with models that are flattened or modularized using groups). Fully-flattened models are considered to better facilitate understanding and to be easier to comprehend than models with sub-processes. These models are regarded as easier to understand even than models that show additional modularization information in flat models using BPMN groups. If modularization is necessary (due to practical reasons), displaying sub-processes within their context rather than as separate models should be preferred.

As for the presentation medium, although using paper or computer does not influence the objectively measured understandability (effectiveness and efficiency), *paper* is practitioners' preferred choice of medium in terms of the degree it facilitates understandability and ease of understanding.

Our work has a number of limitations from which several possible directions for future research emerge. Experimenting with real-life processes and business practitioners has a positive effect on the external validity of our study. This allows us to better generalize the results towards practical implications. However, having participants from a single enterprise reduces this effect. Future research should consider involving practitioners working in diverse business environments.

The specific choice for the modularization of two processes can also be regarded as a further threat to the validity of our findings. It is difficult to verify that the choices for the parts that are structured as sub-processes are optimal (but not arbitrary, which may lead to a flawed modularization [9]). We addressed this risk by requesting domain experts (who also act as process modelers/owners in the case organization) to validate the models including their modularity structures. Yet, future research should experiment the effect of modularity when other (theoretical) modularization approaches (such as Wand & Weber's [16] as in [15]) are employed.

Our experiment was not able to identify any influence of process modeling experience or level of knowledge on understandability (based on the self-reported levels by the participants). Future research should consider using other methods to more objectively operationalize such factors (e.g. in the form of tests to quantify the level of theoretical knowledge on process modeling and notation).

Following a rigorous method in developing, verifying and validating the understandability questions contributes to the accuracy by which the understandability factors are operationalized. This reinforces the construct validity of our work. However, our findings are valid only for BPMN collaboration diagrams, where a number of *pools* are used (each with a single control-flow). To understand the potential effect of using this type of BPMN models, future work should consider experimenting also with BPMN models where a single main control-flow is present (i.e. a single pool potentially with multiple lanes). Future works should also use processes of different size, complexity, and applied level of modularity to better understand the interplay between these factors and contribute to the development of guidelines for applying modularization in business process modeling.

References

1. Dumas, M., La Rosa, M., Mendling, J., Reijers, H.A.: Fundamentals of Business Process Management. Springer, Heidelberg (2013)
2. Reijers, H.A., Mendling, J.: A study into the factors that influence the understandability of business process models. IEEE Trans. Syst. Man Cybern. - Part A Syst. Hum. **41**, 449–462 (2011)
3. Houy, C., Fettke, P., Loos, P.: On the theoretical foundations of research into the understandability of business process models. In: ECIS 2014, pp. 1–38 (2014)

4. Recker, J.: Empirical investigation of the usefulness of Gateway constructs in process models. Eur. J. Inf. Syst. **22**, 673–689 (2012)
5. Sanchez-Gonzalez, L., Garcia, F., Ruiz, F., Mendling, J.: Quality indicators for business process models from a gateway complexity perspective. Inf. Softw. Technol. **54**, 1159–1174 (2012)
6. Zugal, S., et al.: Investigating expressiveness and understandability of hierarchy in declarative business process models. Softw. Syst. Model. **14**, 1081–1103 (2013)
7. Reijers, H.A., Mendling, J.: Modularity in process models: review and effects. In: Dumas, M., Reichert, M., Shan, M.-C. (eds.) BPM 2008. LNCS, vol. 5240, pp. 20–35. Springer, Heidelberg (2008)
8. Moody, D.L.: Cognitive load effects on end user understanding of conceptual models: an experimental analysis. In: Benczúr, A.A., Demetrovics, J., Gottlob, G. (eds.) ADBIS 2004. LNCS, vol. 3255, pp. 129–143. Springer, Heidelberg (2004)
9. Reijers, H.A., Mendling, J., Dijkman, R.M.: Human and automatic modularizations of process models to enhance their comprehension. Inf. Syst. **36**, 881–897 (2011)
10. Figl, K., Koschmider, A., Kriglstein, S.: Visualising process model hierarchies. In: ECIS 2013, p. 180 (2013)
11. Leymann, F., Roller, D.: Workflow-based applications. IBM Syst. J. **36**, 102–123 (1997)
12. van der Aalst, W., van Hee, K.: Workflow Management: Models, Methods, and Systems. MIT Press, Cambridge (2002)
13. Zugal, S., Pinggera, J., Weber, B., Mendling, J., Reijers, H.A.: Assessing the impact of hierarchy on model understandability – a cognitive perspective. In: Kienzle, J. (ed.) MODELS 2011 Workshops. LNCS, vol. 7167, pp. 123–133. Springer, Heidelberg (2012)
14. Houy, C., Fettke, P., Loos, P.: Understanding understandability of conceptual models – what are we actually talking about? In: Atzeni, P., Cheung, D., Ram, S. (eds.) ER 2012 Main Conference 2012. LNCS, vol. 7532, pp. 64–77. Springer, Heidelberg (2012)
15. Johannsen, F., Leist, S., Braunnagel, D.: Testing the impact of wand and weber's decomposition model on process model understandability. In: ICIS 2014, pp. 1–13 (2014)
16. Wand, Y., Weber, R.: A model of systems decomposition. In: ICIS 1989 (1989)
17. Cruz-Lemus, J.A., Genero, M., Manso, M.E., Morasca, S., Piattini, M.: Assessing the understandability of UML statechart diagrams with composite states—A family of empirical studies. Empir. Softw. Eng. **14**, 685–719 (2009)
18. Zugal, S., Soffer, P., Pinggera, J., Weber, B.: Expressiveness and understandability considerations of hierarchy in declarative business process models. In: Bider, I., Halpin, T., Krogstie, J., Nurcan, S., Proper, E., Schmidt, R., Soffer, P., Wrycza, S. (eds.) EMMSAD 2012 and BPMDS 2012. LNBIP, vol. 113, pp. 167–181. Springer, Heidelberg (2012)
19. Wolf, C., Harmon, P.: The State of Business Process Management. BP Trends, Newton (2014)
20. Field, A., Hole, G.: How to Design and Report Experiments. SAGE Publications Ltd., Los Angeles (2003)
21. Mendling, J., Strembeck, M., Recker, J.: Factors of process model comprehension—findings from a series of experiments. Decis. Support Syst. **53**, 195–206 (2012)
22. Melcher, J., Mendling, J., Reijers, H.A., Seese, D., Laue, R., Gadatsch, A.: Measuring the understandability of business process models - are we asking the right questions? In: Muehlen, M., Su, J. (eds.) BPM 2010 Workshops. LNBIP, vol. 66, pp. 37–48. Springer, Heidelberg (2011)
23. Davis, F.D.: Perceived usefulness, perceived ease of use, and user acceptance of information technology. MIS Q. **13**, 319–340 (1989)
24. Venkatesh, V., Morris, M.G., Davis, G.B., Davis, F.D.: User acceptance of information technology: toward a unified view. MIS Q. **27**, 425–478 (2003)

25. Moody, D.L.: The method evaluation model: a theoretical model for validating information systems design methods. In: ECIS 2003 Proceedings, Paper 79 (2003)
26. Recker, J., Rosemann, M., Green, P., Indulska, M.: Do ontological deficiencies in modeling grammars matter? MIS Q. **35**, 57–79 (2011)
27. Field, A.: Discovering Statistics Using IBM SPSS Statistics. SAGE Publications Ltd., Los Angeles (2013)

Towards Quality-Aware Translations of Activity-Centric Processes to Guard Stage Milestone

Julius Köpke[1,2](✉) and Jianwen Su[1]

[1] Department of Computer Science, UC Santa Barbara, Santa Barbara, USA
su@cs.ucsb.edu
[2] Alpen-Adria Universität, Klagenfurt, Austria
julius.koepke@aau.at

Abstract. Current translation approaches from activity-centric process models to artifact-centric Guard Stage Milestone (GSM) models operate on the syntactic level. While such translations allow equivalent traces (behaviors) of executions, we argue that they generate poor GSM models for the intended audience (including business managers and process modelers). A specific deficiency of these translations is their inability to relate to relevant domain knowledge, especially groupings of activities to achieve well-known business goals cannot be obtained by syntactic translations. Ironically, this is a main principle of GSM models. We developed an initial ontology based translation framework [14] that incorporates the missing knowledge for improved translations. In this paper we further extend this framework with two metrics for the assessment of quality aspects of resulting GSM translations with domain knowledge, propose a novel semantic rewriting algorithm that enhances the quality of GSM translations, and provide an evaluation of the achievable quality for different classes of input processes. Our evaluation shows that maximum quality scores are achievable if semantics and structure of the input processes are well aligned. Given poorly aligned input processes, a translation method can optimize one of the metrics but not both.

Keywords: Process translation · Artifact-centric BPM · Guard Stage Milestone · GSM · Quality metrics

1 Introduction

In contrast to the predominant activity-centric modeling methods (e.g. BPMN) that concentrate on the control-flow between activities, Guard Stage Milestone (GSM) [12] is artifact-centric and defines business processes based on data entities and their declarative life-cycles. With the growing adaption of the artifact-centric modeling paradigm, the need for translations between activity-centric

J. Köpke—Research conducted while visiting UCSB and supported by the Austrian Science Fund (FWF) under grant J-3609-N15.

M. La Rosa et al. (Eds.): BPM 2016, LNCS 9850, pp. 308–325, 2016.
DOI: 10.1007/978-3-319-45348-4_18

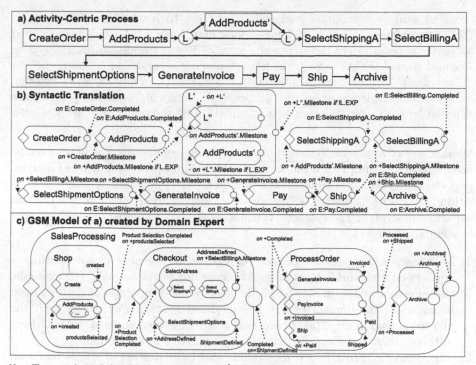

Note: The syntactic translation algorithm creates a stage L' representing the loop (L). The loop is controlled with an additional control-stage L'' that evaluates the loop condition $L.exp$.

Fig. 1. (a) Input process (b) Syntactic translation (c) Translation of domain expert [14]

and artifact-centric process models gains importance. The fact that GSM provides the basis for the new OMG Case Management Standard (CMMN[1]) further extends its importance. Especially for inter-organizational cooperations, translations between both paradigms become vital. Translation of activity-centric models to artifact-centric models has been studied [7,17]. However, these approaches remain on the syntactic level and create completely flat GSM models not following the basic principles and guidelines of GSM.

Guard Stage Milestone (GSM). We highlight the relevant essentials of GSM here and refer the reader to [5,12] for details. A process is modeled in the form of artifacts, where each artifact has a data schema with data attributes and state attributes, and a life-cycle definition. GSM life-cycles are based on *guards*, *stages*, and *milestones*. In the graphical representation (Fig. 1(b) and (c)), guards are depicted as diamonds, stages as rounded boxes with optional labels, and milestones as circles. A guard defines when a particular stage becomes active, a milestone defines when a stage is completed (e.g. a business goal is reached). Stages can be *atomic* or *composite*. Every atomic stage contains a service that is executed when the stage becomes active. A composite stage contains other stages. The idea of composite stages is to group stages that are executed in

---

[1] http://www.omg.org/spec/CMMN/.

order to achieve a common goal collectively, i.e. to reach the milestone(s) of their parent stage. Guards and milestones may have labels and are specified as *sentries*. Sentries are defined in the form of Event Condition (over the data schema) Action (ECA) rules of the form *"on event if condition"*, *"on event"*, or *"if condition"*. Events may be internal (e.g. achieving of a milestone) or external such as the completion event of a service call. Achieving events of sentries are denoted by the prefix "+" and their invalidation by the prefix "−", respectively.

Weaknesses of Syntactic Translations. We discuss weaknesses of syntactic translations with an example. For the activity-centric input process shown in Fig. 1(a), part (b) shows the GSM translation based on a purely syntactic translation algorithm [14]. Part (c) shows a GSM version of (a) potentially created by a domain expert from scratch. The syntactic translation (b) has a number of disadvantages in comparison to (c):

1. Milestones and guards are defined on a solely technical level not relating to any agreed real-world states of data objects nor business goals. For example, the milestone of *Pay* in Fig. 1(b) is defined by the completion of the *Pay* task. In contrast, the domain expert has modeled a stage *PayInvoice* with the milestone *paid* in Fig. 1(c), where *paid* is a well-known state of order objects in the domain and *PayInvoice* is a known activity in the domain.
2. The syntactic translation is mostly flat and lacks nesting of stages based on business goals. In contrast, the domain expert uses nested stages to structure the process based on business goals of the domain. In Fig. 1(c) the activity stages are nested inside the upper-level stages *Shop*, *Checkout*, *ProcessOrder*, and *SalesProcessing*.

The model in Fig. 1(c) not only has advantages for stake-holders, by presenting structured models referring to agreed terms, but also facilitates advanced process monitoring based on abstract stages and business goals of the domain.

From a general perspective, the model in Fig. 1(c) has a higher "quality" [9,16] than that in Fig. 1(b). A main cause of this quality difference is the different expressiveness of the activity-centric model and the GSM model in the following sense. While GSM allows to define business goals and hierarchies of stages to achieve them, this information is missing in the source models. Consequently, it cannot be added through a purely syntactic translation.

Quality of models [9,16] depends on many aspects, some of which may not have technical formulations. In many application domains, a large part of domain knowledge exists in documents or even with semi-formal languages. Examples include housing management [8], travel industry (e.g. http://www.opentravel. org), the financial/accounting domain [15] and of course the medical domain [2]. For applications in these domains, focusing on ontology "alignment" can improve learning/training of process models, as well as monitoring of *key performance indicators*.

In our earlier work [14] an architecture to tackle this problem was developed. The general idea is to provide the missing domain knowledge for meaningful translations in form of an ontology representing the states of business documents and a taxonomy of state changing actions defining typical part of relations of actions in the domain.

Contributions of this paper. We extend our earlier framework with the following specific contributions:

- Quality metrics for assessing the semantic alignment (Sect. 2) and control-flow complexity (Sect. 3) of GSM translations.
- A rewrite algorithm (Sect. 4) for improving the semantic alignment of a translation.
- Our findings based on the evaluation (Sect. 5) are: Maximum quality metrics of translations are achievable for both metrics if input processes are fully aligned with the domain taxonomy. Having poorly aligned input processes, either semantic alignment or control-flow complexity can be optimized but not both at the same time.

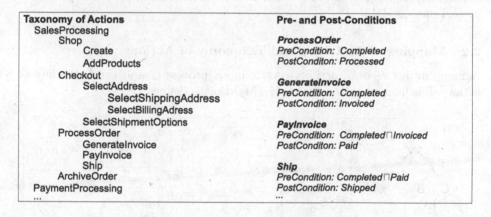

Fig. 2. An example taxonomy of actions [14]

2 Semantic Alignment of a GSM Translation

A core element of our translation framework [14] is a *taxonomy of actions T* that defines relationships between actions in the domain. The key idea was to automatically or manually map activities in an input process to the taxonomy T to allow GSM translations with semantic stage nesting. While [14] focused on how an existing process can be matched with the taxonomy, in this paper we assume such a matching given. We first review the taxonomy from [14] and then present a mapping formalism between activity-centric input processes and the taxonomy. Based on the mapping and the taxonomy, we define a novel quality metric for the semantic alignment of GSM translations.

2.1 Taxonomy of Actions

A taxonomy of actions T describes abstract, well agreed actions that result in state changes (e.g. the achievement of business goals) of business entities. The actions are organized in a rooted tree (whose root node is *root*) representing a *part of* hierarchy. The semantics of T is the following: If an action b is defined as a child-action of some action a where $a \neq root$, then b is considered as potentially contributing to achieving the goal of action a (in GSM reaching a milestone). Action b can be used to achieve the goal of a, but it is not required to use b to achieve a in every process or instance. Therefore, T can be considered as a general glossary of actions that can be reused for different processes of the domain. As described in [14] each node in T is additionally annotated with OWL expressions defining pre- and post-states of each action. The annotations are primarily used for matching activities and actions and are out of scope of this paper. An example taxonomy for our previous example is shown in Fig. 2. We assume that the taxonomy is provided as input. It may be created by employing domain ontologies [2,8,15], or it could be derived from GSM process repositories or goal models [4,13].

2.2 Mapping of Activities and Taxonomy of Actions

A mapping between an activity-centric input process G and the taxonomy of actions T is defined by the tuple (M_1, M_2) that is defined below:

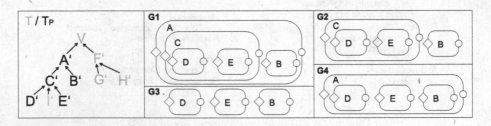

Fig. 3. Taxonomy alignment - correct alignment examples

Definition 1 *(Realizes Mapping)*. M_1 is a set of pairs of the form (s, a), where $s \in G.activitySteps$, $a \in T.actions$, $T.actions$ is the set of actions in the taxonomy T and $G.activitySteps$ refers to the set of activities in the input process. A tuple in M_1 defines that the activity s realizes the action a. Each activity can realize zero or one action in T and each action in T can be realized by zero or one activity (partial bijection).

Not requiring a *1:1* mapping is based on the assumption that the taxonomy is not necessarily complete and should be generic to be applicable for different processes. Definition 1 forbids to map more than one activity in the process model to one action that occurs in the same context (same parent) in the taxonomy. However, this limitation can be lifted by extending the taxonomy with additional actions or parent actions.

Definition 2 *(Contributes to Mapping).* The mapping M_2 is also a set of pairs (s, a), where $s \in G.activitySteps$ and $a \in T.actions$, and specifies that a specific activity contributes to the achievement of some action in T. Every activity that realizes an action also contributes to it $(M_1 \subseteq M_2)$. M_2 further satisfies the following (quantifiers omitted):

- Activities can only contribute to actions they realize or to ancestors thereof: $(s, a) \in M_2 \Rightarrow (s, a) \in M_1 \lor \exists (s, a') \in M_1$, where a is an ancestor of a'.
- Activities must contribute to common ancestors: $\{(a, a'), (b, b'), (a, a'')\} \subseteq M_2 \Rightarrow (b, a'') \in M_2$ if a'' is a common ancestor of a' and b'.
- No skipping of levels in T: $\{(a, a'), (a, a''')\} \subseteq M_2 \Rightarrow (a, a'') \in M_2$, if $a'' \in T.actions$, a'' is a descendent of a''' and an ancestor of a'.

Definition 3 *(Taxonomy Projection).* For each taxonomy T and each mapping M_2, let $project(T, M_2)$ denote a rooted taxonomy (with *root* as the root node) obtained by projecting T onto M_2. A node t of T is also a node of $project(T, M_2)$, if $\exists (x, t) \in M_2$ for any x. The relative hierarchical order of T is preserved in the projection.

2.3 Assessing Taxonomy Alignment of a Translation

Given a GSM translation of some activity-centric input process with a mapping to a taxonomy of actions, we want to assess how well the stage nesting in the translation corresponds to the taxonomy projection.

General Idea of the Taxonomy Alignment Metric. Figure 3 shows four different GSM translations $G1$–$G4$ of some activity-centric input process (not shown). The taxonomy T and the taxonomy projection T_P are shown on the left. Elements of T that are not in T_P are depicted in grey.

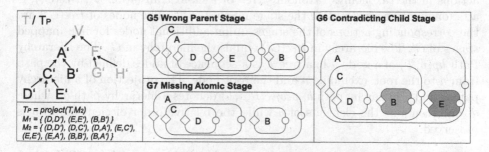

Fig. 4. Taxonomy alignment - contradictions

Translation $G1$ provides the same nesting as defined in T_P. We consider this as a perfect alignment. $G1$ should get the maximum score of 1. $G3$ does not provide any grouping of atomic stages and should get the minimum score of 0. We do not give credits for the existence of mapped activities since they are trivially part of the translation.

$G2$ and $G4$ are partially aligned but parent actions of T_P are missing in the translations. $G4$ perfectly describes the contribution of B. We therefore assign a credit of 1 for B in $G4$. However, the contributions of D and E are only partially described. We assign a credit of 0.5 for the description of D and of E because only 1 of two abstractions is present in $G4$. $G2$ does not describe the contribution of B at all (no credit for B) and the contributions of D and E are only partially modeled (credits 0.5 for D and for E). We argue that $G4$ should be considered as superior to $G2$ because the contribution of the atomic stages is better described in $G4$. Following this principle we calculate the overall metrics by the average credit for each atomic stage: The metrics of $G4$ is $\frac{0.5+0.5+1}{3} = \frac{2}{3}$ and that of $G2$ is $\frac{0.5+0.5+0}{3} = \frac{1}{3}$.

While the previous example only addressed missing hierarchy levels, Fig. 4 shows example translations, where the nesting in the process model contradicts with the one in the taxonomy projection. In process $G5$ the hierarchy is inverted, where C is a child of A in the taxonomy, A is a child of C in the translation. In $G6$, B is nested under C but it should be nested under A. In $G7$, a mapped atomic stage is missing. Stage E contributes to the achievement of C in the taxonomy but this is not reflected in the process model. We consider this as incorrect since the goal of C may never be achieved without executing E. While credits are assigned separately for each atomic stage, contradictions influence the contributions of multiple atomic stages. We assign a credit of 0 to all atomic stages that are nested in a stage that contains contradictions.

Calculating Alignment Metrics. We first provide preliminary definitions: Corresponding Taxonomy Action of an Atomic Stage: Let G' be a GSM translation of an activity-centric process G with a mapping $M = (M_1, M_2)$ to a taxonomy T. Let s be an atomic stage in G' implementing an activity a of G. If $(a, t) \in M_1$, then t is the corresponding action of s. The corresponding taxonomy action of a composite stage is defined by equivalent stage labels and labels of the actions in the taxonomy. Taxonomy Tree of a GSM translation G', $tree(G')$, is a taxonomy tree representing the stage nesting of G'. The nodes of $tree(G')$ are the corresponding actions of the stages union additional nodes for non-mapped stages of G'. The hierarchy in $tree(G')$ equals the hierarchy in G'. The Hierarchy Path $hp(n, T)$ of a node n in a tree T is a sequence of nodes defined by the path from n to the root, excluding n and the root node. The projection of a hierarchy path a and a hierarchy path b, $projectP(a, b)$ denotes a hierarchy path a', where a' only contains the elements of b while the relative order of elements in a is preserved.

Definition 4 (*Correct Nesting* of a mapped atomic stage s in a GSM translation G' under T and $M = (M_1, M_2)$). Let t be the corresponding taxonomy node of the atomic stage s and T_P the taxonomy projection of T under M_2. The atomic stage s is correctly nested into parent stages if $\forall$ action $a \in hp(t, tree(G'))$ where a is an action in $T_P \Rightarrow a$ is an action in $hp(t, T_P)$ and the relative order of actions is equivalent in both paths.

Definition 5 (*Contradiction* of composite stages in G' with the taxonomy projection). A composite stage s_1 contradicts with a taxonomy projection if it contains incorrectly nested atomic stage (Definition 4) or if atomic stages are missing: Let $t_1 \in project(T, M_2)$ be the corresp. taxonomy node of s_1. An atomic stage is missing in s_1 if there exists a descendent t_2 of $t_1 \in project(T, M_2)$, a tuple $(x, t_2) \in M_1$ for some x, but $\nexists s_2$ as a substage of s_1 in G' such that t_2 is the corresp. taxonomy node of s_2.

For calculating the taxonomy alignment score of a (mapped) atomic stage, we assign the value of 0 if the atomic stage is part of a contradicting composite stage. Otherwise, the score is based on the fraction of existing parents in the translation and the number of parents in the taxonomy projection:

Definition 6 (*Taxonomy Alignment* of an atomic stage s). Let G' be a GSM translation of an activity-centric process G and t the corresponding action of s in T under the mapping M_2. If s is part of a composite stage that does not contradict with the taxonomy projection (Definition 5), the score is the fraction of the number of existing mapped abstractions of t in $tree(G')$ and the number of abstractions of t in the taxonomy projection: $SemMetricAtomic(s) = \frac{|\,projectP(hp(t, tree(G')), hp(t, project(T, M_2)))\,|}{|\,hp(t, project(T, M_2))\,|}$ otherwise, the score is 0.

Definition 7 (*Taxonomy Alignment* of a GSM translation). The taxonomy alignment metrics of a translation is the mean of the metrics scores of all mapped atomic stages.

EXAMPLE Calculating the taxonomy alignment for D of $G4$ in Fig. 3:
$$hp(D', tree(G4)) = \langle A \rangle, hp(D', project(T, M_2)) = \langle C, A \rangle$$
$$projectP(\langle A \rangle, \langle A, B \rangle) = \langle A \rangle \rightarrow SemMetricAtomic(D) = \frac{|\langle A \rangle|}{|\langle A, B \rangle|} = \frac{1}{2}.$$
In analogy to D: $SemMetricAtomic(E) = \frac{1}{2}$, $SemMetricAtomic(B) = \frac{1}{1} = 1$. The taxonomy alignment score of $G4$ is: $(\frac{1}{2} + \frac{1}{2} + \frac{1}{1})/3 = \frac{2}{3}$.

Properties of the Metrics: The purpose of the taxonomy alignment metrics is to compare translations of the same input process. The metrics is based on assessing the degree of alignment of each atomic stage. When a translation a achieves better average taxonomy alignment scores for all atomic stages than another translation b, then a gets a better score than b. When the taxonomy projection is balanced this metrics is equivalent to an alternative metrics, which is the number of all provided abstractions of atomic stages divided by the number of possible abstractions of all atomic stages. The result of the alternative approach is different for unbalanced taxonomy projections because atomic stages that are deeper nested have stronger positive or negative impact on the overall alignment score. This behavior should be considered when the metrics is applied to unbalanced taxonomy projections. Which metrics better describes the desired alignment depends on the usage scenario.

We define the quality of a stage nesting (unordered tree) relative to the taxonomy projection (unordered tree). This also makes general tree similarity

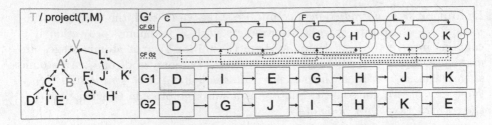

Fig. 5. GSM translation G' for input processes $G1$ and $G2$

approaches such as the tree edit distance (e.g. [1]) possible candidates for metrics. However, beside the problem that the calculation of the minimal tree edit distance is NP-hard for unordered trees, it does not directly produce the desired results: In the example in Fig. 3, the non-weighted tree edit distance between the taxonomy and $G2$ and between the taxonomy and $G4$ are both 1 (adding one node). However, $G4$ better matches the desired stage nesting. Therefore, the edit operations would still need to be weighted based on the number of affected atomic stages and potential contradictions (see Definition 5).

3   Control-Flow Complexity

The previous metrics assesses the existence of stage nestings relative to a taxonomy while ignoring the control-flow between composite stages. However, the control-flow may limit the usefulness of a given stage nesting: frequent switches between sub-processes negatively impact on the understandability of (behaviors of) process models [23,24]. Additionally, the utility of translation for monitoring purposes is limited because numerous stages remain opened at the same time without actually performing tasks in parallel. In GSM switching between sub-processes (composite stages) exists if there is control-flow between atomic stages of different (active) composite stages. To address this, we introduce a "control-flow complexity" metrics of translations. It is based on the usual fan-in and fan-out [11] of modules (stages). We are specifically interested in fan-out of composite stages that are not linked to their closing (non-exit fan-out) and fan-in into already opened composite stages (non-entry fan-in).

EXAMPLE Figure 5 shows a GSM stage hierarchy G' perfectly aligned with the taxonomy projection on the left. If G' is the result of a translation of $G1$, the control-flow is completely in-line with the stage progression of G' (solid arrows in the top part of G' in Fig. 5). The composite stages C, F, and L are executed in a sequence. There is no non-entry fan-in nor non-exit fan-out control-flow. (For the sake of simplicity the example does not contain control-blocks.) If $G2$ is the input for G', the control-flow (dashed arrows in the bottom part of G' in Fig. 5) is scattered over multiple composite stages that are open in parallel without actually executing tasks in parallel. We denote the parent stage of an atomic stage in subscript. C is opened and (D_C, G_F) opens F not closing C. (G_F, J_L)

opens L not closing F. (J_L, I_C) resumes C. (I_C, H_F) resumes F not closing C. (H_F, K_L) closes F and resumes L. Finally, (K_L, E_C) resumes C and closes L. For stage C as one example this leads to the non-entry fan-in control-flows $(J_l, I_C), (K_L, E_C)$ and the non-exit fan-out control-flows $(D_C, G_F), (I_C, H_F)$.

Control-Flow Complexity for GSM. We define fan-in and fan-out of a stage based on the control-flow graph of the activity-centric input process G. A *control-flow* from an activity a to another b exists if a is a predecessor of b in the graph representation of G and there exists a path from a to b that does not contain any other activity.

Definition 8 (*Non-Entry Fan-In of a Stage S*). Let G' be the GSM translation of an activity-centric process G and S be a composite stage of G'. A *fan-in* of S is a control-flow (a, b), where a corresponds to an atomic stage $\notin S$ and b corresponds to an atomic stage $\in S$. A fan-in (a, b) of S is a *non-entry* if for all permissible instantiation of G some activity $\in S$ is executed before a. The set of all non-entry fan-ins of S is denoted $NonEntryFanIn(S)$. *Fan-out* of S and $NonExitFanOut(S)$ are defined correspondingly.

$AvgNonEntryFanIn(G')$ is the arithmetic mean of $|NonEntryFanIn(S)|$ of all composite stages $S \in G'$. $AvgNonExitFanOut(G')$ is defined similarly. The calculation of the control-flow complexity is realized in analogy to coupling metrics [6]. The values are in the interval of $[\geq 0, < 1]$, where 0 indicates no unwanted switching between active composite stages, near 1 indicates very high numbers of switches on average.

Definition 9 (*Control-Flow Complexity* of a GSM translation G').
$$controlComplex(G') = 1 - \frac{2}{1 + AvgNonEntryFanIn(G') + 1 + AvgNonExitFanOut(G')}$$

EXAMPLE In the example in Sect. 3, when considering $G2$ as the input process of G': The non-entry-fan-in of C in G' is $|\{(J, I), (K, E)\}| = 2$, for F and L, we get 1. The non-exit-fan-out of C in G' is $|\{(D, G), (I, H)\}| = 2$, for F and L, we get 1. This leads to an average non-entry-fan-in and non-exit fan-out of $\frac{4}{3}$. Thus, $controlComplex(G') = 1 - 2/(1 + \frac{4}{3} + 1 + \frac{4}{3}) = 0.572$.

When $G1$ is the input we have $controlComplex(G') = 1 - \frac{2}{1+0+1+0} = 0$.

Properties of the Metrics: The purpose of the control-flow complexity metrics is to compare translations with different stage nestings of the same input process regarding unwanted dependencies between active composite stages. Therefore, higher total numbers of non-entry fan-in and non-exit fan-out relative to the number of composite stages must lead to higher complexity values of the metrics. This is guaranteed. The metrics does not assess the control-flow complexity [3,10] of the input process. However, control-blocks in the input process have impact on the potential fan-in and fan-out of composite stages in the translation.

A control-flow is considered non-entry if the stage has certainly been opened before. A more pessimistic and more complex approach would be to calculate

Algorithm 1. Semantic Rewrite of a GSM Translation

1: *Method rewriteTranslation*
Input: TaxonomyNode node
2: **if** (node is not root node) **then**
3:    GsmStage commonAncest = getCommonAncestor(
      getMappedAtomicStages(node));
4:    **for all** (GsmStage s ∈ getMappedAtomicStages(node)) **do**
5:       topStageBefore = ancestorBefore(s,commonAncest);
6:       nestingCandidates ⊎ topStageBefore;
7:       checkAtomic ⊎ topStageBefore.getAllAtomicStages();
8:    **end for**
9:    **if** (allNestable(checkAtomic,getMappedAtomicStages(node)) **then**
10:       nestStages(nestingCandidates,node,commonAncest);
11:    **end if**
12: **end if**
13: **for all** (TaxonomyNode n ∈ node.getChildren()) **do**
14:    rewriteTranslation(node);
15: **end for**

---

non-entry fan-in based on the probability that some stage has already been opened before and to compute non-exit fan-out correspondingly. However, what metrics better describes problematic control-flows still needs to be decided based on a user-study.

4   Semantic Rewrite Algorithm

Based on the taxonomy alignment metrics, we present an algorithm that rewrites a syntactic translation of an activity-centric input process to enhance its metrics score. The algorithm takes as input an activity-centric process G, a (possibly nested) syntactic translation G' of G, a taxonomy of actions T, and a contributes-to mapping M_2.

The core method *rewriteTranslation(TaxonomyNode)* is shown as Algorithm 1. It is first called with the root node of the taxonomy projection and visits the nodes of the taxonomy projection in a depth-first traversal. Unless the current node is the (virtual) root node of the projection it retrieves the common ancestor *commonAncest* stage of all atomic stages that are mapped to the current node of the projection in G'. It then creates the sets *nestingCandidates* and *checkAtomic*, where *nestingCandidates* contains the top-level ancestor stage of each atomic-stage below *commonAncest* and *checkAtomic* contains all atomic stages nested into each stage in *nestingCandidates*. The set *checkAtomic* is used to check if a nesting is possible.

According to the alignment metrics, a nesting is correct if it contains all required atomic stages and it does not contain atomic stages that are not mapped to the current node but to other taxonomy nodes. This check is realized by the Boolean method *nestable()*. If *nestable* returns *true*, a new stage with the label of the current taxonomy node is created as a child stage of the common ancestor and all nodes in *nestingCandidates* are assigned as child stages of the new stage. Finally, guards and milestones are generated for the new stage.

EXAMPLE   Applying Algorithm 1 on $G3$ in Fig. 3, *rewriteTranslation* (project(T, M_2)) $\rightarrow$ *rewriteTranslation*(A'): *CommonAncestor* of D, E, and B is $G3$ itself. The loop in lines 4 to 8 produces the sets *nestingCandidates* = $\{D, E, B\}$ and *checkAtomic* = $\{D, E, B\}$, *allnestable*$(\{D, E, B\}, \{D, E, B\})$ returns *true*. The new stage A' is created under the common ancestor $G3$. The *nestingCandidates*, $\{D, E, B\}$, are set as its child stages. Next, *rewriteTranslation*(C') is called and processed in analogy to A'. Finally, $G3$ equals $G1$ in Fig. 3.

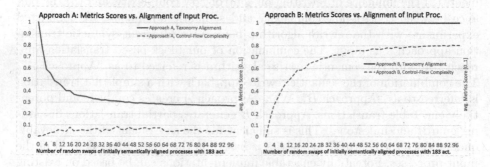

Fig. 6. Metrics scores vs. alignment of input processes. Left: App. A, Right: App. B

Setting Guards and Milestones. Since the rewrite algorithm must not change the permitted traces of executions it should guarantee that every stage that could be opened before the new stage was introduced can still be opened after the new stage is introduced. In GSM, a child stage cannot be opened if the parent stage is closed. Therefore, the new stage must be opened before any of the potentially first executed nested atomic stages may get opened. In principle, we could add a copy of the guards of each potentially first opened stage to the new stage.

When taking a block-structured syntactic translation from [14] as input, control-blocks (xor, par, loops) of the activity-centric input process are represented as composite stages and in a block-structured activity-centric process there is always one block that is evaluated first. Therefore, we use the sentry expression of the substage that represents the first block as the (single) guard sentry expression of the new stage.

For milestones, we apply a similar strategy. In principle, the new stage is completed, e.g. some milestone of it is reached, when no atomic stage within the new stage is open and no atomic stage within the new stage can get opened anymore. However, this may depend on future decisions during the runtime of the process, resulting in potentially complex milestone expressions. In contrast when using the nested syntactic translation of [14] as input there is always one last stage. We use the achievement sentry expression of its milestone as the sentry expression of the new stage's milestone.

Finally, we beautify the generated guards and milestones by rewriting equivalent expressions of child and parent guards/milestones. If a child stage has the exact sentry expression for guards as its parent stage, we update the sentry of the guard to the opening event of the parent stage. If a parent milestone has the exact same sentry condition as a milestone of a child stage, we rewrite the parent milestones sentry to the achieving event of the child milestone.

5   Evaluation

We present an evaluation of achievable metrics scores of the rewrite algorithm (Sect. 4) to assess (1) the influence of existing hierarchy on taxonomy alignment, (2) the influence of rewriting on control-flow complexity, and (3) the balance between control-flow complexity and semantic alignment. We conducted experiments with the rewrite algorithm having two different syntactic translation approaches as input. The combination of our block-based translation approach [14] with the semantic rewrite algorithm is referred to as "Approach A". The combination of the semantic rewrite approach with a simple flat translation is referred to as "Approach B". While Approach A creates complete and potentially enactable translations, Approach B generates partial translations discarding guards and milestones. This is sufficient for the assessment of the achievable quality since the control-flow metrics is based on the control-flow defined in the input processes. Potentially enactable implementations can be based on existing flat translation approaches such as [17,18].

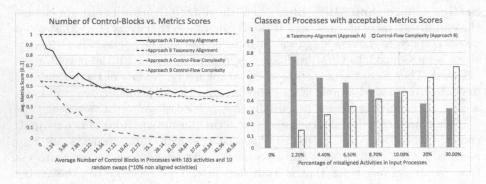

Fig. 7. Left: #control-blocks vs. metrics scores, Right: %-random vs. metrics scores

For our experiments, we have generated semantically aligned block-structured processes and taxonomy mappings based on the *Food Products Chapter* of the well balanced *UN Central Product Classifications Taxonomy*.[2] A block structured input process G is aligned with a taxonomy when each control-block (par, xor, loop) c that contains mapped activities only contains

---

[2] CPC Ver.2.1 http://unstats.un.org/unsd/cr/registry/regdnld.asp?Lg=1.

mapped activities if all are mapped to the same most specific common ancestor action a in the taxonomy (recursively) and only brothers or descendants of c may also contain activities mapped to a.

Experiment 1. We assess the influence of taxonomy alignment of the input process and the achievable metrics scores for Approaches A and B. We have conducted experiments with varied number of misaligned activities by repeatedly swapping two random activities. For each number of swaps (0 to 96 = completely random), we randomly generated 50 fully semantically aligned initial processes with mappings and applied the swaps. Each process contains 183 activities and on average 19 control-blocks (par, xor, loop). The average metrics scores of 50 processes in relation to the number of swaps for Approach A (on the left) and Approach B (on the right) are shown in Fig. 6.

Experiment 2. In the second experiment we investigate the influence of control-blocks in the input processes on taxonomy alignment and control-flow complexity scores. We generated input processes with 183 activities, 0 control-blocks (only sequences) to 183 activities, 59 control-blocks (par, xor, loop). For each number of control-blocks we generated 50 processes with 10 swapped activities (approx. 20 changed activities or 10 % of the activities are not aligned with the taxonomy). The average metrics scores of 50 processes in relation to the number of control-blocks are shown on the left side of Fig. 7.

5.1 Findings

Finding 1: *Maximum taxonomy alignment scores are achievable*
Both approaches can achieve maximum taxonomy alignment scores. Approach A achieves an alignment score of one, if the input processes are fully aligned with the taxonomy (see 0 swaps at left side of Fig. 6) or if the input processes only contain sequences (see left side of Fig. 7). Approach B constantly produces the maximum alignment score of 1 (see right side of Fig. 6 and left side of Fig. 7). In contrast to Approach A, the non-nested GSM translation used as input for Approach B does not impose any restrictions on the required nesting.

Finding 2: *Optimizing taxonomy alignment scores increases control-flow complexity*
When input processes are not aligned with the taxonomy, Approach B still produces perfect taxonomy alignment scores of 1 (right side of Fig. 6 and left side of Fig. 7). However, the semantic grouping results in an increase of control-flow complexity. As shown on the right side of Fig. 6, the control-flow complexity of the translation results of Approach B grows logarithmical with the percentage of misaligned activities in the input processes. A rough estimate for the control-flow complexity is $complex = 0.1936 \ln(x) + 0.1074$, where x is the percentage of misaligned activities in the input processes. This behavior of increased control-flow complexity score due to semantic nesting also applies for Approach A if the processes contain (mostly) of sequences (left side of Fig. 7). The reason is that nested syntactic translation approach does not perform nesting for sequences.

Another interesting behavior is that the control-flow complexity given a fixed number of swapped activities decreases, when the number of control-blocks grows in the processes (left side of Fig. 7, dotted line). The reason for this behavior is that the number of non-entry fan-in and non-exit fan-out decreases, when more (potential) entry fan-ins and exit fan-outs exists due to conditions.

Finding 3: *Optimizing control-flow complexity decreases taxonomy alignment scores*
Where Approach B produces constantly perfect taxonomy alignment scores, Approach A produces very low control-flow complexity scores (left side of Fig. 6). By not modifying existing nestings of the syntactic translation that translates control-blocks to single-entry, single-exit composite stages, the control-flow complexity stays at a very low level (dotted line in Fig. 6). However, near optimal control-flow complexity comes with strongly reduced taxonomy alignment scores of Approach A, if randomness is added to the input processes. The taxonomy alignment scores decrease potentially with a rough estimation of *score* $= 0.8081x^{-0.299}$, where x is the percentage of misaligned activities in the input processes. This exponential decrease is induced by the growing misalignment of two trees: The nesting of the syntactic translation and the best-case semantic nesting defined by the taxonomy projection.

By combining Findings 2 and 3 we conclude that given non-perfectly aligned input processes, a translation approach producing control-flow preserving translations (e.g. permitting the same traces of executions) can either optimize taxonomy alignment scores (as approach B) or minimize control-flow complexity scores but cannot achieve both at the same time.

5.2 Input Processes that Achieve Acceptable Alignment/Complexity Scores

We assume that for real-world applications, a process will mostly follow the domain taxonomy. The right side of Fig. 7 shows the average taxonomy alignment scores for approach A and the average control-flow complexity scores for approach B depending on the percentage of randomly assigned activities in the processes (data from Exp. 1). $2.2\%^3$ randomly assigned activities results in a still very good taxonomy alignment score of 0.77 for approach A and in a very low control-flow complexity score of 0.15 for approach B. 6.5 % random activities results in a still reasonable score of 0.55 for A and 0.35 for B. When 10 % of the activities are randomly assigned, the metrics score is 0.47 for both approaches. To conclude, both approaches still provide good scores (>0.5 for taxonomy alignment and <0.5 for control-flow complexity) when less than approx. 8 % activities in the input processes are not aligned with the taxonomy. We suspect that this class covers a wide range of real-world processes since it is very likely that activities that belong semantically together are also structurally related in the input processes. However, the assumption of acceptable scores (>0.5 / <0.5) requires further empirical validation with experts or practitioners.

---

[3] 2.2 % corresponds to 2 swaps resulting in 4 misaligned activities out of 183 in Fig. 6.

We have created variants of the taxonomy with deeper and flatter hierarchies. Our experiments show, that all findings also apply for these variants. Only the classes of acceptable quality are influenced by the taxonomy depth.

6 Related Work

Translations of activity-centric processes to declarative GSM models have been studied [7,14,17,18]. The approach in [7] generates from UML activity diagrams with data objects and state information as input state machines for data objects, and then translates the state machines into flat GSM models. The translation of Petri nets to GSM was addressed in [17] and applied to mining GSM processes in [18]. The approach is based on calculating pre-condition sets for each activity in order to generate guards of atomic stages. The resulting GSM models are completely flat. To the best of our knowledge, the syntactic translation approach in [14] is the only approach that generates nested GSM models, with nesting based on the block structure of the input process.

A key component of our work is the mapping between input processes and taxonomies. Such a mapping could be obtained by matching pre- and and post-conditions of activities [14]. As an alternative approach to obtain a mapping, processes are matched with a taxonomy based on label similarity [20]. However, this would not take into account (explicit) business goals, which is a key idea of abstractions in GSM. Approaches combining activity-centric modeling and goal modeling such as [4,13] lead to richer input models, which potentially allow to derive the taxonomy and mapping.

The broader context of our quality metrics is framed by the work on quality of conceptual models in general [9,16] and quality of business process models [10,21] in particular. Metrics for business process models were inspired by metrics from software engineering [6,11], namely coupling, cohesion, complexity, modularity and size. Coupling and cohesion in the context of business processes were addressed in [19], where the major goal is to find a proper granularity of activities. The control-flow complexity (CFC) of activity-centric models was studied in [3], where the complexity is measured based on different gateway types and the potential number of states.

There are no quality metrics for GSM processes. We have made a first step with our taxonomy alignment metrics following the basic principles of stage nesting in GSM. The metrics is accompanied with a control-flow complexity metrics to assess unwanted communications between active composite stages. However, in contrast to [3,10] our control-flow complexity metrics does no assess the control-flow complexity of the input process. The core of both metrics developed here is counting existing abstractions or unwanted control-flow between composite stages. This naturally satisfies all 9 properties of Weyuker measures [22] for software programs. The normalized metrics are in-line with all relevant properties of Weyuker measures given that their purpose is to compare different translations of the same input process.

7   Conclusions and Future Work

GSM models allow to group stages based on the fulfillment of business goals. The absence of goals in activity-centric models leads to undesirable syntactic translations. We presented two novel metrics for GSM translations assessing the quality of stage nesting relative to domain taxonomies and assessing the control-flow complexity induced by stage nesting. We developed a semantic rewrite algorithm to enhance the taxonomy alignment metrics of syntactic translations. Experiments show that rewritten translations can achieve reasonable to perfect metrics scores if input processes are well aligned with the domain taxonomies. When input processes are poorly aligned a translation can either achieve optimal alignment scores or low complexity scores but not both.

While we argue that adding semantics nestings to GSM translations will also enhance understandability of the models, this hypothesis still needs to be addressed in further evaluations with end-users. Such a study could also reveal details on the interpretation of the metrics values: What values can be considered good? At which scores do processes actually get uncomprehensible?

Other fields of future work include the study of translations of process models that already partially include (typically structural) groupings (e.g. BPMN sub-processes). Given such models, the taxonomy and mapping creation process may exploit existing groupings. The translation itself can be realized as presented in this paper. Finally, we suppose that processes, where the translations have high control-flow complexity might already have deficits in their activity-centric representation. On the one hand they might themselves by hardly understandable, on the other hand the control-flow may still have room for optimizations. Both questions are interesting future work.

References

1. Bille, P.: A survey on tree edit distance and related problems. Theor. Comput. Sci. **337**(13), 217–239 (2005)
2. Bodenreider, O.: Biomedical ontologies in action: role in knowledge management, data integration and decision support. Yearb. Med. Inf. 67–79 (2008)
3. Cardoso, J.: Control-flow complexity measurement of processes, Weyuker's properties. Int. J. Math. Comput. Phys. Electr. Comp Eng. **1**(8), 366–371 (2007)
4. Cortes-Cornax, M., Matei, A., Dupuy-Chessa, S., et al.: Using intentional fragments to bridge the gap between organizational and intentional levels. Inf. Softw. Tech. **58**, 1–19 (2015)
5. Damaggio, E., Hull, R., Vaculín, R.: On the equivalence of incremental and fixpoint semantics for business artifacts with guard-stage-milestone lifecycles. Inform. Syst. **38**(4), 561–584 (2013)
6. Dhama, H.: Quantitative models of cohesion, coupling in software. J. Syst. Soft. **29**(1), 65–74 (1995). Oregon Metric Workshop
7. Eshuis, R., Van Gorp, P.: Synthesizing data-centric models from business process models. Computing **98**, 345–373 (2015)
8. City Office for Property Management of Hangzhou: 2014 rental subsidies for low income families: processing guidelines, July 2014 (in Chinese)

9. Gemino, A., Wand, Y.: A framework for empirical evaluation of conceptual modeling techniques. Requirements Eng. **9**(4), 248–260 (2004)
10. Gruhn, V., Laue, R.: Complexity metrics for business process models. In: International Conference on Business Information Systems - BIS, vol. 85, pp. 1–12 (2006)
11. Henry, S., Kafura, D.: Software structure metrics based on information flow. IEEE Trans. Softw. Eng. **SE–7**(5), 510–518 (1981)
12. Hull, R., Damaggio, E., De Masellis, R., et al.: Business artifacts with guard-stage-milestone lifecycles: managing artifact interactions with conditions and events. In: Proceedings of DEBS, pp. 51–62. ACM (2011)
13. Koliadis, G., Ghose, A.K.: Relating business process models to goal-oriented requirements models in KAOS. In: Hoffmann, A., Kang, B.-H., Richards, D., Tsumoto, S. (eds.) PKAW 2006. LNCS (LNAI), vol. 4303, pp. 25–39. Springer, Heidelberg (2006)
14. Köpke, J., Su, J.: Towards ontology guided translation of activity-centric processes to GSM. In: Reichert, M., Reijers, H. (eds.) BPM Workshops 2015. LNBIP, vol. 256, pp. 364–375. Springer, Heidelberg (2016). doi:10.1007/978-3-319-42887-1_30
15. McCarthy, W.E.: The REA accounting model: a generalized framework for accounting systems in a shared data environment. Acc. Rev. **57**(3), 554–578 (1982)
16. Moody, D.L.: Theoretical and practical issues in evaluating the quality of conceptual models: current state and future directions. Data Knowl. Eng. **55**(3), 243–276 (2005)
17. Popova, V., Dumas, M.: From petri nets to guard-stage-milestone models. In: La Rosa, M., Soffer, P. (eds.) BPM Workshops 2012. LNBIP, vol. 132, pp. 340–351. Springer, Heidelberg (2013)
18. Popova, V., Fahland, D., Dumas, M.: Artifact lifecycle discovery. Int. J. Coop. Inf. Syst. **24**, 44 (2015). http://dx.doi.org/10.1142/S021884301550001X. 1550001
19. Reijers, H.A., Vanderfeesten, I.T.P.: Cohesion and coupling metrics for workflow process design. In: Desel, J., Pernici, B., Weske, M. (eds.) BPM 2004. LNCS, vol. 3080, pp. 290–305. Springer, Heidelberg (2004)
20. Smirnov, S., Dijkman, R., Mendling, J., Weske, M.: Meronymy-based aggregation of activities in business process models. In: Parsons, J., Saeki, M., Shoval, P., Woo, C., Wand, Y. (eds.) ER 2010. LNCS, vol. 6412, pp. 1–14. Springer, Heidelberg (2010)
21. Vanderfeesten, I., Cardoso, J., Mendling, J., Reijers, H., van der Aalst, W.M.P.: BPM and workflow handbook, chapter quality metrics for business process models, p. 179 (2007)
22. Weyuker, E.J.: Evaluating software complexity measures. IEEE Trans. Softw. Eng. **14**(9), 1357–1365 (1988)
23. Zugal, S., Pinggera, J., Weber, B., Mendling, J., Reijers, H.A.: Assessing the impact of hierarchy on model understandability – a cognitive perspective. In: Kienzle, J. (ed.) MODELS 2011. LNCS, vol. 7167, pp. 123–133. Springer, Heidelberg (2012)
24. Zugal, S., Soffer, P., Haisjackl, C., et al.: Investigating expressiveness and understandability of hierarchy in declarative business process models. Softw. Sys. Model. **14**(3), 1081–1103 (2013)

Runtime Management

Untrusted Business Process Monitoring and Execution Using Blockchain

Ingo Weber[1,2]([✉]), Xiwei Xu[1,2], Régis Riveret[3], Guido Governatori[3],
Alexander Ponomarev[1], and Jan Mendling[4]

[1] Data61, CSIRO, Eveleigh, NSW, Australia
{Ingo.Weber,Xiwei.Xu,Alexander.Ponomarev}@data61.csiro.au
[2] School of Computer Science and Engineering, UNSW, Sydney, Australia
[3] Data61, CSIRO, Spring Hill, QLD, Australia
{Regis.Riveret,Guido.Governatori}@data61.csiro.au
[4] Wirtschaftsuniversität Wien, Vienna, Austria
jan.mendling@wu.ac.at

Abstract. The integration of business processes across organizations is typically beneficial for all involved parties. However, the lack of trust is often a roadblock. *Blockchain* is an emerging technology for decentralized and transactional data sharing across a network of untrusted participants. It can be used to find agreement about the shared state of collaborating parties without trusting a central authority or any particular participant. Some blockchain networks also provide a computational infrastructure to run autonomous programs called *smart contracts*. In this paper, we address the fundamental problem of trust in collaborative process execution using blockchain. We develop a technique to integrate blockchain into the choreography of processes in such a way that no central authority is needed, but trust maintained. Our solution comprises the combination of an intricate set of components, which allow monitoring or coordination of business processes. We implemented our solution and demonstrate its feasibility by applying it to three use case processes. Our evaluation includes the creation of more than 500 smart contracts and the execution over 8,000 blockchain transactions.

Keywords: Business process · Blockchain · Choreography · Orchestration

1 Introduction

The integration of business processes, e.g., along the supply chain, has been found to contribute both to better operational and business performance [4,10]. A lack of trust, however, may hamper the innovativeness of further developing the collaborative process and its performance altogether [13]. Once service-level agreements are in place, it becomes a highly delicate question which partner should serve as a hub for controlling the collaborative process of several parties, or where a mediator process is hosted. While control asymmetries can be avoided

© Springer International Publishing Switzerland 2016
M. La Rosa et al. (Eds.): BPM 2016, LNCS 9850, pp. 329–347, 2016.
DOI: 10.1007/978-3-319-45348-4_19

by a decentralized choreography instead of central orchestration, it does not solve the general problem of trust in controlling the collaborative business process.

The described lack-of-trust problem can be addressed with novel blockchain technology. Instead of agreeing on one trusted party, participants share transactional data across a large network of *untrusted* nodes (i.e., machines). This is achieved using a timestamped list of blocks which record, share, and aggregate data about transactions that have ever occurred within the blockchain network. Cryptographic proofs make this data storage immutable. As long as a majority share of the blockchain is not compromised, transactions can only be inserted; updating or deleting existing transactions is prohibitively expensive, making the blockchain tamper-proof. Blockchain also provides a global computational infrastructure, which can run programs: so-called *smart contracts* [12] execute across the blockchain network and automatically enforce the conditions defined in the transactions to enable, for example, conditional payment.

In this paper, we adopt blockchain technology to address the lack-of-trust problem in collaborative business processes. More specifically, we develop an approach to map a business process onto a peer-to-peer execution infrastructure that stores transactions in a blockchain, offering the following benefits. First, we provide a monitoring facility that integrates an automatic and immutable transaction history. Second, smart contracts can be used as a direct implementation of the mediator process control logic. Third, we obtain an audit trail for the complete collaborative business processes, for which payments, escrow, and conflict resolution can be enforced automatically. Our contribution is the first approach and implementation that leverages blockchain for collaborative process execution and monitoring. We evaluate our approach for feasibility by prototyping three use case processes on top of it. To this end, we ran of more than 500 process instances by creating as many smart contracts, and executed over 8,000 blockchain transactions that interact with the smart contracts.

The paper proceeds with a discussion of the research problem, related work, and blockchain technology in Sect. 2. Section 3 presents the details of our approach. Section 4 evaluates our approach using several real-world business scenarios, and Sect. 5 concludes. Technical details and evaluation use cases are described in a technical report (TR) [23]. Finally, a screencast video is available.[1]

2   Background

This section discusses the research problem we address, related work, and the background of blockchain technology as a solution.

2.1   Challenges of Collaborative Business Process Execution

We illustrate challenges of executing collaborative business processes by the help of a supply chain scenario reported in [3] that we simplify in Fig. 1. The process

---

[1] https://youtu.be/1SNn9c5HHQs.

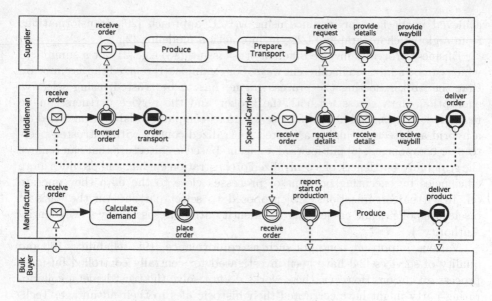

Fig. 1. Supply chain scenario from [3] (simplified)

starts with the Bulk Buyer placing an order with the Manufacturer. The latter calculates the demand and places an order for materials via a Middleman. This Middleman forwards the order to a Supplier and arranges transportation by a Special Carrier. Once the materials are produced, the Carrier picks them up at the Supplier site and delivers them to the Manufacturer. The Manufacturer produces the goods and delivers to the Bulk Buyer. The process is a *choreography* since there is no party that sees all messages. If all messages were sent and received by the Manufacturer, it would be an *orchestration* with the Manufacturer serving as a mediator [7].

Conflict Example. This simple scenario already involves five participants who would likely blame each other in case of delays and errors. Consider the case that the Manufacturer receives the materials three days later than agreed, with eight pallets being delivered instead of ten. The Supplier might argue that this is exactly in line with what was ordered by the Middleman while the Middleman would claim the fault to be on the side of the Supplier. The situation is delicate for the Carrier since the Manufacturer refuses to accept the delivery. The Carrier is now eligible for a compensation by the Supplier or the Middleman depending on who is responsible for the fault.

2.2 Prior Research on Collaborative Business Processes

Prior research on collaborative business processes has intensively investigated different notions of compatibility between the local processes of different partners and between local processes and a global process. Such compatibility can be achieved by design, for instance using a P2P approach [20], transformations from a global choreography [7,22], or interaction modeling [2].

Business processes involve different trust issues (see e.g. [21] for a summary) which can be addressed in different ways. For example, [1] relaxed the assumption that the broker hosting the process engine has to be trusted: using selective encryption, data access for both the broker and the service partners can be restricted. [8] designed a trust service for cross-company collaboration based on a hybrid architecture mixing a trusted centralized control with untrusted peer-to-peer components. [6] put forward an agent-based architecture that can remove the scalability bottleneck of a centralized orchestration engine, and provides more efficiencies by executing portions of processes close to the data they operate on. In virtual organizations, [15] proposed to select partners on the basis of disclosure policies and credentials (i.e. identity attributes issued by a "Credential Authority").

Various important concepts such as conformance [19], reliability [16] and quality of services [24] have been investigated for centrally controlled business process execution. However, these works do not solve the trust issue: a collaborating party might have corrupted their historic files to their advantage. Technologies such as shared data stores provide solutions via consensus protocols to synchronize replicas [5] in a fully trusted environment. In this paper, we build our approach on blockchain technology for reasons explained next.

2.3   Blockchain Technology

Blockchain is the technology that supports Bitcoin [9]. The Bitcoin blockchain is a public ledger, which stores all transactions of the Bitcoin network. This concept has been generalized to distributed ledger systems that verify and store any transactions without coins or tokens [17]. A key feature of a blockchain-based system is that it does not rely on any central trusted authority, like traditional banking or payment systems. Instead, trust is achieved as an emergent property from the interactions between nodes within the network.

The blockchain data structure is an ordered list of blocks. *Blocks* are containers aggregating transactions. Every block is identifiable and linked to the previous block in the chain. *Transactions* are identifiable data packages that store parameters (such as monetary value in case of Bitcoin) and results of function calls in smart contracts. The integrity is ensured by cryptographic techniques. Once created, a transaction is signed with the signature of the transaction's initiator, which indicates e.g. the authorization to spend the money, create a smart contract, or pass the data parameters associated with the transactions.

If the signed transaction is properly formed, valid and complete, it is sent to a few other nodes on the blockchain network, which will further validate it and send it to their peers until it reaches every node in the network. This *flooding approach* guarantees that a valid transaction will reach all the connected nodes in the network within a few seconds. The senders do not need to trust the nodes they use to broadcast the transactions, as long as they use more than one to ensure that it propagates. The recipient nodes do not need to trust the sender either because the transaction is signed. When a transaction reaches a *mining node*, it is verified and included in a block. Blockchain networks rely on miners to aggregate transactions into blocks and append them to the blockchain. Once the transaction is confirmed by a sufficient number of blocks, it becomes a permanent part of the ledger and is accepted as valid by all nodes.

A *smart contract* is a user-defined program executed on the blockchain network [12]. It can be used to reach agreement and solve common problems. Smart contracts can be enforced as part of transactions, and are executed across the blockchain network by all connected nodes. The blockchain platform Ethereum views smart contract as a first-class element, and offers a built-in Turing-complete scripting language for writing smart contracts, called *Solidity*. Its execution environment, the *Ethereum Virtual Machine (EVM)*, comprises all full nodes on the network and executes bytecode compiled from Solidity scripts. Trust in the correct execution of smart contracts extends directly from regular transactions, since (i) they are deployed as data in a transaction, and hence immutable; (ii) all their inputs are through transactions; and (iii) their execution is deterministic. Deployed contracts should be tested. Whether the bytecode can be trusted is a separate matter, which we discuss for our approach in Sect. 4.5.

3 Blockchain-Based Collaborative Process Execution

In the following, we propose a blockchain-based system to address the lack-of-trust problem in collaborative business processes. A number of technical challenges arise during the adoption of blockchain for this purpose. For example, since transactions, computation, and data storage in blockchain platforms are not cost-free, not all aspects of collaborative processes should be dealt with inside smart contracts. However, smart contracts cannot call external APIs outside the blockchain environment or directly create blockchain transactions. This section presents our approach and how it addresses the challenges encountered.

3.1 Overview of the Approach

An overview of our approach is shown in Fig. 2. We use blockchain to facilitate the collaborative processes in either of two ways:

(i) As a *choreography monitor*, it stores the process execution status across all involved participants by observing the message exchanges. In this setting, blockchain serves as an immutable data storage to share the process execution status and create an audit trail. Smart contracts check if interactions are conforming to the choreography model. In addition, a choreography monitor can be used to manage automated payment points and escrow.

(ii) As an *active mediator* among the participants, it coordinates the collaborative process execution. This includes all the above as well as using smart contracts to drive the process and implement data transformation or calculations.

These options are supported by the following main components:

– At design time, a **translator** derives from a process specification described in, e.g., Business Process Model and Notation (BPMN), a smart contract in a script language (such as Solidity). The generated smart contract is a factory for mediators or choreography monitors.

– For Option (i), a **Choreography monitor** or **C-Monitor** uses smart contracts *to monitor* the collaborative business processes. The C-Monitor is split into a factory and case-specific instance C-Monitors. The factory instantiates the case-specific monitors as needed, and contains the blueprint for instance C-Monitors. The C-Monitor instance tracks the interactions of a choreography instance and combines them into a consolidated view of the current state of the execution. Optionally, it can trigger automatic conditional payment from escrow, when certain points in the choreography are reached.

– For Option (ii), an active **mediator** uses a smart contract to *implement* the collaborative business processes. As with the C-Monitor, it is split between a factory and a set of instances and offers a consolidated view of the process state. In contrast to the C-Monitor, the mediator always plays an active role, receiving and sending messages according to the business logic defined in the process model. It also may transform data or execute other computations.

– **Interfaces** or **triggers** connect the process executing on blockchain and the external world. Because smart contracts cannot directly interact with the world outside the blockchain, a trigger plays the role of an organization's agent. It holds confidential information and runs on a full blockchain node, keeping track of the execution context and status of running business processes. The trigger calls external APIs if needed, receives API calls from external components, and updates the process state in the blockchain based on external observations. It further keeps track of data payload in API calls and keeps the data in an external database when appropriate.

By the help of these components, we achieve that (i) participants can execute collaborative processes over a network of untrusted nodes, (ii) only conforming messages advance the state of the process, (iii) payments and escrow can be coded into the process, and (iv) an immutable ledger keeps a log of all transactions, successful or not. Next, we explain the above components in more detail. Additional details are available in a technical report [23].

3.2   Design Time: Translator

The translator is used at design time: it takes an existing business process specification as input and generates smart contracts. These implement the C-Monitor or mediator and can be deployed and executed on the blockchain.

In a collaborative process, this functionality must be split and distributed between the smart contract and the triggers. The translator creates the artifacts in such a way that the triggers and the smart contract can collaborate directly with each other over the blockchain network.

When the translator is called, it may not be known which participants will play which roles. Therefore, the translator outputs only a **factory contract**,

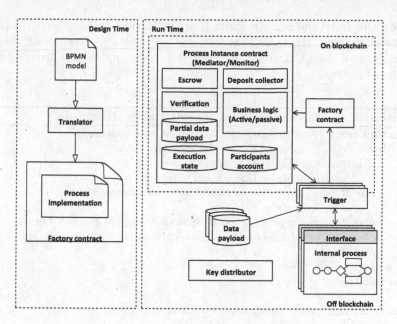

Fig. 2. Overview of our approach

which in turn contains all information needed for instantiating the process. The factory contract includes the methods for instantiation and two types of artifacts: (i) an interface specification per role (e.g., buyer, manufacturer, and shipper) in a collaborative process, to be distributed to the respective triggers, and (ii) a process instance contract, which is deployed to the blockchain when the process is instantiated. The process instance contract contains the implementation of the business logic and takes the form of a C-Monitor or mediator, depending on the content of the original process specification.

The overall translation algorithm has two phases. First, the translator parses the input process model and iterates through all its elements, where it generates two lists per element in the process model: one list of previous elements and one of next elements. Then, the translator translates each element with its respective links, generating Solidity code based on the translation rules for different types of elements as detailed in the TR [23]. Note that, in the current implementation, only some combinations of consecutive gateways can be connected to each other without tasks in between. The previous element list is used by the translator to determine which other elements need to be deactivated when the current element is executed; the next element list specifies which elements need to be activated after the current element is executed.

The selection methods for the two lists are shown in Algorithm 1. *NextElements* of an element includes all the tasks that directly follow the element, or the outgoing edge if the target of that edge is an AND-Join. If a next element is a Split or XOR-Join gateway, the tasks / edges that connect to it are added into *NextElements* through a recursive call. *PreviousElements* of an element includes the element itself. If an XOR-Split gateway $Split_i$ precedes the current element, the tasks that follow it are added to *PreviousElements*. In the case of an AND-Join gateway, all incoming edges are added to *PreviousElements*.

Algorithm 1. Calculating PreviousElements and NextElements.

1: **function** SELECTNEXTELEMENTS(*Element*, *NextElements*[])
2:     **for all** Edge$_j$ $\in$ *outgoingEdges*[*Element*] **do**
3:         **if** Edge$_j$.*targetElement* is Task **then**
4:             *NextElements* $\leftarrow$ *Edge$_j$.targetElement*
5:         **else if** Edge$_j$.*targetElement* is AND-Join gateway **then**
6:             *NextElements* $\leftarrow$ *Edge$_j$*
7:         **else if** Edge$_j$.*targetElement* is Split or XOR-Join gateway **then**
8:             *SelectNextElements*(*Edge$_j$.targetElement*, *NextElements*[])
9:         **end if**
10:    **end for**
11: **end function**
12:
13: **function** SELECTPREVIOUSELEMENTS(*Element*, *PrevElements*[])
14:     *PrevElements* $\leftarrow$ *Element*
15:     **if** *Element* is Task **then**
16:         **for all** Edge$_i$ $\in$ *incomingEdges*[*Element*] **do**
17:             **if** Edge$_i$.*sourceElement* is XOR-Split gateway **then**
18:                 *SelectNextElements*(*Edge$_i$.sourceElement*, *PrevElements*[])
19:             **end if**
20:         **end for**
21:     **else if** *Element* is AND-Join gateway **then**
22:         **for all** Edge$_i$ $\in$ *incomingEdges*[*Element*] **do**
23:             *PrevElements* $\leftarrow$ *Edge$_i$*
24:         **end for**
25:     **end if**
26: **end function**

The **generator** is based on the workflow patterns [18]. Some patterns can be directly translated, some have to be supported off-chain, and other are unnecessary in our case. Our focus is not on supporting all elements of BPMN, but we start from the 5 basic control flow patterns [18], which are among the most frequently used elements in process models [25]. For brevity, we give an overview of the translation rules in Table 1. These make use of the two lists derived above, for activation / deactivation. After generating the smart contracts, the translator also calculates the cost range for executing the resulting smart contract. This serves as an indication of how much crypto-coins have to be spent in order to execute process instances over the blockchain.

Table 1. Translation rule summary. During traversal of the process model, when the translator encounters a pattern (left column), it inserts code according to the right column into the smart contract code. Scope concerns which variants the pattern applies to (M: mediator; CME: C-Monitor with escrow)

BPMN element	Scope	Solidity code summary
All patterns	All	On execution, deactivates itself and activates the subsequent element.
Parallel-Split	All	Executes on activation, activates *all* subsequent elements.
Parallel-Join	All	Executes on activation of *all* incoming edges.
XOR-Split	All	Executes on activation, conditionally activates all subsequent elements. If one of them is executed, it deactivates all others.
XOR-Join	All	Executes on activation of *one* incoming edge.
Choreography Task	All	Executes when the respective message is received (as blockchain transaction), and if the task is activated (message conforms with process). If conforming, the message is forwarded (as smart contract log entry); else, an alert is broadcasted.
Task: Payment	M, CME	Execution and conformance check as above. If conforming, payment into or from escrow is processed. Incoming payment is through a transaction, which has the desired effect already. Outgoing payment is sent to the account of the specified role.
Task: Data Transformation	M	Execution and conformance check as above. Mediator-internal logic on data transformation, to be handled on-chain by the mediator or off-chain by a designated trigger.

3.3 Runtime Environment: Executing Processes as Smart Contracts

The translator generates all artifacts needed for runtime execution. We start by describing C-Monitors, which allow passive monitoring of choreographies and optionally escrow. Active mediators can be seen as an extension of C-Monitors, and the additions are explained subsequently. The third important concept for runtime, the triggers, and the interaction between triggers and smart contracts are covered afterwards. Finally, we describe how technical challenges like key distribution are handled.

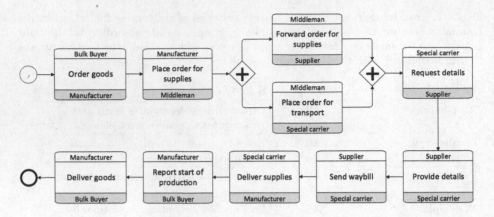

Fig. 3. BPMN choreography diagram of the process in Fig. 1

Choreography Monitor. The first way of facilitating collaborative processes is to use a smart contract as C-Monitor, with optional escrow and conditional payment at certain points of the processes. For a new process instance, an instance contract is generated from the factory contract. Initialization includes registering participants and their public keys to roles. The C-Monitor instance contract contains variables for storing the role assignment and for the process execution status. During execution, the involved participants do not interact with each other directly. Instead, they use the monitor to exchange their input/output data payload and, by doing so, advance the state of the collaborative process. Consider the choreography in Fig. 3, which is another representation of the collaborative process from Fig. 1. All tasks are communication tasks between roles. By exchanging the messages through the C-Monitor, it can check conformance with the choreography and track the status. In this way, conformance checking is done implicitly by the C-Monitor, and all transactions (successful or not) are logged in the blockchain. The handling of escrow is described below.

Mediator. Similar to the C-Monitor, the mediator is implemented as a smart contract, which is generated from the factory contract. It uses the same components as the C-Monitor. It also implements active components, among others to transform data and receive and send messages and payments.

Triggers. The Blockchain is a closed environment, where the deployed smart contracts cannot call external APIs. In our approach, a trigger (or blockchain interface) connects the participants' internal processes with the blockchain. It monitors the process execution status, logically receives messages from smart contracts and calls external APIs, or receives API calls and logically sends messages to smart contracts accordingly.

Triggers are programs running on full nodes of the blockchain network. In the typical setup, every participant operates its own trigger deployed on a node it

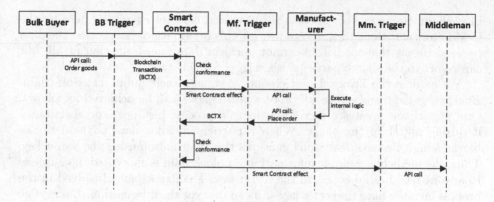

Fig. 4. Sequence diagram for the first two tasks in Fig. 3

controls, and the participant's systems only communicate with its own trigger. We assume that this situation is given. Since the trigger is required to hold private keys for all participants on whose behalf it operates, a high degree of trust into the individual trigger is required.

When a new process instance is created, the participants register their roles and public keys. The public key corresponds to the account address of a participant. All keys and role assignments are passed to all triggers associated with the process instance, so everyone knows which role is played by whom and can verify messages accordingly. With the private key it holds, the trigger can encrypt or sign a message, allowing the contract and the other participants to verify its messages. In this fashion, it can also create payment transactions.

During the process execution, the trigger is receptive to API calls from its owner, as well as to logical messages from the process instance contract. The interaction between internal process implementations, triggers, and the process instance smart contract is shown in simplified form in Fig. 4. When a trigger's API is called from its owner, the trigger translates the received message into a blockchain transaction, and sends the transaction to the instance contract. When the trigger receives a logical message from the instance contract, it updates its local state and calls an external API from the private process implementation.

Finally, the trigger takes care of sizable data payloads. For incoming API calls, it moves the data to secure storage, hashes it, and attaches a URI and the hash to the outgoing transaction. For incoming messages from the blockchain, it retrieves the data via its URI, checks if the hash matches, and sends it on to the internal process implementation.

Encryption and Key Distribution. All the information on the blockchain is publicly accessible to all nodes within the network. We store two types of information on blockchain, namely the process execution status and the data payload (or its URI/hash). To preserve the privacy of the involved participants, we have the option to encrypt the data payload before inserting it into the blockchain. However, the process execution status is not encrypted because the C-Monitors and mediators need to process this information. Encrypting the data payload means that mediators cannot perform data transformation at all, but can resort to the source participant's trigger for this task.

We assume the involved participants exchange their public keys off-chain. *Encrypting data payload for all process participants* can be achieved as follows. One participant creates a secret key for the process instance, and distributes it during initial key exchange. When a participant adds data payload to the blockchain, it first symmetrically encrypts this information using the secret key. Thus, the publicly accessible information on blockchain is encrypted, i.e., useless to anyone who has no access to the secret key. The participants involved in the process instance have the secret key and can decrypt the information. *Encrypting data payload between two process participants,* in contrast, may be desired if two participants want to exchange information privately through the process instance. For this case, the sender can asymmetrically encrypt the information using the receiver's public key; only the receiver can decrypt it with its private key.

Escrow. The C-Monitor or mediator can also work as an escrow for conditional payment at designated points. Similar to an escrow agent, e.g., in real estate transactions, the smart contract receives money from one or more parties, and only releases the money to other parties once certain criteria are met. For the receivers this has the benefit that they can observe that the money is actually there before doing work; and the sender does not have to pay upfront, trusting it will eventually receive the goods or service in return.

In the running example process, the Manufacturer (Mf) needs to pay the Middleman (Mm), Supplier (S) and Carrier (C) when it receives the goods. But S is unwilling to send the goods without some guarantees that it will get paid. Therefore, Mf puts the money in escrow, namely an account held by the process instance contract, when ordering the goods. Later, both C and Mf confirm the delivery of the goods, which triggers automatic payment from the escrow account to Mm, S, and C. The smart contract defines under what conditions the money can be transferred and how the money should be transferred. Thus, when a payment function is triggered, the smart contract automatically checks the defined conditions, and transfers the money according to the defined rules. It is, however, of high importance to specify rules that cover all possible scenarios and the respective outcomes: e.g., what shall happen with money in escrow if Mf and C disagree about the delivery of the goods or their condition?

Gas Money. The computation, data storage, and creation of smart contracts on the blockchain costs crypto-coins. That represents the cost for using the blockchain network, since it is used to pay the miners that execute the smart contracts. Each function call is thus accompanied by cost, but contract creation is relatively much more expensive than a regular function call. For fairness, the participants in a collaborative process may want to decide on a different split of who pays how much, rather than the implicit split from the process.

4 Evaluation

4.1 Evaluation Method, Implementation, and Setup

The goal of our evaluation is to assess the feasibility of the approach. To this end, we implemented proof-of-concept prototypes for the translator and the trigger. The translator, written in Java, accepts BPMN 2.0 XML files, which we parse using the source code of the JBoss BPMN2 Modeller (jbpm-bpmn2 6.3.0). The translator's output are files that comply with the Solidity scripting language, version 0.2.0. Our smart contracts are running on go-ethereum 1.3.5, which is the official Golang implementation of the Ethereum protocol. The trigger is written as a Node.js web application, in JavaScript.

We picked three use case processes of different size, two from the litera-ture and one from an industrial prototype. All three could be used directly as C-Monitor, and we extended one to cover the other options, i.e., C-Monitor with escrow and mediator. The key functionality of the blockchain is to accurately record the shared history of the choreography processes. Therefore, we derived the set of permissible execution traces for each process model, which we called the *set of conforming traces*. Furthermore, we randomly modified these traces to obtain a larger *set of not conforming traces* with the following manipulation operators: (i) add an event, (ii) remove an event, or (iii) switch the order of two events, such that the modified trace was different from all correct traces. Then we tested the ability of the smart contracts to discriminate between correct and incorrect traces. For escrow and the mediator data transformation, we ran a smaller number of experiments where we manually verified the effects.

Finally, during the above experiments we collected data that allows us to analyze important qualities. We focused particularly on cost and latency of using the blockchain in our setting, since these are the two non-functional properties that differ most from traditional approaches, such as trusted third parties. We ran experiments on a private blockchain and the public Ethereum blockchain, which allowed us to compare the effects of different options on these qualities.

4.2 Use Case Processes

For our evaluation, we used the following three processes.

1. Supply chain choreography: This process is discussed throughout this paper as a running example, see Fig. 3, and adapted from [3]. This process has ten tasks, two gateways and two conforming traces. From the 2 possible con-forming traces, we generated 60 randomly manipulated traces. Out of these, 3 were conforming (switched order of parallel tasks) and 57 not.

2. Incident management choreography: This process stems from [11, p.18]. This process has nine tasks, six gateways and four conforming traces. We generated 120 not conforming traces. We implemented it with and without (i) a payment option and (ii) data manipulation in a mediator.
3. Insurance claim handling: This process is taken from the industrial prototype Regorous[2]. Choreographies tend to result in a simplified view of a collaborative process, as can be seen when comparing Figs. 1 and 3. To test the conformance checking feature with a more complex process, we added a third use case which was originally not a choreography. This process has 13 tasks, eight gateways and nine conforming traces. We generated 17 correct and 262 not conforming traces.

4.3   Identification of Not Conforming Traces

For this part of the evaluation, we investigate if our implementation accurately identifies the not conforming traces that have been generated for each of the models. The results are shown in Table 2. All log traces were correctly classified. This was our expectation: any other outcome would have pointed at severe issues with our approach or implementation.

Table 2. Process use case characteristics and conformance checking results

Process	Tasks	Gateways	Trace type	Traces	Correctness
Supply chain process of Fig. 3	10	2	Conforming	5	100 %
			Not conforming	57	100 %
Incident management	9	6	Conforming	4	100 %
			Not conforming	120	100 %
Incident management with payment	9	6	Conforming	4	100 %
			Not conforming	19	100 %
Incident mgmt. with data transformation	9	6	Calculation	10	100 %
			String manipulation	10	100 %
Insurance claim	13	8	Conforming	17	100 %
			Not conforming	262	100 %

4.4   Analysis of Cost and Latency

In this part of the evaluation, we investigate the cost and latency of involving the blockchain in the process execution, since these are the non-functional properties that are most different from solutions currently used in practice.

---

[2] http://www.regorous.com/. A subset of the authors is involved in this project.

Cost. In our experiments on the private blockchain, we executed a total of 7923 transactions, at zero cost. On the public Ethereum blockchain, we ran 32 process instances with a total of 256 transactions. The deployment of the factory contract cost 0.032 Ether, and each run of the Incident Management process, with automatic payments and data transformations, cost on average 0.0347 Ether, or approx. US\$ 0.40 at the time of writing. The data (transactions and contract effects) of the experiment on the public blockchain is publicly viewable from the factory contract's address, e.g. via Etherscan.[3]

Latency. We measure latency as the time taken from when the trigger receives an API call until it sends the response with conformance outcome, transaction hash, block number, etc. A test script iterates over the events in a trace and synchronously calls the trigger for each event. Therefore, the test script sends the next request very soon after receiving a response. This distorts the latency measurement to a degree, since the trigger adds the next transaction to the transaction pool just after the previous block has been mined, and it needs to wait there until mining for the block after the current one is started. Our measurements should thus be regarded as an upper bound, rather than the typical case. A more detailed explanation is given in the technical report [23].

An overview of the latency measurements is shown in Fig. 5[4]. The duration for a block to be mined comes from the complexity of the mining task, which is deliberately designed to be computationally hard. On the public Ethereum blockchain, the *target median time* between blocks at the time of writing is set to around 13 s, with the actual time measured at 14.4 s. On our private blockchain, we can control the complexity mechanism to increase mining time (shown as *Private fast* in Fig. 5) or leave the default implementation in place (*Private uncontrolled*). As can be seen, the variance is high. On the public Ethereum blockchain, the median latency was 23.0 s. In our *private fast* setting we achieved a median latency of 2.8 s, which should be sufficient for many practical deployments. For any application, this *tradeoff* needs to be considered: public blockchains offer much higher trustworthiness in return for higher cost and latency.

4.5   Discussion

Conflict Resolution. Following up on the *conflict example* from Sect. 2.1, we discuss how conflict resolution can be implemented in our approach. Recall that there was disagreement about the amount of supplies ordered. The blockchain inherently provides an immutable audit trail, thus it is trivial to review the original order and waybill messages – the culprit can be identified through such inspection. Say, the Supplier was at fault, but the Manufacturer paid crypto-coins

---

[3] https://etherscan.io/address/0x09890f52cdd5d0743c7d13abe481e705a2706384.

[4] Note that, instead of the typical error bars with *min* and *max* in box plots, we here show the 1st and the 99th percentile, to reduce the effect of the worst outliers. For *Private uncontrolled*, the *max* was 183 s – almost twice as much as the 99th percentile.

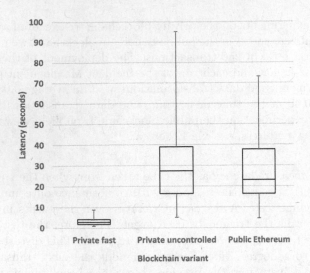

Fig. 5. Latency in seconds, using private blockchain with/without speed modification, and public Ethereum blockchain (box plot)

into escrow – how does it get its money back? The conditions for reimbursement from escrow need to be specified in the smart contract, but then they can be invoked at a later time. For instance, the participants may agree upfront that the Manufacturer gets reimbursed only if the Middleman agrees to that; then the Middleman sends a transaction to that effect, and the Manufacturer's money is transferred back to its account.

Trust. Blockchain provides a trustworthy environment, without requiring trust in any single entity. In contrast, in the traditional model participants who do not trust each other need to agree on a third party which is trusted by all. Blockchain can replace this trusted third party. This is of particular interest in cases of coopetition. If multiple parties come together to achieve a joint business goal, but some of the organizations are in coopetition, it is important that the entity which executes the joint business process is neutral. Say, *Org1*, *Org2*, and *Org3* are in coopetition, but want to have a joint process to achieve some business goal. However, *Org1* would not accept *Org2* or *Org3* to control the process, and neither of those would accept *Org1*. Using our approach, the blockchain can be used, enabling trustless collaboration as it is not controlled by a single entity. Our translator allows the deployment of business processes on blockchain network without the need to manually implement the corresponding smart contract. *Trust in the deployed bytecode* for a process is established as follows: each participant has access to the process model, translates it to Solidity with our translator, and uses an agreed-upon Solidity compiler. This results in the same bytecode, and each participant can verify that the deployed bytecode has not been manipulated. Finally, the *trigger* allows for seamless integration into service-based message exchanges. However, each trigger is a fully trusted party, and by default we assume each organization hosts their own trigger.

Privacy. Public blockchains do not guarantee any data privacy: anyone can join a public blockchain network without permission, and information on the blockchain is public. Thus, for scenarios like collaborative process execution, a permissioned blockchain may be more appropriate: joining it requires explicit permission. Even with permission management, the information on blockchain is still available to all the participants of the blockchain network. While we propose a method to encrypt the data payload of messages, the process status information is publicly available. As such, if *Org1*'s competitor, *Org4*, knows which account address belongs to which participant, it can infer with whom *Org1* is doing business and how frequently. This can be mitigated by creating a new account address for each process instance: the space of addresses is huge, and account creation trivial. However, this method prevents building a reputation, at least on the blockchain.

Off-Chain Data Store. For large data payloads, we propose to store only meta-data with a URI on-chain, and to keep the actual payload off-chain – accessible with the URI. Due to size limits for data storage on current blockchains [14] and associated costs, this solution can be highly advantageous. There are existing solutions that provide a data layer on top of blockchains, such as Factom [14]. Distributed data storage, like IPFS, DHT (Distributed Hash Table), or AWS S3, can also be used in combination with the blockchain to build decentralized applications.

Threats to Validity. There are several limitations to our study. To start, we made some assumptions when implementing our evaluation scenario, which bear threats to validity. First, we considered a supply chain scenario in which seconds of latency are typically not an issue. We expect that scenarios in other industries, such as automatic financial trading, would have stronger requirements in terms of latency, which could limit the applicability of our technique. Second, we worked with a network of limited size. A global network might have stronger requirements in terms of minimal block-to-block latency to ensure correct replication. These threats emphasize the need to conduct further application studies in different settings. Furthermore, there are open questions regarding technology acceptance, including management perception and legal issues of using blockchain technology.

5   Conclusion

Collaborative process execution is problematic if the participants involved have a lack of trust in each other. In this paper, we propose the use of blockchain and its smart contracts to circumvent the traditional need for a centralized trusted party in a collaborative process execution. First, we devise a translator to translate process specifications into smart contracts that can be executed on a blockchain. Second, we utilize the computational infrastructure of blockchain to coordinate business processes. Third, to connect the smart contracts on blockchain with external world, we propose and implement the concept of triggers. A trigger converts API calls to blockchain transactions directed at a smart contract, and receives status updates from the contract that it converts to API calls. Triggers can thus act as a bridge between the blockchain and an organization's private process implementations. We ran a large number of experiments to demonstrate the feasibility of this approach, using a private as well as a public blockchain. While latency is low on a private, customized blockchain, the latency on the public blockchain may be considered too high for fast-paced scenarios. Additional benefits of our approach include the option to build escrow and automated payments into the process, and that the blockchain transactions from process executions form an immutable audit trail.

Acknowledgments. We thank Chao Li for integrating the trigger prototype with POD-Viz and recording the screencast video.

References

1. Carminati, B., Ferrari, E., Tran, N.H.: Secure web service composition with untrusted broker. In: IEEE ICWS, pp. 137–144. IEEE (2014)
2. Decker, G., Weske, M.: Interaction-centric modeling of process choreographies. Inf. Syst. **36**(2), 292–312 (2011)
3. Fdhila, W., Rinderle-Ma, S., Knuplesch, D., Reichert, M.: Change and compliance in collaborative processes. In: IEEE SCC, pp. 162–169 (2015)
4. Flynn, B.B., Huo, B., Zhao, X.: The impact of supply chain integration on performance: a contingency and configuration approach. J. Oper. Manag. **28**(1), 58–71 (2010)
5. Kemme, B., Alonso, G.: Database replication: a tale of research across communities. Proc. VLDB Endow. **3**(1–2), 5–12 (2010)
6. Li, G., Muthusamy, V., Jacobsen, H.A.: A distributed service-oriented architecture for business process execution. ACM TWEB **4**(1), 2 (2010)
7. Mendling, J., Hafner, M.: From WS-CDL choreography to BPEL process orchestration. J. Enterp. Inf. Manag. **21**(5), 525–542 (2008)
8. Mont, M.C., Tomasi, L.: A distributed service, adaptive to trust assessment, based on peer-to-peer e-records replication and storage. In: IEEE FTDCS (2001)
9. Nakamoto, S.: Bitcoin: a peer-to-peer electronic cash system. https://bitcoin.org/bitcoin.pdf. Accessed 19 July 2015
10. Narayanan, S., Jayaraman, V., Luo, Y., Swaminathan, J.M.: The antecedents of process integration in business process outsourcing and its effect on firm performance. J. Oper. Manag. **29**(1), 3–16 (2011)
11. Object Management Group, June 2010. BPMN 2.0 by Example. www.omg.org/spec/BPMN/20100601/10-06-02.pdf. Version 1.0. Accessed 10 Mar 2016
12. Omohundro, S.: Cryptocurrencies, smart contracts, and artificial intelligence. AI Matters **1**(2), 19–21 (2014)

13. Panayides, P.M., Lun, Y.V.: The impact of trust on innovativeness and supply chain performance. J. Prod. Econ. **122**(1), 35–46 (2009)
14. Snow, P., Deery, B., Lu, J., Johnston, D., Kirby, P.: Business processes secured by immutable audit trails on the blockchain (2014)
15. Squicciarini, A., Paci, F., Bertino, E.: Trust establishment in the formation of virtual organizations. In: ICDE Workshops, IEEE Computer Society (2008)
16. Subramanian, S., Thiran, P., Narendra, N., Mostéfaoui, G., Maamar, Z.: On the enhancement of BPEL engines for self-healing composite web services. In: Proceedings of SAINT Symposium, pp. 33–39 (2008)
17. Tschorsch, F., Scheuermann, B.: Bitcoin and beyond: a technical survey on decentralized digital currencies. IACR Cryptology ePrint Archive, 2015, 464 (2015)
18. van der Aalst, W., ter Hofstede, A.H.M., Kiepuszewski, B., Barros, A.P.: Workflow patterns. Distrib. Parallel Databases **14**(1), 5–51 (2003)
19. van der Aalst, W.M.P., Dumas, M., Ouyang, C., Rozinat, A., Verbeek, E.: Conformance checking of service behavior. ACM Trans. Internet Technol. **8**(3) (2008)
20. van der Aalst, W.M.P., Weske, M.: The P2P approach to interorganizational workflows. In: Dittrich, K.R., Geppert, A., Norrie, M. (eds.) CAiSE 2001. LNCS, vol. 2068, pp. 140–159. Springer, Heidelberg (2001)
21. Viriyasitavat, W., Martin, A.: In the relation of workflow and trust characteristics, and requirements in service workflows. In: Abd Manaf, A., Zeki, A., Zamani, M., Chuprat, S., El-Qawasmeh, E. (eds.) ICIEIS 2011, Part I. CCIS, vol. 251, pp. 492–506. Springer, Heidelberg (2011)
22. Weber, I., Haller, J., Mülle, J.: Automated derivation of executable business processes from choreograpies in virtual organizations. Int. J. Bus. Process Integr. Manag. (IJBPIM) **3**(2), 85–95 (2008)
23. Weber, I., Xu, X., Riveret, R., Governatori, G., Ponomarev, A., Mendling, J.: Using blockchain to enable untrusted business process monitoring and execution. Technical report UNSW-CSE-TR-09, University of New South Wales (2016)
24. Zeng, L., Benatallah, B., Ngu, A., Dumas, M., Kalagnanam, J., Chang, H.: QOS-aware middleware for web services composition. IEEE TSE **30**(5), 311–327 (2004)
25. Muehlen, M., Recker, J.: How much language is enough? Theoretical and practical use of the business process modeling notation. In: Bellahsène, Z., Léonard, M. (eds.) CAiSE 2008. LNCS, vol. 5074, pp. 465–479. Springer, Heidelberg (2008)

Classification and Formalization
of Instance-Spanning Constraints
in Process-Driven Applications

Walid Fdhila[✉], Manuel Gall, Stefanie Rinderle-Ma, Juergen Mangler,
and Conrad Indiono

Faculty of Computer Science, University of Vienna, Vienna, Austria
{walid.fdhila,manuel.gall,stefanie.rinderle-Ma,
juergen.mangler,conrad.indiono}@univie.ac.at

Abstract. In process-driven applications, typically, instances share human, computer, and physical resources and hence cannot be executed independently of each other. This necessitates the definition, verification, and enforcement of restrictions and conditions across multiple instances by so called instance-spanning constraints (ISC). ISC might refer to instances of one or several process types or variants. While real-world applications from, e.g., the logistics, manufacturing, and energy domain crave for the support of ISC, only partial solutions can be found. This work provides a systematic ISC classification and formalization that enables the verification of ISC during design and runtime. Based on a collection of 114 ISC from different domains and sources the relevance and feasibility of the presented concepts is shown.

Keywords: Instance-spanning   constraints   ·   Compliance   ·
Process-Aware Information Systems

1 Introduction

Checking and enforcing constraints such as regulations or security policies is the key concern of business process compliance [29]. Enterprises have to invest significantly into compliance projects, e.g., for large companies $4.6 million only for the management of internal controls [31]. BPM research has provided several solutions for compliance at design time, e.g., [6] and runtime (cf. survey in [15]). Despite these large efforts, an important type of constraints has not been paid sufficient attention to, i.e., *Instance-Spanning Constraints (ISC)*. ISC are constraints that refer to more than one instance of one or several process types. Logistics is a domain where ISC play a crucial role for the bundling or rebundling of cargo over several transport processes [4]. Other domains craving for ISC support are health care [7] and security [33]. Specifically, in highly adaptive process-driven applications where processes dynamically evolve during runtime [10] ISC provide the means for ensuring a certain level of control.

© Springer International Publishing Switzerland 2016
M. La Rosa et al. (Eds.): BPM 2016, LNCS 9850, pp. 348–364, 2016.
DOI: 10.1007/978-3-319-45348-4_20

ISC support is scattered over a few approaches [7,13,17,18,27,33], but a *comprehensive* support for ISC formalization, verification, and enforcement is missing. Here, the property *comprehensive* refers to the context of ISC such as multiple instances or processes, the expressiveness, e.g., ISC referring to data or time, and the process life cycle phase the ISC is referring to. For a sufficient understanding of these requirements, a systematic classification of ISC is needed. An ISC formalization can then be chosen based on the ISC classification and additional requirements such as complexity of the verification. The following research questions address these needs:

1. *How to systematically classify ISC?*
2. *How to formalize ISC based on ISC classification?*
3. *Do ISC classification and formalization meet real-world ISC requirements?*

Questions 1–3 will be tackled following the milestones set out in Fig. 1. At first, objectives are harvested from literature that must be met by an ISC classification (*Question 1*) and formalization (*Question 2*). The ISC classification will be created as new artifact. The ISC formalization choice (*Question 2*) is based on an analysis of existing languages. Based on an ISC collection of 114 examples from practice, literature, and experience, relevance and feasibility of the ISC classification are evaluated (*Question 3*). Moreover, the ISC formalization will be validated by formalizing and implementing representatives along the provided ISC classification (*Question 3*). In summary, this work provides an ISC classification and formalization as well as an evaluation based on an extensive meta study on ISC examples (cf. [26] for a complete description and all 114 ISC examples).

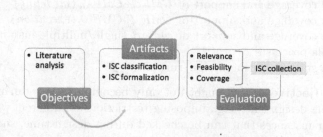

Fig. 1. Milestones following the research methodology in [22]

Section 2 provides ISC objectives and the ISC classification. Section 3 discusses alternatives for formalization languages. In Sect. 4, relevance and feasibility of the ISC classification is evaluated. ISC representatives are formalized and implemented in Sect. 5. Section 6 discusses related approaches and Sect. 7 closes with a summary.

2   ISC Classification

Following the milestones set out in Fig. 1, a collection of objectives on the ISC classification and formalization is harvested from literature. ISC have a strong runtime focus [33] and can thus be estimated as related to compliance monitoring in business processes. In [15], objectives on compliance monitoring have been selected and evaluated as Compliance Monitoring Functionalities (CMF). The CMFs are grouped along *modeling, execution,* and *user* requirements. For the ISC classification the focus is at the moment on modeling and execution requirements. User requirements will play an important role later on when investigating feedback options and handling of ISC violations and conflicts. According to [15], modeling and execution requirements are *CMF 1: Constraints referring to time, CMF 2: Constraints referring to data, CMF 3: Constraints referring to resources, CMF 4: Supporting non-atomic activities, CMF 5: Supporting activity life cycles, CMF 6: Supporting multiple instances constraints.*

Although *CMF 6* suggests the use of CMFs for ISC, the CMF framework does not deal with ISC, but rather with multiple activity instantiations. Hence, we complement the elicitation of objectives by including requirements stated in literature on ISC, i.e., [7,13,17,18,27,33]. These works partly confirm *CMF 1–CMF 6* and extend it by the *context* of a constraint [13,17,18], i.e., whether it refers to a single/multiple processes and/or single/multiple instances. An example for an ISC spanning multiple instances of a single process is a security constraint restricting the loan sum granted by one employee over all her customers [33]. An example for an ISC spanning single instances of multiple processes is imposing an order between two activities of different treatment processes [7].

Concluding, we state as objectives for ISC classification and formalization:

Objective 1: coverage and support of *CMF 1–CMF 3* (*modeling*)
Objective 2: coverage and support of *CMF 4–CMF 6* (*execution*)
Objective 3: coverage and support of *context* single/multiple instances for single/multiple processes
Objective 4: support during design/runtime

Regarding **Objective 4**: ISC might not only become effective during runtime, but also during design time, e.g., imposing restrictions on different process variants and their instances that can be checked during design time, such as static information about roles in a process spanning separation of duty scenario. Thus, support of ISC during design time is added to the objectives.

Figure 2 depicts the proposed ISC classification designed along **Objective 1–4** . **Objective 1** suggests a classification along the modeling requirements time, data and resource. Here, the classification of an ISC into several requirements is conceivable. ISC *A user is not allowed to do t2 if the total loan amount per day exceeds \$1M* [33], for example, can be classified as time and data. For a selective classification, ISC should not fit into multiple categories, but be assigned to exactly one category. For this reason, the modeling requirements are grouped into *single* and *multiple* requirements. Multiple modeling requirements describe ISC for which more than one modeling requirement is existing such as in the example above. An ISC is classified as single modeling requirement if none or one modeling requirement is present. **Objective 2** is not considered for the ISC classification. In turn, the underlying CMFs are relevant for the formalization and for the interplay with a process execution engine which manages task states and multiple instances of a task.

Fig. 2. ISC classification according to objectives.

Objective 3 requires to extend the classification by the spanning property of constraints, e.g., imposing a restriction that must hold across several process instances. In the iUPC logical description [13,17,18,27], for example, the spanning part is described as *context*. ISC can span over processes and/or instances. An ISC is considered *single* spanning if the constraint spans over processes **or** instances and *multi* spanning when the constraint spans across both.

ISC can be enforced during design and run time (**Objective 4**). The proposed ISC classification considers both, but due to the strong runtime focus of ISC design-time will be a single group and run-time is divided into the four classifications provided by modeling requirements and context. A more extensive discussion on design and runtime support of ISC is provided in Sect. 3.1.

3 Analysis of Existing Formalisms for ISC Support

In Sect. 2, we have identified 4 objectives primordial for the classification and formalization of ISC. In the following, we use these 4 objectives to evaluate a list of existing formalisms and compare them to ISC requirements.

3.1 ISC Support During Design and Runtime

We start with a discussion of ISC requirements on verification at design time and runtime (cf. **Objective 4**).

Design time checking aims at verifying the process model compliability with respect to the defined ISC, detecting and resolving conflicts between multiple ISC, and checking the reachable states of the instances with respect to the defined ISC. This might imply generating and combining possible traces to be checked against the ISC. One of the techniques used at design time is model checking. This technique suffers from well known problem of state explosion and is not well suited for checking constraints that refer to runtime data.

Runtime checking becomes necessary as soon as ISC refer to execution data, time, or resources. Moreover, at runtime it is possible to deviate from the original process model, and therefore a monitoring approach to check possible violations becomes primordial. In contrast to design time checking, the process models are not used in the monitoring of constraints (unless for conformance checking), but the runtime events instead. At runtime, we differentiate between two checking possibilities: (i) using partial traces, where events are analyzed against the constraints when they arrive, and (ii) post checking, i.e., using complete traces, which assume that the analyzed instances have completed. ISC span multiple instances. Hence, the fact that an instance or a set of instances satisfy an ISC at the time of their completion does not necessarily ensure that this ISC will not be violated by the executing of future instances, i.e., combined with the completed ones. Consequently, it becomes crucial for ISC monitoring to define correctly the window for analyzing the instances against the constraints.

3.2   Analysis of Formal Languages

In this section, we have analyzed the commonly used formalisms in the areas of business process compliance and concurrent systems as follows.

Event-B is a specification language that describes how the system is allowed to evolve. In particular, it specifies the properties that the system must fulfill [1]. Event-B is mainly used for distributed systems, using artifacts; i.e. blueprints, to reason about the behavior and the constraints of the future system. The main advantage of Event-B is that it allows different level of abstractions through stepwise refinement. Event-B is based on events, expresses the constraints between them, and supports modality; i.e. time operators (CMF 1). In the context of business processes, Event-B has been used for verifying cloud resource allocation and consumption [3] (CMF 2–3).

TLA+ is a syntactic extension of TLA (Temporal logic of Action), a specification language for describing and reasoning about asynchronous, nondeterministic concurrent systems [9]. TLA+ combines temporal logic with logic of action, is suited for reasoning about protocols, and can be used to specify safety and liveness properties. Similarly to Event-B, TLA+ allows different levels of abstraction through refinement.

Both TLA+ and Event-B can be appropriate for specifying and checking ISC at design time. In particular, structural parts of ISC might checked before runtime to detect inconsistencies or incorrect specifications. Both formalisms are very expressive, support time, data and resources (**Objective 1**), and can ensure properties such as liveness, fairness or safety at design time. However, this does not prevent deviations from the specified model at run time. To our knowledge, TLA+ and Event-B are meant to be used for specifying correct and compliant models, but not for monitoring the system properties at run-time; i.e. they does not satisfy **Objective 4**. Both languages are used for distributed and concurrent systems and can support **Objective 3**.

LTL (Linear Temporal Logic) is a formal language, introduced by Pnueli [24], referring to the temporal modality (CMF 1), and used for reactive and concurrent systems. LTL is an extension of propositional logic, and expresses properties of computation traces; i.e., is interpreted over execution traces. Recently, LTL has been used for modeling and checking compliance constraints of business processes at both design and run-time [2,16] (**Objective 4**). While most of the approaches for design time verification would use a Kripke Structure for model checking LTL properties, some monitoring approaches rely on a transformation of the constraints to a monitor (automata) that evaluates the runtime events. Several extensions of LTL have been proposed to cover other aspects not originally considered. For example, DLTL (Dynamic Linear Temporal Logic) strengthen the UNTIL modality with regular expression of the propositional dynamic logic. Similarly, RTL (Regular Temporal Logic) extends LTL with semi-extended regular expressions, and MLTL extends it with metrics.

CTL (Computation Tree Logic), is a branching time logic that, in contrast to LTL, expresses constraints on dynamic evolution of states rather than traces. Unlike LTL, in CTL the evolution of time is nondeterministic, and every instant of time has several successors, rather than, exactly one [32]. While LTL reasons about events along a single computation path, CTL quantifies over paths that are possible from a given state, through a computation tree. LTL and CTL are not really comparable and have different expressive powers; i.e., there are formula that can be expressed in CTL but not in LTL, and inversely. The strong fairness property, which guarantee a fair behavior between concurrent instances cannot be expressed in CTL. While LTL is better in expressiveness, the problem of model-checking CTL formulae of a Kripke structure is of polynomial complexity [32]. Several extensions of CTL has been proposed; e.g. CTRL extends it with regular expressions [19].

CTL* can express all formulae of both LTL and CTL [32]. However, the problem of model checking becomes P-space complete. While LTL can be used for monitoring, CTL and CTL* are mostly used for model checking at design time (**Objective 4**).

PDL is a dynamic logic with several modalities that extends modal logic by associating action to the operators; i.e.; multimodal logic [5]. It particularly expresses formulae of the form: *after executing an action, it is necessary or possible that the proposition holds.* PDL can also express nondeterministic behavior through regular expressions and compound actions. The complexity of PDL decidability is proved to be in deterministic exponential time which makes it not appropriate for monitoring (**Objective 4**).

μ-Calculus is an extension of modal logic with two operators μ and v corresponding to the least and greatest fixpoints operators [14]. μ-Calculus is a superset of CTL* and PDL, and is also used for the formal verification of concurrent systems. Despite its expressive power, the complexity of model checking systems specified with μ-Calculus is considerably high.

Although CTL* and μ-Calculus are powerful branching-time logics, both of which subsume CTL and LTL (μ-Calculus subsumes PDL as well), they are complex to understand and to use by non-experts [19]. ISC can be conveniently and concisely formulated in terms of regular expressions that are not provided

by standard temporal logics such as CTL and LTL [13,18]. Besides, LTL, CTL*
and μ-calculus adopt an inherent qualitative notion of time but when it comes
to quantitative time or metrics they become insufficient (CMF 1) [15]. LTL is
also not suitable for constraints that deal with data and resources (CMF 2–3),
or mult-instances (CMF 6), which are aligned with **Objectives 1–2** of ISC.

EC (Event Calculus) is a general logic programming treatment of time and
change [12]. Event calculus is based on first order predicate logic FOL and
expresses properties in terms of Fluents. A Fluent is a time-varying property
whose valuation is changing according to effect axioms defined in the theory of
the problem domain. The time in EC is linear rather than the branching time
used in other logics, where time is a tree. Accordingly, Fluent valuation is relative to time points instead of successive situations. EC provides an inherent
support for concurrent events [12], where events occurring in overlapping time
intervals, from different sources can be deduced (**Objective 3**). EC has bene-
fited enormously from several extensions; e.g. for expressing different properties
such as non deterministic actions, gradual changes, compound events, indirect
effects, actions with duration or actions with delayed effects [21]. There exist a
multitude of reasoners or solvers for EC; e.g. Discrete Event Calculus reasoner,
F2LP [21]. EC supports abductive reasoning to generate hypothetical events.
In other words, it permits constructing a rule based on the observed events. In
the context of business processes, EC has been widely used for either formalizing
process models, process choreographies (process interactions) [28], or obligations
and compliance rules [20]. As already mentioned in [15,20], EC adopts an explicit
representation of qualitative and quantitative time (CMF 1), and supports the
CMF 2–6 that we pointed as relevant for ISC checking. Moreover EC supports
checking at both design and runtime (**Objective 4**).

Other Languages: In particular, **SQL-like languages** such as PQL or
APQL [8] as declarative languages based upon temporal logic seem to be good
candidates for expressing complex constraints and querying instance events at
runtime. In contrast to the logic based reasoning, they are data-centric and can
deal with the CMFs that we have defined. Currently, PQL is used for querying process model instances. Also **eCRG** (extended Compliance Rule Graph)
is a visual monitoring language for business process compliance which supports control and data flow including time and resource perspectives [11] (CMF
2–3). eCRG is based on FOL and can be used at both, design and runtime
(**Objective 4**).

ISC checking at design-time is not always decidable due to loops or quantification over infinite sets (e.g., time, integer, arbitrary data objects). While
the assumption of finite sets is made implicit for LTL and CTL, and therefore they are considered as decidable at design time, it does not hold for more
expressive language such as EC. The expressive power of EC precludes its decidability at design time, but meanwhile can cope with most ISC specifications.
Since temporal logic properties are decidable over finite-state models, adopting
this assumption makes EC also decidable at design time. LTL, CTL, PDL, EC,
eCRG and SQL-like languages are all decidable at runtime (monitoring) since
they check over traces. However, they have different complexity.

Table 1 elaborates on the above discussion and classifies the studied languages with respect to **Objectives 1–4**. eCRG, SQL-like languages, and EC seem to be good candidates for ISC formalization. SQL-like languages are more data-centric, but remain as a good alternative to support ISC. Overall, EC is adopted for ISC formalization and used as basis for design time checking and runtime monitoring.

Table 1. Evaluation of formalisms with respect to Objectives 1–4

		TLA+	Event B	LTL	CTL	PDL	μ-Calculus	eCRG	SQL-Like	EC
Objective 1		+	+	+/−	+/−	+/−	+/−	+	+	+
Objective 2		+	+	+/−	+/−	+/−	+	+	+	+
Objective 3		+	+	+	+	+	+	+	+	+
Objecjtive 4	Design	+	+	+	+	+/−	+/−	+/−	+/−	+/−
	Runtime	−	−	+	+/−	+/−	+/−	+	+	+

Caption: (Full support (+), Not Supported (−), Partly supported (+/−))

4 Relevance and Feasibility of ISC Classification

114 ISC examples were collected during a meta study described in [26]. Manufacturing, logistics/transport, health care, security and energy/smart grid were identified as relevant application domains which were complemented by other domains such as teaching and insurance during the study. Altogether, 42 % of the ISC examples stem from the energy domain, 16 % from automotive and manufacturing, 10 % from security, 9 % from logistics and transport, 7 % from health care, and 16 % from other domains. Among the analyzed sources were EU and WWTF projects (16 %), regulatory documents (42 %), industry papers (15 %), literature (9 %), as well as ISC examples from experiences; i.e., own working projects (18 %). The complete collection of ISC examples is provided in [26].

In order to show the relevance and feasibility of the ISC classification (cf. Fig. 2), the ISC were manually categorized with respect to the following aspects[1].

- Application: design/runtime
- Context: single/multiple processes/instances
- Modeling requirements: structure, data, time, resource, execution data

Regarding *application*, it can be observed that all examples refer to runtime (except those in category undef). Hence, the classification into *design time* and *runtime* is not reflected by the examples. Nonetheless, ISC examples for design time can be envisaged (e.g., static role assignment), however, the emphasis seems to be ISC support during runtime. *Execution data* [18] can be observed as additional modeling requirement when compared to the CMFs in [15]. *Structure* is present in every ISC (as implicitly also the case for the CMF framework [15]).

---

[1] Note that ISC for which no categorization was possible without further information were categorized as *undef*. The reason behind is that the ISC in many cases did not have a specified connected process model.

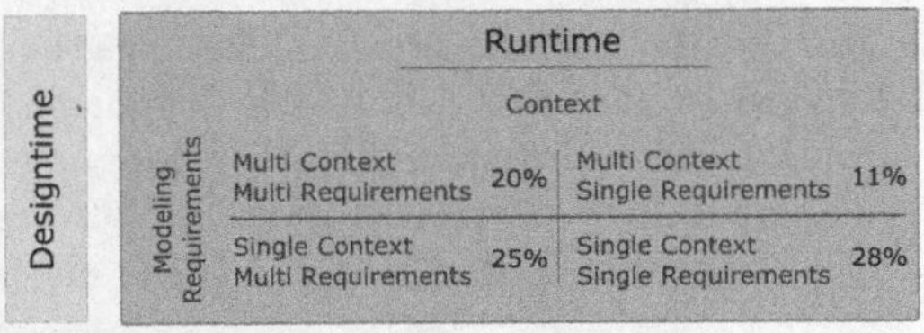

Fig. 3. Distribution of classification

The distribution of the examples with respect to *context and modeling requirements* is depicted in Fig. 3. About 20 % of the examples can be classified as spanning multiple processes, instances, and modeling requirements. 11 % span multiple context and are categorized to fit a single modeling requirement. In total, 53 % of the ISC are classified as single context spanning either processes or instances. 25 % of the ISC in category single context are further categorized as referring to multiple modeling requirements and 28 % as single modeling requirement. 16 % of the examples are not considered due to unclear context (12 %) or missing modeling requirements (4 %). For this data set, each ISC fits exactly one of the classification categories.

To learn more about the modeling requirements, they were plotted against the domain and the source (cf. Fig. 4). *Structure* is a modeling requirement present in every domain (cf. Fig. 4(a)) ranging from about 35 % to 45 %. There are differences for modeling requirements *data*. Specifically, *data* is not present at all for domain energy whereas for the other domains the amount of ISC referring to *data* ranges from about 20 % to 32 %. *Time* plays some role for all domains, but seems to be especially represented for the energy domain (about 38 %) compared to a range from about 6 % to 20 % for all other domains. Looking into the energy examples, many ISC refer to a certain time frame (Service Level Agreements (SLA)). *Resource* is present throughout all domains, again the energy domain shows less ISC referring to *resources* (about 1 %) than the other domains (about 14 % to 29 %). All ISC referring to *execution data* fall into domain energy. *Resources* seem to play a particularly important role in manufacturing and automotive as well as in security. The latter is not very surprising as the assignment of resources is an essential security measure.

For analyzing modeling requirements along source (cf. Fig. 4(b)), it was decided to aggregate sources into categories *practice* (covering projects and regulatory documents), *experience*, and *literature* (covering literature and industry papers) in order to compare practice and research. Industry papers could have also been categorized under practice as these paper mostly describe real-world use cases. Figure 4(b) shows that practice has more emphasis on *time* as literature, whereas literature emphasizes on *resources*. Literature also contains more examples with modeling requirement *data* then the practical examples. Experience seems to balance out modeling requirements from practice, e.g., *time*, and literature, e.g., *data*. Only practice refers to example with *execution data*. One can interpret this as follows: category *practice* is dominated by the energy

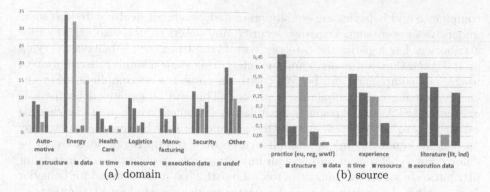

(a) domain   (b) source

Fig. 4. Modeling requirements for domain and source (normalized, grouped barcharts)

domain where *time* plays an important role. Nonetheless, the rather marginal coverage of *time* by literature in contrast to practice is interesting to look into. Also the practice category introduces *execution data* which has not been considered by literature at all. The experience examples intentionally try to resemble a balanced coverage of all modeling requirements.

To round off the explorative analysis of the ISC collection, the *usage* of the ISC examples was analyzed. [18,27] distinguish categories *compliance, attribution, behavior*, and *meta* where compliance refers to checking certain properties, attribution to, for example, runtime assignments, behavior to enforcement of certain actions during runtime such as synchronization, and meta to constraints defined on other constraints. Figure 5 shows the distribution of ISC example usage for the different domains. For automotive and manufacturing, compliance and behavior are present with an emphasis on compliance. Energy refers to compliance, but no other category (except undef). For health care and security

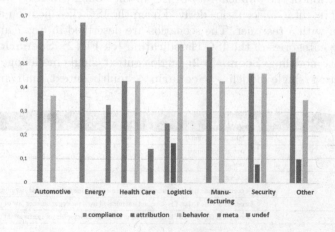

Fig. 5. Usage of ISC examples along domain (normalized, grouped barchart)

compliance and behavior are equally presented, where for health care also some undef cases are present. Logistics, security, and others exhibit also examples for attribution. For logistics the category with highest presence is behavior. Trying an interpretation, automotive and manufacturing show a similar distribution of usage, i.e., compliance and behavior with an emphasis on compliance. For the energy domain, only compliance is present. This can be explained by the sole existence of SLAs in the respective regulatory document which are to be checked rather than to be enforced. For health care and security behavior seems to play an equally important role as compliance because certain regulations are to be enforced or synchronization plays an important role. Security also demands for attribution, e.g., for assignment of roles. Logistics has more demand for behavior (e.g., synchronizing deliveries) and a relatively high demand for attribution.

5 Formalization of ISC Representatives

Preliminaries: As aforementioned, EC is a temporal formalism that can specify properties of dynamic systems in terms of events and the effects of their occurrence on predefined fluents (properties). While fluents are conditions regarding the state of a system, events are occurrence of actions that might change the state of the system and consequently the valuation of the fluents. A typical fluent would indicate that a process variable holds a specific value at a given time. EC mainly defines a set of domain independent predicates, which can be augmented by a domain related predicate. Figure 6 describes a subset of the basic predefined predicates of EC [21]. Specifically, the occurrence of an event e at a time t is represented by the predicate $Happens(e, t)$. This can influence a fluent f by terminating its old valuation that holds until point in time t, and initiating it with a new valuation that holds after t (through the predicates $Terminates$ and $Initiates$ respectively). The reader can refer to [21] for the complete set of domain independent fluents.

As evaluation of the applicability of EC in the context of ISC, we have formalized 4 representative scenarios derived from the ISC classification and implemented them with a reasoner. The scenarios are described in Fig. 7 and refer to the following categories of the ISC classification (cf. Fig. 2): **Scenario 1:** single context/multi modeling; **Scenario 2:** single context/single modeling; **Scenario 3:** multi context/single modeling; **Scenario 4:** multi context/multi modeling.

PREDICATE	MEANING
InitiallyN(f)	f is false at timepoint 0
InitiallyP(f)	f is true at timepoint 0
HoldsAt(f,t)	f is true at time t
Happens(e, t)	e occurs at time t
Initiates(e, f, t)	if e occurs at time t, then f is true and not released from the commonsense law of inertia after t
Terminates(e, f, t)	if e occurs at time t, then f is false and not released from the commonsense law of inertia after t
Release(e, f, t)	if e occurs at time t, then f is released from the commonsense law of inertia after t

Fig. 6. A subset of EC predicates (cf. [21])

SCENARIOS	EVENT CALCULUS	FORMULA
Type: [Single / Multi] "When starting the read-out operation at time t, 99% of all meter readouts should be read out within 6 hours and the read out value does not exceed X."	**EVENTS** GlobalReadoutStart() ReadoutEnd(meter, data) **STATEMENTS** ∀meter, time, counter, value **Happens**(GlobalReadoutStart(), time) => **Terminates**(GlobalReadoutStart(), ReadoutFinished(meter), time)∧ **Initiates**(GlobalReadoutStart(), Value(counter, 0), time) ∧ **Terminates**(GlobalReadoutStart(), Value(counter, value), time) ∧ ¬(value = 0); **FLUENTS** ReadoutFinished(meter) Value(counter, value)	∀time1,time2, meter, data, counter,value **Happens**(GlobalReadoutStart(), time1) ∧ **Happens**(ReadoutEnd(meter, data), time2) ∧ (time2 > time1) ∧ (time2 < time1 + 6) => (data <= X) ∧ **Terminates**(ReadoutEnd(meter, data), Value(counter, value), time2) ∧ **Initiates**(ReadoutEnd(meter, data), Value(counter,value+1), time2) ∧ **Initiates**(ReadoutEnd(meter, data), ReadoutFinished(meter), time2); ∀time, counter, value **Happens**(GlobalReadoutStart(), time) => **HoldsAt**(Value(counter, value), time+6) ∧ (value = n)
Type: [Single / Single] "For 100 (simultaneous) ad hoc readouts of end devices/"activate/deactivate customer interface" readouts/ meter checks, 99 % <= 5 min is required."	**EVENTS** GlobalReadoutStart() ReadoutEnd(meter) **STATEMENTS** **InitiallyP**(Value(counter,0)) **InitiallyP**(Value(violations,0)) ∀meter, time **Happens**(ReadoutStart(meter), time) => **Terminates**(ReadoutStart(meter), ReadoutFinished(meter), time); ∀meter, time2 **Happens**(ReadoutEnd(meter), time2) => ∃time1 **Happens**(ReadoutStart(meter), time1) ∧ (time2 > time1); ∀meter, time1, time2, counter, violations, value1, value2 **Happens**(ReadoutEnd(meter), time2) ∧ **Happens**(ReadoutStart(meter), time1) ∧ (time2-time1 > 5) ∧ **HoldsAt**(Value(counter, value1), time) ∧ (value1 modulo N > 0) => **Initiates**(ReadoutEnd(meter), ReadoutViolation(meter), time2) ∧ **Terminates**(ReadoutEnd(meter),Value(violations, value2),time2) ∧ **Initiates**(ReadoutEnd(meter), Value(violations,value2+1), time2); **FLUENTS** ReadoutFinished(meter) Value(counter, value)	∀time, meter, counter,value1 **Happens**(ReadoutEnd(meter), time) ∧ **HoldsAt**(Value(counter, value1), time) ∧ (value1 modulo N > 0) => **Terminates**(ReadoutEnd(meter), Value(counter, value1), time2) ∧ **Initiates**(ReadoutEnd(meter), Value(counter,value1+1), time2); ∀time1,time2, meter, counter , violations ,value1, value2 **Happens**(ReadoutEnd(meter), time2) ∧ **Happens**(ReadoutStart(meter), time1) ∧ (time2-time1 > 5) ∧ **HoldsAt**(Value(counter, value1), time) ∧ (value modulo N = 0) => HoldsAt(Value(violations,value2), time2)) ∧ (value 2 +1 < (99*N/100)) **Terminates**(ReadoutEnd(meter), Value(violations, value2), time2) ∧ **Initiates**(ReadoutEnd(meter), Value(violations,value2+1), time2); ∀time1,time2, meter, counter , violations ,value1, value2 **Happens**(ReadoutEnd(meter), time2) ∧ **Happens**(ReadoutStart(meter), time1) ∧ (time2-time1 <= 5) ∧ **HoldsAt**(Value(counter, value1), time) ∧ (value modulo N = 0) => HoldsAt(Value(violations,value2), time2)) ∧ (value 2 <(99*N/100)) **Terminates**(ReadoutEnd(meter), Value(violations, value2), time2) ∧ **Initiates**(ReadoutEnd(meter), Value(violations,value2+1), time2);
Type: [Multi / Single] "A user is not allowed to execute more than 100 tasks (of any workflow) in a day."	**EVENTS** TaskStart(user, task) TaskEnd(user, task) **FUNCTIONS** getday(time) : Day **STATEMENTS** ∀user **InitiallyP**(TaskCount(user,0)); ∀user, task, value, time **Happens**(TaskStart(user, task), time) => **HoldsAt**(TaskCount(user, value), time) ∧ (value < n); ∀user, task, value, day, time **Happens**(TaskStart(user, task), time) ∧ **HoldsAt**(LastTaskDay(user, day), time) ∧ (day = getday(time)) => **FLUENTS** TaskCount(user, value) LastTaskDay(user, day)	**Terminates**(TaskStart(user, task), TaskCount(user, value), time) ∧ **Initiates**(TaskStart(user, task), TaskCount(user, value + 1), time); ∀user, task, value, day, time **Happens**(TaskStart(user, task), time) ∧ ¬**HoldsAt**(LastTaskDay(user, day), time) => **Initiates**(TaskStart(user, task), LastTaskDay(user, getday(time), time) ∧ **Terminates**(TaskStart(user, task), TaskCount(user, value), time) ∧ **Initiates**(TaskStart(user, task), TaskCount(user, value + 1), time); ∀user, task, value, day, time **Happens**(TaskStart(user, task), time) ∧ **HoldsAt**(LastTaskDay(user, day), time) ∧ (day < getday(time)) => **Terminates**(TaskStart(user, task), LastTaskDay(user, day), time) ∧ **Initiates**(TaskStart(user, task), LastTaskDay(user, getday(time), time) ∧ **Terminates**(TaskStart(user, task), TaskCount(user, value), time) ∧ **Initiates**(TaskStart(user, task), TaskCount(user, 0), time);
Type: [Multi / Multi] "Print similar jobs together."	**EVENTS** PrintStart(printer, queuetype) PrintEnd(printer, queuetype) **STATEMENTS** ∀printer, queuetype **InitiallyP**(PrintQueue(printer, queuetype, 0)) ∧ **InitiallyN**(Printing(printer, queuetype)); ∀printer, queuetype1, queuetype2, integer, time **Happens**(PrintStart(printer, queuetype1), time) ∧ ¬**HoldsAt**(Printing(printer, queuetype1), time) ∧ ¬**HoldsAt**(Printing(printer, queuetype2), time) ∧ (queuetype1 != queuetype2) => **HoldsAt**(PrintQueue(printer, queuetype1, integer), time) => **Initiates**(PrintStart(printer, queuetype1), Printing(printer, queuetype1), time) ∧ **Initiates**(PrintStart(printer, queuetype1), PrintQueue(printer, queuetype1, integer + 1), time); ∀printer, queuetype1, queuetype2, integer, time **Happens**(PrintStart(printer, queuetype1), time) ∧ ¬**HoldsAt**(Printing(printer, queuetype1), time) ∧ **HoldsAt**(Printing(printer, queuetype2), time) ∧ (queuetype1 != queuetype2) => **HoldsAt**(PrintQueue(printer, queuetype1, integer), time) => **Initiates**(PrintStart(printer, queuetype1), PrintQueue(printer, queuetype1, integer + 1), time); **FLUENTS** Printing(printer, queuetype) PrintQueue(printer, queuetype, integer)	∀printer, queuetype, integer, time **Happens**(PrintStart(printer, queuetype), time) ∧ **HoldsAt**(Printing(printer, queuetype), time) ∧ **HoldsAt**(PrintQueue(printer, queuetype, integer), time) => **Terminates**(PrintStart(printer, queuetype), PrintQueue(printer, queuetype, integer), time) ∧ **Initiates**(PrintStart(printer, queuetype), PrintQueue(printer, queuetype, integer + 1), time); ∀printer, queuetype, integer, time **Happens**(PrintEnd(printer, queuetype), time) ∧ **HoldsAt**(Printing(printer, queuetype), time) ∧ **HoldsAt**(PrintQueue(printer, queuetype, integer), time) => **Initiates**(PrintEnd(printer, queuetype), PrintQueue(printer, queuetype, integer - 1), time); ∀printer, queuetype1, queuetype2, integer, time **Happens**(PrintEnd(printer, queuetype1), time) ∧ **HoldsAt**(Printing(printer, queuetype1), time) ∧ ¬ **HoldsAt**(Printing(printer, queuetype2), time) ∧ (queuetype1 != queuetype2) => **HoldsAt**(PrintQueue(printer, queuetype1, 0), time) ∧ **HoldsAt**(PrintQueue(printer, queuetype2, integer), time) ∧ (integer > 0) => **Terminates**(PrintEnd(printer, queuetype1), Printing(printer, queuetype1), time) ∧ **Initiates**(PrintEnd(printer, queuetype1), Printing(printer, queuetype2), time);

Fig. 7. ISC scenarios based on [26] and formalized using EC

Scenario 1: The scenario is taken from the energy domain and adapted from the engergy domain, and states that when starting the readout operation at time t, 99 % of all meter readouts should be read within 6 h and the readout values not exceeding X. The ISC includes time as well as data and concerns all instances of the same meter readout process (Single/Multi). First, we define the events that have to be caught by the ISC checker, which are the starting action for launching meter readouts and an event related to each meter readout that finished. Note that the readouts of the different meters are simultaneous. If we assume n as the number of all meters, then the checker needs to wait for all instances to complete until 6 h from the start time, in order to check whether the condition of 99 % is met. The status of each meter is represented by the fluent $ReadoutFinish(meter)$, whose value is set to true if the readout is finished and false otherwise. The fluent $Value(counter, value)$ is used to check the value of the counter; i.e., number of finished readouts, after 6 h. Each event of type $ReadoutFinish(meter)$; i.e. Happens(ReadoutEnd(meter, data), time2), increments the value of the counter by terminating the old valuation of the fluent $Value(counter, oldvalue)$ to false; i.e., $Terminates(ReadoutEnd(meter, data), Value(counter, value), time2)$, and initiating the fluent $Value(counter, oldvalue + 1)$ to true:

$$Initiates(ReadoutEnd(meter, data), Value(counter, value + 1), time2).$$

Scenario 2: The second scenario (Single/Single) removes the data constraint from the first one but extends it by limiting the constraint to each 100 finished instances, which requires to reinitialize the counter after each 100 readouts. For each group of 100 finished readouts, 99 % of the instances should have finished within 5 min. This makes the constraint selective, since it selects the first 100 completed readouts first, than applies the deadline constraint. To this endeavor, we have added a violation counter that increments each time a readout takes more than 5 min to finish. We use the modulo function to reinitialize the number of violations after 100 readouts. If the number of violations exceeds 99 %, the last statement will evaluate to false. It is possible to consider another fluent for each meter to express if its readout exceeded 5 min; e.g., $Readoutviolation(meter)$.

Scenario 3 is of type Multi/Single and states that a user is not allowed to execute more than 100 tasks of the same or different workflows in the same day. The ISC clearly spans multiple processes, but here we assume that a user can instantiate each process only once. For the formalization (cf. Fig. 7), we use a predefined function $getday(time)$ that extracts the day as an integer value from the given discrete time. At each new day, the counter is reset allowing the user to execute more tasks for the day. A simple counter is incremented on the execution of a task.

Scenario 4: is of type Multi/Multi and states that similar jobs of different processes are printed together (cf. Fig. 7). The modeling requirements are resource for the printers as well as data for the print job type. Scenario 4 can be interpreted in various ways. For this simple implementation, we have opted to represent a queuing system, incremented as new print jobs of the same type are added. Each job type is added to an associated queue. Only the currently active job type represented in the *Printing*(*printer, queuetype*) fluent are worked on by the limiting resource. Jobs are finished in batches and printing jobs are switched as the queue empties at a *PrintEnd*(*printer, queuetype*) event. To improve the queuing system, an additional time-based counter could be added.

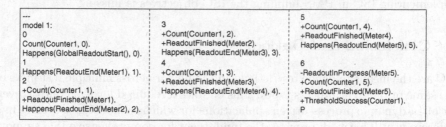

Fig. 8. ISC scenarios checking results with Decreasoner

Implementation. Each of the representative scenarios has been formalized with EC, and implemented and simulated with Decreasoner (Discrete Event Calculus Reasoner)[2]. Decreasoner uses discrete time representation, and transforms the problem into a satisfiability problem (SAT). Since the examples have been taken from the aforementioned domains; e.g., energy or healthcare, where no processes were provided, we have simulated the generation of the events in a separate module. These events are represented as *Happens*(*event*(..), *time*). statements, applicable for each scenario. We specified event occurrences at different times and with different data. This replaces the simulation using a replay of the process models or logs. Checking results of the first scenario are depicted in Fig. 8. In particular, it shows the trace for one model, where it shows the valuations of the fluents as well as events occurrence at different time points. A fluent preceded by a "+" means that the fluent is evaluated to true, while a fluent preceded by "−" means that it is evaluated to false.

6   Related Work

A multitude of approaches for business process compliance exist that can be mainly categorized into design time, e.g., [6,29] and runtime approaches (see, for example, the survey on compliance monitoring approaches in [15]). However, there are only a few approaches that directly deal with ISC. Heinlein [7] addresses ISC at structural level only, i.e., offering means to define constraints on process activities between different instances. Other approaches focus on certain usage scenarios for ISC in Process-Aware Information Systems (PAIS) such as access control [33], batching [25], and queuing [23,30]. These usage scenarios provide

---

[2] http://decreasoner.sourceforge.net.

valuable input for the objectives and evaluation of a comprehensive approach for ISC support in PAIS.

The iUPC approaches [13,17,18,27] provide a comprehensive logical description for constraints in general, i.e., the iUPC framework. Moreover, the design and enactment of ISC in PAIS are preliminarily addressed in [13]. A special kind of ISC usage, i.e., for synchronization is formalized and implemented in [17]. However, a systematic and integrated approach for formalizing, verifying, and implementing ISC in PAIS fulfilling the ISC objectives is missing.

7 Conclusion and Outlook

ISC are the means to define restrictions and behavior across multiple instances of the same or different process types. This enables a required level of control, even for ultra-dynamic process-driven applications for which each instance evolves in a different way. This work provides the fundament for comprehensive ISC support in process-driven applications by an ISC classification and a corresponding ISC formalization based on Event Calculus. The feasibility is evaluated based on a collection of 114 ISC examples from different domains and resources. It could be observed that ISC requirements exist for many domains from manufacturing to health care and can be harvested from different sources such as regulatory documents or project deliverables. Future work will include user requirements in ISC support as well as an integration with existing process engines.

Acknowledgment. This work has been funded by the Vienna Science and Technology Fund (WWTF) through project ICT15-072.

References

1. Abrial, J.R.: Modeling in Event-B: System and Software Engineering, 1st edn. Cambridge University Press, New York (2010)
2. Awad, A., Weidlich, M., Weske, M.: Consistency checking of compliance rules. In: Abramowicz, W., Tolksdorf, R. (eds.) BIS 2010. LNBIP, vol. 47, pp. 106–118. Springer, Heidelberg (2010)
3. Boubaker, S., Gaaloul, W., Graiet, M., Hadj-Alouane, N.B.: Event-b based approach for verifying cloud resource allocation in business process. In: International Conference on Services Computing, pp. 538–545 (2015)
4. Cabanillas, C., Baumgrass, A., Mendling, J., Rogetzer, P., Bellovoda, B.: Towards the enhancement of business process monitoring for complex logistics chains. In: Lohmann, N., Song, M., Wohed, P. (eds.) BPM 2013 Workshops. LNBIP, vol. 171, pp. 305–317. Springer, Heidelberg (2014)
5. Fischer, M.J., Ladner, R.E.: Propositional dynamic logic of regular programs. J. Comput. Syst. Sci. **18**(2), 194–211 (1979)
6. Ghose, A., Koliadis, G.: Auditing business process compliance. In: International Conference on Service-Oriented Computing, pp. 169–180 (2007)
7. Heinlein, C.: Workflow and process synchronization with interaction expressions and graphs. In: International Conference on Data Engineering, pp. 243–252 (2001)

8. ter Hofstede, A.H.M., Ouyang, C., La Rosa, M., Song, L., Wang, J., Polyvyanyy, A.: APQL: a process-model query language. In: Song, M., Wynn, M.T., Liu, J. (eds.) AP-BPM 2013. LNBIP, vol. 159, pp. 23–38. Springer, Heidelberg (2013)

9. Joshi, R., Lamport, L., Matthews, J., Tasiran, S., Tuttle, M., Yu, Y.: Checking cache-coherence protocols with TLA+. Form. Methods Syst. Des. **22**(2), 125–131 (2003)

10. Kaes, G., RinderleMa, S., Vigne, R., Mangler, J.: Flexibility requirements in real-world process scenarios and prototypical realization in the care domain. In: OTM Workshops, pp. 55–64 (2014)

11. Knuplesch, D., Reichert, M., Kumar, A.: Visually monitoring multiple perspectives of business process compliance. In: International Conference on Business Process Management, pp. 263–279 (2015)

12. Kowalski, R., Sergot, M.: A logic-based calculus of events. New Gener. Comput. **4**(1), 67–95

13. Leitner, M., Mangler, J., Rinderle-Ma, S.: Definition and enactment of instance-spanning process constraints. In: International Conference on Web Information Systems Engineering, pp. 652–658 (2012)

14. Lenzi, G.: The modal μ-calculus: a survey. Task Q. **9**(3), 293–316 (2005)

15. Ly, L.T., Maggi, F.M., Montali, M., Rinderle-Ma, S., van der Aalst, W.M.P.: Compliance monitoring in business processes: functionalities, application, and tool-support. Inf. Syst. **54**, 209–234 (2015)

16. Maggi, F.M., Montali, M., Westergaard, M., van der Aalst, W.: Monitoring business constraints with linear temporal logic: an approach based on colored automata. In: Rinderle-Ma, S., Toumani, F., Wolf, K. (eds.) BPM 2011. LNCS, vol. 6896, pp. 132–147. Springer, Heidelberg (2011)

17. Mangler, J., Rinderle-Ma, S.: Rule-based synchronization of process activities. In: Commerce and Enterprise Computing, pp. 121–128 (2011)

18. Mangler, J., Rinderle-Ma, S.: IUPC: identification and unification of process constraints. CoRR abs/1104.3609 (2011). http://arxiv.org/abs/1104.3609

19. Mateescu, R., Monteiro, P.T., Dumas, E., de Jong, H.: Ctrl: extension of CTL with regular expressions and fairness operators to verify genetic regulatory networks. Theoret. Comput. Sci. **412**(26), 2854–2883 (2011)

20. Montali, M., Maggi, F.M., Chesani, F., Mello, P., van der Aalst, W.M.P.: Monitoring business constraints with the event calculus. ACM Trans. Intell. Syst. Technol. **5**(1), 1–30 (2014)

21. Mueller, E.T.: Commonsense Reasoning: An Event Calculus Based Approach. Morgan Kaufmann, Burlington (2006)

22. Peffers, K., Tuunanen, T., Rothenberger, M.A., Chatterjee, S.: A design science research methodology for information systems research. J. Manag. Inf. Syst. **24**(3), 45–77 (2007)

23. Pflug, J., Rinderle-Ma, S.: Dynamic instance queuing in process-aware information systems. In: Symposium on Applied Computing, pp. 1426–1433 (2013)

24. Pnueli, A.: The temporal logic of programs. In: Annual Symposium on Foundations of Computer Science, pp. 46–57 (1977)

25. Pufahl, L., Herzberg, N., Meyer, A., Weske, M.: Flexible batch configuration in business processes based on events. In: Franch, X., Ghose, A.K., Lewis, G.A., Bhiri, S. (eds.) ICSOC 2014. LNCS, vol. 8831, pp. 63–78. Springer, Heidelberg (2014)

26. Rinderle-Ma, S., Gall, M., Fdhila, W., Mangler, J., Indiono, C.: Collecting examples for instance-spanning constraints. Technical report, arXiv:1603.01523 (2016)

27. Rinderle-Ma, S., Mangler, J.: Integration of process constraints from heterogeneous sources in process-aware information systems. In: International Workshop on Enterprise Modelling and Information Systems Architectures, pp. 51–64 (2011)
28. Rouached, M., Fdhila, W., Godart, C.: A semantical framework to engineering WSBPEL processes. Inf. Syst. e-Bus. Manag. **7**(2), 223–250 (2008)
29. Sadiq, W., Governatori, G., Namiri, K.: Modeling control objectives for business process compliance. In: Alonso, G., Dadam, P., Rosemann, M. (eds.) BPM 2007. LNCS, vol. 4714, pp. 149–164. Springer, Heidelberg (2007)
30. Senderovich, A., Weidlich, M., Gal, A., Mandelbaum, A.: Queue mining – predicting delays in service processes. In: Jarke, M., Mylopoulos, J., Quix, C., Rolland, C., Manolopoulos, Y., Mouratidis, H., Horkoff, J. (eds.) CAiSE 2014. LNCS, vol. 8484, pp. 42–57. Springer, Heidelberg (2014)
31. Ulfelder, S.: Building a compliance framework. Compt. World **38**(27), 34–35 (2014)
32. Vardi, M.Y.: Branching vs. linear time: final showdown. In: Margaria, T., Yi, W. (eds.) TACAS 2001. LNCS, vol. 2031, p. 1. Springer, Heidelberg (2001)
33. Warner, J., Atluri, V.: Inter-instance authorization constraints for secure workflow management. In: Symposium on Access Control Models and Technologies, pp. 190–199 (2006)

Value at Risk Within Business Processes: An Automated IT Risk Governance Approach

Oscar González-Rojas[✉] and Sebastian Lesmes

Systems and Computing Engineering Department, School of Engineering,
Universidad de los Andes, Bogotá, Colombia
{o-gonza1,s.lesmes798}@uniandes.edu.co

Abstract. Business processes are core operational assets to control firms' efficiency in value generation. However, the execution and control of business processes is increasingly dependent on Information Technology (IT). Therefore, the risks that arise from relying on IT in business processes must be quantified. This paper proposes the adaptation of the Value at Risk (VaR) financial technique to measure the level of risk within a process portfolio. This is done by quantifying the impact resulting from changes in the performance of IT services. The probability of IT risks is measured daily in order to model the volatility of IT services, especially when they are flexible and changeable. The proposed method enables predicting and estimating the losses of IT risks and their effect on dependent business processes over a time horizon. The incorporation of risk management mechanisms enriches business processes with organizational management capabilities.

Keywords: Risk analysis · Process portfolio · IT assets · Value at risk

1 Introduction

Business processes are core operational assets to control firms' efficiency in value generation. However, they are also carriers of operational risks, particularly when their execution and control is highly dependent on Information Technology (IT). The inherent volatility of IT services generates volatility and continuous changes in the value delivered by business processes. Therefore, IT risks quantification becomes a critical mechanism to manage operational risks [12].

We have identified a gap on tools for monitoring and forecasting the value of business processes when analyzing IT-related operational risks. Seddon et al. [15] discuss different methods used for valuating the impact of IT on business concerns (*e.g.* net present value, probability of project completion). Despite this, we have not found mechanisms that allow quantifying IT risks by considering: (1) their occurrence probability, and (2) the impact of IT failures taking into account different time horizons (*i.e.* daily, n-day) and confidence levels. Moreover, a mechanism to explicitly link IT risks to value delivery within business processes is missing. Suriadi et al. [17] present two main research gaps on Risk-aware Business Process Management (R-BPM): the limited capabilities for risk

© Springer International Publishing Switzerland 2016
M. La Rosa et al. (Eds.): BPM 2016, LNCS 9850, pp. 365–380, 2016.
DOI: 10.1007/978-3-319-45348-4_21

analysis at runtime and post-execution process stages to detect, quantify and manage risk events; and, the need to apply existing risk analysis techniques to perform a richer formal analysis on the impact of process risks.

This paper presents the specialization of the Value at Risk (VaR) financial technique [10] to measure and forecast the level of risk within a process portfolio. The proposed method is named BP-VAR and is composed of three algorithms that navigate among dependencies of process and IT service architectures to quantify risks. The first algorithm quantifies the current value of a particular business process by measuring changes on the performance of the leveraging IT services. The current value of an IT service for a process portfolio is already quantified in terms of the expected incomes of business processes, losses caused by the materialization of threats, service level agreement losses, and income affectation due to service degradation [6]. The second algorithm quantifies the value at risk (expected value) of process and IT assets by modeling the parameters required to quantify the VaR metric (*i.e.* a mathematical distribution, deviations, confidence levels, and historic values). The third algorithm forecasts the losses of IT risks and their effect on dependent business processes over a given time horizon and by considering multiple pessimistic and optimistic risk scenarios. This is done by measuring and analyzing the daily IT risk probability that results from the inherent volatility of IT services. Measuring the value at risk within a process portfolio allows decision makers to define strategies to control risks in business processes.

The organization of this paper is as follows. Section 2 introduces the core terminology, a case study to motivate the need for our business processes valuation approach, and the methodological approach. Section 3 gives a brief overview of the general VAR approach and the proposed specialization within process and IT portfolios. It also describes the proposed algorithms and tool support to quantify value at risk. Section 4 shows the results of applying the proposed BP-VAR method to the presented case study. Section 5 introduces multiple approaches for managing risks on business processes in order to position the research presented in this work. Lastly, conclusions and future work are presented in Sect. 6.

2   Background and Motivation

The main concepts involved in the business processes valuation approach are *process architecture, IT services architecture, risk quantification,* and *IT governance.* An architecture is defined as "the fundamental organization of a system embodied in its components, their relationships to each other, and to the environment" [9]. Therefore, a Business Process Architecture (BPA) involves elements such as value chain activities, process specifications, and tasks. An IT services architecture links software and hardware components, data structures, etc.

We refer to risk quantification (*e.g.* value at risk metric) as the total loss exposure of business processes that is generated by risk events on leveraging IT services. The inherent volatility of IT services can be caused by the materialization of threats, the variable costs on service providers, the degradation of quality attributes, among others. Weill and Ross define IT Governance as "specifying the decision rights and accountability framework to encourage desirable behavior in the use of IT" [19]. IT Risk Governance (ITRG) is a wealth-protecting form that seeks to prevent IT-related disasters or to minimize their consequences for the business [12]. The remainder of this article deals with monitoring and controlling operational mechanisms defined to ensure accountability for the ITRG's commitments on both process and IT assets.

2.1   Requirements for the Valuation of Risks in Business Processes

We use the following case study throughout the paper to present our risk quantification approach. Figure 1 illustrates a simplified process portfolio of a Latin American University. Both business processes (*i.e.* Admission, Course inscription) were selected because they are critical for the organization due to their impact on business strategies, amount of incomes, losses volume, number of affected users, and the amount of dependent business processes. This figure also illustrates a simplified IT services architecture, and the dependencies between the aforementioned business processes and critical IT services supporting them (*i.e.* banner system, database manager, and authentication system).

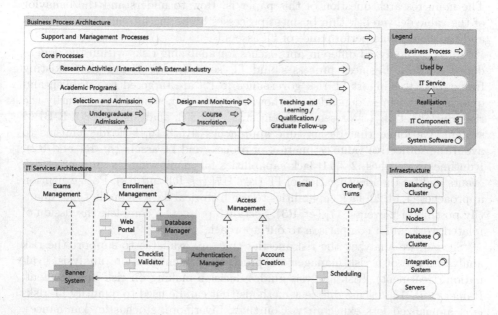

Fig. 1. Dependencies between a process portfolio and IT services.

Both business processes are highly dependent on IT services for their execution and control (*i.e.* 11 application services are supported by 26 software components). The high volatility associated to these services (*e.g.* 10 identified threats with 120 materializations) generates volatility within business processes. We identified the following requirements to valuate business processes.

- *R1. Quantify the risk of a business process.* This requires quantifying the level of financial risk associated with each IT service supporting the business process. Performing this quantification will allow answering common organizational questions: Is the business process able to operate properly without IT services?, Which IT services are critical to the business processes?.
- *R2. Quantify the risk of an IT service for a process portfolio.* This requires measuring the expected incomes of business processes, the probability for IT threats, and the changes on the performance of its quality attributes.
- *R3. Forecast the expected value for business processes.* Besides analyzing the current affectation of IT risks, this requires analyzing historic events to quantify the impact of IT failures depending on different time horizons (*i.e.* daily, n-day) and confidence levels (occurrence probability).

Measuring the value at risk within process portfolios allows decision makers to define strategies to control risks during business process execution.

2.2 Methodology

The main research question of this paper is: How to understand the behavior of the value delivered within business processes by taking into account the risks and the changeable performance of IT assets?.

First, we analyzed different approaches for analyzing risks within the dependency between business processes and IT services. We found that existing frameworks to support IT risk governance [6,12] are targeted to establish and quantify IT-business dependencies, however, they do not intend to quantify the risk. Suriadi et al. [17] present different stages for risk analysis within a R-BPM system. We found that design-time approaches [1,5,8,16] lack mechanisms to avoid the subjective value estimation of process and IT assets (*cf.* R1 and R2). Runtime approaches [2,3,11] lack capabilities for monitoring the impact of risk events and for the identification of IT risks [17] (*cf.* R1 and R2). Post-execution approaches [4,14,20] lack capabilities to use historical data to predict and quantify possible risk events [17] (*cf.* R3). Section 5 presents a complete discussion of related work and a comparison to our approach.

Second, we analyzed the risk metrics that are available to support the risk analysis stage of a risk management process (*cf.* identification, analysis, evaluation, treatment). Risk analysis guides decision-making on risk management. Rainer et al. [13] discuss different methods that can be used to quantify IT risks (*i.e.* annualized loss expectancy, Courtney, Livermore, stochastic dominance). Within the stochastic dominance, the value of an IT asset can be considered as a stochastic event where the impacts of IT risks on the organizational elements that are liable to losses are analyzed over time. We decided to analyze the impacts of IT risks on business processes by considering them the integrator asset of all organizational elements (*e.g.* incomes, customers, costs, products and services, resources).

We selected the VAR financial technique [10] since it allows a stochastic analysis to quantify a daily loss, but also due to its additional characteristics to fulfill the identified requirements for the valuation of business processes (*cf.* Sect. 2). In particular, the VAR specialization (from financial risk within a firm to operational risk within process and IT portfolios) allows organizations (i) to quantify the total value of IT services leveraging a process portfolio (*i.e.* involving the occurrence of multiple event losses), (ii) to model the daily volatility of IT assets as a continuous distribution of independent events to quantify a risk closer to reality and with higher accuracy (*cf.* deterministic probabilities within risk metrics), and (iii) to forecast the value of process and IT assets and to quantify a loss amount within a time horizon higher than one day and with a given confidence level (*i.e.* under a probabilistic distribution). VAR integrates different methods to calculate the potential loss of an asset portfolio (*i.e.* historical, variance, and Monte Carlo).

Risk metrics must reach a consensus regarding the value of analyzed assets and probability estimates. Therefore, we defined concrete algorithms to measure the value of process and IT assets in order to avoid subjectivity for risk-based decision-making (*cf.* Delphi technique), and to forecast the value at risk for these assets (*cf.* Sect. 3). The adopted quantitative technique is used to improve the accuracy of the results of a risk analysis.

The process and IT services architectures for the aforementioned case study were modeled by using an existing method that supports the quantification of dependencies [6]. We took the models that were created for these architectures as the initial dataset to perform our business process valuation approach. We focused on the dependencies that were quantified between critical business processes and IT services. This dataset contains approximately 13500 elements among which are business architecture elements, IT architecture elements, dependencies, and analysis data associated with IT assets (*i.e.* costs, threat materialization, agreement losses, criticallity, degradation of quality attributes). This dataset also contained one year of historic data related to the behavior of critical IT services in terms of performance, integrity, availability, and capacity. Additional historic data of the value of IT services and processes was gathered during six months in order to analyze the results of applying the BP-VAR method.

3 BP-VAR: Value at Risk for Process and IT Portfolios

The VAR (Value At Risk) methodology is explained in general terms as "a measure of the maximum potential change in value of a portfolio of financial instruments with a given probability over a pre-set horizon" [10]. The VAR principle is based on the *Market Risk* concept defined as the uncertainty in the movement of the diverse market variables. The Market Risk brings a high volatility over enterprise incomes, and which may in turn result in significant losses (*Downside Risk*) or winnings (*Upside Risk*) over time. The position of an *enterprise financial asset* is measured through an estimation of its own volatility, based on a series of *discrete events* (*i.e.* the daily stock price).

Figure 2 illustrates the specialization of the main elements of the VAR for process and IT assets. If the asset is in the day t_0 (Date0) with a value v_0 (Current value), the variance on this value will depend on the available information regarding disruptive events. Therefore, the asset value (Expected value) for the day t_{0+1} (Date+1) may vary according to the area under the curve of a normal distribution that is assumed as the confidence level, plus an error ε_{0+1}, with mean v_0 and variance σ^2, making v_0 the most probable value for the next day.

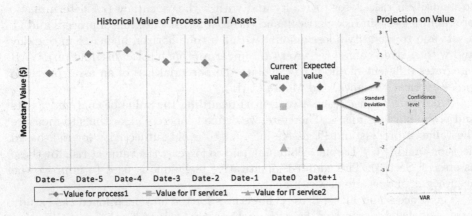

Fig. 2. Value and expected value within business processes.

The following definitions scope the specialization performed to the VAR:

1. An *Operational Asset* is an IT Service and its monetary value, or a business process and its monetary value (*cf.* financial asset).
2. *Operational Risk*, which is increasingly related to IT risk for digital organizations, is the group of external events (*cf.* Market Risk) able to generate volatility over the value of operational assets. For example, an increase in IT operation costs may be originated by exchange rate fluctuations or by a regulation for information protection, changes in IT services may originate from new IT tendencies or lower prices from market suppliers, degradation in IT service provision may be originated by late support from suppliers, and so on. Moreover, the risks that are internal to the organization but external to the business unit that is accountable for the business process are also considered as external events (*e.g.* management decisions on investment and security policies). The uncertainty in the changing environment causes volatility in the enterprise's IT assets, and therefore potential losses (*e.g.* costs, incomes per downtime) or winnings (*e.g.* incomes per efficiency) on business processes over time. Internal and external IT risks are treated as equal since both of them generate volatility on business processes.
3. The *Downside risk* on business processes is analyzed in terms of the expected value of leveraging IT services, whereas the upside is related to the increasing support of IT to business processes. The downside risk on IT services is

analyzed through the levels reached regarding quality attributes, service level agreements, costs, and process incomes. For example, the non-compliance with an agreed service level for an IT service (*e.g.* 0.99 on availability) will degrade the process value in terms of the expected incomes, penalties applied on service level agreements, and financial impacts on threat materialization.

4. *Discrete Events* refer to the continuous (at least daily) monitoring, simulation and storing of the relevant information related to service/process monetary values. The series of discrete events allows modeling the continuous behavior of the operational assets. Therefore, this historical data is used to improve the prediction of expected values.

3.1   Quantification of Current and Expected Value Within Processes

Calculate the Process Value. This algorithm computes the current value of a business process (pV) by adding a portion of the current value of each IT service that supports process execution. We implemented the algorithm as follows:

$$pV = \sum_{i=1}^{n}(sV_i * cr_i) \tag{1}$$

- sV_i represents the value of an IT service i, which is computed by using the algorithm described in [6] in terms of: expected incomes of supported business processes, income affectation due to quality attributes degradation, costs of threat materialization, and losses for penalties on service level agreements. The impact of these variables is dependent on a degradation factor computed by considering the non-compliance with levels agreed for the IT service's quality attributes (*i.e.* availability, capacity, performance, integrity). The value of an IT service is computed for a process portfolio for which dependency information (*e.g.* incomes, risks) was gathered.
- cr_i represents the criticality of service i against process p (a percentage from 0 to 100). This criticality is automatically calculated from the dependencies previously established among architectures. The portion taken of an IT service value is relative to its support and criticality to the entire process portfolio (*cf.* current value in Fig. 2).

Calculate Process VAR. The expected value of a business process ($VAR - p$ in Eq. 2a) is computed from an aggregation of the expected value of leveraging IT services ($VAR - it$ in Eq. 2b). We implemented the algorithm as follows:

$$VAR - p = \sum_{i=1}^{n}(VAR - it_i * cr_i) \tag{2a}$$

$$VAR - it_{v_t} = [N^-1(0, \sigma_{ITs}) * \sigma_{ITs}] * v_t$$

$$\sigma_{ITs} = \sqrt[2]{\sum_{i=1}^{n}(mu_{Qa_i} * Qa_iW * \sigma_{Qa_i}^2)^2} \tag{2b}$$

- cr_i represents the criticality of service i against process p.
- n is the number of services that support process p.
- $VAR - it_i$ represents the projection of values for service i in a time horizon of 1-day (d_{t+1}) from the date d_t and their corresponding probabilities of occurrence (cf. VAR in Fig. 2). This projection is based on the service value v_t in the date d_t, and on a set of historical data for the same service.
- $N^-1(0, \sigma_{ITs})$ represents the inverse function of the normal distribution for the service (ITs), with a given confidence interval. We took standard deviations given by the most statistically relevant confidence intervals (e.g. 99.7%, 99%, 95%, 68%) For example, adding and subtracting n times the standard deviation (e.g. $n = 2,326342$ to calculate the confidence level of 99%) to a normal distribution with mean $(\mu = 0)$ and deviation (σ), will result in the area under the curve representing a 99% probability of occurrence of the future value to fit within the deviation interval (cf. confidence level in Fig. 2).
- σ_{ITs} represents the *weighted deviation* of the service value from the mean value. A comparative factor Qa_iW given by the mean between the mean of the historical service values (μ_{ITs}) and the mean of the historical values of a quality attribute i (μ_{Qa_i}) represents the possible impact of the quality attribute on the service (a value from 0 to 1). This comparative factor is used to calculate the relative deviation $((mu_{Qa_i} * Qa_iW * \sigma^2_{Qa_i}))$ of the service against the selected quality attribute i. $\sigma^2_{Qa_i}$ represents the variance of the normalized historical values of quality attribute i. Finally, the total deviation of the IT service σ_{ITs} must include all the quality attributes related to the service. Since the relative deviations are not linear measures, but dispersion measures over the mean, all the deviations were squared to calculate the variance (a linear measure that can be added normally calculating a total variance). This way of quantifying the deviation is important to understand the deviation of the values that historically generate the IT service's volatility.

The continuous calculation, monitoring and storing of service values (at least daily) is crucial to generate accurate historical data that serves as an input to calculate the expected values for process and IT assets.

Calculate the N-Day VAR. This algorithm is used to extrapolate the expected value to a desired number of days (n) higher than 1. As the weighted deviation used to calculate the 1-day $VAR - p$ is not a linear measure, it cannot be added or multiplied normally, so the algorithm needs to be adjusted as follows:

$$N - Day - VAR = (VAR - p) * \sqrt[2]{n} \tag{3}$$

Nevertheless, the results will always be more accurate whenever n is closer to 1, because a long term estimation does not incorporate the daily updated scores in the values of the quality attributes related to the service.

3.2   Automated Implementation

Currently, all the algorithms and calculations presented in this work are completely implemented within a web application. These algorithms run on existing process and IT service models. Some of the main features provided by the application are the following:

– Service Volatility Simulation: Based on a set of values for each of the quality attributes related to a given service, a simulation can be performed to calculate a new service value based on the changes defined by the user. This can be useful, for example, to simulate service quality scenarios, generate historical data, or document real operational scenarios, while always keeping the service value records updated.
– Projection-Value Analysis: Based on historical data, value-graphs can be generated from different periods of time, summarizing services, processes or a combination of both (service-value graphs discriminated by processes, and process-value graphs discriminated by services). This can be useful, for example, to continue monitoring the performance of IT services, and to assess the convenience or risks associated with a strong dependency between elements (*e.g.* a process that depends a 95 % on 1 particular service).

The following section illustrates these features in terms of the enterprise modeling dataset presented as a case study.

4   Application of the BP-VAR to the Case Study

4.1   Results of Quantifying Risk for Process and IT Assets

This section discusses the results of quantifying risk for the *Undergraduate Admission* process and its dependent IT services (*cf.* case study in Sect. 2.1). We analyzed three types of risk behaviours: a stable scenario, where the process value was constant over time; an upside risk scenario, where the process value increased over time; and a downside risk scenario, where the process value decreased over time. Pessimistic and optimistic estimations are analyzed for each of these scenarios. Having almost a thousand records of quality attributes (*i.e.* availability, integrity, capacity, and performance) for each related IT service (corresponding to 18 months of business operation with almost a daily monitoring), the BP-VAR was calculated with accurate results and projected continuously.

Figure 3a illustrates the evolution of the current value of the Undergraduate Admission process throughout a 15-day time horizon. This process value is discriminated by service (adding up the relative values contributed by the process to all of the services that support it). The stable and pessimistic risk scenarios are also illustrated in the current value for the ninth and twelfth dates. Figure 3b presents the projection of the process value, calculated on a particular date (the ninth day was selected from Fig. 3a), and with a confidence level of 65 %. The area under the curve delimited by the point marked in the graph, represents the probability of occurrence of the process increasing/decreasing its value to a value within the range delimited by this area.

Historic Process Value – Distribution by Service

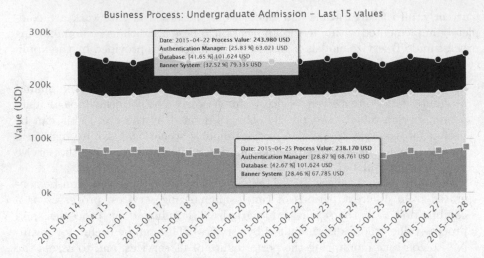

Business Process: Undergraduate Admission – Last 15 values

Date: 2015-04-22 Process Value: 243.980 USD
Authentication Manager: [25.83 %] 63.021 USD
Database: [41.65 %] 101.624 USD
Banner System: [32.52 %] 79.335 USD

Date: 2015-04-25 Process Value: 238.170 USD
Authentication Manager: [28.87 %] 68.761 USD
Database: [42.67 %] 101.624 USD
Banner System: [28.46 %] 67.785 USD

■ Authentication Manager   Database   ■ Banner System

(a) Historic values of a business process discriminated by values of IT services

Value Projection for Process: Undergraduate Admission

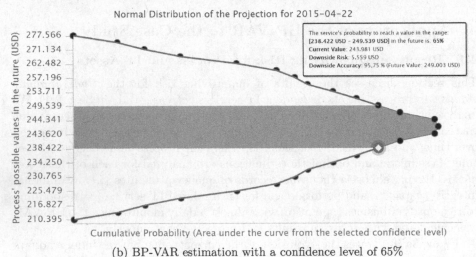

Normal Distribution of the Projection for 2015-04-22

The service's probability to reach a value in the range:
[238.422 USD - 249.539 USD] in the future is. 65%
Current Value: 243.981 USD
Downside Risk: 5.559 USD
Downside Accuracy: 95,75 % (Future Value: 249.003 USD)

Cumulative Probability (Area under the curve from the selected confidence level)

(b) BP-VAR estimation with a confidence level of 65%

Fig. 3. Risk quantification for the undergraduate admission process.

BP-VAR Results for a Stable Scenario. We analyzed a stable scenario of operation taking into account four days, from 2015-04-20 to 2015-04-23. During that short period of time the set of recorded values of the process experienced a low variation, mainly produced by the constant behaviour of the quality attributes levels. Figure 3 illustrates a 1-day VAR projection from 2015-04-22 with a confidence value of 65 %. The VAR was estimated within the range from 238.422 USD to 249.539 USD, whereas the current value stored at 2015-05-23 was 249.003 USD. This results in 95.7 % accuracy for downside risk and 99.7 % accuracy for upside risk estimations. The downside risk for a pessimistic scenario (given by a confidence level of 99 %) is estimated in 243.620 USD (97.8 % accuracy).

BP-VAR Results for a Downside Risk Scenario. We analyzed an operation scenario with a negative variation on process value for two days, from 2015-04-24 to 2015-04-25. During that short period of time the process experienced a great decreasing variation, due to the degradation of a leveraging IT service (Banner System). The variation on the quality attribute capacity (from 89 % to 67 %) generated value affectations in terms of service degradation and costs due to SLA's penalties. The value of the service decreased 25 % of its own value, an abrupt change for a day-to-day evolution. On 2015-04-24, the BP-VAR projected a future value within the range from 249.001 USD to 260.538 USD, with a confidence value of 65 % (an optimistic scenario). However, the current stored value was 238.171 USD, which generates a deviation of 4,54 % from the projection limits. However, the downside risk for a pessimistic scenario (given by a confidence level of 99 %) was estimated in 219.797 USD (92 % of accuracy).

BP-VAR Results for an Upside Risk Scenario. We analyzed an operation scenario with a positive variation on process value for two days, from 2015-04-16 to 2015-04-17. During that period of time, process value experienced a great increasing variation, mainly produced by the stable value of its three underlying services. At this time, the quality attributes of these services were within the expected agreements (*e.g.* the availability of the service increase from 94.9 % to 97.3 %); therefore there was lower affectation through service degradation and the avoidance of SLA's penalties. The services' value increased between 8–10 %, an important non-constant change for a day-to-day evolution. On 2015-04-17, the BP-VAR projected a future value within the range from 237.056 USD to 248.154 USD, with a confidence value of 65 %. The current stored value was 255.895 USD thus generating a deviation of 3,02 % from the limits of the projected value. However, the upside risk for an optimistic scenario with confidence level of 99 % was estimated in 276.133 USD (92.6 % of accuracy).

We observe that in scenarios with a great variation (positive and negative) of values, the BP-VAR accuracy can be compromised for optimistic estimations and close to the limits for pessimistic estimations. Nevertheless, the calculated percentage deviation was not significant at all and, taking into account that abrupt events (like the one treated in this scenario) are not as frequent inside organizations, the model behavior remains within an adequate accuracy level.

N-Day BP-VAR Results for a Process Portfolio. The values of the service *Banner System* evidence a continuous degradation for the first 6-days thus generating volatility for the *Undergraduate Admission* process (*cf.* a decrease of the service value from 83.535 USD to 73.035 USD in Fig. 3a). This service represents a 50 % criticality for this process from the prioritized IT service portfolio (the service value decreased from 167.070 USD to 146.070 USD). Then, we performed an N-Day VAR calculation (with a confidence interval of 80 % and a time-horizon of 6 days from the beginning of the degradation) to compare the results among real and predicted values. The results show that the N-Day VAR behavior is not as expected, given the fact that the real value was stored as 73.035 USD, and the predicted value was calculated as 43.473 USD. The variation from the real value was important (40,47 %), explicitly showing the main failure of this calculation: the need of continuously monitoring and storing the series of values to guarantee that the daily-occurred events affecting the service value are taken into account. However, we highlight the decreasing trend calculated through the N-Day VAR which, although highly accelerated, was properly identified.

4.2   Limitations

To guarantee a higher level of accuracy for risk analysis, the BP-VAR should be replicated for all business processes within the process portfolio and for all critical IT services within the IT portfolio. The BP-VAR quantifies the value at risk for a business process without considering the loss impacts generated by other interconnected business processes. Therefore, further research is required to examine how the VAR flows through a business portfolio. This can be done by integrating the BP-VAR with existing approaches for modeling spillover effects of alignment between business processes [18] and also for quantifying the level at which alignment assets create value [7].

We assumed a 1-day recovery time from the occurrence of an IT risk by considering regular threats to IT assets (*e.g.* low performance), but not catastrophes on them (*e.g.* loss of a datacenter). Accordingly, temporal restrictions can be incorporated to the BP-VAR to support a non lineal analysis. Moreover, since BP-VAR averages regular events, the loss associated with major disasters exceeds the VAR and is not quantified.

5   Related Work

This section discusses related work within the following stages of the lifecycle of an R-BPM system as presented by [17]: design-time analysis, runtime analysis, post-execution analysis. The proposed BP-VAR presents an approach to support risk analysis at these stages and also deals with its automation.

Table 1 summarizes specific gaps for risk analysis at these stages and presents a comparison of related work with the proposed approach.

Risk Analysis at Design-Time. At this stage, business processes are analyzed to identify opportunities for improvement. The authors in [1] use two risk metrics (VAR and Conditional VaR) to quantify risks based on the financial consequences of data error propagation in the information flows and to compute the optimal distribution of control procedures (minimizing risks and costs) along the

Table 1. Specific gaps on R-BPM systems tackled by the BP-VAR approach.

Stage/approaches	Specific gaps	BP-VAR approach
Design-time analysis		
Bai et al. [1] Fill [5] Han et al. [8] Suh and Han [16]	– Lack of a formal estimation of assets' value – Low degree of implementation semantics and tools	– Software implementation of risk quantification (It supports the three stages) – Quantification algorithms to valuate process and IT assets
Runtime analysis		
Caron et al. [2] Kang et al. [11] Conforti et al. [3]	– Limited support to quantify risks – Limited identification of risks not identified in the design stage – Lack of IT risk analysis	– Measurement of process value on IT performance variations – Formalization of process risk semantics – Simulation on disruptive events – Analysis of consequences of risk events – Identification of new risks
Post-execution analysis		
Conforti et al. [4] Wickboldt et al. [20] Sackmann and Syring [14]	– Few support to analyze risks using historical data and with existing risk metrics	– Formal method to quantify risk (VAR) – Continuous distribution of events to model IT assets volatility – Traceability on risk events

process' activities. Despite the formal approach to quantify value, there is a gap for defining and implementing the semantics of the proposed analysis perspectives (processes, control procedures, and risks). The propagation of events can be used to extend the BP-VAR capabilities to analyze process value at the different stages. The author in [5] uses inference rules for the risk annotations defined in process models to create process configurations with an expected return and variance. The authors in [8] present a framework to design and evaluate delegation policies (based on measurable risks) to establish a risk level to assess the hypothetical role delegation at any stage of a workflow system. These annotations and policies can be formalized by the BP-VAR to enrich the capabilities of quantifying value not only with IT risk but also with process-specific risks (*e.g.* participants, control flows). The authors in [16] calculate the annual loss expectancy for information systems with a relative importance on the assets (*e.g.* processes) supporting business functions. The BP-VAR complements this approach of quantifying IT assets by daily monitoring the performance of IT services in terms of their quality attributes. In contrast to other approaches where the value of assets is defined by subjective estimations (*e.g.* Delphi), the selection of IT services to support business processes is guided by current information on service performance and also from past information on service volatility. Additional security-aware processes and IT investments required to protect process and IT assets should be considered for risk analysis.

Risk Analysis at Runtime. At this stage, potential problems that were not identified during design-time can be identified and handled accordingly during the processes' execution. Caron et al. [2] use process mining to evaluate, monitor, and respond to risks by checking the compliance with process execution rules (functional, control flow, organizational, and data). Kang et al. [11] propose a runtime risk monitoring technique to estimate the probability of a process instance to reach a nonexpected termination state. Conforti et al. [3] propose an executable language to annotate process models with risk conditions (organizational, structural, data), which are monitored during process execution to estimate the occurrence probability of risk events and to generate risk alerts. In contrast to the BP-VAR, these approaches do not analyze IT risks, they do not quantify the impact of the risk nor the variance in the value of process and IT assets. Additionally, the BP-VAR defines new constructs to compute the current value of an IT service, the current value of a business process, and the value at risk of IT and process assets. The semantics of these constructs is defined by a set of algorithms that take as input the variations on quality attributes performance for each IT service. The quantification of risks can be improved by combining the runtime information of IT services with runtime information of process instances to evaluate the risks of running process instances. Although the BP-VAR does not respond to risks automatically, the values of these constructs can be graphically analyzed within the software tool through real or simulated risk events (associated with a particular activity through an IT service affectation). Therefore, the process risks and their consequences can be identified in order to plan how to deal with them in the present moment and in the future.

Risk Analysis at Post-execution. At this stage, historical data generated from the execution of the business processes is analyzed to understand their behaviour over time. Conforti et al. [4] present a recommendation system for predicting the most likely progression (with lower risk-level) based on historical logs of process executions (*e.g.* involved resources, task durations). The authors in [20] compare past workflow executions from predefined risk constructs to classify and quantify risks for future executions. Sackmann and Syring [14] model different cause-effect relationships between IT risks and a business process instance within a historical loss database. Changes in these relationships are continuously stored within an adjusted loss database to analyze risks when they are assessed for an automated business process. Our process valuation approach can be used to complement those approaches with a formal risk analysis technique to forecast the value of IT and process assets, based on their historical analysis. This facilitates a precise and unambiguous way of analyzing risk with a continuous distribution of events that impacts process volatility. The use of current and historical information obtained from process-specific systems can enrich the data obtained from the execution of IT services. In contrast to the event-type raw data these approaches use for risk analysis, the BP-VAR uses IT risks (*i.e.* IT threats, degradation on IT services quality attributes, costs, criticality dependencies) to quantify and forecast the value at risk on process and IT assets.

6   Conclusions and Future Work

The incorporation of a mathematical technique that is highly used for financial analysis on firm investments is a novel approach within both, business process management and IT risk governance disciplines. The proposed method contains formal mechanisms and tool support to understand the behavior of the current and expected values delivered within business processes over time and according to the behavior of IT assets. These measures help the process management team to identify specific business processes that are most susceptible to operational risks. Therefore, process managers avoid spending greater time and attention on broad IT issues for the complete process portfolio. A high level of accuracy was obtained when comparing the expected value of assets estimated by the BP-VAR and the actual value obtained in subsequent days.

Generating simulation scenarios on IT services performance shows process management teams where operational problems are likely to occur. Executing these scenarios will graphically demonstrate the value at risk within business process assets. Although the expected value can help process managers to promote contingency plans, they have to be aware that the quantitative analysis cannot define them. The governance of the IT services leveraging these processes is an effective way to reduce risk and to create stable process value.

The BP-VAR process valuation method is expected to be used in combination with enterprise modeling approaches. The main reason for this is the wide amount of process and IT assets, as well as the large amount of analysis information within their dependencies (e.g. (risks, costs, incomes)) that must be modeled before quantifying the value of business processes.

Multiple improvements of the presented approach are considered for further research. First, risk quantification on IT services must compute the loss on service degradation by considering different weights to combine the value deviations generated for each quality attribute (e.g. integrity, availability). We plan to estimate these weights by using a correlation analysis among quality attributes levels and IT service values. Second, additional risk metrics such as the conditional VAR have to be integrated with the BP-VAR to quantify losses that are beyond a certain threshold. Finally, further investigation is required to support the correlation analysis of VAR among assets that have an implicit interconnection between them (process-process, process-IT service, IT service-IT service).

Acknowledgments. The authors would like to thank Fabian Arias who collaborated in the validation of this work.

References

1. Bai, X., Krishnan, R., Padman, R., Wang, H.J.: On risk management with information flows in business processes. Inform. Syst. Res. **24**, 731–749 (2013)
2. Caron, F., Vanthienen, J., Baesens, B.: Comprehensive rule-based compliance checking and risk management with process mining. Decis. Support Syst. **54**(3), 1357–1369 (2013)

3. Conforti, R., Fortino, G., La Rosa, M., ter Hofstede, A.H.M.: History-aware, real-time risk detection in business processes. In: Meersman, R. (ed.) OTM 2011, Part I. LNCS, vol. 7044, pp. 100–118. Springer, Heidelberg (2011)
4. Conforti, R., de Leoni, M., Rosa, M.L., van der Aalst, W.M., ter Hofstede, A.H.: A recommendation system for predicting risks across multiple business process instances. Decis. Support Syst. **69**, 1–19 (2015)
5. Fill, H.G.: An approach for analyzing the effects of risks on business processes using semantic annotations. In: ECIS 2012 Proceedings, p. Paper 111. ESADE/AIS, Barcelona (2012)
6. González Rojas, O.: Governing IT services for quantifying business impact. In: Matulevičius, R., Dumas, M. (eds.) BIR 2015. LNBIP, vol. 229, pp. 97–112. Springer, Heidelberg (2015)
7. González-Rojas, O., Ochoa-Venegas, L., Molina-León, G.: Information security governance: valuation of dependencies between IT solution architectures. In: Repa, V., Bruckner, T. (eds.) BIR 2016. LNBIP, vol. 261. Springer, Heidelberg (2016, in Press)
8. Han, W., Ni, Q., Chen, H.: Apply measurable risk to strengthen security of a role-based delegation supporting workflow system. In: IEEE International Symposium on POLICY 2009, pp. 45–52. IEEE, London (2009)
9. IEEE Architecture Working Group: Std 1471-2000. Recommended practice for architectural description of software-intensive systems. Technical report, IEEE (2000)
10. J.P. Morgan and Reuters: RiskMetrics - technical document. Technical report, 4th edn. JP Morgan and Reuters, New York, December 1996
11. Kang, B., Cho, N.W., Kang, S.H.: Real-time risk measurement for business activity monitoring (BAM). Int. J. Innov. Comput. I **5**(11), 3647–3657 (2009)
12. Parent, M., Reich, B.H.: Governing information technology risk. Calif. Manag. Rev. **51**(3), 134–152 (2009)
13. Rainer Jr., R.K., Snyder, C.A., Carr, H.H.: Risk analysis for information technology. J. Manag. Inform. Syst. **8**(1), 129–147 (1991)
14. Sackmann, S., Syring, A.: Adapted loss database - a new approach to assess IT risk in automated business processes. In: Santana, M., Luftman, J.N., Vinze, A.S. (eds.) AMCIS 2010 Proceedings, p. Paper 374. AIS, Lima (2010)
15. Seddon, P.B., Graeser, V., Willcocks, L.P.: Measuring organizational IS effectiveness: an overview and update of senior management perspectives. SIGMIS Database **33**(2), 11–28 (2002)
16. Suh, B., Han, I.: The IS risk analysis based on a business model. Inf. Manag. **41**(2), 149–158 (2003)
17. Suriadi, S., Wei, B., Winkelmann, A., ter Hofstede, A., Adams, M., Conforti, R., Fidge, C., La Rosa, M., Ouyang, C., Pika, A., Rosemann, M., Wynn, M.: Current research in risk-aware business process management-overview, comparison, and gap analysis. Commun. ACM **34**(1), 933–984 (2014)
18. Tallon, P.P.: Value chain linkages and the spillover effects of strategic information technology alignment: a process-level view. J. Manag. Inf. Syst. **28**(3), 9–44 (2011)
19. Weill, P., Ross, J.: IT Governance: How Top Performers Manage IT Decision Rights for Superior Results. Harvard Business School Press, Boston (2004)
20. Wickboldt, J.A., Bianchin, L.A., Lunardi, R.C., Granville, L.Z., Gaspary, L.P., Bartolini, C.: A framework for risk assessment based on analysis of historical information of workflow execution in IT systems. Comput. Netw. **55**(13), 2954–2975 (2011)

Prediction

PRISM – A Predictive Risk Monitoring Approach for Business Processes

Raffaele Conforti[1], Sven Fink[2], Jonas Manderscheid[2(✉)],
and Maximilian Röglinger[3]

[1] Queensland University of Technology, Brisbane, Australia
raffaele.conforti@qut.edu.au
[2] FIM Research Center, University of Augsburg, Augsburg, Germany
sven.fink@student.uni-augsburg.de,
jonas.manderscheid@fim-rc.de
[3] FIM Research Center, University of Bayreuth, Bayreuth, Germany
maximilian.roeglinger@fim-rc.de

Abstract. Nowadays, organizations face severe operational risks when executing their business processes. Some reasons are the ever more complex and dynamic business environment as well as the organic nature of business processes. Taking a risk perspective on the business process management (BPM) lifecycle has thus been recognized as an essential research stream. Despite profound knowledge on risk-aware BPM with a focus on process design, existing approaches for real-time risk monitoring treat instances as isolated when detecting risks. They do not propagate risk information to other instances in order to support early risk detection. To address this gap, we propose an approach for predictive risk monitoring (PRISM). This approach automatically propagates risk information, which has been detected via risk sensors, across similar running instances of the same process in real-time. We demonstrate PRISM's capability of predictive risk monitoring by applying it in the context of a real-world scenario.

Keywords: Business process management · Risk-aware BPM · Risk propagation · Predictive risk monitoring

1 Introduction

The pressing need for organizations to increase productivity, to achieve operational excellence, and to save costs has been and still is one of the driving forces for the adoption of business process management (BPM) methods and technologies [1]. Due to an increasingly complex and dynamic business environment as well as the organic nature of processes, organizations are exposed to severe operational risks (e.g., the violation of the four-eye principle or a payment default of a customer engaged in multiple instances) when executing their business processes [2, 3].

In the attempt of solving this problem, industry and academia have proposed several solutions. From an industry perspective, there are legislative initiatives such as Basel II [4] and Sarbanes-Oxley Act [5]. In the academic world, previous research

© Springer International Publishing Switzerland 2016
M. La Rosa et al. (Eds.): BPM 2016, LNCS 9850, pp. 383–400, 2016.
DOI: 10.1007/978-3-319-45348-4_22

recognized the importance of incorporating a risk perspective in all activities of the BPM lifecycle [3, 6, 7]. A detailed analysis of research conducted in the area of risk-aware BPM is presented by Suriadi et al. [8]. Accordingly, the effort of the academic world shows a bias toward the process design phase of the BPM lifecycle [9]. Beyond risk-aware process design, there are also works that take a risk perspective when valuating and comparing process models [10, 11]. Therefore, Suriadi et al. [8] particularly highlight the need for research on risk-informed process execution. This need is supported by Recker and Mendling [12], who point to a lack of research on real-time process monitoring and controlling. Although recent studies attempt to address this gap regarding risk-informed process execution and monitoring via approaches for real-time risk or deviance monitoring [13, 14], risk mitigation [15], and the avoidance of risk during runtime [16], the timely detection of process risks still is an open challenge.

Current approaches to real-time risk detection monitor running instances via sensors [13]. Such sensors operate at the level of process instances, using information about running instances and log data from completed process instances. Although risk eventuation in process instances is not necessarily affected by other running instances, external factors (e.g., customer behavior, characteristics of process inputs) play an influential role for the eventuation of risks. Due to such factors, risk monitoring at process instance-level may not be sufficient when instances are considered in isolation [17]. To the best of our knowledge, there are no approaches that share risk information across multiple process instances for the predictive monitoring and early detection of risks.

Against this background, we propose an approach for predictive risk monitoring (PRISM), which builds on and extends the work of Conforti et al. [13]. The PRISM approach aims at supporting early risk detection by automatically propagating risk information, which has been detected by sensors, across similar running instances of the same process in real-time. To do so, the PRISM approach uses a similarity-weighted process instance graph (PING) and a risk propagation algorithm.

The remainder of this paper is organized as follows: Sect. 2 discusses related work in the areas of risk-aware BPM and process similarity. Section 3 presents the PRISM approach, elaborating on the PING and the risk propagation algorithm. Section 4 illustrates PRISM's effectiveness when used in the context of a real-life scenario. Section 5 concludes the paper, discusses limitations and future work.

2 Theoretical Background and Preliminaries

In this section, we compile theoretical background on risk-aware BPM and on previous work related to process similarity.

2.1 Risk-Aware Business Process Management

Risk management techniques found their way into many different fields. At the strategic level, risk management standards prescribe general guidelines for identifying, analyzing, evaluating, and handling risks [18, 19]. Though being of great importance, such guidelines are mostly meta-models, sketchy, and fail to provide specific guidance on how to operationalize risk management strategies in business processes. Conforti et al. [13, 15, 16] thus proposed to enrich the traditional BPM lifecycle [9] with elements of risk management. This enables the four phases of the BPM lifecycle, i.e., *process design*, *process implementation*, *process enactment*, and *process analysis*, to become risk-aware. The resulting risk-aware BPM lifecycle is shown in Fig. 1.

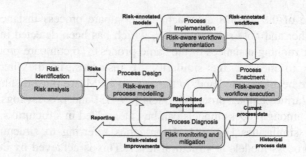

Fig. 1. Risk-aware BPM lifecycle [16]

The risk-aware BPM lifecycle starts with the *risk identification* phase. In this phase, risks that may eventuate during the execution of a business process are identified. The output of this phase is a set of risks, expressed as risk conditions, which are then mapped to process model-specific aspects in the *process design* phase. This mapping results in risk-annotated process models. In the *process implementation* phase, a more detailed assignment of risks and faults to specific aspects of a process model, e.g., the content of data variables and resource states, is conducted. A risk-aware process engine then executes this process model in the *process enactment* phase. Finally, based on the input of current and historical process data, risk conditions are analyzed in the *process diagnosis* phase, leading to risk-related improvements.

Considering the risk-aware BPM lifecycle, most approaches proposed for risk-aware BPM fall into the design phase. Among these approaches, we can distinguish between approaches that focus on the analysis and modeling of process risks via new risk constructs [3, 20–22] or based on the use of existing risk analysis methods [6, 23–25]. We refer to the work of Suriadi et al. [8] for a comprehensive discussion. Regarding the process diagnosis phase, we find the works of Pika et al. [26] and Suriadi et al. [27], who analyze process data to retrieve risk information. Pika et al. [26] propose an approach that uses statistical analysis to predict overtime risks, whereas Suriadi et al. [27] use classification algorithms to conduct a root cause analysis of risks.

In light of the need for research on risk-informed process execution/enactment [8], it is important to focus on risks that can be identified within the boundaries of a process. Thereby, a process risk is the chance of something happening that will impact the objectives of a process and is measured in terms of likelihood and consequence [28]. The work of Conforti et al. [13] focuses on real-time risk detection. The approach, which is based on sensors, detects risks via real-time monitoring of risk conditions.

Though being capable of monitoring a process instance using current and historical information, sensors consider process instances as independent. This limits the capabilities of the approach since it is unable to detect the eventuation of process risks based on information about process risks that eventuate in other instances. Nonetheless, it offers a good starting point for addressing the problem.

2.2 Similarity Measures in BPM

For the purpose of the PRISM approach, we compare process instances in order to determine whether and how strongly a risk, which has been detected in one instance, influences other running instances of the same process. To compare process instances, it is necessary to measure the similarity of instances. In the literature, several approaches have been proposed and, in the area of BPM, we must distinguish between measuring similarities among process models [29–33] and process logs [34].

Similarities among process models can be categorized in structural similarities [29] and behavioral similarities [30, 31]. Approaches referring to structural similarities compare two process models at structural level. This is achieved by determining the number of structural changes required (e.g., flows, gateways, and tasks) for two process models to match. Approaches that deal with the behavioral similarity of process models require more advanced techniques. Two process models are compared regarding the set of possible executions that can be generated using these models. A similar approach is used by similarity measurement that operates on process logs [35], while in this case the set of possible executions is already contained in the log. For these forms of similarity, two characteristics need to be kept in mind: first, instances belonging to the same process model make structural similarity pointless and, second, multiple completed instances are required in order to reasonably compare logs.

As an approach for measuring the similarity of process logs, Song et al. [34] rely on trace profiles. Trace profiles are vectors, containing several items that describe the trace from a specific perspective (e.g., case attributes or involved tasks). Trace profiles build on historical data from process logs in order to obtain their information. In light of their multi-perspective vectorial representation, trace profiles can be easily compared using string similarity techniques [36, 37]. Song et al. [34] show how a similarity measure based on trace profiles enhances discovering process models. This is why the PRISM approach builds on the work of Song et al. [34].

3 The Predictive Risk Monitoring Approach

We now present the PRISM approach that builds on and extends the work of Conforti et al. [13]. The approach encompasses a similarity-weighted PING and a risk propagation algorithm. For the sake of completeness, we first sketch the approach of Conforti et al. [13].

3.1   The Sensor-Based Approach to Risk Detection

In the sensor-based approach of Conforti et al. [13], a fault is an undesired state of a process (e.g., a process violating a service level agreement). In order to minimize the negative effects of faults, it is important to detect the risk of a fault as early as possible. Conforti et al. [13] achieve this through the use of digital risk sensors. However, the approach would also be suitable in the case of physical sensors [38].

Sensors are defined at design time on top of an executable process model. Each sensor is associated with a risk condition that captures the situation in which the risk related to a distinct fault may occur. A risk condition combines a risk likelihood (henceforth referred to as risk $r_i(t)$ in instance i at a given point in time t), i.e., the probability of the fault to occur, and a threshold TRE, i.e., a risk value that an organization is willing to tolerate. As process models can contain several sensors referring to different faults with individual risk conditions, each sensor must be treated separately.

At execution time, when a new instance is created, the sensors associated with the process model are enabled. The sensors monitor the process instance by evaluating the associated risk condition. A risk condition is evaluated either based on a given sampling rate or on the occurrence of a specific event by looking into historical and current process execution data. Finally, whenever a risk is detected the system automatically triggers a notification to the process administrator, who will act accordingly.

The PRISM approach builds on top of and extends the work of Conforti et al. [13]. It is based on the idea that similar process instances feature a similar risk exposure. We thus assume that identical instances have the same risk exposure. As other approaches (e.g., case-based reasoning or adaptive case management) rely on similarity measures to determine similar instances [39, 40], we adopted similarity as a proxy to estimate the risk exposure of other currently running instances. On this assumption, we use the sensor-based detection of a risk in a distinct instance as a trigger for checking whether the risk is likely to eventuate in similar process instances, too. This is achieved by propagating information about the detected risk from the process instance for which the risk has been detected to other currently running instances. To determine to which instances a detected risk should be propagated and how strongly the related effect should be, the PRISM approach compares different instances regarding their similarity. The risk propagation triggers a manual evaluation of the corresponding sensor from the receiving instance, taking the propagated risk as well as the similarity between the source and the receiving instance as input for evaluating the risk condition.

Figure 2 illustrates the idea behind the PRISM approach for two running instances using a single sensor as example. In this example, the sensor is monitoring an *unfulfillment risk*. This sensor relates to a situation where a process instance executes a distinct task too many times, with the related risk condition checking for loops. We assume that both instances here have a high risk exposure and are similar. In the following, we refer to instance 1 as source. Accordingly, the source's unfulfillment risk sensor detects a risk that exceeds the given threshold at time $t = 2$. This calculation is based on available historical data (i.e., already executed log traces), enabling to analyze past executions of the process in focus. In Fig. 2, the bold dashed line from the source to instance 2 visualizes the risk propagation, triggered by the detection of the unfulfillment risk. The propagation leads to rechecking the risk conditions in instance 2. In our example, the unfulfillment risk is detected in instance 2 triggered by the risk propagation. PRISM therefore enables detecting the unfulfillment risk in instance 2 earlier, i.e., in $t = 2$ instead of $t = 3$, than the sensors of instance 2 would have done without risk propagation.

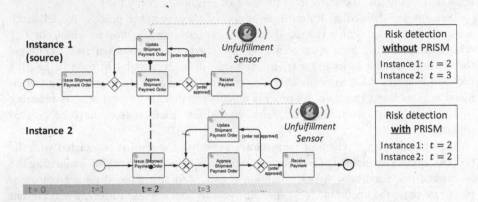

Fig. 2. Example of time advantage through the PRISM approach with two instances

As there usually is more than one running instance of the same process, the PRISM approach propagates risk information among these instances to enable early risk detection. In order to perform the risk propagation, the PRISM approach uses a similarity-weighted PING and a risk propagation algorithm whenever a sensor detects a risk. We introduce both concepts below.

3.2   Similarity-Weighted Process Instance Graph

To propagate risk information among running instances of a process, we rely on a similarity-weighted PING. The PING virtually links instances using their similarity as edge weights. The PING can be interpreted as a temporal snapshot of all process instances, which we use to determine whether and how strongly a risk detected in the source instance influences other instances of the same process.

Formally, the PING is a graph $PING = (V, E)$, where $V = (1, \ldots, n)$ is the index set of all running instances with index 1 representing the source, i.e., the instance that triggers the creation of the PING. Further, $E(t) \in \mathbb{R}^{n \times n}$ is the triangular adjacency matrix that captures the similarity $s_{i,j}(t)$ of two instances at a distinct point in time. The adjacency matrix relates to a distinct point in time as the similarity of instances may change over time when their execution is progressing. Each time a PING is created, the process instances receive a new index. As running instances terminate and new instances begin, $E(t)$'s dimensionality changes constantly. By assigning new indexes, we ensure that, for a distinct point in time, only running instances are considered and that no unnecessarily large data structures must be handled in real-time.

$$E(t) = \begin{pmatrix} s_{1,1}(t) & \cdots & s_{1,n}(t) \\ \vdots & \ddots & \vdots \\ s_{n,1}(t) & \cdots & s_{n,n}(t) \end{pmatrix}, s_{i,j}(t) \in [0,1] \tag{1}$$

The adjacency matrix $E(t)$ is symmetric except for those elements that contain the source, i.e., $s_{i,j}(t) = s_{j,i}(t) \forall i,j \in V \backslash \{1\}$. The source instance only propagates risk information, i.e., $s_{i,1}(t) = 0$. The source needs not receive any risk information as one of its sensors has initially detected the risk that triggered the creation of the PING. For the same reason, all other instances do not propagate risk information to themselves, i.e., $s_{i,i}(t) = 0$. In all other cases, $s_{i,j} = 0$ if two instances are absolutely different and $s_{i,j} = 1$ if the instances are perfectly equal according the similarity measure.

In the PRISM approach, we calculate the similarity of instances in line with Song et al. [34], i.e., based on trace profiles (Sect. 2.2). We build trace profiles based on explicit information (e.g., names of tasks) and on derived information (e.g., number of events in a trace). Each instance can be characterized by multiple profiles. A profile is an n-dimensional vector where n indicates the number of items extracted from a log. A profile $c_{p,i}$ refers to a vector $\langle a_{i,1}, a_{i,2}, \ldots, a_{i,n} \rangle$, where $a_{i,k}$ denotes the amount of item k's appearances in instance i for profile p. For each profile p, the similarity of two instances $s_{p,i,j}(t)$ is calculated as shown in Eq. (2).

$$s_{p,i,j}(t) = 1 - \frac{d(c_{p,i}(t), c_{p,j}(t)) - d_{\min}}{d_{\max}(t) - d_{\min}} = 1 - \frac{\sqrt{\sum_{k=1}^{n} |a_{i,k}(t) - a_{j,k}(t)|^2}}{\max_{j \in V} \left\{ \sqrt{\sum_{k=1}^{n} |a_{i,k}(t) - a_{j,k}(t)|^2} \right\}} \tag{2}$$

To determine the similarity of instances i and j for profile p, the respective normalized distance is subtracted from 1. We assume $d_{\min}$ to be 0 as instances can be identical. As an increasing value is needed to capture more similarity, we subtract the normalized distance from 1. In order to calculate the distance, it is possible to apply different distance measures (e.g., Euclidean, Hamming, or Jaccard) as shown by Song et al. [34]. We decided in favour of the Euclidean distance, which led to good results when used for trace clustering [34]. As the focus of this paper is not on the identification of the best similarity measures, other distance could have been used as well. We will get back to this issue in the critical reflection. To normalize the distance between two instances, an operation necessary to compare the distance between any pair of instances, we divide the distance of the respective trace vectors by the maximum distance available.

To derive a single value that represents the similarity of two instances across all trace profiles in focus, we determine an overall similarity by calculating the weighted average of all profiles that relate to the involved instances. We thus integrate the similarity of all profiles based on their relative importance for the estimation of risks. In Eq. (3), w_p represent the weights of all profiles p with $\sum_{p \in P} w_p = 1$.

$$s_{i,j}(t) = \sum_{p \in P} w_p \cdot s_{p,i,j}(t) \qquad (3)$$

3.3   Risk Propagation Algorithm

In case a sensor in a distinct instance detects a risk (i.e., the risk condition evaluates to true because the risk probability exceeds the threshold), the risk propagation algorithm cascades this information across all currently running instances. To do so, the risk propagation algorithm builds on the PING and estimates the eventuation probability (i.e., the probability that the risk condition of the other instances also evaluates to true) of the detected risk in other instances using similarities, inspired by the signal/collect programming model [41]. The risk propagation algorithm follows a two-phase approach, i.e., initial propagation and re-propagation. If a propagation is successful, we refer to the state of the respective instance as "at risk."

In the initial propagation phase, the source propagates the detected risk (i.e., a risk likelihood that exceeds a given threshold) to all other instances (see black solid lines in Fig. 3a). The propagation accounts for the source's similarity with other running instances. Acting on the assumption of a proportional relationship between similarity and risk exposure, we estimate the risk of a receiving instance $r_j(t)$ at a distinct point in time according to Eq. (4).

$$r_j(t) = \begin{cases} s_{i,j}(t) \cdot r_i(t) & \text{if } s_{i,j}(t) \cdot r_i(t) > TRE \\ 0 & \text{else} \end{cases} \qquad (4)$$

If the risk multiplied with the similarity of the propagating instance (i.e., the source instance in the initial propagation phase) and the receiving instance exceeds the threshold pre-defined for a sensor, the respective product is assigned to the receiving instance in terms of a signal/collect procedure. If the threshold is not exceeded, the product is 0. As instances typically are different and thus do not feature the same risk exposure, not all instances receive the same propagated risk. As we look at pairwise similarity, we do not cumulate received risk values in an instance during propagation, as this would result in an overestimation. In Figs. 3 and 4, the results of the initial propagation are written into the table below the graph (even if the threshold is not exceeded) to illustrate the risk received in an instance. Figure 3a shows the situation when the source detects risk and propagates the risk value to all other running instances (see black solid lines). As not for all instances the propagated risk (i.e., similarity times risk of the source) exceeds the threshold, only instances 3 and 5 reach the "at risk" state (Fig. 3b).

For all instances whose product of risk and similarity exceeds the sensor's threshold, the iterative re-propagation phase is triggered (Fig. 4). This phase and the iterative character are necessary as a process instance can get into the "at risk" state by receiving risk transitively propagated from the source (e.g., the similarity between the

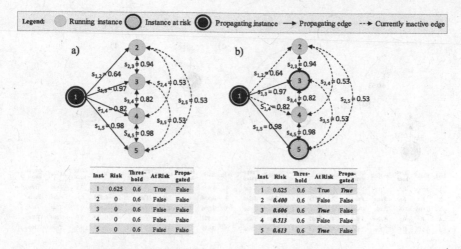

Fig. 3. Visualization of the initial propagation phase

source and instance 4 is rather low, but much higher between instances 5 and 4). As the risk is getting smaller with each re-propagation (i.e., $s_{ij} < 1$), we account for "paths" from the source to other nodes with a maximum length of 2. Using longer "paths" for risk propagation than assumed is possible and provides experts with the ability to customize the PRISM approach to their needs.

In the re-propagation phase, all instances that have been classified as "at risk" in the initial propagation or a previous re-propagation are sorted according to their risk exposure. We start with the instance that has the highest risk exposure. From the initial propagation (Fig. 3) to the re-propagation (Fig. 4), we can see that instance 5 with the highest received risk is considered first. The instance's received risk is used for the first re-propagation to all instances that have not yet been classified as "at risk". As, for example, the re-propagation from instance 5 to 4 exceeds the threshold of instance 4, instance 4 is classified as "at risk" after the re-propagation (Fig. 4d). The sorting of the instances "at risk" is not mandatory. However, starting with the highest risk, the algorithm terminates faster. All instances that went into the "at risk" state due to the current re-propagation are then added to the set of instances to be considered in the next re-propagation (e.g., instance 4 after the re-propagation of instance 5). Instances that already re-propagated need not be considered further (e.g., instance 5). This iterative procedure continues until there are no more "at risk" instances that have not yet re-propagated or until the specified maximum number of re-propagations is reached.

Although, in Fig. 4, instance 4 is added to the relevant instances for re-propagation, instance 3 still has the highest risk of the remaining "at risk" instances. Thus, the algorithm starts the second re-propagation with instance 3 (Fig. 4e). As no further instance exceeds the threshold based on the re-propagation, the algorithm terminates after the re-propagation of instance 4 (Fig. 4f). As result, the PRISM approach classifies four out of five instances as "at risk".

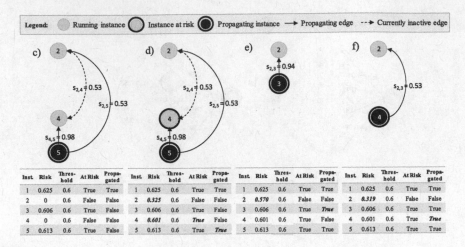

Fig. 4. Visualization of the re-propagation phase

Inst.	Risk	Threshold	At Risk	Propagated
1	0.625	0.6	True	True
2	0	0.6	False	False
3	0.606	0.6	True	False
4	0	0.6	False	False
5	0.613	0.6	True	False

Inst.	Risk	Threshold	At Risk	Propagated
1	0.625	0.6	True	True
2	0.325	0.6	False	False
3	0.606	0.6	True	False
4	0.601	0.6	True	False
5	0.613	0.6	True	True

Inst.	Risk	Threshold	At Risk	Propagated
1	0.625	0.6	True	True
2	0.570	0.6	False	False
3	0.606	0.6	True	True
4	0.601	0.6	True	False
5	0.613	0.6	True	True

Inst.	Risk	Threshold	At Risk	Propagated
1	0.625	0.6	True	True
2	0.319	0.6	False	False
3	0.606	0.6	True	True
4	0.601	0.6	True	True
5	0.613	0.6	True	True

4 Demonstration

To demonstrate its effectiveness, we apply the PRISM approach to a process for a personal loan or overdraft application in the context of a real-world scenario from a Dutch financial institute. The corresponding log data was released as part of the BPI Challenge held in conjunction with the 8th International Workshop on Business Process Intelligence 2012 [42]. As a prerequisite for our demonstration, we implemented the PRISM approach as an extension of the workflow management system Camunda.[1] Below, we first present the process model and data from process execution. After that, we outline how we operationalized the sensors and similarity measures. Finally, we compare the results of the PRISM approach with the sensor-based approach by Conforti et al. [13].

4.1 Demonstration Design and Data Set

The application process for a personal loan or overdraft (Fig. 5) starts with the submission of an application. The financial institute may already decline the application at this point in time, a decision that will bring the process to a quick end. The financial institute may pre-accept the application for further processing. In this case, one of the financial institute's employees first adds missing information until the application is completed. The employee then selects and creates an offer, sends the offer to the customer, and adds this information to the application. After that, the employee calls the customer periodically. After the customer made her decision, the application will be finally assessed while adding still missing information.

---

[1] http://www.camunda.com/. The authors are happy to provide the source code upon request.

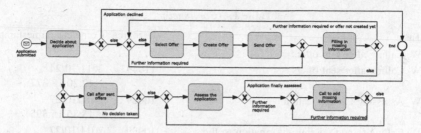

Fig. 5. Filtered process model of the personal loan and overdraft application process

The corresponding log contains traces with events that cover a period of six months, i.e., from October 2011 to March 2012. Each line of the log corresponds to an executed task that relates to a distinct instance. The log also includes the resource that executed the task, the timestamp of task completion as well as the loan or overdraft amount requested by the customer. As an example, Table 1 shows the trace of the process instance with the CaseID 175585 with a requested amount of 22,000 EUR.

To improve its quality, we pre-processed the log via a two-phase filtering approach. In the first phase, we removed infrequent labels, applying the "Filter Log using Simple Heuristics" plugin of ProM with a boundary of 90 %. In the second phase, we removed infrequent behavior from the log based on the approach by Conforti et al. [43]. The pre-processed log contained 11 unique tasks and 9,350 instances resulting in 91,500 events. Having pre-processed the log, we extracted the process model used for our demonstration (Fig. 5).

Table 1. Log trace for CaseID 175585

#	Task	Resource	Complete_Timestamp
1	START	artificial	2011/10/08 14:50:02.113
2	A_SUBMITTED	112	2011/10/08 14:50:02.113
3	A_PARTLYSUBMITTED	112	2011/10/08 14:50:02.243
4	A_PREACCEPTED	112	2011/10/08 14:50:42.639
5	O_SELECTED	11000	2011/10/08 14:56:37.300
6	O_CREATED	11000	2011/10/08 14:56:39.224
7	O_SENT	11000	2011/10/08 14:56:39.271
8	W_Filling in information for the application	11000	2011/10/08 14:56:41.605
9	W_Calling after sent offers	11000	2011/10/08 14:57:16.346

(Continued)

Table 1. (*Continued*)

#	Task	Resource	Complete_Timestamp
...	W_Calling after sent offers	...	...
18	W_Calling after sent offers	11049	2011/10/24 12:20:18.377
19	W_Assessing the application	10629	2011/10/27 13:35:15.895
20	W_Calling to add missing information to the application	10939	2011/10/27 18:42:05.333
21	W_Assessing the application	10629	2011/10/28 08:38:08.642
22	END	Artificial	2011/10/28 08:38:08.643

In our demonstration, we measured how often the PRISM approach was capable of predicting the eventuation of a risk measured by a sensor. To substantiate the advantage gained by applying PRISM, we determined how long before the risk's eventuation the prediction was made. Additionally, we measured how often PRISM was unable to predict a risk detected by a sensor or produced an erroneous prediction where no risk has been detected before. To perform the demonstration and to ensure its replicability, we replayed the execution of process instances according to the log data.

4.2   Operationalization for PRISM Demonstration

Before starting the replay, we implemented one sensor in the application process. This sensor monitors the *unfulfillment risk* as introduced in Conforti et al. [13]. This risk occurs if an instance executes a task too often, a situation that occurs in loops. To avoid slowdowns and livelocks during execution, a task is assigned a maximum amount of executions per instance (*MAE*), which may be defined as part of an internal regulation or service level agreement. In our demonstration, we monitor the unfulfillment risk with respect to the "*W_Calling after sent offers*" task with $MAE = 10$. As the process log did not come with any additional information on a defined maximum time or maximum amount of executions, we had to estimate a sensible value. We expected that not more than 10 % of the instances are faulty and set $MAE = 10$, as it represents the 92 % quantile of the *MAE* distribution contained in the log. The instance from Table 1, for example, reached this amount as the task "*W_Calling after sent offers*" is executed 10 times. The unfulfillment risk sensor monitors the risk according to the risk condition shown in Eq. (5), whenever an instance executes the "*W_Calling after sent offers*" task.

$$\min\left\{\frac{\#instances \geq MAE}{\#instances \geq current\ amount\ of\ task\ execution}; 1\right\} > TRE \qquad (5)$$

Accordingly, we divide the amount of instances that executed the task at least as often as the defined *MAE* by the amount of instances that executed the task at least as often as the instance that triggered the sensor calculation. In case an instance already executed the task more often than the defined *MAE*, the left value of the risk condition must not exceed 1, as it reflects the probability that the instance exceeds the specified maximum amount of executions. Whenever the probability exceeds the defined threshold *TRE*, the PING is created and the risk propagation algorithm is triggered. We chose *TRE* = 0.6 to capture a risk-neutral setting. The threshold can also be adapted to reflect more risk-averse or risk-seeking settings. As the sensor calculates the risk based on the already executed instances of a process, we had to ensure that a sufficient amount of instances has already been executed before the first risk propagation is triggered. We thus started 40 instances of the log in order not to perform the sensor's calculation on an empty database. This amount of instances shaped up as sufficient in some scenarios.

To derive the similarity values used for risk propagation, we used two profiles. The first profile builds on case attributes from the log, the second considers the amount of executed tasks of a distinct instance. However, the log only offers two attributes, i.e., the requested amount of money and resource executing a task, whereby the resource is missing for many tasks. We decided to calculate the distance vector of the first profile with just one element, i.e., the difference of the requested amounts of money. For the second profile, we used the amount of executions per task. For both profiles, the maximum distance vector was determined based on instances in the snapshot (e.g., instances that were currently running when the risk was detected, as explained for the PING in Sect. 3.2). The maximum distance vector we choose for normalizing the distance values must not exceed the average distance from the snapshot by 80 %. We decided for this assumption to minimize the effect of outliers, which would cause many false positives. To further reduce the number of false positive risk propagations, we limited the amount of instances taken into consideration for propagation. We reduced the running instances by those who have already passed the task our sensor is attached to. Instances that proceeded to the task *"W_Assessing the application"* cannot be faulty anymore. At least the sensor related to their instance would have had to indicate potential risk.

The calculation of both profiles is performed according to Eq. (2). We take the profiles' result and their weights in order to derive a similarity for two distinct instances (Eq. 3). As the log contained almost no case attributes, we selected the task profile as the leading profile. We thus assigned a weight of 0.6 to the task profile and 0.4 to the attribute profile as shown in Eq. (6).

$$s_{i,j}(t) = \sum_{p \in P} w_p \cdot s_{p,i,j}(t) = 0.4 \cdot s_{\text{attribute},i,j}(t) + 0.6 \cdot s_{\text{task},i,j}(t) \qquad (6)$$

4.3   Results of the Replay and Discussion

To show a successful implementation and validate the PRISM approach, we selected instances that started between October 1st and 11th 2011. This set of instances captures an average workload per week from the process log, including a sufficiently large number of instances to train the PRISM approach. As declined loan requests would lead to negligible similarity values and receive no risk propagation, we only looked at instances with accepted loan requests. With the replay of the resulting 241 instances, we gained the results as illustrated in Table 2.

Table 2. Contingency table for predicting risk with PRISM

	Sensor detected risk	Sensor detected no risk
PRISM risk predicted	13/14 = 92.86 %	31/227 = 13.66 %
PRISM no risk predicted	1/14 = 7.14 %	196/227 = 86.34 %

In this setting, the PRISM approach predicted with an accuracy of 86.72 % (209 out of 241 instances). In the used log data, the sensor detected a risk for 14 instances. Out of these instances, 13 where correctly identified as being "at risk" before the respective instances' own sensors detected the risk. The instance with the missing prediction appeared due to propagation algorithm. The algorithm triggers the risk propagation upon the detection of risk in a sensor. Thus, the first instance that runs into a risk and triggers the first propagation cannot receive any information from an earlier propagation.

When we look into details, the time saved by the PRISM approaches averages 4 days 18 h compared to a risk detection without risk propagation among similar instances. The average execution time of the covered 241 instances amounted to 65 days 12 h. For our example trace (i.e., CaseID 175585) in Table 1, the unfulfillment risk was identified in task 16 with the 8th execution of task "W_Calling after sent offers" and caused a time advantage of 5 days 20 h.

Finally, we critically reflect on the results of the demonstration, as we made some assumptions when operationalizing the PRISM approach (e.g., similarity measure, normalization of the distance vectors). The different profiles of a process allow for different perspectives on similarity and provide high flexibility. The process log we used for the replay, however, only contained very few attributes we could use for building profiles. Thus, it needs to be checked how the availability of more attributes influences the demonstration results. Further, the relation of missing to false predictions is influenced by the risk conditions, thresholds, and the maximum number of re-propagations. These properties can be adapted according to a process manager's risk attitude. Nevertheless, we were able to demonstrate the effectiveness of the PRISM approach as we gained good results based on limited information. In addition, we only analyzed instances that started in a limited time period. Although this set of instances represented an average work week, it covers only a subset of the log data. We deliberately restricted the demonstration to a smaller subset to better understand what is happing during risk propagation. Thus, a next step would be to further develop the prototype and to apply the PRISM approach to the entire log.

5 Conclusion and Critical Discussion

In this paper, we proposed the predictive risk monitoring (PRISM) approach that automatically propagates risk information, detected by risk sensors, across similar instances of the same process in real-time. On the assumption that similar process instances have a similar risk exposure, the PRISM approach uses a similarity-weighted process instance graph (PING) that can be interpreted as a snapshot of all currently running instances. The PING virtually links all currently running instances and uses the similarity of these instances as edge weights. Based on the PING, a risk propagation algorithm then determines whether and how strongly a detected risk influences other instances. The PRISM approach intends to detect risks earlier than approaches without risk propagation. In the context of a real-world scenario, we demonstrated that the similarity assumption holds true and that the PRISM approach is indeed able to detect risks earlier than the approach of Conforti et al. [13].

Although we were able to demonstrate the effectiveness of the PRISM approach and the feasibility of the underlying assumptions based on real-world data, the approach is beset with limitations that stimulate future research. First, the PRISM approach is based on a distinct similarity measure as well as on the assumption of a proportional relation between similarity and risk exposure. Future research should analyze whether other similarity measures and other relation types help achieve better risk prediction results. Second, it is time-consuming to parameterize the PRISM approach. Currently, the parameterization needs to be strongly geared toward the properties of the process log at hand. Future research should explore into methods that help parameterize the PRISM approach. Third, the information we use as input for the PRISM approach grounds on risk information triggered by risk sensors. We do not consider other input than log data. It might be useful to account for information from outside the process such as the context in which the process is executed (e.g., market fluctuations) or organizational risks (e.g., dependencies on third parties) to enhance predictive risk detection. Ideas may be derived from risk monitoring approaches applied in other domains as well as from more sophisticated propagation algorithms (e.g., belief propagation). This can help overcome current shortcomings of the PRISM approach (e.g., the re-propagation sequence and the termination rule). Likewise, the PRISM approach would benefit from further evaluation by means of sensitivity analyses, robustness tests, and case studies. Case studies would also help gain experience with estimating the needed parameters.

Acknowledgements. This research is partially funded by the ARC Discovery Project DP150103356 and was partially carried out in the context of the Project Group Business and Information Systems Engineering of the Fraunhofer Institute for Applied Information Technology FIT.

References

1. van der Aalst, W.M.P.: Business process management: a comprehensive survey. ISRN Softw. Eng. **2013**, 1–37 (2013)
2. Beverungen, D.: Exploring the interplay of the design and emergence of business processes as organizational routines. Bus. Inf. Syst. Eng. **6**, 191–202 (2014)
3. zur Muehlen, M., Rosemann, M.: Integrating risks in business process models. In: 16th Australasian Conference on Information Systems, pp. 62–72. Association of Information Systems (2005)
4. Basel Committee on Banking Supervision: Basel II: International Convergence of Capital Measurement and Capital Standards (2006)
5. Oxley, M.G., Sarbanes, P.: Sarbanes Oxley Act of 2002, 745–810 (2002)
6. Mock, R., Corvo, M.: Risk analysis of information systems by event process chains. Int. J. Crit. Infrastruct. **1**, 247–257 (2005)
7. Betz, S., Hickl, S., Oberweis, A.: Risk-aware business process modeling and simulation using XML nets. In: 13th Conference on Commerce and Enterprise Computing, pp. 349–356. IEEE (2011)
8. Suriadi, S., Weiß, B., Winkelmann, A., ter Hofstede, A.H.M., Adams, M., Conforti, R., Fidge, C.J., La Rosa, M., Ouyang, C., Pika, A., Rosemann, M., Wynn, M.: Current research in risk-aware business process management - overview, comparison, and gap analysis. Commun. Assoc. Inf. Syst. **34**, 933–984 (2014)
9. Dumas, M., La Rosa, M., Mendling, J., Reijers, H.A.: Fundamentals of Business Process Management. Springer, Heidelberg (2013)
10. Bolsinger, M.: Bringing value-based business process management to the operational process level. Inf. Syst. E-bus. Manag. **13**, 355–398 (2015)
11. Buhl, H.U., Röglinger, M., Stöckl, S., Braunwarth, K.S.: Value orientation in process management. Bus. Inf. Syst. Eng. **3**, 163–172 (2011)
12. Recker, J., Mendling, J.: The state of the art of business process management research as published in the BPM conference. Bus. Inf. Syst. Eng. **58**, 55–72 (2016)
13. Conforti, R., La Rosa, M., Fortino, G., ter Hofstede, A.H.M., Recker, J., Adams, M.: Real-time risk monitoring in business processes: a sensor-based approach. J. Syst. Softw. **86**, 2939–2965 (2013)
14. Manderscheid, J., Reißner, D., Röglinger, M.: Inspection coming due! How to determine the service interval of your processes! In: Motahari-Nezhad, H.R., Recker, J., Weidlich, M. (eds.) BPM 2015. LNCS, vol. 9253, pp. 19–34. Springer, Heidelberg (2015)
15. Conforti, R., ter Hofstede, A.H., La Rosa, M., Adams, M.: Automated risk mitigation in business processes. In: Meersman, R., et al. (eds.) OTM 2012, Part I. LNCS, vol. 7565, pp. 212–231. Springer, Heidelberg (2012)
16. Conforti, R., de Leoni, M., La Rosa, M., van der Aalst, W.M.P., ter Hofstede, A.H.M.: A recommendation system for predicting risks across multiple business process instances. Decis. Support Syst. **69**, 1–19 (2015)
17. Krumeich, J., Werth, D., Loos, P.: Prescriptive control of business processes. Bus. Inf. Syst. Eng. **7**, 1–40 (2015)
18. Association Information Systems Audit and Control: COBIT 5: A Business Framework for the Governance and Management of Enterprise IT (2013)
19. AXELOS: Information Technology Infrastructure Library. https://www.axelos.com/best-practice-solutions/itil

20. Jakoubi, S., Goluch, G., Tjoa, S., Quirchmayr, G.: Deriving resource requirements applying risk-aware business process modeling and simulation. In: 16th European Conference on Information Systems, pp. 1542–1554. AIS (2008)
21. Sienou, A., Karduck, A.P., Lamine, E., Pingaud, H.: Business process and risk models enrichment: considerations for business intelligence. In: 2008 IEEE International Conference on e-Business Engineering, pp. 732–735. IEEE (2008)
22. Singh, P., Gelgi, F., Davulcu, H., Yau, S.S., Mukhopadhyay, S.: A risk reduction framework for dynamic workflows. In: 2008 IEEE International Conference on Services Computing, pp. 381–388. IEEE (2008)
23. Rotaru, K., Wilkin, C., Churilov, L., Neiger, D., Ceglowski, A.: Formalizing process-based risk with value-focused process engineering. Inf. Syst. E-Bus. Manag. 9, 447–474 (2011)
24. Karagiannis, D., Mylopoulos, J., Schwab, M.: Business process-based regulation compliance: the case of the Sarbanes-Oxley Act. In: 15th IEEE International Requirements Engineering Conference, pp. 315–321. IEEE (2007)
25. Lambert, J.H., Jennings, R.K., Joshi, N.N.: Integration of risk identification with business process models. Syst. Eng. 9, 187–198 (2006)
26. Pika, A., van der Aalst, W.M., Fidge, C.J., ter Hofstede, A.H., Wynn, M.T.: Predicting deadline transgressions using event logs. In: La Rosa, M., Soffer, P. (eds.) BPM Workshops 2012. LNBIP, vol. 132, pp. 211–216. Springer, Heidelberg (2013)
27. Suriadi, S., Ouyang, C., van der Aalst, W.M., ter Hofstede, A.H.: Root cause analysis with enriched process logs. In: La Rosa, M., Soffer, P. (eds.) BPM Workshops 2012. LNBIP, vol. 132, pp. 174–186. Springer, Heidelberg (2013)
28. Standards Australia and Standards New Zealand: ISO 31000:2009, Risk Management — Principles and Guidelines (2009)
29. van Dongen, B.F., Dijkman, R., Mendling, J.: Measuring similarity between business process models. In: Bellahsène, Z., Léonard, M. (eds.) CAiSE 2008. LNCS, vol. 5074, pp. 450–464. Springer, Heidelberg (2008)
30. Armas-Cervantes, A., Baldan, P., Dumas, M., García-Bañuelos, L.: Diagnosing behavioral differences between business process models: an approach based on event structures. Inf. Syst. 56, 304–325 (2016)
31. Polyvyanyy, A., Weidlich, M., Weske, M.: Isotactics as a foundation for alignment and abstraction of behavioral models. In: Barros, A., Gal, A., Kindler, E. (eds.) BPM 2012. LNCS, vol. 7481, pp. 335–351. Springer, Heidelberg (2012)
32. Dijkman, R.M., Dumas, M., van Dongen, B.F., Käärik, R., Mendling, J.: Similarity of business process models: metrics and evaluation. Inf. Syst. 36, 498–516 (2011)
33. Beheshti, S.-M.-R., Benatallah, B., Sakr, S., Grigori, D., Motahari-Nezhad, H.R., Barukh, M.C., Gater, A., Ryu, S.H.: Process Analytics - Concepts and Techniques for Querying and Analyzing Process Data. Springer International Publishing, Switzerland (2016)
34. Song, M., Günther, C.W., van der Aalst, W.M.: Trace clustering in process mining. In: Ardagna, D., Mecella, M., Yang, J. (eds.) Business Process Management Workshops. LNBIP, vol. 17, pp. 109–120. Springer, Heidelberg (2009)
35. van Beest, N.R.T.P., Dumas, M., García-Bañuelos, L., La Rosa, M.: Log delta analysis: interpretable differencing of business process event logs. In: Motahari-Nezhad, H.R., Recker, J., Weidlich, M. (eds.) BPM 2015. LNCS, vol. 9253, pp. 386–405. Springer, Heidelberg (2015)
36. Hamming, R.W.: Error detecting and error correcting codes. Bell Syst. Tech. J. 29, 147–160 (1950)
37. Jaccard, P.: The distribution of the flora in the alpine zone. New Phytol. 11, 37–50 (1912)

38. Daniel, F., Eriksson, J., Finne, N., Fuchs, H., Karnouskos, S., Montero, P.M., Mottola, L., Oertel, N., Oppermann, F.J., Picco, G. Pietro, Römer, K., Spieß, P., Tranquillini, S., Voigt, T.: makeSense: real-world business processes through wireless sensor networks. In: 4th International Workshop on Networks of Cooperating Objects for Smart Cities, CONET/UBICITEC, pp. 58–72 (2013)

39. Minor, M., Bergmann, R., Görg, S.: Case-based adaptation of workflows. Inf. Syst. **40**, 142–152 (2014)

40. Motahari-Nezhad, H.R., Bartolini, C.: Next best step and expert recommendation for collaborative processes in IT service management. In: Rinderle-Ma, S., Toumani, F., Wolf, K. (eds.) BPM 2011. LNCS, vol. 6896, pp. 50–61. Springer, Heidelberg (2011)

41. Stutz, P., Bernstein, A., Cohen, W.: Signal/collect: graph algorithms for the (semantic) web. In: Patel-Schneider, P.F., Pan, Y., Hitzler, P., Mika, P., Zhang, L., Pan, J.Z., Horrocks, I., Glimm, B. (eds.) ISWC 2010, Part I. LNCS, vol. 6496, pp. 764–780. Springer, Heidelberg (2010)

42. van Dongen, B.F.: BPI Challenge 2012.xes.gz. http://data.3tu.nl/repository/uuid:3926db30-f712-4394-aebc-75976070e91f

43. Conforti, R., La Rosa, M., ter Hofstede, A.H.M.: Filtering out Infrequent Behavior from Process Event Logs (2015)

Predictive Business Process Monitoring
with Structured and Unstructured Data

Irene Teinemaa[1,2]($\boxtimes$), Marlon Dumas[1], Fabrizio Maria Maggi[1],
and Chiara Di Francescomarino[3]

[1] University of Tartu, Tartu, Estonia
{irheta,marlon.dumas,f.m.maggi}@ut.ee
[2] STACC, Tartu, Estonia
irene.teinemaa@gmail.com
[3] FBK-IRST, Trento, Italy
dfmchiara@fbk.eu

Abstract. Predictive business process monitoring is concerned with continuously analyzing the events produced by the execution of a business process in order to predict as early as possible the outcome of each ongoing case thereof. Previous work has approached the problem of predictive process monitoring when the observed events carry structured data payloads consisting of attribute-value pairs. In practice, structured data often comes in conjunction with unstructured (textual) data such as emails or comments. This paper presents a predictive process monitoring framework that combines text mining with sequence classification techniques so as to handle both structured and unstructured event payloads. The framework has been evaluated with respect to accuracy, prediction earliness and efficiency on two real-life datasets.

Keywords: Process monitoring · Predictive monitoring · Text mining

1 Introduction

Business process monitoring is concerned with the analysis of events produced during the execution of a process in order to assess the fulfillment of its compliance requirements and performance objectives [7]. Monitoring can take place offline (e.g., based on periodically produced reports) or online via dashboards displaying the performance of currently running cases of a process [3].

Predictive business process monitoring [15] refers to a family of online process monitoring methods that seek to predict as early as possible the outcome of each case given its current (incomplete) execution trace and given a set of traces of previously completed cases. In this context, an outcome may be the fulfillment of a compliance rule, a performance objective (e.g., maximum allowed cycle time) or business goal, or any other characteristic of a case that can be determined upon its completion. For example, in a sales process, a possible outcome is the placement of a purchase order by a potential customer, whereas in a debt recovery process, a possible outcome is the receipt of a debt repayment.

© Springer International Publishing Switzerland 2016
M. La Rosa et al. (Eds.): BPM 2016, LNCS 9850, pp. 401–417, 2016.
DOI: 10.1007/978-3-319-45348-4_23

Existing approaches to predictive process monitoring [5,13,15,16] consider that a trace consists of a sequence of events with a structured data payload, such as a payload consisting of attribute-value pairs. For example, in a loan application process, one event could be the receipt of a new loan application. This event may carry structured data such as the name, date of birth and other personal details of the applicant, the type of loan requested, and the requested amount and valuation of the collateral. Each subsequent event in this process may then carry additional or updated data such as the credit score assigned to the applicant, the maximum loan amount allowed, the interest rate, etc.

In practice, not all data generated during the execution of a process is structured. For example, in said loan application process, the customer may include a free-text description of the purpose of the loan. Later, a customer service representative may attach to the case the text of an email exchanged with the customer regarding her employment details, while a credit officer may add a comment to the loan application following a conversation with the customer. Comments like these ones are common for example in application-to-approval processes, issue-to-resolution and claim-to-settlement processes, where the execution of the process involves unstructured interactions with the customer.

This paper studies the problem of jointly exploiting unstructured (free-text) and structured data for predictive process monitoring. The contribution is a predictive process monitoring framework that combines text mining techniques to extract features from textual payload, with (early) sequence classification techniques for structured data. The proposed framework is evaluated on two real-life datasets: a debt recovery process, where the outcomes are either a (partial) repayment or the referral of the case to an external agency for encashment, and a lead-to-contract process, where the outcome conveys whether or not a sales contract is signed with a potential customer.

The rest of the paper is structured as follows. Section 2 introduces the text mining techniques upon which our proposal builds. Section 3 presents the predictive process monitoring framework, while Sect. 4 presents the evaluation. Section 5 discusses related work while Sect. 6 summarizes the contribution and outlines future work directions.

2   Background: Text Mining

The central object in text mining is a *document* — a unit of textual data such as a comment or an e-mail. Natural language processing can be used to derive representative feature vectors for individual documents, which can thereupon be used in various (predictive) data mining tasks. In order to construct reasonable representations, the textual data should be preprocessed. Firstly, the text needs to be *tokenized* — segmented into meaningful pieces. In the simplest approach, text is split into tokens on the white space character. More sophisticated tokenization techniques can be used to obtain multi-word tokens (e.g., "New York") or to separate words such as "it's" into two tokens "it" and "is".

Tokens can also be *normalized* so that tokens with small differences (e.g., "e-mail" and "email") are equated. In addition, inflected forms of words can be grouped together using *stemming* or *lemmatization*. For instance, lemmatization can group words "good", "better", and "best" under a single *lemma*.

A document can be represented by using frequencies of single words as features. For example, the document "The fox jumps over the dog" is represented as {"the":2, "fox":1, "jumps":1, "over":1, "dog":1}. This representation ignores the order of words – a limitation that can be overcome by using sequences of two (*bigrams*), three (*trigrams*), or n (*n-grams*) contiguous words instead of or in addition to single words (*unigrams*). The bigrams in the above document are: {"the fox":1, "fox jumps":1, "jumps over":1, "over the":1, "the dog":1}. Features that are constructed based on words that occur in the document are called *terms*, while the corresponding representation is called *bag-of-n-grams* (BoNG).

Terms that occur frequently in a document collection are not representative of a particular document, yet they receive misleadingly high values in the basic BoNG model. This problem can be addressed by normalizing the term frequencies (tf) with the *inverse document frequencies* (idf) — the number of all documents divided by the number of documents that contain the term, scaled logarithmically. Thus, rare terms receive higher weights, while frequent words (like "with" or "the") receive lower weights. In text classification scenarios, weighing the term frequencies with *Naive Bayes* (NB) log count ratios may improve the accuracy of the predictions [19]. The BoNG model also suffers from high dimensionality, as each document is represented by as many features as the number of terms in the *vocabulary* (the set of all terms in the document collection). Common practice is to apply *feature selection* techniques, such as mutual information or Chi-square test, and retain only the most relevant terms.

Alternative approaches to the BoNG model are *continuous representations* of documents. These techniques represent text with real-valued low-dimensional feature vectors, where each feature is typically a *latent* variable — inferred from the observed variables. One such approach is *topic modeling*, which extracts abstract *topics* from a collection of documents. The most widely used topic modeling technique, Latent Dirichlet Allocation (LDA) [1], is a generative statistical model, which assumes that each document entails a mixture of topics and each word in the document is drawn from one of the underlying topics.

Continuous representations of words using neural network-based language models have also shown high performance in natural language processing tasks. These language models are trained to predict a missing word, given its *context* — words in the proximity of the word to be predicted. Techniques have been proposed that extend these approaches from word-level to sentence-, or document-level. For instance, *Paragraph Vector* (PV) [12] generates fixed-length feature representations for documents of variable length.

3   Framework

The proposed framework takes as input a set of traces and a labeling function that assigns a label (e.g., positive vs.negative) to each trace. Given this labeled set of traces, and the incomplete trace of a running case, it returns as output a prediction on the outcome (label) of the running case. Each trace consists of a sequence of events carrying a payload consisting of structured and unstructured data. For example, the following is a possible event (*Call*) in a debt collection process, carrying structured data (*revenue* and *debt_sum*) and unstructured data (the associated textual description).

$$Call \{revenue : 34555, debt\_sum : 500\} \{\text{Please send a warning. 1234567: "Gave} \\ \text{extension of 5 days and issued a warning about sending it to encashment.} \\ \text{An encashment warning letter sent on the 06/10, 11:10 deadline."}\} \tag{1}$$

The framework embodies two different components. An *offline component* uses historical traces to train classifiers that are used to make predictions about running cases through an *online component*. The following subsections explain each of these components in more detail.

3.1   Offline Component

Figure 1 illustrates the offline component of our proposed predictive monitoring framework. At the core of the framework, there are *text models* and *classifiers*. Both are trained using prefixes of historical cases. In particular, one text model and one classifier is trained for each possible *prefix length* (from 1 to *m*). From all prefixes of a certain length, unstructured sequences (sequences of events with their associated textual description) and structured sequences (sequences of events with their structured data payload) are extracted (*Extract sequences* in Fig. 1). A textual model is trained by using the unstructured data (*Construct text model* in Fig. 1). The purpose of a textual model is to transform a variable length textual description associated to an event into a fixed length numerical feature vector. Each textual description extracted from the considered prefixes is translated into a feature vector (*Extract textual features* in Fig. 1). A classifier is then trained by encoding each prefix as a *complex sequence*, combining (i) control flow, (ii) structured data payload, and (iii) features extracted from textual data. Therefore, the number of features depends on the prefix length k (from 1 to m) and thus different classifiers need to be trained for different prefix lengths. We now describe in more detail the main phases in the offline component.

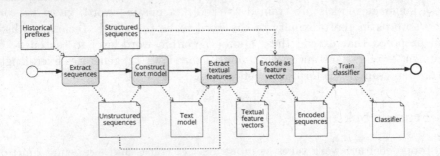

Fig. 1. The **offline** component of the proposed framework

Construct Text Models and Extract Textual Features: In the proposed framework, the text associated to each event is considered as a document and a feature vector is extracted from it. We compare 4 different techniques for extracting feature vectors from text: BoNG model with and without NB log count ratios, LDA topic modeling, and PV.

Before feature extraction, some preprocessing is done on the unstructured data. We start with tokenizing the documents, using simple white space tokenization. In the case of the running example (1), the tokenization produces a vector of tokens, e.g., "Please", "send", "a", "warning", ... Moreover, we generate equivalence classes for different types of numerals by replacing them with a corresponding tag (phone number, date, or other). For example, in (1), token "1234567" would be replaced by token "phone number", token "06/10" by "date" and token "11:10" by "time". Lastly, we *lemmatize* the text, i.e., we group together different inflected forms of a word and we refer to such a group with its base form or *lemma*. For example, in our running example, tokens "send", "sent" and "sending" will be clustered together into a "send" cluster (where "send" is the lemma), whereas "deadlin" is the base form of "deadline" and "deadlines".

In the following paragraphs, we illustrate in detail the techniques for extracting feature vectors from text we use in this paper.

Bag-of-n-grams (n, idf): This method is based on the BoNG model and takes as inputs two parameters: n, which is the maximum size of the n-grams; and *idf*, that is a boolean variable specifying whether the BoNG model is normalized with idf. In this method, the documents from historical prefixes are used to build a vocabulary of n-grams, $V(n)$. Given a vocabulary $V(n)$ of size $|V(n)| = v$, a document j is represented as a vector $\mathbf{d}^{(j)} = (g_{t_1}^{(j)}, g_{t_2}^{(j)}, ..., g_{t_v}^{(j)})$, where:

$$g_{t_i}^{(j)} = \begin{cases} tfidf(t_i^{(j)}) & \text{if } idf \\ f_{t_i}^{(j)} & \text{otherwise} \end{cases}$$

$f_{t_i}^{(j)}$ represents the frequency of n-gram t_i in document $\mathbf{d}^{(j)}$, i.e., $f_{t_i}^{(j)} = tf(t_i^{(j)})$.

For instance, in our running example (1), if $n = 1$, $idf = false$ and the vocabulary is $V(1) = \{about, agenc, collect, commun, date, deadlin, encash, extens, gave, issu, letter, number, phonenumb, pleas, send, time, warn, warning\}$, the vector encoding the textual description would be:

$$d^{(\bar{j})} = (1, 0, 0, 0, 0, 1, 1, 1, 1, 1, 1, 1, 1, 1, 3, 1, 1, 3) \tag{2}$$

where the word "send" (and its variations) occur three times in the document, the word "about" occurs once and the word "agency" does not occur.

Naive Bayes log count ratios (n, α): In this method, features are still based on the BoNG model, but they are weighted with NB log count ratios, $\mathbf{d}^{(j)} = (f_{t_1}^{(j)} \cdot r_1, f_{t_2}^{(j)} \cdot r_2, ..., f_{t_v}^{(j)} \cdot r_v)$. The parameter α is a *smoothing parameter* for the weights [19], while n is, as in BoNG, the maximum size of the n-grams. For instance, if the vocabulary (and hence the term frequency) is the same as the one in (2) and the NB log count ratios vector is $\mathbf{r} = (0.85, 1.02, 0.76, 0.76, 1.52,$ $2.03, 1.19, 1.02, 0.45, 0.89, 1.02, 1.4, 1.39, 0.41, 1.02, 1.38, 1.27, 1.83)$, $\mathbf{d}^{(j)}$ would be:

$$\mathbf{d}^{(j)} = (0.85, 0, 0, 0, 1.52, 2.03, 1.19, 1.02, 0.45, 0.89, 1.02, 1.4, 1.39, 0.41, 3.06, 1.38, 1.27, 5.49) \quad (3)$$

Latent Dirichlet Allocation topic modeling (num_topics, idf): In this method, the text model is represented by *topics* covered by the documents. The method takes as input the *number of topics* to be obtained and, similarly to BoNG, a boolean parameter *idf* that determines whether the term frequencies should be weighted with *idf* before applying topic modeling. A topic is expressed as a probability distribution over words, where words that are characteristic to a particular topic possess higher values. Each document is represented as a probability vector over topics, $\mathbf{d}^{(j)} = (p_1^{(j)}, p_2^{(j)}, ..., p_c^{(j)})$, where c is the number of topics and $p_i^{(j)}$ is the probability that document j concerns topic p_i. For instance, if the three following topics have been identified by applying topic modeling to the textual descriptions of the historical unstructured data:

topic1 :$(immediately : 0.4, phone : 0.2, pay : 0.1, ...)$ $(immediate\ payment)$

topic2 :$(mobile : 0.3, answer : 0.2, switched : 0.15, off : 0.15, ...)$ $(not\ accessible\ by\ phone)$

topic3 :$(send : 0.35, letter : 0.2, warning : 0.1, ...)$ $(warning\ letter\ sent)$

(each topic can be abstracted by using textual descriptions like the ones reported on the right-hand side of the list of topics), the textual description in (1) will be represented as a vector of three items. Each item corresponds to the probability that the document concerns *topic*1, *topic*2 and *topic*3, respectively. In particular, the document is not very related to *topic*1, a bit more to *topic*2 and closer to the warning letter scenario. The resulting vector is:

$$d^{(j)} = (0.1, 0.2, 0.7) \qquad (4)$$

Paragraph Vector (vector_size, window_size): In this method, not only terms but also the sequence of terms are exploited for the construction of the model. Namely, the method slides a window of size *window_size* over the documents, using each of such windows of words as the context. Once trained, the model is able to provide for each document a vector of features of a fixed length (specified by *vector_size*).

For the methods based on the BoNG model with and without NB log count ratios, before the textual features can be used for the complex sequence encoding, a *feature selection* step is required to reduce the number of features extracted. In particular, for the method based on the basic BoNG model the Chi-square test is used, while for the method based on the BoNG model with NB log count ratios the most discriminative features (i.e., the terms that achieve the top lowest and top highest NB log ratio scores) are selected. Both these feature selection techniques take as input the number of features to select, so that BoNG and NB also require such a number as additional input parameter.

Encode as Feature Vector: Our approach utilizes the index-based encoding for complex sequences [13]. This encoding scheme differentiates between static and dynamic (structured) data. Case attributes are static since they do not change as the case progresses. On the other hand, dynamic attributes may take new values during the execution of a case. Event attributes can hence be considered either as static (only the most recent value is used) or dynamic (the sequence of values up to a given point is used). Given a sequence σ_i of length k, with u static features $s_i^1, ..., s_i^u$, and r dynamic features $h_i^1, ..., h_i^r$, the index-based feature vector g_i of σ_i is:

$$g_i = (s_i^1, ..., s_i^u, event_{i1}, ..., event_{ik}, h_{i1}^1, ..., h_{ik}^1, ..., h_{i1}^r, ..., h_{ik}^r).$$

We enhance the index-based encoding with textual features by concatenating them to the feature vector. Textual data can be of both static and dynamic nature. When text contains static information, the derived v features $t_i^1, ..., t_i^v$ are added to the feature vector of σ_i as follows:

$$g_i = (s_i^1, ..., s_i^u, event_{i1}, ..., event_{ik}, h_{i1}^1, ..., h_{ik}^1, ..., h_{i1}^r, ..., h_{ik}^r, t_i^1, ..., t_i^v).$$

On the other hand, if textual data changes throughout the case, it should be handled in the same way as dynamic structured data:

$$g_i = (s_i^1, ..., s_i^u, event_{i1}, ..., event_{ik}, h_{i1}^1, ..., h_{ik}^1, ..., h_{i1}^r, ..., h_{ik}^r, t_{i1}^1, ..., t_{ik}^1, ..., t_{i1}^v, ..., t_{ik}^v).$$

For instance, if the case containing the event in the example (1) does not contain any static structured and unstructured data, using the topic model vector in (4), the complex sequence would be:

$$g^i = (..., call, ..., 34555, 500, ..., 0.1, 0.2, 0.7, ...) \tag{5}$$

Train Classifier: We use *random forest* [2] and *logistic regression* [9] to build the classifiers. Random forest has been shown to be a solid classifier in various problem settings, including credit scoring applications [14]. On the other hand, logistic regression, one among the most popular linear classifiers in text classification tasks, suites well to cases in which data are very sparse (this is the case when the BoNG model is used).

3.2   Online Component

The structure of the online component of our predictive monitoring framework is presented in Fig. 2. When predicting the outcome for a running case of prefix length k, the pre-built textual model and classifier for length k are retrieved and applied to the running case at hand. If the prefix length of the running case is larger than the maximum prefix length m used in the training process, only the first m events of the running case are used.

Threshold *minConf* is an input parameter of the framework. If the classifier returns a probability higher than minConf for the *positive* class, the framework outputs a *positive* prediction. If the probability is lower than the threshold, no

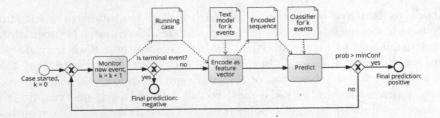

Fig. 2. The **online** component of the proposed framework

prediction is made and the framework continues to monitor the case. When the observed event is a terminal event, the final prediction is *negative*.

This setting, where the framework focuses only on making positive predictions, follows closely most real-life scenarios. Indeed, it is important for the stakeholders to filter the cases that may become deviant in the future, so that preventive actions can be taken. On the other hand, in cases that will likely have a normal outcome, no specific action is taken and they are allowed to continue in their own path. Still, our framework is easily extensible to early prediction of both positive and negative outcomes.

4   Evaluation

We have implemented the proposed methods in Python[1] and evaluated their performance on two datasets using an existing technique for predictive process monitoring with structured data as a baseline [13]. Below we describe the datasets, evaluation method and findings.

4.1   Datasets

We evaluated our framework on two real-life datasets pertaining to: (i) the debt recovery (DR) process of an Estonian company that provides credit management service for its customers (creditors), and (ii) the lead-to-contract (LtC) process of a due diligence service provider in Estonia.

The debt recovery process starts when the creditor transfers a delinquent debt to the company. This means that the debtor has already *defaulted* — failed to repay the debt to the creditor in due time. Usually, the collection specialist makes a phone call to the debtor. If the phone is not answered, an inquiry/reminder letter is sent. If the phone is answered, the debtor may provide an expected payment date, in which case no additional action is taken during the present week. Alternatively, the specialist and the debtor can agree on a payment schedule that outlines the repayments over a longer time period. If the collection specialist considers the case to be irreparable, she makes a suggestion to the creditor

---

[1] Scripts available at https://github.com/irhete/PredictiveMonitoringWithText.

about forwarding the debt to an outside debt collection agency (*send to encashment*) or about sending a warning letter to the debtor on the same matter. The final decision about issuing an encashment warning to the debtor and/or sending the debt to encashment is made by the creditor. If there is no advancement in collecting the debt after 7 days (e.g., the payment was not received on the provided date or the debtor has neither answered the phone nor the reminder letter), the procedure is repeated.

It is in the interest of the creditor to discover, as early as possible, cases that will not lead to any payment in a reasonable timeframe. The earlier the debt is recovered, the more value it entails for the creditor. Moreover, such cases are likely irreparable and could be sent to encashment without further delay. Therefore, our prediction goal is to determine cases where no payment is received within 8 weeks after the beginning of the debt recovery process.

The lead-to-contract process is logged through a customer relationship management system (CRM). The process begins when the sales manager selects companies as "cold leads" and loads them into CRM. Based on personal experience, the sales manager selects leads that qualify for an opportunity, or alternatively, makes a phonecall to the company in order to determine qualification. Then, when a case is in the *qualification stage*, a phonecall is initiated with the purpose of scheduling a meeting with the potential customer's representatives. If a meeting is scheduled, the opportunity enters the *presentation stage*. The goal of a sales person is to get the contract signed during the presentation. If she succeeds, the opportunity is marked as *won* and the case terminates. If the offer made during the meeting was acceptable, but the signing of the contract is postponed, the opportunity enters the *contract stage*. If the offer was not accepted during the meeting, an offer is sent via e-mail, and the opportunity moves to the *offer stage*. Any time during the process additional phonecalls can be made and follow-up meetings scheduled. When it becomes clear that the company is not interested in collaboration, the opportunity is marked as *lost*.

The number of potential customers is very high and it is not feasible for the sales people to deeply explore all of the possible leads. Thus, the process would benefit from a support system that estimates if an opportunity will likely end with a signed contract (opportunity won) or not (opportunity lost). If an opportunity is likely to be lost, the sales person can close it at an early stage (or assign it a lower priority), becoming able to focus on other leads with higher potential. Given this motivation, in the following experiments we aim at predicting, as early as possible, if an opportunity will be lost.

Table 1. Evaluation datasets

Data	# Normal cases	# Deviant cases	Avg. # words/doc	# Lemmas
DR	13608	417	11	11822
LtC	385	390	8	2588

In the debt recovery dataset, events are not explicitly logged. Instead, this information is captured in the *collector's notes*, which are written down in unstructured textual format. The collector's notes constitute a dynamic feature, which may describe the activity taken by the collection specialist, as well as the answer of the debtor and the assessment of the specialist. In the second dataset, the phonecall summaries are written down in unstructured format. The text in both datasets is written in Estonian language. Statistics about both datasets are given in Table 1.

Based on the structured data available, we identify 8 static and 69 dynamic features in the debt recovery dataset, and 3 static and 65 dynamic features in the lead-to-contract dataset. The static features are general statistics about the company, for instance, *the size of equity*, *the net profit*, and *field of activity*. The dynamic features in the first dataset are mostly related to the debt, e.g., *the number of days past due*, *the expected repayment amount until the next 7 days*, and *the sum of other debts of the debtor*. In the second dataset, the dynamic features include *activity name*, *resource*, and *expected revenue*. For both datasets, we use dynamic features that reflect the company's (either the debtor's or the potential customer's) risk score, calculated at 6 different months prior to the given event. Moreover, as the first dataset contains a considerable amount of missing values, additional 16 (static) features are added that express whether the value of a particular feature is present or missing. In the given datasets, we decide to use unstructured data as static information, i.e., to encode only the last available text, given a specific prefix length.

4.2   Research Questions and Evaluation Measures

In our evaluation, we address the following three research questions:

RQ1 Do the features derived from textual data (using different methods) increase the prediction *accuracy* of index-based sequence encoding?

RQ2 Do the features derived from textual data (using different methods) increase the prediction *earliness* of index-based sequence encoding?

RQ3 Is the proposed predictive monitoring framework *efficient*?

For evaluating prediction accuracy (**RQ1**) of our framework, we use *precision*, *recall*, and *F-score*, as suggested in [16]. We do not use *accuracy*, as it can lead to misleading results in case of imbalanced data [18]. Also, we do not report about *specificity*, as our main goal is to predict the positive class as accurately as possible. All metrics are based on the possible combinations of actual and predicted outcomes. True positives (TP) are positive cases, which are correctly predicted as positive. True negatives (TN) are negative cases, which are correctly predicted as negative. False positives (FP) are negative cases, which are incorrectly predicted as positives. False negatives (FN) are positive cases, which are incorrectly predicted as negatives. Given these notions, precision is defined as $TP/(TP+FP)$, recall as $TP/(TP+FN)$, and F-score as $2 \cdot precision \cdot recall/(precision+recall)$.

To answer **RQ2**, we measure the *earliness* of predictions [6]. Earliness is calculated for cases that are predicted as positive, as the ratio of *length of the* *case when the final prediction was made/total length of the case.* For instance, if the case was predicted as positive after 2 events, while the actual total length of the case was 8 events, *earliness* = 0.25. Low earliness values are better, as the aim of predictive monitoring is to provide predictions as early as possible.

Finally, the *computation time* is measured in order to estimate the efficiency of the framework (**RQ3**). For evaluating the offline component of the framework, we differentiate between the time for data processing (text model construction, textual feature extraction, and sequence encoding) and classifier training. Times are summed up over all prefix lengths, in order to evaluate the total time that is needed to set up the framework. For evaluating the online component, we combine the time for encoding the running case as a feature vector and the time for prediction. Times are averaged over the total number of processed events.

4.3 Evaluation Procedure

We split each dataset randomly in two parts, so that 4/5 of it is used for training the offline component, while the remaining 1/5 is used for testing the online component. For tuning the parameters of the text modeling methods, we perform a grid-search over all combinations of selected parameter values using 5-fold cross-validation on the training set. In the DC dataset, where only 3 % of cases are deviant, we use oversampling on the training data in order to alleviate the imbalance problem. The final Paragraph Vector models are trained for 10 epochs. The optimal parameters are chosen based on F-score, for each combination of text modeling method, classification method, and confidence threshold. The computation times are calculated as the average of 10 equivalent executions with $minConf = 0.6$. The probability estimates returned by the classifier are used as confidence values.

The optimal parameters found when using random forest and logistic regression are different. However, in the following, we discuss the values obtained using random forest only, since random forest performs better than logistic regression in all cases. We optimize the parameters described in Sect. 3 and use the default values for all the parameters not mentioned.

For the method based on the basic BoNG model, we explore 43 parameter settings (varying maximum *n-gram size*, *idf*, and *number of selected features*). In most cases, tf-idf weights perform slightly better than simple tf. Moreover, bigrams and trigrams gain similar performance, while both are better than unigrams. The best number of selected features stays between 100 and 1000. In the DR dataset, only 100 features are often sufficient to gain a good accuracy, while more features are needed in the LtC dataset (usually 750 or 1000).

For the method based on the BoNG model with NB log count ratios, we try 84 combinations of parameters (varying α, maximum *n-gram size* and *number of selected features*). Changing the α value has almost no effect on the results, usually a small value (either 0.01 or 0.1) is chosen. The best number of selected features tends to be higher than in the BoNG case, usually between 250 and 1000 features in the DR dataset and between 1000 and 5000 in the LtC dataset. In most cases, trigrams outperform bi- and unigrams.

In case of LDA (we vary the *number of topics* and *idf*), we try 6 different numbers of topics (12 combinations in total). In general, the larger the confidence, the higher the number of topics that achieves the best results. In the DR dataset, idf normalization does not improve the outcome, while changing the parameters has very little effect on the results in the LtC dataset.

For PV, we explore 91 combinations, varying the *size of the feature vector* and the *window size*. The best results are obtained with a small 10- or 25-dimensional vector. The optimal window size varies a lot across the experiments, but stays between 5 and 9, in general.

Experiments were run in Python 3.5 using scikit-learn (BoNG and classifiers), gensim (LDA and PV) and estnltk (lemmatization) libraries on a single core of a 64-bit 2.3 GHz AMD Opteron Processor 6376 with 378 GB of RAM.

4.4   Results

The F-scores of the random forest classifiers are shown in Fig. 3a (debt recovery dataset) and c (lead-to-contract dataset). We observe that in both datasets, the methods that utilize unstructured data almost always outperform the baseline. In the DR dataset, BoNG and NB achieve considerably better results than the other methods, while in the LtC dataset, the best results are produced by LDA. Although the proportion of unstructured vs. structured data in the LtC dataset is much smaller than in the DR dataset, the improvement of the results is still substantial. The highest F-score in the DR dataset (0.791) is achieved by NB with $minConf = 0.55$, while LDA achieves F-score of 0.753 with $minConf = 0.65$ in the LtC dataset.

Figure 3b and d show the prediction earliness achieved with random forest. The model with the best F-score in the DR dataset tends to make predictions when 59 % of a case has finished, while the best model in the LtC dataset is predicted after 40 % of a case has been seen.

In order to further explore the importance of unstructured data in making predictions, we performed additional experiments using unstructured data only. In the DR dataset, the NB model achieves F-score of 0.66 (instead of 0.791 as in Fig. 3a), while in the LtC dataset, the LDA model reaches F-score of 0.70 (instead of 0.75 as in Fig. 3c). In both datasets, the model trained with only structured data (the baseline) outperforms all unstructured data models in terms of precision, while falls behind in terms of recall. Thus, unstructured features have some predictive power on their own, but in order to get the most out of the data, they should be combined with structured data. In addition, we observe that using the best model (NB, conf = 0.55) of the DR dataset, 3 out of the top 5 features ranked according to Gini impurity are derived from textual data. On the other hand, in the LtC dataset (LDA, conf = 0.65), the first 9 features according to importance are structured features. This implies that in best model of the LtC dataset, textual features are less relevant than structured features.

Table 2 reports the computation time required by the offline component for data processing and for classification, as well as the computation time required by the online component for providing a prediction with a minimum confidence

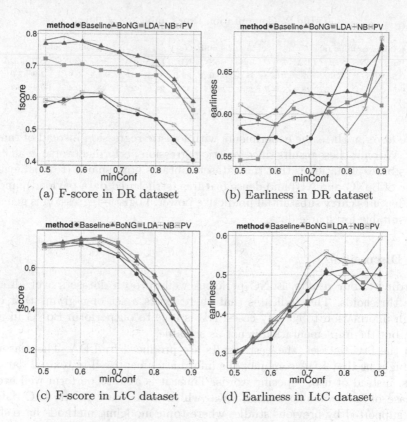

Fig. 3. Predictive monitoring results with random forest

of 0.6. The most expensive technique, in terms of computation time for setting up the offline component, is LDA, which requires more than 4 min for data processing in the DR dataset and 28 s in the LtC dataset (Table 2). The difference between the time required by the two datasets is likely due to their different size. In case of PV, the processing time of the offline component depends highly on the number of epochs used for training the paragraph vectors. In our experiments, we used 10 epochs, which results in relatively high processing time. BoNG is the most efficient method, taking only little over a second in the smaller dataset and over 5 s in the larger one. On the other hand, the current implementation of NB does not scale well as the size of the data increases.

Classifier training times remain between 24 and 83 s, depending on the dataset size and number of features. In the online component, all the methods are extremely fast in processing a running case (in the order of milliseconds per event). The slowest is LDA which takes 7 ms on average in the DR dataset.

Depending on the application, some additional time may be needed to prepare the data into a suitable format. Preprocessing the entire dataset took 2.3 min in case of DR and 14 s in case of LtC. The most time-consuming procedure was lemmatization that took 1.5 min in DR (12 s in LtC).

Table 2. Computation times, minConf = 0.6

	total_proc_offline (s)					total_cls_offline (s)					avg_online (ms)				
Data	Base	BoNG	NB	LDA	PV	Base	BoNG	NB	LDA	PV	Base	BoNG	NB	LDA	PV
DR	0.5	5.1	54.0	262	212	41.3	50.0	53.9	83.6	61.3	0.1	0.4	2.9	7.0	2.0
LtC	0.5	1.4	1.7	28.0	14.7	28.1	29.9	35.2	24.5	27.3	0.3	0.4	0.5	0.7	0.5

We also ran the same experiments with logistic regression instead of random forest. We omit these results since logistic regression performed worse in all cases. A possible explanation is that the dataset contains both sparse (textual features in case of BoNG and NB) and dense features (structured data payload), and the dense features carry substantial predictive power. Logistic regression is generally more suitable for sparse data.

4.5   Discussion

According to our results, BoNG performs well on both datasets over all confidence thresholds. This indicates that there exists a set of n-grams that carry enough information to classify cases. NB is able to outperform BoNG in a few cases, but the implementation is not as scalable.

In the LtC dataset, the best results are produced by LDA. The reason for this might be that LDA combines the information captured in textual data into topics, instead of using specific words. Thus, it is able to perform well even in the case of few available textual data, which is the case in the LtC dataset. Also, supported by previous studies where topic modeling methods have shown to perform well on short texts, such as tweets [10], LDA is less affected by the fact that individual notes in the LtC data set contain only 8 words on average.

A possible reason for PV performing worse than the other methods is that PV computes the feature vector for an unseen document via inference. Therefore, in order to produce reliable results, it requires a fairly large document collection for training. Moreover, the benefits of PV become more evident in heterogenous datasets, where a variety of words is used to express similar concepts.

One limitation of our evaluation is its low generalizability. While the evaluation datasets come from two real-life processes with different deviant case ratios (balanced vs. imbalanced), the textual notes in both datasets are written by members of a small team of debt recovery specialists and salespeople respectively. The observations might be different if these notes were written by a larger team or if they included emails sent by customers (higher heterogeneity). Also, the results may be affected by the amount of textual data available. Another limitation is the reduced set of classification algorithms employed (random forest and logistic regression). While these algorithms are representative and widely used in text mining, other classifiers might be equally or more suitable.

5   Related Work

Predictive monitoring is relevant in a range of domains where actors are interested in understanding the future performance of a system in order to take preventive measures. Predictive monitoring applications can be found in a wide range of settings, including for example industrial processes [11] and medical diagnosis [4]. One recurrent task addressed in this field is that of failure prediction [18] – i.e., detecting that a given type of failure will occur in the near-term.

While the predictive monitoring problems addressed in the above fields share common traits with the problem addressed in this paper, business process event logs have a specific characteristics that call for specialized predictive monitoring methods, chiefly: (i) business process event logs are structured into cases and each case can have a different outcome; hence, the problem is that of monitoring multiple concurrent streams of events rather than one; (ii) every event in a case refers to a given activity or external stimulus; (iii) every event has a payload; (iv) the payload may contain both structured data and text, and the structured part of the data includes both discrete and numerical attributes. In contrast, in other application domains [4,11,18], events in a given stream are generally of homogeneous types and carry numerical attributes (e.g., measurements taken by a device), this requiring a different type of techniques compared to predictive business process monitoring.

A range of methods have been proposed in the literature to deal with this specific combination of characteristics. These methods differ in terms of the object of prediction, the type of data employed, and the approach used for feature encoding. With respect to the former, some approaches focus on predicting time or other performance measures. For example, [17] uses stochastic Petri nets to predict the remaining execution time of a case, while [16] addresses the problem of predicting process performance violations in general and deadline violations in particular. Other approaches focus on predicting the outcome of a process, such as predicting failures or other types of negative outcomes (a.k.a. *deviance*). For example, [5] presents a technique to predict risks, while [15] focuses on predicting binary outcomes (normal vs. deviant cases).

Predictive process monitoring approaches also differ depending on the type of data they use. Some approaches only use control-flow data [16,17], others use control-flow and structured data [5,8,13,15]. When building predictive process monitoring models that take into account both control-flow and data payloads, a key issue is how to encode a given trace in the log (or a prefix thereof) as a feature vector. In this respect, a comparison feature encoding approaches is given in [13], which empirically shows that an index-based encoding approach provides higher performance.

None of the above studies have taken into account textual data. Yet, textual data is generated in a range of customer-facing processes and as shown in this paper, can enhance the performance of predictive process monitoring models.

6   Conclusion

We outlined a framework for predictive process monitoring that combines text mining methods to extract features from textual documents, with (early) sequence classification techniques designed for structured data. We studied different combinations of text mining and classification techniques and evaluated them on two datasets pertaining to á debt recovery process and a sales process.

In the reported evaluation, BoNG and NB, in combination with random forest, outperform other techniques when the amount of textual data is sufficiently large. In the presence of a smaller document collection, LDA exhibits better performance. An avenue for future work is to further validate these observations on other datasets exhibiting different characteristics, for example, datasets containing longer or more heterogeneous documents. Another future work avenue is to produce interpretable explanations of the predictions made, so that process workers and analysts can understand the reasons why a given case is likely to end up with a given outcome. Last but not least, we are planning to integrate our tool in the operational support of the process mining tool ProM to provide predictions starting from an online stream of events.

Acknowledgments. This research is funded by the EU FP7 Programme (project SO-PC-Pro) and by the Estonian Research Council and by ERDF via the Software Technology and Applications Competence Centre (STACC).

References

1. Blei, D.M., Ng, A.Y., Jordan, M.I.: Latent Dirichlet allocation. J. Mach. Learn. Res. **3**, 993–1022 (2003)
2. Breiman, L.: Random forests. Mach. Learn. **45**(1), 5–32 (2001)
3. Castellanos, M., Casati, F., Dayal, U., Shan, M.: A comprehensive and automated approach to intelligent business processes execution analysis. Distrib. Parallel Databases **16**(3), 239–273 (2004)
4. Clifton, L.A., Clifton, D.A., Pimentel, M.A.F., Watkinson, P., Tarassenko, L.: Predictive monitoring of mobile patients by combining clinical observations with data from wearable sensors. IEEE J. Biomed. Health Inf. **18**(3), 722–730 (2014)
5. Conforti, R., de Leoni, M., Rosa, M.L., van der Aalst, W.M.P., ter Hofstede, A.H.M.: A recommendation system for predicting risks across multiple business process instances. Decis. Support Syst. **69**, 1–19 (2015)
6. Di Francescomarino, C., Dumas, M., Maggi, F.M., Teinemaa, I.: Clustering-Based Predictive Process Monitoring. arXiv preprint (2015)
7. Dumas, M., La Rosa, M., Mendling, J., Reijers, H.A.: Fundamentals of Business Process Management. Springer, Heidelberg (2013)
8. Folino, F., Guarascio, M., Pontieri, L.: Discovering context-aware models for predicting business process performances. In: Meersman, R., Panetto, H., Dillon, T., Rinderle-Ma, S., Dadam, P., Zhou, X., Pearson, S., Ferscha, A., Bergamaschi, S., Cruz, I.F. (eds.) OTM 2012, Part I. LNCS, vol. 7565, pp. 287–304. Springer, Heidelberg (2012)
9. Freedman, D.: Statistical Models: Theory and Practice. Cambridge University Press, Cambridge (2005)

10. Hong, L., Davison, B.D.: Empirical study of topic modeling in Twitter. In: Proceedings of the First Workshop on Social Media Analytics, pp. 80–88. ACM (2010)
11. Juriceka, B.C., Seborga, D.E., Larimore, W.E.: Predictive monitoring for abnormal situation management. J. Process Control **11**(2), 111–128 (2001)
12. Le, Q.V., Mikolov, T.: Distributed representations of sentences and documents. arXiv preprint arXiv:1405.4053 (2014)
13. Leontjeva, A., Conforti, R., Di Francescomarino, C., Dumas, M., Maggi, F.M.: Complex symbolic sequence encodings for predictive monitoring of business processes. In: Motahari-Nezhad, H.R., Recker, J., Weidlich, M. (eds.) BPM 2015. LNCS, vol. 9253, pp. 297–313. Springer, Switzerland (2015)
14. Lessmann, S., Baesens, B., Seow, H.V., Thomas, L.C.: Benchmarking state-of-the-art classification algorithms for credit scoring: an update of research. Eur. J. Oper. Res. **247**(1), 124–136 (2015)
15. Maggi, F.M., Di Francescomarino, C., Dumas, M., Ghidini, C.: Predictive monitoring of business processes. In: Jarke, M., Mylopoulos, J., Quix, C., Rolland, C., Manolopoulos, Y., Mouratidis, H., Horkoff, J. (eds.) CAiSE 2014. LNCS, vol. 8484, pp. 457–472. Springer, Heidelberg (2014)
16. Metzger, A., Leitner, P., Ivanovic, D., Schmieders, E., Franklin, R., Carro, M., Dustdar, S., Pohl, K.: Comparing and combining predictive business process monitoring techniques. IEEE Trans. SMC **45**(2), 276–290 (2015)
17. Rogge-Solti, A., Weske, M.: Prediction of remaining service execution time using stochastic petri nets with arbitrary firing delays. In: Basu, S., Pautasso, C., Zhang, L., Fu, X. (eds.) ICSOC 2013. LNCS, vol. 8274, pp. 389–403. Springer, Heidelberg (2013)
18. Salfner, F., Lenk, M., Malek, M.: A survey of online failure prediction methods. ACM Comput. Surv. (CSUR) **42**(3), 10 (2010)
19. Wang, S., Manning, C.D.: Baselines and bigrams: simple, good sentiment and topic classification. In: Annual Meeting of the Association for Computational Linguistics, pp. 90–94 (2012)

P³-Folder: Optimal Model Simplification for Improving Accuracy in Process Performance Prediction

Arik Senderovich[1], Alexander Shleyfman[1], Matthias Weidlich[2(✉)],
Avigdor Gal[1], and Avishai Mandelbaum[1]

[1] Technion–Israel Institute of Technology, Haifa, Israel
{sariks,alesh}@tx.technion.ac.il,
{avigal,avim}@ie.technion.ac.il
[2] Humboldt-Universität zu Berlin, Berlin, Germany
matthias.weidlich@hu-berlin.de

Abstract. Operational process models such as generalised stochastic Petri nets (GSPNs) are useful when answering performance queries on business processes (e.g. 'how long will it take for a case to finish?'). Recently, methods for process mining have been developed to discover and enrich operational models based on a log of recorded executions of processes, which enables evidence-based process analysis. To avoid a bias due to infrequent execution paths, discovery algorithms strive for a balance between over-fitting and under-fitting regarding the originating log. However, state-of-the-art discovery algorithms address this balance solely for the control-flow dimension, neglecting possible over-fitting in terms of performance annotations. In this work, we thus offer a technique for performance-driven model reduction of GSPNs, using structural simplification rules. Each rule induces an error in performance estimates with respect to the original model. However, we show that this error is bounded and that the reduction in model parameters incurred by the simplification rules increases the accuracy of process performance prediction. We further show how to find an optimal sequence of applying simplification rules to obtain a minimal model under a given error budget for the performance estimates. We evaluate the approach with a real-world case in the healthcare domain, showing that model simplification indeed yields significant improvements in time prediction accuracy.

1 Introduction

Performance analysis is an important pillar of business process management initiatives in diverse domains, reaching from telecommunication, through healthcare, to finance. Taking healthcare as an example, it involves the ability to answer questions such as 'how long will it take for a patient to get treatment?', and 'how many nurses do we need to staff to accommodate the incoming demand?'. Answers to these questions are key in running an organization successfully and deliver value to its clients [1].

© Springer International Publishing Switzerland 2016
M. La Rosa et al. (Eds.): BPM 2016, LNCS 9850, pp. 418–436, 2016.
DOI: 10.1007/978-3-319-45348-4_24

Operational process models such as generalised stochastic Petri nets and queueing networks are useful in answering the aforementioned performance questions [2,3]. In particular, these models enable testing of re-design and improvement initiatives with respect to the as-is model. For instance, by changing staffing levels and altering the control-flow, the impact of operational changes on the performance characteristics of the process can be explored.

Process mining enables automatic discovery and enrichment of operational process models from logs, which record process executions [4]. Data-driven model discovery improves beyond the manual model elicitation in its ability to reflect the process as it is actually executed. However, automatically discovered models tend to incorporate infrequent process executions, which may result in over-fitting with respect to the originating log. Recently proposed discovery algorithms attempt to balance between over-fitting and under-fitting in the control-flow dimension [5–7,35]. Yet, the question of how to avoid over-fitting in terms of performance annotations of operational models has not been addressed in the literature.

This work approaches the problem of over-fitting of operational process models with P^3 − Folder, a method for automated simplification of generalised stochastic Petri nets (GSPNs) for process performance prediction. Starting with an over-fitting GSPN discovered from a log, the idea behind P^3 − Folder is that simplification reduces the number of model parameters. This, in turn, increases the accuracy of performance estimates, even though simplification generalises the model by introducing an estimation error regarding the original model. More specifically, our contribution is twofold. As a first step, P^3 − Folder defines a set of structural simplification rules for GSPNs, referred to as *foldings*. Unlike existing proposals for model simplification [8], these rules are local (affecting only a subnet of the GSPN), come with formal bounds regarding the introduced estimation error, and their applicability is identified automatically by structural decomposition of the GSPN. Second, P^3 − Folder formulates model simplification as an optimization problem that aims at attaining a minimal model for a given budget for the introduced estimation error. This problem is cast as an Integer Linear Programming (ILP) problem, which enables efficient computation of the optimal sequence of folding operations.

We evaluate P^3 − Folder with a case in the healthcare domain. Our experiments show that simplification of a GSPN discovered from a real-world log yields a significant improvement in time prediction accuracy compared to the original GSPN.

The remainder of the paper is structured as follows. The next section discusses the methods and challenges in performance-oriented process mining. Section 3 recalls the GSPN formalism. Foldings of GSPNs are introduced in Sect. 4. The model simplification problem and its encoding as an ILP program is proposed in Sect. 5. Evaluation results are presented in Sect. 6. Section 7 reviews related work, before Sect. 8 concludes the paper.

2   Background: Performance-Oriented Process Mining

Process Mining for Operational Analysis. We consider a setting in which a log L of recorded process executions is given and analysis questions regarding the performance of process execution shall be answered. Specifically, let Y be a performance measure, e.g., the total runtime of a process instance. Further, let $q(Y)$ be a performance query over Y, e.g., the expected value of Y, which we aim at answering based on L. In general, we distinguish two types of process mining techniques to quantify $q(Y)$.

First, machine learning (ML) techniques may be exploited. That is, process executions (including their data) are encoded as a feature vector X. Common ML methods such as regression or decision trees are used to construct an estimator $\hat{q}(Y)$ conditioned on X. Examples for such methods are found in [9–11]. While such an approach is often accurate in predicting $q(Y)$, it has two major drawbacks. Given a performance measure Z that is not directly observable in the log, one needs to quantify $q(Z)$, since ML methods require labelled observations of $q(Z)$ in the training phase. For instance, Z may be the waiting time for a specific resource. If it is not recorded in the log, $q(Z)$ must be estimated. This estimation procedure may introduce an error, which will reduce the accuracy of the learning technique. In addition, exploring to-be processes and sensitivity analysis of current process parameters is impossible due to lack of data that describes the effect of X on Y under the new terms.

A second angle to answer performance question is to use operational process models. Given the log L, operational models such as GSPNs can automatically be discovered and enriched with performance information [12,13]. To quantify $q(Y)$, a corresponding query $q_M(Y)$ is evaluated over the model, e.g., with the help of simulation [13] or queueing theory approximations [3,8]. A model-based approach overcomes the aforementioned limitations. It supports queries for measures that were not directly recorded in the log and enables to-be performance analyses and sensitivity analysis (e.g., by changing the control-flow and altering activity durations).

However, a model-based approach also suffers from a major drawback, namely *over-fitting* of the estimated $q(Y)$ with respect to L [8]. ML-based methods balance over-fitting of $\hat{q}$ to L by means of regularization methods (e.g., pruning the regression tree [10]). A model-based approach for regularizing, in turn, does not exist.

We illustrate this problem with two models that were discovered from a real-world case in the healthcare domain (see our evaluation results for details). Figure 1 depicts the two process models discovered using the Inductive Miner [14] with different noise thresholds: 0 % for model (a) and 20 % for model (b). We observe that noise filtering balances over- and under-fitting of the control-flow regarding the log, yielding a more sequential model when filtering more noise events. However, the trade-off between over- and under-fitting is not addressed for the performance perspective. Enriching both models with performance information based on [12] and testing them against a month of operational data not

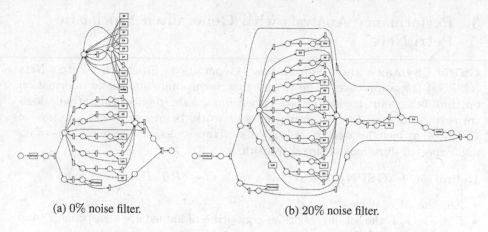

(a) 0% noise filter.   (b) 20% noise filter.

Fig. 1. Automatically discovered model of a hospital process.

used in model construction shows that model (b) is only slightly more accurate than model (a). As we later demonstrate experimentally, a principled approach based on model simplification, in turn, alleviates over-fitting in the performance dimension, thereby significantly improving prediction accuracy.

Resolving Performance Overfitting by Model Simplification. The idea followed in this work is to avoid over-fitting in the performance dimension by model simplification. We balance model size (number of model parameters) and proximity of the performance estimates of the simplified model to those of the original model (and thus the log).

To explain this idea in more detail, we adopt a statistical perspective on discovery and enrichment of operational process models. We assume that the performance measure Y is governed by a (parametric and stochastic) process model M, i.e., $Y \sim M$. Then, an estimation of $q(Y)$ translates into an estimation of $q(M)$. Hence, it is sufficient to estimate the model M to obtain $q(Y)$.

Common process discovery and enrichment techniques yield an initial model M_0 of the model parameters. Then, our $\mathsf{P}^3 - \mathsf{Folder}$ method applies a sequence of simplification rules to M_0, each introducing an estimation error with respect to $q(Y)$. What prevents the model from collapsing into a single node is an error budget B. $\mathsf{P}^3 - \mathsf{Folder}$ generates a model M^* as the most simple one in terms of size that is still with the specified error bound from M_0 with respect to $q(Y)$. Tuning the error budget B for a specific measure Y is performed via a cross-validation procedure on L. The resulting model M^* 'enjoys' the benefits of a model-based performance analysis, while being more general compared to M_0. As such, $\mathsf{P}^3 - \mathsf{Folder}$ can be viewed as a regularization of process models, transferring the analogy of machine learning into the world of model-based performance analysis.

3   Performance Analysis with Generalised Stochastic Petri Nets

GSPN Syntax and Semantics. Generalised Stochastic Petri Nets (GSPNs) [15] are a class of Petri nets that incorporate stochastic information on time behaviour: transitions are either *immediate*, representing atomic logical actions, or *timed*, representing units of work. Below, we recall a notion of GSPNs that includes weights of immediate transitions, and resource capacities and expected durations of timed transitions.

Definition 1 (GSPN). A GSPN is a tuple $G = \langle P, T, F, \gamma, \delta, \omega \rangle$ where:

- P is the set of places,
- $T = T_i \cup T_t$ is the set of transitions consisting of immediate transitions T_i and timed transitions T_t, respectively,
- $F \subseteq (P \times T) \cup (T \times P)$ is the flow relation,
- $\gamma : T_t \to \mathbb{R}_0^+$ assigns capacities to timed transitions (work units per time unit).
- $\delta : T_t \to \mathbb{R}_0^+$ assigns expected durations to timed transitions.
- $\omega : T_i \to [0, 1]$ assigns weights to immediate transitions.

We refer to the tuple $\langle P, T, F \rangle$ as the *structure* of the GSPN, and to $\langle \gamma, \delta, \omega \rangle$ as its *functional component*. The set $X = P \cup T$ denotes all *nodes* and the *size* of a GSPN is defined as $|X|$. For a node x, $\bullet x = \{y \in X \mid (y, x) \in F\}$ and $x \bullet = \{y \in X \mid (x, y) \in F\}$ denote its *preset* and *postset*, respectively. Further, F^* is the transitive closure of F.

Semantics of a GSPN are defined as a 'token game': A *marking* $M : P \to \mathbb{N}_0$ assigns to each place a number of *tokens*, thereby representing a GSPN state. A transition $t \in T$ is *enabled* in M, if all places in its preset are marked, i.e., $\forall\, p \in \bullet t : M(p) > 0$.

An immediate transition that is enabled, can *fire*. Firing of a timed transition t depends on its capacity and expected duration: Once it is enabled, a single exponential clock with rate $\lambda(t) = \frac{\gamma(t)}{\delta(t)}$ is started and the transition can *fire* when the clock is elapsed. That is, we assume a single-server semantics: there is one exponential clock per enabling.

Firing a transition t in a marking M yields a marking M', such that $M'(p) = M(p) - 1$ for all $p \in \bullet t \setminus t\bullet$; $M'(p) = M(p) + 1$ for all $p \in t \bullet \setminus \bullet t$; and $M'(p) = M(p)$ otherwise. Although tokens are indistinguishable, for performance analysis, we shall assume that the tokens that enable a timed transition are selected on a First-Come First-Served (FCFS) policy. Since first-order performance measures (e.g., average waiting times and average number of tokens in a place) are indifferent to the selection policy [15], the assumed FCFS policy is indeed plausible.

Semantics of a GSPN further depend on types of transitions and their assigned rates (capacity over expected duration) and weights as follows. Let $t_1, ..., t_k \in T$ be transitions that are enabled in a marking M, i.e., they compete for firing. If transitions $t_1, ..., t_k$ are either all immediate or all timed, the assigned rates or weights determine the likelihood of each of the transitions being fired. This likelihood is defined for transition t_j, $1 \leq j \leq k$, as $\frac{\lambda(t_j)}{\sum_{i=1}^{k} \lambda(t_i)}$ (only timed transitions) or $\frac{\omega(t_j)}{\sum_{i=1}^{k} \omega(t_i)}$ (only immediate transitions), respectively. If some transitions are immediate and some are timed, the immediate transitions have priority and the likelihood model is applied only to the immediate transitions.

Process Performance Analysis. A business process is described by an *open GSPN*, which is a GSPN $G = \langle P, T, F, \gamma, \delta, \omega \rangle$ that has a dedicated timed transition $\tau_0 \in T_t$, called *arrival transition*, which represents external arrivals into the system [16]. Specifically, it holds that $\bullet\tau_0 = \emptyset$ (and for all $t \in T_t \setminus \{\tau_0\}$ it holds $\bullet t \neq \emptyset$), $\gamma(\tau_0) = 1$, and $\delta(\tau_0) = \frac{1}{\beta_0}$, so that β_0 represents the *arrival rate* of the open GSPN. In the remainder, we assume all GSPNs to be open GSPNs.

The arrival transition τ_0 is enabled in any marking and thus, also in the *empty marking* M_0 with $M_0(p) = 0$ for all $p \in P$, which serves as the *initial marking*. Then, the *reachability graph* of G is a graph comprising all *reachable markings*, denoted $\mathcal{R}(M_0)$, i.e., markings that can be obtained by firing of transitions of G, starting in M_0 (here, the empty marking). To perform steady-state analysis, it was shown that the reachability graph of a GSPN is isomorphic (after reduction) to a Continuous-Time Markov Chain (CTMC) [15]. The transition rates between the CTMC states correspond to the rates $\lambda(t) = \frac{\gamma(t)}{\delta(t)}$ assigned to the respective timed transitions in the GSPN. Exploiting this transformation, performance analysis of a GSPN is based on techniques of CTMC analysis: global balance equations of the CTMC are solved or, to alleviate the complexity of solving these equations, queueing theory approximations can be used. In this work, we use such an approximation technique presented in [17].

4 Foldings of GSPN

P³ – Folder employs folding operations (aka foldings) to simplify GSPNs. We first elaborate on the general notion of foldings, before providing a detailed discussion of an exemplary folding. Finally, we show how to identify applicable foldings based on structural decomposition of a GSPN.

4.1 The Notion of a Folding

A folding operation is a contraction of a GSPN, which yields a GSPN that is equal or smaller in size. Yet, not all contractions are reasonable when aiming at improved accuracy of performance prediction. It is important that foldings preserve *stability* to ensure that the resulting model has a finite expected waiting time value. In GSPN terminology, a timed transition $t \in T_t$ of a GSPN $G = \langle P, T, F, \gamma, \delta, \omega \rangle$ is *stable*, if the marking $M_h(p) = 0$,$\forall p \in \bullet t$ is a home marking for M_0 in G, i.e., $\forall M' \in \mathcal{R}(M_0) : M_h \in \mathcal{R}(M')$. We call G *stable*, if all its timed transitions T_t are stable.

Let $\mathcal{G}$ be the universe of GSPNs. Then, we define foldings as follows:

Definition 2 (Folding). A folding is a function $\psi : \mathcal{G} \rightarrow \mathcal{G}$, such that for all $G \in \mathcal{G}$ it holds that $|\psi(G)| \leq |G|$. A folding ψ is called *proper*, if for all $G \in \mathcal{G}$ it holds that G being stable implies that $\psi(G)$ is stable.

The preservation of stability, termed *properness*, can be seen as a correctness criterion for the definition of foldings. Aiming at a contraction of the original GSPN, however, most foldings are actually abstractions that imply a certain bias in any performance analysis done with the resulting model. To control the application of foldings, therefore, we assign each folding a *cost* that bounds the possible estimation error. Clearly, this cost is specific to a particular performance measure and, thus, the type of performance analysis that shall be conducted with the folded model. As a prominent example measure, we consider the sojourn time of a GSPN: the total time it takes for the tokens produced by a single firing of the arrival transition τ_0 to reach a deadlocking marking (a marking in which no transition is enabled).

Let G be a GSPN and $G' = \psi(G)$ for some folding ψ. Let S and S' be random variables for the sojourn times of G, and G', respectively. The cost of applying folding ψ to G is defined as the absolute deviation in expectation between the sojourn times: $c(G, \psi) = |\mathbb{E}S' - \mathbb{E}S|$. Note that, since firing delays are given in the GSPN, the main challenge in evaluating sojourn times is obtaining good estimates for waiting times.

In this work, we consider five foldings: (1) sequence-folding, (2) race-folding (3) XOR-folding, (4) AND-folding, and (5) loop-folding. These foldings relate to common behavioural structures in business process models [18]. Each of them yields a simple GSPN comprising the arrival transition and a second timed transitions, as illustrated in Fig. 2. Note that the race-folding and XOR-folding relate to different semantic concepts: the former folds a net that represents resources working in parallel on jobs that arrive as tokens in the respective place. The XOR-folding, in turn, relates to probabilistic selection of activities, i.e., a probabilistic selection among different timed transitions.

All the five foldings are proper and their costs can be computed by exploiting results from queueing theory. Due to space limitations, however, we limit the discussion of properness and costs in this work to XOR-folding.

4.2   The XOR-folding

The XOR-folding, denoted by ψ_X, takes as input a GSPN $G = \langle P, T, F, \gamma, \delta, \omega \rangle$ of the structure visualised in Fig. 2(D): it comprises the τ_0 transition (with rate β_0), a single place p_i with $\bullet p_i = \{\tau_0\}$ and a single place p_o with $p_o \bullet = \emptyset$ that are connected by sequential structures, each comprising two immediate transitions and a timed transition.

Applying the folding yields a GSPN $G' = \psi_X(G) = \langle P', T', F', \gamma', \delta', \omega' \rangle$, where the structure $\langle P', T', F' \rangle$ is a trivial net comprising the τ_0 transition ($\gamma'(\tau_0) = \gamma(\tau_0)$ and $\delta'(\tau_0) = \delta(\tau_0)$), and two places that are connected via a timed transition, t, see Fig. 2.

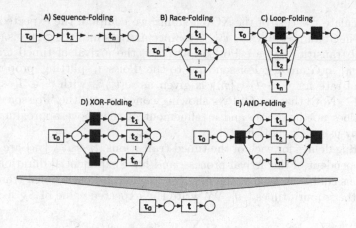

Fig. 2. Overview of foldings.

The functional part of G', that is $\langle \gamma', \delta', \omega' \rangle$, is constructed as follows. First, weights (ω') become irrelevant, since G' does not contain immediate transitions. The capacity (γ) and expected duration (δ) of the timed transition t of G' are set as:

- $\gamma'(t) = \sum_{t_t \in T_t \setminus \{\tau_0\}} \gamma(t_t)$, i.e., the new transition is allocated the total capacity of the internal timed transitions in G;
- $\delta'(t) = \sum_{t_t \in T_t \setminus \{\tau_0\}, t_i \in T_i, (t_i, t_t) \in F^*} w(t_i) \delta(t_t)$, i.e., the new transition is assigned an expected duration that is the weighted average of the durations of the timed transitions in G, where the weights stem from the respective immediate transitions.

Theorem 1 ascertains the XOR-folding properness.

Theorem 1 *If G is stable, then $\psi_X(G)$ is stable.*

Proof By [19], the stability condition for G is that for all $t_t \in T_t \setminus \{\tau_0\}$ it holds that $\beta_0 w(t_i) < \frac{\gamma(t_t)}{\delta(t_t)}$ with $t_i \in T_i$ such that $(t_i, t_t) \in F^*$. Hence, the sum of these inequalities yields $\beta_0 < \sum_{t_t \in T_t \setminus \{\tau_0\}} \frac{\gamma(t_t)}{\delta(t_t)}$. Due to

$$\sum_{i=1}^{n} \frac{a_i}{b_i} < \frac{\sum_{i=1}^{n} a_i}{\sum_{i=1}^{n} b_i},$$

for $a_i, b_i > 0$, we arrive at

$$\sum_{t_t \in T_t} \frac{\gamma(t_t)}{\delta(t_t)} < \frac{\sum_{t_t \in T_t \setminus \{\tau_0\}} \gamma(t_t)}{\sum_{t_t \in T_t \setminus \{\tau_0\}, t_i \in T_i, (t_i, t_t) \in F^*} w(t_i) \delta(t_t)},$$

which proves stability of G'. $\qquad\square$

To calculate the cost of the XOR-folding, we compute the expected sojourn times, S_X in G, and S'_X in $G' = \psi_X(G)$. Since arrivals into the systems (by firing the arrival transition τ_0) are Poisson arrivals, the arrival of timed transitions $t_t \in T_t \setminus \{\tau_0\}$ in G are also Poisson (due to the 'Poisson splitting' property [26]). The arrival rate for $t_t \in T_t \setminus \{\tau_0\}$ is given as $w(t_i)\beta_0$ with $t_i \in T_i$ such that $(t_i, t_t) \in F^*$. Note that for GSPNs showing concurrency, the 'Poisson splitting' property does not hold true and a refinement of the above approximation can be made by using Eq. (24) in [17].

The firing delays for each of the timed transitions, $t_t \in T_t \setminus \{\tau_0\}$ are assumed to be independent of the arrival process, and have exponential durations. These assumptions enable the use of the $M/M/1$ formula for each timed transition to calculate the sojourn times [16]. We write the expected value of S_X as:

$$\mathbb{E}S_X = \sum_{t_t \in T_t \setminus \{\tau_0\}, t_i \in T_i, (t_i, t_t) \in F^*} w(t_i)\mathbb{E}S_X^{t_t}, \tag{1}$$

Since it is known that

$$\mathbb{E}S_X^{t_t} = \frac{1}{\lambda(t_t) - w(t_i)\beta_0} = \frac{\delta(t_t)}{\gamma(t_t) - \beta_0 w(t_i)\delta(t_t)}, \tag{2}$$

for $t_t \in T_t \setminus \{\tau_0\}, t_i \in T_i, (t_i, t_t) \in F^*$, see [16], the sojourn time is given by:

$$\mathbb{E}S_X = \sum_{t_t \in T_t \setminus \{\tau_0\}, t_i \in T_i, (t_i, t_t) \in F^*} \frac{w(t_i)\delta(t_t)}{\gamma(t_t) - \beta_0 w(t_i)\delta(t_t)}. \tag{3}$$

We now turn to the calculation of the sojourn time S'_X for $G' = \psi_X(G)$:

$$\mathbb{E}S'_X = \frac{1}{\lambda'(t) - \beta_0}, \tag{4}$$

with $\lambda'(t) = \frac{\gamma'(t)}{\delta'(t)}$. In primitives of G, the expected sojourn time is given as:

$$\mathbb{E}S'_X = \frac{\sum_{t_t \in T_t \setminus \{\tau_0\}, t_i \in T_i, (t_i, t_t) \in F^*} w(t_i)\delta(t_t)}{\sum_{t_t \in T_t \setminus \{\tau_0\}, t_i \in T_i, (t_i, t_t) \in F^*} \gamma(t_t) - \beta_0 w(t_i)\delta(t_t)}. \tag{5}$$

The resulting cost for the XOR-folding is: $c(G, \psi) = |\mathbb{E}S'_X - \mathbb{E}S_X|$, which is easy to compute as it comprises only of primitives of G, the originating GSPN.

4.3 Finding Foldings by GSPN Decomposition

So far, we discussed the foldings shown in Fig. 2 as a transformation of a complete GSPN of the according structure. However, P^3 − Folder employs foldings also to transform parts (aka subnets) of a GSPN, which may enable iterative application of foldings. This holds in particular, as the foldings can be applied to any part of a GSPN that has one of the structures shown in Fig. 2, when removing the arrival transitions τ_0. The reason is that the rate of token arrival into the structures, as encoded by the arrival transitions, can be precomputed by solving the (linear) 'traffic equations' [17,20], which tie the external arrival rate of the entire GSPN to the internal arrival rates of places of the GSPN.

Observing that the structures in Fig. 2, once the arrival transitions have been removed, correspond to common *single-entry/single-exit (SESE)* controlflow structures, P³ − Folder employs structural decomposition of the GSPN to identify applicable foldings. Specifically, the Refined Process Structure Tree (RPST) [21,22] is used to parse a GSPN into a hierarchy of SESE *fragments*. Then, the RPST is a containment hierarchy of *canonical* fragments of the graph, which is unique and can be computed in linear time [22]. Fragments can be classified to one out of four structural classes: trivial fragments consists of a single edge; polygons (P) that are sequences of fragments; bonds (B) that are collections of fragments that share entry and exit nodes; and rigids representing any other structure.

To identify which of the foldings outlined in Fig. 2 can be applied to a given GSPN, we rely on the RPST of the GSPN as follows:

Sequence-Folding: The folding can be applied to any polygon fragment that has only trivial fragments as children and comprises at least two timed transitions. Assuming that the GSPN has been normalised (immediate transitions may occur only as the first child, as they are redundant at any other position in a polygon), the folding applies to the maximal sequence of timed transitions.

Race-Folding/XOR-Folding/AND-Folding: The foldings apply to place-bordered (Race, XOR) or transition-bordered (AND) bond fragments that contain only polygons of single timed transitions (Race, AND) or polygons of

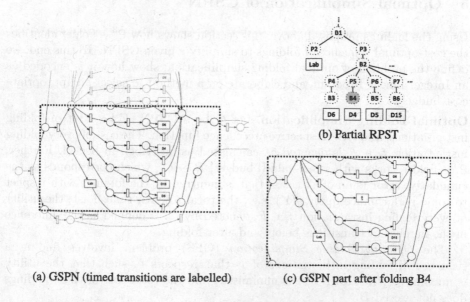

(a) GSPN (timed transitions are labelled)   (b) Partial RPST

(c) GSPN part after folding B4

Fig. 3. Example for the decomposition of a GSPN using the RPST.

three children, a timed transitions that is preceded and succeeded by immediate transitions (XOR).

Loop-Folding: The folding applies to place-bordered bonds that are cyclic and part of a polygon. The bonds needs to be followed by an immediate transition in the parent polygon and show the structure visualised in Fig. 2. That is, the children of the bond are polygons of single transitions that are either immediate (if flows in the child lead from the bond entry to the bond exit) or timed (otherwise).

The above rules identify foldings iteratively: whenever an applicable folding was found, the respective part of the GSPN is replaced by a timed transition and the rules are checked again. This way, given a GSPN, $\mathsf{P}^3 - \mathsf{Folder}$ obtains a set of *folding instantiations* $F = \{f_1, \ldots, f_n\}$, each being defined by a folding and the GSPN that is folded. Further, a precedence function $\nu : F \to (\wp(F) \cup \emptyset)$ defines, given $f \in F$, the set of all folding instantiations that must be applied before f, to generate the GSPN on which f is applied.

We illustrate this approach with a GSPN derived by annotating the model of Fig. 1b. Figure 3a shows an excerpt of this model. The RPST of the highlighted part is depicted in Fig. 3b. Here, loop-foldings can be applied to all the bond fragments $B3$-$B6$, since they comprise polygons of single transitions of the required types. Applying the loop-folding to bond $B4$ yields the net partially shown in Fig. 3c. Once loop-foldings have been applied to bonds $B3$-$B6$, an XOR-folding can be applied to bond $B2$, which now comprises polygons, each built of an immediate transition followed by a timed transition.

5   Optimal Simplification of GSPN

Using the foldings proposed above, this section shows how $\mathsf{P}^3 - \mathsf{Folder}$ identifies the cost-optimal sequence of foldings to simplify a given GSPN. To this end, we define the problem of optimal folding simplification, show how it is encoded as an Integer Linear Program, and elaborate on a method to select an appropriate cost budget.

Optimal Folding Simplification. Let G be a GSPN, F be a set of folding instantiations, and ν the respective precedence function. The cost of every folding instantiation $f_i \in F$ is denoted c_i, calculated as described in Sect. 4. Further, $\mathsf{P}^3 - \mathsf{Folder}$ works with a real-valued budget, $B \in \mathbb{R}^+$, which corresponds to the cumulative error (sum of all costs) that is incurred by the foldings with respect to some performance query $q(Y)$, e.g., the total sojourn time. Last, the utility of every folding instantiation $f_i \in F$, denoted by u_i, is defined as the difference in the number of transitions before and after folding.

The *Optimal Folding Simplification* (OFS) problem involves finding a sequence of folding instantiations of F that respects ν, such that the utility is maximised (the GSPN size is minimised) and the total cost of these foldings does not exceed B.

ILP Encoding. OSF is a tree-knapsack problem, a generalised 0-1 knapsack problem, that is known to be $\mathcal{NP}$-complete. In this problem all items are subjected to a partial ordering represented by a rooted tree [23]. In our case, this partial ordering is induced by the precedence function defined over the folding instantiations.

In what follows, we show a simple reduction from the tree-knapsack problem to an Integer Linear Program (ILP). The ILP problem is well-studied and many tools exist for its solution. We instantiate the ILP as follows. Let x_i be a decision variable that receives 1 if the folding instantiation f_i is applied to G, and 0 otherwise. Then, the ILP representation of the OSF problem is:

$$\underset{x_i}{\text{maximize}} \sum_{i=1}^{n} u_i x_i$$

$$\text{subject to:} \sum_{i=1}^{n} c_i x_i \leq B \quad \wedge \quad \forall\, i,j \in \{1, \ldots, n\}, f_j \in \nu(f_i) : x_i \geq x_j.$$

Here, the score function ensures that total utility is maximized, while the constraints ensure that folding errors do not exceed budget B and that the precedence ν is respected.

Budget Selection. The only input of the OSF problem that is not based on the originating model, G, is the budget B. The budget can be interpreted as the amount of trust in G: B should be small if trust is high, and vice versa.

When applying $P^3 - \text{Folder}$ to a model G that was constructed based on some event log L, the budget can be set in the spirit of model selection techniques that are often used in machine-learning [24]. Specifically, one may elicit the 'best' budget for a given log via K-fold cross-validation [24, Ch. 7]: The event log is partitioned into K parts, and the budget is determined based on random $\frac{K-1}{K}$ parts that are treated as training logs, and tested on the remaining part. All budgets between 0 (no folding) and $\sum_{i=1}^{n} c_i$ (unlimited folding) are considered and the budget that yields the most accurate answer to the performance query $q(Y)$ under a certain criteria (e.g., sampled root-mean squared error) is selected for the OSF problem.

6 Evaluation

We evaluated $P^3 - \text{Folder}$ with a real-world case from the healthcare domain. $P^3 - \text{Folder}$ [1] is implemented in the Python programming language, and uses Gurobi [36], for solving the ILP. The input is a process model (GSPN), and an event log; the method produces a folded GSPN model. Our results indicate that our simplification technique helps to avoid over-fitting of GSPN. $P^3 - \text{Folder}$ yields up-to a 15 % improvement in accuracy when predicting the total sojourn times, with respect to a GSPN discovered from log data using state-of-the-art mining algorithms.

---

[1] https://github.com/ArikSenderovich/P3Folding/.

6.1 Datasets and Setup

Our experiments were based on five months (April–August, 2014) of real-world operational data stemming from the treatment process of a large outpatient hospital in the United States. The hospital treats approximately 1000 patients a day, with patients arriving and leaving on the same day. The average length-of-stay per visit is 4.4 h (standard deviation of 2 h) with the highest number of patients arriving between 8:00 and 11:00 in the morning. The dataset includes the following attributes: case identifier, activity start time, activity end time, and resource performing the activity.

We selected April as our training set for discovering a GSPN and enriching it with data, as well as for the error budget selection (outlined in Sect. 5). The other four months were used as separate test sets, to validate the results.

To discover an initial Petri net, we applied the Inductive Miner [14] on the training set, with resources being treated as activities and a 20 % noise threshold (see Fig. 1b). We enriched the model based on the training set using the techniques described in [12], thus turning it into the initial GSPN.

As the performance query $q(Y)$, we selected the determination of total sojour times. To estimate $q(Y)$ for a given GSPN, we implemented a GSPN-to-queueing networks transformation and used the queueing network analyzer [17].

We focused on three evaluation aspects: (1) We explored the impact of the error budget on the accuracy of the resulting models. To this end, we varied the budget between 0 (no folding) and $\sum_{i=1}^{n} c_i$ (unlimited folding). (2) We studied the sensitivity of the approach to patient volumes, i.e., exploring the improvement in prediction accuracy caused by foldings as a function of time-of-day. We varied the time periods for which the original GSPN was obtained and then selected the best budget with respect to the training set by cross-validation (Sect. 5). (3) We considered the interplay of methods to over-fitting in the control-flow dimension (i.e., noise filtering in the initial GSPN discovery) and our approach. We altered the noise filtering threshold in the Inductive Miner, and estimated the prediction accuracy of an unfolded model. We compared the obtained results to those achieved with a folded model.

To quantify the accuracy of models, we used the sample root-mean squared error (sRMSE), which is a standard statistical accuracy measure, defined as follows. Let $\{Y_k\}_{k=1}^{K}$ be the sample of K total sojourn times as observed in the log (training or test). Then, the sRMSE is defined as:

$$sRMSE = \sqrt{\frac{1}{K} \sum_{i=1}^{K} [\hat{q}(Y) - Y_k]^2}.$$

As a baseline method, we used the historical average, which is an unbiased estimator. For the total sojourn time query $q(Y)$, it is the standard deviation of the length of stay, 120 min for the entire five months. In sum, controlled variables in our experiments were the budget, the time-of-day, and the noise filtering threshold of the Inductive Miner, while the sRMSE is the response variable.

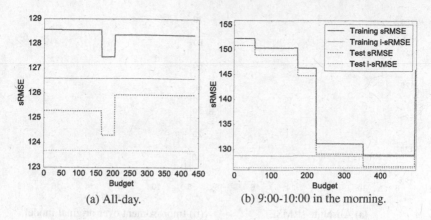

(a) All-day.   (b) 9:00-10:00 in the morning.

Fig. 4. sRMSE in relation to the error budget used for folding.

6.2 Results

First, even though the tree-knapsack problem is known to be $\mathcal{NP}$-complete [23], modern ILP solvers enable efficient reasoning on the OFS problem. Specifically, the run-time of P^3 − Folder when considering the entire days of the training data and all budget configurations, turned out to be 152 s. This run-time is in the same range as the model discovery, which demonstrates feasibility of the approach.

Next, we turn to the evaluation of the accuracy improvement achieved by P^3 − Folder . Figure 4 shows the sRMSE as a function of the error budget for two time frames, namely all-day and 9:00–10:00 in the morning. Here, the solid blue line corresponds to the training data (April) and the dashed red line to one of the test datasets (May). We demonstrate a single test month, since for fixed time-of-day intervals we did not observe a difference in sRMSE shape or value for all four months used as test datasets. The two additional flat lines correspond to the irreducible sRMSE (i-sRMSE) for the training and test sets, respectively. The irreducible error represents a bound for the prediction as it is essentially the noise, the variance of the total sojourn time in the data. Consequently, one cannot improve the sRMSE beyond the i-sRMSE without adding additional predictive features to the model (e.g. number of patients in the system or patient attributes).

We observe that the shape of sRMSE as a function of budget differs for the different time frames. For the all-day scenario, we observe that while low-budget folding improves the sRMSE, high budget folding causes the accuracy to deteriorate. On the other hand, for the busy period of 9:00–10:00, we notice a monotone improvement in the sRMSE as the budget grows and more folding is allowed (with 15 % improvement for the maximal budget). Furthermore, for the busy period, our method is able to approach the irreducible error. Lastly, we see that the model trained on the April data has a higher accuracy for the May data, which indicates that P^3 − Folder does not suffer from over-fitting the log.

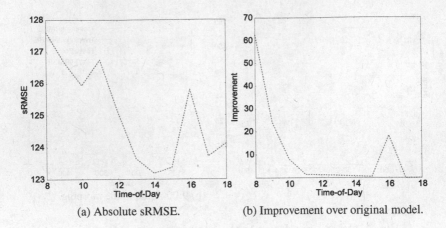

(a) Absolute sRMSE.   (b) Improvement over original model.

Fig. 5. sRMSE in relation to time-of-day.

Further, we select the error budget by cross-validation using the training dataset and explore the sensitivity to patient volumes. Figure 5a depicts the sRMSE as a function of the time-of-day. Figure 5b shows the absolute improvement in sRMSE, i.e., the difference (in %) between the sRMSE of the original and the folded model. The sRMSE changes over the day. Specifically, Fig. 5b illustrates that our technique is most effective during the morning hours, where the load is highest. This can be the result of our queueing approximation technique [17], as it has accuracy guarantees for heavy-traffic periods.

Finally, we explore the impact of noise filtering in the initial discovery (balancing over-fitting and under-fitting in control-flow) on our method. We alter the noise threshold for the Inductive Miner between 15 % and 40 % and compute the sRMSE of its unfolded prediction for the 9:00–10:00 interval, and compare the result to the sRMSE of the model obtained by $P^3 - $Folder when folding the 20 % noise model. Figure 6 illustrates that the sRMSE for the unfolded

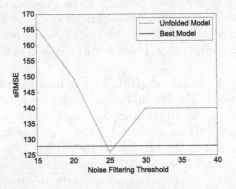

Fig. 6. sRMSE in relation to noise filtering threshold in initial model discovery.

model improves and deteriorates, while the sRMSE of the model obtained by P^3 − Folder (Best Model) remains constant. Hence, P^3 − Folder finds the optimal level of generalisation for answering the respective performance query.

7 Related Work

Previous work on business process simplification (synonymous to abstraction), considers manual ad-hoc rules that simplify the model while preserving similarity to the originating model [25]. Works on automated model simplification proposed to aggregate and eliminate components according to user-defined rules [27]. These rules were concerned mainly with visualization, and preserving behavioural relations between the various components. In [28], process abstraction is consistent, automatic, and preserves behavioural similarities, while in [35] the authors rely on Petri net unfolding into branching processes to balance behavioural over-fitting and under-fitting of a discovered model. However, none of these works considered performance preserving simplifications. Another related approach is to filter the data, prior to applying automated discovery, therefore creating simple models based on partial set of the data [14].

Existing performance-oriented model simplification techniques approximate typical process patterns (e.g., sequence, choice) via queueing theory, and guaranteed certain notion of equivalence between the original model and the resulting simplifications [29,30]. However, these techniques did not propose a method of locating typical patterns, and thus were not automated. Moreover, these works did not suggest how to order the simplifying operations, and some of the proposed performance bounds are not well-grounded [30].

Manual simplification of GSPN models has been considered before. In [31], GSPNs are simplified by using ad-hoc rules, not providing any error bounds. A simplification technique that provides bounds for specific performance measures between the original model and the resulting simple model includes decomposition and aggregation of the GSPN [32,33]. The first step (decomposition) refers to partitioning the GSPN into subnets, such that the subnets are weakly dependent. Every subnet can then be efficiently analysed without unfolding the underlying CTMC [30,34]. The second step (aggregation) aggregates the subnet according to performance-preserving rules.

Our approach takes up the ideas of model aggregation based on folding steps [8]. However, the steps in [8] incorporate ad-hoc assumptions and violating them may yield an unbounded estimation error with respect to the original model. In this work, we formulate an optimization problem aiming at a maximal number of folding instantiations, subject to guarantees regarding an error budget. This enables us to balance performance fitness and generalization of the resulting model in a principled manner.

8 Conclusion

In this work, we presented P^3 − Folder as a novel technique for automated simplification of models that aim at improving performance analysis of business processes. Specifically, we proposed foldings of GSPNs and showed how to find an optimal sequence of applying them to obtain a minimal model under a given error budget for the performance estimates. This results in a model that generalises in the performance dimension, while preserving the process perspective of the original model. The evaluation of our technique showed a significant increase in the model's predictive power, with respect to the unfolded model that was discovered from a real-world event log. The proposed technique can be viewed as regularization method for process models, in analogy to pruning and other model selection methods in machine learning.

In future work, we aim at integrating behavioural fitness and performance fitness. Specifically, optimal simplification can be modified to include both the control-flow and time perspective. We further aim at testing the accuracy improvements achieved by our technique on other queries, such as outcome prediction and resource utilisation.

Acknowledgments. This work was partially supported by the German Research Foundation (DFG), grant WE 4891/1-1.

References

1. Dumas, M., Rosa, M.L., Mendling, J., Reijers, H.A.: Fundamentals of Business Process Management. Springer, Heidelberg (2013)
2. Rogge-Solti, A., Weske, M.: Prediction of remaining service execution time using stochastic petri nets with arbitrary firing delays. In: Basu, S., Pautasso, C., Zhang, L., Fu, X. (eds.) ICSOC 2013. LNCS, vol. 8274, pp. 389–403. Springer, Heidelberg (2013)
3. Senderovich, A., Weidlich, M., Gal, A., Mandelbaum, A.: Queue mining – predicting delays in service processes. In: Jarke, M., Mylopoulos, J., Quix, C., Rolland, C., Manolopoulos, Y., Mouratidis, H., Horkoff, J. (eds.) CAiSE 2014. LNCS, vol. 8484, pp. 42–57. Springer, Heidelberg (2014)
4. van der Aalst, W.M.P.: Process Mining: Discovery, Conformance and Enhancement of Business Processes. Springer, Heidelberg (2011)
5. van der Aalst, W.M.P., Rubin, V., Verbeek, H., van Dongen, B.F., Kindler, E., Günther, C.W.: Process mining: a two-step approach to balance between underfitting and overfitting. Softw. Syst. Model. **9**(1), 87–111 (2010)
6. Buijs, J.C.A.M., van Dongen, B.F., van der Aalst, W.M.P.: On the role of fitness, precision, generalization and simplicity in process discovery. In: Meersman, R., Panetto, H., Dillon, T., Rinderle-Ma, S., Dadam, P., Zhou, X., Pearson, S., Ferscha, A., Bergamaschi, S., Cruz, I.F. (eds.) OTM 2012, Part I. LNCS, vol. 7565, pp. 305–322. Springer, Heidelberg (2012)
7. van Zelst, S.J., van Dongen, B.F., van der Aalst, W.M.P.: Avoiding over-fitting in ILP-based process discovery. In: Motahari-Nezhad, H.R., Recker, J., Weidlich, M. (eds.) BPM. LNCS, vol. 9253, pp. 163–171. Springer, Heidelberg (2015)
8. Senderovich, A., Rogge-Solti, A., Gal, A., Mendling, J., Mandelbaum, A., Kadish, S., Bunnell, C.A.: Data-driven performance analysis of scheduled processes. In: Motahari-Nezhad, H.R., Recker, J., Weidlich, M. (eds.) BPM. LNCS, vol. 9253, pp. 35–52. Springer, Heidelberg (2015)

9. van der Aalst, W.M.P., Schonenberg, M., Song, M.: Time prediction based on process mining. Inf. Syst. **36**(2), 450–475 (2011)
10. de Leoni, M., van der Aalst, W.M., Dees, M.: A general process mining framework for correlating, predicting and clustering dynamic behavior based on event logs. Inf. Syst. **56**, 235–257 (2016)
11. Leontjeva, A., Conforti, R., Di Francescomarino, C., Dumas, M., Maggi, F.M.: Complex symbolic sequence encodings for predictive monitoring of business processes. In: Motahari-Nezhad, H.R., Recker, J., Weidlich, M. (eds.) BPM, vol. 9253, pp. 297–313. Springer, Heidelberg (2015)
12. Rogge-Solti, A., van der Aalst, W.M., Weske, M.: Discovering stochastic petri nets with arbitrary delay distributions from event logs. In: Lohmann, N., Song, M., Wohed, P. (eds.) BPM 2013, vol. 171, pp. 15–27. Springer, Heidelberg (2013)
13. Rozinat, A., Mans, R., Song, M., van der Aalst, W.M.P.: Discovering simulation models. Inf. Syst. **34**(3), 305–327 (2009)
14. Leemans, S.J., Fahland, D., van der Aalst, W.M.: Discovering block-structured process models from event logs containing infrequent behaviour. In: Lohmann, N., Song, M., Wohed, P. (eds.) BPM Workshops, vol. 171, pp. 66–78. Springer, Heidelberg (2014)
15. Marsan, M.A., Balbo, G., Conte, G., Donatelli, S., Franceschinis, G.: Modelling with Generalized Stochastic Petri Nets. Wiley, Hoboken (1994)
16. Bolch, G., Greiner, S., de Meer, H., Trivedi, K.S.: Queueing Networks and Markov Chains - Modeling and Performance Evaluation with Computer Science Applications. Wiley, Hoboken (2006)
17. Whitt, W.: The queueing network analyzer. Bell Syst. Tech. J. **62**(9), 2779–2815 (1983)
18. van der Aalst, W.M., Ter Hofstede, A.H., Kiepuszewski, B., Barros, A.P.: Workflow patterns. Distrib. Parallel Databases **14**(1), 5–51 (2003)
19. Hall, R.W.: Queueing methods for services and manufacturing (1990)
20. Balsamo, S., Marin, A.: Composition of product-form generalized stochastic petri nets: a modular approach. In: Proceedings of the ESM, pp. 26–28 (2009)
21. Vanhatalo, J., Völzer, H., Koehler, J.: The refined process structure tree. Data Knowl. Eng. (DKE) **68**(9), 793–818 (2009)
22. Polyvyanyy, A., Vanhatalo, J., Völzer, H.: Simplified computation and generalization of the refined process structure tree. In: Bravetti, M. (ed.) WS-FM 2010. LNCS, vol. 6551, pp. 25–41. Springer, Heidelberg (2011)
23. Shaw, D.X., Cho, G.: The critical-item, upper bounds, and a branch-and-bound algorithm for the tree knapsack problem. Networks **31**(4), 205–216 (1998)
24. Hastie, T., Tibshirani, R., Friedman, J.: The Elements of Statistical Learning. Springer Series in Statistics. Springer New York Inc., New York (2001)
25. Smirnov, S., Reijers, H.A., Weske, M., Nugteren, T.: Business process model abstraction: a definition, catalog, and survey. Distrib. Parallel Databases **30**(1), 63–99 (2012)
26. Resnick, S.I.: Adventures in Stochastic Processes. Springer Science & Business Media, New York (2013)
27. Günther, C.W., van der Aalst, W.M.P.: Fuzzy mining – adaptive process simplification based on multi-perspective metrics. In: Alonso, G., Dadam, P., Rosemann, M. (eds.) BPM 2007. LNCS, vol. 4714, pp. 328–343. Springer, Heidelberg (2007)
28. Mafazi, S., Grossmann, G., Mayer, W., Schrefl, M., Stumptner, M.: Consistent abstraction of business processes based on constraints. J. Data Semant. **4**(1), 59–78 (2014)

29. Zerguini, L.: On the estimation of the response time of the business process. In: 17th UK Performance Engineering Workshop, University of Leeds. Citeseer (2001)

30. Zerguini, L., van Hee, K.M.: A new reduction method for the analysis of large workflow models. In: Promise, pp. 188–201 (2002)

31. Balbo, G., Bruell, S.C., Ghanta, S.: Combining queueing networks and generalized stochastic petri nets for the solution of complex models of system behavior. IEEE Trans. Comput. **37**(10), 1251–1268 (1988)

32. Ciardo, G., Trivedi, K.S.: A decomposition approach for stochastic petri net models. In: Petri Nets and Performance Models, pp. 74–83. IEEE (1991)

33. Woodside, C.M., Li, Y.: Performance petri net analysis of communications protocol software by delay-equivalent aggregation. In: Petri Nets and Performance Models, pp. 64–73. IEEE (1991)

34. Freiheit, J., Billington, J.: New developments in closed-form computation for GSPN aggregation. In: Dong, J.S., Woodcock, J. (eds.) ICFEM 2003. LNCS, vol. 2885, pp. 471–490. Springer, Heidelberg (2003)

35. Fahland, D., Van Der Aalst, W.M.P.: Simplifying discovered process models in a controlled manner. Inf. Syst. **38**(4), 585–605 (2013)

36. Gurobi Optimization Inc: Gurobi Optimizer Reference Manual (2015). http://www.gurobi.com

Author Index

Printed in the United States
by Bookmasters

Printed in the United States
By Bookmasters